The Lexicon-Encyclopedia Interface

Current Research in the Semantics/Pragmatics Interface

Series Editors:
K.M. Jaszczolt, University of Cambridge, UK
K. Turner, University of Brighton, UK

Related Elsevier books

In this Series:
TURNER (ed.)   The Semantics/Pragmatics Interface
                            from Different Points of View

JASZCZOLT   Discourse, Beliefs and Intentions

GEURTS   Presuppositions and Pronouns

JASZCZOLT (ed.)   The Pragmatics of Propositional
                            Attitude Reports

Related Elsevier journals

Journal of Pragmatics
Editor: Jacob Mey

Language and Communication
Editors: Roy Harris and Talbot J. Taylor

Language Sciences
Editor: Nigel Love

Lingua
Editors: Johan Rooryck and Neil Smith

Free specimen copies available on request

For further information on the CRiSPI series and for
details of how to submit a proposal go to:
www.elsevier.nl/locate/series/crispi

THE LEXICON-ENCYCLOPEDIA INTERFACE

Edited by **Bert Peeters**
University of Tasmania, Australia

2000
ELSEVIER

Amsterdam - Lausanne - New York - Oxford - Shannon - Singapore - Tokyo

ELSEVIER SCIENCE Ltd
The Boulevard, Langford Lane
Kidlington, Oxford OX5 1GB, UK

First edition 2000

100210 279 8

Library of Congress Cataloging in Publication Data
A catalog record from the Library of Congress has been applied for.

British Library Cataloguing in Publication Data
A catalogue record from the British Library has been applied for.

T

ISBN: 0 08 043591 2

⊗ The paper used in this publication meets the requirements of ANSI/NISO Z39.48-1992 (Permanence of Paper).
Printed in The Netherlands.

Current Research in the Semantics/Pragmatics Interface (CRiSPI)

Series Editors: K.M. Jaszczolt, University of Cambridge, UK, and
K. Turner, University of Brighton, UK

The aim of this series is to focus upon the relationship between semantic and pragmatic theories for a variety of natural language constructions. The boundary between semantics and pragmatics can be drawn in many various ways, the relative benefits of each gave rise to a vivid theoretical dispute in the literature in the last two decades. As a side-effect, this variety has given rise to a certain amount of confusion and lack of purpose in the extant publications on the topic.

This series provides a forum where the confusion within existing literature can be removed and the issues raised by different positions can be discussed with a renewed sense of purpose. The editors intend the contributions to this series to take further strides towards clarity and cautious consensus.

Acknowledgements

I wish to thank all the contributors whose papers follow, whether they showed their interest in the project when it was first mentioned on the Linguist list in early 1998, or whether they joined at a later date after being invited to contribute. I am very grateful indeed for the numerous new contacts that were made and that will hopefully not prove to be ephemeral. I am delighted to have been in a position to learn so much in such a short time: nothing opens up the intellectual horizons of a linguist more than the responsibilities of an editing assignment.

I thank the contributors for their patience, often sorely tested. Certain editorial practices were not universally appreciated, and led to situations that I would rather not go through again. I acknowledge the help of the many colleagues who assisted in the peer-review process; the end-result is a work that no doubt remains imperfect, but that nonetheless is a whole lot better than it would have been without their feedback.

I am grateful for the assistance lent to me by the staff of several university and other libraries: the librarians and other staff at the Morris Miller library of the University of Tasmania in Australia on the one hand, and at the Department of Linguistics library of the Katholieke Universiteit Leuven and the Aarschot (Belgium) municipal library on the other hand, all went out of their way to ensure that I could pursue work on this project under the most favourable circumstances. I thank the CRiSPI editorial team, esp. Ken Turner, and the Elsevier linguistics team, esp. Chris Pringle, Leighton Chipperfield, and Melanie Wheeler, for making the right suggestions and providing the right information at the right time.

Finally, I owe more than I can tell to my wife Monina and her aunt Josephine Wong alias Hajjah Maryam Abdullah of Kuching (Sarawak, East-Malaysia). Their patience has been very much appreciated, as has been my parents' hospitality while, for several months during the project, I was based in Belgium. Monina dear, this is for you. Even though you are not a linguist, even though you will find it difficult to relate to the contents of this book, I am sure you will be pleased that it is now off my plate and on the market. I love you.

Bert Peeters

Hobart, 20 March 2000

Table of contents

Bert Peeters

    Setting the scene: Some recent milestones in the lexicon-encyclopedia
    debate   1

I.   ASSESSMENTS   53

Anne Reboul

    Words, concepts, mental representations and other biological categories   55

Carlos Inchaurralde

    Lexicopedia   97

John Taylor

    Approaches to word meaning: The network model (Langacker) and the
    two-level model (Bierwisch) in comparison   115

    Afterword   135

II.   UNDERSTANDING UNDERSTANDING   143

Pierre Larrivée

    Linguistic meaning, knowledge, and utterance interpretation   145

Keith Allan

    Quantity implicatures and the lexicon   169

William Croft

    The role of domains in the interpretation of metaphors and metonymies   219

    Afterword   251

III.   WORDS, WORDS, WORDS   257

Richard Hudson & Jasper Holmes

    Re-cycling in the encyclopedia   259

Eva Born-Rauchenecker

    Towards an operationalisation of the lexicon-encyclopedia distinction:
A case study in the description of verbal meanings in Russian   291

M. Lynne Murphy

    Knowledge *of* words versus knowledge *about* words: The conceptual
basis of lexical relations   317

Heidi Harley & Rolf Noyer

    Formal versus encyclopedic properties of vocabulary: Evidence
from nominalisations   349

IV.   GRAMMAR   375

Joseph Hilferty

    Grammar, the lexicon, and encyclopedic knowledge: Is there such a
thing as informational encapsulation?   377

Rob Pensalfini

    Encyclopedia-lexicon distinctions in Jingulu grammar   393

V.   FURTHER AFIELD   433

Susanne Feigenbaum

    Lexical and encyclopedic knowledge in an ab initio German reading
course   435

Victor Raskin, Salvatore Attardo & Donalee H. Attardo

    Augmenting linguistic semantics descriptions for NLP: Lexical
knowledge, encyclopedic knowledge, event structure   463

    Afterword (by Victor Raskin)   481

Index   487

Subject Index   493

Language Index   499

Setting the scene:
Some recent milestones in the lexicon-encyclopedia debate[1]

Bert Peeters

*University of Tasmania, School of English and European Languages and
Literatures, GPO Box 252-82, Hobart TAS 7001, Australia
E-mail: Bert.Peeters@utas.edu.au*

0. Introduction

Questions about the exact nature of linguistic as opposed to non-linguistic knowledge have been asked for as long as humans have studied language, be it as linguists,
philosophers, psychologists, language teachers, semioticians, cognitive scientists,
whatever. The distinction has been maintained and defended by some, attacked and
abandoned by others. Those who have maintained and defended the distinction have
drawn the line in many different ways. Very solid arguments have been advanced in
both camps; in the course of a) editing this volume, and b) doing the research leading up to the present paper, I have seen so many that in the end, no longer sure of my
own thoughts on the matter, I had to reluctantly decide to cancel my own contribution, or at least to hold it over until I would have had enough time for further re-
flexion. I had intended to look at the sort of knowledge that is required for the exact
understanding of phrases involving the verb *begin* immediately followed by a direct
object (i.e. phrases of the type *begin a book*). I had intended to use French as my

---

[1] I am grateful to Susanne Feigenbaum, Joe Hilferty, Dick Hudson, Pierre Larrivée, Victor Raskin,
and Anne Reboul for comments on an earlier version of this essay.

target language, since that is the field in which I do all my teaching and a sizeable proportion of my research. I need more time to figure out whether native speakers rely on linguistic (lexical) or non-linguistic (encyclopedic) knowledge to determine that an utterance such as *Jean a commencé un nouveau livre* is most likely to refer to a reading or a writing event, although various other events are by no means excluded. I need more time to figure out how they know that a certain set of interpretations (e.g. wounding, drinking) are once and for all impossible. The same questions have been asked – and answered in more ways than one – by various scholars, especially in the last ten years, even though none has framed them in terms of the lexicon-encyclopedia debate. *That* was going to be *my* contribution. It would of course have been an appropriate addition to this volume, but for now at least it has not seen the light of day.[2]

It has been said that, as a result of the spread of prototype semantics and the increased reliance on descriptive tools such as frames, scenes, and scripts, the distinction between lexical (or linguistic) and encyclopedic (or world) knowledge is now defunct.[3] A significant majority of the papers brought together here show that nothing is further removed from the truth. They also illustrate the inevitable fact, referred to above, that the distinction, when made, is not being made along the same lines by everyone with an interest in the matter. The present volume does not aim at resolving the issue: it is most unlikely that *any* issue in linguistics will ever be resolved to everyone's satisfaction. The various contributors to this volume toe very different lines. Some work within frameworks (e.g. Cognitive Linguistics, Word Grammar) that reject the distinction; they either advance reasons why it should not be made or show through detailed case studies how much can be gained from not making it. Others were trained in the generative tradition (more particularly in Distributed Morphology), and demonstrate how a very theory-specific split between a list of so-called vocabulary items (the "Vocabulary") and a list of meanings (the "Encyclopedia") may clarify particular issues. Most are active in areas (e.g. pragmatics, language teaching, machine translation) where, for practical (but typically very different) reasons, one or the other distinction, more radical in some cases than in others, appears to be mandatory.

If so many people, all of a sudden, can come up with good reasons for a split, why is it that the view according to which the distinction is no longer made in contemporary linguistics could be upheld in the first place? My own view is that it has a lot to do with the fact that those who argue against a distinction have been increasingly

---

[2] For an overview of the literature, including discussion, criticism, and new directions, see Kleiber (1999:149-209).

[3] At the time of writing (October 1999), this view was expressed on a University of Leicester website, in a research essay written around 1992 by Brigitte Nerlich ("Semantic Development and Semantic Change, with Special Reference to Metaphor and Metonymy. An Overview of Theories from 1950 to 1990", http://www.le.ac.uk/psychology/metaphor/semdev.html).

vocal over the last few years, so much so that the opposite view was typically drowned in a sea of adverse opinion. The most vocal camp has been that of Cognitive Linguistics, an approach to language and linguistics looked at in section 1. Section 2 compares older writings of George Lakoff and Charles Fillmore, both currently associated with the Cognitive Linguistics movement, with more recent output. Section 3 identifies Haiman (1980) as the preferred source for the view that has been predominant in Cognitive Linguistics, and looks at responses by William Frawley and especially Anna Wierzbicka. Victor Raskin's contribution to the debate is revisited in section 4. Section 5 shows some striking similarities between selected aspects of James Pustejovsky's *Generative Lexicon* model and earlier work by scholars who took a stand on the issue of lexical vs. encyclopedic knowledge. Section 6 looks at the disappearance of the lexicon in *Distributed Morphology* and the subsequent inflation of the encyclopedic component. Section 7 returns to the past, paying particular attention to Katz & Fodor's "Structure of a semantic theory" (1963) as well as to some of the waves it made among linguists and philosophers. Section 8 closes the loop and brings us back to the Cognitive Linguistics camp – or rather, to a famous precursor who does not appear to have been recognised as such, at least not among (most) linguists, namely Umberto Eco. Summaries of the papers included in the present volume follow in section 9.[4]

1. Cognitive Linguistics

I must disagree with Goddard (1998:15), who says that it is a "minority view, but an important (and perhaps ascendant) one, [that] denies the existence of any boundary between real-world and linguistic knowledge". Goddard's assessment, followed by the inevitable reference to Haiman (1980), is a clear understatement of the facts: Cognitive Linguistics (which is the "minority view" he refers to) is *no longer* a minority view.[5] Goddard goes on to say that "theorists like Charles Fillmore and Ronald Langacker believe that knowledge of all kinds is integrated in the mind to such an extent that it doesn't make any sense to partition it into two distinct realms".

---

[4] Some contributors, in addition to putting their own views, refer to (sometimes highly relevant) work that is not mentioned in this introductory essay. On the other hand, I felt I had to insert a couple of "late footnotes" to acknowledge other relevant work that I failed to read (or reread). It might have been worthwhile to try and go back further than I did; still, in all likelihood it would have turned out to be impossible to report in a meaningful and informative way on work that stretches out over too many decades. Since exhaustivity was not my aim, it is not an exaggeration to say that the full history of the lexicon-encyclopedia debate remains to be written.

[5] For an assessment of Cognitive Linguistics, with special reference to its "cognitive import", see Peeters (1998, forthcoming a). Recent introductions to Cognitive Linguistics include Ungerer & Schmid (1996) and Dirven & Verspoor (1999).

Langacker, as is well known, is one of the founding fathers of Cognitive Linguistics as it exists today – together with George Lakoff, Gilles Fauconnier and Len Talmy. Fillmore is now also very much a part of the Cognitive Linguistics enterprise, even though Lakoff, for instance, has his doubts (cf. Pires de Oliveira forthcoming).

Few have put the Cognitive Linguistics position as emphatically as Langacker (1987:154-166). He claimed – and still does – that the distinction between semantics and pragmatics (which he equates with that between linguistic and extralinguistic knowledge) is "largely artifactual": there is only one "viable conception" of linguistic semantics, namely the one that a) *avoids* "false dichotomies" such as those just referred to, and b) adopts an unashamedly *encyclopedic* perspective. The second feature follows from the first. According to Allan (1995:294), concepts such as Fauconnier's "mental spaces" (e.g. Fauconnier 1994), Lakoff's "idealised cognitive models" (or ICM's; e.g. Lakoff 1987), and Fillmore's "frames" (e.g. Fillmore 1982, 1985) "are by no means all identical, but they call extensively upon encyclopedic knowledge" (cf. also Allan 1992:357).[6]

According to Geeraerts (1988a), the need to abandon the distinction between lexicon and encyclopedia is a direct result of the necessity to study lexical concepts as an integral part of human cognition in general, instead of as part of an autonomous language structure within human cognition. This goes against the structuralist hypothesis of a lexicon containing a strictly semantic structure that exists independently of the general cognitive organisation of the human mind. The structuralist belief that it was the task of semantics to reveal that independent semantic structure implies that semantics itself is an autonomous discipline. This is not at all what Cognitive Linguistics (and Cognitive Semantics in particular) takes to be the case: its position is that the only appropriate way to study lexical concepts is with constant reference to the general cognitive abilities of humans. There is no separate, specifically linguistic or semantic organisation of knowledge. Research in lexical semantics can therefore not be carried out in an autonomous fashion, or in isolation. It must be carried out in strict cooperation with other disciplines with an interest in the human mind (such as psychology, artificial intelligence, neuropsychology and cultural anthropology).

Geeraerts (1988a) puts the distinction between lexical and encyclopedic knowledge on a par with that between essence and accidence, or that between analytic and synthetic. Both of these, and a few more, had also been cited by Haiman (1980), in his demonstration of the theoretical impossibility of a distinction between dictionaries and encyclopedias (cf. section 3). Haiman is not a lexicographer, but Geeraerts is. In fact, he was one even before he closed ranks with Lakoff and Langacker, and before

---

[6] Allan's observation is not quite correct in the case of Fillmore (1975), mentioned alongside with Fillmore (1982) and Fillmore & Atkins (1992). Hilferty (this volume) errs along the same lines. Cf. section 2. Allan also incorporates in his list a number of concepts developed in artificial intelligence, to which Cognitive Linguistics owes a substantial debt. The AI concepts include Minsky's (1975) "frames" and Schank & Abelson's (1977) "scripts".

he became the founding editor of the journal *Cognitive Linguistics*. It is interesting to note that, as a lexicographer, he published at least one paper (Geeraerts 1985) in which he happily juxtaposed dictionaries, encyclopedias, and encyclopedic diction- aries, and saw no reason to abandon the distinction. I do not believe that Geeraerts would feel his more recent theoretical stance to be contrary to his earlier work. Al- though he does not appear to have said so anywhere in print, it seems that his posi- tion is not unlike that of Haiman (1980), who is mentioned in Geeraerts (1988a) but not in Geeraerts (1985). In other words, there is no *theoretical* justification for a dis- tinction, but in practice it does not work out that way.[7]

2. Lakoff and Fillmore... before and after

Four years before Lakoff & Thompson (1975) first used the term *cognitive linguis- tics* to refer to a programme which remains very much that of Cognitive Linguistics today (cf. Peeters forthcoming a for details), Lakoff (1971:329), at the time a gen- erative semanticist, claimed that Chomsky's original notion of "strict grammaticality (or degrees thereof)", which he applied to sentences in isolation, had to be supple- mented with a notion of "relative well-formedness", applied to utterances produced in a context, utterances said to be well-formed relative to "certain presuppositions about the nature of the world".[8] Lakoff declared **The salami is sleeping* ill-formed with respect to our "knowledge of the world", which is one in which salamis do not sleep; **I went Boston to*, on the other hand, involved a breach of the rules of gram- mar, and therefore was a case of straight ungrammaticality. He then went on to say (ibid.):

> It should be pointed out at the outset that [my] claim does *not* constitute a position that linguistic knowledge cannot be separated from knowledge of the world. On the contrary, it is a claim that the general principles by which a speaker pairs a sentence with those presuppositions required for it to be well-formed are part of his linguistic knowledge.

This almost sounds like Lakoff talking to us in a previous life. Cognitive Linguistics is not too far away, though – both historically speaking (cf. above) and from an ideological point of view. Indeed, Lakoff's assumption, as Keesing (1979:16) very aptly remarked just over twenty years ago, was that "information about cultural and

---

[7] ["Late footnote"] There are several interesting observations from a cognitive (though not necessar- ily Cognitive Linguistics) point of view on the lexicon, the encyclopedia, knowledge of language, and knowledge of the world in Nuyts (1992). For a review, see Peeters (1996).

[8] Instead of *supplement*, Lakoff used the verb *replace*. I am not entirely sure whether that is what he really meant.

sociolinguistic conventions required to interpret grammatical patterns [could] be incorporated by *stretching* formal grammatical theory" (emphasis added). Lakoff was not yet ready to "break down the boundary between a speaker's 'knowledge of the language' and his/her 'knowledge of the world'", but he was starting to widen the boundary of the former (Keesing 1979:17). In an interview published in 1974, Lakoff clearly marked his awareness of what had been happening:

> We have found that one cannot just set up artificial boundaries and rule out of the study of language such things as human reasoning, context, social interaction, deixis, fuzziness, sarcasm, discourse types, fragments, variation among speakers, etc. Each time we have set up an artificial boundary, we have found some phenomenon that shows that it has to be removed. That is not to say that there are no bounds on the study of linguistics. I only suggest that at this point in history the boundaries are disappearing daily, and one should not be too surprised if the domain of the field continues to expand. (Lakoff 1974:178)

Cognitive Linguistics was basically the natural outcome of this ongoing process: boundaries kept disappearing – at least in the eyes of Lakoff and those who worked alongside him – until it was realised that there were none left. Of course, there were many who would have no bar of it. Hence, Lakoff's lengthy criticism, in what for a linguistics text was a remarkable best-seller with a remarkable title (*Women, fire, and dangerous things*, Lakoff 1987), of what he referred (and still refers) to as the "objectivist paradigm in linguistics", a paradigm he once belonged to, but as a Cognitive Linguist no longer does. Lakoff's current view remains identical to the one he defended in 1987, when he pointed out that the "*dictionary-encyclopedia* distinction", or the objectivist linguists' distinction between *definitional knowledge* of words (i.e. knowledge that "corresponds to the *essential* properties of the entities and categories that the words designate") and *encyclopedic knowledge* of words (i.e. knowledge that "corresponds to the *contingent* properties of the entities and properties [sic] that the words designate"), is a "technical distinction, induced by the rest of the objectivist paradigm", a consequence of "the objectivist paradigm extended to include language as a matter of objective institutional fact" (Lakoff 1987:172). Elsewhere in the same volume, Lakoff (1987:138) confirmed his previous affiliation with the objectivist paradigm by referring to an earlier paper (Lakoff 1972) where he had made a distinction between *definitional properties* and *characteristic but incidental properties*. "This – he added – corresponds to the semantics-pragmatics distinction in the objectivist paradigm, the distinction between what the word 'really means' and encyclopedic knowledge that you happen to have about the things the word refers to".

In the case of Fillmore, it is a similar story. He used the terms *dictionary* and *encyclopedia* from the very beginning. The former was supposed to contain "lexical information about words", the latter "non-lexical information about things" (Fillmore

1969:124). The need to distinguish the two kinds of information was taken for granted, and illustrated by means of two examples, one of which will be left for later (section 5). The other example was based ·on observations made by Bierwisch (1967), whose name became eventually associated with what has been called "the two-level model", in which lexicon and encyclopedia are rigorously kept apart (cf. Taylor, this volume; Born-Rauchenecker, this volume; see also my comments on Taylor in section 9 below). Fillmore's observations deserve to be quoted at length.

> Let us examine some of the ways in which users of English speak of the horizontal dimensions of pieces of furniture. If we consider a sofa, a table, and a chest of drawers, we note first of all that a sofa or a chest of drawers has one vertical face that can be appropriately called its *front*, but the table does not. For a non-vertically-oriented oblong object that does not have a natural front, its shorter dimension is spoken of as its WIDTH, the longer dimension as its LENGTH. For the two items that do have a front, the dimension along that front is the WIDTH (even though it may be the longer of the two dimensions), the dimension perpendicular to the front is its DEPTH.
>
> Objects with fronts, furthermore, are typically conceived of as confronted from the outside, as is the case with the chest of drawers, or as viewed from the inside, as with the sofa. The terms LEFT and RIGHT are used according to this inner or outer orientation. Thus the left drawer of a chest of drawers is what would be to our *left* as we faced it, the left arm of a sofa is what would be to our *right* as we face it.
>
> This information is clearly related to facts about the objects themselves and the ways in which they are treated in our culture, and cannot be something that needs to be stated as lexically specific information about the nouns that name them. It seems to me, therefore, that the truly lexical information suggested by these examples is the information that must be assigned to the words LEFT, RIGHT, WIDE, LONG and DEEP (and their derivatives), and that the facts just reviewed about the items of furniture are facts about how these objects are treated by members of our culture and are therefore proper to an encyclopedia rather than a dictionary. (Fillmore 1969:124-125)

Throughout the seventies, Fillmore remained convinced of the need for a distinction between *linguistic* and *encyclopedic information*. He raised the topic in Fillmore (1977a), using the terms that I have just indicated, as well as those he had used in 1969 (*dictionary* and *encyclopedia*). Unlike before, he also turned his attention to *real* dictionaries and *real* encyclopedias (Fillmore 1977a:132-133):

> A frequent topic of discussion among semanticists is the issue of where and how to draw the line between linguistic information about the meanings of words and real-world information about the properties of things. This issue usually takes the form of the question "What is the difference between a dictionary and an encyclopedia?" The famous Spanish Academy definition of *dog*, as the species in which the male urinates by raising one leg, or the

common dictionary definitions of *left* and *right*, which speak of the side of a
person facing south or north when that person is facing west, clearly are not
conceptual analyses of their definienda, but rather serve as recognition tests
for people who need to make sure what kinds of things the words designate.
It is frequently assumed by linguistic semanticists that the linguist's job is
to determine the purely linguistic information about word meanings, and
that a distinction between a dictionary and an encyclopedia can in principle
be established. A more realistic view might be something like this: there are
things in the world, there are typical event types that one can observe in the
world, and there are institutions and cultural values that make human en-
deavors interpretable; for a very large part of the vocabulary of our languages, the only form a definition can take is that of pointing to these things
and actions and institutions and indicating the words used for naming and
describing parts and aspects of them.

Fillmore did not conclude that the job of a lexicographer cannot be distinguished
from that of an encyclopedist; in fact, as I foreshadowed in my introduction to Fillmore (1977a) a moment ago, he emphasised that, notwithstanding the blurred nature
of the distinction between dictionaries and encyclopedias in daily lexicographical
practice, the distinction between linguistic and encyclopedic information is a necessary one. Haiman (1980), three years later, would reach a dramatically different conclusion (cf. sections 1 and 3): namely, that the distinction between dictionaries and
encyclopedias works very well in practice, even though there is no theoretical basis
for a distinction between lexical and encyclopedic knowledge. Fillmore, however,
thought that the latter distinction was necessary first of all to provide a convincing
account of the interpretative process:

> It seems clear, at any rate, that any attempt to relate a person's knowledge
> of word meanings to a person's abilities to interpret texts will have to rec-
> ognize the importance of nonlinguistic information in the interpretation
> process. We get clearly different interpretations from the sentences "The fly
> was on the wall" and "The cat was on the wall", just because we know dif-
> ferent possibilities for stable positions for these two kinds of animals and
> because we know that the same word – *wall* – can be used to refer to a ver-
> tical surface of a room or building and to a high-relief boundary around a
> place. Generally this kind of disambiguation is thought of as a use of se-
> mantic competence, but in this case it surely involves information of the
> kind that cannot be sensibly incorporated in the definitions of the associated
> words. (Fillmore 1977a:133)

The distinction was also necessary to make sense of metaphorical statements (ibid.):

> If we hear something like "Harry is a pimple on the face of the commu-
> nity", we do not use peculiarly linguistic information to interpret what has
> been said. We know enough about people, pimples, and communities to
> know that a coherent scene cannot be constructed out of that sentence taken

literally. From that detection of a mismatch, we know that we should make use of the psychocultural information that people are embarrassed by and want to get rid of a pimple, and we assume that the speaker intended us to believe that the members of the community have feelings like that about Harry.

A quick look at the extensive Cognitive Linguistics literature on prepositions and on metaphor is enough to indicate that, in the seventies, Fillmore was anything but a Cognitive Linguist in waiting. He did end up joining them, though. To understand how that happened we must look at how *frame semantics* evolved from an enterprise involving *frames* and *scenes* (cf. in the quote above the clause "a coherent scene cannot be constructed") to one involving (possibly) *frames*, *scenes*, *schemas* and *models*, and finally to one in which no mention is made of *scenes* and *schemas*, because nothing else matters but (redefined) *frames*.

In at least four papers published in the seventies (Fillmore 1975, 1976, 1977a, 1977b), *frames* coexisted with *scenes*. The following passage (Fillmore 1977b:63) shows the difference, but also indicates the author's dissatisfaction with the latter of the two terms:

> I want to say that people, in learning a language, come to associate certain scenes with certain linguistic frames. I intend to use the word scene – a word I am not completely happy with – in a maximally general sense, to include not only visual scenes, but familiar kinds of interpersonal transactions, standard scenarios, familiar layouts, institutional structures, enactive experiences, body image; and, in general, any kind of coherent segment, large or small, of human beliefs, actions, experiences, or imaginings. I intend to use the word frame for referring to any system of linguistic choices – the easiest cases being collections of words, but also including choices of grammatical rules or grammatical categories – that can get associated with prototypical instances of scenes.

Scenes and frames activated each other: upon activation by a word belonging to a certain frame, the corresponding scene would help the addressee activate the word's meaning. Frames were also associated with other frames, and scenes with other scenes: in the former case, the association would come about "by virtue of shared linguistic material"; in the latter case, it would come about "by virtue of sameness or similarity of the entities or relations or substances in them or their contexts of occurrence" (ibid.).

The notion of "scene" was further expanded in Fillmore (1977a), which is a more recent text than Fillmore (1977b). Towards the end of that more recent text, the author finally admitted that the term *scene* had been given "too much work to do". Additional distinctions were necessary (Fillmore 1977a:126-127):

In the first place, we need to recognize the real-world scenes in terms of which people have learned categories and distinctions, and in terms of which people have acquired their original awareness of the objects and experiences that the world has to offer, as well as the real-world scenes that are the contexts and causes of ongoing perceptions and behavior.

Secondly, there are memories and distillations of real-world scenes in people's minds, possibly restructured in ways provided by their participation in a particular community, possibly with some aspects of them forgotten or suppressed and others enhanced.

Thirdly, there are schemata of concepts, stereotypes of familiar objects and acts, and standard scenarios for familiar actions and events that can be spoken of independently of given individuals' memories of experiences.

Fourthly, there is the imagined scene of the speaker as he is formulating his text; and fifthly there is the imagined scene of the interpreter as he is trying to construct a model of the world that matches the text he is interpreting.

And lastly there are the sets of linguistic choices that a given language provides and the ways in which these activate or are activated by particular conceptual schemata.

To identify each of these, Fillmore ended up borrowing some of the terms that had been proposed in artificial intelligence.[9] How exactly he proposed to define *scenes*, *schemata*, *frames*, and *models* is not all that important, however (see Fillmore 1977a:127 for details), because he soon realised that the best way forward was to make no distinctions at all. The only term left in the eighties and beyond (e.g. Fillmore 1982, 1985; Fillmore & Atkins 1992) was *frame*. In Fillmore's current thinking, frames provide the conceptual underpinning, the underlying conceptual structure required for all forms of interpretation. Frames, which have become very much part of the conceptual apparatus of Cognitive Linguistics, are comprehensive but stereotypical knowledge stores where the distinction between lexical and encyclopedic knowledge is no longer made. Fillmore has come to share with just about every other Cognitive Linguist under the sun the view referred to by Langacker (1997) as the "doctrine of encyclopedic semantics".[10]

---

[9] An impressive list, unfortunately without bibliographic references, is provided in Fillmore (1977a:127).

[10] Fillmore's latest research project is called *FrameNet*. Further information is available on the world-wide-web (http://www.icsi.berkeley.edu/~framenet/).

3. Haiman, Frawley, and Wierzbicka

For the careful onlooker, it should be clear that *some* Cognitive Linguists have re-fused to get "indoctrinated". One of them is Anna Wierzbicka, who is among the most original thinkers in semantics and pragmatics of the last thirty years. Her rele-vant work is reviewed in what follows, together with that of John Haiman and Wil-liam Frawley.

Cognitive Linguists typically appear to assume that the first author to have argued in favour of an overhaul of the distinction between lexical and encyclopedic knowledge is Haiman (1980). In the present volume, Joe Hilferty, who recently co-authored a Spanish-language introduction to Cognitive Linguistics (Cuenca & Hilferty 1999), is quite explicit about it. As we shall see, the reality is that Haiman was by no means the first, even though his often-quoted study on dictionaries and encyclopedias is probably the first scholarly paper that was entirely devoted to the topic. In it, he asked what exactly should be mentioned in a dictionary (what is linguistic or lexical knowledge), and what ought to be reserved for the encyclopedia (what is world or encyclopedic knowledge). The view that "knowledge of (the semantics of) a lan-guage – properly codified in a dictionary – is distinct from that knowledge of the real world which belongs in an encyclopedia alone" was referred to as an "article of faith" held by many linguists and philosophers, an "apparently uncontroversial dis-tinction" that, in spite of earlier attacks, was "still very far from being a dead horse" (Haiman 1980:330).[11]

Ironically, it was Wierzbicka's (1972:54) definition of the word *horse* (!) as "an animal called 'horse'", among other similar definitions of natural kind terms pro-vided by the same author and by several others, that had incited Haiman to investi-gate the matter in more detail than had ever been done before. Haiman found himself in agreement with the thesis that it was impossible to add anything to the definition without turning it from a dictionary definition into an encyclopedia definition. In fact, he went one step further, claiming that "perhaps the linguistically most impec-cable definition of elephants, as of all other words, is simply the most austere: *ele-phant* NP", and that all the rest "is contingent on knowledge of the world" (Haiman 1980:342). Of course, dictionaries do add a lot more – their definitions typically only start where according to Haiman they should end – which is why, in the author's view, dictionaries *are* in fact encyclopedias (Haiman 1980:331). The con-clusion ran as follows (Haiman 1980:355):

> Having demonstrated that dictionaries are not in principle different from encyclopedias, I do not, in my wildest dreams, expect that sales and pro-duction of either one or the other will come to an end. Part of the reason for

---

[11] Surprisingly, Lakoff (1971) is listed among earlier opponents of the distinction. Cf. section 2 for evidence to the contrary. Keesing (1979) is mentioned as well (cf. below).

this is that the distinction between dictionaries and encyclopedias, while theoretically untenable, has the happy property of working very well in practice.

It was perhaps unavoidable that this conclusion would be questioned in the very pages of the journal that had accepted Haiman's paper. Frawley (1981) published a rejoinder "in defense of the dictionary", to which Haiman (1982) issued a short (and, one presumes, rather hastily written) reply. Haiman blamed Frawley for having missed the point he had been trying to make. I am not absolutely convinced. What Frawley did was show that Haiman's argumentation had been basically flawed: there was nothing wrong with the various distinctions that either *had been* – or looked as though they *might be* – invoked to motivate the distinction between linguistic and encyclopedic knowledge, and that Haiman had said were unsustainable. There were six such distinctions:

- *sense* vs. *denotation* (also referred to by Haiman 1980 as the distinction between *linguistic knowledge* and *cultural knowledge*, no doubt under the influence of Keesing 1979; I am not sure whether the two distinctions *are* identical);[12]

- *subjective* vs. *objective* fact (a distinction apparently upheld in Wierzbicka's early work, especially in her claim that natural kind terms – because they correspond to objective categories in the world – cannot be linguistically defined);

- *essence* vs. *accidence* (or core knowledge vs. peripheral knowledge, à la Bierwisch; not to be confused with core and periphery in prototype semantics – cf. Haiman's 1982 rebuff of Frawley 1981; cf. also the afterword to Taylor, this volume);[13]

- *semantics* vs. *pragmatics* (a distinction abandoned by Cognitive Linguists, as shown in section 1);

- *analytic* vs. *synthetic* statements (this distinction will be revisited in section 7);

---

[12] In fact, contrary to what Haiman indicated (cf. previous note), Keesing did not argue *against* the distinction of what he called linguistic knowledge and cultural knowledge. He viewed the latter as "*part of*, and in the same epistemological plane as, cultural knowledge" (Keesing 1979:15; emphasis in the original). He saw linguistic knowledge as "contingent on" and "taking for granted" a culturally defined model of the universe (ibid.). Keesing (1979:14) suggested that "some of the difficulties that beset grammatical theory derive from trying to analyze native speakers' linguistic knowledge as a self-contained system", and he argued that "this has obscured the ways in which language rests on and draws on cultural premises about the world in which speech takes place".

[13] There is a proposal, in Klinkenberg (1984:1173), to make a distinction at word level between a so-called *noyau sémique* – a 'semic core' instituted (*fourni*) by a genuine linguistic competence – and the remaining *sèmes latéraux* (or *sèmes périphériques*) – 'lateral/peripheral semes' instituted by encyclopedic knowledge. Klinkenberg has advised (personal communication) that his memory of the concepts is fairly hazy.

- *proper names* vs. *common names* or *definite descriptions* (on "what names tell about the lexicon and the encyclopedia", see Allan 1995, and also this volume).

Haiman's thesis that the traditional distinction between lexical and encyclopedic knowledge had been motivated by one or more of these allegedly unsustainable distinctions led him to the conclusion that it, too, was unsustainable – and, with it, at least from a theoretical point of view, the distinction between dictionaries and encyclopedias. What he failed to see, and what Frawley did not observe either, is that there were perhaps other ways of justifying the distinction. Wierzbicka eventually confirmed that this was indeed the case. It is probably quite correct to say that Haiman's paper convinced the Polish-born Australian linguist that her earlier claim regarding natural kind terms (cf. Wierzbicka 1972, 1980) had been misguided. She set out to show that natural kind terms do have a fair amount of *linguistic* knowledge associated with them, that therefore they *can* be linguistically defined in a far more satisfactory way than she had assumed before, and that it is entirely legitimate to oppose linguistic and encyclopedic knowledge.

Wierzbicka's views set her apart from her colleagues in the Cognitive Linguistics movement. She condemns the claim that it is "impossible to draw a line between 'meaning' and 'knowledge' or between 'dictionaries' and 'encyclopaedias'" for the "unfortunate effect" that it has had on the study of the lexicon (Wierzbicka 1996:336). Similarly, the "belief that a dictionary definition represents nothing other than a selection from a (real or imaginary) encyclopaedia entry, with the choice being determined by practical considerations and having no theoretical justification, leads to stagnation in lexical semantics" (ibid.). Remarks such as these have not prevented Wierzbicka from being considered by many Cognitive Linguists as one of them. Others are noncommittal or question her belonging. In other words, it is not entirely clear whether she is best described as "friend, foe, or fellow traveller" (Goddard forthcoming).

Perhaps, it is fair to consider Wierzbicka a co-opted member rather than a founding member of the Cognitive Linguistics movement, even though she was in Duisburg in the spring of 1989 for a symposium (organised by René Dirven) that was later said to have "marked the birth of cognitive linguistics as a broadly grounded, self-conscious intellectual movement" (Langacker 1990:1). It was at that symposium that, in Langacker's words, "initiation of the journal *Cognitive Linguistics* was announced", that "plans were made to form the International Cognitive Linguistics Association", and that "agreement was reached to launch the monograph series Cognitive Linguistics Research" (ibid.). Wierzbicka's contribution to the Duisburg symposium immediately follows Brygida Rudzka-Ostyn's introduction to the third volume in that series (Geiger & Rudzka-Ostyn 1993). A very thought-provoking paper of hers (now revised and expanded as chapter 10 of Wierzbicka 1996) appears in the very first issue of the journal (Wierzbicka 1990).

Langacker (1990:2) judges Wierzbicka's work to be "entirely compatible" with his own. Lakoff (1990:45-46), on the other hand, just pages before Wierzbicka's own article referred to above, spends considerable time explaining how much he disagrees with her (cf. also Lakoff 1987:278-280), how much he learnt from her, and how important it is for all of us to have an ongoing dialogue with people whose work we can partly, but not totally, endorse. Interestingly, in two recent interviews (Pires de Oliveira 1998, forthcoming), Lakoff's tone is quite different. He does no longer consider Wierzbicka a Cognitive Linguist. In the first interview, she is described as an "idealist", whereas Cognitive Linguistics is about "the *embodiment* of meaning", about "the lack of separation between mind and body". In the second interview, Lakoff categorically states that Wierzbicka "does not look empirically at the same range of data that cognitive linguists do". He adds that "her analyses sometimes capture some aspects of meaning, but they miss an awful lot", and that "they do not fit with what we know of the mind and the brain". At the same time, in the same interview, talking about the building blocks for non-universal concepts and metaphor systems, he takes on a clearly Wierzbickian perspective – but without saying so.[14]

Wierzbicka has come in for a good deal of criticism from at least one other Cognitive Linguist of the early days, viz. Dirk Geeraerts (cf. section 1). In his review of Wierzbicka (1985), Geeraerts (1988b) does show a lot of restraint; he is slightly more critical in Geeraerts et al. (1994), and outspokenly negative in his recent pastiche of Ancient Greek philosophical discourse (the dialogue between teacher and pupil; cf. Geeraerts 2000).[15] The Belgian linguist is less dismissive, though, than his American counterpart. He does not bar Wierzbicka from the Cognitive Linguistics fold, but opposes within it two methodological extremes, summarised as follows by Goddard (forthcoming):

---

[14] There can be little doubt that Lakoff wrote down his initial impressions about the Wierzbickian enterprise with, at the back of his mind, Wierzbicka's detailed (1986) criticism of Lakoff and Johnson (1980), and perhaps also her rather disparaging description of Lakoff (1987) as a "particularly speculative" work "which runs over six hundred pages and which is supported by just three original examples ('case studies'), taken from one language: English" (Wierzbicka 1988:20). It may be useful to add that two of Wierzbicka's colleagues (Goddard 1989 and Peeters 1991) have published fairly critical reviews of Kövecses (1986), a metaphor study written in an overtly Lakoff-Johnson type framework.

[15] In my review of Geeraerts et al. (1994), I comment as follows on the lexicon/encyclopedia debate (cf. Peeters 1997:360): "Il convient à mon avis de 'revisiter' la distinction entre lexique et encyclopédie, rejetée par la plupart des adhérents de la linguistique cognitive, mais extrêmement utile pour distinguer ce qui est linguistique et relève de la *valeur* des mots de ce qui est non linguistique et relève du niveau *référentiel* et *conceptuel*" ['It may be appropriate to revisit the distinction between lexicon and encyclopedia rejected by supporters of Cognitive Linguistics, but extremely useful to distinguish what is linguistic and pertains to word *value* from what is non-linguistic and pertains to the *referential* and *conceptual* levels']. Prophetic words, written at a time when the present volume had not yet been conceived...

In the "good corner" there are the data-driven, empirically-minded linguists doing psycholinguistics, neurophysiological modelling and corpus analysis. In the "bad corner" there is the "idealistic tendency" represented by Wierzbicka and her colleagues, with their appeals to intuition and platonistic views about universal conceptual primes.

The data-driven, empirically-minded linguists reject the idea of a distinction between lexicon and encyclopedia, whereas the "idealistic tendency" subscribes to the opposite view. Two publications of Wierzbicka's deserve to be singled out for further comment in this regard. In her assessment of Wierzbicka (1985), Lehrer (1988:236) writes that Wierzbicka "draws a distinction between a dictionary (what a proper definition contains) and an encyclopedia (additional information about the world)". She then adds that where Wierzbicka "draws that line is considerably different from that of other lexicologists". I for one have the feeling that this has not been sufficiently recognised. Born-Rauchenecker (this volume), for instance, points out that Wierzbicka separates the two domains of knowledge, but that – unlike some others – she describes encyclopedic knowledge as far as possible. The so-called encyclopedic knowledge that Wierzbicka describes is encyclopedic knowledge as understood by Born-Rauchenecker, not by Wierzbicka herself. Allan's (1992:356) observation (repeated in Allan 1995:293) according to which "Wierzbicka (1985) developed semantic descriptions *very reminiscent* of those in an encyclopedia" (emphasis added) is more accurate than Born-Rauchenecker's statement: while Wierzbicka claims to be describing linguistic knowledge, the fact remains that some of the detail she provides has a distinctive encyclopedic flavour (Lehrer 1988:236; cf. also the afterword to Taylor, this volume).[16]

The 1985 book contains a lot of rather lengthy lexicographical definitions, mostly of natural kind terms and of cultural kind terms, far too long for the average dictionary, but nonetheless consisting exclusively of what Wierzbicka takes to be linguistic information. In her view, an important difference between linguistic and encyclopedic knowledge (the latter term is used quite sparingly) is that "linguistic knowledge is essentially shared between all the speakers of a language, whereas real-world knowledge is not" (Goddard 1998:14). This leaves of course a lot of uncertainty regarding so-called "common knowledge", e.g. "that dogs have four legs, bark, and wag their tails" (ibid.). What sort of knowledge is this? Wierzbicka's answer is that the meaning of the word *dog* (to take but one example) coincides with the folk knowledge surrounding dogs. This folk knowledge includes among other things the features quoted by Goddard. "The linguistic concept of *dog*, for instance, includes barking, tail-wagging, and much more besides" (Goddard 1998:15).

---

[16] There is an unfortunate, but isolated, reference to a cultural *encyclopedia* in Wierzbicka (1985:221). Its entries come however with full *lexical* definitions of names of plants and animals, definitions that can be very long but do not duplicate botanical and zoological descriptions.

Wierzbicka's position is perhaps more clearly stated in her 1995 paper (revised reprint in Wierzbicka 1996), where terms such as *encyclopedia* and *encyclopedic knowledge* are no longer rare occurrences:

> I am using the words "dictionary" and "encyclopaedia" in a metaphorical sense, referring to language-related "folk knowledge" (everyday knowledge) and to language-independent scientific knowledge (and certainly not to any concrete reference works such as the *Oxford English Dictionary* or the *Encyclopaedia Britannica*). (Wierzbicka 1996:337)

According to Wierzbicka, there is linguistic evidence that the human mind itself draws a distinction between a "mental dictionary" and a "mental encyclopedia".[17] The nature of the available linguistic evidence is neatly summarised in Taylor (forthcoming). He argues that "acquisition is not a process of building up a concept from its constituent parts", but that it consists in the "gradual elaboration of a knowledge network". He then goes on as follows:

> Wierzbicka's definition of *mouse* is instructive in this respect. The definition, as mentioned, extends over almost two pages, and includes such information as the characteristic size, shape, and colour of mice, their habitat, their manner of moving, and the sounds they make. Also included is the fact that mice are (or are thought of as being) timid, quiet, and inconspicuous; that cats chase them; that they are fond of eating cheese; that they live near humans; that they are regarded as pests; and that people try to get rid of them. (Surprisingly, the fact that some people – stereotypically women – have a phobic terror of mice, is not included in the definition.) Wierzbicka motivates the contents of her definition largely on linguistic grounds. A cat can be 'a good mouser'; poor quality Cheddar cheese can be called (or used to be called) 'mousetrap cheese'; a shy, timid, and inconspicuous person (usually female) can be called 'a mouse' (or 'a grey mouse'); and so on. Idioms ('as poor as a church mouse') and nursery rhymes ('Three blind mice') are also called in evidence. Excluded from the definition are 'encyclopedic' facts about mice that are *not* reflected in everyday linguistic usage, such as their geographical distribution, the length of the gestation period of the female mouse, the size of the mouse litter, and such like.

Wierzbicka's *linguistic* definition of *mice*, first attempted in Wierzbicka (1985:175-176), later revised in Wierzbicka (1995, 1996:340-341), "sums over a range of conventionalised uses of the word *mouse*; these include idioms, fixed expressions, typi-

---

[17] Another phrase used by Wierzbicka is that of *cultural dictionary* (comparable no doubt to the "cultural encyclopaedia" mentioned in the previous footnote). The cultural dictionary (Wierzbicka 1996:344) aims at "capturing what is psychologically real and linguistically relevant". It explicates "everyday concepts".

cal collocations, standard metaphorical uses, and so on" (Taylor forthcoming).[18] The differences between the 1985 and 1995/1996 definitions are quite remarkable, and would in themselves be worthy of detailed study. Why, for instance, does the 1985 version (which Taylor clearly did not consult) refer to the fact that "people say that women are often frightened of contact with them" (Wierzbicka 1985:176), whereas no mention is made of this in the later definition?

4. Raskin

Wierzbicka's view that lexical and encyclopedic knowledge should be kept apart is shared by Victor Raskin who, apart from being a contributor to the present volume, is the author of a paper on linguistic and encyclopedic knowledge in text processing (Raskin 1985a).[19] Major topics in the area of text processing and in that of text linguistics at large are cohesion and coherence (cf. Peeters 1994); although there is a lot of confusion in the literature as to what each of these concepts covers, the fact remains that they are necessary ingredients of a text (and of course also of single utterances).[20] At times, cohesion and/or coherence result from linguistic knowledge, as in (1), at other times they result from encyclopedic knowledge, as in (2). Both (1) and (2) are taken from Raskin (1985a:93).

(1)   I did not like the spoon. The bowl was too small.

(2)   I did not like the spoon because of the ornament.

How do we know that native speakers use *linguistic* knowledge to attribute coherence to (1), and *encyclopedic* knowledge to do the same in the case of (2)? Raskin's answer is based on what one typically finds in a lexicographical definition. Since dictionary entries are intended by lexicographers to represent the meaning of words, and since a typical dictionary entry for the word *spoon* refers to an 'eating or cooking implement consisting of a small shallow bowl with a handle', without adding

---

[18] It is quite conceivable that, in fact, Haiman (1980) unwittingly provided Wierzbicka with the basis for her about-face, and therefore with ammunition against his own thesis: in the opening paragraphs of his paper, he mentioned, with reference to a previously quoted dictionary definition of the word *horse*, that "the dictionary leaves out a great deal of information which most speakers of English seem to have about horses, *if commonly accepted idioms and metaphors are to be used as evidence*" (Haiman 1980:329; emphasis added, B.P.).

[19] Another paper (Raskin 1985b) published in the same year is less relevant, in spite of its title.

[20] [Late footnote] For other relevant work in text linguistics, see for instance Petöfi (1976), Neubauer & Petöfi (1981), and Hatakeyama et al. (1984). Regretfully, these publications came to my attention too late to be given full consideration in the present essay.

anything on the ornaments that one sometimes finds on spoons, the attribution of coherence to (1) involves linguistic knowledge, whereas the attribution of coherence to (2) involves encyclopedic knowledge. Linguistic knowledge is defined as knowledge "internalized by the native speaker of a language by virtue of his/her knowing the language in question"; it includes "familiarity with the meanings of the words and of the ways the words can be combined together". Encyclopedic knowledge, on the other hand, is defined as "what the native speaker knows about the world he/she lives in and what is not included in his/her linguistic knowledge" (Raskin 1985a:92).

Raskin lists a number of arguments *against* the distinction followed by a number of arguments *in favour* of it. Since references are not always provided, it is not clear whether all or only a selection were gleaned from the available literature. Raskin (1985a:99) does find, though, that most of them "are not easily defensible". In what follows, I only reproduce the more interesting ones, with the additional exclusion of arguments from within artificial intelligence, an area to which Raskin has made important contributions (see section 9.5 below).

Because of the widespread belief that frame structures (cf. section 1 and footnote 5) provide a convenient format (perhaps the most convenient format) for the representation of both linguistic and encyclopedic knowledge, it has been argued (e.g. by Hudson 1985) that no distinction should be made. The opposite belief, namely that encyclopedic knowledge cannot be as easily represented by means of frames as linguistic knowledge (for instance because frames are too rigid or too formal), may lead to the view that a distinction is after all in order. The two arguments do not only cancel one another out; according to Raskin, they are faulty. Identical representation does not necessarily preclude differences along other dimensions, and divergent representations do not necessarily rule out the existence of a different format of representation that suits both kinds of knowledge to perfection, and that therefore makes their identity obvious.[21]

- Lexicography requires a distinction between linguistic and encyclopedic knowledge for practical reasons: dictionary entries must be finite and reasonably succinct. The lexicographer's task is not feasible, unless a limit is placed on the amount and the sort of information that is allowed to appear in a dictionary. Linguists such as Eva Born-Rauchenecker and Anna Wierzbicka (cf. section 3, as well as Born-Rauchenecker, this volume) also argue that, in lexicography, the distinction is an important one. Raskin (1985a:99), however, rejects the lexicographer's demands. Lexicography, he says, is "anecdotal, circular, and devoid of any scholarly value"; it has ignored semantics for centuries, and has no right to demand anything now.

---

[21] Hudson & Holmes (this volume) do not refer to Hudson's earlier paper. It was only after the completion, peer-review and revision of their text that Hudson was reminded of its existence – and only because I asked him for a copy. He tells me he continues to endorse what he said at the time.

- Variations from one subject to another (a natural consequence of the inevitably variable size of their respective vocabularies) appear to make it impossible to decide once and for all which pieces of knowledge are linguistic. Moreover, it seems rather unlikely to suggest that, when a new word is acquired by a speaker, particular pieces of knowledge that were already available to that speaker would change their status (i.e. move from encyclopedic to linguistic knowledge). According to Raskin (1985a:100), this argument must be rejected on the grounds that a similar one would have to lead to the denial of the existence of English (or of course any other language). No two people speak in exactly the same way, yet to think in terms of the language of a certain speech community, irrespective of any idiosyncracies and individual variations, is far more than a useful fiction.

The reason why, in Raskin's opinion, "theoretical linguistics should be concerned about the distinction in question while the applied fields [especially lexicography and artificial intelligence, B.P.] can continue feigning nonchalance about it" (Raskin 1985a:100) is not covered in the above list of arguments: basically, the amount of semantic information allowed to take part in any formal procedure of semantic interpretation associated with a formal semantic theory has to be limited "simply because such a theory is likely to be a mechanical symbol-manipulation device and such a device cannot manipulate infinite sequences of symbols" (ibid.). Raskin proposes a theory "which, in principle, can accommodate and represent both linguistic and encyclopedic information but which can also distinguish between them and only use the former for semantic calculation" (Raskin 1985a:101). At the same time, he strongly believes that the applied fields should in fact not be too dismissive of what is happening in linguistic theory. More than many others, Raskin is aware of the fact that theoretical distinctions that are of no practical use should not be made in the first place. The fact that he makes the distinction strongly suggests that he believes it ought to be made, for theoretical as well as for practical reasons. In his co-authored contribution to the present volume, he shows that in machine translation a distinction is most definitely required.

5. Pustejovsky, Fillmore (bis), and Klinkenberg

Several contributors to this volume (Reboul, Taylor [afterword], Larrivée, Allan, Murphy) acknowledge the impact that James Pustejovsky's *Generative Lexicon* model (most forcefully expounded in Pustejovsky 1995) appears to have had in the last decade. His work has been rightly noted and hotly debated in natural cognition as well as artificial cognition. One of the most stinging and effective critiques of Pustejovsky's model is arguably contained in Nirenburg & Raskin (1996). According to Reboul (this volume), the model "has done much to revive the controversy around the boundary between lexical and encyclopedic knowledge". In fact, the boundary he refers to is "between what we formally take to be linguistic or lexical knowledge and that what is sometimes referred to as 'commonsense knowledge'" (Pustejovsky 1995:232). What exactly is meant by the latter term is not entirely clear. It seems, though, that a lot of encyclopedic knowledge, as usually defined, is not exactly shared by everyone, or even by a majority, and therefore does not qualify as commonsense knowledge. At best, the latter seems to be a subset of the former. Reboul further points out, and quite rightly so, that Pustejovsky's originality lies in his decision to treat as part of the (generative) lexicon various pieces of knowledge that lexicologists before him used to almost automatically relegate to the encyclopedia.[22]

As a first illustration, let us revisit Fillmore (1969) (for more, see section 2 above). Building on work done by Katz (1964), Fillmore defined *evaluative features* as those features that describe from what point of view someone or something is evaluated as being good or bad, poor or excellent, etc. He argued that there are several clear-cut instances where "the evaluative feature can be automatically specified from the function-identifying part of a definition" (Fillmore 1969:123). Fillmore cited the case of agentive and instrumental nouns, whose definition refers to one or the other activity. A pilot is someone who *navigates* an air vessel. This is Fillmore's gloss, not mine; it is lexical knowledge, it gives us the meaning of the word *pilot*. By default, a "good pilot" will be someone who is "good at navigating air vessels". Similarly, a knife is an instrument used to *cut* things. A "good knife" is a knife that "cuts well". On the other hand, Fillmore (1969:124) also believed that there are clear-cut instances where "the evaluative feature apparently needs to be specified separately". Nothing in the lexical definition of the words *food* or *photograph* specifies in a direct or immediate way what it means for food or for a photograph to be called *good* (its nutritional value or palatability in the case of food, its clarity or ability to "elicit positive esthetic responses in the viewer" in the case of a photograph). Fillmore (ibid.) clearly thought that these were important matters, because they raise an important question:

> The question a lexicographer must face is whether these matters have to do with what one knows, as a speaker of a language, about the words in that language, or what one knows, as a member of a culture, about the objects, beliefs and practices of that culture. Do we know about books that they are used in our culture to reveal information or elicit certain kinds of esthetic appreciation, or do we know about *the word* BOOK that it contains evaluative features that allow us to interpret the phrase A GOOD BOOK? Do we understand the expression GOOD WATER (as water that is safe for drinking) be-

---

[22] Wierzbicka's work (section 3) goes very much into the same direction: although, ideologically, she is about as far removed from Pustejovsky as one can possibly be, she too considers as lexical large chunks of information that others would take to be encyclopedic. Cf. the afterword to Taylor (this volume).

cause its semantic description has set aside that one use of water as the use in terms of which water is to be generally evaluated, or because we know that for most purposes (e.g., watering the grass, bathing) any kind of water will do, but for drinking purposes some water is acceptable and some is not? These are serious questions, but we can of course avoid facing them by making, with the typical lexicographer, the decision not to insist on a strict separation between a dictionary and an encyclopedia. (Fillmore 1969:124)

The impression one gets from reading Fillmore is: a) that he was unsure whether addressees rely on lexical or on encyclopedic knowledge to work out the meaning of noun phrases such as *a good book*, or *good water*; b) that he thought that interpreting noun phrases such as *a good pilot* and *a good knife* involves lexical knowledge; and c) that encyclopedic knowledge is needed to make sense of noun phrases such as *good food* and *a good photograph*.

What is Pustejovsky's view on the matter? Before I answer that question, I would like to point out that, although included in the bibliography, Fillmore (1969) does not appear to be quoted anywhere in Pustejovsky's text.[23] However, very similar examples are used: *a good car, a good meal, a good knife* in Pustejovsky (1995:ch.3); *a good umbrella, a good meal, a good teacher* in Pustejovsky (1995:ch.4). Then, in chapter 7, a generative mechanism called *selective binding* is introduced, which treats the adjective as a function and applies it to a particular "quale" or semantic role within the noun that it qualifies (cf. Pustejovsky 1995:76-81, or Reboul, this volume, for further details on a noun's *qualia structure*). This is followed by the statement that the same interpretive mechanism allows us to account for the contextualised senses of adjectives in general. In other words, the only knowledge that is needed is lexical.

Type coercion is another generative mechanism that operates in the generative lexicon (Pustejovsky 1995:106-122). Like selective binding, it appears to allow for the view that the interpretation of certain phrases, instead of relying on encyclopedic (or rather commonsense) knowledge, involves only lexical knowledge. Type coercion is very similar to what happens, according to Klinkenberg (1983, 1984), when so-called *allotopy* leads to reassessment in order to restore the *isotopy* induced by a verb. The crucial difference is that, when allotopy occurs, *encyclopedic knowledge* is used to reestablish isotopy. The terminology will be explained in a moment; first, I wish to express my surprise at the fact that neither Reboul (this volume), nor various other French-speaking authors who have commented on Pustejovsky (e.g. Danièle Godard, Jacques Jayez, Georges Kleiber; cf. Godard & Jayez 1993a, 1993b, Jayez 1996, Kleiber 1997, 1999) or collaborated with him (e.g. Pierrette Bouillon; cf. Pustejovsky & Bouillon 1995), appear to be aware of Klinkenberg's work – or of

---

[23] Pustejovsky does quote Fillmore's source (Katz 1964), apart from other material – but Fillmore himself is not mentioned.

that of the so-called *Groupe μ* to which he belongs. The time has come to make that work better known outside the semiotic-rhetorical circles where it was originally conceived.[24]

One year before Haiman (1980) saw the light of day, Klinkenberg spoke about semantic and encyclopedic knowledge at a Vienna semiotics conference. He argued, unlike Haiman, that the two were distinct. Parts of the conference paper, published five years after the event (Klinkenberg 1984) were used in another relevant text (Klinkenberg 1983), published the year before. I will mainly refer to the latter. Klinkenberg's (1983:295) demonstration revolves around the French utterance *Je viens de relire Greimas* 'I have just been rereading Greimas'. The verb *lire* 'read' carries an isotopy requirement: its direct object must refer to a written item. Since the object perceived by the addressee does not meet the isotopy requirement, it is allotopic and in need of reassessment. The reassessment process produces a so-called *conceived degree* (*un degré conçu*), namely 'written item emanating from Greimas', which is superposed onto the original so-called *perceived degree* (*degré perçu*). Both are part of what may be conventionally called the *Greimas universe*, which includes items such as 'writings' by Greimas, 'classes' he teaches, 'views' he defends, 'disciples' – and of course Greimas as a 'person' is in it as well. Commutation of the item 'person' with any of the others allows the formation of utterances such as *I have reread the whole of Greimas*, meaning 'I have reread all his writings', *I've got Greimas this afternoon* 'I am attending one of his classes', *That's typically Greimas* 'that's one of the views he defends' etc.

According to Klinkenberg, the deployment during interpretation of an utterance with an allotopic object reveals that, predating the utterance, there has to be a representation of the world, a representation that implies among other things one's acquaintance with a person called Greimas, a knowledge of writings, and their attribution to that person. All of these are non-linguistic elements. Klinkenberg hesitates to refer to them as "elements of knowledge", since he believes that the word *knowledge* has too much of a passive connotation. He qualifies 'attributing some piece of writing to a person' as a highly complex operation that entails a decision on the person, one on the written piece, one on the relationship between the person and the written piece, even one on the attribution (itself a complex operation). The common belonging of the various items to a coherent universe is not at all a given, even less a linguistic given: it is nothing short of a set of decisions that aim to lend coherence to what are basically isolates.

---

[24] The concept of isotopy is originally due to Greimas (1966). It has evolved in many different directions (cf. Rastier 1987 for a summary up to the mid-eighties). The concept of allotopy is an innovation of the members of the *Groupe μ* (e.g. Groupe μ 1976, 1977), who have also reinterpreted the original concept of isotopy for their own ends and purposes.

The same sort of remark applies to the articulation or structuration of the preexisting universe. Not all commutations within it are equally felicitous. Greimas being of Lithuanian origin, 'Lithuania' is no doubt part of the Greimas universe, but the utterance *I'm going to Greimas* is not very likely to trigger an interpretation of the type 'I'm going on a pilgrimage to Greimas' birthplace'. The various items in a universe are not merely juxtaposed, but organised in intricate ways, according to certain relations of implication, subordination, etc. That organisation, as well as the common belonging referred to in the previous paragraph, are derived from our knowledge of the world: this is, according to Klinkenberg, encyclopedic knowledge situated "en deça du composant sémantique" 'beneath the semantic component', and to be embedded in the linguistic description (because it is part of the speaker's competence; cf. section 9.2). Technically, the "encyclopedic component" stores knowledge "accepted" by the language community, and therefore always determined by social and historical factors. This, in turn, explains a major originality of Klinkenberg's encyclopedia, namely the fact that it *explicitly* allows for the storage of contradictory pieces of knowledge. There are two opposing perspectives: a practical one which is mostly linked with immediate perception, and a theoretical one where the link with perception is more tenuous. When we talk about a fire, we often visualise and/or conceptualise it together with the smoke that escapes from it: in practical terms, the smoke is "part of the fire", together with the flames, the heat, the combustion etc. On the other hand, it is equally possible, though perhaps not so obvious, to keep the fire and the smoke separate. For more details, see Klinkenberg (1983:296-297).[25]

Pustejovsky's examples of type coercion are not identical to Klinkenberg's, but they are close. True to the generative tradition of linguistics, Pustejovsky distinguishes between a deep and a surface level of syntax. At the deep level, predicates assign *semantic types* to their arguments. The verb *begin*, for instance, assigns the type 'event'. Type coercion explains why it is nonetheless possible, at surface level, to have constructions of the type "NP_1 *begin* NP_2", where the latter NP appears to be of the wrong type ('object' instead of 'event'). The mechanism is entirely controlled by the predicate. It does not apply when *begin* is followed by an infinitive (as in *John began to read the book*), because the infinitive already refers to an event. When there is no infinitive, and *begin* is followed by a noun complement, type coercion *may* apply. It does only if the NP is of the object type; in that case, another type (viz. 'event') is superimposed upon it. In other words, the NP is *coerced* to refer to an event rather than to an object. Obviously, if the NP is of the correct type (as is the case in, e.g., *begin a class* (said of a teacher; a class is an event), no type coercion is required.

---

[25] The reader may have noticed that Klinkenberg's views are rendered in the present, whereas those of Fillmore were rendered in the past. Fillmore has changed his mind, whereas (in spite of what was said in footnote 10) there is no evidence to suggest the same for Klinkenberg.

The question is: when a new type is generated, how exactly does this happen? In Pustejovsky's model, type coercion critically relies on lexical information associated with the noun complement. Again, as previously illustrated with reference to selective binding, what is exploited is the so-called *qualia structure* of the noun. In the case of a noun such as *book*, there is a *telic quale* identifying what books are for (they are meant to be read); there is also an *agentive quale* identifying who is at the origin of the object *book* (a writer). Depending on the context, either the verb *read* or the verb *write* are "drawn" from the qualia structure associated with the noun *book*, and their type (which is the expected one after a verb such as *begin*) is superposed upon the type of the NP *book*. For relevant criticism, cf. Reboul (this volume), as well as the various "French sources" mentioned above (except, of course, Pustejovsky & Bouillon 1995).

6. Distributed Morphology

Whereas Pustejovsky stores in the lexicon information that many would rather treat as encyclopedic, those behind another fairly new model have done the exact opposite. The model, which goes back to the early 1990s, is known as *Distributed Morphology*, and is basically the brainchild of Morris Halle and Alec Marantz. No single authoritative book-length presentation of its basic principles is as yet in existence, even though there is a substantive body of research that has already been carried out.[26] A crucial tenet of the theory is that there is no lexicon as understood by most if not all forms of generative grammar practiced in the 1970s and beyond. In the absence of a unique lexicon, there are also no lexical items, and there is no lexical knowledge. Marantz (1997:203) explains that "Distributed Morphology explodes the Lexicon and includes a number of *distributed*, non-computational lists as Lexicon-replacements". Harley & Noyer (forthcoming) point out that "the jobs assigned to the Lexicon component in earlier theories are *distributed* through various other components". Statements such as these go a long way towards explaining how the model arrived at its name.

Distributed Morphology distinguishes two types of meaning (syntactic and encyclopedic). The various abstract morphosyntactic features (e.g. [Det], [1st], [CAUSE], [+ pst], [Root], [pl], etc.) combined by the syntax into so-called syntactic terminals or nodes have no meaning other than *syntactic*. They constitute what might be called a "narrow lexicon", which "most directly replaces the Lexicon as it provides the units that the syntax operates with" (Marantz 1997:203). The same features are also part of so-called *vocabulary items*. These may be identical in size to what is traditionally

---

[26] The most important papers, for those who want an overview, are Halle & Marantz (1993, 1994), Marantz (1997), and Harley & Noyer (forthcoming).

referred to as words, but also either smaller or larger. Vocabulary items are the building blocks of morphophonology. Here, the role of the features is to indicate where (in which syntactic terminals or nodes) particular items may be inserted. Items of a given category "compete" for insertion into a node belonging to the same category. The vocabulary item that presents the best match against the features of a specific node wins out.

Importantly, vocabulary items consist of nothing more than a phonological string (e.g. /dɔg/) combined with feature bundles, and therefore syntactic meaning, of the sort referred to (in the case of /dɔg/: [Root], [+ count], [+ animate]). They do not in themselves have any other meaning, but are associated with an *encyclopedic entry*. Encyclopedic entries provide full details regarding the second type of meaning distinguished within Distributed Morphology, namely *encyclopedic meaning*. This second type of meaning plays no role whatsoever in the syntax. The encyclopedic entry for the vocabulary item *dog* specifies, among other things, that dogs are four-legged canine pets that may bite and that enjoy chasing balls. There is a comparable encyclopedic entry for, say, *cat* – which entails, among other things, that the meaning components that distinguish *cat* from *dog* are encyclopedic. Encyclopedic knowledge is basically non-linguistic knowledge, which means that in Distributed Morphology there is no *linguistic* difference between the items *dog* and *cat*.[27] Encyclopedic knowledge also specifies, for instance, that, in the environment *let sleeping ___ lie, dog* refers to a discourse entity that is better left alone. The precise relationship between what are basically the three Lexicon-replacements – i.e. the *encyclopedia*, or sum total of all encyclopedic entries, the *vocabulary*, or set of all vocabulary items, and the *narrow lexicon* (cf. above) – remains a topic of discussion (cf. Marantz 1997, and also Harley & Noyer, this volume).[28]

---

[27] In the mid-sixties, Baumgärtner (1967) argued that the difference in meaning between words such as *spaniel, poodle, bulldog* etc. is not linguistically relevant: sentences do not become semantically unacceptable if, instead of using the word *dog*, one uses words such as *spaniel* etc. This comes close to the Distributed Morphology view, were it not for the fact that Baumgärtner also held the view that the only *linguistically* relevant features are those that distinguish the words *dog* and *cat*, so that, for instance, an utterance such as *The cat barks* is unacceptable for linguistic reasons.

[28] Other issues that remain unresolved include the question of how Distributed Morphology might best deal with the distinction between the two kinds of morphological processes traditionally called *productive* and *non-productive*. Harley & Noyer (forthcoming) recall that "the earliest work in generative morphology such as Halle (1973) postulated a Dictionary which effectively licensed the use of expressions formed by non-productive word-formation rules". They then note that "the question of whether the DM Encyclopedia can or should perform this licensing function, or how, if at all, expressions formed by 'non-productive' mechanisms of the grammar are to be specially treated, is currently under investigation".

7. Katz & Fodor's legacy

Allan (1992:356 = 1995:293) notes that, before the 1980s, it was "normal practice" to favour "parsimonious dictionary knowledge" against "elaborated encyclopedic knowledge". This is perhaps a slight overstatement, but it can be seen as a direct reference to Katz & Fodor (1963), and to other related work such as Katz & Postal (1964) and Katz (1966), none of which is referred to explicitly. What Katz and colleagues (esp. Fodor) had to say was important, though, as clearly recognised by Raskin (1985a:97-98):

> It would be fair to say that the issue [of linguistic vs. encyclopedic knowledge; B.P.] was brought into contemporary semantic theory by Katz and Fodor [1963] who made a strong and clear claim about the boundary between one's knowledge of language and one's knowledge of the world. Not only did they claim the existence and necessity of such a boundary but they also declared that the boundary served another important purpose – it separated the object of semantic theory from all the rest. Katz and Fodor believed that it was impossible for any formal semantic theory to account for the meaning of any sentence in any context because, according to them, that would amount to the formal description of one's entire knowledge of the world, the goal which they considered axiomatically unattainable. The object of semantic theory for them was the meaning of the sentence in isolation, and what it took to calculate it was linguistic knowledge while the rest was not.

Raskin (1985a:100) endorsed the need for a clear delimitation (cf. section 4), but rejected Katz & Fodor's reasons, arguing that to narrow the scope of semantic theory to the "more feasible but almost entirely uninteresting task of accounting for the meaning of the sentence in isolation" is absurd. He went on to say that if the goal of semantic theory is "to match the native speaker's semantic competence", Katz & Fodor's proposals had to be "self-defeating": no native speaker ever deals with sentences in isolation. However, for Katz & Fodor, all that mattered was the *dictionary*, their name for the semantic subcomponent in the theory responsible for linking linguistic forms and meanings.

As it turns out, the integrity of the model was remarkably short-lived. One of the reasons why it came in for a lot of criticism fairly early in the piece has no doubt to do with what many perceived as the spurious distinction between so-called *markers* and so-called *distinguishers*. For Bolinger (1965), who listed a string of problems left unaddressed by Katz & Fodor, it was one of two unjustified dualisms, the other one being that between *knowledge of the language* and *knowledge of the world*. Both deserve a closer look: contrary to appearances, both are relevant for the lexicon-encyclopedia debate.

First to markers and distinguishers. Before reiterating what Bolinger had to say about them, I should point out, with Allan (1986:306-314), that between 1963 and 1972 Katz shifted ground on a number of occasions: the definition of what was a marker and what was a distinguisher did not remain unchanged.[29] Allan also notes that the term *distinguisher* vanished from Katz's work after 1972. It was in his *Semantic theory* that, for the last time, Katz sought to clarify what the much-maligned distinction between markers and distinguishers had intended to achieve. No reference at all is made in the relevant pages (Katz 1972:82-88) to encyclopedic information or world knowledge, which strongly suggests that markers and distinguishers were both intended to identify linguistic information. Both were supposed to be *semantic* features, with a distinguisher being whatever is left over of a given sense within a word once all the markers have been taken care of. Square brackets were used to identify the former, round brackets to identify the latter, as in the following oft-quoted semantic description of the English word *bachelor*, taken from Katz & Fodor (1963).

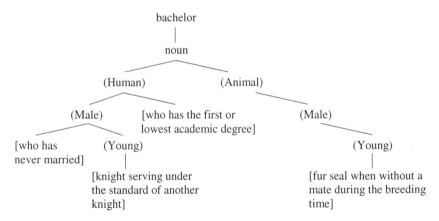

Returning to Bolinger now, we may note that he used the above *bachelor* analysis to argue that markers and distinguishers could be shown to be one and the same thing, with all the distinguishers reducible to markers (Bolinger 1965:558-562). Importantly, though, in the course of the argument the author granted the possibility of "a spot for distinguishers, or something like them", situated "a bit to one side" of where Katz & Fodor had placed them (Bolinger 1965:561). More specifically, distinguishers could be used to refer to knowledge of the world. This suggestion, abandoned later in the paper, was to be revived on several occasions (cf. e.g. Stachowiak 1982:15, and Klinkenberg 1983:298 = 1984:1173). According to Bolinger, it had the

---

[29] Ten years after the publication of my review (Peeters 1989) of Allan (1986), I am rather pleased with the amount of detail Allan chose to provide. Ironically, I was not so impressed back then.

advantage of reducing two dualisms to one, but the disadvantage of leaving the re-maining one intact. The author's reasons to also reject the second dualism were as follows (Bolinger 1965:568):

> The speaker's 'knowledge of the world' comes in at the point where two possible theories of disambiguation are pitted against each other, one a the-ory (the common one) that ambiguities are resolved by the context of situa-tion, the other that they are resolved by rules operating on markers that are part of the linguistic apparatus of a sentence. K-F do not deny the role of the nonlinguistic context in resolving many ambiguities; what they deny is that any tightly constructed theory can be built that will reflect its operation, be-cause it involves too much; nothing less, in fact, than everything we know. The example offered to illustrate the point is *Our store sells alligator shoes* vs. *Our store sells horse shoes.* Our knowledge of the world tells us that al-ligators do not wear shoes, hence the first of these cannot mean 'shoes for alligators', but that horses do, whence the second probably does not mean shoes made of horsehide. (...) In other words, we achieve a disambiguation by way of something that is not a semantic marker.
>
> But why is it not a semantic marker? Where do markers like (Animal), (Physical Object), (Young), and (Female) come from if not from our knowledge of the world? What is strange about (Shoe-wearing) as a seman-tic marker – not as general, surely, as (Female), but general enough? The discalced branch of Carmelite monks is identified by it, and it crops up every now and then as a mark of status, like horse-riding: 'A Methodist, it was said, is a Baptist who wears shoes...'[30]

Although they do receive a mention in his writings, Katz does not appear to have taken Bolinger's remarks as seriously as those of language philosopher Neil L. Wil-son, who is virtually unknown in linguistic quarters. In his review of Katz (1966), Wilson (1967:63) observed that "there is no sharp line between what properly be-longs in a dictionary and what properly belongs in an encyclopedia". In a footnote, he acknowledged that, for this "neat formulation", he was indebted to some "oral remarks of Katz's". The statement was as much a condemnation of Katz & Fodor's conception of the *dictionary* as it was a gloss of Quine's (1953) dismissal of a *sharp* boundary between analytic truths (which are "grounded in meanings independently of matters of fact", and therefore – according to Wilson – linguistic in nature) and

---

[30] Few others have raised the question of the origin of semantic markers ("Where do markers [...] come from if not from our knowledge of the world?") as clearly as Bolinger. Cavazza & Zweigen-baum (1995:342), who work in artificial intelligence, come close: they termed Katz & Fodor's ap-proach *referential*, "because the components used by Katz and Fodor were in fact properties of the *referent*, hence incorporating encyclopedic knowledge into an endless description". They added that this "also explains why the dictionary-encyclopedia controversy is active in Katz and Fodor's [1963] paper". For more criticism of the *horse shoe* (or *horseshoe*? – as opposed to *alligator shoe* vs. **alligatorshoe*) example, see Bolinger (1965:570).

synthetic truths (which are "grounded in fact", and therefore – again according to Wilson – encyclopedic in nature). The link between the dictionary-encyclopedia and the analytic-synthetic debates has been with us ever since (cf. Haiman 1980, Silingardi 1983:305 and Marconi 1997, among others, as well as the brief remarks in section 3).[31]

Katz (1972:73) construed Wilson's criticism – which, as I have mentioned, he seems to have found more worthy of a reply than Bolinger's – as an attempt to *replace* his dictionary entries with encyclopedia-like entries which present the "common core of factual beliefs about the referents of a word". This he found unacceptable. He defended at length his views of the *dictionary* and of what *dictionary entries* were supposed to look like (Katz 1972:68-82), and he continued to argue that there was no need for encyclopedic information or an encyclopedic component in a semantic theory. The following passage summarises his argumentation (for full details, see Katz 1972:ch.6):

> The proper question to ask is by what criterion are we to decide when a piece of information is correctly represented in the dictionary entry for a word as part of the dictionary's account of a sense of the word and when a piece of information is correctly excluded from lexical readings. (...) The criterion can be thought of as an answer to the following question: how do we make a justified choice between two lexical readings R_1 and R_2 for the word W if they are exactly the same except that R_2 but not R_1 contains a symbol or symbols that (*ex hypothesi*) represent information of the sort that properly belongs in an encyclopedia entry for the thing(s) to which W refers, i.e., information of a factual and purely contingent nature about everything to which W refers? (...) The answer, roughly, is that we are to choose R_2 over R_1 if the incorporation of R_2 in the dictionary of the semantic component as the lexical reading of W enables us to predict a range of semantic properties and relations of sentences (for example, their semantic ambiguity, synonymy, semantic anomaly, redundancy) that cannot be predicted by incorporating R_1 in the dictionary in place of R_2, and we are to choose R_1 over R_2 if the incorporation of R_2 in the dictionary entry for W does *not* enable us to predict anything that is not already predicted on the basis of R_1. What this criterion says, then, is that if the information represented in the symbol(s) that constitutes the only formal difference between R_2 and R_1 plays a role in predicting *semantic* properties and relations of sentences (...), then this information is dictionary information, information about meaning; but if we can simplify the dictionary entry for W by not including the symbol(s) that distinguish R_2 from R_1 without the semantic

---

[31] It might be useful to recall that the opposition between *analytic* and *synthetic* has in fact never been very precise, not among philosophers, and not among logicians and linguists either. For a recent review of a series of philosophical and linguistic debates, among which the one regarding the analytic-synthetic distinction, see Marconi (1997:29-56). Like Haiman, but unlike Silingardi, he reaches the conclusion that the distinction between lexical and encyclopedic knowledge cannot be upheld.

component's losing any predictive power, then this information is not dictionary information but encyclopedia information, factual information about the referent of W. (Katz 1972:76)

It appears as though Katz has never renounced the view that there is no place for encyclopedic knowledge in a semantic description, and that the distinction between "dictionary information" and "encyclopedia information" is an essential one. Chomsky, on the other hand, did not stick to his guns – and this may come as news to many. After the ringing endorsement in Chomsky (1965) came a change of mind that has apparently never been noted, which is surprising since remarks made by Chomsky usually do *not* go unnoticed. Unless they are uninformative, they are quoted and interpreted by friend and foe alike, to the point where they virtually start a life of their own (cf. Peeters forthcoming b). The statement I have in mind seems to have slipped through the net. Although it is far from being uninformative, I have seen it reported only once, namely by Silingardi (1983:305), who does not refer to either Katz & Fodor (1963) or Chomsky (1965). She does refer to one of four (!) identical publications in which Chomsky recognises that "a full dictionary cannot be distinguished in a principled way from an encyclopedia" (Chomsky 1977:36; cf. also Chomsky 1975a, 1975b, 1975c). The adjective *full* is of course important: it indicates that, according to Chomsky, writing in the seventies, a dictionary such as Katz & Fodor's was in fact an abridged encyclopedia, or part of an encyclopedia. Jackendoff, whose views are often close to Chomsky's, would later suggest that information in the lexical entry "shades toward 'encyclopedia' rather than 'dictionary' information, with no sharp line drawn between the two types" (Jackendoff 1983:139-140; cf. Wilson's formulation cited above).

The boundary problem raised by Bolinger (1965) and by Wilson (1967) has pushed some to adopt the view that, *where it exists*, encyclopedic knowledge is simply "more detailed" than lexical knowledge. The originality of this position, most clearly expressed in Leiss (1986:80), resides in the added comment. Leiss referred to the oft-discussed question "ob semantische Merkmale nur sprachlicher Art sind, oder ob auch sogenanntes Weltwissen, also enzyklopädisches Wissen Bestandteil der semantischen Merkmalsbündel ist", i.e. 'whether semantic features are exclusively linguistic in nature, or whether so-called knowledge of the world, in other words encyclopedic knowledge, may also be part of semantic feature bundles'. She then went on to say:[32]

---

[32] What follows is my own English translation of the German original. Leiss (1986) is a reply to Ziegler (1984), whose approach of the lexicon as a "catalogue of human knowledge about the world" she condemned as a form of "behaviourist regression" (Leiss 1986:76). Ziegler's concept of the lexicon had to be "the most uneconomical one that could be imagined". He "confuses lexicon and encyclopedia", but fails to see that "semantics is not the same thing as knowledge of the world" (ibid.).

Sprengel (1980), for instance, asks how sentences such as *The elephant had eighty legs* could be rejected as nonsensical. To reject such sentences, should he allow for an additional feature /+ four-legged/ in the word *elephant*? And how many more additional semantic features ought to be identified in the end to guarantee semantically correct utterances? The fact of the matter is that nouns, and in particular essentially referential terms, could not be adequately described without "knowledge of the world". As a result, the entries for *elephant* in a lexicon and in an encyclopedia are comparable, the only difference being that the encyclopedia provides even more information. The situation is different with respect to the closed class of relational terms [on this concept, see Born-Rauchenecker, this volume; B.P.]; as a general rule, they are not to be found among the entries in an encyclopedia, even though they will be found in a lexicon (...).

Sprengel's (1980) example of an elephant with eighty legs is strangely similar to Leech's (1981:84) example of a dog with eighty legs.[33] Leech pleaded against the inclusion of encyclopedic knowledge in semantic descriptions: he was of the opinion that "the oddity of propositions like 'The dog had eighty legs' is something that zoology has to explain rather than conceptual semantics". In Keith Allan's work, there are at least two different comments on this statement; they show, in a subtle way, that Allan's thoughts on the lexicon-encyclopedia interface have evolved over the years. Allan currently defends a view similar to that of Chomsky in the nineteen seventies and Leiss in the nineteen eighties (cf. below). Here is his first assessment of Leech's claim (Allan 1992:357):

Leech is mistaken, or rather he puts the wrong case: whereas we should look to zoology to explain why genera of higher animals have no more than four limbs, we should look to linguistic semantics to recognize that, if the speaker or writer is speaking of a world identical with or similar to ours, the statement *The dog had eighty legs* is either false or identifying an incredibly abnormal creature. If we are interested in properly accounting for discourse coherence (i.e., in the grammar of texts larger than a sentence), then this is surely a matter that an adequate linguistic semantics should recognize – and for exactly the same kinds of reasons that it recognizes the animacy of a dog (...).

Now, here is the same author, in a paper published a few years later (Allan 1995:294):

Leech is surely correct, but there has to be path from the listeme [= lexicon entry, B.P.] to directly access encyclopedic information about dogs (or whatever) because of Hearer's ability to 'shadow' a text very rapidly – that

---

[33] Sprengel's paper was originally delivered at a conference in Wuppertal (Germany) in 1977. One wonders whether Leech was there as well...

is, to begin understanding it and making appropriate inferences milliseconds after Speaker has presented it (cf. Marslen-Wilson 1985, 1989). Consequently, we might presume that

> The lexicon entry is one access point into the isomorphic set of encyclopedia entries, all of which are activated by recognition of the listeme.

> If the encyclopedia is a data-base, then the lexicon forms an integral component of the encyclopedia.

Given the entirely different assessment, it is perhaps not entirely surprising that there is no reference to Allan (1992) in Allan (1995). The new conclusion was however foreshadowed in a postscript (dated October 1991; Allan 1992:372-373), in which Allan *hypothesises* "that the lexicon is either part of, or closely associated with, the mental encyclopedia (or knowledge base)", before *suspecting* "that the encyclopedia incorporates not only a lexicon, but other linguistically relevant components". One such component uses encyclopedic information to abstract connotations, which are often crucial for the interpretation of non-literal meanings. Allan goes on to say that "yet another component that needs to be networked with the lexicon and the encyclopedia is one that stores metalinguistic information about expressions, their stylistic characteristics, and alternatives to them". Allan (1992) was about "something that rhymes with *rich*" (as a description of certain people). I take the author as saying, in the main body of his text, that Hearer (to use Allan's terminology) has typically no difficulty in retrieving the word *bitch*, because the information 'rhymes with *rich*' is part of "a complete semantic representation in the dictionary". I take him as saying, in his postscript, that that same piece of information is in fact retrieved from one of the linguistically relevant components of the encyclopedia other than the dictionary (namely, the one that stores metalinguistic information). I take him as saying, in Allan (1995) (which seems to be his current position; cf. Allan, this volume), that it is lexical knowledge after all, inasmuch as each lexical item in the lexicon has three kinds of specification (formal, morpho-syntactic, and semantic); "rhymes with *rich*" falls under formal specification (more particularly, of a phonological nature).

8. Eco

We are nearing the end of our survey of recent milestones in the lexicon-encyclopedia debate. Umberto Eco's work is often overlooked by linguists, possibly because he is not quite a linguist, but a semiotician. He is however among the most important critics of Katz & Fodor, and therefore deserves our attention. Eco (1976:98) endorsed Wilson's (1967) view that Katz & Fodor's model represented "the ideal competence of an ideal speaker". He added that "in the last analysis it can only lead to the making of a very elementary dictionary unable to explain social competence in all its living combinations". For Eco, the difference that mattered was that between the "abstract dictionary" and the "concrete encyclopedia". In fact, he appears to have gone further than that, claiming that *each meaning* conceals an encyclopedia of its own (Eco 1976:112-114). Whether he really meant to say that is an open question (for criticism, see Rastier 1987:258).

In more recent work, Eco (1984) has devoted an entire chapter on the lexicon-encyclopedia issue.[34] Again, he claimed that there was a need to go beyond semantic models that are based on a dictionary. No specific models were singled out, but it is clear that people such as Katz, Fodor and Postal once again bore the brunt of the attack. The arguments remained the same: however rigorous, a dictionary could not begin to account for situational meaning and for the manifold ways in which words may be used for communicative purposes. Eco pointed out that the sort of model needed was one that would integrate, either in part or in full, the respective domains of semantics and pragmatics.[35] The author called for the replacement of the idea of a relatively succinct dictionary with that of a complex system of encyclopedic competencies. He argued that semanticists had to wake up to the fact that a dictionary is nothing short of an unavowed (but very incomplete and inconsistent) encyclopedia, in other words an encyclopedia in disguise. This is in agreement with Haiman's (1980) critique, approved of by Eco (1984).

For those who believe that, in the first half of the eighties, Eco was engaging in Cognitive Linguistics *avant la lettre*, there is more to come.[36] Using language strangely reminiscent of later work by dozens of Cognitive Linguists, Eco (1984) proposed to organise encyclopedic knowledge in terms of the scenes, frames, scripts, etc. that had started to invade philosophy, linguistics and artificial intelligence. Apart from such scenes etc., the encyclopedia had to provide lexical meanings in the form of instructions for contextual insertion. To illustrate how an encyclopedic semantic model would work, Eco alleged several examples. For instance, to determine whether a speech act is an order or a request, we use encyclopedic knowledge. There is a workplace script that stipulates that bosses give orders to workers rather than the other way round. If the speaker is higher up in the hierarchy than the addressee, he or she is most likely issuing an order. Journalists, on the other hand, know for a fact

---

[34] All five chapters in Eco (1984), a work published at the same time in Italian and in English, are expanded and revised versions of entries originally written in Italian for the *Einaudi* encyclopedia.

[35] The study of presupposition (see also Lakoff in section 2 above), often seen as part of the brief of pragmaticians, is part of Eco's encyclopedic semantics, as described in Eco (1984).

[36] As an aside, I should point out that Eco's tone in his 1984 volume appears to be more moderate than that of many Cognitive Linguists. His conclusion at the time was that, once one has recognised the inevitability of an encyclopedic representation, nothing should prevent a return to a dictionary model, for practical reasons, in specific situations. As far as he was concerned, the encyclopedia was bound to remain a "semiotic postulate", because it cannot possibly be described in its entirety, and because it is not fully shared by all.

(it is part of their encyclopedic knowledge) that an evasive answer from a magistrate is indicative of the fact that the information sought is not yet available for public consumption. As for metaphors such as the one that I have just used (i.e. information for public consumption), their interpretation also relies on encyclopedic knowledge, as does the waiter's interpretation of my room service order of a hamburger with mustard. The waiter uses encyclopedic knowledge to gather that I am after a standard-sized hamburger, not one that is a mile long, nor one packed in a plastic container that I would have to smash with a hammer. The room service example is one borrowed by Eco from Searle (1979).[37]

9. Summaries and comments[38]

We have come a long way. I started off (section 1) with Cognitive Linguistics, then looked at the evolution of Lakoff's and Fillmore's thought (section 2). Haiman (1980) was identified as the source of the Cognitive Linguistics position, and of Wierzbicka's current views (section 3). I moved closer to the present time with Raskin (section 4), Pustejovsky (section 5), and Marantz (section 6). I finally returned to the golden days of generative grammar, and to the views that were put forward in the wake of Katz & Fodor's seminal paper on the structure of a semantic theory (sections 7 and 8). The time has come to have a closer look at what the contributors to the present volume have to offer. The headings that follow reflect the five parts of the book.

9.1. "Assessments"

The papers contributed by Reboul, Inchaurralde, and Taylor are either largely or exclusively meant as assessments. Reboul's paper is a nice illustration of the fact that "history repeats itself, with variations" (opening sentence of Bolinger 1965). I do not mean this in any negative way, but could not help being struck by Bolinger's *conclusion* to his critical appraisal of Katz & Fodor (1963). He stated, albeit conditionally, that "the theory of K-F is at best a partial theory of the semantics of a natural language, though it may be a very good theory of how to program for mechanical translation" (Bolinger 1965:573). This is very much how Reboul feels about Puste-

---

[37] According to Eco, not all inferences can possibly be based on encyclopedic knowledge. When someone talks to me about a soccer match, I may conclude that this person is lying to me, either because I saw the match and know that certain things reported did not happen, or because I know from experience that the person talking to me is a liar. It is not clear what sort of knowledge intervenes here, if not encyclopedic.

[38] This section relies to a considerable extent on multiple readings of all the papers that follow; it also relies on abstracts provided by the various authors. I do hope that, in the process of condensing these abstracts even further, I have not misrepresented anyone.

jovsky's *Generative Lexicon*. Inchaurralde, on the other hand, evaluates the evidence that decades of research have provided in favour of what Cognitive Linguists call the "encyclopedic view". The proposal to use the term *lexicopedia* to refer to a lexicon which is encyclopedic in contents and outlook appears set to make history. Taylor, finally, assesses the relative merits of the Cognitive Linguistics view and that of the "two-level model" associated with the work of Manfred Bierwisch, Ewald Lang and colleagues in Germany. Like Inchaurralde, he opts for the former.

* *Reboul*

Anne Reboul ("Words, concepts, mental representations, and other biological categories") assumes that both words and concepts are mental representations, albeit of a different kind. The former should be seen as a mode of access to the latter. Reboul's assumption leads to the formulation of a hypothesis on the boundary between lexical and encyclopedic knowledge that for now remains untested, even though it is claimed to be testable, both through standard psycholinguistic experiments, and against what is known about various types of language-impairment, whether hereditary or acquired. In other words, the author takes an empirical view of the distinction between lexicon and encyclopedia, as opposed to a methodological one. On the methodological view, the distinction is used mainly to help draw boundaries between domains of scientific investigation: it helps determine what is a proper topic for linguistics (namely, the lexicon), and what is not (namely, the encyclopedia). On the empirical view, the distinction is taken to be susceptible of empirical investigation; the immediate problem is to draw it in a way which is sufficiently precise to allow for empirical evaluation. Reboul bases much of her argument on an assessment of Pustejovsky's *Generative Lexicon* (cf. section 5); however, rather than to assess it on its merits as a model in artificial cognition (where it clearly belongs), she chooses to construct a model in natural cognition (her own side of the fence) that incorporates all the crucial features of Pustejovsky's model, without losing sight of what is important in natural cognition, namely psychological (and especially neurological) reality. Reboul's conclusion is that the *Generative Lexicon* model appears to have a brighter future in artificial cognition than it does in natural cognition, and that Pustejovsky has not drawn the line between lexicon and encyclopedia where it ought to be drawn.[39]

---

[39] There seems to be no general recognition yet of the implications that work on language pathologies may have for the lexicon-encyclopedia debate. Stachowiak (1982) is perhaps the only author to have actually *relied* on neurolinguistic experimentation to examine whether lexical meanings and encyclopedic knowledge have separate mental representations, instead of simply *suggesting* that this is the way to go. His conclusion is that the distinction is a legitimate one. There is no reference in Reboul's work to Stachowiak's research (see also Stachowiak 1979).

• *Inchaurralde*

According to Carlos Inchaurralde ("Lexicopedia"), the available evidence suggests that what he decides to call the "lexicon perspective" (illustrated in Reboul's paper, as well as in a number of other papers in the present volume) is in fact less attractive than the encyclopedic view of meaning espoused by most Cognitive Linguists (who do *not* seek to distinguish lexical and encyclopedic knowledge). Inchaurralde argues that, although there is *some* psycholinguistic evidence to support the so-called *conduit metaphor* (Reddy 1979), which he claims inspires work done within the lexicon perspective, other observations appear to lend further support to the idea of a "lexicopedia" (hence the title of the paper). Connectionist models, specifically of the PDP (parallel distributed processing) type, on the one hand, and Pribram's holographic brain theory, on the other hand, are said to have a better chance of accounting for the truly distributed – and encyclopedic – nature of the lexicopedia in our minds than computational simulations that, by integrating different layers of information within individual lexical entries and subsequently linking them by means of different kinds of networks, do provide helpful insights, but at a cost: the simulations referred to are generally rather unrealistic from a psychological point of view. Inchaurralde's previous experience in both natural and artificial cognition add, I believe, considerable poignancy to his claims.

• *Taylor*

John R. Taylor ("Approaches to word meaning: The network model (Langacker) and the two-level model (Bierwisch) in comparison", originally published in René Dirven & Johan Vanparys (ed.), *Current approaches to the lexicon*, Frankfurt, Peter Lang, 1995, pp. 3-26) compares two theoretical frameworks situated on opposite ends of the spectrum. In his title, he refers to them as the "network model" and the "two-level model". Only the latter label has a certain currency in linguistics, even though the author whose approach is being described (Manfred Bierwisch) has never used the term himself. The former is not at all common; reference is in fact made to Cognitive Linguistics, more specifically to Ronald Langacker's version of it, usually called Cognitive Grammar. The two-level model is based on a rigorous separation of lexical and encyclopedic knowledge, whereas the network model rests on the assumption that no such separation is either needed or indeed feasible. Taylor's paper is followed by a newly written afterword in which the author revisits and updates his earlier findings.[40]

---

[40] [Late footnote] In an early co-authored paper not mentioned by Taylor (Bierwisch & Kiefer 1969), there are a number of interesting observations on linguistic and encyclopedic knowledge. One of the examples used involves the word *spoon*, also used later by Raskin (1985a) (cf. section 4).

9.2. *"Understanding understanding"*

More than the other papers in the present volume, those of Larrivée, Allan, and Croft deal with utterance interpretation, an area of scholarly endeavour that very few linguists these days would reject as irrelevant to their concerns. In the seventies, the situation was still markedly different. Almost two decades ago, Klinkenberg (1983:297-298 = 1984:1173-1174) observed that if linguists were ever to account in a satisfactory way for "rhetorical effects" such as metaphor, metonymy, and synecdoche, linguistics itself had to give up part of its "theoretical purity" and become a theory of utterance interpretation. Klinkenberg then went on to quote Ruwet (1975:372), who several years earlier had indicated what such a theory might consist of. Ruwet listed the following five components: a) a semantic theory for utterance interpretation; b) a theory of reference; c) a speech act theory; d) a theory on the effects of context, discourse, and situation; and e) an encyclopedia. He defined component a) as being fully linguistic, did not believe that the role of linguistics in components b) to d) was clear at all, and was convinced that component e) (that is, the encyclopedia) had nothing to do with linguistics whatsoever. Klinkenberg did not endorse Ruwet's opinion: he did not think the exclusion of the encyclopedia was at all warranted (cf. section 5). Larrivée, Allan, and Croft share that view, each in their own individual ways. They do not refer to either Ruwet or Klinkenberg.

- *Larrivée*

Pierre Larrivée ("Linguistic meaning, knowledge, and utterance interpretation") shows that, from an analytical point of view, the knowledge that speakers have of their own experience must be distinguished from linguistic meaning, which is underspecified. In support of his claim, Larrivée examines various instances of distortion between literal and situational meaning, before undertaking a brief study of focus phenomena.[41] Importantly, though, distinction does not preclude interaction: Larrivée goes on to show that, in utterance interpretation, knowledge and meaning must be viewed as closely interacting with one another to yield the correct understanding of linguistic sequences. The inferential process that takes place is exemplified with reference to the previously considered focus phenomena. Larrivée concludes that the interpretation of linguistic utterances is the result of the interaction of distinct yet interconnected levels of representation.

- *Allan*

Keith Allan ("Quantity implicatures and the lexicon") argues that there is a division of labour between the lexicon and the encyclopedia: the lexicon contains formal, morphosyntactic, and semantic specifications of lexical items (called *listemes* by the author) and the encyclopedia contains other kinds of information about them, such as their etymology, and information about their denotata. Implicatures, on the other

---

[41] For more on focus phenomena, see now Bosch & van der Sandt (1999).

hand, are pragmatic: they arise from the use of language in particular contexts. They differ from entailments in being defeasible. Even though some could be said to be at the interface between the lexicon and the encyclopedia, Allan's claim is that quantity implicatures (where *quantity* refers to Grice's 1975 maxim of quantity) have a place in the lexicon. Consider the NP *three birds*. It is part of the lexical knowledge of the language user that the lexical meaning of *three* includes both the indefeasible (logical) meaning 'greater than or equal to three (at least three)' and the defeasible quantity 1 implicature identifying the default meaning 'equal to three (exactly three)'. The lexical meaning of *bird* includes both an indefeasible part identifying the class of creatures, and a defeasible part 'capable of flight' – a quantity 2 implicature. The difference between Q1 and Q2 implicatures is that the former involve some sort of downscaling, whereas the latter involve augmentation. Surveying many examples of quantity implicature, Allan finds that all Q implicatures based on a single lexical item are noted in the lexicon entry. Nonlexical implicatures arise from collocations of lexical items and can perhaps be located within the encyclopedia of which the lexicon is a part.

- *Croft*

In "The role of domains in the interpretation of metaphors and metonymies" (originally published in *Cognitive Linguistics* 4, 1993, and reprinted here with a newly added afterword), William Croft shows some of the advantages that an encyclopedic approach such as the one taken by Cognitive Linguists may have for the study of metaphor and metonymy. He argues that metaphorical and metonymical interpretation of individual words is determined by the interpretation of the entire construction in which those words are found. The entire construction provides clues as to the *domain* in which the words are to be interpreted. Croft's domains are comparable to the frames, mental spaces, scripts etc. referred to above (section 1). Whereas metaphor consists of a mapping of conceptual structure from one domain to another, metonymy is based on the highlighting of a particular domain in a domain matrix. The processes of domain mapping and domain highlighting are subjected to detailed study. The afterword looks at recent claims made by Geoffrey Nunberg, whose earlier research is covered in the body of the paper.[42]

---

[42] Croft's position regarding metaphor and metonymy is not the only possible one in a tradition that argues that linguistic knowledge is necessarily encyclopedic. It appears to be rather different from the view expressed, for instance, by Dirven (1993). The most important difference has to do with metonymy, which is defined in terms of domain *annexation*. Metonymy involves the linking of adjacent or contiguous domains (in some cases subdomains, or parts of domains) that are being juxtaposed (rather than superimposed or mapped), and reconstructed as one. Metaphor, on the other hand, remains a question of domain mapping, combined with suppression or annihilation of the source domain by the target domain. Metaphorical mapping involves contrasting rather than similar domains. In metaphor, what is exploited is conceptual distance. In metonymy, conceptual closeness is exploited instead. A confrontation of opposing views such as those of Dirven and Croft should convince us of one thing at least: namely, the pressing need for a clarification of the notion of "domain" (cf. Dirven

9.3. "Words, words, words"

The four papers in the third part of the present volume deal with strictly lexical matters. While Hudson & Holmes, who adopt Word Grammar as their theoretical framework, reject the need for a division, Born-Rauchenecker points out that in lexicography there *is* a need for a principled distinction. Murphy zooms in on the distinction between lexical and encyclopedic knowledge of words *irrespective* of their referents, thereby restricting lexical knowledge to a far greater extent than is usually done. Harley & Noyer's "vocabulary" is also extremely restricted, in line with the general principles of Distributed Morphology.

- *Hudson & Holmes*

Adopting Word Grammar (Hudson 1990, Hudson & Van Langendonck 1991) as the general framework for their study, Richard Hudson & Jasper Holmes ("Re-cycling in the lexicon") revisit the linguistic world of bicycles described fifteen years ago by Wierzbicka (1985). Whereas Wierzbicka distinguished dictionary information from encyclopedic information, with the former including details on the parts of a bicycle, their relationship, their use, and how the bicycles themselves are to be operated, and the latter details on history, production, and development, together with technical information, Hudson & Holmes adopt the view that dictionary and encyclopedia are not to be distinguished: language, for them, is a knowledge network (for which Word Grammar has devised a particular representation) where no clear boundary exists between different areas of knowledge, for instance between lexicon and grammar, or between linguistic meaning and encyclopedic knowledge. The idea is one taken over from early work in Cognitive Linguistics, and is held to reflect the facts of language.

In the title of their paper, Hudson & Holmes refer to the principle of "recycling". Concepts are recycled rather than duplicated. At the interface between the encyclopedia and the lexicon, this means that a concept may serve both as the meaning of a word and also as part of ordinary non-linguistic cognition; for example, the ordinary concept "bicycle" which we use in everyday life in classifying experiences is also the sense of the noun *bicycle*, and similarly for the concept "cycling", which is the sense of the verb *cycle*. Hudson & Holmes offer a partial analysis of both these concepts which illustrates the difficulty, and pointlessness, of trying to separate lexical and encyclopedic properties. The recycling principle also means that wherever possible meaning of words should be recycled in the definitions of other words. It is therefore wrong in principle to try to define all word meanings in terms of a universal semantic vocabulary. On this score, Hudson & Holmes disagree quite dramatically with Wierzbicka. They show, for example, how "cycling" must be defined in

---

1993:12, and Nerlich forthcoming). A closer look at synecdoche, often "subsumed under metonymy" (as pointed out by Croft, with respect to the part-whole synecdoche), may be an attractive strategy to help achieve that aim (Nerlich ibid.).

terms of concepts such as "bicycle", which must in turn be defined in terms of "pedal", "pedalling" and so on.

- *Born-Rauchenecker*

Eva Born-Rauchenecker ("Towards an operationalisation of the lexicon-encyclopedia distinction: A case study in the description of verbal meanings in Russian") argues that a principled distinction between lexical and encyclopedic knowledge is crucial in the field of lexicography. She points out that a largely encyclopedic approach such as is now common in Cognitive Linguistics brings with it a demarcation problem: when linguists describe synchronic semantic variation (polysemy) or diachronic semantic variation (semantic change), they still need to decide whether any new usage of a word constitutes a new sense or is a contextually determined variant. The semantic description of any lexical item will involve (or reflect) the application of a number of criteria for separating encyclopedic from semantic knowledge. Three such criteria are proposed, based on a detailed study of lexicographical practice concerning one particular kind of relational lexical item, namely concrete transitive action verbs in Russian.

- *Murphy*

M. Lynne Murphy ("Knowledge *of* words vs. knowledge *about* words: the conceptual basis of lexical relations") draws the line between lexical and encyclopedic knowledge in a rather original way. Traditional divisions of lexicon and encyclopedia have associated the former with knowledge relative to a word's meaning and the latter with knowledge relative to its referents. Murphy, on the other hand, is interested in encyclopedic knowledge speakers may have of words (regardless of their denotata). The sort of questions she asks may be exemplified as follows: Which of the following facts about the word *dog* belong in the encyclopedic realm? That its opposite is *cat*? That my cousin pronounces it strangely? Its frequency in crossword puzzles?

Murphy's paper considers two frameworks for knowledge about lexical items. The first takes knowledge structure to be modular – which means that there is a distinction between lexicon and encyclopedia. This does not mean that lexical relations such as antonymy are stored in the lexicon. Murphy would not buy Cavazza & Zweigenbaum's (1995) definition according to which, in the dictionary approach, "a word is defined through *linguistic* knowledge, for instance with the help of relations to other words like synonymy-antonymy, or hyperonymy-hyponymy". Lexical relations have nothing to do with our knowledge *of* words: they constitute knowledge *about* words, which is part of our knowledge of the world. Lexical relations are non-arbitrary, and the lexicon only contains arbitrary information. In the second framework, lexical knowledge is a subtype of conceptual knowledge – which means that there is no separate lexicon. Relations among words are generated through and derivable from two general and interrelated cognitive principles. Rather than linguistic knowledge *of* words, they constitute again conceptual knowledge *about* them. Murphy finds most promise in the latter framework: it allows for a good explanation of behaviour in psycholinguistic tests (such as free word association), as well as for a variety of factors to come into play in judgements of word-relatedness. The model accounts for different levels of rigidity or context-sensitivity in antonymic pairings or synonymic groupings, since the relations may be learned through experience or derived from other concepts. Murphy concludes by showing that her findings are compatible with a variety of current positions on whether semantic content can be represented in the lexicon.

- *Harley & Noyer*

Heidi Harley and Rolf Noyer ("Formal versus encyclopedic properties of vocabulary: Evidence from nominalisations") point out that theories of syntax emerging from the Government and Binding tradition rely on a Lexicon to construct morphophonologically complex objects – words – which form the atoms of syntactic representation. Distributed Morphology (cf. section 6) departs radically from the above. Phrase-markers are constructed freely out of abstract categories defined by universal features, including such "functional" features as tense, number, person, definiteness and so forth. Phonological expressions called *vocabulary items* are inserted into syntactic structures at Spell-Out after syntactic operations. Instead of a Lexicon, there are a number of Lexicon-replacements, one of which is the Encyclopedia, where specific meanings are stored.

Harley & Noyer defend the view that argument structure alternations arise when vocabulary items are underspecified for the syntactic structure which licenses them. They see different argument structures as determined by different syntactic configurations and not by vocabulary items themselves. For example, the VI *break* is licensed in both an ergative and an unaccusative syntax. They develop an account of licensing which predicts the correct class of observed alternations. Second, they examine whether the ill-formedness of expressions such as #*John's growth of tomatoes* or #*I saw three oxygens in the kitchen* derives from grammatical properties strictly speaking or from extragrammatical knowledge speakers have about the meaning of the vocabulary items inserted in these structures. Throughout their paper, # is used to signal pragmatic anomaly; * is reserved for downright ungrammaticality. Harley & Noyer conclude that the theory of syntax proper should not account for the anomalousness of these expressions.

9.4. "Grammar"

The papers contributed by Hilferty and Pensalfini are very different both in outlook and in content. Whereas the first is written from within a Cognitive Linguistics perspective, the second builds on the tenets of Distributed Morphology. Both papers are data-driven: Hilferty works on Spanish data, and Pensalfini describes facts found in Jingulu (an Australian aboriginal language).

- *Hilferty*

To illustrate the reality of direct interaction between world knowledge, grammar and the lexicon, Joseph Hilferty ("Grammar, the lexicon, and encyclopedic knowledge: is there such a thing as informational encapsulation?") singles out a case of verb complementation (namely, Spanish *tener* 'have' followed by a bare NP) the intricacies of which, in his view, can only be explained by invoking underlying encyclopedic-knowledge structures. The interaction of such disparate types of information has obvious repercussions for modular conceptions of language: Hilferty claims that the notion of syntax as an informationally encapsulated process is basically flawed. In light of the evidence at hand, it is argued that an interactionist view affords a more adequate depiction of the relationship between grammar, the lexicon, and encyclopedic knowledge. The ball is in the modularists' court: if we find phenomena that can be naturally explained if we do accept interaction, then it is up to the modularist to prove that another explanation is possible which does not imply such interaction.

- *Pensalfini*

Like Harley & Noyer (cf. above), Rob Pensalfini ("Encyclopedia-lexicon distinctions in Jingulu grammar") adopts the theoretical framework of Distributed Morphology. The chosen topic is however vastly different: English makes room for Jingulu. Pensalfini uses the DM distinction between formal and encyclopedic features to give a principled account of a range of phenomena including nonconfigurational syntax, but also word formation and phonological behaviour. He shows how a range of apparently disparate and individually quite bizarre phenomena in one language all derive from the same distinction in the grammar. Pensalfini has done extensive research on Jingulu, leading to a PhD thesis and a forthcoming article in *Natural language and linguistic theory* (for precise references, see the bibliography at the end of Pensalfini's paper). The study presented in this volume is a synthesis of the theoretical sections of the PhD, although at least some of the ideas put forward here are somewhat advanced from the way they were presented there.

9.5. *"Further afield"*

The two final contributions to the present volume approach the lexicon-encyclopedia debate from further afield. Feigenbaum's paper is, as far as I can tell, the first ever to canvass the need for and the implications of a distinction in the area of second language learning. In natural language processing quarters, on the other hand, the distinction is well-known and has received considerable attention.[43] Raskin's work in the area contributes in a very important way to current debates in artificial cognition.

---

[43] The lexicon of most AI systems has included lexical *and* encyclopedic knowledge. How else would these systems be able to cope with the inferences that humans seem to make so effortlessly? Nonetheless, a distinction is perhaps in place after all, to limit the potentially infinite number of inferences

• *Feigenbaum*

Susanne Feigenbaum ("Lexical and encyclopedic knowledge in an *ab initio* German reading course") argues that world knowledge may *support* but not *replace* linguistic knowledge. Even with the support of contextual inferences based on world knowledge, communication by means of deficient vocabulary is severely hampered. Feigenbaum also hypothesises that there are several forms of encyclopedic knowledge which interact with the lexicon. The author's observations are based on the performance of students enrolled in an *ab initio* reading course. From the outset, such students must use lexical and encyclopedic knowledge strategies alternately so as to compensate for lacking vocabulary. Foreign language learners in comprehensive courses, on the other hand, start with lexical knowledge strategies and abandon the latter in favour of world knowledge as their vocabulary expands. The advantages and disadvantages of the combined method are discussed, with particular reference to sources of errors and stages in the learning process.

• *Raskin, Attardo & Attardo*

The centerpiece of the paper co-authored by Victor Raskin, Salvatore Attardo & Donalee H. Attardo ("Augmenting linguistic semantics descriptions for NLP: Lexical knowledge, encyclopedic knowledge, event structure", reprinted from *Machine translation* 9, 1994) is SMEARR, an enriched and augmented lexical database with a database management system and several peripherals. The authors show that, to be usable in natural language processing, linguistic semantic descriptions have to be reformalised and considerably expanded. They are led to question the validity of the original descriptions, and raise the issue of whether the SMEARR entries are still exclusively lexical in nature. It is argued that NLP specialists may not particularly care about the origin of specific pieces of information.[44] Not to ask such questions is dangerous for lexical theorists, though, because it opens the door to unlimited polysemy and to either under- or overspecification. Raskin et al. suggest that lexical knowledge may range from a minimum to a maximum value. How exactly both values may be determined is the topic of research reported on in Raskin's afterword, newly added to the reprint of the original article.

---

a computer might otherwise come up with. Cavazza & Zweigenbaum (1995) argue that the construction of large multi-purpose encyclopedic lexicons for natural language understanding is an intractable task. They therefore opt for a "dictionary approach", and look for means to describe relevant linguistic information associated with given words.

[44] Cf. Raskin (1985a:96-97): "Whenever scholars in this area address the issue, which does not happen frequently because, generally, the interest to theory there is very weak for lack of material stimulation and linguistic sophistication, they almost invariably deny the existence of any boundary between the two kinds of knowledge, insisting that the two are handled in an exactly identical way in their systems". Cf. also section 4 above.

References

Allan, Keith. 1986. *Linguistic meaning* (2 vol.). London: Routledge & Kegan Paul.

Allan, Keith. 1992. "Something that rhymes with rich". In Adrienne Lehrer & Eva F. Kittay (ed.), *Frames, fields, and contrasts. New essays in semantic and lexical organization.* Hillsdale: Lawrence Erlbaum. 355-374.

Allan, Keith. 1995. "What names tell about the lexicon and the encyclopedia". *Lexicology* 1. 280-325.

Baumgärtner, Klaus. 1967. "Die Struktur des Bedeutungsfeldes". In Hugo Moser (ed.), *Satz und Wort im heutigen Deutsch. Probleme und Ergebnisse neuerer Forschung.* Düsseldorf: Schwann. 165-197.

Bierwisch, Manfred. 1967. "Some semantic universals of German adjectivals". *Foundations of language* 3. 1-36.

Bierwisch, Manfred; Kiefer, Ferenc. 1969. "Remarks on definitions in natural language". In Ferenc Kiefer (ed.), *Studies in syntax and semantics.* Dordrecht: Reidel. 55-79.

Bolinger, Dwight. 1965. "The atomization of meaning". *Language* 41. 555-573.

Bosch, Peter; van der Sandt, Rob (ed.). 1999. *Focus. Linguistic, cognitive, and computational perspectives.* Cambridge: Cambridge University Press.

Cavazza, Marc; Zweigenbaum, Pierre. 1995. "Lexical semantics. Dictionary or encyclopedia?". In Patrick Saint-Dizier & Evelyne Viegas (ed.), *Computational lexical semantics. Studies in natural language processing.* Cambridge: Cambridge University Press. 336-347.

Chomsky, Noam. 1965. *Aspects of the theory of syntax.* Cambridge: M.I.T. Press.

Chomsky, Noam. 1975a. "Questions of form and interpretation". In Robert Austerlitz (ed.), *The scope of American linguistics.* Lisse: Peter de Ridder. 159-196.

Chomsky, Noam. 1975b. *Questions of form and interpretation.* Lisse: Peter de Ridder.

Chomsky, Noam. 1975c. "Questions of form and interpretation". *Linguistic analysis* 1. 75-109.

Chomsky, Noam. 1977. *Essays on form and interpretation.* New York: North-Holland.

Cuenca, Maria Josep; Hilferty, Joseph. 1999. *Introducción a la lingüística cognitiva.* Barcelona: Ariel.

Dirven, René. 1993. "Metonymy and metaphor. Different mental strategies of conceptualisation". *Leuvense bijdragen* 82. 1-28.

Dirven, René; Verspoor, Marjolijn (ed.). 1999. *Cognitive exploration of language and linguistics*. Amsterdam: John Benjamins.

Eco, Umberto. 1976. *A theory of semiotics*. Bloomington: Indiana University Press.

Eco, Umberto. 1984. *Semiotics and philosophy of language*. Bloomington: Indiana University Press.

Fauconnier, Gilles. 1994 [1985]. *Mental spaces. Aspects of meaning construction in natural language*. Cambridge: Cambridge University Press.

Fillmore, Charles J. 1969. "Types of lexical information". In Ferenc Kiefer (ed.), *Studies in syntax and semantics*. Dordrecht: Reidel. 109-137.

Fillmore, Charles J. 1975. "An alternative to checklist theories of meaning". In Cathy Cogen, Henry Thompson, Graham Thurgood, Kenneth Whistler & James Wright (ed.), *Proceedings of the first annual meeting of the Berkeley Linguistics Society*. Berkeley: Berkeley Linguistics Society. 123-131.

Fillmore, Charles J. 1976. "Frame semantics and the nature of language". In Steven R. Harnad, Horst D. Steklis & Jane Lancaster (ed.), *Origins and evolution of language and speech*. New York: Annals of the New York Academy of Sciences. 20-32.

Fillmore, Charles J. 1977a. "Topics in lexical semantics". In Roger W. Cole (ed.), *Current issues in linguistic theory*. Bloomington: Indiana University Press. 76-138.

Fillmore, Charles J. 1977b. "Scenes-and-frames semantics". In Antonio Zampolli (ed.), *Linguistic structures processing*. Amsterdam: North-Holland. 55-81.

Fillmore, Charles J. 1982. "Frame semantics". In Linguistic Society of Korea (ed.), *Linguistics in the morning calm*. Seoul: Hanshin. 111-137.

Fillmore, Charles J. 1985. "Frames and the semantics of understanding". *Quaderni di semantica* 6. 222-254.

Fillmore, Charles J.; Atkins, Beryl T. 1992. "Toward a frame-based lexicon. The semantics of RISK and its neighbors". In Adrienne Lehrer & Eva F. Kittay (ed.), *Frames, fields, and contrasts. New essays in semantic and lexical organization*. Hillsdale: Lawrence Erlbaum. 75-102.

Frawley, William. 1981. "In defense of the dictionary. A response to Haiman". *Lingua* 55. 53-61.

Geeraerts, Dirk. 1985. "Les données stéréotypiques, prototypiques et encyclopédiques dans le dictionnaire". *Cahiers de lexicologie* 46. 27-43.

Geeraerts, Dirk. 1988a. "Cognitive grammar and the history of lexical semantics". In Brygida Rudzka-Ostyn (ed.), *Topics in cognitive linguistics*. Amsterdam: John Benjamins. 647-677.

Geeraerts, Dirk. 1988b. Review of Wierzbicka (1985). *Language in society* 17. 449-455.

Geeraerts, Dirk. 2000. "Idealistic tendencies in cognitive linguistics". In Theo Janssen & Gisela Redeker (ed.), *Cognitive linguistics. Foundations, scope, and methodology.* Berlin: Mouton de Gruyter. 211-242.

Geeraerts, Dirk; Grondelaers, Stefan; Bakema, Peter. 1994. *The structure of lexical variation. Meaning, naming, and context.* Berlin: Mouton de Gruyter.

Geiger, Richard A.; Rudzka-Ostyn, Brygida (ed.). 1993. *Conceptualizations and mental processing in language.* Berlin: Mouton de Gruyter.

Godard, Danièle; Jayez, Jacques. 1993a. "Towards a proper treatment of coercion phenomena". *Proceedings of the sixth conference of the European Chapter of the Association for Computational Linguistics.* Morristown: Association for Computational Linguistics. 168-177.

Godard, Danièle; Jayez, Jacques. 1993b. "Le traitement lexical de la coercion". *Cahiers de linguistique française* 14. 123-149.

Goddard, Cliff. 1989. Review of Kövecses (1986). *Lingua* 77. 90-98.

Goddard, Cliff. 1998. *Semantic analysis. A practical introduction.* Oxford: Oxford University Press.

Goddard, Cliff. Forthcoming. "Verbal explication and the place of NSM semantics in cognitive linguistics". In June Luchjenbroers (ed.), *Cognitive linguistics investigations across languages, fields, and philosophical boundaries.* Amsterdam: John Benjamins.

Greimas, Algirdas Julien. 1966. *Sémantique structurale.* Paris: Larousse.

Grice, H. Paul. 1975. "Logic and conversation". In Peter Cole & Jerry L. Morgan (ed.), *Speech acts (Syntax and semantics,* vol. 3). New York: Academic Press. 41-58.

Groupe μ. 1976. "Isotopie et allotopie. Le fonctionnement rhétorique du texte". *Versus* 14. 41-65.

Groupe μ. 1977. *Rhétorique de la poésie.* Bruxelles: Complexe.

Haiman, John. 1980. "Dictionaries and encyclopedias". *Lingua* 50. 329-357.

Haiman, John. 1982. "Dictionaries and encyclopedias again". *Lingua* 56. 353-355.

Halle, Morris. 1973. "Prolegomena to a theory of word formation". *Linguistic inquiry* 4. 3-16.

Halle, Morris; Marantz, Alec. 1993. "Distributed morphology and the pieces of inflection". In Kenneth L. Hale & Samuel Jay Keyser (ed.), *The view from building 20.* Cambridge: M.I.T. Press. 111-176.

Halle, Morris; Marantz, Alec. 1994. "Some key features of Distributed Morphology". In Andrew Carnie & Heidi Harley (ed.), *Papers on phonology and morphology (M.I.T. working papers in linguistics*, 21). Cambridge: MITWPL. 275-288.

Harley, Heidi; Noyer, Rolf. Forthcoming. "State-of-the-article. Distributed Morphology". *Glot international* 4.

Hatakeyama, Katsuhiko; Petöfi, János S.; Sözer, Emel. 1984. "Text, Konnexität, Kohäsion, Kohärenz". In Maria-Elisabeth Conte (ed.), *Kontinuität und Diskontinuität in Texten und Sachverhalts-Konfigurationen. Diskussion über Konnexität, Kohäsion und Kohärenz.* Hamburg: Buske. 1-55.

Hudson, Richard. 1985. "Some basic assumptions about linguistic and non-linguistic knowledge". *Quaderni di semantica* 6. 284-287.

Hudson, Richard. 1990. *English word grammar.* Oxford: Blackwell.

Hudson, Richard; Van Langendonck, Willy. 1991. "Word grammar". In: Flip G. Droste & John E. Joseph (ed.), *Linguistic theory and grammatical description.* Amsterdam: John Benjamins. 307-336.

Jackendoff, Ray. 1983. *Semantics and cognition.* Cambridge: M.I.T. Press.

Jayez, Jacques. 1996. "Référence et aspectualité. Le problème des verbes dits 'aspectuels'". *Cahiers de linguistique française* 18. 275-298.

Katz, Jerrold J. 1964. "Semantic theory and the meaning of 'good'". *Journal of philosophy* 61. 739-766.

Katz, Jerrold J. 1966. *The philosophy of language.* New York: Harper & Row.

Katz, Jerrold J. 1972. *Semantic theory.* New York: Harper & Row.

Katz, Jerrold J.; Fodor, Jerry A. 1963. "The structure of a semantic theory". *Language* 39. 170-210.

Katz, Jerrold J.; Postal, Paul M. 1964. *An integrated theory of linguistic description.* Cambridge: M.I.T. Press.

Keesing, Roger M. 1979. "Linguistic knowledge and cultural knowledge. Some doubts and speculations". *American anthropologist* 81. 14-36.

Kleiber, Georges. 1997. "Prédicat et coercion. Le cas de *commencer*". *Sémiotiques* 13. 179-199. Updated reprint: Kleiber (1999:173-209).

Kleiber, Georges. 1999. *Problèmes de sémantique. La polysémie en questions.* Villeneuve d'Ascq: Presses Universitaires du Septentrion.

Klinkenberg, Jean-Marie. 1983. "Problèmes de la synecdoque. Du sémantique à l'encyclopédique". *Le français moderne* 51. 289-299.

Klinkenberg, Jean-Marie. 1984. "Le rôle du composant encyclopédique en linguistique". In Tasso Borbé (ed.), *Semiotics unfolding. Proceedings of the second congress of the International Association for Semiotic Studies*, vol. 3. Berlin: Mouton. 1169-1174.

Kövecses, Zoltán. 1986. *Metaphors of anger, pride and love. A lexical approach to the structure of concepts*. Amsterdam: John Benjamins.

Lakoff, George. 1971. "Presupposition and relative well-formedness". In Danny D. Steinberg & Leon A. Jakobovits (ed.), *Semantics. An interdisciplinary reader in philosophy, linguistics and psychology*. Cambridge: Cambridge University Press. 329-340.

Lakoff, George. 1972. "Hedges. A study in meaning criteria and the logic of fuzzy concepts". In Paul M. Peranteau, Judith N. Levi & Gloria C. Phares (ed.), *Papers from the eighth regional meeting of the Chicago Linguistic Society*. 183-228. Chicago: Chicago Linguistic Society. Also in *Journal of philosophical logic* 2 (1973). 458-508.

Lakoff, George. 1974. Interview with Herman Parret. In Herman Parret (ed.), *Discussing language*. The Hague: Mouton. 151-178. Also in Charles J. Fillmore, George Lakoff & Robin Lakoff (ed.). 1974. *Berkeley studies in syntax and semantics*, vol. 1. Berkeley: Institute of Human Learning & Department of Linguistics, UCB. XI-1 – XI-44.

Lakoff, George. 1987. *Women, fire and dangerous things*. Chicago: Chicago University Press.

Lakoff, George. 1990. "The invariance hypothesis. Is abstract reason based on image-schemas?". *Cognitive linguistics* 1. 39-74.

Lakoff, George; Johnson, Mark. 1980. *Metaphors we live by*. Chicago: University of Chicago Press.

Lakoff, George; Thompson, Henry. 1975. "Dative questions in cognitive grammar". In Robin E. Grossman, L. James San and Timothy J. Vance (ed.), *Papers from the parasession on functionalism*. Chicago: Chicago Linguistic Society. 337-350.

Langacker, Ronald W. 1987. *Foundations of cognitive grammar*, vol. 1. *Theoretical prerequisites*. Stanford: Stanford University Press.

Langacker, Ronald W. 1990. *Concept, image, and symbol. The cognitive basis of grammar*. Berlin: Mouton de Gruyter.

Langacker, Ronald W. 1997. "The contextual basis of cognitive semantics". In Jan Nuyts & Eric Pederson (ed.), *Language and conceptualization*. Cambridge: Cambridge University Press. 229-252.

Leech, Geoffrey. 1981 [1974]. *Semantics. A study of meaning.* Harmondsworth: Penguin.

Lehrer, Adrienne. 1988. Review of Wierzbicka (1985). *Studies in language* 12. 235-239.

Leiss, Elisabeth. 1986. "Das Lexikon ist keine Enzyklopädie. Antwort auf J. Ziegler, LB 93 (1984)". *Linguistische Berichte* 101. 74-84.

Marantz, Alec. 1997. "No escape from syntax. Don't try morphological analysis in the privacy of your own lexicon". In Alexis Dimitriadis, Laura Siegel, Clarissa Surek-Clark & Alexander Williams (ed.), *Proceedings of the 21st annual Penn linguistics colloquium (U. Penn working papers in linguistics* 4:2). Philadelphia: University of Pennsylvania. 201-225.

Marconi, Diego. 1997. *Lexical competence.* London: Bradford.

Marslen-Wilson, William D. 1985. "Speech shadowing and speech comprehension". *Speech communication* 4. 55-73.

Marslen-Wilson, William D. 1989. "Access and integration. Projecting sound onto meaning". In William D. Marslen-Wilson (ed.), *Lexical representation and processing.* Cambridge: M.I.T. Press. 3-24.

Minsky, Marvin L. 1975. "A framework for representing knowledge". In Patrick H. Winston (ed.), *The psychology of computer vision.* New York: McGraw Hill. 211-277.

Nerlich, Brigitte. Forthcoming. "Synecdoche. A trope, a whole trope, and nothing but a trope?". In Neal R. Norrick & Armin Burckhardt (ed.), *Tropical truth.* Amsterdam: John Benjamins.

Neubauer, Fritz; Petöfi, János S. 1981. "Word semantics, lexicon systems, and text interpretation". In Hans-Jürgen Eikmeyer & Hannes Rieser (ed.), *Words, worlds, and contexts. New approaches in word semantics.* Berlin: Walter de Gruyter. 343-377.

Nirenburg, Sergei; Raskin, Victor. 1996. *Ten choices for lexical semantics* (Computing Research Laboratory monograph MCCS-96-304). Las Cruces: New Mexico State University. Also available at http://omni.cc.purdue.edu/~raskin/Choices.pdf.

Nuyts, Jan. 1992. *Aspects of a cognitive-pragmatic theory of language.* Amsterdam: John Benjamins.

Peeters, Bert. 1989. Review of Allan (1986). *Canadian journal of linguistics* 34. 119-122.

Peeters, Bert. 1991. Review of Kövecses (1986). *Australian journal of linguistics* 11. 229-232.

Peeters, Bert. 1994. "The things we do to make things make sense". *Pragmatics & cognition* 2. 357-380.

Peeters, Bert. 1996. Review of Nuyts (1992). *Word* 47. 105-109.

Peeters, Bert. 1997. Review of Geeraerts et al. (1994). *Canadian journal of linguistics* 42. 358-361.

Peeters, Bert. 1998. "Cognitive musings". *Word* 49. 225-237.

Peeters, Bert. Forthcoming a. "Does Cognitive Linguistics live up to its name?". In René Dirven, Bruce Hawkins & Esra Sandikcioglu (ed.), *Language and ideology*, vol. 1. *Cognitive theoretical approaches*. Amsterdam: John Benjamins.

Peeters, Bert. Forthcoming b. "*Vouloir* et obviation en français". *Romance philology*.

Petöfi, János S. 1976. "Lexicology, encyclopaedic knowledge, theory of text". *Cahiers de lexicologie* 29. 25-41.

Pires de Oliveira, Roberta. 1998. "Cognitive semantics. In the heart of language. An interview with George Lakoff". *Fórum lingüístico* 1. 83-118.

Pires de Oliveira, Roberta. Forthcoming. "'In the name of science'. Language and ideology. Interview with George Lakoff". In René Dirven, Bruce Hawkins & Esra Sandikcioglu (ed.), *Language and ideology*, vol. 1. *Cognitive theoretical approaches*. Amsterdam: John Benjamins.

Pustejovsky, James. 1995. *The Generative Lexicon*. Cambridge: M.I.T. Press.

Pustejovsky, James; Bouillon, Pierrette. 1995. "Aspectual coercion and logical polysemy". *Journal of semantics* 12. 133-162. Reprinted (1996) in James Pustejovsky & Branimir Boguraev (ed.), *Lexical semantics. The problem of polysemy*. Oxford : Clarendon Press. 133-162.

Quine, Willard V.O. 1953. *From a logical point of view*. Cambridge: Harvard University Press.

Raskin, Victor. 1985a. "Linguistic and encyclopedic knowledge in text processing". *Quaderni di semantica* 6. 92-102.

Raskin, Victor. 1985b. "Once again on linguistic and encyclopedic knowledge". *Quaderni di semantica* 6. 377-383.

Rastier, François. 1987. *Sémantique interprétative*. Paris: Presses universitaires de France.

Reddy, Michael J. 1979. "The conduit metaphor. A case of frame conflict in our language about language". In Andrew Ortony (ed.), *Metaphor and thought*. London: Cambridge University Press. 284-324.

Ruwet, Nicolas. 1975. "Synecdoques et métonymies". *Poétique* 23. 371-388.

Schank, Roger C.; Abelson, Robert P. 1977. *Scripts, plans, goals and understanding. An inquiry into human knowledge structures.* Hillsdale: Lawrence Erlbaum.

Searle, John R. 1979. *Expression and meaning. Studies in the theory of speech acts.* Cambridge: Cambridge University Press.

Silingardi, Germana. 1983. "La catégorie du contenu conceptuel dans la distinction classique synecdoque - métonymie". *Le français moderne* 51. 300-308.

Sprengel, Konrad. 1980. "Über semantische Merkmale". In Dieter Kastovsky (ed.), *Perspektiven der lexikalischen Semantik.* Bonn: Bouvier. 145-173.

Stachowiak, Franz-Josef. 1979. *Zur semantischen Struktur des subjektiven Lexikons.* München: Fink.

Stachowiak, Franz-Josef. 1982. "Haben Wortbedeutungen eine gesonderte mentale Repräsentation gegenüber dem Weltwissen? Neurolinguistische Überlegungen". *Linguistische Berichte* 79. 12-29.

Taylor, John R. Forthcoming. "Concepts, or: what is it that a word designates?". Manuscript, University of Otago.

Ungerer, Friedrich; Schmid, Hans-Jörg. 1996. *An introduction to cognitive linguistics.* London: Longman.

Wierzbicka, Anna. 1972. *Semantic primitives.* Frankfurt: Athenäum.

Wierzbicka, Anna. 1980. *Lingua mentalis. The semantics of natural language.* Sydney: Academic Press.

Wierzbicka, Anna. 1985. *Lexicography and conceptual analysis.* Ann Arbor: Karoma.

Wierzbicka, Anna. 1986. "Metaphors linguists live by: Lakoff & Johnson contra Aristotle". *Papers in linguistics* 19. 287-313.

Wierzbicka, Anna. 1988. *The semantics of grammar.* Amsterdam: John Benjamins.

Wierzbicka, Anna. 1990. "The meaning of colour terms. Semantics, culture, and cognition". *Cognitive linguistics* 1. 99-150.

Wierzbicka, Anna. 1993. "The alphabet of human thoughts". In Richard A. Geiger and Brygida Rudzka-Ostyn (ed.), *Conceptualizations and mental processing in language.* Berlin: Mouton de Gruyter. 23-51.

Wierzbicka, Anna. 1995. "Dictionaries and encyclopedias. How to draw the line". In Philip W. Davis (ed.), *Alternative linguistics. Descriptive and theoretical modes.* Amsterdam: John Benjamins. 289-315.

Wierzbicka, Anna. 1996. *Semantics. Primes and universals.* Oxford: Oxford University Press.

Wilson, Neil L. 1967. "Linguistical butter and philosophical parsnips". *Journal of philosophy* 64. 55-67.

Ziegler, Jürgen. 1984. "Gibt es lexikalische Lücken?". *Linguistische Berichte* 93. 66-79.

Part One

ASSESSMENTS

Part One

Words, concepts, mental representations, and other biological categories[1]

Anne Reboul

Institut des Sciences Cognitives, CNRS UPR 9075,
67 boulevard Pinel, F-69675 Bron cedex, France
E-mail: reboul@isc.cnrs.fr

0. Introduction

The distinction between *lexical knowledge* and *encyclopedic knowledge*, familiar to most linguists, has recently been submitted to considerable criticism. Its very validity has been questioned. In this paper, I shall attempt to show that the distinction is necessary, not only for methodological reasons, but also from an empirical point of view. I first discuss a phenomenon that has come to be seen as a crucial ingredient in the current lexical knowledge debate, arguing that *polysemy*, even though any theory of either lexical or encyclopedic knowledge must account for it, has no major role to play in determining the boundary between lexical and encyclopedic knowledge. I then describe a way of approaching the distinction from a pragmatic point of view, namely that of post-Gricean relevance theory. I make comparisons with various other distinctions in the fields of linguistics and pragmatics, concluding that, like most of them, the lexicon-encyclopedia distinction should be made sense of in a cognitive rather than a purely linguistic framework. I distinguish two types of cognition, natural and artificial, and proceed with a brief presentation of Pustejovsky's

---

[1] Bert Peeters has made a number of editorial comments on an earlier version of this paper, for which I am thankful.

Generative Lexicon model (Pustejovsky 1995), a model for artificial cognition that has done much to revive the controversy around the boundary between lexical and encyclopedic knowledge. After a short, pragmatics-based, criticism of Pustejovsky's model, I turn to evidence from natural cognition (mainly, though not exclusively, from the extensive neurolinguistic literature on language pathologies) to indicate what such evidence suggests about the lexicon-encyclopedia divide. I propose a few leads as to what a natural cognition test of Pustejovsky's model might look like, raising doubts in the process on its validity for natural cognition.[2] Finally, I outline my own version of the divide, relying on the neurolinguistic data previously described, as well as on notions such as *specific* and *ad hoc* concepts, and offering a few suggestions for testing it in natural cognition.

1. What, if anything, is polysemy?

Although it is not crucial for the distinction between lexical and encyclopedic knowledge, polysemy has played a prominent role in many discussions of the lexicon. The important thing to note is that lexical ambiguity may come from either homonymy or polysemy. It may be worthwhile to formally distinguish the three notions as follows:

- Definition of lexical ambiguity

Lexical ambiguity occurs when the same phonological or written form can be understood as corresponding to different meanings.

- Definition of homonymy

Homonymy occurs when different words with different meanings happen to share the same phonological or written form.

- Definition of polysemy

Polysemy occurs when a single word gives access to several different but related meanings.

Let us look at a few examples:

    (1a)   He went for a walk on the *banks* of the Thames.

    (1b)   He had savings accounts in several *banks*.

---

[2] Its validity for artificial cognition is not in doubt.

(2a)   Open the *door*, it's hot in here.

(2b)   Go through the *door*, and turn to your left.

In the examples under (1), we are dealing with a clear-cut case of homonymy, according to the definition above. It just happens to be the case that, in English, a single form corresponds to two different words, *bank₁* and *bank₂*, with two unrelated meanings, 'the land along the side of a river' and 'a place where money is kept and paid out' (*Oxford Advanced Learner's Dictionary of Current English*, 1961). On the other hand, in the examples under (2), polysemy comes into the picture. In (2a), the hearer is told to push against a solid panel (the *door*) so as to create an aperture while, in (2b), the hearer is told to go through the aperture itself (also called the *door*).

What is the distinction between homonymy and polysemy based on? What grounds are there for saying that the meanings are unrelated in (1) and related in (2)? A brief examination of examples (3) and (4) may be useful at this stage:

(3a)   He went for a walk on the banks of the Thames. ?The cashier looked old and bored.

(3b)   He had savings accounts in several banks. ?The water was dirty.

(3c)   He went for a walk on the banks of the Thames. ?He had savings accounts in more than one.

(4a)   He opened the door. The man was still sitting on the steps.

(4b)   He went through the door. The man was still sitting on the steps.

(4c)   Open the door. Go through it, and turn to your left.

(3a), (3b) and (3c) are bizarre, to say the least. By contrast, (4a), (4b) and (4c) make perfect sense. A distinction between homonymy and polysemy, provided it can be accommodated in either a model of the structure of the lexicon or a model of the structure of the encyclopedia, may account for the difference between the examples under (3) and those under (4).

Other phenomena have also been described in terms of polysemy. Some authors have postulated polysemy, not on the basis of whole sentences, but on the basis of lists of complex NPs with a common word thought to be polysemous, such as, for instance, the list for *mother* below (borrowed from Lakoff 1987):

(5)   stepmother, adoptive mother, birth mother, natural mother, foster mother, biological mother, surrogate mother, unwed mother, genetic mother

Lakoff describes these complex NPs as denoting subcategories of *mother*. Assuming that subcategories are to categories what subsets are to sets, it seems reasonable to suppose that where a given category delimites an extension (a set), its subcategories delimit subsets of that set. The problem is that, although this works well enough in some cases, it certainly does not work across the board. Granted, unwed mothers form a subset of mothers, but do surrogate mothers form a subset of mothers?

Approaches such as this raise a methodological problem. It is generally the case that a modifier (*step-, adoptive, birth, natural, foster, biological, surrogate, unwed, genetic*) modifies the extension of its head noun. This is not in itself contradictory with Lakoff's hypothesis in terms of subcategorisation, but for the hypothesis to stand the modifiers would have to delimit subsets, not alternative sets. The latter do seem to eventuate in some of Lakoff's examples, however. This, in turn, leads to a more general point of criticism. We can speak of *black cats, tabby cats, siamese cats, persian cats*, etc. All of these correspond to a restriction of the extension of *cat*, i.e. they delimit subsets of the set of cats. It does not follow that *cat* is polysemous. Relying on paradigms of complex NPs just yields what one should expect it to, namely compositionality. It does not yield insights on polysemy. This is not to say that polysemy is unimportant. In fact, it is a rather pervasive factor in natural language. It is indeed among the causes of one specific, general feature of natural languages that has attracted a lot of attention in contemporary pragmatics, namely underdetermination.[3]

2. Linguistic underdetermination and the pragmatic scene at the dawn of the third millennium

The border between lexical and encyclopedic knowledge is particularly crucial in the branch of pragmatics to which I belong, namely post-Gricean, relevance-oriented pragmatics. At the basis of all pragmatic investigations lies the distinction between *sentence* and *utterance*, and (conjointly) between *sentence meaning* and *utterance interpretation*. Utterances communicate more than the corresponding sentences say.

The most common type of examples used to justify the distinction between sentence and utterance involves indexicals, as in (6):

(6)   My cat is on the mat.

Depending on speaker, time, location, etc. (6) has different interpretations, e.g. 'Jonas is on the mat by the front-door of the old presbytery in Sainte-Cécile, France, on May 11, 1999' or 'Pussy is on the mat in front of the fire in the parlour of the

---

[3] For more on polysemy and, more generally, on vagueness in natural languages, as well as on the pragmatic treatment of such issues, see Reboul (1989, 1993).

White Horse pub in Cumnor, England, on December 31, 1900', etc. The same sentence may be given many more interpretations. However, none seem to be reducible to the sentence meaning of (6). Instead, all appear to be the result of a combination of sentence meaning and the circumstances in which the sentence is uttered (thereby becoming an utterance). In other words, an utterance is what is produced by the enunciation of a given sentence in specific circumstances, including speaker, spatio-temporal location, etc. A sentence, on the other hand, always has the same meaning (or meanings, if it is syntactically or semantically ambiguous), though the corresponding utterances may and generally *do* have different interpretations. The interpretation of a sentence, yielding its meaning, is carried out with linguistic means (where linguistics is defined as phonology, syntax and semantics). The interpretation of the corresponding utterances, which (as we have just seen) is not equivalent and cannot be reduced to the meaning of the sentence, rests on an enrichment of sentence meaning, using pragmatic and generally inferential (i.e. non-linguistic) means.

In general, there is a degree of linguistic underdetermination: the intentions of a speaker are often not entirely clear from the sentence used to communicate them. Nor do they have to be, because of the versatility of natural language, i.e. the ability of utterances to communicate more than the corresponding sentences say (as illustrated above; cf. the notion of "efficiency of natural languages" in Barwise & Perry 1983). The versatility of natural language is due to ambiguity, polysemy, and the use of inference relying on both linguistic and non-linguistic information to enrich sentence meaning. Let us look at an example taken from Sperber & Wilson (1995:194):

> (7a)   Peter: Would you drive a Mercedes?

> (7b)   Mary: I wouldn't drive any expensive car.

Anyone living in a Western culture instantly recognises Mary's utterance in (7b) as an answer to Peter's question in (7a). Yet, Mary does not say either *Yes, I would drive a Mercedes* or *No, I wouldn't*. She simply says that she would not drive any expensive car. To recognise her answer as such, the additional information needed is that Mercedes are expensive cars, allowing the inference below:

> (8)   Mary would not drive any expensive car.
>
>   Mercedes are expensive cars.
>
>   --
>
> ∴   Mary would not drive a Mercedes.

Knowledge of this kind has typically been considered as encyclopedic rather than linguistic. It has been assumed that there are two kinds of knowledge, namely lexical knowledge, accessible from the words of natural languages and determining their meanings, and encyclopedic knowledge, all and any information a given cognitive agent has on the world. Traditionally, linguistic knowledge is supposed to be available at a linguistic level of analysis, while encyclopedic knowledge comes into play at the pragmatic level, where sentential meaning is enriched to yield the complete interpretation of the utterance. To put it differently, the distinction between lexical and encyclopedic knowledge parallels the distinction between linguistics and pragmatics.

3. Linguistics vs. pragmatics, lexical vs. encyclopedic knowledge and some parallel distinctions

The distinction between lexical and encyclopedic knowledge is not the only distinction traditionally made to justify the linguistics-pragmatics divide. A few other distinctions, not necessarily equivalent but somehow running parallel, are *word* vs. *concept, procedural* vs. *conceptual* content, *grammaticality* vs. *truth conditionality*, and *explicit* vs. *implicit* communication. Throwing some light on each of them may actually help us clarify the boundary between lexical and encyclopedic knowledge.

- *Word* and *concept*

The distinction between *word* and *concept* is presumably nearer to that between *lexical* and *encyclopedic knowledge* than any other distinction we shall look at. It should be noted that, if words and concepts are all we have, the notion of "word" should be enlarged to encompass at least some linguistic knowledge over and above phonological form: knowledge regarding syntactic category, argument structure (for verbs, prepositions, and some nouns), and possibly morphology. This is sometimes seen to imply that all there is to the *meaning* of a given word (which might be roughly defined as extension + intension) would be contained in the corresponding concept. Alternative accounts incorporate in the word at least some of its meaning, though exactly how much is being incorporated differs from one model to the next. There is an important caveat, though: the correspondence between words and concepts is not necessarily one-to-one.

- *Conceptual* and *procedural content*

Lexical items are often said to have either *conceptual* content (defined, very much along the above lines, in terms of extension and intension, though with encyclopedic knowledge added), or *procedural* content (defined as outlining procedures that apply to either conceptual content or compositional conceptual content, i.e. propositions or, possibly, propositional functions.[4] Classes of words arranged according to con-

---

[4] The working of prepositions as described in Pustejovsky (1995) may be taken as a nice example of procedural content applying to conceptual content, even though it is not described as such. Blakemore (1987), in her analysis of connectives, gives a good description of what procedural content applying

tent (*conceptual* and *procedural*) seem to correspond to classes of words arranged according to grammar (*open* and *closed*): the distinction between conceptual and procedural content closely parallels that between open and closed classes of words.[5] The distinction between conceptual and procedural content cuts across that between words and concepts: both procedural and conceptual contents presumably have to do with concepts, which can have either a procedural or a conceptual content.

- *Grammaticality* and *truth-conditionality*

Grammaticality has mainly to do with language, that is with lexical knowledge and grammar (i.e. lexicon and syntax), while *truth-conditionality* has to do with language use, i.e. with encyclopedic knowledge and its processing (semantics and pragmatics). In other words, no matter how much is treated as word meaning, there is some linguistic indeterminacy; the meaning of a sentence may well fall short of the sense of a corresponding utterance (its truth-conditions) and may have to be supplemented by an inferential system operating with encyclopedic knowledge. The relationship with the previous distinctions is as follows: words appear to be on the grammaticality side of the border, and concepts in the truth-conditionality domain; conceptual and procedural knowledge are both on the truth-conditionality side, but they make different contributions to the processing of utterance truth-conditions.

- *Explicit* and *implicit communication*

The distinction between explicit and implicit communication cuts across the previous distinctions in manifold ways, depending on whether it is understood in traditional, Gricean or post-Gricean terms.

1. In *traditional* terms, it might be said that explicit communication corresponds to what is asserted, while implicit communication corresponds to what is presupposed. Both *assertion* and *presupposition* correspond to lexical/semantic meaning, since presupposition is considered a *result* of lexical meaning.[6] This implies a mildly extended notion of "word", including a fair amount of meaning that does not belong at the conceptual level (cf. the distinction between word and concept above). It is not clear how the distinction between assertion and presupposition relates to that between conceptual and procedural content.

2. In *Gricean* terms, (non-natural) meaning could be defined as a triadic notion consisting of *literal meaning* (i.e. meaning that is *explicitly* communicated with-

---

to compositional conceptual content would be. For extensions of her analysis to French, see Luscher (1994, 1998) and Moeschler (1989).

[5] As is well known, open classes are those to which new words can be freely added (nouns, verbs and adjectives, at least). Closed classes cannot be added to with the same freedom (pronouns, connectives, prepositions, but possibly also tenses, are obvious examples).

[6] In fact, convincing arguments have been advanced against the idea that presupposition is lexically encoded (see Wilson 1975, Kempson 1975 for details).

out violation of cooperative maxims), *conversational implicatures* (these are *implicit*), and *conventional implicatures* (they occupy an uneasy position between explicit and implicit communication).

- Literal meaning is part of lexical/semantic meaning. It seems to imply a fairly extended notion of word meaning encompassing at least extension + intension. Presumably, it would mainly fall on the conceptual side of the distinction between conceptual and procedural content.

- Conventional implicatures are also part of lexical/semantic meaning. They exist on either side of the procedural vs. conceptual meaning divide. They, too, seem to imply an extended notion of word meaning, encompassing not only extension + intension but procedure as well; in fact, those that appear to be due to procedural meaning presumably make up a significant proportion of the total.

- Conversational implicatures are clearly part of encyclopedic meaning: on no account could they be thought to derive from word meaning, irrespective of how the latter is defined. They are non-linguistic. In neo-Gricean terms, they would involve both conceptual and procedural content, as well as content that is neither conceptual nor procedural according to the definitions above.[7]

3. In *post-Gricean* terms (see Sperber & Wilson 1995), language is seen as essentially underdetermined: it conveys *explicitly* far less than speakers intend to communicate (cf. above). Sentence processing is an entirely linguistic affair. It involves lexicon and syntax, and yields the *logical form* of the corresponding utterance. That logical form is a structured sequence of concept addresses, and a means of access to non-lexical knowledge, which may itself involve conceptual (i.e. generic or specific) as well as procedural content. According to Sperber and Wilson, an utterance's logical form is hardly ever identical to its *propositional form*. The latter is complete inasmuch as it may be assessed on its truth value. It still falls short of being the entire informational content that the speaker wanted to put across, but it is much richer than mere logical form. The propositional form is accessed through pragmatic inferential processes that enrich the logical form. The inferential processes bear on premises of which most come from encyclopedic, i.e. non-lexical, conceptual knowledge.

---

[7] They involve content that may be seen as either propositional or conceptual specific (the former in the sense of DRT or *Discourse Representation Theory*, cf. Kamp & Reyle 1993; of SDRT or *Segmented Discourse Representation Theory*, cf. Asher 1993; or of FCS or *File Change Semantics*, cf. Heim 1982). Conceptual specific content (cf. section 11 below) is content relative to specific objects, content that cannot be found in the usual, generic, concepts or conceptual contents.

4. An institutional vs. empirical boundary

The distinction beween lexical and encyclopedic knowledge may be seen as (quasi-) equivalent to that between words and concepts. The other distinctions reviewed in section 3 are drawn from various models that are preoccupied in their own individual ways with defining the boundary between what is a legitimate part of word / lexicon / lexical knowledge and what is a legitimate part of concept / encyclopedia / encyclopedic knowledge – or, in more negative terms, between what is a legitimate part of the lexicon and what is dumped into the (widely rumoured to be untractable) wastebasket of encyclopedia.

Tracing the boundary between *word* and *concept, lexicon* and *encyclopedia, lexical knowledge* and *encyclopedic knowledge* is important because it helps those who do not reduce linguistic inquiry to phonology, syntax and non-lexical semantics determine the legitimate domain of their scholarly endeavours. That is, the boundary is mainly *methodologieal* or, to put it more bluntly, *institutional*. It enables people to decide whether what they are doing is or is not linguistics: if it has to do with lexical knowledge, it is linguistics; if it has to do with encyclopedic knowledge, it is not linguistics – though it may be pragmatics, in a post-Gricean sense. It provides them with a justification to ignore work that deals with what they take to be encyclopedic knowledge (if they consider themselves linguists) or with what they take to be lexical knowledge (if they do not consider themselves linguists but, e.g., pragmaticians).

In recent times, the institutional boundary has been undercut by another one that may be termed *empirical*. The empirical boundary is the immediate result of the cognitive turn in language studies. The latter term is supposed to be neutral between linguistics and pragmatics. The cognitive turn – an expression *not* taken to refer exclusively to so-called *Cognitive Linguistics* or *Cognitive Grammar* – reveals itself through developments in two different areas.

- Research in *artificial cognition* seeks to model cognitive abilities (including language). Computer implementation is an immediate or less immediate goal. Realism with regard to human cognitive processes may be sacrificed to *operationality*.

- Research in *natural cognition* aims at describing the mechanisms of human cognition. It tries to be as realistic as possible. Production of hypotheses is governed, directly or indirectly, by *experimental testability*.

In terms of contemporary linguistics, Pustejovsky's *Generative Lexicon* and most of dynamic semantics (DRT, SDRT, FCS, etc.; cf. note 7) appear to fall under *artificial cognition*, whereas Generative Linguistics, Cognitive Linguistics and Relevance Theory fall under *natural cognition*. However, the boundary between the two should be seen as being permeable: there is no reason in principle why a model developed in natural cognition could not be implemented, or why a model developed in artificial cognition could not be tested experimentally, on animals – including humans (subject, of course, to all the obvious ethical limits).

Why should the boundary between lexical and encyclopedic knowledge be seen differently in view of the cognitive turn? The answer has to do with the multidisciplinarity of cognitive sciences. Cognitivists may not want to draw boundaries mainly or only for institutional reasons. The way they may want to draw them is more likely to depend on whether they are working in artificial cognition or in natural cognition.

Those who are interested in artificial (computer) modelling, i.e. those who want to model the processing and production of a possibly unlimited number of grammatical sentences, will take as belonging to lexical knowledge everything required by their respective models to process and produce grammatical sentences, apart from syntax. They will have a syntax operating on words, and put in word meaning everything that is clearly not syntactic but needed nonetheless. This is what *lexical knowledge* will mean to them. Anything else they might need, should they wish to extend their model of sentence processing and production to discourse processing and production, will be treated as encyclopedic knowledge.

In contrast, those who are interested in natural cognition may still want to have a model of sentence production and interpretation, and be able to say what difference (if any) there is between word and concept, but they are not free to put into word meaning anything they need, regardless of how natural human production and interpretation of language actually works. They are constrained by a goal or rule of *realism*: it is not the case that anything goes, provided it works. Hypotheses may be proposed, but they will have to be tested. The question is: how could that be done?

Let us assume three levels of sentence processing; two are linguistic (syntax and lexicon), and the remaining one is conceptual. The three levels are independent of each other, though mutually interacting. In other words, they are not merely types of information, but *modules* (in the sense of Fodor 1983; for details, cf. section 10, and particularly note 16). The validity of the distinction between syntax and lexical knowledge, and that of the distinction between lexical and conceptual knowledge, could be tested through *double dissociation*. A process or information store has a good chance of being a module if it can be doubly dissociated from all other processes and information stores, that is iff:

1. it may be impaired while *all other processes* are functioning correctly;

2. all other processes are impaired while *it* is functioning correctly.

To show that syntax is independent of lexical knowledge, it must be demonstrated that syntax can function while lexical knowledge is impaired and vice versa. To show that lexical and conceptual knowledge are independent, it must be demonstrated that the lexicon can function while conceptual knowledge is impaired and vice versa. Experiments involving double dissociation between lexical and conceptual knowledge should not only show whether or not the distinction itself makes sense in natural cognition; they should also help draw the boundary between the two types of knowledge, though this is by no means a straightforward task. Moreover, the possibility of disturbed access and interaction between presumed modules makes it harder to demonstrate double dissociation. Access and interaction between modules is an additional level (additional to what happens inside every module) where sentence processing and production may go wrong.

To summarise, drawing the boundary between lexical and encyclopedic knowledge may be an *institutional* aim, with no other goal than to delimit the academic domain of linguistics (or pragmatics). The same boundary may also be seen in *empirical* terms. The various models that draw it may be tested either in artificial cognition, where they are assessed for efficiency through implementation, or in natural cognition, where they are assessed through experiments trying to elicit double dissociation. Pustejovsky's *Generative Lexicon* model falls squarely on the side of artificial cognition. It has been much publicised of late, and has revived the controversy around the boundary between lexical and encyclopedic knowledge.

5. The *Generative Lexicon* model

Pustejovsky's *Generative Lexicon* (see Pustejovsky 1995) has been at the core of most discussions in lexical semantics for the past few years. There are several reasons for this, chief among which the fact that it is more ambitious than most other models in lexical semantics: it attempts to account in an explicit way for the creative use of words in novel contexts (a topic of which a majority of older models fought shy), and for compositionality. Though most previous lexical models pay lip service to compositionality, it is hard to see what exactly they have put in place to deal with it, apart from argument structure. Pustejovsky's lexicon incorporates lexical entries that are at the same time richer in informational content (cf. below), and more richly structured. It relies on *generative operations*, among which *type coercion* and *co-compositionality*.

According to Pustejovsky, the distinction between lexical meaning and background knowledge in natural languages is a necessary one. There is no such thing in natural languages as a one-to-one correspondence between words and meanings, nor is there an unrestricted correspondence between words and background knowledge. To put it differently, natural languages are neither *monomorphic* nor *unrestrictedly polymorphic*. Instead, they are *weakly polymorphic*: to one word may correspond several lexical meanings (*ambiguity*), and to several words may correspond a single lexical meaning (*synonymy*). Whereas most lexical models have treated ambiguity as a single and fairly straightforward phenomenon that could be more or less reduced to *homonymy* (one word form for several word meanings), Pustejovsky distinguishes two types:

1. *contrastive ambiguity* (≈ homonymy); and

2. *complementary polysemy*, itself comprising two subtypes:

   a) *non-logical polysemy*, which involves a change of syntactic type (e.g. the verb *cut* 'make an incision' vs. the noun *cut* 'the incision itself');

   b) *logical polysemy*, which involves no change of syntactic type (e.g. *window* 'aperture' vs. *window* 'physical object').

Complementary polysemy should not so much be described in terms of ambiguity as in terms of *sense alternations*. These include *count* vs. *mass* alternations (*lamb*), *container* vs. *containee* alternations (*cup*), *figure* vs. *ground* alternations (*window*), *product* vs. *producer* alternations (*newspaper*), *plant* vs. *food* alternations (*fig*), *process* vs. *result* alternations (*examination*), *place* vs. *people* alternations (*city, village*). According to Pustejovsky, all of these are usually treated in the same way as truly ambiguous (homonymous) words such as *bank* ('side of a river' or 'financial institution') or *plant* ('industrial building' or 'living vegetable entity'). Each of the complementary senses of a complementarily polysemous word is treated as a different lexical item, as if there was no logical link between, for instance, a window qua aperture and a window qua physical object. Pustejovsky calls formal lexicons that adopt this practice *Sense Enumeration Lexicons* (*SELs*), and finds that they are in fact predominant in the existing formal research on lexical knowledge. In his opinion, three basic arguments can be levelled against SELs: namely, that (unlike his own model) they cannot account for the permeability of word senses, the existence of multiple syntactic forms (for instance, inchoative-causative alternations: *The bottle broke* vs. *John broke the bottle*), and the creative use of words in novel contexts.

In contrast, Pustejovsky's *Generative Lexicon* aims to deal with exactly these three problems, as well as with the polymorphic structure of language, the semanticality (vs. grammaticality) of natural language utterances, and the co-compositionality of semantic representation. For each lexical item, there are in fact four levels of representation, of which two are particularly relevant in the present context:

1. ARGUMENT STRUCTURE states the number and type of logical arguments of an item, and indicates their syntactic realisation;

2. EVENT STRUCTURE specifies whether a lexical item or phrase denotes a *state*, a *process* or a *transition*, and indicates sub-eventual structure;

3. QUALIA STRUCTURE includes FORMAL, CONSTITUTIVE, TELIC, and AGENTIVE roles;

4. LEXICAL INHERITANCE STRUCTURE identifies relations between a lexical structure and other structures in the lattice type, and its contribution to the global organisation of the lexicon.

Generative devices include the following semantic transformations:

- *Type coercion*, which involves the selection of a semantic interpretation without a change of syntactic type;

- *Selective binding*, which occurs when a lexical item operates on the substructure of a phrase without changing the overall type in the composition;

- *Co-composition*, where multiple elements behave as functors generating enrichment, as in *manner co-composition, feature transcription* and *light verb specification*.

The backbone of any contemporary lexicon, namely the strong link between lexical items and *semantic types*, has been kept by Pustejovsky. To deal with at least some complementarily polysemous words, and in strong contrast with established practice in SELs, Pustejovsky introduces *meta-entries*. A meta-entry (or *lexical conceptual paradigm, lcp*) conflates different word senses in a single lexical item. This means that a single complementarily polysemous word can be related to several different types in its lcp. For reasons of space, I shall not develop this aspect of Pustejovsky's proposals in the present paper. Instead, I shall discuss what may be his most original proposal with regard to the lexicon-encyclopedia distinction, namely the introduction of what he calls the QUALIA STRUCTURE of a lexical item. That structure specifies four aspects (or QUALIA) of word meaning:

1. The CONSTITUTIVE QUALE indicates the relation between an object and its constitutive parts (material, weight, parts, and component elements);

2. The FORMAL QUALE distinguishes it within a larger domain (orientation, magnitude, shape, dimensionality, color, position);

3. The TELIC QUALE indicates its purpose or function (the purpose that an agent has in performing the act, and the built-in function or aim that specifies certain activities);

4. The AGENTIVE QUALE identifies the factors involved in its origin or realisation (creator, artefact, natural kind, causal chain).

By and large, QUALIA STRUCTURES are the reason why Pustejovsky's *Generative Lexicon* model has revived the controversy around lexical and encyclopedic knowledge: though the FORMAL QUALE is fairly classic, and the CONSTITUTIVE QUALE might pass muster with some lexicologists, TELIC and AGENTIVE QUALIA clearly incorporate in the lexicon information that had traditionally been thought to belong to encyclopedic knowledge. Pustejovsky's justification for the inclusion of QUALIA STRUCTURES in the lexicon is that they help account for *semanticality*, which is to semantics what *grammaticality* is to syntax: "semanticality refers to the semantic well-formedness of expressions in a grammar" (Pustejovsky 1995:40). To illustrate, consider the material provided in (9) below:

(9a)   Mary began the book.

(9b)   ?John began the dictionary.

(9c)   ??Mary began the rock.

Semanticality ratings do not reflect degrees of grammaticality (or syntactic well-formedness), as shown by the various direct objects in (9), all of which belong to the same syntactic type (they are all full NPs). The ratings reflect degrees of semanticality, accounted for by Pustejovsky in terms of *type coercion* (possible in (9a), difficult in (9b), impossible in (9c)). Type coercion rests on information stored in the QUALIA STRUCTURE, and involves the selection of a semantic interpretation without a change of syntactic type. Very roughly, type coercion happens when, for instance, the ARGUMENT STRUCTURE of a verb demands that its complement be of the **event**-type (which is the case for *begin* in the examples above). A noun such as *book* is of two different types, namely **physical object** and **information** (i.e. the lexical item is a meta-entry or lcp), neither of which agrees with the type required for the complement of *begin*. However, in the QUALIA STRUCTURE of *book*, and more specifically in its TELIC and AGENTIVE QUALIA, **events** (respectively of **reading** and of **writing**) are indicated. Under those circumstances, type coercion is possible: it changes the type of *book* to that of either its TELIC or AGENTIVE QUALIA, yielding the right type for the complement of *begin* in (9a). On the other hand, the TELIC ROLE for *dictionary* is not **read**, but **consult**, an activity instead of an accomplishment. Type coercion is difficult, hence the relative anomaly of (9b). Finally, *rock* does not have any clear TELIC or AGENTIVE ROLE: type coercion is impossible, hence the even higher anomaly of (9c).

The notion of *type coercion* has been criticised (cf. Godard & Jayez 1993). I for one am not interested so much in its validity as I am in its impact on the distinction between lexical and encyclopedic knowledge. In the next section, I examine whether Pustejovsky's defence of his model as a model of lexical as opposed to one of encyclopedic knowledge (resting as it does on the notion of *semanticality*) can be criticised *a priori*, on a principled basis.

6. A criticism of the *Generative Lexicon* model, with special reference to the distinction between lexicon and encyclopedia

Pustejovsky's model is certainly the most elegant model to date for lexical semantics. It sheds new light on a significant proportion of the problems he aims to address, particularly the creative use of words, complementary polysemy and co-composition. On the other hand, it is a matter of speculation whether the notion of *semanticality*, on which he relies to establish his own divide between lexical and encyclopedic knowledge, is really as clear-cut as he thinks.

Apart from the fact that the semanticality ratings of utterances do not appear to include the classic asterisk to signal asemanticality (in contrast with their grammaticality ratings, which do include the asterisk to signal agrammaticality), it is not entirely clear that coercion does not work on encyclopedic-pragmatic as well as on lexical-semantic information. If it does (as I hope to establish below), then serious consideration should be given to the hypothesis of a continuum between more or less accessible information rather than a clear-cut line between non-syntactic lexical knowledge (including TELIC and AGENTIVE QUALIA) and encyclopedic knowledge. I hope to show, on the basis of a few examples, that what we have is indeed a continuum, and not a clear-cut line. Let us consider examples (10a) and (10b):

(10a)   Mary began her book.

(10b)   Virginia Woolf began her book.

On the assumption that the most easily accessible interpretations for (11a) and (11b) are *Mary began **reading** her book* (TELIC QUALE) and *Virginia Woolf began **writing** her book* (AGENTIVE QUALE), the following question must be raised. Why is it that we choose in the first case the TELIC and in the second case the AGENTIVE QUALE, if not because *encyclopedic* knowledge leads us to the conclusion that, Virginia Woolf being a writer, she is more likely to write than to read a book?[8] Information pertaining to Mary and to Virginia Woolf is *not* lexical knowledge: it is associated with mental representations of individuals rather than with the lexical contents of words. The choice in QUALIA between TELIC and AGENTIVE is mediated by that non-lexical, encyclopedic, knowledge. This does not in itself disqualify the idea of type coercion, but it does weaken the view that it is essentially or only a lexical semantic operation. Its range seems to extend well beyond lexical knowledge, into encyclopedic knowledge.

Given that Pustejovsky himself recognises the need for some commonsense reasoning (based on encyclopedic knowledge), there seems to be a good case for a continuum rather than a clear-cut distinction between lexicon and encyclopedia. This seems to agree with the remarks on semanticality above. Semanticality, if indeed it exists in the sense defended by Pustejovsky, appears much less clear-cut than grammaticality, as is shown by the contextualisations for (9b) and (9c) in (11) below. Because the original material was not agrammatical, in which case contextualisation

---

[8] Considering that most serious writers, irrespective of the number of books they write, presumably write far less than they read, this is a disturbing instance of what can go wrong in information processing, especially in the interpretation of isolated utterances.

would not generally have the sort of effect it has here, semantic acceptability is increased.

> (11a)   John had been thinking that his vocabulary was so poor that he should improve it. He could think of no better idea than to read the entire OED. He began the dictionary on a sunny afternoon...

> (11b)   Mary had been a sculptor for years. On one of her visits to a nearby quarry, she picked up a rock that seemed ideal for a long-delayed project. She began the rock on a sunny afternoon...

While certainly not as anomalous as (9c), (11b) is not quite as good as (11a) (which seems to be about perfect). This could be because the linguistic context in (11a) has changed the TELIC role in the QUALIA STRUCTURE of *dictionary* from **consult** to **read**. A change of that nature is anything but straightforward, though: if the QUALIA STRUCTURE is essentially lexical, we need an account of how it can be changed pragmatically. Such an account is still outstanding.[9]

It should also be noted that, though the distinction between complementary polysemy and straightforward ambiguity advocated by Pustejovsky seems convincing, alternative accounts have been proposed (see, e.g., Nunberg 1995).

As a general summary of how things stand in the matter, we might say that, as long as Pustejovsky's *Generative Lexicon* is considered to belong to artificial cognition, adequacy tests may be limited to the purely operational kind. If it is found that it can deal efficiently with a greater number and a greater range of sentences than other models, it may be considered provisionally adequate, i.e. adequate until another, more efficient, model is put forward. It should be remembered though that, despite its merits, Pustejovsky's model has not yet been implemented. Hence, it may well be worth turning to natural cognition to further assess it, especially in view of the difficulties outlined above with respect to the boundary between lexical and encyclopedic knowledge.

7. The distinction between lexical and encyclopedic knowledge in natural cognition

The *Generative Lexicon* model does not seem to address the gradualness of class or category membership as established over the past twenty years in Rosch's research

---

[9] The qualia structure would have to be reproduced in a peculiar type of encyclopedic knowledge, namely one that has to do not with dictionaries as a generic kind, but with dictionaries as perceived by John as he sets out to improve his vocabulary.

(the so-called *typicality effect*). This, by the way, is not specific of Pustejovsky's work: it is quite general in lexical semantics, excluding Cognitive Linguistics. Another thing not taken into account by Pustejovsky is the (apparently contradictory) finding that very young children tend to be essentialists about natural categories though not about artefacts. As a theory belonging to artificial cognition, the *Generative Lexicon* clearly does not have to take either of these into account; however, if the model is assessed on the basis of criteria used in natural cognition, this may be seen as a serious shortcoming. We shall now look at each of these points in more detail.

What can work in natural cognition tell us about the distinction between lexical and encyclopedic knowledge?[10] Even though details may differ considerably, there appears to be general agreement on a four-stage model of verbal lexical processing:

1. *lexical contact*, which results from the extraction of a phonological representation from the acoustic waveform;

2. *activation of lexical entries* corresponding with that phonological representation;

3. *selection of the appropriate lexical entry* among the possible candidates;

4. *access to the entire information* behind the lexical entry.

Strictly speaking, this model seems to *erase* the distinction between *lexical* knowledge (in the sense of lexical semantics) and *encyclopedic* knowledge. The first two steps (lexical contact and activation of lexical entries) appear to involve nothing but phonological form. The third step may imply phonological form as well as minimal access to the information below, as it is also able to rely on context (both syntactic constraints and more semantic or pragmatic content). In contrast, accessing the entire information behind a lexical entry seems to imply access, on the one hand, to syntactic category (if selection of the appropriate lexical entry has not already involved reference to context), and, on the other hand, to what Pustejovsky and most lexical semanticists would call *lexical information*, AND to what they would call *encyclopedic information*. Far more important than the distinction between lexicon and encyclopedia is the above-mentioned dissociation between phonological information, which essentially plays the role of an address (i.e. a means of access to all the other information), and the other information itself (including syntactic, so-called lexical and so-called encyclopedic information). If this were rephrased in terms of the distinction between *word* and *concept*, **word would correspond to phonological information** (i.e. means of access), while *concept* **would correspond to more or less all other information** (*syntactic*, *lexical* and *encyclopedic* under the traditional distinction).

---

[10] Experimental work that deals more specifically with language pathologies will be reviewed in section 8.

The picture is however rather more complex than this first approximation would suggest. For one thing, conceptualisation is not only linked to language. It is also linked to categorisation and, notably, to discrimination through visual perception: words are not the only means of access to concepts. On the other hand, natural cognition cannot ignore the typicality effects discovered and studied under the impulse of Rosch's work (see Rosch 1973a, 1973b, 1975, Rosch & Mervis 1975). In the traditional approach to conceptualisation and categorisation, inherited from Aristotle, a concept stands for a list of properties that apply to all members of the corresponding category, while the meaning of a word corresponds to a list of features that are singly necessary and jointly sufficient. If this is the case, membership of a given category is a matter of all-or-nothing, with no room whatsoever for gradualness: something either is or is not a bird. However, Rosch's experiments have established the existence of widespread typicality effects, i.e. of a tendency to rate members of a given category (e.g. *bird*) along a membership scale, with, for instance, sparrows or robins being rated as "better birds" or "more birdy" than, e.g., chickens, penguins or ostriches. Findings like this appear to be in direct contradiction with the predictions of the classical model. Moreover, they come with a rather troublesome implication, namely that categorisation rests on probabilistic criteria.

There is some contradictory evidence, however: it has been shown (e.g. by Keil 1989 and Gelman & Markman 1987) that children tend to be essentialist about natural kinds, though not about artefacts. This raises the interesting question whether typicality effects might be explained without prejudice for the classical model, which could then be preserved. Some psychologists have attempted to formulate such an explanation: according to them, typicality effects result from the inclusion of non-necessary features in categorisation. This has led them to postulate a *core definition* of the concept (consisting of necessary and sufficient conditions of membership), as well as an *identification procedure* (through which exemplars are identified). The identification procedure must involve not only abstract non-necessary features and visual or more general perceptual information, but also functional information for artefacts. Typicality effects would then be explained as a by-product of the identification procedure: "if we assume that the identification procedure related to a concept is more readily accessible than the core definition of that concept, we can argue that semantic categorization tasks are often not performed by looking up core features but by comparing the features in the identification procedure of the target and those associated with the probe item" (Caplan 1992:72). Conversely, children tested for permanency of categorisation or of necessary characteristics would use the core meaning rather than the identification procedure, giving rise to essentialism.

Approaches to concepts in terms of core meaning and identification procedure have been corroborated by psychological experiments (see Armstrong et al. 1983). On the face of it, the distinction between lexicon and encyclopedia could thus be revived and reapplied, with core meaning corresponding to lexical meaning and identification procedure linked with encyclopedic knowledge. However, there are again several reasons why this cannot be the whole story. First of all, the core meaning of a concept gathers all necessary and sufficient features (and nothing but them), which does not seem to correspond exactly to the notion of *lexical meaning* as defined by lexical semanticists. For instance, it is doubtful that the information listed in Pustejovsky's lexical entries is sufficient for the core meaning of a concept, while at the same time it is clear that part of the information stored there rather belongs to identification procedure (e.g., TELIC and AGENTIVE QUALIA). Secondly, lexical information must obviously include syntactic category and argument structure, which seem to be pieces of linguistic information rather than of information related to the core meaning of the corresponding concept. We might be tempted to conclude that, although there is obviously a very valid distinction to be made between core meaning (including necessary features only) and identification procedure (involving frequent but non-necessary features), it may be sufficient to lump all the relevant information together in a "global" concept including less accessible core meaning as well as more accessible identification procedure.

A number of theorists, working on the assumption of a one-to-one correspondence between words and concepts, see the former as including four types of information. Two of these belong to the word's lemma, and the other two to its morpho-phonological form. Specifically, words comprise:

1. a *lemma*, which incorporates

    a) the word's *meaning* (i.e. the corresponding concept, including core meaning and identification procedure);

    b) the word's *syntax* (i.e. its syntactic category and, possibly, its argument structure);

2. a *morpho-phonological form*, which incorporates

    a) the word's *morphology*;

    b) the word's *phonology*.

Briefly, in terms of the four stages of word processing discussed above, one could see *processing* as going through the analysis of the acoustic waveform, yielding first lexical contact, and then through activation of lexical entries. These two steps would involve phonological information only. Selection of the appropriate lexical entry would follow, involving phonological information, and possibly morphological or syntactic information as well (e.g. agreement or syntactic category), or even some meaning. Access to the entire information would come as a last step. The *production* of words would first involve meaning and then access to syntactic information, to morphology and phonology, before reaching the final stage of articulation.

8. Aphasias

After the literature review in section 7, it will be useful to look more specifically at the work that has been done on language pathologies. We should first of all remind ourselves that the latter come in a bewildering variety; *aphasia* is the general term used to refer to any language processing deficit. An important distinction must be made between *primary aphasic impairments*, which have to do with language processing itself, and *secondary aphasic impairments*, which have to do with disorders of memory, attention, perception, motor functions, etc. that could impact on language processing. Unfortunately, whether a given impairment is language-related or involves a different type of disturbance is not always easy to determine.[11]

Conclusions drawn about patients depend on four performance features:

1. ability in one given language-related task, coupled with inability in another (this is evidence for a selective deficit);

2. poor performance in two language-related tasks (this is evidence for a single underlying processing deficit);

3. graded performance, on the basis of comparisons of groups of patients involving different types of linguistic stimuli in a given task (this allows for the determination of relative difficulties for individual patients);

4. error types (their analysis allows for the description of a patient's impairments).

No conclusion reached on the basis of these performance features is entirely foolproof. More importantly, evidence of double dissociation may not be enough to determine which functions are affected.

The most important disorders of language processing involve the recognition of spoken words, the meaning of words, the production of spoken words, the reading and writing of single words, the recognition and the production of morphologically complex words, sentence comprehension and sentence production. The last two will not be reviewed here, since most of the relevant work has concentrated on syntactic factors.

- *Impaired recognition of spoken words*

There seems to be clear evidence that speech is not processed in the same way as non-speech: "one of the most important aspects of auditory processing for speech is that the auditory system rapidly distinguishes speech from nonspeech sounds, and appears to process speech sounds differently than nonspeech sounds" (Caplan 1992:32). Apart from disturbances of auditory processing that are not specific to the

---

[11] For instance, a patient's inability to name objects when shown visual stimuli may come from a disturbance of the visual system rather than from a disturbance of the lexical or conceptual modules.

recognition of linguistic items, but that may nonetheless affect such recognition, some other disturbances exist that are genuinely specific to acoustic-phonetic processing. They are identified through a few specific inabilities or difficulties of patients: the inability to discriminate and/or label stops,[12] repetition performances associated with a much milder speech output disturbance, and poor auditory comprehension. The latter may be explained through a disturbance in auditory processing, with an impairment of auditory processing leading to an impairment in lexical access, which will itself render access to the information stored in the concept difficult or impossible and induce bad performance. It has been pointed out that results achieved up to now have suffered from the nature of the comprehension tests used, while other tests (such as lexical decision, word monitoring and gating), all of which could have shed light on the relation between phonological processing disturbances and auditory word comprehension, have not (yet) been used.

- *Impaired recognition of word meaning*

Impaired access to concepts (i.e. the meaning of words as defined at the end of section 7) may be tested either through single word comprehension or through naming tasks. The latter may involve verbal definitions or visual stimuli. However, even though no definitive answer has been reached on the existence of either a single amodal store for both visual and non-visual information or several modal stores, it should be clear that accessing concepts will involve different processes depending on the nature of the stimuli. The chief difficulty in establishing whether a patient suffers a semantic deficit lies in distinguishing *loss* of conceptual representations from *disturbed access* to such representations, on the one hand, and in identifying partial semantic or access impairments. In fact, "naming deficits in aphasic patients often result from a disturbance affecting the retrieval or production of the form of a word rather than a failure to determine semantic description of the target" (Caplan 1992:77). Nevertheless, some fairly clear cases have been described, and these have occasionally had a further interesting feature: in some instances, impairment may be restricted to classes of concepts relating to objects with similar semantic properties (e.g. animals, inanimate objects, artefacts or abstract notions), whereas other classes of concepts, with different semantic properties, are preserved. That is, a patient may perform correctly on a naming task involving, say, vegetables, but very poorly on a naming task involving animals – or vice versa.

- *Impaired production of spoken words*

This common impairment in aphasic patients can have different origins: informational loss in the corresponding concepts, impaired access to word forms, impaired transfer of word forms to motor neurons, and articulatory impairment. A lot has been

---

[12] All three possibilities are found: some patients can discriminate but not label, others are capable of both, and a third group fails to discriminate *and* to label. The dependence of labelling on discrimination explains why there are no patients who can label but not discriminate.

learned from research involving investigations of normal speakers' speech errors, such as tip-of-the-tongue phenomena, malapropisms, and slips of the tongue. In tip-of-the-tongue phenomena, though subjects are unable to produce the right word, they typically have some phonological information, including word onset, number of syllables and sometimes the end of the word. In malapropisms, the word pronounced in error is a real one, without any relation in meaning to the proper word, but closely related to it in pronunciation. Slips of the tongue affect only a portion of the sound structure of the word; they frequently involve phoneme substitution. The general conclusion drawn from these cases, where informational loss in the concept or access to the concept is *not* the problem (remember that reference here is to research involving normal subjects who have already accessed a particular concept, but fail to access the complete phonological form), is that "different aspects of phonological form are computed at different stages of processing" (Caplan 1992:117). Experiments on word recognition and word production, which both involve the recovery of phonological form (in recognition as a means of access to the concept, and in production as an intermediary step between concept retrieval and articulation), support a double lexicon hypothesis as far as phonological form is concerned, i.e. a store of phonological forms for recognition and a (distinct) store of phonological forms for production.

Disturbances in accessing phonological form (rather than in semantic or phonological processing) can be tested through word production tasks from semantic stimuli (pictures or definitions). For instance, the *inability* to name an object shown on a picture, combined with an *ability* to answer questions about the object and to repeat words or read them aloud, seems to indicate that no significant semantic or phonological impairment exists, though access from concept to phonological form is impaired.

- *Impaired reading and writing of single words*

There are two major tendencies in reading and writing studies: either reading and writing imply the activation of phonological codes, or they do not. Those who adopt the former view hold that the recognition of spoken words and that of written words imply basically the same mechanisms; those who adopt the latter view hold that different mechanisms are implied. Good evidence is available for the existence of written word forms (i.e. no letter-by-letter phonetic processing), though phonology may be useful in accessing the meaning of written words. Theories of reading and writing have been based on the various known forms of dyslexia:

1. *Phonological dyslexias* – patients are unable to read even simple nonsense words, but have no difficulties with regular words; the dissociation between words and non-words may be complete.

2. *Surface dyslexias* – nonsense words are read correctly but patients have great difficulty with real words, often failing to recognise and pronounce them completely; surface dyslexics usually have no difficulty in understanding the words

they can read, but irregularly written words elude them, as their lexical access through reading is impaired.

3. *Non-semantic reading* – adequate performance in whole word reading is offset by a disturbance in meaning representation.

4. *Deep dyslexias* – which come in a variety of forms: patients presented with a written word may pronounce a semantically related word, they may be worse at reading abstract words than concrete ones, function words may be read with errors, and inflected or derived words may be read with substitution of affixes.

5. *Letter-by-letter reading* may be the only reading process available to some patients, who may not have any difficulty in writing or spelling words but whose problem appears to originate in the inability of accessing or building written word forms.

Agraphias also come in different forms:

1. *Phonological agraphias* – patients are impaired in their ability to write nonsense words but not in their ability to write existing words; this is good evidence in favour of independent activation of spoken and written word forms.

2. *Dissociations between written and spoken naming* – patients who are unable to produce the spoken form of an object name can nonetheless write it.

3. *Category-specific phonological agraphias* – performance under dictation differs depending on whether the words are abstract or concrete; function words are generally impaired; this disturbance does not entail a semantic disturbance.

4. *Surface or lexical agraphias* – the agraphia equivalents to letter-by-letter reading.

5. *Asemantic writing* – patients unable to write spontaneously manage to write under dictation.

Although the evidence is not entirely clear, all of the above may suggest the existence of dual systems (input and output) for reading and writing.

- *Impaired recognition and production of morphologically complex words*

Two types of morphologically complex words must be distinguished: those derived through inflectional morphological processes (e.g. agreement and tense), and those derived through derivational word formation processes. This raises two questions, one at word level, the other at sentence level. Are morphologically complex words recognised and produced as such, and are they understood and computed through the meaning of the words they are derived from? What does the information contained in the affixes contribute to higher-order syntactic and semantic structures?

With respect to the recognition of morphologically complex words, three positions compete. According to the first (the *decomposition model*), constituent morphemes are recognised individually. According to the second, morphologically complex words are recognised as units in themselves. The third position is a mix of the first and the second. It seems that the data support the decomposition model for regularly inflected forms. For irregularly inflected forms and for derived words, the evidence rather suggests that they are recognised as units. The picture for production of morphologically complex words is much less clear.

Disturbed *processing* of morphologically complex words in single word tasks seems to indicate that the reading of affixes involves spelling-sound correspondence rather than whole-word reading. In auditory *recognition*, studies on agrammatic patients seem to corroborate the distinction between derivational and inflectional affixes made above: patients fare better on the former than on the latter. Research on disturbed *production* of morphologically complex words by agrammatic subjects during single word tasks (reading, writing, and repetition) show a similar discrepancy.

9. A proposal for a model in natural cognition based on the *Generative Lexicon*

The insights from natural cognition summarised in section 8 appear to suggest that the phonological form of a word provides information leading to the recognition and production of the spoken word, as well as access to all other information (which is not necessarily equally accessible). In Pustejovsky's model, on the other hand, words involve form as well as meaning. But this equation ("word = form + meaning") is anything but a central feature of Pustejovsky's model, and need not concern us in the following (tentative) proposal for a model in *natural* cognition based on the *Generative Lexicon* model and testable via the usual processes in natural cognition. Since Pustejovsky defines natural languages as being weakly polymorphic, i.e. as not involving a one-to-one correspondence between words and concepts, a model in which phonological form is represented separately from lexical meaning would presumably not upset him.[13] What of other, more central characteristics?

The three main features that, together with its ambitious scope, make Pustejovsky's model stand out are as follows:

1. it insists on a strict separation of lexical meaning and encyclopedic knowledge;
2. it insists on the necessity of lcps, i.e. on the need to treat complementarily polysemous words as units, instead of dividing them in as many entries as there are meanings;

---

[13] Phonological form is in fact *not* taken into account in his model (nor is it in most other models in lexical semantics). One might posit the existence of a level separate from that of the lexical meaning for which his lexicon is designed. Phonological form would be represented at this additional level, with access *from* that level and from the representations therein *to* the lexical level and to the representations therein.

3. it insists on making TELIC and AGENTIVE QUALIA, which most lexicologists would relegate to encyclopedic knowledge, part of lexical meaning.

All of these are important enough to be taken into account in our proposal. The first feature, a strong separation of lexicon and encyclopedia, is not very easy to model. Encyclopedic meaning could certainly be put on a par with identification procedure (as defined in section 7), but it should be clear that, in the psychologists' model, identification procedure is readily accessible under the words themselves: it can be immediately accessed through phonological form (in fact, it is more readily accessible than core meaning).[14] It is not clear how this would tally with Pustejovsky's strong feelings about the divide between lexicon and encyclopedia. Moreover, it may well be the case that Pustejovsky, like most linguists, would want the encyclopedia to be less accessible than the lexicon (or, on the equivalence suggested above, identification procedure to be less accessible than core meaning). A further problem has been pointed out above: lexical meaning according to Pustejovsky presumably falls short of core meaning; it is certainly not a list of singly necessary and jointly sufficient features. To see this, let us revisit example (11a), reproduced here as (12):

(12)   John had been thinking that his vocabulary was so poor that he should improve it. He could think of no better idea than to read the entire OED. *He began the dictionary* on a sunny afternoon...

In section 6, the semantic acceptability of the italicised part of (12) was explained through a pragmatic change in the TELIC quale of *dictionary*, from **consult** to **read**. Such a change would be problematic if the various pieces of information included in the QUALIA STRUCTURE as well as in the ARGUMENT, EVENT and INHERITANCE STRUCTURES were singly necessary: none of them could be changed by whatever means.[15] Taken collectively, they will probably fall short of being jointly sufficient to determine membership. In all likelihood, there is thus no direct correspondence between Pustejovsky's model and the core meaning vs. identification procedure model outlined above.

Should we be surprised? Should we now cast doubt on the validity of Pustejovsky's model? The answer to both questions is negative. After all, it is a linguistic model (hence its insistence on a distinction between lexical and encyclopedic knowledge), proposed to solve problems of linguistics (syntactic and semantic compositionality) rather than of categorisation. In other words, the lexical structure proposed by Pustejovsky would come under the lemma, and the overall structure might look something like this:

---

[14] If the distinction between core meaning and identification procedure is to account for typicality effects, identification procedure *has to be* more accessible.

[15] Some bits and pieces in the qualia structure may *not* be singly necessary. As pointed out in section 7, they may have to be included under identification procedure.

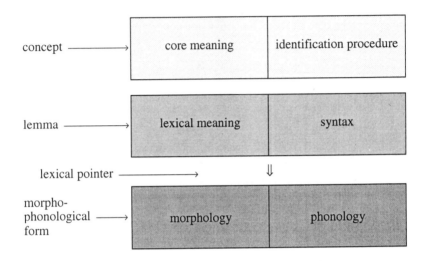

Lexical meaning (in Pustejovsky's sense) and syntactic information would be the only data stored under the lemma, with all conceptual knowledge stored at another level, not necessarily accessed for linguistic processing. On the other hand, categorisation would take place entirely at the conceptual level, and would not imply any linguistic information, whether syntactic or lexical. The problem, though, is that this cannot be completely right, as we are able to name objects on the basis of either a definition or visual perception. It would be prudent to suppose some kind of shortcut between conceptual knowledge and morpho-phonological knowledge, as follows:

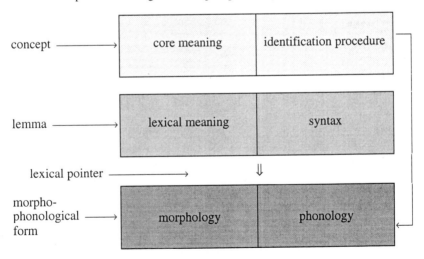

No provision has been made for a shortcut between lemma and conceptual level. As lexical meaning would *not* be sufficient for single word comprehension in the usual sense, the same shortcut as is used for categorisation would be used here (processing would go directly from the phonological form to the conceptual level). The lemma would be used only or mainly for sentence interpretation, which comes to include rather more than most contemporary pragmaticians would allow. This, in turn, begs the question of the role of *encyclopedic* information in *utterance* processing, for instance in examples such as (12) above.

Be that as it may, in which way could it be said that lexical knowledge is more accessible than encyclopedic knowledge? Clearly, the operations of syntax and lexical compositional semantics are automatic and entirely unconscious in the cognitive sense: they do not seem to be accessible at all to consciousness or introspection. Categorisation, too, seems to be an automatic and unconscious process. What is more, the information in the core meaning at conceptual level does not appear to be accessible to introspection any more than information in the lemma. By contrast, though the use of encyclopedic information drawn from the identification procedure is largely unconscious and automatic in utterance interpretation, this information nevertheless seems much more accessible to consciousness. Thus, something appears to be right in the idea of a linguistic level (the lemma) that would be used in sentence interpretation, but not in utterance interpretation, categorisation, or single word understanding.

The second feature, regarding lcps, is among the most interesting and convincing of Pustejovsky's proposals. It clearly sets him apart from the mainstream of lexical semantics. We have pointed out that, in SELs (sense enumeration lexicons), each sense gives rise to a different item. In our terms, that would mean a separate three-layered representation for each. In the case of *sonata*, separate items (and representations) would exist for the *score* sense, for the *informational* sense, for the *record* sense, for the *performance* sense. In Pustejovsky's model, all of these are gathered in a single item. To verify whether this is the right way to go in natural cognition, cogent tests would have to be designed that measure relative accessibility of word meanings. If, given one meaning of a complementarily polysemous word, the other meanings are more clearly accessible than are, given the meaning of a non-polysemous word, the meanings of semantically related words (as, for instance, names of different birds) or those of truly homonymous words, we would have a rather good indication (apart from common sense, which in this instance clearly plays in favour of Pustejovsky) of the existence of lcps rather than different items, or at least of very strong links between the senses of complementarily polysemous words.

The third feature concerns the insertion of TELIC and AGENTIVE QUALIA in lexical meaning. If information stored in these QUALIA does indeed belong to a linguistic level that has the characteristics mentioned above (automaticity and inaccessibility to consciousness), tests aimed at determining their accessibility to consciousness will obviously not be conclusive, especially in view of the fact that some of the information under lexical meaning could quite well be duplicated in conceptual knowledge, even if it is represented there in another format, and serves a different purpose. However, this is where the generative devices could come into play. *Type coercion, selective binding* and *co-composition* all rely on information in the structures that are constitutive of lexical meaning, among them TELIC and AGENTIVE QUALIA. Testing could apply at that level.

10. Testing Pustejovsky's *Generative Lexicon* in natural cognition

Having provided a brief sketch of how a model of the *Generative Lexicon* could be developed in natural cognition, I would like to say a little more than I have done so far about testing, though I shall stay on very general ground.

The model presented here integrates several information stores that may well correspond to modules in the Fodorian sense, and therefore be subject to double dissociation. There are two potential modules at each level: core meaning and identification procedure at the conceptual level, lexical meaning and syntactic information at the linguistic level (lemma), morphological information and phonological information at the morpho-phonological level. Let us see first how they measure up against Fodor's criteria for modularity.[16]

1. *Core meaning* has most of the cognitive characteristics of a Fodorian module. It has domain specificity (it applies only to the members of the corresponding category), obligatory firing (one cannot decide not to recognise an object one can recognise), inaccessibility to consciousness, fast performance and informational encapsulation (in this model at least). It presumably has a characteristic ontogenic course. It seems to have specific breakdown patterns (as shown by the existence of category-specific loss of conceptual information). Whether the core meaning "module" has shallow outputs is less clear.

2. *Identification procedure* is not quite as good a candidate for a Fodorian module. It is not entirely clear whether it has domain specificity: a good case could be made for the hypothesis that a given concept can provide access to other concepts,[17] and, given the more modular nature of core meaning, identification procedure would be a good candidate for where this happens. For the same reasons, it is not so sure that identification procedure has informational encapsulation. It

---

[16] Fodor (1983) defines a *module* as having *domain specificity, encapsulation, obligatory firing, shallow outputs, speed, inaccessibility to consciousness, a characteristic ontogenic course, a dedicated neural architecture* and a *characteristic pattern of breakdown*. Cf. Hilferty, this volume. The neurological criteria will not be taken into account in what follows.

[17] This would be an alternative to lcps.

presumably has obligatory firing, though it is doubtful whether its output is shallow. It has fast performance but, as said above, it is probably relatively accessible to consciousness. For the other modular characteristics, much the same remarks as given for core meaning apply.

3. *Lexical meaning*, by contrast, would have all of the cognitive characteristics of a Fodorian module. It has domain specificity, informational encapsulation, obligatory firing, shallow outputs, fast performance, and it is inaccessible to consciousness. It may have a characteristic ontogenic course, but this requires further study. Whether it has specific breakdown patterns is precisely what should be tested.

4. *Syntax* is also a Fodorian module, in the usual sense, but it is not the topic of this paper.

5. It is a matter for discussion whether the two information stores at the morpho-phonological level are modules in the Fodorian sense. They seem to allow more interpenetration than would be the case, for instance, between lexical meaning and syntax.

All of this is summed up in the following table:

	core meaning	identification procedure	lexical meaning	syntax	morphology	phonology
domain specificity	+	?	+	+	?	?
encapsulation	+	?	+	+	?	?
obligatory firing	+	+	+	+	+	+
shallow outputs	?	?	+	+	+	+
fast performance	+	+	+	+	+	+
limited conscious access	+	—	+	+	+	+

characteristic ontogenic course	+	+	+	+	+	+
specific breakdown patterns	+	+	+	+	+	+

The ultimate test for modularity lies in double dissociation (cf. section 4). Here, problems soon arise. It seems difficult, for instance, to test whether double dissociation is possible between core meaning and identification procedure, i.e. whether either can work when the other one is impaired. We need to ask ourselves whether full functionality at the level of core meaning would be at all possible in the case of impairment at the level of identification procedure. It would be, if the shortcut from phonological form to conceptual level could access *either* core meaning *or* identification procedure.

Let us assume that this is the case and that we want to test for correct performance in a core meaning task in the absence of correct performance in an identification procedure task: how could it be done? As its name indicates, identification procedure could be tested by means of naming tasks, provided other tests have established no disturbance to phonological access, visual perception, or word recognition. In other words, a patient who would perform poorly on a naming task (that is, who would not be able to produce the right name when presented with a visual stimulus or a definition) while these other capacities are preserved, could be said to suffer a disturbance in identification procedure. Such a patient might then be tested for core meaning abilities. On the assumption that essentialism in natural categories comes from core meaning, a good test would appear to consist in a reproduction of the experiments that brought essentialism to light. However, a lower than normal performance in such a test would not necessarily mean that core meaning does not function adequately: it might also mean that the assumption of a link between essentialism and core meaning is wrong. On the other hand, if a patient whose performance corresponds to the description provided above (i.e. a naming deficit combined with normal performances in phonological access, visual perception, and word recognition) performed normally in the essentialism experiments, this could indicate that core meaning may be preserved while identification procedure is impaired. Testing the reverse (impaired core meaning and intact identification procedure) would be possible if patients could be found who perform normally in naming tasks and typicality rating experiments but not in essentialism experiments.

For our purposes, by far the most interesting part of the testing procedure would be an exploration of whether lexical meaning is susceptible of double dissociation from the two conceptual level components. The existence of patients whose syntax is impaired (so-called agrammatic patients) but who remain in a position to access some meaning through inferences based on encyclopedic knowledge has been well-documented. The type of patient one would have to work with would have a normal performance in sentence interpretation and production (i.e. full functionality at the lexical level), but an impaired performance in conceptual tasks, for instance single word understanding. Since, as we have seen, lexical meaning (in the natural cognition model derived from the *Generative Lexicon*) is a module in the Fodorian sense, the only way to test performance at that level is presumably by means of a sentence interpretation task that would involve the generative operations. If the sentence interpretation task implied lexical meaning, with generative operations involving TELIC or AGENTIVE QUALIA, good performance levels would show, first of all, that there is double dissociation between lexical meaning and components at the conceptual level, and secondly, that TELIC and AGENTIVE QUALIA do have a legitimate place in lexical meaning. However, it must be pointed out that, though agrammatic patients who perform satisfactorily at the conceptual level have been described, as have patients with an adequate grammatical performance level but with impaired performance in naming tasks, patients with correct sentence processing and production, not only at the level of syntax, but also at the level of lexical meaning, while suffering an impairment at the conceptual level, have not.[18] I should probably also insist on the fact that none of the tests or experiments summarily sketched above would be easy to organise or interpret.

In conclusion, even though at this point in time several details of the model proposed above as a possible equivalent in natural cognition to the *Generative Lexicon* model in artificial cognition could be discussed and contested, new evidence, experiments and tests would be necessary to show its full validity or otherwise. On the face of it, it is not the most likely model in natural cognition to date for the divide between lexical knowledge and encyclopedic knowledge. Nevertheless, it has to be remembered that the *Generative Lexicon* is an artificial cognition model and that even if it were invalidated for natural cognition, this in itself would not disqualify it for use in artificial cognition.

11. *A woman begins a book* vs. *Virginia Woolf begins "The Waves"*: generic vs. specific knowledge

An important question that must be raised if, indeed, it is hard or impossible in natural cognition to separate encyclopedic knowledge (including core meaning and identification procedure) from lexical meaning (in Pustejovsky's sense) is where exactly, or when, semantic composition is done. If, excluding purely linguistic features (syntactic category and argument structure for instance), all meaning is conceptual,

---

[18] The existence of "blatherers", i.e. mentally retarded individuals with intact linguistic capacities (see Curtiss 1989), is inconclusive: blatherers are not specifically deficient at the conceptual level.

whether it falls under core meaning or identification procedure, it does not seem to make much sense to posit a linguistic procedure of semantic composition independent of conceptual meaning. In other words, there would be no meaning other than conceptual; all lexical semantic operations (including those postulated in the *Generative Lexicon*, namely selective binding, type coercion, and co-composition) would be pragmatic devices operating on conceptual or encyclopedic knowledge. How likely would that be?

Some arguments have been given above in favour of a more pragmatic view of type coercion (cf. section 6). I would like to add another, important, argument linked to a subject alluded to before, but not developed at that stage, namely *specific encyclopedic information* (SEI). What could specific encyclopedic information be? Let us accept as it stands Kripke's (1980) view according to which proper names are rigid designators (they refer to the same individual in all possible worlds) that do not have senses, even though they have referents. This does not mean that it is impossible to hold information relative to the referent of a proper name: it merely means that such information, even if it is uniquely identifying, cannot replace the proper name in a proposition. That is, the claim that a proper name has no sense pertains to logico-philosophical semantics. It is not directly linked to natural cognition. What is relevant to us here is that the information relative to the bearer of a proper name is not lexical in any sense. Rather, it may help identify the bearer of a given proper name.[19] The issue is the status of that information: it is clearly not lexical, since a) proper names do not belong to the lexicon, and b) the information is not the meaning of the corresponding proper names. But then, what is it? In what terms should we describe the information that, e.g., *Bill Clinton is the present President of the United States*? To clarify the matter, I propose a distinction between two kinds of encyclopedic knowledge :

I. on the one hand, encyclopedic knowledge relative to categories, i.e. classes of individuals who share the same necessary and sufficient properties, represented in the core meaning of the corresponding concepts, and identifiable through the properties represented in the identification procedure of those concepts;

II. on the other hand, encyclopedic knowledge relative to individuals.

The first type of encyclopedic knowledge, i.e. knowledge relative to classes, is clearly conceptual. I would like to claim that the second type of encyclopedic knowledge is conceptual as well, but in a different way. There are similarities and dissimilarities. We shall call the first type *generic encyclopedic knowledge*, and speak of the corresponding concepts as *generic concepts*; we shall call the second

---

[19] As Kripke (1980) himself has pointed out, this is not incompatible with the notion of a rigid designator: proper names are rigid designators because they cannot be replaced with coreferential expressions and because they are causally linked (through baptism, for instance) with their bearers. These may however be identified by means of other information.

type *specific encyclopedic knowledge*, and speak of the corresponding concepts as *specific concepts*.

Information regarding what it means to be the president of the United States, irrespective of the incumbent at any given time, may safely be considered to be GEI. The information that Bill Clinton is the president of the United States is SEI that may be found under a specific concept, specifically that linked to the individual who goes by the name Bill Clinton. To be clear on what that specific concept consists of (and on what specific concepts in general consist of), the first thing to note is that the individual (Bill Clinton) presumably falls under a category (for instance, he is a man). It may be safely assumed that the conceptual information under the corresponding generic concept is either copied onto the specific concept or directly accessible from it. Secondly, although all individuals in a given category share by definition the totality of their necessary and sufficient properties, they all have specific properties shared with *some* other individuals in the same category (but also possibly with individuals of other categories), and they may have unique properties, too (e.g., place and date of birth, a particular set of parents). These specific properties, or rather, those that are known, should also enter the specific concept corresponding to the individual. Some of them may be permanent (i.e. exist as long as the individual exists), while others may not be. A highly individuating factor is the personal history of the individual, that is the temporally ordered list of its individual properties or states. Thirdly, individuals should be recognised, and visual and spatial information would be important on that count. Such perceptual properties should be accessible from the specific concept. Finally, individuals can be spoken of (language is certainly a very important source of individuating information about individuals), and the expressions (possibly including a proper name) used to refer to them or to describe them should be stored.[20]

So far so good, but what of the distinction between generic and specific concepts? How should it affect the distinction between lexical and encyclopedic knowledge? As pointed out above, knowledge under specific concepts cannot possibly be lexical: it can only be encyclopedic. But in Pustejovsky's model an independant level of linguistic interpretation, which might be called *lexical compositional semantics*, is postulated: it should work on lexical meaning only,[21] and the operations of lexical compositional semantics should presumably occur before any pragmatic treatment

---

[20] The model outlined here is known as the *Theory of Mental Representations* (Reboul 1997, 1999, forthcoming). It was designed to account for reference resolution, relying on the idea that most so-called discourse anaphora are not linguistic phenomena, but rather depend on conceptual knowledge of the kind described above. For such a goal and, notably, for pronoun resolution, keeping track of previous referential expressions may well be crucial.

[21] That it may be supplemented by encyclopedic knowledge and/or pragmatic operations is not relevant here.

occurs. In the light of these remarks, it may be interesting to compare the following two examples:

(13a)   A woman begins a book.

(13b)   Virginia Woolf begins *The Waves*.

There are nothing but generic concepts in (13a). It seems reasonable to surmise that type coercion will select the TELIC QUALE of *book*. In (13b), there are two specific concepts, corresponding to *Virginia Woolf* (the author) and *The Waves* (one of her books), as well as a generic concept, corresponding to *begin*. There is no reason to believe that the specific concept corresponding to *The Waves* does not include the same information as the generic concept of *book*, i.e. TELIC and AGENTIVE QUALIA. But this cannot be lexical meaning in the sense of the *Generative Lexicon*, if only because specific concepts, though they may be accessible through linguistic information (as well as through any other perceptual information, including olfaction), are not lexical and do not give access to lexical meaning. The best case one could mount for lexical meaning accessible from specific concepts would rest on the claim that the properties indicated under a specific concept provide access to the corresponding generic concepts, which themselves would provide access to the lexical meaning linked to them. However, as we saw above, there seems to be no use in Pustejovsky's model for a link between lexical meaning and conceptual level, although there is certainly a link between conceptual meaning and morpho-phonological level, and between lemma and morpho-phonological level. Such a derivative access to lexical meaning would imply longer delays for the interpretation of utterances with specific concepts than for the interpretation of utterances with generic concepts. Pending investigations, this does not seem to be the case. Finally, the tortuous access between specific concept and lexical meaning in Pustejovsky's sense would presumably still violate the idea of a modular lexical meaning and that of a linguistic interpretation step occurring before any type of pragmatic processing, and accounting for composition.

In brief, the existence of non-lexical, specific, knowledge pleads in favour of a view of compositional interpretation that occurs at pragmatic level and implies non-lexical knowledge, i.e. encyclopedic knowledge. If this is the case, there seems to be no reason to postulate lexical meaning over and above the encyclopedic knowledge accessible under the corresponding concept. I shall now briefly outline how a model working along these lines would function.

12. A pragmatics-based account of compositional interpretation, encyclopedia and lexicon

As pointed out above, Pustejovsky's model and the operations it involves are attractive, as is his structural organisation of lexical meaning. What I am about to say does not contradict the hypothesis that most of his account is right as far as compositional operations and the organisation of knowledge are concerned. It will however reject the existence of any lexical knowledge over and above syntactic knowledge and argument structure. All knowledge relative to the meaning of words (extension and intension) will be considered as being conceptual and not lexical.

The first thing to note, as Sperber & Wilson (1998) did, is that there is no one-to-one correspondence between words and concepts – not only, as pointed out by Pustejovsky, because of homonymy and complementary polysemy, but because it is possible to have concepts without having words that correspond to them. Sperber & Wilson's example is that of the concept corresponding to the English word *siblings*, which does not have a corresponding word in French, though nothing would suggest that the French do not have such a concept. This is an example of a generic concept that is presumably fairly general. Sperber & Wilson point out that we can also build generic concepts based on our individual personal experience – *ad hoc* concepts for which no public words exist, even though the concepts do (see Barsalou 1987).

Thus, natural languages are indeed at least weakly polymorphic, although I would rather understand this to mean, not that there is no one-to-one correspondence between words and lexical meanings, but rather that there is no one-to-one correspondence between words and concepts. Words are a means of *accessing* concepts, whether they are generic, *ad hoc*, or specific.

My remarks in what follows will be squarely based on Sperber & Wilson's (1995) account of utterance interpretation. According to them, utterance interpretation follows a hierarchical model. The first step involves linguistic processing by a linguistic module. This yields a logical form, i.e. a structured sequence of concept addresses. The logical form is the input of the second, pragmatic, step in processing, for which the central system of mind takes responsibility. The mind relies on inferences, taking as premises the logical form of the utterance as well as other information under propositional form, of which at least some is encyclopedic information accessed through the concepts in the logical form.

The relevance of this account for the distinction between lexical and encyclopedic knowledge depends on what is understood by the notion of a structured sequence of concepts. It appears safe to hypothesise that the structure in question is largely derived from syntax, that is syntactic structure and binding. The rest consists of concepts, or rather concept addresses. How one accesses concept addresses is not transparent in Sperber & Wilson's model, which presumably, at the time, dealt mainly with generic concepts. Despite the absence of a one-to-one correspondence between words and concepts, it seems reasonable to assume that, as described above (section 7), the phonological forms of words give access to generic concepts, subject to the remarks on one-to-many correspondence formulated above. But access to *ad hoc* and to specific concepts may be more complex than that. *Ad hoc* concepts, though they should be accessible through words, are certainly not accessible in a straightforward manner, given that at least some of them are presumably fairly private. Specific concepts may be accessed through words, although access may be quite different depending on the words used.

It would be purely gratuitous to assume that specific concepts correspond to objects (individuals or things) only. All the ontological types generally considered to be individuals (including events, states, properties) may indeed give rise to specific concepts. For the sake of simplicity, we shall concentrate on specific concepts corresponding to concrete objects. Quite a big range of expressions may provide direct or indirect access to specific concepts corresponding to individual concrete objects. These expressions are generally called referential or referring expressions, for the rather good reason that they are used to refer to the individual concrete objects in question.[22] Referential expressions are varied: personal pronouns, demonstrative pronouns, definite descriptions, demonstrative NPs, proper names, etc. They all provide access to the corresponding specific concepts, but may do so in different ways. For instance, whereas proper names are presumably a direct means of access to a specific concept, with, fairly frequently, a one-to-one correspondence between a given proper name and a given concept, this certainly would not be the case for personal or demonstrative pronouns (which should be seen as encoding procedural content rather than as giving direct access to concepts, either generic or specific). Even definite descriptions or demonstrative NPs cannot function as labels for specific concepts. They are compositional, which means that they probably identify their referent as the object corresponding to the specific concept that, in a given context, satisfies the properties described in their head nouns and its modifiers. This context is itself a small subset of all specific concepts existing at a given time (the *domain of reference*). It is built through (linguistically given) procedural information *and* through pragmatic (relevance-theoretic) considerations. That is, identification is context-relative, but it also depends on a match between the information provided linguistically and the information represented in the specific concepts in the domain of reference.

A very general and tentative schematic representation of the model of lexical vs. conceptual knowledge sketched above might take the following form:

---

[22] Indeed, it is a (strong) hypothesis of the Theory of Mental Representations that mental representations (i.e. specific concepts) are a kind of hinge between linguistic expressions (referring expressions) and concrete objects.

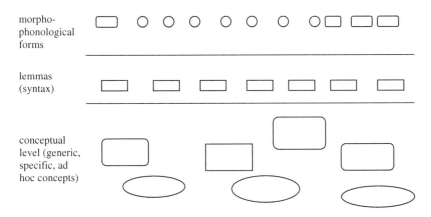

Two of the three levels (morpho-phonological form and syntax) are linguistic and fairly simple. Syntax (from a lexical viewpoint) includes syntactic category and argument structure (if any). The third level is the conceptual level; it gathers much if not all of what is usually meant by word or lexical meaning. The argument structure in the lemma may be safely assumed to be very close or even equivalent to Pustejovsky's ARGUMENT STRUCTURE. His EVENT, QUALIA and INHERITANCE STRUCTURES, on the other hand, all fall squarely under conceptual (or encyclopedic) meaning. At the morpho-phonological level, proper names are shown as rectangles with rounded angles, while ordinary nouns or NPs (remember that we have focused our attention on concrete objects) are represented by circles. Lemmas, at the second level, are represented as rectangles. At the conceptual level, generic concepts are represented as ellipses, specific concepts as rectangles with rounded angles and *ad hoc* concepts as normal rectangles. Relations between the three levels may be portrayed as follows:

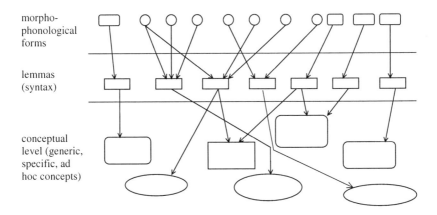

There is no one-to-one correspondence between any two levels, even though we get close in the case of proper names. Finally, it should be obvious that, although the figure describes word understanding in the interpretation of utterances, a direct link from the morpho-phonological to the conceptual level does not contradict it.

A question that remains is how this model might be tested (granted that, if anything, it is a model of natural cognition). Quite a few of the pointers given above (section 10) for testing Pustejovsky's model in natural cognition could be adopted here in reverse. For intance, the absence of any patient who would have impaired conceptual knowledge but intact sentence processing at the level of semantic compositionality, while it does not prove me right (for all we know, such a patient might appear one day), weakens Pustejovsky's position and reinforces mine (as a matter of fact, this would be true for any test of Pustejovsky's model that would not yield a positive result). As no such patient seems to exist at this point in time, and pending further investigation, the pragmatic model that has just been outlined looks quite promising, at least in the area of natural cognition. In artificial cognition, on the other hand, Pustejovsky's model may be a better candidate because it may well be easier to implement.

13. Conclusion

This paper has *not* tried to demonstrate that Pustejovsky's *Generative Lexicon* model is wrong: I am inclined to think that, as a model for *artificial* cognition, it is indeed very interesting – and highly promising. My aim was rather to show the urgent need, in *natural* cognition, for a larger number of experimental, psycho-linguistically oriented tests aimed at determining the validity (or at least the provisional validity) of certain models. Establishing the precise point where knowledge ceases to be lexical and becomes encyclopedic would gain a lot from such renewed experimental research, which could exploit the fact that linguistic disorders are so numerous and so varied. Instead of relying on tests that remain to be devised, I have here used examples to illustrate, in a more traditionally linguistic way, that Pustejovsky's approach does not draw the line between lexical and encyclopedic knowledge where it should be drawn.

References

Armstrong, Sharon Lee; Gleitman, Lila R; Gleitman, Henry. 1983. "What some concepts might not be". *Cognition* 13. 263-308.

Asher, Nicholas. 1993. *Reference to abstract objects in discourse*. Dordrecht: Kluwer.

Barsalou, Lawrence W. 1987. "The instability of graded structure. Implications for the nature of concepts". In Ulrich Neisser (ed.), *Concepts and conceptual development. Ecological and intellectual factors in categorization*. Cambridge: Cambridge University Press. 101-140.

Barwise, Jon; Perry, John. 1983. *Situations and attitudes*. Cambridge: M.I.T. Press.

Blakemore, Diane. 1987. *Semantic constraints on relevance*. Oxford: Blackwell.

Caplan, David. 1992. *Language, structure, processing and disorders*. Cambridge: M.I.T. Press.

Curtiss, Susan. 1989. "The independence and task-specificity of language". In Marc H. Bornstein & Jerome S. Bruner (ed.), *Interaction in human development*. Hillsdale: Lawrence Erlbaum. 105-138.

Fodor, Jerry A. 1983. *The modularity of mind. An essay on faculty psychology*. Cambridge: M.I.T. Press.

Gelman, Susan; Markman, Ellen. 1987. "Young children's inductions from natural kinds. The role of categories and appearances". *Child development* 58. 1532-1540.

Godard, Danièle; Jayez, Jacques. 1993. "Towards a proper treatment of coercion phenomena". *Proceedings of the sixth conference of the European Chapter of the Association for Computational Linguistics*. 168-177.

Heim, Irene. 1982. *The semantics of definite and indefinite noun phrases*. Amherst: Graduate Linguistic Student Association.

Kamp, Hans; Reyle, Uwe. 1993. *From discourse to logic. Introduction to modeltheoretic semantics of natural language, formal logic and discourse representation theory*. Dordrecht: Kluwer.

Keil, Franck. 1989. *Concepts, kinds and conceptual development*. Cambridge: M.I.T. Press.

Kempson, Ruth. 1975. *Presupposition and the delimitation of semantics*. Cambridge: Cambridge University Press.

Kripke, Saul. 1980. *Naming and necessity*. Oxford: Blackwell.

Lakoff, George. 1987. "Cognitive models and prototype categories". In Ulrich Neisser (ed.), *Concepts and conceptual development. Ecological and intellectual factors in categorization*. Cambridge: Cambridge University Press. 63-100.

Luscher, Jean-Marc. 1994. "Les marques de connexion. Des guides pour l'interprétation". In Jacques Moeschler, Anne Reboul, Jean-Marc Luscher & Jacques Jayez, *Langage et pertinence. Référence temporelle, anaphore, connecteurs et métaphore*. Nancy: Presses Universitaires de Nancy. 175-227.

Luscher, Jean-Marc. 1998. *Eléments d'une pragmatique procédurale*. Unpublished PhD dissertation, Université de Genève.

Moeschler, Jacques. 1989. *Modélisation du discours. Représentation de l'inférence argumentative*. Paris: Hermès.

Nunberg, Geoffrey. 1995. "Transfers of meaning". *Journal of semantics* 12. 109-132.

Pustejovsky, James. 1995. *The Generative Lexicon*. Cambridge: M.I.T. Press.

Reboul, Anne. 1989. "Relevance and argumentation. How bald can you get". *Argumentation* 3. 285-302.

Reboul, Anne. 1993. "Le poids des pères, le choc des fils: prédicats de phase, modificateurs et identification". *Cahiers de linguistique française* 14. 229-246.

Reboul, Anne. 1997. *Le projet CERVICAL. Représentations mentales, référence aux objets et aux événements*. Unpublished manuscript.

Reboul, Anne. 1999. "Reference, evolving reference and the theory of mental representations". In Martine Coene, Walter De Mulder, Patrick Dendale & Yves D'Hulst (ed.), *Traiani Augusti vestigia pressa sequamur. Studia lingvistica in honorem Lilianae Tasmowski*. Padova: Unipress. 601-616.

Reboul, Anne. Forthcoming. "A relevance theoretic approach to reference". To appear in the proceedings of the Relevance Theory workshop held at the University of Luton (U.K.), 8-10 September 1998.

Rosch, Elaine. 1973a. "On the internal structure of perceptual and semantic categories". In Timothy E. Moore (ed.), *Cognitive development and the acquisition of language*. New York: Academic Press, 11-144.

Rosch, Elaine. 1973b. "Natural categories". *Cognitive psychology* 4. 328-350.

Rosch, Elaine. 1975. "Cognitive representations of semantic categories". *Journal of experimental psychology: General* 104. 192-233.

Rosch, Elaine; Mervis, Carolyn. 1975. "Family resemblance. Studies in the internal structure of categories". *Cognitive psychology* 7. 573-605.

Sperber, Dan; Wilson, Deirdre. 1995 [1986]. *Relevance. Communication and cognition*. Oxford: Blackwell.

Sperber, Dan; Wilson, Deirdre. 1998. "The mapping between the mental and the public lexicon". In Peter Carruthers & Jill Boucher (ed.), *Thought and language*. Cambridge: Cambridge University Press. 184-200.

Wilson, Deirdre. 1975. *Presuppositions and non-truth-conditional semantics*. London: Academic Press.

Lexicopedia[1]

Carlos Inchaurralde

Universidad de Zaragoza, Departamento de Filología Inglesa y Alemana,
E-50009 Zaragoza, Spain
E-mail: inchaur@posta.unizar.es

0. Introduction

Linguists have always enjoyed drawing parallels with physics, which for many is the "mother of all sciences", universally accepted as "providing an explanation of the real physical world". When it comes to the distinction between lexicon and encyclopedia, the temptation is once again irresistible. If we ask a physicist where matter ends and energy begins (or vice versa), there is a good chance we will be told that they are two sides of the same coin.[2] If we ask a quantum physicist about light, there is an equally good chance we will be told it appears as both discrete quanta and analogue waves. Similarly, in linguistics, the distinction between lexicon and encyclopedia depends on the perspective adopted by the observer and on the practical needs of the research or the application that any previously gathered data may be used for. On the one hand, we have the "lexicon perspective", which tries to fix in a small descriptive piece of knowledge a great deal of the semantically-and-grammatically relevant information associated with a lexical item and useful for its linguistic analysis or linguistic use. Langacker (1987) reminds us that the lexicon

---

[1] I gratefully acknowledge the observations of an anonymous reviewer, as well as Bert Peeters' help in reshaping this contribution.

[2] Einstein, as is well-known, wrote a famous equation linking the two.

perspective is guided by the *conduit metaphor* (Reddy 1979), "which views lexical items as containers for meaning":

> [M]eaning is stored in these containers, and it is carried along with the lexical items as a linguistic expression is conveyed from the speaker to the hearer. This metaphor leads to the natural conclusion that all facets of the linguistic meaning of a lexical item are carried along together. (Langacker 1987:162)

As we shall see in a few moments, the conduit metaphor is also supported by some psycholinguistic facts. However, these do not seem to be strong enough in the light of other observations that favour a more "encyclopedic view" of meaning, where the meaning of words is strongly linked to extensive world knowledge. These pages are an attempt to throw more light on the topic; they are a psycholinguistic journey into this "encyclopedia in the lexicon" or "lexicopedia".

1. From form to meaning

It should be intuitively clear to everyone that the words we need to identify, understand or use can be processed individually: we have a lexical "entry list" in which they can be looked up, and each entry has information of some sort attached to it. But is that the only way human "word processing" works? It soon appears that the process is not as straightforward as it might have seemed: there may be *external* information that is equally relevant. Nonetheless, empirical evidence supports to some extent the existence of a matching process.[3]

In the literature, two different hypotheses have been formulated about access routes to lexical information. They have to do with different ways of representing information. According to the first (Forster & Chambers 1976, Morton & Patterson 1980, etc.), access to our mental lexicon differs depending on whether we are considering visual or auditive information, i.e. written or spoken words. Whereas spoken words are processed directly, written words may be processed in one of two ways: either directly, in which case there is a separate visual representation of the way the word is written, or indirectly, in which case the orthographic code is first translated into a phonological representation. Hence, there are two access routes. The second hypothesis is based on the idea that the convergence between visual and auditive information is carried out *before* access to the mental lexicon takes place, so that in fact we use a pre-lexical access code (Coltheart 1978, McCusker et al. 1981; etc.). In the latter case there is only one access route.

---

[3] It is important to make it clear that this matching process takes place mainly with "content" words, as opposed to functional words, which have a more grammatical role.

Some empirical research has been undertaken to test which of the two hypotheses is the most plausible one. Evidence gathered both from normal and impaired (e.g. dyslexic) subjects favours the hypothesis of the dual route (cf. Garnham 1985, Forster 1990, Seidenberg et al. 1984, Patterson et al. 1985, Sartori et al. 1984, Coltheart et al. 1980, etc.). In the experiments mentioned in the literature, some problems and intriguing facts appear that may throw some light on how the matching process is carried out.

First, it is of considerable interest to see that, even though under normal circumstances it takes very little time to find the information associated with a word that we need to identify or use, high-frequency words tend to be recognised much sooner than words that are less commonly used. There are longer reaction times with less frequent words, both in decision-taking and naming tasks. This variation affects open-class words more than closed-class words, which are functional in most cases and tend to be identified in relation with their syntactic significance and role.

A second observation, which substantiates the claim that information associated with words is necessarily accessed through form (be it phonological or orthographic) rather than directly, thereby underscoring the importance of form in lexical representations, is that it takes longer for subjects to reject a pseudo-word when it resembles a real word or uses a valid sequence of phonemes or letters for the language considered. Apparently, this has to do with the fact that subjects rely on a search process that starts immediately, but takes longer to complete, since it searches exhaustively all the entries in the lexicon before giving up.

Thirdly, there is the proven influence that certain lexical stimuli (primes) that are presented before a given lexical item may have on the reaction times reported in experimental tasks concerning the identification of that item. Among the most frequent priming effects are *repetition priming* (Scarborough et al. 1977), *semantic priming* (Meyer & Schvaneveldt 1971), and *contextual priming* (which is triggered by a group of words).

Last but not least, experimental work clearly demonstrates the role played by lexical ambiguity in a considerable number of cases. We normally assume that the linguistic and extralinguistic context help in determining the right meaning. A fundamental problem that has troubled psycholinguists has to do with whether we activate all the meanings of a word whenever we find ambiguity or whether we only activate one meaning because context guides us before we even start out on the search for senses. None of the models for word recognition that have been proposed could have possibly avoided taking into account this antagonism (initial autonomy vs. continued interactivity). As a result, different authors have taken different sides.

Morton (1979) and Patterson & Shewell (1987) propose an interactive model in which each word is represented in the lexicon by a device that is sensitive to certain types of information. The various devices receive that information from the sensory-acoustic input as well as from the linguistic context (in the form of syntactic and semantic data). Recognition of lexical items takes on the form of a competition. Different entries are simultaneously exposed to cumulative activation, until one of them crosses a threshold that guarantees selection. Elman & McClelland's (1984, 1986) TRACE model involves a network in which the various nodes (which represent acoustic features, phonemes, and words) are exposed to certain levels of activation that propagate throughout, via connections that may be either excitatory or inhibitory. The word that in the end attains the highest level of activation is the one that is recognised. Word nodes do not become activated until there is enough activation at the lower levels (acoustic features and phonemes); once the upper (word) level is reached, activation increases steadily. This is a typical connectionist model; it is interactive since it uses information from different sources to identify lexical units.[4]

On the other hand, there are the so-called "autonomous" models. One example will suffice. For Forster (1976, 1990), lexical identification is carried out in two different steps. First, the perceptual representation of the stimulus is compared with its phonological or graphical representation. Three different entry lists are used: phonological, orthographical, and semantic (only for word production, not for recognition). The matching process is carried out through an exhaustive search of the lexical entry in the lists. Once the word is found, a second step involves looking up syntactic and semantic information in a main database. Each of the two steps in this serial process has a high degree of autonomy.

Both the interactive and the autonomous approaches offer explanations for the problems and facts listed above. Interactive models explain frequency effects in terms of the different levels of activation that lexical units may reach. Autonomous models, on the other hand, have frequent words appear first in the mental lists. As for priming effects, they are easily explained, not only in interactive models, but also in autonomous ones, since the interaction can be carried out in the database at a post-access stage. The time it takes to reject a "pseudo-word" can be explained as a consequence of an exhaustive search in the lists.

It should come as no surprise that models with mixed approaches have also been proposed (e.g. Marslen-Wilson 1987). Whatever approach is adopted, the point is that words are identified as units and that, as such, the information they carry is considered to be encapsulated, "contained" so to speak (as per the conduit metaphor). Words, or rather lexical items, tend to be unequivocally identified in a certain mental checklist, and some information is associated with them. But what is the nature of that information? Can we hope to find something that is both very well encapsulated and easy to handle? The way things are, it rather seems to be the opposite. Indeed, by "meaning" of a lexical item we may understand a great many different things.

---

[4] More information on activation and connectionist modelling is provided in section 2 below.

2. What is in the meaning of a word?

The familiar distinction between denotation and connotation provides a nice place from where to continue our journey. Denotation has to do with "reference", and is said to be an "objective" kind of meaning. Connotation, on the other hand, is "subjective" and has to do with the evaluative content of words. Denotation seems to be a very simple notion: the denotation of a word is what it refers to. Nonetheless, for various reasons, this is a very problematic definition. Does a word refer to just one thing? Does it refer to a class of things? Does it always, i.e. in all circumstances, refer to that entity or class, or does it do so only in certain cases? Is the denotation of a word as perceived through our senses independent of that word, or can it only exist as long as it remains linked to that word? Is denotation simple to describe? Or is it something that goes beyond any description? The last two questions nicely summarise the debate surrounding the dictionary-encyclopedia interface. And then there is connotation, which is also part of meaning. Or is it not? Connotation is highly dependent on individuals or groups of individuals (so is denotation, but to a lesser extent). As connotation has no clear referential or truth-value content, can it be considered to be meaning proper? Let us try to examine some facts that may help clarify these questions.

First of all, it is important to see where (denotational) meaning comes from. A widely accepted view in psychology is that all the information that we have in our minds is stored in different kinds of memory (Tulving 1979). Permanent information is stored in *long-term memory* (as opposed to *short-term memory*, which only stores information that is useful for a while). In long-term memory, we must distinguish *episodic memory* (related to concrete situations in which the subject participated) from *semantic memory* (not related to any situation in particular, except via episodic memory; semantic memory is the kind of memory that stores a large number of knowledge structures about anything in the world). It seems that it is only through interaction with external reality that children learn to use their language and that they acquire the vocabulary they need (cf. Nelson 1985). That means that episodic memory gets a lot of information that helps build the knowledge networks present in semantic memory.

The more exposure one has to different manifestations of the denotational meaning of a word (together with the actual use of that word), the more clearly established the semantic content of that word will be in the end. I call this acquisition mode "cognitive *extension*". By means of this apparently rather unscientific term, I am basically suggesting that our world knowledge is created through interaction with our environment through our senses.[5] On the other hand, when we learn new concepts in

---

[5] Work by Barsalou and various associates gives some support to the assumptions followed here. References are provided at the end of the present section.

formal training at school, we often only receive concise explanations of the meaning of words. This I call "cognitive *intension*". The distinction is relevant when we consider the knowledge of specialised domains; it is also relevant to the discussion about dictionary and encyclopedia. Most of our vocabulary is learnt through cognitive extension, which leads to a very encyclopedic configuration of meaning, as opposed to what can be found in dictionary entries (information to be learned through cognitive intension).

For a long time, the prevailing opinion was that, if we want to study meaning, or even just talk about it, it has to be made manageable (presumably because it was felt that it was not). As a result, meaning was usually cut down, shrunk to what were perceived to be manageable proportions. Approaches to meaning were traditionally "intensional", i.e. based on the dictionary entry model. Denotational meaning was usually talked about in terms of (discrete) features or similar categories, articulated in different ways. This has not been without raising many representational problems. The outcome was inevitable: it became clear that meaning *does not* consist of discrete features that are supposed to be sufficient and necessary (cf. Geeraerts 1988). But proving that it does not is not enough. It was equally clear that meaning *is* structured, albeit in a different way. Meaning has indeed a very complex structure that grows with time and creates multiple links and possibilities not only inside one's own mental networks, but also in its characterisation as a collective construct. Starting from basic core senses, words may carry with them new meanings that appear in different sentential contexts.

Over the last fifteen to twenty years, to grasp the wide range of possible uses that words may have, concepts such as "variation" and "polysemy" have regained in theoretical importance.[6] In cognitive linguistics, one notion that has helped clarify the issue is the concept of a "core meaning" from which different meaning extensions originate. For instance, Lakoff (1986:144ff.) mentions a case of meaning extension that is cognitively rooted and based on image-schemas: a *path-focus schema* (e.g. *Sam walked **over** the hill*) may be transformed into an *end-point-focus schema* (e.g. *Sam lives **over** the hill*), a *multiplex schema* (e.g. ***All** men are mortal*) into a *mass schema* (e.g. ***All** gold is yellow*), a *one-dimensional trajector schema* (e.g. *Sam ran **through** the forest*) into a *zero-dimensional moving trajector schema* (e.g. *There is a road **through** the forest*), a *non-reflexive schema* (e.g. *He rolled over me*) into a *reflexive schema* (e.g. *He rolled over*), and so on. The main idea behind this approach is that conceptual categories have a radial structure (Lakoff 1987a:436). All members of a category are networked around a single core member.

Radial structures have not been universally accepted. Cruse (1986) has pointed out that certain meaning structures do pose problems when conceived of as networks.

---

[6] It has been often remarked that the boundary between the two is quite fuzzy (cf. Cruse 1986:55ff., Geeraerts 1993, and also Tuggy 1993).

When there is a connection between meanings along a continuum, normally developed in the course of time by metaphorical or metonymical processes, the idea of a "sense-spectrum" may be more accurate. Cruse's own example is that of the *mouth of a river*, where the relevant meaning of *mouth* is just one of several along a spectrum (*mouth of a person, mouth of a fish, mouth of a sea-squirt, mouth of a bottle, mouth of a cave, mouth of a river*). He adds that, as such, "a full sense-spectrum is not a satisfactory lexical unit: it does not, for instance, enter into any recognised lexical relations" (Cruse 1986:73). In other words, each of the meanings in the spectrum has to be further enriched. Going back to the earlier example, *mouth of a river* illustrates different meaning relations: opposites (*mouth* vs. *source*), part-whole (*mouth* vs. *river*), coordinate parts (*mouth* vs. *bed*), superordinate-hyponym (*mouth* vs. *estuary*), etc.

Cruse's findings are important, and have had repercussions for cognitive linguistics. The established view remains that different related meanings do not *need* to be graded along a continuum. On the contrary, the most common arrangement *is* a radial network in which the different extensions surround the main meaning. This configuration is geometrically similar to the family resemblance relations observed in prototype theory (Rosch 1973a, 1973b, 1975). For each category, there is a central example, and several peripheral instances that share only some characteristics (not necessarily the same throughout). This is the standard view. In the "extended" version of prototype theory (on the difference, cf. Kleiber 1991), the possibility of configurations similar to Cruse's sense-spectra is acknowledged. In any case, what is immediately apparent here is that meaning is not structured in "boxes" of content (the conduit metaphor), but rather scattered in various directions and among lexical items. Meaning is something more encompassing than structural semanticists conceded. It has a "distributed quality".

Let us move on. Another aspect of meaning is what has been referred to as the "connotations" of lexical items. What we have been looking at up to now had to do mainly with denotational meaning, i.e. referential objective meaning. There is a subjective dimension that has to be considered as well and that, more importantly, may also influence "objective" meaning. The pioneering work in this area, and still one of the most important references, is Osgood's research into what he calls "semantic space". Osgood (1976) confronted a large number of subjects with a vocabulary sample, to which they had to assign different values on several bipolar scales made up of qualifying adjectives. A factorial analysis of the data revealed three main dimensions (*evaluation, potency*, and *activity*), which reflected connotational configurations of the lexical items involved in the sample. This, too, is meaning. But where does it come from? It has an evaluative content that can only be explained through the cumulative experience that the subject has of interaction with the proper use of the lexical item in different contexts.

Apart from denotation and connotation, other types of "meaning" have been identified from a psycholinguistic point of view. For instance, we have norms about features like "familiarity", "concreteness" or "imagery", obtained through extensive sampling among speakers (Gilhooly & Logie 1980, Paivio et al. 1968, Toglia & Battig 1978; cf. Quinlan 1992). Combinations of such psycholinguistically relevant features, all of which have a different weight, may lead to lists of words organised according to principles that may be useful for teaching "basic English" vocabulary to children, second language learners, or people with language disorders (e.g. aphasics; cf. the PSET project referred to by Carroll et al. 1998).

Clearly, things are not as simple as they seemed to be at first. And we have not even mentioned encyclopedic information, i.e. information about the world that goes beyond the simple label, the set of features or the referential link that can be provided in a mental "dictionary". This is real "world knowledge", it is part of the communicative context and it exists inside our minds, in the form of semantic memory. Its role in language can be seen not only in inference processes, such as presuppositions, implicatures, etc., but also in the understanding of many idiomatic expressions and creative metaphors. Any speaker of Spanish who has some knowledge about bull-fighting and all the "actors" and elements involved in this activity is able to understand not only the entirely lexicalised expressions related to bull-fighting, but also creative idioms and metaphors that use this fragment of world knowledge. I have given relevant examples elsewhere (Inchaurralde 1997); they include, e.g., *salir al ruedo* ('to go into the arena') when one starts something challenging, *dar la alternativa* ('to give the alternative') when we give somebody new to the job an opportunity to prove his/her worth, *vestirse de luces* ('to dress in lights', 'to wear a bullfighter's costume') when we mean 'to make a good impression on others', etc.

Descriptions of how this encyclopedic information deep in our minds can be used and linked to single words appear in the work of some cognitive authors. Langacker (1987:162) suggests that lexical units are merely points of access, and that therefore "concepts are simply entrenched cognitive routines". More precisely:

> The entity designated by a symbolic unit can (...) be thought of as a *point of access* to a network. The semantic value of a symbolic unit is given by the open-ended set of relations – simple and complex, direct and indirect – in which this *access node* participates. Each of these relations is a cognitive routine, and because they share at least one component the activation of one routine facilitates (...) the activation of another. (Langacker 1987:163)

Langacker does not suggest this description out of nowhere. It is based on proposals by psychologists and computer scientists for models that involve semantic networking. The main hurdle is how to determine, for every access node, the extent of the corresponding conceptual network. Since it is possible to think of a network in terms of an unending chain of associations between nodes, there must be some mechanism, congruent with current psychological evidence, that helps determine which nodes get a place in the network, or in other words which nodes are "relevant". The keyword here is *activation*. This is a term used in connectionism to designate the degree of strength that the different nodes in a neural network may have.

Models of cognition that incorporate connectionist ideas use this term profusely. Anderson (1983), for instance, in his ACT model, distinguishes *declarative memory* from *production memory* and *working memory*. To retrieve information from declarative memory so that we can use it in our working memory, a certain amount of energy is needed in the form of activation. There are three routes to activation: *perception*, *spreading activation*, and *focusing*. Hearing a word or seeing an object may activate the corresponding access node: this form of awareness is called *perception*. In the case of an object, the corresponding access node may be that of the word denoting it. *Spreading activation* refers to what happens when an active concept spreads its activity to related concepts in the network; it may be either *convergent* (when one concept receives activation from many others) or *divergent* (when there is strong competition for activation among different nodes) (cf. Deane 1992:35). *Focusing* refers to the conscious, forceful concentration of activation on one concept that does not receive enough activation either from perception or from spreading activation. The various modes of activation for concepts in a network explain the link between words and encyclopedic knowledge dynamically.

Also from psychology come the now well-established assumptions of so-called "schemata" theories (Bartlett 1932, Rumelhart & Ortony 1977, Rumelhart 1980) according to which everything we know about the world is stored in large mental knowledge structures. Different labels have been used to refer to these structures, depending on the type of information and the way it is stored: "frames", "scenarios", "scripts", "situations", "idealised cognitive models", and so on (Minsky 1975, Schank & Abelson 1977, Sanford & Garrod 1981, Fillmore 1982, Lakoff 1987b, etc.) are all equally useful to understand how people use vocabulary in context. For instance, Wierzbicka (1994, 1997) has pointed to the existence of different "scripts" for interaction in different cultures and has drawn attention to how words have uses and meanings highly dependent on culturally-shared knowledge structures.

The numerous models that have been proposed strongly suggest that knowledge structures and the individual concepts associated with them are *dynamically constructed*. A systematic theory of how cognition is grounded in perceptual mechanisms, and how concepts are created dynamically has been gradually constructed by Barsalou and a team of co-workers (e.g. Barsalou 1982, Barsalou & Sewell 1984, Barsalou 1993, Barsalou *et al.* 1993, Barsalou & Prinz 1997, among others). The implication is that it is necessary to leave behind us the fixed-entry approach provided by a dictionary perspective on the lexicon.

3. Facing the facts from a computational perspective

If we take a computational perspective, we have different ways of approaching the various representational problems that have been mentioned. One approach consists in merely providing lists of data, structured in such a way that somehow we manage to reflect the richness of the phenomena involved. In Inchaurralde (1994), I made an attempt at setting up different data structures that could account for facts commonly related to knowledge structures and lexical sets. The different structures I suggested were the following:

- Scripts, i.e. conventionalised situations normally associated with verbs:

VERB script = (S_{case} VERB O_{case}; <CONSEQU: cns_1, ..., cns_n>; <CAUSES: $caus_1$, ..., $caus_n$>; <SETTING: set_1, ..., set_n>; <SUPERCHAIN: spc_1, ..., spc_n>; <SUBCHAIN: sbc_1, ..., sbc_n>)

Legend: VERB = verb, S = subject, S = object, CONSEQU = consequences of the action expressed by the verb, CAUSES = causes of the action, SETTING = setting, SUPERCHAIN = larger scripts that contain VERB script, SUBCHAIN = shorter scripts that contain VERB script.

- Frames, i.e. schematic information of a more static kind (with part-whole relationships):

X meron = (<MAIN: mn_1, ..., mn_n>; <PARTS: prt_1, ..., prt_n>; <LOC: loc_1, ..., loc_n>)

Legend: MAIN = main entities that may contain or possess X, PARTS = parts of X, LOC = location of X with respect to the different possibilities of MAIN.

e.g. *head* meron = (<MAIN: body>; <PARTS: eye(s), nose, ear(s), forehead, eyebrow(s), eyelash(es), chin, cheek, mouth, lip, hair, ...>; <LOC: loc *body*>)

- Hierarchies:

X hierarchy = (<HYPER: hyper>; <HYPO: $hypo_1$, ..., $hypo_n$>)

Legend: HYPER = hyperonym, HYPO = hyponyms.

e.g. *animal* hierarchy = (<HYPER: living thing>; <HYPO: vertebrate, invertebrate>)

- Chains:

X chain = (<CHAIN: ch_1, ..., ch_n>; <TYCH: [ch], [cycl]>)

Legend: CHAIN = chain of items, TYCH = type of chain, [ch] = chain with first and last elements, [cycl] = cycle.

e.g. *colour* chain = (<CHAIN: red, orange, yellow, green, blue, purple>; <TYCH: cycl>)

- Gradation:

X grad = (<ORDER: grd_1, ..., grd_n>; <TYGR: [cngr], [cnngr], [disc]>)

Legend: ORDER = list of ordered items, TYGR = type of gradation, [cngr] = continuous-gradable, [cnngr] = continuous-nongradable, [disc] = discontinuous.

e.g. *second* grad = (<ORDER: first, second, ..., fourth, ...>; <TYGR: disc>)

There can be little doubt that such representations (including others similar to these) are very helpful when trying to emulate our understanding of meaning relationships on a machine. However, they are very poor from a psychological point of view. Several problems are immediately apparent:

- The selected features are not the only possible ones for the meaning structures that are represented. In fact, their types and number may differ greatly.

- Scripts are highly variable and speaker-dependent.

- Scripts normally have a prototypical and fuzzy structure that is not adequately represented here.

- The representations do not say anything about the role of the context in the recovery of material related to the words involved.

- The configurations represent the relational structure, but say nothing about the relationship between lexical interpretation and production and our senses and memory.

- The representations do not provide any clue as to what is in fact the meaning of words (that is, their ontological foundation).

Some of these problems are easily solved in a connectionist parallel computational paradigm of the sort referred to above, i.e. revolving around the concept of activation.[7] In such paradigms, the system is claimed to behave in a way very similar to that of the human brain, since its "architecture" is based on neural networks, typically consisting of a number of "neurons" or cells. These cells are interconnected, normally forming layers. One layer receives the input and then gives signals to another layer, and so forth, proceeding through the network. After going through one or several layers of cells, there is an output pattern "on the other side".

---

[7] It has to be granted, though, that neuronal nodes are not quite identical to the "concept" nodes in, say, Anderson's ACT model.

Because they are conscious attempts at recreating the workings of the brain, the paradigms referred to allow for a better understanding of why it is that the human brain produces conceptual categories with a fuzzy or prototypical structure. They also solve the problem of discovering the prototypical features of a category, a task that is in fact far more problematical than would appear at first: no features are available to the outside observer, there are only weights on different neurons. In addition, the interface with the senses and the body is easily explained because allowance is made for different kinds of input that have access to the neural network at different points and that therefore modulate the information flow. Varied input also helps us understand why context is so important in our interaction with the world.

Not surprisingly, PDP (parallel distributed processing) connectionist models are congruent with psycholinguistic research that supports interaction with context information and a less modular approach (as opposed to Fodor's modular view in which different levels of linguistic processing are carried out through different "modules", independent from general cognitive capacities; cf. Fodor 1983). It is obvious that if the activation and firing of the different neurons propagate throughout the whole network without a clear distinction between different modules or sections in which different kinds of information are processed, PDP is very promising indeed for non-modular approaches, because it convincingly explains how the same information is distributed in many places in the brain at the same time. This is precisely a key issue in an encyclopedia approach, where concepts are assumed to be interrelated and interconnected in an infinitely complex way.

There are alternative models to explain the psychological modalities of the interaction between our internal lexicon and encyclopedic information in a manner that is isomorphic with the neural connectionist paradigm. A very promising model, one that has not attracted much research yet, is the holographic brain theory proposed by Pribram (1971). This model assumes that information stored by the brain is comparable to information stored in holograms, i.e. images that normally preserve the three-dimensionality of the objects that are being represented, and that can therefore be viewed from different points in space, with viewing results fully dependent on the viewing angle, as though genuine three-dimensional objects were being viewed rather than images. The technicalities are difficult to explain in detail; suffice it to say that a hologram is in fact an "interference pattern" formed when light originating from a defined source meets light reflected by an object. The interference pattern is stored on a light-sensitive emulsion. The brain also stores interference patterns rather than direct representations. The patterns produced are very rich representations and have a great deal of information stored in very little space. It is typical of holograms that if a slice is cut out of one, the slice still contains the entire image. According to Pribram's theory, the brain is continuously carrying out correlation processes that involve cutting slices out of holographic patterns. This is the way links between concepts are established; this is also how we build complex encyclopedic networks around the vocabulary that we have acquired. The brain is a finite device, but apparently it has an unlimited capacity for information storage, carried out by processes that can be mathematically modelled in the form of Fourier transformations. The act of remembering would then be the subjective result of applying the inverse of a Fourier transformation or something similar.

Pribram's model is compatible with available evidence (cf. e.g. Prideaux 1998 for references related to vision); it is coherent with the phenomena that occur when we store and retrieve vocabulary. There is no localised image stored in the brain, but there are correlations and associations achieved by different parts of the brain projecting on certain groups of cells. If we add to this the many limitations inherent in approaches that take the brain to be a conventional computational device (cf. e.g. Penrose 1994, Rosen 1991, Kampis 1991, Pattee 1995), it may well be that Pribram's theory is set to provide a sounder basis for a true understanding of the workings of the brain in years to come. The crucial thing for us here is that the model is entirely compatible with the way our "lexicopedia" works. Relations across semantic networks, or sets of neural weights (according to connectionist models), may be thought of as interference patterns that are as simple or as complicated as the amount of information they store.

4. Conclusion

We are so used to thinking of words as discrete units which "contain" meaning that it is not at all surprising that we normally favour the dictionary approach to meaning. But meaning is a complex reality, with pointers to events and entities in the external world that build up complex associative networks of concepts with different degrees of concreteness or abstraction, and also of judgements and impressions. Our store of words is fundamentally based on experience and, as a result, it has a strong encyclopedic nature, with a strong distributed structure in terms of what individual items refer to. It is now well established that the meaning structure of words cannot be conceived of as simply a container for features but should rather be thought of as a diffuse and dynamic complex. Yet, what is still not completely understood is how this network of meaning originates. We have shown how naïve an assumption it is to think of meaning only in referential, compositional terms, with no relation to our entire mental storage of knowledge about the world. Practical solutions emulating the behaviour of meaning structures from a serial computational point of view may be useful for certain concrete applications, but in no way do they reproduce the manner in which our mental lexicon works. Connectionism and the holographic brain theory seem to be more faithful to the distributed and encyclopedic nature of our mental "lexicopedia".

References

Anderson, John R. 1983. *The architecture of cognition*. Cambridge: Harvard University Press.

Barsalou, Lawrence W. 1982. "Context-independent and context-dependent information in concepts". *Memory and cognition* 10. 82-93.

Barsalou, Lawrence W. 1993. "Flexibility, structure and linguistic vagary in concepts. Manifestations of a compositional system of perceptual symbols". In Alan F. Collins, Susan E. Gathercole, Martin A. Conway & Peter E. Morris (ed.), *Theories of memory*. Hillsdale: Lawrence Erlbaum. 29-101.

Barsalou, Lawrence W.; Prinz, Jesse J. 1997. "Mundane creativity in perceptual symbol systems". In Thomas B. Ward, Steven M. Smith & Jyotsna Vaid (ed.), *Creative thought. An investigation of conceptual structures and processes*. Washington, D.C.: American Psychological Association. 267-307.

Barsalou, Lawrence W.; Sewell, Daniel R. 1984. "Constructing representations of categories from different points of view". *Emory Cognition Project technical report* 2. Atlanta: Emory University.

Barsalou, Lawrence W.; Yeh, Wenchi; Luka, Barbara J.; Olseth, Karen L.; Mix, Kelly S.; Wu, Ling-Ling. 1993. "Concepts and meaning". In Katharine Beals, Gina Cooke, David Kathman, Sotaro Kita, Karl-Erik McCullough & David Testen (ed.), *Papers from the 29th regional meeting of the Chicago Linguistic Society*, vol. 2. *Parasession on conceptual representations*. Chicago: University of Chicago. 23-61.

Bartlett, Frederick C. 1932. *Remembering. A study in experimental and social psychology*. Cambridge: Cambridge University Press.

Carroll, John; Minnen, Guido; Canning, Yvonne; Devlin, Siobhan; Tait, John. 1998. "Practical simplification of English newspaper text to assist aphasic readers". Paper presented at the *AAAI-98 workshop on integrating artificial intelligence and assistive technology*, Madison, Wisconsin (U.S.A.).

Coltheart, Max. 1978. "Lexical access in simple reading tasks". In Geoffrey Underwood (ed.), *Strategies of information processing*. London: Academic Press. 151-216.

Coltheart, Max; Paterson, Karalyn; Marshall, John C. 1980. *Deep dyslexia*. London: Routledge & Kegan Paul.

Cruse, D. Alan. 1986. *Lexical semantics*. Cambridge: Cambridge University Press.

Deane, Paul D. 1992. *Grammar in mind and brain. Explorations in cognitive syntax*. Berlin: Mouton de Gruyter.

Elman, Jeffrey L.; McClelland, James L. 1984. "The interactive activation model of speech perception". In Norman Lass (ed.), *Language and speech*, vol. 10. New York: Academic Press. 337-374.

Elman, Jeffrey L.; McClelland, James L. 1986. "Exploiting lawful variability in the speech wave". In Joseph S. Perkell & Dennis H. Klatt (ed.), *Invariance and variability in speech processes*. Hillsdale: Lawrence Erlbaum. 360-385.

Fillmore, Charles J. 1982. "Frame semantics". In Linguistic Society of Korea (ed.), *Linguistics in the morning calm*. Seoul: Hanshin. 111-137.

Fodor, Jerry A. 1983. *The modularity of mind. An essay on faculty psychology.* Cambridge: M.I.T. Press.

Forster, Kenneth I. 1976. "Accessing the mental lexicon". In Roger J. Wales & Edward C.T. Walker (ed.), *New approaches to language mechanisms*. Amsterdam: North Holland. 257-287.

Forster, Kenneth I. 1990. "Lexical processing". In Daniel N. Osherson & Howard Lasnik (ed.), *Language. An invitation to cognitive science*, vol. 1. Cambridge: Bradford-M.I.T. Press. 95-131.

Forster, Kenneth I.; Chambers, Susan M. 1973. "Lexical access and naming time". *Journal of verbal learning and verbal behavior* 12. 627-635.

Garnham, Alan. 1985. *Psycholinguistics. Central topics.* London: Methuen.

Geeraerts, Dirk. 1988. "On necessary and sufficient conditions". *Journal of semantics* 5. 275-291.

Geeraerts, Dirk. 1993. "Vagueness's puzzles, polysemy's vagaries". *Cognitive linguistics* 4. 223-272.

Gilhooly, Kenneth J.; Logie, Robert H. 1980. "Age of acquisition, imagery, concreteness, familiarity and ambiguity measures for 1944 words". *Behavioural research methods and instrumentation* 12. 395-427.

Inchaurralde, Carlos. 1994. "Schematicity in lexical representations". In Carlos Martin-Vide (ed.), *Current issues in mathematical linguistics*. Oxford: Elsevier. 249-258.

Inchaurralde, Carlos. 1997. "What is behind a word. Cultural scripts". In Martin Pütz (ed.), *The cultural context in foreign language teaching*. Frankfurt: Peter Lang. 55-66.

Kampis, George. 1991. *Self-modifying systems in biology and cognitive science.* New York: Pergamon Press.

Kleiber, Georges. 1991. "Prototype et prototypes. Encore une affaire de famille". In Danièle Dubois (ed.) *Sémantique et cognition. Catégories, prototypes, typicalité.* Paris: CNRS.

Lakoff, George. 1986. "Cognitive semantics". *Versus* 44. 119-154.

Lakoff, George. 1987a. *Women, fire, and dangerous things. What categories reveal about the mind.* Chicago: University of Chicago Press.

Lakoff, George. 1987b. "Cognitive models and prototype theory". In Ulric Neisser (ed.), *Concepts and conceptual development. Ecological and intellectual factors in categorization.* Cambridge: Cambridge University Press. 63-100.

Langacker, Ronald W. 1987. *Foundations of cognitive grammar*, vol. 1. *Theoretical prerequisites.* Stanford: Stanford University Press.

Marslen-Wilson, William D. 1987. "Functional parallelism in spoken word recognition". *Cognition* 25. 71-102.

McCusker, Leo X.; Hillinger, Michael L.; Bias, Randolph G. 1981. "Phonological recoding and reading". *Psychological bulletin* 89. 217-245.

Meyer, David E.; Schvaneveldt, Roger W. 1971. "Facilitation in recognizing pairs of words. Evidence of a dependence between retrieval operations". *Journal of experimental psychology* 90. 227-234.

Minsky, Marvin L. 1975. "A framework for representing knowledge". In Patrick H. Winston (ed.), *The psychology of computer vision.* New York: McGraw-Hill. 211-277.

Morton, John. 1979. "Word recognition". In John Morton & John C. Marshall (ed.), *Psycholinguistics series*, vol. 2. *Structures and processes.* London: Elek. 107-156.

Morton, John; Patterson, Karalyn E. 1980. "A new attempt at an interpretation, or an attempt at a new interpretation". In Max Coltheart, Karalyn E. Patterson & John C. Marshall (ed.), *Deep dyslexia.* London: Routledge & Kegan Paul. 91-118.

Nelson, Katherine. 1985. *Making sense. The acquisition of shared meaning.* New York: Academic Press.

Osgood, Charles. 1976. *Focus on meaning*, vol. 1. *Explorations in space.* The Hague: Mouton.

Paivio, Allan; Yuille, John C.; Madigan, Stephen A. 1968. "Concreteness, imagery and meaningfulness values for 925 words". *Journal of experimental psychology. Monograph supplement* 76 (1:2).

Pattee, Howard H. 1995. "Evolving self-reference. Matter, symbols, and semantic closure". *Communication and cognition. Artificial intelligence* 12. 9-27.

Patterson, Karalyn E.; Marshall, John C.; Coltheart, Max. 1985. *Surface dyslexia. Neuropsychological and cognitive studies of phonological reading.* Hillsdale: Lawrence Erlbaum.

Patterson, Karalyn E.; Shewell, Christina. 1987. "Speak and spell. Dissociations and word-class effect". In Max Coltheart, Giuseppe Sartori & Remo Job (ed.), *The cognitive neuropsychology of language.* Hillsdale: Lawrence Erlbaum. 273-294.

Penrose, Roger. 1994. *Shadows of the mind. A search for the missing science of consciousness.* Oxford: Oxford University Press.

Pribram, J. Karl. 1971. *Languages in the brain. Experimental paradoxes and principles in neuropsychology.* Englewood Cliffs: Prentice-Hall.

Prideaux, Jeff. 1998. "Comparison between Karl Pribram's holographic brain theory and more conventional models of neuron computation". Unpublished paper.

Quinlan, Philip T. 1992. *The Oxford psycholinguistic database.* Oxford: Oxford University Press.

Reddy, Michael J. 1979. "The conduit metaphor. A case of frame conflict in our language about language". In Andrew Ortony (ed.), *Metaphor and thought.* London: Cambridge University Press. 284-324.

Rosch, Eleanor. 1973a. "Natural categories". *Cognitive psychology* 4. 328-350.

Rosch, Eleanor. 1973b. "On the internal structure of perceptual and semantic categories". In Timothy E. Moore (ed.), *Cognitive development and the acquisition of language.* New York: Academic Press. 111-144.

Rosch, Eleanor. 1975. "Cognitive representations of semantic categories". *Journal of experimental psychology: General* 104. 192-233.

Rosen, Robert. 1991. *Life itself. A comprehensive inquiry into the nature, origin, and fabrication of life.* New York: Columbia University Press.

Rumelhart, David E. 1980. "Schemata. The building blocks of cognition". In Rand J. Spiro; Bertram C. Bruce & William F. Brewer (ed.), *Theoretical issues in reading comprehension. Perspectives from cognitive psychology, linguistics, artificial intelligence, and education.* Hillsdale: Lawrence Erlbaum. 33-58.

Rumelhart, David E.; Ortony, Andrew. 1977. "The representation of knowledge in memory". In Richard C. Anderson, Rand J. Spiro & William E. Montague (ed.), *Schooling and the acquisition of knowledge.* Hillsdale: Lawrence Erlbaum. 99-135.

Sanford, Anthony J.; Garrod, Simon C. 1981. *Understanding written language.* New York: John Wiley.

Sartori, Giuseppe; Barry, Christopher; Job, Remo. 1984. "Phonological dyslexia. A review". In R.N. Malatesha & Harry A. Whitaker (ed.), *Dyslexia. A global issue.* The Hague: Nijhoff. 339-356.

Scarborough, Don L.; Cortese, Charles; Scarborough, Hollis S. 1977. "Frequency and repetition effects in lexical memory". *Journal of experimental psychology: Human perception and performance* 3. 1-17.

Schank, Roger C.; Abelson, Robert P. 1977. *Scripts, plans, goals and understanding. An inquiry into human knowledge structures.* Hillsdale: Lawrence Erlbaum.

Seidenberg, Mark S.; Waters, Gloria S.; Sanders, Michael; Langer, Pearl. 1984. "Pre- and postlexical loci of contextual effects on word recognition". *Memory & cognition* 12. 315-328.

Toglia, Michael P.; Battig, William F. 1978. *Handbook of semantic word norms.* New York: Lawrence Erlbaum.

Tuggy, David. 1993. "Ambiguity, polysemy, and vagueness". *Cognitive linguistics* 4. 273-290.

Tulving, Endel. 1979. "Relation between encoding specificity and levels of processing". In Laird S. Cermak & Fergus I.M. Craik (ed.), *Levels of processing in human memory.* Hillsdale: Lawrence Erlbaum. 405-428.

Wierzbicka, Anna. 1994. "Cultural scripts. A new approach to the study of cross-cultural communication". In Martin Pütz (ed.), *Language contact, language conflict.* Amsterdam: John Benjamins. 69-87.

Wierzbicka, Anna. 1997. *Understanding cultures through their key words. English, Russian, Polish, German, and Japanese.* Oxford: Oxford University Press.

Approaches to word meaning: The network model (Langacker) and the two-level model (Bierwisch) in comparison[1]

John R. Taylor

University of Otago, School of Languages, PO Box 56, Dunedin, New Zealand
E-mail: john.taylor@stonebow.otago.ac.nz

0. Introduction

In this paper I compare two approaches to the study of word meaning, and make some proposals for their evaluation. The approaches under consideration are the "network model", due to Ronald Langacker, and the "two-level model" of Manfred Bierwisch.

Langacker regards it as a normal state of affairs that lexical units – especially frequently used lexical units – are polysemous, i.e. exhibit a range of established, yet interrelated senses (whence the term "network model"). Each of the established senses is characterised "encyclopedically", relative to one or more cognitive domains, i.e. knowledge structures of varying degrees of complexity and sophistication

---

[1] [Editor's note] This paper was first published in René Dirven & Johan Vanparys (ed.), *Current approaches to the lexicon*, Frankfurt, Peter Lang, 1995, pp. 3-26. Permission to reprint was granted by Peter Lang and is gratefully acknowledged. The author was asked and kindly agreed to write an afterword, which is printed immediately after the main text. Apart from a few editorial changes and bibliographical updates, the latter is identical to the 1995 original.

(cf. Croft, this volume). The network model – or variants of it – has been employed by Brugman (1988), Herskovits (1986), Lakoff (1987), Schulze (1991), and others.[2]

In contrast, Bierwisch makes a clean distinction between a word's purely linguistic meaning, and the interpretation that a word may have relative to conceptual knowledge; the term "two-level" alludes precisely to the distinction between a linguistic-semantic level of meaning, and an essentially non-linguistic, conceptual level of interpretation.[3] On the two-level model, polysemy tends to be seen as a consequence of alternative conceptual interpretations of a unitary semantic representation. The two-level model has been adopted by a number of linguists, especially in German-speaking countries, including Herweg (1988), Lang (1990, 1991), and Wunderlich (1991, 1993).[4]

There are several reasons why I have selected just these two approaches for comparison. From the above brief remarks, it will be apparent that in spite of fundamental differences, the two approaches do address much the same kinds of issues. Foremost amongst these are the questions – central to any study of meaning – of meaning variation, and of the role of conceptual, or encyclopedic knowledge in the determination of meaning. A more immediate reason is that some adherents of the two-level model have themselves invited the comparison, in that in various places they have polemically distanced themselves from Langacker's approach.[5]

Taking a wider perspective, the two approaches invite comparison in that they both have been dubbed, by their progenitors and adherents, as "cognitive linguistic" approaches.

Cognitive linguistics, broadly understood, is characterised by commitment to the thesis that language is a mental, i.e. cognitive phenomenon (Schwarz 1992:36). The goal of linguistic analysis is a descriptively adequate account, not only of language behaviour, but of the mental states and processes that cause the behaviour. A grammar is meant, quite literally, as a model, or hypothesis, of what a person who knows a language actually knows, and of what a speaker or listener actually does when speaking and listening.

The cognitive commitment, as just outlined, is highly programmatic and does not, of itself, dictate a specific research strategy. The approaches of Langacker and Bier-

---

[2] For an exposition of Langacker's Cognitive Grammar, see Langacker (1987, 1991). A brief presentation of Langacker's view of word meaning may be found in Langacker (1988a).

[3] The term has been popularised especially by Lang, e.g. Lang (1990, 1991). Bierwisch himself has not used it.

[4] The two-level model is presented in Bierwisch (1981, 1983); for a recent statement, see Bierwisch & Schreuder (1992). The most extensive implementation of the model is in Bierwisch & Lang (1989). For a critical discussion of some aspects of the model, see Taylor (1992, 1994).

[5] See, e.g. Lang (1991:145); Herweg (1988:53ff *et passim*); Wunderlich (1993:111).

wisch invite comparison precisely because they represent very different implementations of the cognitive commitment.

Broadly speaking, the approach of Langacker, Lakoff, etc. has been to constrain linguistic description by psychological considerations. Lakoff (1987), for example, has appealed to prototype categorisation – a phenomenon independently established by Rosch (1978) – in his analysis of a wide range of linguistic phenomena; whilst Langacker motivates his Cognitive Grammar largely by appeal to what one might call "common sense psychology" – aspects of mental experience that are said to be "mostly self-evident" (Langacker 1987:99), and presumably readily accessible to conscious introspection. It is on the basis of "common sense psychology" that Langacker rejects many features of the contemporary linguistic landscape, such as mathematical-logical formalism as a model of linguistic semantics, and the idea that there might be layers of abstract structure hidden beneath the overt linguistic form of an utterance.

An alternative approach – implemented by Chomsky, Bierwisch, and others – has been to use linguistic analyses as input to the construction of hypotheses about cognition. Consider the issues of autonomy and modularity, i.e. the notion that a person's linguistic competence is independent of other cognitive abilities, and that linguistic competence itself is the product of an interaction of a number of autonomous modules. Autonomy and modularity did not have the status of independently discovered facts of cognition, around which linguistic theories were built, nor can the issues be appraised by appeal to common sense intuitions. Autonomy and modularity are hypotheses, put forward, by linguists, to explain linguistic phenomena, as these have been analysed within certain linguistic theories.

In spite, then, of their commitment to cognitive realism, cognitive linguists have made incompatible assumptions about the mental representation and processing of language. Of course, cognitive linguists are, first and foremost, linguists, not cognitive scientists. Linguistic theories, even cognitive linguistic theories, tend to be evaluated, first and foremost, by linguistic criteria: explanatory power (with respect to linguistic data, in all their variety and complexity), as well as economy, explicitness, and internal consistency. But if appeal to cognitive realism is not to be completely vacuous, it is essential to consider ways in which conflicting cognitive linguistic analyses might, after all, be validated.

1. Meaning variation and encyclopedic knowledge

Let us begin by looking at the two issues mentioned earlier, i.e. meaning variation, and the role of encyclopedic knowledge in the determination of meaning.

It is commonplace that a word can denote different kinds of entities, or different kinds of states of affairs, according to the context in which it is used. To put it another way: depending on context, the word may make different contributions to the truth conditions of the sentences in which it occurs. The phenomenon is ubiquitous, and could be illustrated on just about any item randomly selected from the dictionary. Below are some examples, mostly taken (slightly adapted) from the two-level literature.

(1a)   John left the University at 4 pm yesterday.

(1b)   John left the University in 1980.

(1c)   John left the University a short time ago.

(Cf. Bierwisch & Schreuder 1992:31)

(2a)   John is in the telephone booth.

(2b)   John is in the telephone book.

(Cf. Langacker 1990:189)

(3a)   the water in the vase

(3b)   the crack in the vase

(3c)   the flowers in the vase

(Cf. Herweg 1988:15 *et passim*)

(4a)   She ran round the lake.

(4b)   She swam round the lake.

(Cf. Wunderlich 1993:127)

(5a)   Sam opened the window.

(5b)   Sam painted the window.

(5c)   The surgeon opened the wound.

(Cf. Searle 1983:145)

On its normal interpretation, (1a) means that John moved away from the university building, or campus, while (1b) means that John severed a relation of association with the university, e.g. he graduated, or resigned his position. Both readings are available for (1c), whereby *a short time ago* can invoke different time scales: 'not many minutes/hours ago' vs. 'not many months/years ago'. Note in particular that the two readings of *university* ('building' vs. 'institution') co-vary with two readings of *leave* ('move away from' vs. 'sever a relation with'). We could even say that *John* has slightly different readings. (1a) is about John *qua* physical object, whereas (1b) is about John *qua* rational being.

Different readings of *John* are also evinced by (2). (2a) is about the physical person, while in (2b) *John* denotes a printed representation of John's name, address, and telephone number.

Different *in*-relations are documented in (3). In (3a), the water is located in a hollow internal region of the vase, while in (3b) the crack is located in the material substance of the vase. (3c) is different yet again, in that the flowers are not just located with respect to the vase, they are supported, or held in position, in virtue of the containment of the lower part of their stems in the hollow region of the vase. Different readings of a prepositional phrase – *round the lake* – are also at issue in (4).

The contrasts in (5) are perhaps more subtle. A moment's thought, however, shows that what is opened, in *open the window*, is different from what is painted, in *paint the window*; also that the activity of opening a window is different in kind from opening a wound. You do not, for example, open a window by making incisions in it with a scalpel!

These few examples only scratch the surface of the phenomenon of meaning variation, even with respect to the words that have been discussed. On the basis of even these few examples, however, we may make the following observations.

This is that the interpretation of a sentence is rather closely tied up with encyclopedic, or conceptual knowledge, for example, knowledge of what water, cracks, vases, lakes, windows, wounds etc. actually are. If you run round the lake, then, obviously, the route that you take is external to the boundary of the lake. But given what we know of lakes and swimming, if you swim round the lake, your path has got to be internal to the boundary of the lake. And given what we know about windows, it is evident that when you open a window the part of the window that you manoeuvre is a different part from the one which you paint when you paint a window. Sometimes, quite extensive background knowledge is invoked. Consider the interpretations of (1). We know that the kinds of relation that a person may have with a university – as a student, or as an employee – are typically fairly long-term, measured in years and months, while a person's physical presence in a building is typically a matter of hours and minutes. The more coarse-grained temporal phrase (*in 1980*) is therefore more suited to relations of association with an institution, while the more fine-grained phrase (*at 4 pm yesterday*) is more appropriate when speaking about a person's physical presence in a building.

The role of encyclopedic knowledge may go further, in that it may enable us to draw various inferences from an expression. In (3a) and (3c), for example, we would infer that the vase was in its canonical position, while in (3b) the vase could be in any position whatsoever. We infer from (1b) that John used to be associated with the University in the capacity of a student or employee (though not in the capacity of a sponsor or benefactor). No such inference may be drawn from (1a). John could have been a member of the general public, who had taken a short cut by walking through the University premises.

That the interpretation of an expression is typically tied up with conceptual knowledge is, I take it, uncontroversial. But the above examples raise two further issues, whose treatment is by no means so straightforward.

The first concerns the possibility, and desirability, of a unified treatment of meaning variation, as exhibited in (1-5). For example, we might want to say that the two readings of *round* in (4) are not only mutually incompatible, they are sufficiently different to justify, perhaps, a claim that *round* is polysemous between 'external to boundary of landmark entity' and 'internal to boundary of landmark entity'. With respect to (1), one might want to say that (1b) exemplifies the "basic" meaning of *university* ('kind of educational institution'), while (1a) exemplifies a metonymic extension of this basic sense ('building in which the institution is housed'). On the other hand, few people, I imagine, would want to say that *window* is polysemous between 'movable panel' and 'frame'.[6] An even clearer case is *a short time ago*, which is simply indeterminate with respect to different time scales. With regard to the uses of *in* in (3) the situation is perhaps less clear. Do we want to say that *in* has only a general meaning 'containment', or do we want to recognise distinct senses of *in*: 'containment in hollow internal region', 'containment in material substance', and 'support by partial containment'?

Our answers to these questions will depend crucially on our approach to the second issue. To understand an expression, a person needs to draw, not only on encyclopedic knowledge, but also on knowledge of the language in which the expression is encoded. Our concern here is with just one aspect of a person's language knowledge – knowledge of the meanings of the words of which an expression is composed. But what does a person who "knows the meanings of the words" actually know? Does knowing the meaning of (say) the verb *(to) open* involve knowing the kinds of activities one performs when one opens entities of various kinds (windows, wounds, not to mention books, parcels, penknives, and bank accounts)? This would be Langacker's position, and it is one which could entail a high degree of polysemy in the

---

[6] Lakoff (1987:416), though, does seem to regard 'opening in a wall' and 'glass-filled frame' as polysemes of *window*.

mental lexicon. Alternatively, is this kind of encyclopedic knowledge only supplied in the act of interpreting the word in context, the word meaning itself being under-determined with respect to its possible interpretations in different kinds of context? This would be Bierwisch's position, which would tend to severely limit polysemy in the mental lexicon, and treat instances of meaning variation as effects of conceptual interpretation.

2. Langacker's "encyclopedic" approach to word meaning

Let us first look at Langacker's approach. For Langacker, no principled distinction is drawn, or drawable, between "linguistic semantics" and "encyclopedic knowledge". Meaning, quite simply, is equated with conceptualisation. A word gets its semantic value by the relation of a profile to a base. The profile is what a word designates – the conceptual entity it refers to – while the base (or "base of predication") is the context necessary for the conceptualisation of the profile. *Radius* and *hypotenuse* both designate a line segment. Yet the two words are not synonymous, and both dif-fer in meaning from *line*. Crucially, *radius* presupposes (has as its base) the concep-tion of a circle (as well as other geometrical concepts), whilst *hypotenuse* presup-poses the conception of a right-angled triangle. Divorced from knowledge of circles and right-angled triangles, the semantic values of *radius* and *hypotenuse* would be vacuous.

The base of predication is in principle open-ended, in that it may comprise every-thing a person knows about the concept. This is not to say that all such knowledge is equally central, or intrinsic to the concept, nor that each facet of conceptual knowl-edge is always relevant to each use of the word. In fact, variations in the relevance of a domain is one important way in which Langacker's semantic theory is able to account for some of the meaning variation in (1-5). In *swim round the lake,* the no-tion of a lake as an expanse of water is clearly very prominent, whilst in *run round the lake* the lake may be conceptualised simply as a bounded region. Likewise, *wa-ter in the vase* and *flowers in the vase* activate knowledge of the function of vases, whilst *crack in the vase* activates knowledge that vases are typically made of fragile material.

Different contexts may also cause shifts in the profile of a linguistic unit. Cruse (1986:52-53) speaks of "contextual modulation", while Langacker (1990) handles these effects by means of the notion of "active zone". *Window* profiles an entity of a certain shape, function, manner of construction, etc., against background knowledge pertaining to buildings, their ventilation, illumination, etc. In different contexts, dif-ferent facets of the profile may be involved in a predication. In *paint a window,* only the wood or metallic portion is involved, in *break a window,* only the glass portion is affected, and so on. More dramatic variations in active zone go under the traditional name of metonymy. Such is the case of *university*. On different occasions of its use, the word could profile the institution *(He works in the University)*, the daily activities in the institution *(He's bored with the University)*, the people associated with the institution *(The University protested)*, the building *(We live near the University)*, and so on.

Langacker's encyclopedic approach allows for the possibility that a word may have a one-off interpretation, as determined by the unique circumstances of its use in a context. In contrast with the two-level approach, however, the network model also allows for the possibility that a contextually determined interpretation may become entrenched, or "routinised", for a speaker, leading to the establishment of a separate sense for the word. The process, clearly, is a gradual one. Consequently, meaning variation due to shifts in active zone and full-fledged polysemy are end-points on a continuum, rather than fully distinct phenomena.

It is worth mentioning (and on this point also Langacker's Cognitive Grammar differs substantially from Bierwisch's approach) that while word meanings, for Langacker, are cognitively complex (in the sense that they invoke many facets of a person's encyclopedic knowledge), they are not strictly compositional, in the sense that they are products of conceptually simpler elements (Langacker 1987:21-22). Bierwisch (1981:344, 1983:90), for example, decomposes the transitive predicates *melt* and *wake up* into structures that contain the primitive element CAUSE. On an encyclopedic approach, it is certainly allowed that some predicates may be construed, by speakers of a language, as similar, in various respects, to other predicates; also, that these perceived similarities may have important consequences for linguistic usage. *Melting the ice* may be perceived as similar, in certain ways, to *boiling the water, killing the fly, waking up Eva,* and even *teaching the students.* One might even say that the similarity involves the notion of "causation". But this is a very different matter to incorporating a semantic primitive, such as CAUSE, into the semantic entries for *melt, boil,* etc. At the very least, "cause" would itself be construed, within Langacker's approach, as a highly differentiated, and cognitively complex notion, characterised against a number of cognitive domains (purposeful activity, rational explanation, etc.).[7]

3. Bierwisch's two-level model

Whereas Langacker integrates encyclopedic knowledge into the lexicon, Bierwisch insists on the need to make a clean distinction between a purely linguistic level of meaning, and a non-linguistic level of conceptual representation. The distinction is

---

[7] See Dirven (1995) for a study of the differentiation of the concept "cause", as expressed by prepositional phrases in English, German, and Dutch.

justified on various grounds. It is claimed, for example, that an identification of linguistic-semantic knowledge with conceptual knowledge would make the factually incorrect prediction of a pre-established congruence between conceptualisations and semantic structures (Bierwisch & Schreuder 1992:28).[8] It is pointed out further (ibid.:31) that a person may have various kinds of knowledge that in no way impinge on the semantic system of his language; thus, what I know of a certain John is irrelevant to the linguistic meaning of *John*, which is merely to refer to a person who is called John. On the other hand, linguistic expressions may have interpretations that are clearly not part of their purely linguistic meaning. *A short time ago*, in (1c), illustrates the phenomenon. Bierwisch & Schreuder (1992:32) cite, as further examples, the context-determined interpretations of possessives (my *chair*) and deictics (*over there*). Further arguments for the two levels are based on theory-internal and metatheoretical considerations. Thus Herweg (1988:66) points out that a separation of semantic and conceptual principles leads to greater economy in the mental lexicon: lexical entries do not become "unnötig komplex" (i.e. unnecessarily complex; ibid.:55), and rampant polysemy ("Polysemie-Inflation", ibid.) is avoided.

The separation of the levels is closely bound up with the thesis of modularity, according to which a person's linguistic knowledge constitutes an encapsulated mental module, independent of other skills and knowledge. Given such a conception of linguistic competence, it is necessary to posit a bridge, or interface, which links the linguistic system to the conceptual system. The semantic level serves just this function, in that the semantic entry for a lexical item points in two directions. On the one hand, the entry contains specifications which permit the item to enter into syntagmatic relations with other items. The entry also contains specifications which make it possible for the word to identify conceptual units at the conceptual level.

In order for a semantic entry to fulfil this dual function, Bierwisch proposes semantic representations which decompose a word's meaning into predicate-argument format. On the one hand, the predicate-argument structure determines the combinatorial possibilities of the lexical item (i.e. its valence potential). The semantic representation also contains open variables. These are parameters whose values can be fixed at the conceptual level, as determined by context. The semantic entry thereby specifies "sets of conditions for the identification of conceptual elements" (Lang 1991:146).

To see how this works, let us look at a couple of examples from the two-level literature. Consider, first, Bierwisch's account of words like *university, school, mu-*

---

[8] Note that Langacker's theory does not entail such a pre-established congruence between linguistic meanings and conceptualisations. Langacker (1991:109) characterises semantic structure as conventionalised conceptual structure. That is to say, conceptualisations typically need to be shaped so as to conform with the semantic resources made available by a given language.

seum. For these kinds of words, Bierwisch (1983:86) suggested semantic entries of the following general format.

(6) $^\wedge$X [PURPOSE[X, W]]

PURPOSE has the status of a semantic primitive. The value of W varies according to lexical item, and serves to identify a conceptually complex unit (akin, perhaps, to the domain-based knowledge of Langacker's model). For *university,* one might suggest something like the following:

(7) $^\wedge$X [PURPOSE[X, W] & ADVANCED STUDY AND TEACHING[W]]

The value of X is determined only at the conceptual level. To this end, Bierwisch proposed an inventory of functions, of the following kind:

(8a) $^\wedge$X [INSTITUTION[X] & PURPOSE[X, W]]

(8b) $^\wedge$X [BUILDING[X] & PURPOSE[X, W]]

The effect of these functions is to assign to X in (6) the value 'institution' or 'building'. The unitary semantic representation of *university* thus comes to be interpreted, on the conceptual level, as a kind of institution, or as a kind of building.[9] Bierwisch therefore denies that *university* in (1) is polysemous, and neither does his account involve reference to metonymy. Both the institution and the building readings of the word are derived, by analogous means, from the same semantic entry.

As already noted, a general feature of the two-level approach is that it seeks to relegate polysemy, or much of what passes as polysemy, to the conceptual level, where unitary semantic representations are mapped into conceptual interpretations. Consider, for example, Herweg's (1988:74) account of the preposition *in.* He suggests the following semantic entry:

(9) $^\wedge$Y $^\wedge$X [LOC [X, PLACE [Y]]]

According to (9), the location of X (the located object, or trajector) is PLACE [Y], where PLACE [Y] is defined as the space that Y (the reference, or landmark object) occupies. Note especially that (9) is neutral with respect to the different readings in (3), i.e. with respect to whether X is located in a hollow region defined by the exte-

---

[9] Actually, the application of the functions in (8) to the formula in (7) is far from unproblematic. It may make sense to say that a university *qua* institution has purpose W. But the building does not have purpose W; its purpose, rather, is to house the institution that has purpose W. The "conceptual interpretations" of (7) are thus compromised, not only by the fact that the building sense is derivative on the institution sense, but also by the fact that the semantic primitive PURPOSE itself turns out to have context-conditioned interpretations – to be, if one will, polysemous!

rior sides of Y (*the water in the vase*), whether X is contained in the material substance of Y (*the crack in the vase*), or whether X is held in position by partial containment in Y (*the flowers in the vase*). These different possibilities are therefore not part of the semantic meaning of *in*. How *in* is interpreted, in a given context, depends on conceptual knowledge of the topological properties of the objects X and Y – cf. Lang's (1990) "object schemata" – and on our knowledge of the typical configuration of objects with respect to each other.[10]

In a similar spirit, Wunderlich (1993) proposed the following unitary semantic entry for the German preposition *um* 'round':

(10) $^\wedge Y \, ^\wedge X \, [\text{LOC}[X, \text{EXT}[Y]] \, \& \, \text{ENCL}[D[X], Y]]$

According to this formula, the trajector entity X is located in a region external to Y, also D[X], i.e. a closed line that encircles X, encloses Y.

That *um*, like *round*, can, in apparent contradiction to (10), denote a path interior to the reference object (cf. *She swam round the lake*), is explained by Wunderlich in terms of a shift of conceptual focus. The device is similar, perhaps, to Langacker's notion of "active zone", with the difference that for Wunderlich focus shift is a conceptual, not a linguistic-semantic phenomenon. Thus, if you run round the lake, you adopt an external perspective on the lake, such that (10) applies unproblematically. But if you are swimming round the lake, you adopt a different perspective, whereby the lake is conceptualised as the interior, central region of the lake. Your swimming is thus located in the shallow edge of the lake, external to this central region, again fully in accord with (10).

Wunderlich outlines some further principles of conceptual interpretation, whereby *um* (the principles would apply equally to English *round)* can denote only partial encirclement (*go round the corner*), and avoidance (*drive round the obstacle*). In brief, Wunderlich sees no reason to regard *um* as polysemous at all, on the semantic level.

4. Polysemy vs. unitary meanings

There is a long and important tradition in twentieth century linguistics which is highly sceptical of polysemy. In proclaiming, as a "heuristic principle", that different readings of a word are to be covered as much as possible by unitary semantic

---

[10] Conventional expectations may, of course, be overridden. Consider *the splinter in my hand* (cf. Herweg 1988:75). Although this expression would normally be taken to refer to the splinter in the flesh of my hand, given conceptual knowledge that a hand may be "cupped", and may thus define a hollow containing region, the expression may also denote the splinter that I am holding in my hand.

representations, Bierwisch (1983:76) and Wunderlich (1991:593) are merely restating the structuralist Saussurian doctrine of "one form – one meaning" (cf. Jakobson 1971, García 1991). Indeed, sympathisers with the two-level approach have seen its treatment of polysemy as a major strength of the approach.[11] Furthermore, they have explicitly contrasted the parsimony of the two-level approach with the rampant polysemy tolerated by "prototype semantics", as represented by the work of Lakoff, Langacker, Herskovits, etc.[12]

It needs to be borne in mind, however, that the possibility of a monosemous representation obviously depends on the facts of the case.

On the one hand, there are homophones like *bank,* which uncontroversially do need more than one entry in the lexicon. The same, presumably, goes for words like *board.* It is easy to see, if prompted, how the senses 'food' (as in *board and lodging*) and 'group of people' (*board of directors*) might be related to the sense 'plank of wood', in virtue of the use of the plank of wood as the top of a table, at which people ate, or around which people sat (the senses, that is, would be related by metonymy). But what once, perhaps, may have been one-off extensions of a unitary meaning, have now acquired the status of independent senses, which the modern speaker, under normal circumstances, probably does not perceive as being related at all.

In contrast, there are items like the preposition *in,* discussed earlier, where it might well be plausible, at a certain level of analysis, to bring the different readings exemplified in (3) under a single common denommator ('containment'). The possibility of such an analysis, however, by no means entails that the more specific readings of *in* are not stored, by speakers of English, in the mental lexicon. I return to this point later.

The really problematic cases for the monosemy-polysemy issue are lexical items whose different readings are related, in a fairly transparent manner, and for which it might even be possible to identify a common semantic core, but whose different readings are significantly richer in semantic content than any putative unitary meaning. Furthermore, the specificity of the different readings goes beyond what might be determined by context. For an example, we need go no further than the verb *leave.* The verb exhibits a wide range of contextual variants. Here are some possibilities:

(11a)   He stood up and left the room.

(11b)   He left home when he was 16.

---

[11] See the references in footnote 5.

[12] The term *prototype semantics* is actually rather misleading, at least with respect to Langacker. This is not to deny that the notion of "prototype" does play a crucial role in Langacker's Cognitive Grammar, or that his network model can tolerate a large amount of polysemy.

(11c)   He left the communist party.

(11d)   If you leave your things on the floor, they'll get trodden on.

(11e)   I left my briefcase in the car.

(11f)   He left all his work for me to do.

(11g)   There's no money left ('it's all been spent').

(11h)   He left his books to the library ('bequeathed').

(11i)   He left a wife and two children ('was survived by').

(11j)   Where did I leave my car-keys?

(11k)   He left the door open ('didn't close it').

(11l)   He ate the potatoes, but left the peas ('didn't eat').

(11m)   Leave it alone ('don't touch it').

(11n)   Leave me alone ('don't disturb me').

The various uses of the verb cluster in three groups:

(i)   Firstly, there is the sense already exemplified in (1a), i.e. 'move away from', as in *leave the room.*

(i')   On a metaphorical construal of motion, *leave* can denote the severing, or termination of a relation: *leave the communist party.* Note that in some cases the literal and metaphorical senses may both be present; the one, in fact, entails the other. If you *leave home at 16*, you both move away from, and sever a relation with, your parents' home.

(ii)   A second group of uses have the sense 'not to take (some object, or possession) with one (when one moves away from a place)': *I left my briefcase in the car.* The senses 'bequeath' (11h) and 'be survived by' (11i) reflect a metaphorical construal of death as a departure.

(ii')   I may fail to take something with me either intentionally, or out of forgetfulness, or carelessness. In the latter case, *leave* acquires the nuance 'mislay' (*Where did I leave my car-keys?*).

(iii)   As a generalisation of (ii), *leave* can have the sense 'not to do something (to some entity) that one might have been expected to do', where the nature of the omitted activity is determined by context: *leave the door open* (instead of closing it), *leave the tap running, leave the light on, leave it to me* (instead of doing it yourself). A situation is "left" as it is, it is not interfered with. Hence the readings 'not to touch' (*Leave it alone!*), or 'not to disturb' (*Leave me alone!*).

Consider now the possibility of bringing these (obviously related) senses under a single common denominator. On the one hand, all the variants do involve the notion of "lack of contact", or "lack of involvement", either in a spatial or a more abstract domain. But to postulate, say, 'not to have contact with' as the unitary entry for *leave* would miss the distinctive contribution of *leave* in many contexts. The first group of senses involve lack of contact as the result of movement away from some place or region, while the third group denote lack of contact (or lack of involvement) as the consequence of a failure to interact with an entity. Alternatively, we could regard the first group as a special instance of 'fail to do something (that one might have been expected to do)'. This approach would miss the essential fact that whereas the omitted activity in *leave the peas* ('not to eat', 'not to cook', 'not to plant', etc.) can be specified only relative to a context, the interpretation of *leave the room* ('not to remain in the room') is very specific, regardless of context. In brief, the proposed unitary representations would fail utterly as a basis for predicting the diverse readings of the verb.

A final comment on these examples. The very possibility of relating the different uses of *leave* rests on the availability of conceptual knowledge, regarding, for example, the fact that people normally take certain of their possessions with them when they move around, that failure to take certain things with you may be analogous to a failure to turn off a light or to close a door. In other words, the examples provide compelling evidence of the inseparability of conceptual and linguistic-semantic knowledge.

5. The network model

Langacker (1988b:133-140) proposes that the different senses of a lexical item may be linked by two kinds of relation. Recursive application of these relations can give rise to networks of considerable complexity:

(i) The first kind of relation is the relation of extension. Sense [B] is an extension of sense [A] if [B] is perceived to be similar, in some respects, to [A]. Similarity may be based on many factors. Certain specifications associated with [A] may be relaxed in [B]; [B] may be related metaphorically or metonymically to [A]; or [A] and [B] may be related in virtue of the fact that each instantiates a more schematic sense [C].

(ii) The second is the relation of instantiation or, conversely, schematicity. Sense [A] instantiates sense [C], or sense [C] is schematic for sense [A], if [A] is specified in more detail than [C].

These relations are pictured in figure 1, where a broken line represents a relation of extension, a solid line a relation of instantiation.

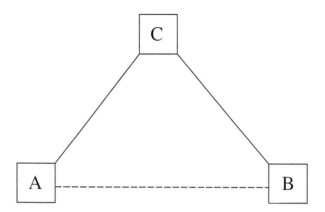

Figure 1: Network relations

To illustrate on the example of *leave*: the sense 'not to do something (which one might have been expected to do)' is schematic for the readings 'not to close' (as in *leave the door open*) and 'not to switch off' (as in *leave the light on*). 'Not to close' and 'not to switch off' are related through similarity – whereby the similarity plausibly resides in the presence of the more abstract schema. Note that in this particular case there may be no reason to attribute priority to either of the senses 'not to close' and 'not to switch off'. But other examples are more clearly directional. The sense 'move away from' (*leave the room*) is plausibly regarded as the source for the metaphorical 'sever a relationship' (*leave the communist party*), while both senses could be brought under the more schematic sense 'distance oneself from', unspecified with respect to the domain of instantiation (space vs. social institutions).

Some observations on the network model:

(a) Content of the nodes

Recall that for Langacker, meanings are conceptualisations, which are characterised encyclopedically. This goes for the more schematic, higher level nodes as much as for the more specific, lower level nodes. The mere fact that a conceptualisation is vague, or underdetermined with respect to detail, by no means conflicts with the encyclopedic nature of semantic representations. It is perfectly possible to entertain a vague conceptualisation, e.g. of a relation of containment, which is underdetermined with respect to the shape, material substance, density, boundedness, relative size, etc., of the containing and contained entities.

(b) Possibility of a "superschema"

The network model certainly foresees the possibility of a "superschema" – a single node which is schematic for all the more specific uses of a lexical item. As already noted, the uses of *in* exemplified in (3) could well be brought under a single schematic node 'containment' (construed, possibly, in image-schematic terms, cf. Johnson 1987). The network model and two-level model differ, however, in various respects. A first difference has to do with the cognitive status of the unitary representation. On the network model, a schema and its instantiations differ only in richness of detail, while on the two-level model the unitary representation is a different kind of entity from its more specific elaborations, i.e. it is a linguistic-semantic entity, while its elaborations are essentially non-linguistic, conceptual entities. A second difference concerns processing mechanisms. On the two-level model, the interpretation of an expression emerges through the interaction of the unitary semantic representation with conceptual information, relative to a context. Word meanings must therefore be accessed at the unitary semantic level. If it were allowed that specific interpretations of a lexical item could be stored and accessed, the two-level model would be indistinguishable from the network model! The network model, namely, foresees the possibility that an expression may be understood through accessing of more specific representations, without regard for the superschema. Indeed, a network which lacks a superschema still constitutes a coherent and operationally viable category.

(c) Conventionality

A related issue is that a network may embody a high degree of conventionality. Even though it might be possible to postulate very general, schematic representations for (some) word meanings, a person may still have to learn which instantiations of the schema are sanctioned in the language. The schema does not of itself "generate", or "make available" to the language user the full range of possible instantiations. It is, for example, a matter of linguistic convention that in English you book a seat *on* a plane, not *in* a plane, contrary to what one might expect, given only the most schematic characterisations of *in* and *on*. *On a plane* instantiates a "local schema", which sanctions the use of *on* with respect to conveyance by scheduled means of transportation: *on a plane*, *on a bus*, *on an ocean liner*, but *in a car*, *in a taxi*, *in a rowing-boat*.

(d) Number of senses

The claim that a word is polysemous raises questions concerning the number of different senses, and the criteria by which these are established and demarcated. The two-level approach seeks to by-pass these questions by maintaining that (barring obvious cases of homonymy) each word has only one entry in the lexicon. The network model, on the other hand, suggests that the number of distinct senses of a word might not be determinable in principle (cf. Geeraerts 1993). The number of meanings that one recognises will depend on the schematicity, or, alternatively, the delicacy of one's analysis, whereby a more schematic analysis is in principle no more (or less) "correct" than a more delicate analysis; each in fact is needed as a complement to the other (Geeraerts 1992).

(e) Psychological reality of the network

A network is meant to have psychological reality, i.e. it is meant to capture aspects of a speaker's knowledge of a word's meaning. This raises the question of how the structure of a network, with respect to the identity and the content of the nodes, may be empirically determined.

The issue has been subject to relatively little investigation. As it is, published network structures appear to have been constructed largely on the basis of their authors' intuitions. That different linguists can have somewhat different intuitions is readily apparent from a comparison of figures 2 and 3.

These figures (taken, incidentally, from the same collected volume) purport to represent the structure of the same lexical item, American English *run*. While Langacker's proposal is less detailed than Tuggy's, and although Tuggy fails to indicate relations of extension, and in spite of substantial agreement on "central" aspects of the network, there are also some significant differences between the proposals. Even allowing for the possibility, fully recognised by Langacker (1987:376), that two speakers of a language – in this case Messrs. Langacker and Tuggy – need not share exactly the same mental representations of the words in their language, these examples do point to the need for empirical justification of network structures.

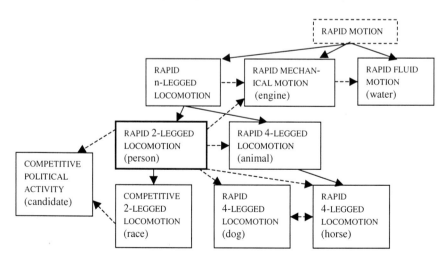

Figure 2: A network for *run* (Langacker 1988b:135)

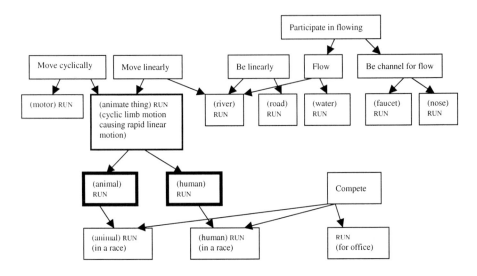

Figure 3: A network for *run* **(Tuggy 1988:588)**

One strategy might be to build on the established fact that speakers of a language are able to make quite reliable judgements on the perceived degree of similarity between different senses of a word (Durkin & Manning 1989). Schulze (1991), in his investigation of the preposition *(a)round*, has subjected similarity judgements to hierarchical cluster analysis, the results of which may be used to confirm a network structure. Some further aspects of psychological reality are discussed below.

(f) Prototypes

Not all the nodes in a network are equally salient.[13] Salience can be characterised in terms of accessibility. Amongst the behavioural correlates of accessibility is the probability that a person, when required to cite an instance of a lexical item, will construct a sentence which instantiates the most easily accessible node. The most salient node in the network may be regarded as the prototype, or prototypical sense of the lexical item (cf. Williams 1992).

(g) Point of access

Whereas the prototype, by definition, is the node that is activated in a neutral, or zero context, specific usage events may require other nodes to be accessed. A general problem, here, concerns the level of schematicity at which meanings are proc-

---

[13] In figures 2 and 3, highly salient nodes are represented by heavy boxes, lack of salience by broken boxes.

essed. Take the example of *running tap*. Is this expression understood with reference to a rather specific sense of *run* – the sense associated specifically with taps – or is a more schematic sense activated (Tuggy's 'be channel for flow', or even 'participate in flowing'), of which *running tap is* an instance? The answer to this question bears not only on the network model, but also on an evaluation of the two-level and other monosemous approaches. For, as already pointed out, the two-level model predicts that word meanings will always be accessed at the most schematic level.

6. Concluding remarks

The above discussion of the network model has raised a number of empirical issues, concerning the shape of a network, the "depth" of a network, and the point of access into the network. I want to conclude by considering some further issues that might bear on an evaluation of the network model vis-à-vis the two-level approach. The following remarks will be brief and schematic, and are meant more as suggestions for further research, than as a conclusive evaluation.

(a) Acquisition

Langacker's Cognitive Grammar and Bierwisch's two-level approach are both meant as psychologically real models of the competence of a mature native speaker. But as Chomsky has taught us, an account of competence is incomplete without a proposal for how this competence could be plausibly acquired by the language learner. On Langacker's model, acquisition would entail the gradual "growth" – both horizontally and vertically – of a network, on the basis of an ever widening database of usage events, and the child's increasingly sophisticated conceptual knowledge. For the two-level model, the central issue would be the acquisition – again, on the basis of exposure to specific usage instances, in interaction with the child's cognitive development – of unitary semantic representations, and of the principles by which the range of conceptual variants can be generated. Although a good deal of research on the acquisition of word meamngs does seem broadly compatible with the network model, there have, to my knowledge, been no acquisition studies carried out explicitly within the framework of the model, neither have the implications of Langacker's Cognitive Grammar for acquisition ever been spelled out.[14] Concerning the two-level model, some very general issues are discussed in Bierwisch (1981). What is lacking is a sufficiently explicit statement of the implications of the model, which would permit non-trivial predictions on the course of acquisition to be formulated.

---

[14] [Editor's note] This assessment is no longer accurate, as Taylor recognises in his afterword.

(b) Language change

Another requirement on any linguistic theory is that it must be able to accommodate known facts of language change. On the network model, semantic change can be straightforwardly represented by the addition of nodes to the network (as well as, of course, by the loss of nodes) and shifts in salience within the network, resulting, possibly, in the emergence of new prototypes. Much of the detailed work on diachronic semantics (e.g. by lexicographers and philologists) does seem broadly compatible with this approach. Indeed, several studies (e.g. Geeraerts 1983, Winters 1989) explicitly invoke a prototype model. With regards to the two-level model, no proposals have been made, to my knowledge, for the treatment of diachronic change. Whether the two-level model can offer insightful accounts therefore remains open.

One important issue would concern the emergence of conventionalised metaphorical senses. These often have to be seen as extensions, not of a highly schematic sense, but of a rather specific reading. This fact in turn suggests that specific readings must enjoy a stable representation in the mental lexicon. For example: *Get round a person* ("manipulate") and *get round a problem* ("overcome") exemplify (slightly different) metaphorical extensions of the spatial sense illustrated in *drive round an obstacle* ("avoid by tracing a roughly semi-circular path"). Even if we accept Wunderlich's claim that the reading of *drive round an obstacle* has the status of a conceptual interpretation of the formula in (10), the metaphorical expressions cannot be derived directly from (10), and cannot therefore be seen as conceptual interpretations of (10).

(c) Cross-language differences

It is commonplace that a word in one language rarely has exactly the same range of uses as a word in another language, even in a historically closely related language. Consider, for example, how the different uses of *leave* in (11) might be rendered in other languages. The only partial overlap between word uses in different languages is easily accommodated on the network model. The situation could, however, be problematic for the two-level model, in that semantic representations would have to be sufficiently similar so as to determine the overlapping uses, whilst at the same time distinct in just those respects that concern divergent uses.

(d) Flexibility

The network model implies that learning the meaning of a word could be a lengthy, even a life-long process, whilst on the two-level model the learning of (the linguistically relevant aspects of) a word's meaning is finalised once the word's semantic representation enters the mental lexicon, presumably at a fairly early stage in a person's life. Some might find the notion of life-long language learning unacceptable, and thus be inclined to favour the two-level approach. I would see things differently. We can observe, almost on a day-to-day basis, how familiar words get used in new ways, in response to new demands that are placed on a speaker's linguistic resources. At the same time, familiar usage patterns may get dated, and gradually fall into disuse. The very flexibility of the network model is surely to be seen as a major empirical strength (Geeraerts 1985). And there is a further aspect. This is that the learning process need not be identical for each speaker in a linguistic community. Again – and this is especially true with respect to the lexicon – it is a common observation that speakers of the "same" language often do differ in the details of their linguistic knowledge.

There are many other areas of investigation where predictions of the network model and the two-level model might be put to the test – areas such as language loss and language pathology, also foreign language learning, in both controlled and naturalistic settings, in addition to the possibility of psycholinguistic study of lexical access. The issues, I would like to stress again, are empirical. What does a person who knows the meaning of a word actually know? Which aspects of this knowledge are activated in acts of speaking and hearing? And how are these aspects processed? Unitary semantic representations (to the extent that these can be postulated at all) may be economical, a division of labour between linguistic and conceptual knowledge may be descriptively elegant, while the network model may be messy. But economy, tidiness, and descriptive elegance may not be the appropriate criteria for settling empirical issues.

Afterword

The two models discussed in this chapter – the "network model" (Langacker) and the "two-level model" (Bierwisch) – offer radically different proposals for the contents of word meanings. The two-level model separates linguistic knowledge proper from conceptual and encyclopedic knowledge. On this model, linguistic meanings are minimalist representations, consisting of semantic units (whether semantic primitives, or variables, which get filled out by conceptual knowledge), and functions which relate the units. On the network model, word meanings are abstracted from usage events, and typically contain rather rich specifications of an encyclopedic nature. Not surprisingly, the two-level model tends to minimise polysemy (with respect to the purely linguistic meanings of words), whereas the network model (as its name suggests) allows meanings to cluster in relations of schematicity and extension, along the lines diagrammed in figures 1 to 3.

It may be useful to think of the two-level and the network models as maximally differentiated approaches to the issue of word meaning. Indeed, many contemporary approaches to lexical semantics can be located somewhere between these two extremes. Jackendoff's *conceptual structures* (in spite of their name!) correspond rather closely to Bierwisch's semantic structures; they are supplemented with content derived from non-linguistic modules (Jackendoff 1983, 1990; Taylor 1996). On the other hand, Pustejovsky's lexical semantic structures already incorporate quite a lot of encyclopedic knowledge, concerning, for example, how an object typically comes into being, what it is used for, what it is made of. The range of interpretations of complex expressions, such as *start a novel*, rests crucially on this aspect of lexical representations (Pustejovsky 1995). Or consider the word definitions proposed by Wierzbicka (1996). Although Wierzbicka herself insists on distinguishing the dictionary from the encyclopedia, her word definitions in fact contain a very great deal of shared, common-sense knowledge about the world. Thus, her definition of *mouse* (Wierzbicka 1996:340-341) provides a rich pool of knowledge, which can be selectively activated on any particular use of the word.

In spite of the radical differences between the network and the two-level models, it is important also to emphasise the commonalities. As noted in the text above, both models seek to address the phenomenon of meaning variation. Moreover, both attempt to come to terms with what is an indisputable fact of language use. This is, that every utterance needs be interpreted relative to the particulars of the context in which it occurs. Often, the interpretation will exploit transient aspects of the situation, and a speaker's construal of that situation, which obviously cannot be captured in a word definition, no matter how "encyclopedic" this may be. The approaches differ with respect to the "distance" between the linguistically encoded meaning and the specifics of a particular usage event, and, of course, with respect to the strategies for linking the one to the other.

Langacker's model handles the specifics of usage events in a fairly straightforward manner, without the need to bring in additional theoretical apparatus (Langacker 1999). The application of a sentence to a specific situation, located in time and space, involves an act of categorisation; the speaker's conceptualisation of the situation is assessed with respect to conceptualisations conventionally symbolised in the language. The sentence-utterance distinction is simply a case of the schema-instance relation, depicted in figure 1. Actually, the same goes for the phonological pole of linguistic expressions, too. Whether we care to represent the sound pattern of an expression by means of a "broad" phonemic transcription (or some latter-day variant), or by a narrow phonetic transcription, there is still a gap between the expression's representation and the particularities of its utterance. Again, the one is schematic for the other; the utterance gets categorised to the extent that it can be regarded as an instance of the stored representation.

Modular approaches, as typified by the two-level model, have the property, that they tend to generate ever more modules (and interfaces between the modules), in order to cope with facts that lie outside the scope of already postulated modules.[15] Indeed, Bierwisch's two-level model is actually inadequate to account for pragmatically de-

---

[15] Jackendoff (1997) nicely illustrates that process.

termined interpretations. In addition to semantic form and conceptual interpretation, there is a need for a third level, communicative interpretation. We ought, therefore, to be talking about a three-level, or even a multi-level, model (Taylor 1994:7).

Confronted with different models which aim to account for the same range of facts, what is a linguist to do? One may, of course, appeal to such criteria as the elegance, economy, and internal consistency of a theory. Still, it is legitimate to ask for evidence that one or other of the models is true. Here, the question of psychological reality looms large, but conclusive pointers (let alone answers) are hard to find.

Croft (1998) presents some methodological criteria for determining the appropriate level of schematicity for representing word meanings. While the criteria may help set a lower boundary for the degree of specificity of a lexical entry, they are of little help for setting the upper boundary, that is, the degree of schematicity. Thus, with respect to figures 2 and 3, there may be compelling empirical reasons for including lower level representations, but none for including (or excluding) the higher-level schemas. Sandra (1998), in a reply to Croft, concludes, pessimistically, that linguistic evidence one way or the other is hard to come by.

For my part, I suspect that a useful line of approach may be found in studies of acquisition. Modular approaches (and the highly schematic linguistic-semantic representations that these approaches usually entail) need to explain how the knowledge state of the mature native speaker comes to be acquired. The standard answer is that the general "architecture" of linguistic knowledge is genetically determined by Universal Grammar, hence, does not have to be learned. Interestingly, even adherents to the generative paradigm are now beginning to question the explanatory power of Universal Grammar (Culicover 1999). The network model, on the other hand, provides a clear hypothesis for the course of acquisition, namely, from the particular to the general, from usage event to schematic representation.

My statement, in the chapter reproduced here, that acquisition researchers have not taken account of the implications of Cognitive Grammar, is now no longer valid. At least one prominent acquisition researcher, Tomasello (1995), is sympathetic to the Cognitive Grammar position, and his studies of the acquisition of syntax certainly seem to confirm the hypothesis that syntactic constructions are learned on a verb-by-verb basis, with schematic generalisations over different verbs emerging only later.

Where does this leave us with the distinction between the dictionary and the encyclopedia? While Bierwisch strenuously insisted on the distinction, it should be noted that scholars as diverse as Pustejovsky and Wierzbicka incorporate quite a lot of encyclopedic knowledge into their lexical-semantic representations, suggesting that for these scholars at least, the distinction between dictionary and encyclopedia may be, at best, fuzzy, and perhaps not even needed at all.

Of course, the fact that one cannot draw a clean line between dictionary knowledge and encyclopedia knowledge is not in itself a reason to reject the distinction. Nowadays, I dare say, most linguists (and, indeed, most practitioners in the other human and social sciences) are accustomed to working with theoretical categories which are referentially fuzzy. The fuzziness of a category, however, by no means renders the category unusable. For example, it might be difficult to decide whether a complex word-form is an instance of derivation or inflection, but this fact does not, of itself, render the concepts of inflection and derivation theoretically vacuous. We are still able to understand these concepts on the basis of good, clear examples, and most linguistic practitioners can continue to make good use of them.

We can certainly think of clear cases of encyclopedic knowledge that is independent of language knowledge. Consider what it takes to know how to change a car tyre; language knowledge is surely irrelevant to the task. The difference between dictionary and encyclopedia, however, immediately blurs, if we consider what it takes to know how to describe, in language, how to change a tyre (as, for example, when giving instructions to a novice). One cannot describe the process, unless one knows how to do it, and one cannot use language appropriate for describing the operation, unless one has the appropriate encyclopedic knowledge.

A possible response here is that describing how to change a tyre involves technical vocabulary, and technical vocabulary needs to be distinguished form the "core" lexicon. Core vs. periphery is yet another of those fuzzy distinctions. I suggest, however, that what goes for talk about changing car tyres goes for talk about almost everything else. To be able to talk about anything at all rests on knowledge about the potential referents of the language that is used. This is just as true of "core" vocabulary items as it is of "technical" terms. True, you can only talk meaningfully about a carburettor if you know what a carburettor is. Equally, use of the preposition *in* rests on knowledge of the concept of containment, and encyclopedic familiarity with the properties of containment. While there is certainly encyclopedic knowledge that is independent of language knowledge, I suspect that the converse is rarely, if ever, the case. Linguistic meanings have got to be encyclopedic in scope.

References

Bierwisch, Manfred. 1981. "Basic issues in the development of word meaning". In Werner Deutsch (ed.), *The child's construction of language*. London: Academic Press. 341-387.

Bierwisch, Manfred. 1983. "Semantische und konzeptuelle Repräsentation lexikalischer Einheiten". In Rudolf Růžička & Wolfgang Motsch (ed.), *Untersuchungen zur Semantik*. Berlin: Akademie-Verlag. 61-99.

Bierwisch, Manfred; Lang, Ewald. 1989. *Dimensional adjectives. Grammatical structure and conceptual interpretation*. Berlin: Springer.

Bierwisch, Manfred; Schreuder, Robert. 1992. "From concepts to lexical items". *Cognition* 42. 23-60.

Brugman, Claudia. 1988. *The story of Over. Polysemy, semantics, and the structure of the lexicon.* New York: Garland.

Croft, William. 1998. "Linguistic evidence and mental representation". *Cognitive linguistics* 9. 151-173.

Cruse, D. Alan. 1986. *Lexical semantics.* Cambridge: Cambridge University Press.

Culicover, Peter W. 1999. *Syntactic nuts. Hard cases, syntactic theory, and language acquisition.* Oxford: Oxford University Press.

Dirven, René. 1995. "The construal of cause. The case of cause prepositions". In John R. Taylor & Robert E. MacLaury (ed.), *Language and the cognitive construal of the world.* Berlin: Mouton de Gruyter. 95-118.

Durkin, Kevin; Manning, Jocelyn. 1989. "Polysemy and the subjective lexicon. Semantic relatedness and the salience of intraword senses". *Journal of psycholinguistic research* 18. 577-612.

García, Erica. 1991. "Grasping the nettle. Variation as proof of invariance". In Linda R. Waugh & Stephen Rudy (ed.), *New vistas in grammar. Invariance and variation.* Amsterdam: John Benjamins. 33-59.

Geeraerts, Dirk. 1983. "Prototype theory and diachronic semantics. A case study". *Indogermanische Forschungen* 88. 1-32.

Geeraerts, Dirk. 1985. "Cognitive restrictions on the structure of semantic change". In: Jacek Fisiak (ed.), *Historical semantics.* Berlin: Mouton de Gruyter. 127-153.

Geeraerts, Dirk. 1992. "The semantic structure of Dutch *over*". *Leuvense bijdragen* 81. 205-230.

Geeraerts, Dirk. 1993. "Vagueness's puzzles, polysemy's vagaries". *Cognitive linguistics* 4. 223-272.

Herskovits, Annette. 1986. *Language and spatial cognition. An interdisciplinary study of the prepositions in English.* Cambridge: Cambridge University Press.

Herweg, Michael. 1988. "Zur Semantik einiger lokaler Präpositionen des Deutschen. Überlegungen zur Theorie der lexikalischen Semantik am Beispiel von 'in', 'an', 'bei' und 'auf'". Stuttgart: LILOG, IBM Deutschland.

Jackendoff, Ray. 1983. *Semantics and cognition.* Cambridge: M.I.T. Press.

Jackendoff, Ray. 1990. *Semantic structures.* Cambridge: M.I.T. Press.

Jackendoff, Ray. 1997. *The architecture of the language faculty.* Cambridge: M.I.T. Press.

Jakobson, Roman. 1971 [1936]. "Beitrag zur allgemeinen Kasuslehre. Gesamtbedeutungen der russischen Kasus". In Roman Jakobson, *Selected writings*, vol. 2. The Hague: Mouton. 23-71.

Johnson, Mark. 1987. *The body in the mind. The bodily basis of meaning, imagination, and reason.* Chicago: University of Chicago Press.

Lakoff, George. 1987. *Women, fire, and dangerous things. What categories reveal about the mind.* Chicago: University of Chicago Press.

Lang, Ewald. 1990. "Primary perceptual space and inherent proportion schema. Two interacting categorization grids underlying the conceptualization of spatial objects". *Journal of semantics* 7. 121-141.

Lang, Ewald. 1991. "A two-level approach to projective prepositions". In Gisa Rauh (ed.), *Approaches to prepositions.* Tübingen: Narr. 127-167.

Langacker, Ronald W. 1987. *Foundations of cognitive grammar*, vol. 1. Stanford: Stanford University Press.

Langacker, Ronald W. 1988a. "A view of linguistic semantics". In Brygida Rudzka-Ostyn (ed.), *Topics in cognitive linguistics.* Amsterdam: John Benjamins. 49-90.

Langacker, Ronald W. 1988b. "A usage-based model". In Brygida Rudzka-Ostyn (ed.), *Topics in cognitive linguistics.* Amsterdam: John Benjamins. 127-161.

Langacker, Ronald W. 1990. *Concept, image, and symbol. The cognitive basis of grammar.* Berlin: Mouton de Gruyter.

Langacker, Ronald W. 1991. *Foundations of cognitive grammar*, vol. 2. Stanford: Stanford University Press.

Langacker, Ronald W. 1999. "A dynamic usage-based model". In his *Grammar and conceptualization.* Berlin: Mouton de Gruyter. 91-145.

Pustejovsky, James. 1995. *The Generative Lexicon.* Cambridge: M.I.T. Press.

Rosch, Elaine. 1978. "Principles of categorization". In Elaine Rosch & Barbara Lloyd (ed.), *Cognition and categorization.* Hillsdale: Lawrence Erlbaum. 27-48.

Sandra, Dominiek. 1998. "What linguists can and can't tell you about the human mind. A reply to Croft". *Cognitive linguistics* 9. 361-378.

Schulze, Rainer. 1991. "Getting round to *(a)round.* Towards the description and analysis of a 'spatial' predicate". In Gisa Rauh (ed.), *Approaches to prepositions.* Tübingen: Narr. 253-274.

Schwarz, Monika. 1992. *Einführung in die kognitive Linguistik*. Tübingen: Francke.

Searle, John R. 1983. *Intentionality. An essay in the philosophy of mind*. Cambridge: Cambridge University Press.

Taylor, John R. 1992. "How many meanings does a word have?" *Stellenbosch papers in linguistics* 25. 133-168.

Taylor, John R. 1994. "The two-level approach to meaning". *Linguistische Berichte* 149. 3-26.

Taylor, John R. 1996. "On running and jogging". *Cognitive linguistics* 7. 21-34.

Tomasello, Michael. 1995. "Language is not an instinct". *Cognitive development* 10. 131-156.

Tuggy, David. 1988. "Náhuatl causative/applicatives in Cognitive Grammar". In Brygida Rudzka-Ostyn (ed.), *Topics in cognitive linguistics*. Amsterdam: John Benjamins. 587-618.

Wierzbicka, Anna. 1996. *Semantics. Primes and universals*. Oxford: Oxford University Press.

Williams, John N. 1992. "Processing polysemous words in context. Evidence for interrelated meanings". *Journal of psycholinguistic research* 21. 193-218.

Winters, Margaret. 1989. "Diachronic prototype theory. On the evolution of the French subjunctive". *Linguistics* 27. 703-730.

Wunderlich, Dieter. 1991. "How do prepositional semantics fit into compositional syntax and semantics". *Linguistics* 29. 591-621.

Wunderlich, Dieter. 1993. "On German *um*. Semantic and conceptual aspects". *Linguistics* 31. 111-133.

Part Two

UNDERSTANDING

UNDERSTANDING

Linguistic meaning, knowledge, and utterance interpretation[1]

Pierre Larrivée

Aston University, School of Languages and European Studies, Birmingham B4 7ET,
United Kingdom
E-mail: P.Larrivee@aston.ac.uk

0. Introduction

Languages appear to be animated by the fundamental duality of being both *structured entities* with a coherent and to some respect autonomous organisation, and *efficient tools* whose function it is to provide ways to convey a speaker's physical or mental, real or imaginary experience. The duality referred to emerges with exceptional clarity in linguistic debates such as the one surrounding the distinction investigated in this volume between linguistic and encyclopedic representations in the study of lexical properties of words. Those who make such a distinction will for instance consider common words like *dog*, *jog*, and *red*, and attempt to determine which units of meaning belong to the realm of real-world knowledge and which ones are associated with the linguistic units themselves. These are by no means easy questions to answer: they inevitably raise such further fundamental issues as the nature of "linguistic" and "world" representations, the theoretical relevance of the distinction, the practical difficulties that must be resolved before the two kinds of rep-

---

[1] I wish to express my heartfelt thanks to Beverly J. Adab, André Bourcier, Patrick J. Duffley as well as an anonymous referee for their enlightening comments upon a preliminary version of this paper. Many thanks also to Rita Woods and Bert Peeters for their linguistic revision of the final version. Of course, the usual disclaimers apply.

resentations can be distinguished, the relationship that holds between them (if indeed they are distinct), and many more.

The present paper seeks to reflect on these selected issues, not by investigating lexical phenomena, but by looking at the interpretation of sentential sequences, with special reference to the interpretation of focusing operators such as *not, even, almost*, and *only*. The choice of a sentential phenomenon is motivated by the fact that its inherent abstractness, as compared to the relative concreteness of lexical phenomena, is likely to provide a better platform from which to evaluate the relevance of a distinction between linguistic semantic representations on the one hand, and world knowledge representations on the other hand, especially in view of the fact that the meaningfulness of syntactic structures is not necessarily accepted without contention by all.

Section 1 discusses the main postulates on which the analysis rests. It will be argued that linguistic units possess a schematic semantic value separate from the information about the world that these units may contribute to evoke; that this distinction also applies to linguistic *sequences*, and not just to words; and that it may be drawn by separating what remains constant across the occurrences of a sequence and what accidentally holds by virtue of that sequence's relation to a given denotation. Sections 2 and 3 describe some key manifestations of focus relationships involving the selected operators (for more details, cf. Larrivée 1998, forthcoming). It is proposed that these manifestations may be explained with reference to the schematic meaning of the focus relationships. Section 4 explores the relation between the schematic meaning of focus relationships and world knowledge representations, and illustrates how the two levels of representation interact in the process of interpretation. The aim of this article is to illustrate the analytically necessary distinction yet processually necessary interaction between different categories of cognitive representation that are relevant to the meanings expressed by language, and that explain the complexity of those meanings.

1. Levels of semantic representation

Language users often appear to assume that the meaning of linguistic sequences may be equated with the knowledge associated with the events or states that these sequences allow them to denote. Such a naïve model of meaning is in fact challenged by the examination of just about any piece of linguistic evidence. Consider a simple everyday utterance such as the following, borrowed from Récanati (1997:109) (cf. also Allan, this volume):

(1)   He stopped the car.

This sequence may actually be used to denote a variety of events, such as a driver bringing his car to a halt either by pressing down the brake pedal or by turning off the ignition key, a police officer signalling a speeding car to slow down and pull over, even Superman using sheer force to prevent an approaching vehicle from going any further. In a similar fashion, the nominal counterpart of the verb *stop* may be used to denote a series of heterogeneous realities. It may refer to the interruption of a process, as in (2); a place where public transport buses pick up passengers, as in (3); a graphical sign indicating the end of a linguistic unit, as in (4); a device on some musical instruments, as in (5); or a type of consonant characterised by particular phonological features, as in (6).

(2)   Let's put a stop to it at once!

(3)   They have been waiting at the bus stop in front of their house for half an hour!

(4)   You must put a full stop at the end of a sentence.

(5)   The clarinet maker replaced the stops on this instrument.

(6)   English possesses several stops.

Examples such as these illustrate and underscore the sharp contrast between the heterogeneity of real or imaginary experiences that may be evoked, and the identity of the linguistic units used to evoke them. The very existence of a contrast of this sort implies that world knowledge and linguistic meaning *must* be different aspects of cognition, and that representations belonging to each are susceptible of a variety of relationships. Polysemy, as illustrated above, is one such relationship, where the same linguistic units are related to a set of different experiences. Another one is paraphrase, which entails communication of a single experience through a variety of different signs. The three sequences below could be used indiscriminately to denote a situation in which a person driving a vehicle brings that vehicle to a halt:

(1)   He stopped the car.

(7)   He turned off the engine.

(8)   He parked.

Each of these utterances could in turn be applied to a series of quite distinct situations: for instance, turning off the engine may be done without parking and parking without turning off the engine. This last remark further illustrates the necessity to recognise the distinction between meaning of linguistic units and knowledge about the world.

Thus, in the same way that linguistic units are claimed to be associated with representations such as a phonological form, some morphological information, and a grammatical category, it is proposed here that, in addition, they are associated with a semantic form distinct from the world knowledge information that, through their use, they can contribute to evoke. Not only do we have to assume that meaning and information belong to distinct cognitive levels: we have to add that no direct one-to-one relationship obtains between units of knowledge and units of linguistic meaning belonging to those distinct levels. Methodologically, the assumption of such a direct relationship between units of different levels would amount to a subordination of language to experience, and jeopardise the study and understanding of the systematic body that language is presumed to constitute on the basis of its creativity, its ease of use, as well as its rapid and systematic acquisition, as convincingly argued by Bouchard (1995) and Pustejovsky (1995). From an analytical point of view, Pustejovsky also suggests that such a subordination does not allow for any distinction between polysemy, where the same linguistic unit evokes different experiences, and homonymy, where different experiences are rendered by two or more linguistic units that happen to share the same form. Failure to make that distinction again obscures the proven creativity and systematicity of language.

While the claim that representations of world knowledge on the one hand and linguistic units on the other hand belong to different cognitive levels appears to be well founded, a question often raised in this context concerns the criteria on the basis of which the distinction is to be drawn. The naïve model of meaning mentioned at the beginning of this section would certainly have it that if linguistic units are to possess a meaning of their own, it should be as easy for linguists to define that meaning as it is for language users to point to instances of realities that can be denoted by such units. This assumption is challenged by linguistic practice, which has yet to come up with easy and rapid procedures allowing for the provision of definitions corresponding to meanings. Even so, it is possible to distinguish what belongs to language from what belongs to world knowledge; all that is needed is an appropriate definition of the way or ways *meaning* is perceived as being distinct from *information*.

Let us consider the following French example:

(9)   Il   est arrivé   avec le   café.

it/he is   arrived with the coffee

'It / He arrived with the coffee'

This sequence may refer to a person who arrives at an unspecified place in the possession of coffee, or to someone who arrives exactly when coffee is being served by a waiter in a restaurant; it may be said of an arrival occurring at the moment that coffee comes out of the expresso percolator or starts dripping down from the filter. As was the case in (1), the linguistic units themselves do not offer any description of the precise reference of the noun *café*, whether it be beans, ground coffee or liquid coffee in a perk, in a cup or in a bowl. They provide no indication of the way the person arrived or of how this arrival was related to that of the coffee, except to say that the arrivals were simultaneous. The only information communicated by the sequence *in its own right* is that a being classified as grammatically masculine was at the origin of a past action of arrival, accompanied by another being that can be referred to as coffee. These schematic indications appear to describe the *meaning* of the sequence, by virtue of which the latter can be used to evoke different states of affairs.

Here are some additional examples, taken from Pustejovsky (1995:45), and originally numbered as (15a), (15b), and (15c):

(10a) Mary wants another cigarette.

(10b) Mary wants a beer.

(10c) Mary wants a job.

Pustejovsky (1995:46) provides the following comment:

> If the goal of a semantic theory is to determine the well-formedness of an expression and then provide the interpretation of that expression, then we must somehow account for how we interpret the sentences in (15) [= (10)]. Clearly, there is contextual variability at play with such a verb as *want*, such that in (15a) [= (10a)] it means "want to smoke," in (15b) [= (10b)] it means "want to drink," and in (15c) [= (10c)], it **presumably** assumes a general "want to have" interpretation. Of course **any of these interpretations are defeasible** (...). (Emphasis added, P. L.)

Several remarks are in order as soon as Pustejovsky's observations are examined in the light of our discussion so far. First of all, it appears inappropriate to attribute the notions of *smoke, drink*, and *have* to the verb *want* or for that matter to the nouns *cigarette, beer* or *job*, since these specific notions appear only when both the verb and its particular object occur together (for discussions of cases where interpretation is induced by cooccurrence of items rather than by one specific item, see Cummins 1998). Similarly, assigning a 'want to smoke a cigarette' interpretation to the example *Mary wants a cigarette* unduly narrows the denotative potential of the sequence; it could be used felicitously to refer to a magician who goes by the name of Mary and who requests a cigarette from the audience to perform a trick, or to a lecturer who goes by that same name and who requires a cigarette that is to be cut into two in preparation of an outline of the principle behind filters.

Pustejovsky recognises all this in the emphasised part of the above quotation by saying that the suggested interpretations are in fact "defeasible". But this may not be the right way to go. While it is true that the prototypical activity engaged in with cigarettes is an activity called *smoke*, and while this information proves essential to understand why, if someone said "I want a cigarette", it would and could be conversationally entailed by the addressee that this person wishes to smoke, it does *not* seem to be entirely adequate to store that information in the linguistic semantic representation of the noun *cigarette*. This strongly suggests that representations belonging to linguistic units should be identified as those and only those that make up the fragments of meaning that remain constant throughout their various denotations, and that therefore are not subject to defeasibility.

Applying this to example (10a), we might say that the linguistic semantic representation of this sentence is that of a person known as Mary, who wishes for the realisation of an event involving herself and the entity denoted by the object nominal. Such a schematic description holds for any and all other examples of *want* modified by a nominal complement, and any further specification as to the concrete nature of that event has to come from compatible world knowledge. Similarly, the linguistic meanings expressed in (9) and in (1), as previously suggested, could be roughly described as the fact that a being classified as grammatically masculine is at the origin of a past action of arrival, accompanied by another being that can be referred to as coffee, and as the fact that a being of masculine gender was at the source of the event of stopping another being known as a car. These indications hold across different denotative usages, which means that they are *not defeasible*. The same holds true in the case of the noun *stop*, whose meaning is not to be found in the comparison of heterogeneous objects (a sentence, a clarinet, a bus route, etc.) but in the property or properties related to the end or the interruption of a process.

In conclusion, I am suggesting that, from an analytical point of view, linguistic units provide a series of schematic indications acting as landmarks to describe or to denote various experiences. There appears to be no continuity between world knowledge and linguistic meaning; what does exist, though, are relations of convergence between two systems of representation. From a processing point of view, the schematic linguistic meaning is only one aspect of the interpretative event. Far from being isolated, it interacts with components such as knowledge of the typical interpretations of linguistic items, cotext, context of interaction, and knowledge of the world. From an analytical point of view, these levels of representation must be carefully distinguished if we are to reach a better understanding of each and, eventually, of their interaction. I do not wish to consider in this paper the genetic relationship that could be said to hold between information about the world and linguistic meaning through the social or individual development of language, but only the relations between the two levels at the mature stage of a particular language.

The following sections set out to determine what is linguistic and what is encyclopedic in the focus relationships established by negation (section 3) and by some adverbs (section 2). The aim is to define how (linguistic) meaning can explain some puzzling manifestations of these relationships, and to show how (linguistic) meaning interacts with information about the world to yield the correct interpretation of a sequence.

2. Adverbial focus

Adverbs such as *even, almost* and *only* are known to impact in interesting ways on the interpretation of the utterances in which they occur. I am thinking of utterances such as the following:

(11a)   Jennifer even talked to *William.*

(11b)   Monica almost talked to *Kenneth.*

(11c)   Hillary only talked to *members of the grand jury.*

Closer inspection reveals that, at the level of interpretation, the adverbs in pre-verbal position affect a constituent other than the one they *syntactically* modify. Although they modify the verb *talked*, the adverbs *even, almost* and *only* bear on the prosodically highlighted noun phrases *William, Kenneth,* and *members of the grand jury,* respectively. This is reflected directly in the implications that derive from these utterances. The fact that *even* is referentially linked to *William* in (11a) explains the utterance's implication that Jennifer talked to a number of people and that she managed to talk to William as well, a person who is judged for whatever reason to be an unexpected addressee, as suggested by the following contexts of use:

(12a)   She talked about this thing to her friends and to a series of lawyers, but she was so desperate that she even talked about it to *William,* who, as you know, is a complete dork.

(12b)   She was upset and she told lawyers and even some prosecutors, but last week, she got so desperate about the whole thing that she even talked to *William* himself, who, as you know, is the most dangerous advisor on their team.

Similarly, the fact that *almost* is referentially linked to *Kenneth* in (11b) explains the inference that Monica possibly talked to a number of people but that, despite getting close, she certainly did not talk to Kenneth, who is again thought for whatever reason to be a most unexpected addressee, as illustrated by the contextualisations in (13):

(13a)   She talked about this thing to her friends and to a series of lawyers, but she was so desperate that she almost talked about it to *Kenneth,* who is such a geek.

(13b)   She was upset and she told lawyers and even some prosecutors, but last week, she got so desperate about the whole thing that she almost talked to *Kenneth* himself, who is such a dangerous advisor!

It is worth noting that the implications brought about by *almost* contradict the oft-repeated claim that focus-related implications do not change the truth value of the sequence in which they occur. Such a claim makes the patently false prediction that (11b) should *denote* that Monica talked to Kenneth while *implying* that she did not. This again shows that linguistic meaning is not structured so as to provide a description of what is true in the world, but rather so as to provide indications of what aspects of the speaker's experiential world are being evoked.

Lastly, the referential link between *only* and *members of the grand jury* in example (11c) implies that Hillary could have talked to a variety of people, but that she restricted herself to exchanges with grand jury members. In this instance, no legitimate inference can be made regarding the predictability or otherwise of the exchanges.

On the basis of the various implications provided above for each of the utterances in (11), it is possible to formulate paraphrases such as those suggested in (14):

(14a)   Jennifer managed to talk to none other than William.

(14b)   Monica didn't talk to Kenneth, but she came close.

(14c)   It's only members of the grand jury that Hillary talked to.

(14c')   Hillary didn't talk to anyone else but members of the grand jury.

Focusing relationships, and consequently any resulting implications and paraphrases, are however subject to conditions of various kinds. The referential links in the first examples of this section stem from *prosodic stress* being applied to the relevant noun phrases. The absence of this stress feature cancels the obligatory nature of the relationship, as illustrated by the following examples:

(15a)   Jennifer even talked to William.

         (≠ ?*Jennifer talked to even William)

         (≈ Talk to William, Jennifer even did *that*)

(15b)   Monica almost talked to Kenneth.

         (≠ *Monica talked to almost Kenneth)

         (≈ Talk to Kenneth, that's almost what Monica did)

On the other hand, focus relationships with a verb complement may be achieved *without* any prosodic support, provided appropriate lexical conditions are present, as in (16):

(16a)   Monica almost talked to every presidential lawyer.

(≈ Monica talked to almost every presidential lawyer)

(≠ Monica talking to every presidential lawyer is almost what happened)

(16b)   Hillary only talked to three members of the grand jury.

(≈ Hillary talked to no more than three grand jury members)

(≠ Talk to three members of the grand jury is all Hillary did)

The distribution of the same lexical support with the wrong adverb, as in (17), makes these relationships quite difficult to establish:[2]

(17a)   Jennifer even talked to three members of the grand jury.

(??= ?*Jennifer talked to even three members of the grand jury)

(≈ Talk to three members of the grand jury, Jennifer even did *that*)

(17b)   Hillary only talked to every presidential lawyer.

(??= Hillary talked to no more than every presidential lawyer)

(≈ Talk to every presidential lawyer is all Hillary did)

Before the reasons behind the effect of prosodic and lexical conditions on adverbial focus relationships can be explained, another type of relationship must be considered.

3. Negative focus

Exactly like focus particles such as *even* and *almost*, negation is known to have the ability to affect one specific constituent in its scope. This focus relationship bears again on the interpretation of a sequence and on its implications, thereby determining the acceptable paraphrases of the original utterance.

In the examples in (18), the negative form *didn't* attached to the verb extends its scope over the entire sentence: it is a sentential negation. Yet, at the level of interpretation, it basically affects the noun phrases *Jeremy* in (18a) and *professors* in (18b) rather than the entire utterances.

---

[2] "??=", here and elsewhere, is to be glossed as 'can hardly be interpreted as meaning'.

(18a)   Miranda didn't talk to *Jeremy* (, but to *his brother*).

(18b)   Miranda didn't talk to *professors* (, but (only) to *lecturers*).

The fact that negation affects particular constituents rather than entire sentences yields the implication that Miranda talked to people other than Jeremy and professors, and the initial sequences can therefore be paraphrased by sentences where the subject and past verb are asserted, leaving only the complement to be negated, as illustrated in the following:

(19a)   Miranda did talk to someone, but that wasn't Jeremy, it was his brother.

(19a')   Miranda talked to Jeremy's brother, not to Jeremy himself.

(19b)   Miranda did talk to some members of staff. They weren't professors though, they were (only) lecturers.

(19b')   Miranda (only) talked to lecturers, not to professors.

As was the case with adverbial focus, the actualisation of a focus relationship depends on factors such as prosodic stress or lexical environment. Prosodic stress is at work in the examples in (18); in its absence, the relationship becomes very difficult to establish, as illustrated in the examples in (20):

(20a)   Miranda didn't talk to Jeremy.

         (≠ It's not Jeremy that Miranda talked to)

         (≈ Talk to Jeremy, Miranda didn't do that)

(20b)   Miranda didn't talk to professors.

         (≠ It's not professors that Miranda talked to)

         (≈ Talk to professors, Miranda didn't do that)

Here, sentential negation affects the whole of the utterance at the level of interpretation. There is no implication that Miranda engaged in any form of talk with anyone else but Jeremy or professors. Legitimate paraphrases are provided in (21):

(21a)   It's not the case that Miranda talked to Jeremy.

(21b)   As for professors, I don't think that Miranda talked to them.

As before, stress-related indications are not a necessary condition for focus relationships to obtain, as long as appropriate lexical conditions are met. Let us look at a few examples:

(22a)   Miranda didn't talk to everybody.

(≈ It's not everybody that Miranda talked to)

(≠ Talk to everybody, Miranda carefully avoided that)

(22b)   Miranda didn't (even) talk to three professors.

(≈ It's not (even) three professors that Miranda talked to)

(≠ Talk to (?*even) three professors, Miranda carefully avoided that)

In (22), sentential negation focuses on the quantifiers *everybody* and *three*, validating the inference that Miranda did talk, in the first case to some people, but not to every person belonging to the relevant set, and in the second case to less than three professors.

(23a)   It's not the case that Miranda talked to everyone, she talked only to some people.

(23b)   As for professors, I think that Miranda managed to talk to some, but definitely less than three.

The interesting thing is that certain lexical specifications are able to *break* the potential relationship between negation and quantifiers, thereby informing us on the conditions that govern it. Consider the real-life examples in contemporary standard French reproduced in (24b) and (25b) (from Larrivée 1998:159), and their English counterparts, presented in (24a) and (25a):

(24a)   All the advice in the world won't ever tell you how to raise your child.

(≠ It's not all the advice in the world that will ever tell you how to raise your child)

(≈ Tell you how to raise your child is something that all the advice in the world will for ever fail to do)

(24b)   Tous les conseils du   monde ne pourront jamais vous
        All   the advice in_the world   ne can_will never to_you

        indiquer la   façon exacte d' élever   votre enfant.
        indicate the way   precise of to_raise your child

(25a) All the ceremonies in the world won't manage to hide the situation
       of the Russian military.

       (≠ It's not all the ceremonies in the world that will manage to hide
       the situation of the Russian military)

       (≈ Hide the situation of the Russian military is something that all
       the ceremonies in the world will fail to do)

(25b) Tout le   cérémonial du   monde ne peut pas cacher la
       All   the ceremonial of_the world ne *can   not hide   the*

       situation des   militaires russes.
       situation of_the military   Russian

Adding the noun complement *du monde* 'in the world' extends the interpretative target of a universally quantified noun phrase to a level of generality and indefiniteness
that severs the focus relationship between the negation and the quantifier. The implication, illustrated by the paraphrases in (26), is that all potential advice with respect
to child rearing will for ever remain insufficient, and that no ceremony of any shape
or form will be able to hide the allegedly poor conditions in the Russian military:

(26a) All the advice in the world could in no way ever tell you how to
       raise your child.

(26b) All the ceremonies in the world would not suffice to hide the situa-
       tion of the Russian military.

In a case like this, no intonation or stress pattern can restore the focus relationship
between negation and quantifier. (27) still means exactly the same thing as (24),
which shows that no modification of the interpretation of these examples is possible
in the existing lexical circumstances.

(27a) *All the advice in the world* won't tell you how to raise your child.

(27b) *Tous les conseils du monde* ne pourront pas vous indiquer la façon
       exacte d'élever votre enfant.

Syntactic movement cannot modify the interpretation either. For instance, floating of
the quantifier to postverbal position, which generally clarifies how narrow the focus
of a syntactically sentential negation effectively is, only yields uninterpretable sequences. This is due to the fact that (28a) and (28b) contain at the same time syntactic indications of a focus relationship between the negation and the quantifier, and
lexical indications of the absence of such a relationship.

(28a) *The ceremonies in the world won't all manage to hide the situation of the Russian military.

(28b) *Les cérémonies du   monde ne cacheront pas toutes la

  The   ceremonies of_the world   ne hide-will   not all   the

  situation des   militaires russes.

  situation of_the military   Russian

The problem disappears as soon as *du monde* and *in the world* are removed from the original sequences:

(29a) *All the advice* won't tell you how to raise your child.

  (≈ It's not all the advice that will tell you how to raise your child)

  (≠ Tell you how to raise your child is something that all the advice will fail to do)

(29b) *Tous les conseils* ne pourront pas vous indiquer la façon exacte d'élever votre enfant.

(30a) The ceremonies won't all manage to hide the situation of the Russian military.

  (≈ It's not all the ceremonies that will manage to hide the situation of the Russian military)

  (≠ Hide the situation of the Russian military is something that all the ceremonies will fail to do)

(30b) Les cérémonies ne cacheront pas toutes la situation des militaires russes.

In conclusion, a maximally generic, virtual, and indefinite extension of a universal quantifier by means of the expressions *du monde* and *in the world* makes it impossible for that quantifier to be the sole focus in the scope of the negation: the extension severs the relationship between the quantifier and its complementary existential value *only some*.

The following examples illustrate another case where, as a result of explicit lexical specification, the focus relationship between negation and universal quantifier turns out to be impossible. (31b) is taken from Larrivée (1998:159).

(31a) All the worldly possessions together aren't worth one single joy of the heart.

(≠ It's not all the worldly possessions together that are worth one single joy of the heart)

(≈ Being worth one single joy of the heart is something that all the worldly possessions fail to achieve)

(31b)   Tous [les biens] ensemble ne valent   pas une jouissance

        All   [the goods] together   ne are_worth not a   joy

        du   cœur...

        of-the heart

        (*Lettres d'amour de Mirabeau*. Paris: Garnier, 1926, p. 223)

(32a)   All the ceremonies together didn't cost £1,000.

        (≠ It's not all the ceremonies together that cost £1,000)

        (≈ Cost £1,000 is something that all the ceremonies together failed to do)

(32b)   Toutes les cérémonies ensemble n' ont   pas coûté 1000

        All   the ceremonies together ne have not cost 1,000

        livres.

        pounds

Underscoring the comprehensiveness of the quantification by means of the noun complements *ensemble* and *together* seems once again to dissolve the focus relationship between negation and quantifier.[3] Neither intonation nor syntactic movement can restore that relationship. (33) means exactly the same as (31), and floating of the quantifier as in (34) produces uninterpretability:

---

[3] This is independently confirmed by the following elicited examples, almost identical to those brought to my attention by the anonymous referee.

    a.   All the volumes of this encyclopedia together aren't worth a grand, but separately they sell for over twelve hundred bucks.

    b.   Tous les tomes de cette encyclopédie ensemble ne coûtent pas 1000 dollars, mais séparément ils coûtent plus de 1200 dollars.

The quantified subject phrase in the first clause of each coordination serves as an interpretative basis for the anaphorical subject pronoun in the second clause. This is generally indicative of the fact that the quantifier is not singled out for focus in the scope of the negation, as a quantifier can hardly have its integral reference at the same time denied and referred to by an anaphor. This analysis is borne out by the fact that the first clauses imply, as do the full utterances in (32), that the whole set of what the subject refers to is worth less than the amount evoked by the post-verbal complement, on which the negation focuses.

(33a)   *All the worldly possessions together* aren't worth a joy of the heart.

(33b)   *Tous les biens ensemble* ne valent pas une jouissance du cœur.

(34a)   *The ceremonies together didn't all cost £1,000 pounds.

(34b)   *Les cérémonies ensemble n'   ont   pas toutes coûté 1000
        The   ceremonies   together   ne   have   not   all   cost   1,000
        livres.

        pounds

Upon removal of the complements *ensemble/together*, the problem disappears:

(35a)   *All the worldly possessions* aren't worth one single joy of the heart.

        (≈ It's not all the worldly possessions that are worth one single joy
        of the heart)

        (≠ Being worth one single joy of the heart is something that all the
        worldly possessions fail to achieve)

(35b)   *Tous les biens* ne valent pas une jouissance du cœur.

(36a)   The ceremonies didn't all cost £1,000.

        (≈ It's not all the ceremonies that cost £1,000)

        (≠ As for amounting to £1,000, all the ceremonies failed to)

(36b)   Les cérémonies n'ont pas toutes coûté 1000 livres.

Lexically specifying the comprehensiveness of the quantification makes it impossible for the quantifier to be the sole focus in the scope of the negation. The focus relationship between the universal quantifier and its complementary existential value is again suspended. As before, focus cannot possibly be restricted to the quantifier, because it rests on the availability of such a relationship.

Let us consider one last piece of evidence. It involves the dissolution of the focus relationship between negation and numerals, illustrated by example (22b), reproduced below:

(22b)   Miranda didn't (even) talk to three professors.

        (≈ It's not (even) three professors that Miranda talked to)

        (≠ Talk to (?*even) three professors, Miranda carefully avoided
        that)

Dissolution may be achieved through syntactic manipulation, as illustrated in (37):

(37a)   Miranda didn't (even) talk to five of these Russian forensic profes-
        sors.

        (≈ It's not even five of these professors that Miranda talked to)

        (≠ Talk to (?*even) five of these professors, Miranda just didn't)

(37b)   Miranda didn't (even) talk to these five Russian forensic professors.

        (≠ It's not even these five professors that Miranda talked to)

        (≈ Talk to (*even) these five professors, Miranda just didn't)

In (37a), the numeral identifies a subset of professors. The focus relationship under
discussion obtains, resulting in the following paraphrase:

(38)   As for these Russian forensic professors, I think Miranda managed
        to talk to some, but less than five for sure.

On the other hand, in (37b), the numeral simply provides a description of the size of
a definite group of people; the bond between the numeral and the set of complementary inferior numbers is severed, and no focus relationship with the negative
marker can be established:

(39)   As for these five Russian forensic professors, I think Miranda
        didn't manage to talk to them.

Where does all this lead us? The examination of the various instances of negative
focus discussed so far suggests that a common linguistic semantic value underlies all
of them. Whenever, at the level of interpretation, negation affects the noun phrase in
the verb complement, as in examples (18), (22), and (37a), reproduced below:

(18a)   Miranda didn't talk to *Jeremy* (, but to *his brother*).

(18b)   Miranda didn't talk to *professors* (, but to *lecturers*).

(22a)   Miranda didn't talk to everybody.

(22b)   Miranda didn't (even) talk to three professors.

(37a)   Miranda didn't (even) talk to five of these Russian forensic profes-
        sors.

the common result is for the focused item negated at the level of interpretation to
refer to a *complementary value*. In (18), the sentential negation conveys rejection of
the assertion that a given person or a specific group of people were addressed by

Miranda, while the focus relationship leads to the inference that some other person or group of people were talked to. In (22), the negative morpheme forces the quantifiers *everybody* and *three* into an implied existential quantification and a set of inferior numbers as complementary values, respectively. In (37), a similar complementary value is inferred from the focus relationship between negation and the partitive quantifier.

It must be noted that while the nature of the complementary value may be established either by lexical determination, as in (22) and (37) (where the negation is purely descriptive), or by full contextual explicitation, as in (18) (where the negation is therefore argumentative), the complementarity is a necessary consequence of the focus relationship, as suggested in different frameworks by Gabbay & Moravcsik (1978), Jackendoff (1972), and Rooth (1996), to name but a few. On the other hand, the impossibility to establish such a relationship may follow from an item's failure to evoke such a complementary value. A closer examination of the examples in (20), reproduced below, provides evidence in support of this hypothesis.

(20a)   Miranda didn't talk to Jeremy.

(20b)   Miranda didn't talk to professors.

Remember that the utterances in (20) are parallel to those in (18), except for the absence of prosodic stress and the descriptive use of negation, so that no focus relationship between the negation and the noun phrases *Jeremy* and *professors* obtains. The absence of focus relationship between the descriptive negation and the unstressed complement may be attributed to the fact that, unlike the quantifiers *everybody* and *three*, the nouns *Jeremy* and *professors* do not in themselves possess a definite complementary value, thus making them ineligible for focus in descriptive conditions.

Further evidence is contained in the examples reproduced below:

(24a)   All the advice in the world won't ever tell you how to raise your child.

(25a)   All the ceremonies in the world won't manage to hide the situation of the Russian military.

(31a)   All the worldly possessions together aren't worth one single joy of the heart.

(32a)   All the ceremonies together didn't cost £1,000.

(37b)   Miranda didn't (even) talk to these five Russian forensic professors.

As has been pointed out, the quantifiers in these examples have their relationship with their lexically determined complementary value severed by contextual indications. The absence of negative focus on the universal quantifier was shown to result from the modification of the noun phrase by expressions such as *in the world* and *together*; by stressing the generic indefinite extension of the quantification in the first case, and in the second the comprehensiveness of that quantification, these expressions make it impossible, if the sequence is to be coherent, for the quantifiers to be singled out for focus in the scope of the negation. On the other hand, the absence of negative focus on the numeral quantifier was suggested to follow from the inclusion of the quantifier in the scope of the demonstrative, so that reference turned out to be to a specific group of people whose properties include, among other things, that of being five in number. As a result, the quantifier does not entertain the relationship to the set of lower numbers that it can only entertain when it has a partitive interpretation, much in the same way as proper names are not crucially organised in complementary series but rather in terms of reference potential. It follows that no narrow focus obtains.

The principle according to which the linguistic semantic parameter of complementary values acts not only as a consequence but also as a condition to be met by expressions if they are to be singled out for focus finds further validation in the examination of the focusing behavior of the adverbs considered in section 2. The relevant examples are repeated below.

(11a)   Jennifer even talked to *William*.

(11b)   Monica almost talked to *Kenneth*.

(11c)   Hillary only talked to *members of the grand jury*.

As in the case of negation, the focus relationship at the level of interpretation between the adverbs *even, almost*, and *only* on the one hand, and the noun phrases in the prepositional complements of the verb *talk* on the other hand, depends on the ability of these NPs to refer to a complementary value. The adverbs affect the prosodically stressed material, which leads to inferences consistent with the lexical value of each focusing particle: namely, that Jennifer talked to William and to somebody else, that Monica might have talked to other people but did not talk to Kenneth, and that Hillary talked to members of the grand jury and refrained from talking to other people although she could have done just that. The same inferences can be derived from similar sentences without prosodically highlighted material, although they then do not possess the compelling character that they have with stressed nouns, since the latter, as a result of being stressed, evoke a complementary set.

The adverbs in question may also bear on quantifiers, as in (16):

(16a)   Monica almost talked to every presidential lawyer.

(16b)   Hillary only talked to three members of the grand jury.

Inferences in (16) include the fact that Monica talked to some of the presidential lawyers, could have talked to all but did not, and that Hillary talked to three members of the grand jury, could have talked to more but did not. In each case, there are clearly identifiable complementary values.

How do we explain the difficulty for focus particles to affect, at the level of interpretation, the nominal in the prepositional complement phrases of the following cases, discussed earlier?

(17a)   Jennifer even talked to three members of the grand jury.

(17b)   Hillary only talked to every presidential lawyer.

The answer goes as follows. While in (16a) the quantified expression *every presidential lawyer* provides an appropriate reference point with respect to which a lower complementary value can easily be situated, the noun phrase *three members of the grand jury* in (17a) does not quite occupy a superlative enough position to achieve the same end. In (16b), *three members of the grand jury* refers to a subgroup that may be defined as restricted against complementary occurrences, thus making focus by means of *only* fully permissible. On the other hand, focus by means of *only* is hardly possible when, as in (17b), with the universally quantified phrase *every presidential lawyer*, no complementary value is readily made available: restriction against such a value then becomes problematic.

What all these facts vividly illustrate is not only that the expression targetted by focus must have a complementary value before it can be so affected, but also that the nature of that value depends on that of the focusing element. The latter observation provides an explanation for the discordances observed in the focusing behaviour of different adverbs (Jackendoff 1972, Ross & Cooper 1979), and supports the idea that interpretation of an utterance is established by the convergence of its constitutive elements.

By way of summary, the empirical data examined in this and the previous section demonstrate that at least some syntagmatic interpretative phenomena (namely adverbial and negative focus) can be analysed as possessing a meaning that characterises them as linguistic phenomena. It is suggested that this general meaning is the capacity to imply complementary values. This linguistic semantic parameter explains the limitations on the manifestations of focus, and it underlies the distinct representations of the world that may be referred to by the appropriate linguistic utterances. The data to be discussed in the next section show that these levels of representation interact in the process of interpretation to produce the appropriate reading from among the various semantic manifestations related to focus.

4. The dynamic interpretation of focus

In the two previous sections, I discussed cases where linguistic indications steer interpretation in certain directions, leaving little possibility for alternative interpretations to be arrived at. Such cases of saturated interpretation were found with stressed noun phrases in complement position, which in the examples considered earlier seem to attract focus, as well as with unstressed proper names, which, in the cases envisaged, cannot constitute the focus of descriptive negation. Overdeterminacy of meaning also occurs with universal quantifiers whose extension is emphasised by expressions such as *in the world* and *together*, and with numerals contributing to the description rather than to the quantification of a specific nominal set. By contrast, most utterances in most contexts are semantically underdetermined, leaving room for several interpretations to be actualised. The following example, adapted from a sequence attributed to Tobler by Bally (1965:173), constitutes an excellent illustration of interpretative underdeterminacy:

(40)   All these jewels aren't worth £1,000.

In itself, the example can invoke for a given group of jewels that either (i) some but not all are sold at a thousand pounds, (ii) none of the jewels considered individually are worth the mentioned amount, or (iii) the whole of the group of jewels under consideration is judged as not adding up to the suggested price. Nothing in the value of either the universal quantifier or the negation, and nothing in the linguistic nature of the focusing relationship, favours one interpretation over the other. This means that other factors must intervene to steer the choice of interpretation that speakers make effortlessly in real interactions. Of course, semiological indications such as prosody will play a crucial role in the determination of interpretations in oral communication, and a final rising or falling intonation or appropriate emphasis on the quantifier can attribute to (40) a definite reference. Of greater interest to our argument is that different types of knowledge about the world can determine the selection of the appropriate interpretation. For instance, if the external appearance of all the considered jewels was patently poor, this could suggest interpretation (iii); if the utterance were given as an answer to a request by a customer to see pieces under the mentioned price, interpretation (ii) would be favoured; if it were visible to the interacting speakers that some but not all of the jewels considered are priced at £1,000 or more, only interpretation (i) could be validated as a contribution consistent with that knowledge.

The contribution of real-world information to the interpretation of semantically underdetermined utterances is further illustrated by the following example:

(41)   Hillary wouldn't spend £250 a month on clothes.

As discussed by Jespersen (1917) with reference to similar cases, depending upon one's expectations as to how much money a person needs to spend on clothes, and how much the mentioned amount represents with respect to that expectation, (41) may mean, for instance, that Hillary would only be willing to spend less than £250 on clothes in the provided frame of reference, which is really very little money; or that Hillary would never spend such an enormous sum of money on clothes in such a short period of time. In the first case, negation focuses on the quantifier, whereas in the second case no such focus relationship exists.

Certain pieces of real-world information may create conditions buttressing otherwise unlikely interpretations. For instance, out of context, it is difficult to see how the adverb *even* in (42) could focus on the noun phrase *books*: little in the knowledge that is generally associated with the noun *book* lends itself to the idea that books are unlikely objects for students to read.

(42)   Some of my undergraduate students even read books.

On the other hand, if the prevailing mood is one of sarcasm or cynicism, (42) may well mean that, in the speaker's mind, his or her students read so little that for them to read something as big as a book is a remarkable thing. Furthermore, if the context of interaction or the cotext itself includes explicit reference to some situation in which for instance books are an optional and quantitatively limited part of a list of required readings otherwise containing articles, web pages, encyclopedia extracts, and other shorter pieces of scientific wisdom, then the relative (un)importance of books in the set warrants the focusing interpretation of (42). Focus can obtain without particular rhetorical effect (e.g. sarcasm), due to the convergence between the situation and the meaning indications provided by focus relationships, as well as to the nature of the particular focus particles and of the constituants singled out for focus.

A similar contribution of situational knowledge leads to the selection of the appropriate interpretation of the utterances in (43):

(43a)   The president doesn't appear to be Mr. Purasneti (, but it is not Mr. Béalard either).

(43b)   The president doesn't appear to be Mr. Rasputin (, but it is not Mr. Abélard either).

As seen in (20), and again in (43a), descriptive negation does not normally focus on proper names, because in their denominative function such nouns do not evoke a definite complementary value but rather a referential perspective. By contrast, in cases such as (43b), the proper names are indeed defined in a network of complementary values. Used in a descriptive role, they evoke paragon examples of properties like debauchery or chastity. They can therefore be singled out for focus.

The upshot of all this is that information about the world that is not linguistic in essence can play an important role in determining the interpretation of linguistic sequences whose meaning is not already saturated by syntactic or lexical indications.[4] This information, whether contextual, cotextual or called up by some linguistic units, acts as a landmark for the interpretative stabilisation of semantically underdetermined linguistic sequences, much in the same way as this world knowledge and knowledge about the typical interpretations of a word will help fix the value of a polysemous item in a sequence containing several polysemes (for a thorough discussion of the calculation of the interpretation of polysemous items in contexts of multiple polysemes, see Victorri & Fuchs 1996). Therefore, while being analytically distinct, meaning and information interact with each other, enabling to correctly interpret linguistic sequences against general principles of consistency.

5. Conclusion

In this paper, I have argued that at least some linguistic manifestations are endowed with semantic representations that characterise them as constitutive parts of a linguistic system. Linguistic semantic representations are analytically distinct from world knowledge representations; even so, the two interact to yield coherent understanding and appropriate interpretation of linguistic sequences. I hope to have shown that focus is structured on the basis of the schematic linguistic representation of complementary values, both at the level of the meaning of the focusing operators and at the level of the meaning of the focused constituents. That complementarity can then be contextually instantiated by converging encyclopedic and linguistic information. The study of focus phenomena appears to establish that, at least in some cases, it is necessary to distinguish world knowledge from knowledge associated with linguistic units. Such a distinction is crucial to understanding both the proper structuration of linguistic semantics and the complexity of the contextual calculation of utterance meaning.

References

Bally, Charles. 1965 [1932]. *Linguistique générale et linguistique française*. Berne: Francke.

---

[4] Which is not to say of course that these linguistic factors are absent in the utterances considered in this section, only that they are insufficient by themselves to single out one interpretation.

Bouchard, Denis. 1995. *The semantics of syntax. A minimalist approach to grammar.* Chicago: University of Chicago Press.

Cummins, Sarah. 1998. "Le mouvement directionnel dans une perspective d'analyse monosémique". *Langues et linguistique* 24. 47-66.

Gabbay, Dov; Moravcsik, Julius. 1978. "Negation and denial". In Franz Guenthner & Christian Rohrer (eds), *Studies in formal semantics.* Amsterdam: North-Holland. 251-265.

Jackendoff, Ray. 1972. *Semantic interpretation in generative grammar.* Cambridge: M.I.T. Press.

Jespersen, Otto. 1917. *Negation in English and other languages.* København: Munksgaard.

Larrivée, Pierre. 1998. *La portée des négations en français contemporain.* Unpublished PhD dissertation, Université Laval.

Larrivée, Pierre. Forthcoming. *L'interprétation des séquences négatives. Portée et foyer des négations en français.*

Pustejovsky, James. 1995. *The Generative Lexicon.* Cambridge: M.I.T. Press.

Récanati, François. 1997. "La polysémie contre le fixisme". *Langue française* 113. 107-123.

Rooth, Math. 1996. "Focus". In Shalom Lappin (ed.), *The handbook of contemporary semantic theory.* Oxford: Blackwell. 271-293.

Ross, John R.; Cooper, William E. 1979. "*Like* syntax". In William E. Cooper & Edward C. T. Walker (eds), *Sentence processing. Psycholinguistic studies presented to Merril Garrett.* Hillsdale: Erlbaum. 343-418.

Victorri, Bernard; Fuchs, Catherine. 1996. *La polysémie. Construction dynamique du sens.* Paris: Hermès.

Quantity implicatures and the lexicon[1]

Keith Allan

Department of Linguistics, Monash University, Clayton VIC 3168, Australia
E-mail: keith.allan@arts.monash.edu.au

0. Introduction

This paper is about the conversational implicatures (hereafter referred to simply as *implicatures*) that result from the two maxims of quantity identified by Grice (1975) and subsequently discussed by (amongst others) Atlas & Levinson (1981), Horn (1984), and Levinson (1995). The question I seek to resolve is whether Q implicatures should be entered in the lexicon, or whether they constitute encyclopedic information. In other work (Allan 1999, forthcoming), Q1 implicatures, deriving from the first maxim of quantity, are included in lexical entries. I shall argue that what Jackendoff (1983, 1985, 1990) refers to as *preference conditions* on lexical items are implicatures deriving from the second maxim of quantity augmented with the Atlas & Levinson principle of informativeness, a combination here referred to as Q2. Jackendoff incorporates preference conditions within his lexical entries. But is it always the case that Q implicatures are located in the lexicon, and exactly how are they to be represented? This is the question for the present paper. It begins with brief discussion of the respective functions of and relationship between a lexicon and an encyclopedia, and continues with the cooperative principle, common ground, conversational implicature, Q implicatures, and Jackendoff's preference conditions.

---

[1] I am grateful to an anonymous reviewer for many valuable observations. All remaining faults are mine.

These preliminaries completed, I turn to the proper statement of generalised quantity implicatures.

1. Proper names, the lexicon, and the encyclopedia

In Allan (1995a), I argued for a clear division of labour between lexicon and encyclopedia with respect to proper names and terms for both natural and nonnatural kinds. The lexicon stores the meanings of listemes – those language expressions whose meanings are not determinable (computable) from the meanings (if any) of their constituents. An encyclopedia contains information about what listemes are used to refer to (cf. Katz 1977). Allan (1995a) argues that a lexicon entry has just three major connected components: formal specification is connected to morpho-syntactic specification, and the morphosyntactic specification is connected to semantic specification in the following manner: F_f — $_fM_s$ — $_sS$. The indices function like bidirectional connectors in a network (cf. figure 1).

Figure 1: The specification network

The encyclopedia functions as a data-base containing exhaustive information either on all branches of knowledge – if there is just one encyclopedia – or on a particular subject area in each one of multiple specialised and cross-referenced encyclopedias.[2]

Consider sentences (1-2).

(1)   I know four Annas.

(2)   Anna just called to ask us to a party.

In (1) there is no need for the hearer to know any of the women bearing the name Anna that the speaker is referring to; all that is required of the hearer is the lexical knowledge that *Anna* is a proper name for a female. *Anna* is located in the English lexicon with some semantic specification. What is the evidence for this?

Many people share the same family name, more share the same given name, some share their entire proper name with others; the *Elizabeth Taylor* listed in the 1989

---

[2] In any human community there are people with widely different areas of specialised knowledge and the vocabulary to go with it. This can be modelled by a bank of encyclopedias, each containing a lexicon, and all accessible to one another.

Tucson AZ phone directory was not the frequently husbanded British-born movie-star. What do language users do about this state of affairs? Well, take *London, Ontario* versus *London, England*, or *Boulder, Utah* versus *Boulder, Colorado*. The strategy used in the proper identification of incomplete names is to add further information to the proper name, thus turning it into a more complete and explicit name with some descriptive material to fix the reference.

If many proper names are shared by different name bearers, there must be a stock of proper names. This stock must surely be located either partially or wholly in the lexicon. Further evidence is to be had from the anomaly of the strings in (3) compared with those in (4-5).

(3a)   *John washed herself.

(3b)   *Mary washed himself.

(4a)   John washed himself.

(4b)   Mary washed herself.

(5a)   Robin washed himself.

(5b)   Robin washed herself.

The gender of the pronoun is normally determined by attributes of the referent. The anomalies in (3) derive directly from semantic incompatibility of the proper name and its clause-mate reflexive pronoun, and indirectly from the fact that the typical denotatum of *John* is male and the name is therefore of masculine gender, whereas *Mary* typically denotes a female and is feminine.[3] *Robin* may denote either a male or a female, and so is semantically compatible with a pronoun of either gender. There are quite general gender constraints on names, as shown in (6-7).

(6)   *Richard is lactating.

(7a)   Mary's just had a baby.

(7b)   John's just had a baby.

---

[3] The terms *reference* and *denotation* and their derivatives are used differently by different writers. They are used here in accordance with the definitions in Allan (forthcoming). Roughly speaking: referring is something that a speaker (writer) does; denoting is the relation that words have to worlds irrespective of any particular utterance.

(6) is anomalous. (7a) normally means that Mary has given birth, whereas (7b) means that John's female partner has given birth. The most significant characteristic of a personal proper name is that it identifies the gender of the name bearer.

> Based on a comparison of sixty societies, Alford (1988:66-68) finds that the sex of an individual is the most common item of information conveyed by first names. This is certainly the case for the United States, where names typically convey gender. Androgynous names are relatively uncommon even at present: In New York State not one of the leading 100 boys' names overlaps with the leading 100 girls' names. (Lieberson & Mikelson 1995:933)

Gender expectations need to be indicated among the semantic specifications of the lexicon entry.

From a lexicological viewpoint, alternative spellings and pronunciations of names should be included, too. For example, the lexicon might contain something like the following entries. The position of the subscripts relative to what they index is of no consequence. The subscript indices indicate links between components of the lexicon, the numbers can be thought of as addresses.

(8) $_{f150}$**Robin** ∨ $_{f151}$**Robyn** / ˈrɒbɪn / — $_{f150-1}$N$_{s250-1}$ — 'bearer of the name $_{f150}$*Robin*, either male or female'$_{s250}$ ∨ 'bearer of the name $_{f151}$*Robyn*, normally female'$_{s251}$

(9) $_{f160}$**Graeme** ∨ $_{f161}$**Graham** / ˈgreiəm / — $_{f160-1}$N$_{s260}$ — 'bearer of the name $_{f160}$*Graeme* ∨ $_{f161}$*Graham*, normally a male'$_{s260}$

(10) $_{f170}$**Colin** / ˈkɒlɪn / ∨ $_{f171}$/ ˈkoulɪn / — $_{f170-1}$N$_{s270}$ — 'bearer of the name $_{f170-1}$*Colin*, normally male'$_{s270}$

Returning to (1), *I know four Annas*, and (2), *Anna just called to ask us to a party*, the lexical knowledge required for proper interpretation of (1) is comparable to that relevant to the interpretation of *computers* in (11):

(11)   I have four computers.

By contrast, (2) is only felicitous if H does have some knowledge of the name bearer; if s/he does not already do so, it would normally be asked for. This is not lexical, but encyclopedic knowledge. As Kripke (1972) rightly said, contra Frege (1966:57), the name *Aristotle* does not have the sense 'the pupil of Plato and teacher of Alexander the Great ... who was born in Stagira': these are encyclopedic facts about one bearer of the name. Kripke did not believe that names have senses at all. For the reasons already advanced, I think this is wrong – though the objection to Frege is not. Where I concur with Kripke's thesis is that within a community of speakers K a particular referent R or a class of denotata D is "baptised" with a name *N*, and afterwards is known within K as *N* (Kripke 1972:302,309). Many Rs and Ds are baptised with more than one *N*, each of which is a *rigid designator*.[4] Some names are initially descriptive, but after the baptism they become rigid designators. The form of *N* may change over time, or when borrowed into another language, cf. Αριστοτέλης = Aristotle. There are usually contextual constraints on which *N* is applicable in the world and time spoken of (Kripke says little about this; see Allan 1995a, forthcoming for much more). Life would be tough for a boy named *Sue*; it was even tough for the American who had his name changed to *One Zero Six Nine*. Once a rigid designator exists in the language, there is presumed to be an historical chain stretching back through users of the name to the original baptism (Kripke 1972:302). The notion of the historical chain is a variation on a long established view that a history of conventional usage characterises the vocabulary in the language and allows successive generations to communicate easily. The historical chain explains as well as anything does how a listeme *N* becomes conventionalised within a community. The motivation for Kripke's historical chain conjecture is that the proper name persists in time denoting just the name-bearer, whereas common names denote a class of entities each of which is distributed in time. However, the class or kind persists, and Kripke (1972:328) does propose that kind terms are rigid designators. The common name *a cat* necessarily names something animal, but the proper name *Martha* only most probably names a female. Baptisms of the same natural kind are likely to be different among different language communities, which is why the thing called *dog* is also called *chien, Hund, pies, ájá, kare, mbwa,* and many other names besides. The reference is fixed for a rigid designator by ostension, definition, or description which constitute part of the encyclopedic information about the referent (ostension is included for an "encyclopedia" that represents visual or auditory images – as our mental encyclopedias surely do). Kripke never refers to anything like an "encyclopedic entry for the name"; but he does talk about evidence for fixing the reference of the rigid designator, and the evidence is composed from exactly the kind of information that goes into the encyclopedia entry.

Information about people is stored in the encyclopedia and one means of access will be via a person's proper name. (The whole encyclopedia entry can be accessed through part of the information in it, enabling the name and further information about the referent to be retrieved.) (12) sketches the encyclopedia entry for *Aristotle*.

(12)   [1]**Aristotle** *proper name* of an ancient Greek philosopher, born in Stagira in C4 BCE. Author of *The Categories, On Interpretation, On Poetry,* ... Pupil of Plato and teacher of Alexander the Great ...

[2]**Aristotle** *proper name* of **Aristotle Onassis**, C20 CE Greek shipping magnate ...

---

[4] I maintain Kripke's term. In my preferred terms, *rigidly designate* would be *rigidly denote*.

[3]**Aristotle** *proper name* of **Ari Papadopoulos**, friend whose phone
number is 018 111 …

The information here is clearly not of the kind that anyone should expect to find in a
lexicon because it is not lexicographical information about a name in the language.
Instead, it is encyclopedic information about particular name bearers. Similarly for
information about things, whether natural kinds such as gold and dogs, or nonnatural
kinds such as polyester and computers. It is far from obvious why Kripke did not
include the names for nonnatural kinds as rigid designators – not that he explicitly
excludes them. The process of naming a new human being, a new town, a newly
discovered mineral, and a new invention seem broadly similar. The way that the
names are transmitted through an historical link is exactly parallel. If there are philosophical problems with nonnatural kinds (cf. Schwartz 1980, Pulman 1983:ch.7), the
linguistic facts seem to force a comparison with natural kind terms.

Rigid designators name referents, they do not classify them. The semantic specification of natural kind terms locates them in a natural taxonomy, but is otherwise similar to the semantic specification of a proper name. The *S.O.E.D.* entry for *cat* describes it as "a carnivorous quadruped" and in the context of zoology "a member of
the genus *Felis* or *Panthera*". Both senses are followed by lists of species, i.e. encyclopedic information. *Gold* is also given a largely encyclopedic entry in the
S.O.E.D.: "The most precious metal; characterised by its yellow colour, non liability
to rust, high specific gravity, and great malleability and ductility. Chemical symbol
Au". Clearly these are guides to fixing the appropriate denotation – which is a good
practical aim for a dictionary. Defining the cat as a "carnivorous quadruped" merely
describes what cats are, it does not give a semantic description of the word *cat*. Consider Putnam's (1975) notion that cats may turn out to be alien automata that we
humans (and our dogs) have been hoodwinked into believing are animals: in this circumstance, is *cat* truly a rigid designator? Kripke says "Cats are in fact animals!",
the alien automata would be automata "in a cat-like form" (1972:321). Though Putnam disagrees, Kripke seems to be right. The unnatural history of such cats is surely
part of the encyclopedia entry. Putnam and Kripke are discussing an outlandish possibility; there is in fact a good deal of renaming in the various branches of biology
when research leads to life-forms being relocated in new tribes, or families, or super-
families, and so forth; or else a new variety or subspecies is recognised. This is
straightforwardly indicated in reference books:

> *Stribolanthes* species (syn[onymous with] *Goldfussia*)
>
> *Tibouchina* species (formerly *Lasiandra*)   (Moore et al. 1980:220,221)

> **Australian chats** Family Epthianuridae [The molecular biology work of
> Sibley & Ahlquist indicates the chats *are* true honeyeaters and they include
> them in the prior Family Meliphagidae. We separate them in this classifica-
> tion for the present.] (Simpson & Day 1993:347)

The encyclopedia will record the changes, and the lexicon will record some of them, too. E.g. the entry for *lasiandra* should be cross-referenced with *tibouchina* and, perhaps in future, *Epthianuridae* with *Meliphagidae*. Because animacy is both semantically and syntactically relevant in the English language, it will need to be indicated in the lexicon; so, given the Putnam-Kripke scenario, if cats turn out to be automata yet continue to display all the characteristics of animates (e.g. they are born, breathe, nurture themselves, die), then at least some automata can be grammatically classified along with animates! Proper names may also be changed over time. Constantinople became Istanbul; St Petersburg became Leningrad and then, once again, St Petersburg. People change names for a variety of reasons. In some communities women get a new name on being married. Transsexuals change their name as they change sex. None of this presents a problem: each name is the rigid designator of an entity over a certain period of time.

It was shown in Allan (1995a) that encyclopedic data on the denotata of listemes is closely networked with their lexicon entries. Indeed, lexical information is heavily dependent on encyclopedic information. Many scholars believe that encyclopedic information about listemes should be considered part of the lexicon (cf. Langacker 1987, Boguraev & Briscoe 1989:5, Pustejovsky 1995). The alternative, argued for in Allan (1995a), is that a lexicon is part of an encyclopedia. The lexicon stores information about the formal, morphosyntactic, and semantic specifications of listemes; but etymological and stylistic data about them is encyclopedic, external to the lexicon yet connected with the appropriate lexicon entries. With respect to proper names, the lexicon will contain lexicographical information about a name in the language, and the encyclopedia holds information about particular name bearers. Allan (1995a) concluded that entries in the combined lexicon and encyclopedia form a quadruple of formal (F), morphosyntactic (M), semantic (S), and encyclopedic (E) specifications as represented by the network in figure 2. The networked F, M, and S constitute the lexicographical information. A fragment of the network for *Aristotle* is given in figure 3.

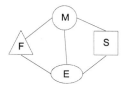

Figure 2: The lexicon–encyclopedia interface

In this section I have argued for an augmentation of Kripke's notion that names are rigid designators. Proper names as well as common ones are listed in the lexicon along with their semantic specifications. On the problems that arise with family names and foreign names, see Allan (1995a, forthcoming). Whereas the lexicon contains lexical information about listemes, the encyclopedia contains information about the denotata of listemes – including name bearers. It is suggested that the lexicon forms a component of the encyclopedia, and furthermore that there are many lexica and many encyclopedias.

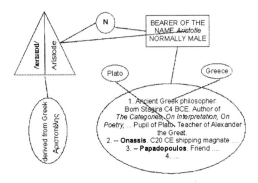

Figure 3: Networked fragment of the combined lexicon-encyclopedia entry for
Aristotle

2. Cooperation, common ground, and implicature

Like other social activities, language interchange requires participants to mutually recognise certain conventions (in the sense of Lewis 1969). Among them are the conventions that Grice (1975:45) described as maxims of the cooperative principle.

> Make your conversational contribution such as is required, at the stage at which it occurs, by the accepted purpose or direction of the talk exchange in which you are engaged. One might label this the COOPERATIVE PRINCIPLE.

Grice identified four categories of maxims: quantity, quality, relation, and manner. We are concerned only with the first of them:

> The category of QUANTITY relates to the quantity of information to be provided, and under it fall the following maxims:
>
> 1. Make your contribution as informative as is required (for the current purposes of the exchange).
>
> 2. Do not make your contribution more informative than is required. (ibid.)

Such maxims are not laws to be obeyed, but reference points for language interchange – much as the points of the compass are conventional reference points for identifying locations on the surface of the earth. The Grice quantity implicatures can be usefully augmented with Atlas & Levinson's (1981:40-50) informativeness principle, paraphrased in Levinson (1983:146f) as "read as much into the utterance as is consistent with what you know about the world". For the purpose of this paper, the augmented Grice implicatures are revamped as follows:

- Q1 enjoins S, the speaker, to make the strongest claim possible consistent with his or her perception of the facts.

- Q2 enjoins S to give no more and no less information than is required to make his or her message clear to hearer H.

Complementing these is a principle of interpretation by H:

- Given the semantic content of the utterance and H's perception of the contextually relevant facts, the strongest inference possible is to be drawn from the utterance.

I shall return to Q1 and Q2 following a brief discussion of implicature. Conversational implicature is the pragmatic counterpart to the semantic relations of entailment and conventional implicature (for the claim that conventional implicature is semantic, see Lyons 1995:276 and Allan forthcoming).

- In the formula $\Phi \vartriangleright \Psi$, Ψ is a conversational implicature of Φ,[5] which is a part (or perhaps the whole) of S's utterance U made in context C under conventional co-operative conditions. Ψ is a pragmatic inference calculated from the meaning of U considered in the light of: (i) the cooperative principle, (ii) the context C, and (iii) encyclopedic knowledge. A conversational implicature is defeasible (can be canceled) without contradicting the utterance which implicates it.

It is defeasibility that distinguishes conversational implicature from entailment and conventional implicature.

Conversational implicature depends upon common ground (Stalnaker 1973, 1974; Clark 1996). S and H are mutually aware that, normally, their interlocutor is an intelligent being. S does not need to spell out those things which are

(a) obvious to the sensory receptors of H, or

(b) which H can very easily reason out on the basis of

    (i)   knowing the language and the conventions for its use, and

    (ii)   using the knowledge that each of us develops from birth as we experience the world around us.

---

[5] Although Levinson has used +>, there is no standard symbol meaning 'conversationally implicates'. I shall use ▷ (empty arrowhead).

These constitute common ground. Much of our understanding rests on an assumption of common ground. Pointing to something and saying *Isn't that nice?* rests on the assumption that H understands English and can also see the referent of *that*; similarly, saying *Let's go to Paris* rests on the assumption that *Paris* will be understood as referring to a certain city. Some common ground is universal, e.g. knowledge of sun, rain, the physiological differences between the sexes; some common ground is very restricted, e.g. between a couple who use *the Hobgoblin* to refer to the man's first wife. S can usually readily assess the probable common ground with H, and choose his or her words accordingly. A simplified definition is:

- Common ground for any community K of two or more people is that:

  (a) every member, or almost every member, of K knows or believes some fact or set of facts F; and

  (b) a member is presumed to know or believe F by (almost) every other member of K; and

  (c) a member of K knows that both (a) and (b) are true.[6]

When a member of K applies knowledge of F in order to interpret P, a state of affairs or something said, s/he can presume that others in the community will also apply knowledge of F in order to interpret P. The existence of F, P, and the application of knowledge of F to interpreting P is common ground for members of the community K. Once attended to, P becomes part of F, incrementing the common ground.

Common ground allows meaning to be underspecified by S, so that language understanding is a constructive process in which a lot of inferencing is expected from H. Take for example the following interchange:

(13)   [*The doorbell to Maggie and Frank's apartment rings*]

Maggie [*voice off*]:   Did you hear the doorbell, dear? I'm in the bathroom.

Frank: I'll get it.

---

[6] This is similar to Lewis's (1969:78) definition of convention. Roughly speaking, a convention is a regularity of behaviour to which, in a given situation, almost everyone within a population conforms and expects almost everyone else to conform. Moreover, almost everyone prefers this state of affairs to an alternative. This is not to say that the convention is immutable: if people cease to conform to a particular regularity and prefer to cease to conform to it, it will cease to remain a convention; and if they gradually adopt another regularity in behaviour, this will become a convention when almost everyone in the population conforms to it and almost everyone prefers this state of affairs to the alternative. In my definition of common ground, F includes not only behaviours but also manifest facts such as what can be seen and heard, etc. by the interlocutors.

First of all Maggie draws Frank's attention to P_1, the fact that the doorbell has been rung, by asking whether Frank has heard it. By asking the question of him, P_2, she demonstrates that she assumes that Frank is not deaf: this is a generalised implicature attached to all spoken questions (part of F). It also suggests that she thinks that he might have heard the doorbell himself (P_1 has become part of F): this is a particularised implicature relevant to this particular context. Maggie could, in principle, justify these implicatures on the basis of what she assumes to be common ground with Frank: he speaks English and knows the conventions for using it (part of F); the doorbell to their apartment has rung (P_1) and it is loud enough for people like them with sufficiently good perceptual and cognitive abilities to recognise that if one of them has heard it the other one will have most probably have done so too (part of F). It follows that Maggie expects Frank to infer (as we do) that she is implying that the caller (part of F recognised from P_1) needs to be attended to (more of F). This is another generalised implicature, but it would usually be described as the illocutionary point of this part of the utterance (Austin 1975; Searle 1969, 1979; Allan 1994a, 1994b). Secondly, Maggie announces she is in the bathroom, thereby implying that she is unable to open the door herself (more of F). The large amount of contextual inferencing that Maggie expects from Frank is typical of normal language interchange (cf. Sperber & Wilson 1995). In (13), Frank takes the hint (P_3): again by a process of implication, we, along with Maggie, recognise the statement *I'll get it* as a promise (yet more F). If Frank's promise is sincere – which is our normal expectation – he will act upon it. We conclude that, because S expects H to make constructive inferences, s/he produces his or her utterance accordingly.

Many of the inferences we draw from (13) are conversational implicatures:

(a) The generalised implicature attached to all spoken questions that H is not deaf (or can lipread).

(b) The particularised implicature that Maggie is presumably aware that Frank probably heard the doorbell himself.

(c) Maggie's implicature that the caller needs to be attended to.

(d) The implicature arising from the cooperative presumption that Maggie has some reason for saying that she is in the bathroom, and that it has particular relevance to the fact that there is someone at the door – from which we conclude that she is unable to open the door herself.

(e) The implicature that Frank's statement *I'll get it* is a promise to answer the door more or less immediately.

Conversational implicatures are the principal device allowing S to minimise the quantity of language expressed and, conversely, are the principal device H must use to augment what is said in order to understand what is meant.

From what we have seen of implicatures so far, they are not conspicuous candidates for a lexicon. Conversational implicatures arise from exploitation of the cooperative principle; they are pragmatic and are not part of the semantics of an expression as are entailments and conventional implicatures. For this reason they are defeasible. Although implicatures are often discussed as though they arise only when FLOUTING the cooperative maxims, in any consistent account of implicature they must also arise from OBSERVING the maxims. This is obvious from an interchange like (14) (taken from Hepworth & McNamee 1989:125):

> (14)   QUESTIONER   You did some time at Yale, didn't you?
>
>   ABBEY   Two weeks. I went to Yale in the fall of '54.

There is a generalised conversational implicature that a questioner seeks a relevant answer. We the readers, like the Questioner, make the assumption that Abbey is responding truthfully: we could legitimately say: " In (14) we have Abbey's word for it that he went to Yale for two weeks in the fall of 1954". Another way to put this is that we have a certain amount of confidence in the credibility of the proposition *Abbey went to Yale for two weeks in the fall of 1954*. The traditional binary conception of truth (true $\underline{\vee}$ false, $\{1,0\}$) in logical systems from Aristotle to Montague's successors is insufficient as a metric for ordinary language use. A three-term system inspired by Strawson (1950) and Quine (1960) which has a truth value gap we might dub *indeterminable* is but a slight improvement. The truth value of a proposition p hinges on whether or not p is, was or will be the case. What matters to language users (at least in our culture) is not so much what is true, but what they believe to be true, i.e. what is credible. The credibility of p is what S and H believe with respect to the truth of p, or believe they know, or do in fact know of its truthfulness. A proposition like *I wouldn't lie to you* is evaluated for truth on the basis of what is known about S; *China is a democracy* is evaluated against what one knows of China and believes is the meaning of *democracy*. Because most so-called "facts" are propositions about phenomena as interpreted by whomever is speaking, we find that "experts" differ as to facts about e.g. the economy or what should be done about narcotics (cf. Shapin 1994). Today, (15a) is taken to be "false" and (15b) "true".

> (15a)   The Earth is roughly flat.
>
> (15b)   The Earth is roughly spherical.

This is the reverse of the assumed "truth" values in the 13th century, when (15a) was credible but (15b) not. The incredibility of (15b) was determined on the basis of experience of things falling off spherical objects and no compensating knowledge of the Earth's gravitational force that attracts things to it. Thus, whether ordinary language users judge a proposition "true" or "false" depends on how credible it is; and this is reflected in the way that they use and understand language. Linguists (though perhaps not philosophers) need a credibility metric such as that in table 1, in which complete confidence that a proposition is true rates 1, represented CRED = 1, and complete confidence that a proposition is false rates CRED = 0; indeterminability is midway between these two – CRED = 0.5. Other values lie in between.

1	Undoubtedly true
0.9	Most probably true
0.8	Probably true
0.7	Possibly true
0.6	Just possibly true
0.5	Indeterminable
0.4	Just possibly false
0.3	Possibly false
0.2	Probably false
0.1	Most probably false
0	Undoubtedly false

Table 1: The credibility metric for a proposition

In reality, one level of the metric overlaps an adjacent level so that the cross-over from one level to another is more often than not entirely subjective; levels 0.1, 0.4, 0.6, 0.9 are as much an artefact of the decimal system as they are independently distinct levels in which I have a great deal of confidence. Nonetheless, it has long been clear to me (cf. Allan 1986) that some variant of the credibility metric exists and is justified by the employment of the adverbials *probably* and *possibly* in everyday speech. This metric is needed in some lexical entries.

Horn (1972) identified a category of scalar implicatures (cf. Horn 1989:232, Gazdar 1979:55-62, Levinson 1983:134).

- Given any scale of the form $\langle e_1, e_2, e_3, ..., e_n \rangle$, if S asserts e_i then s/he potentially conversationally implicates that it is not the case that e_{i-1} holds nor e_{i-2} nor any e higher up the scale.

  <all, most, many / much, some, a few / little, a(n)>

  $\langle n \geq 6, 5, 4, 3, 2, 1 \rangle$

  <no, not all, few / little>

  <excellent, good>

  <cold, cool>

<always, often, sometimes>

<succeed in doing A, try to do A, want to do A>

<know that *p*, believe that *p*>

<necessarily / certainly *p*, probably *p*, possibly *p*>

<and, or>

Scalar implicatures are negative upscale, or Q1, implicatures. If S says *I have two children*, this implicates that s/he has no more than two children. In the case that, say, Ed asserts *I have two children* when in fact he has five, he utters a logical truth and yet can be accused of speaking "falsely" because he has failed to observe the conventions for the normal use of language and misled H by ignoring the communicative significance of Q1 implicatures.

Scalar implicatures are, of course, defeasible.

(16)	Q:	Did some of the students come to his talk?
	A_1:	Yes [some of them came], in fact all of them.
	A_2:	Yes, at least some, if not all.

In the answers A_1 and A_2, the truth of *some* is admitted, but the implicature is canceled (strictly speaking, suspended in A_2 pending possible cancellation) by the correction to an item upscale of *some*. In the contrary state of affairs, it is necessary to deny the truth of Q's supposition, as we see from a comparison of the acceptable answer (17)A_3 with the unacceptable (17)A_1-A_2.

(17)	Q:	Did all of the students come to his talk?
	A_1:	*Yes [all of them came], in fact some of them.
	A_2:	*Yes, at least all, if not some.
	A_3:	No [not all of them came], but some did.

I have already said that Q1 results in negative upscale implicature:

(18a)	some	$\triangleright$	not most	<most, some>
(18b)	three	$\triangleright$	no more than three	<n ≥ 4,3>
(18c)	*p* or *q*	$\triangleright$	not both *p* and *q*	<and, or>
(18d)	I ran over a dog at the weekend	$\triangleright$	The dog was not mine or yours	<definite, indefinite>
(18e)	Sally went out with a man last night	$\triangleright$	The man was not her partner	<definite, indefinite>

(18f) Kim had the ability ▷ S doesn't know that Kim   <do A, have an ability
       to win that race   did win that race   to do A>

With Q2 implicature, because S has not indicated otherwise, H is expected to make the default interpretation, cf. (19). Q2 implicatures can be thought of as common ground (including shared knowledge of language and its use) which H uses to expand upon what is actually said. There are many more Q2 than Q1 examples.

(19a)   It's a bird ▷ It's capable of flight (if it's alive)

(19b)   Sally climbed and climbed ▷ Sally used her legs and feet and
                                                 went upwards

(19c)   Kim was able to win that race ▷ Kim won that race [cf. (18f)]

(19d)   Emma got pregnant and ▷ Emma got pregnant and then later
                        married George   married George

(19e)   Sam and Jack bought a house ▷ They bought it together

(19f)   If you mow the lawn, (then) ▷ I'll give you $15 only if you mow
                        I'll give you $15   the lawn

(19g)   Jack ate the cookies ▷ Jack ate all the cookies

(19h)   I don't believe we've met ▷ I believe we have not met

(19i)   Jack backed a horse ▷ It was a racehorse

(19j)   Sam broke an arm ▷ Sam broke his arm [cf. (18d-e)]

(19k)   The driver stopped the car ▷ by applying the footbrake

What I am here calling Q2 implicatures, Jackendoff (1983:ch.7-8, 1985, 1990:35ff) refers to as *preference conditions*:

> A preference rule system is a collection of features or conditions on a category judgment, any single one of which, under proper circumstances, is sufficient for a positive judgment. In the absence of evidence against any such feature in an item that has already been categorized on the basis of other features, the feature is assumed present by default. The more of the preference features that can be satisfied in a particular instances, the more secure the judgment, and the more stereotypical the instance will be judged.

> On the other hand, any of the preference features may be subject to exception; that is, none of them is necessary. But if *none* of the preference features in the system can be satisfied, a negative judgment results. (Jackendoff 1985:287)

For example:

(20)

TERM	PREFERENCE CONDITION
bird	something which can fly [cf. (19a)]
climb	climb upward and use feet [cf. (19b)]
walk	walk forward using legs and feet
go	go forward
X sees Y	X's gaze makes contact with Y & X has visual experience of Y

Let us consider each of these in more detail, starting with (21):

(21) I'm looking at a bird.

Especially when unaided by a natural context, (21) denotes a bipedal creature with beak and feathers that can fly. Even though some chicks are naked when they come out of the egg, and penguins and emus do not fly, these are all members of the category Bird. Jackendoff (1983:144) represents the condition that a typical bird can fly as (22).

(22)
$$\begin{bmatrix} \text{TYPE} \\ \text{BIRD} \\ \text{P(CAN FLY)} \end{bmatrix}$$

Preference conditions are common to reasoning in many areas of cognitive processing: scripts and frames (cf. Schank & Abelson 1977, Schank 1982, 1984, 1986, Fillmore 1982, Fillmore & Atkins 1992, Barsalou 1992) are examples; they operate in the perceived groupings of notes and chords in musical scores (Jackendoff 1983:131f, Lerdahl & Jackendoff 1982:ch.3); and in visual perception. In figure 4, for example, there is a preference condition that A continues behind B as indicated by the dotted line.

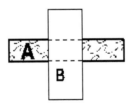

Figure 4

Of course, the invited inference could be wrong: there may be a V-shaped contour in A that is masked by B; or A might end behind B and what appears to be a continuation to the right may be another rectangle. As common sense surely predicts, semantics is not autonomous from other aspects of cognition.

Preference conditions arise from reasonable expectations about the way the world is. The preference conditions exemplified in (20) are Q2 conversational implicatures. All conversational implicatures arise from the cooperative principle which identifies our normal expectations of the way people will behave when speaking to one another. Preference conditions are implicated whenever the common ground (including what S says) gives no indication to the contrary. Like all conversational implicatures, preference conditions are open to cancellation; for instance, preference condition (23) permits (24) without contradiction.

(23) $\forall$x[**bird'**(x) $\triangleright$ **can'**(x,[**fly'**(x)])]

(24) $\forall$x[**emu'**(x) $\rightarrow$ **bird'**(x) $\wedge$ ¬[**can'**(x,[**fly'**(x)])]]

Now take the verb *climb* (with grossly simplified semantics):

(25) $\forall$x[**climb'**(x) $\rightarrow$ **go_upward'**(x)
$\vee$ **move_in_a_vertical_axis_using_ feet'**(x)]

$\forall$x[**climb'**(x) $\triangleright$ **go_upward'**(x)
$\wedge$ **move_in_a_vertical_axis_using_ feet'**(x)]

Hence (where A ⊩ B symbolises "A entails B", A ⊮ B "A does not entail B", A ⊪ B "A is synonymous with B", A ⫢ B "A is not synonymous with B"):[7]

(26a) Bill climbed the mountain ⊪ Bill climbed up the mountain

(26b) Bill climbed the mountain ⫢ Bill climbed the mountain on his knees

(27) Bill climbed down the mountain ⫢ Bill climbed the mountain

(28a) Bill climbed the valley.

(28b) Bill climbed down into the valley.

(28c) Bill climbed out of the valley.

---

[7] If A and B are sentences of the object language and their respective semantic descriptions are respectively *a* and *b*, then A ENTAILS B, A ⊩ B, iff *a* $\rightarrow$ *b* in all possible worlds. If A and B are sentences of the object language and their respective semantic descriptions are respectively *a* and *b*, then A IS SYNONYMOUS WITH B, A ⫢ B, iff *a* $\longleftrightarrow$ *b* in all possible worlds.

Snakes, airplanes, and ambient temperature lack feet they can use when climbing (presumably a metaphorical extension with these actors), hence:

(29a)   The snake climbed the tree.

(29b)   ??The snake climbed down the tree.

(30a)   The airplane climbed to its cruising altitude.

(30b)   ??The plane climbed down to land.

(31a)   The temperature climbed to 42.

(31b)   ??The temperature climbed down to -10.

Jackendoff's (1985:288) lexicon entry for *climb* is given in (32).

$$
(32) \quad
\begin{bmatrix}
\text{climb} \\
+\,V,-N \\
[\_\_\_(XP_j)] \\
\begin{bmatrix}
GO(i, \begin{bmatrix} \{j\} \\ \begin{Bmatrix} \text{TO TOP OF } [_{\text{Thing}}\, j] \\ \text{VIA } [_{\text{Place}}\, \text{ON } [_{\text{Thing}}\, j]] \end{Bmatrix} \\ _{\text{Path}}\, P(\text{UPWARD}) \end{bmatrix}) \\
_{\text{Event}}\, P([_{\text{Manner}}\, \text{CLAMBERING}])
\end{bmatrix}
\end{bmatrix}
$$

In (32), "climb" is the formal specification, "+V,-N" the morphosyntactic specification, "[___(XP$_j$)]" is the strict subcategorisation containing an optional "category-neutral subcategorisation feature"; it is optional because *climb* may be either transitive or intransitive; being category-neutral it ranges over either NP or PP. The index "i" identifies the subject and theme location and "j" the thing climbed – hence "[$_{\text{Thing}}$ j]". Climbing is an "[$_{\text{Event}}$]". So, in Jackendoff's metalanguage:

(33)   *Bill climbed* ⟷ CLIMB(BILL,[$_{\text{Path}}$])

(34)   *Bill climbed that* ⟷ CLIMB(BILL,[$_{\text{Path}}$THAT$_j$])

(35)   *Bill climbed the mountain* ⟷ CLIMB(BILL,[$_{\text{Path}}$ TO TOP OF [$_{\text{Thing}}$ MOUNTAIN$_j$]])

(36)   *Bill climbed along the roof* ⟷ CLIMB(BILL,[$_{\text{Path}}$ VIA [$_{\text{Place}}$ ON [$_{\text{Thing}}$ ROOF$_j$]]])

The two preference conditions in (32) are P(UPWARD) and P(CLAMBERING) – the second one being Jackendoff's counterpart to my **move_in_a_vertical_axis_ using_feet′** in (25).[8]

The verb *walk* potentially implicates "walk forward", any other direction must be made explicit. *Go* works in the same way. (37) implicates that the car went in frontwards.

> (37)   She drove the car into the garage
>
> $\forall$x,y[**do′**(x,[**drive′**(x,y)]) $\triangleright$ **go_forward′**(y)]

Consequently there is no need for a verb *front* to be used as in (38), it is blocked by (37); but there is a need for a special verb *back* in (39).

> (38)   ?*She fronted the car into the garage.

> (39)   She backed the car into the garage.

Finally, consider the conditions on the verb *see*.

> (40) $\forall$x,y[**see′**(x,y) $\longleftrightarrow$ x's gaze makes contact with y $\vee$ x has visual experience of y]
>
> $\forall$x,y[**see′**(x,y) $\triangleright$ x's gaze makes contact with y $\wedge$ x has visual experience of y]

Hence:

> (41a)   Bill saw a movie.

> (41b)   Bill looked straight at me, but he didn't see me.

> (41c)   Bill saw a vision.

> (41d)   *Bill saw a vision, but he didn't notice it.

We have seen that (at least some of) Jackendoff's preference conditions on lexemes invite inferences that are Q2 implicatures. Together with the necessary semantic properties, preference conditions identify the typical attributes of the denotatum. Preference conditions enable a rational explanation to be given for the application of a single lexeme to denotata with diverse characteristics such as birds that fly and others that do not. It is a lesson in capturing the flexibility of natural language in a principled manner. The question that arises is whether all Q2 implicatures can be

---

[8] Jackendoff apparently took CLAMBERING from Fillmore (1978).

accommodated in the lexicon or whether some should be located in the associated encyclopedia.

This section introduced conversational implicature as pragmatic inference that is contextually defeasible. The Q1 and Q2 implicatures discussed in this paper are amalgamations of Grice's quantity implicatures and Atlas & Levinson's informativeness-based implicatures. Despite the fact that the semantic specifications in a lexicon traditionally identify just the logically necessary components of lexical meaning, if the linguist's lexicon is to model the language user's mental lexicon it needs to include at least some default, i.e. probabilistic, components of lexical meaning. For instance, many people find it counterintuitive that *three* (e.g. in *three birds*) is logically "≥ 3, greater than or equal to three". If we are intent on capturing in the lexicon the normal language user's interpretation of *three* we need to add into the semantic specification of *three* that its default interpretation is "= 3 (exactly three)", a Q1 implicature. Similarly, as Jackendoff recognises, the entry for *bird* should indicate that a typical bird is capable of flight, a Q2 implicature, even though this does not apply to day-old chicks of any species (which is encyclopedic information) or to emus and penguins (which is lexical information in respect of entries for *emu* and *penguin*). My initial hypothesis is that Q implicatures are (or are among) the default propositions that need to be added to the logically necessary meaning components in the semantic specification of at least some lexicon items. The question for the present paper, then, is whether or not a larger sample of Q implicatures can be accommodated in the lexicon as proposed, or whether they must appear elsewhere in the encyclopedia.

3. Lexical entries for Q implicatures

The Q1 implicatures in (18) can be straightforwardly incorporated into the lexicon. The semantics for (18a), repeated below, is as in (42). $| \alpha |$ is a measure function on α; it gives the quantity (not necessarily cardinality) of α.

(18a)   three ▷ no more than three

(42) $[three \ y: y \subseteq [PL_Q \ x: \mathbf{cat'}(x)]](\mathbf{grey'}(y)) \longleftrightarrow | c \cap g | \geq 3$

     $[three \ y: y \subseteq [PL_Q \ x: \mathbf{cat'}(x)]](\mathbf{grey'}(y)) \rhd | c \cap g | = 3$

(42) is the semantics for *Three cats are grey*. $[PL_Q \ x: \mathbf{cat'}(x)]$ is a restrictive quantifier in which $\mathbf{cat'}(x)$ functions as a restrictor on the scope of the plural indicated by the morphology of *cats*. This in turn functions as a restrictor on the quantifier *three*.

x and y are ensembles rather than individuals.[9] | c ∩ g | is the quantity of the overlapping ensembles denoted by the predicates **cat′** and **grey′**. In colloquial English, | c ∩ g | means 'the number of cats which are grey'. Thus the two lines of (42) may be informally glossed as follows:

> (42′)   In the particular situation in the world and time spoken of, *three cats are grey* is true only if the number of cats which are grey is at least three; and *three cats are grey* implicates that the number of cats which are grey is exactly three.

The truth statement identifies what must be the case for a proper use of the quantifier *three*, and the conversational implicature identifies what is probably the case, i.e. the way *three* will be understood in default of any contrary evidence. An alternative formalisation for the implicature in (42) is (43), where ≯ means 'not greater than':

> (43)   [*three* y: y ⊆ [PL$_Q$ x: **cat′**(x)]](**grey′**(y)) ▷ | c ∩ g | ≯ 3

(42) is simpler because (43) relies on the semantics of *three* to disallow that the quantity of grey cats is less than three. (42-43) can be generalised by substituting any grammatically appropriate restrictor for **cat′** and any grammatically appropriate predicate for **grey′**.

If the lexicon contains redundancy rules, the Q1 of cardinal quantifiers can be determined as follows:

- Where Φ is a formula containing a cardinal quantifier Q_i; i is a member of the set of natural numbers, | N |; and α is the ensemble denoted by the scope of Q_i:

  If $\Phi \rightarrow | \alpha | \geq$ i, then Φ ▷ | α | = i

Now turning to *some*:

> (18b)   some ▷ not most

> (44)   [*some* y: y ⊆ [∅$_Q$ x: **butter′**(x)]](**salty′**(y)) ⟷ | b ∩ s | ≠ 0
>
>   [*some* y: y ⊆ [∅$_Q$ x: **butter′**(x)]](**salty′**(y)) ▷ | b ∩ s | < | b − b ∩ s |

[∅$_Q$ x: **butter′**(x)] reflects the null number marking on *butter*. The gloss for (44) is:

---

[9] Ensemble theory is described in Bunt (1985) upon which Allan (1999, forthcoming) relies. It is essentially a meronymic theory founded on set theory in which the primitive relation is *part of* rather than *member of*. An ensemble is a set just in case its parts are atomic and cannot be further subdivided.

(44′)   In the particular situation in the world and time spoken of, *some butter is salty* is true only if the quantity of butter that is salty is non-null; and *some butter is salty* implicates that the quantity of butter that is salty is less than the quantity of butter which is not salty.

Some is a very vague quantifier that does no more than claim existence: if all butter were salty it would be true that some butter is salty; it is only false when no butter is salty. The implicature, however, ranges it in the lower half of the quantity scale; hence

(45)   some ▷ not most ∧ not all

(45) is an informal inference from the implicature in (44). As noted in Horn (1972), negation of the upper endpoint is most strongly implicated – *not all* in (45). Lexical redundancy rules will be inefficient with noncardinal quantifiers.

There is no reason why the lexical entry for *or* should not include its Q1 implicature, cf. (18c) and (46):

(18c)   *p* or *q* ▷ not both *p* and *q*

(46)   Φ *or* Ψ ⟷ Φ ∨ Ψ

        Φ *or* Ψ ▷ Φ ⊻ Ψ

(46′)   In the particular situation in the world and time spoken of, if *Φ or Ψ* is grammatical, *Φ or Ψ* is true only if it is true that either Φ is true or Ψ is true or both Φ and Ψ are true. *Φ or Ψ* implicates that either Φ or else Ψ is true, but not both and not neither.

Inclusive disjunction is usually indicated by *and/or* in English; *or* on its own has the default meaning "or else". Thus an alternative formalisation of the implicature is ¬(Φ∧Ψ) ∧ ¬(¬Φ ∧ ¬Ψ); but being deducible from (40), no such formula need be included in the lexicon.

The cases of (18d-e) are more complicated. Contrast them with (47a-b).

(18d)   I ran over a dog at the weekend ▷ The dog was not mine or yours

(18e)   Sally went out with a man last night ▷ The man was not her partner

(47a)   I ran over the dog at the weekend.

(47b)   Sally went out with her man last night.

In Allan (1999, forthcoming), the indefinite and definite are contrastively defined as follows:

- The INDEFINITE requires H to create an ensemble x from an ensemble y such that $x \subset y$.

- The DEFINITE picks out the ensemble x for H by equating it with ensemble y such that x = y (which is what universals do), or naming it, for example $[h/x]\Phi$ where [h=Harry] and x is a variable in formula Φ.[10]

Thus the definite is used whenever S presupposes that the reference is identifiable to H. The conditions on identifiability are complex and I will not try to describe them here (see Allan op.cit., DuBois 1980, Hawkins 1978, Lewis 1979, Givón 1984, Lambrecht 1994, among others). Like other quantifiers, the definite article can be formalised as a restrictive quantifier: [*the* x: Fx] is semantically $\exists!x[x \subseteq f \rightarrow x = f]$ to be read "there is exactly one ensemble x and if it is a subensemble of f, then x is identical with f" which can be paraphrased by "there is exactly one ensemble f at the relevant world and time spoken of". In a clause, the simplified formulation is (48):

(48) $[\textit{the } x: Fx](Gx) \longleftrightarrow \exists!x[x \subseteq f \cap g \rightarrow x = f]$

(48), sketched in figure 5, says *the f is g* is true in the world spoken of only if there is exactly one ensemble f identical with the ensemble of f which is g.[11]

Figure 5: Sketch of (48)

The conditions on the indefinite are described above. The semantics of indefinite *a(n)* is identical with that for *one*; but the implicature is not, because being an article, *a(n)* is in contrast with *the* (its Saussurean *valeur*). The semantics of *one* is given in (49), that for *a(n)* in (50).

(49) $[\textit{one } y: y \subseteq [\varnothing_Q x: Fx]](Gy) \longleftrightarrow |f \cap g| \geq 1$

  $[\textit{one } y: y \subseteq [\varnothing_Q x: Fx]](Gy) \vartriangleright |f \cap g| = 1$

---

[10] "$[h/x]\Phi$" means 'replace every variable x in formula Φ by h'. "[h=Harry]" illustrates the device that introduces proper names to the calculus for quantification.

[11] Diagrams are imprecise illustrations. For instance, neither the formula in (48) nor the English it represents are specific about whether $f \subset g$ (as in figure 5) or f = g. Incidentally, there is nothing significant about the shape of ensemble boundaries in figures 5 and 6.

(50) $[a(n)$ y: y $\subseteq [\varnothing_Q$ x: Fx]](Gy) $\longleftrightarrow$ | f $\cap$ g | $\geq$ 1

      $[a(n)$ y: y $\subseteq [\varnothing_Q$ x: Fx]](Gy) $\triangleright$ | f $\cap$ g | = 1 $\wedge$ ¬∃!y[y $\subseteq$ f $\to$ y = f]

Because (49-50) are indefinite, for both: $\forall y \exists z[y \subseteq f \wedge z \subset f \wedge z \neq y]$, cf. figure 6.

Figure 6: Sketches of indefinites such as (49-50)

The second conjunct of the implicature in (50), ¬∃!y[y $\subseteq$ f $\to$ y = f], says that it is not the case that there is exactly one ensemble y which, if it is a subensemble of f, is identical with f. This contrasts with a definite – as graphically demonstrated by comparing figure 5 with figure 6. Whenever possible, a definite is preferred to an indefinite, so the indefinite implicates that the definite is not applicable, and the relevant inferences are drawn. When applied to the particular context, it is this second conjunct of the implicature in (50) that gives rise to the implicatures in (18d-e). This condition applies with very different effects in respect of sentences like (19j), *Sam broke an arm* – by implication, his own. Such cases are discussed later. The implicature given in each of (18d) and (18e) is just one of several possible lexicalisations of ¬∃!y[y $\subseteq$ f $\to$ y = f] in the context of the implicating sentence.

Finally, consider the Q1 implicature in

      (18f)   Kim had the ability to win that race $\triangleright$ S doesn't know that Kim
              did win that race

The negative implicature is not valid for a non-past: neither sentence in (51-52) implicates that Kim will not win that race – but they do entail that s/he has not yet done so.

      (51)   Kim has the ability to win this race ⊮ Kim has not yet won this
              race.

      (52)   Kim will have the ability to win that race ⊮ Kim has not yet won
              that race.

Win is a telic achievement verb in the sense that something effects winning (i.e. superceding competitors) as its conclusion. The winner may play an active part, as in (53a), or not, as in (53b) (x is the winner and $\varnothing$ is a dummy argument that can be lexicalised as *something*).

(53a) **do′**(x,[**effect′**(x,[**win′**(x, *a_race*)])])

(53b) **effect′**(∅,[**win′**(x, *a_lottery*)])

(53a) can be glossed as 'the winner does something to effect winning a race', and (53b) as 'something happens with the effect that the winner wins a lottery'. When winning is the achievement of effort, there are the entailments in (54-55):

(54) Kim won that race ⊩ Kim was able to win that race [= (19c)]

(55) Kim was able to win that race ⊩ Kim had the ability to win that race [= (18f)]

It follows from (54-55) that *Kim didn't have the ability to win that race* ⊩ *Kim wasn't able to win that race* ⊩ *Kim didn't win that race.* (55) shows that despite their incompatible implicatures, (19c) ⊩ (18f), a fact I will return to. If Kim won, then s/he proved her ability to win (whether honestly or corruptly); so if S is speaking felicitously, the first conjunct of (56) must be uttered before S is aware that Kim has won. In the present tense, the difference between *have the ability to* and *be able to* is neutralised.

(56) $_{[\Phi}$ Kim { has the ability / is able } to win that race $_{\Phi]}$ and, in fact, $_{[\Psi}$ she has won $_{\Psi]}$.

If sentence Φ in (56) is felicitous at time t_i then Ψ is only felicitous at time t_{i+1}, where $t_i \prec t_{i+1}$ and $A \prec B$ symbolises 'A precedes B'. In *Kim had the ability to win,* S entertains the possibility of Kim's having been capable of winning and the possibility would normally have been resolved by the facts of whether or not Kim won. To speak felicitously, S should have chosen one of the sentences in (54), *Kim won that race* or *Kim was able to win that race* [=(19c)] if s/he knows that Kim won, hence the lefthand side of (18f) implicates that S does not know that Kim won – or in other words, admits the possibility that Kim did not win. In (57), **N** is the present tense operator and ◊Φ symbolises "it be possible that Φ".[12]

(57) **N**[◊[**P**[**be_able′**(*Kim*,[**do′**(*Kim*,[**effect′**(*Kim*,[**win′**(*Kim*, *that_race*)])])])]]]
▷ **N**[◊[**P**[¬[**do′**(*Kim*,[**effect′**(*Kim*,[**win′**(*Kim*, *that_race*)])]])]]][13]

---

[12] The possibility operator can fall within the scope of **P**; compare *It is possible that Kim was able to win* with *It was possible that Kim was able to win.*

[13] The location of the negative appears to have the following effects: ¬**do′**... is the most neutral denial of winning; ¬**effect′**... seems to indicate a lack of effort on Kim's part; ¬**win′**... suggests Kim threw the race.

The semantics of the entailing sentence of (51), *Kim has the ability to win this race*, is (58), which can be paraphrased as *It is possible that Kim is able to win this race*.

(58)   N[◊[N[**be_able′**(*Kim*,[**do′**(*Kim*,[**effect′**(*Kim*,[**win′**(*Kim, this_race*)])])])]]]
       ▷ There are reasonable grounds for the belief that Kim has the ability to win this race

A reasonable ground might be Kim's performance in comparable races. The implicature arises from the precondition for felicitous utterances.[14] It is clear that the different implicatures of (18f) and (51-52) are a function of the tense operator that scopes over *have the ability to*. The question arises: Is this the kind of information to be noted in a lexicon?

I shall answer affirmatively, but before doing so, let us turn our attention to (19c), *Kim was able to win that race*. The precondition for felicitous utterance of nonpast *Kim is able to win this race* gives rise to the same implicature as in (58). The grounds for such a belief in a race already run only justify the statement about Kim's capability if s/he did win; hence, the Q2 implicature that Kim did win.

(59)   **P**[**be_able′**(*Kim*,[**do′**(*Kim*,[**effect ′**(*Kim*,[**win′**(*Kim, that_race*)])])])]
       ▷ **P**[**do′**(*Kim*,[**effect′**(*Kim*,[**win′**(*Kim, that_race*)])])]

Looking back to (54-55), we can identify the following relations.[15]

Kim won that race ⊩ *Kim was able to win that race* ⊩ *Kim had the ability to win that race*

outcome of ability   exercise of ability   potential ability

The exercise of ability is, by default, expected to lead to a successful outcome, hence the Q2 implicature in (19c) and (59). Potential ability, however, has unknown outcome; hence the Q1 implicature in (18f) and (57). The implicatures can be included in the lexicon as shown in (60) and (61), where **T** is a variable over tenses.

(60)   *be able to* → **T**[**be_able′**(x,[**do′**(x, ...)])]

       IF **T** = **P**

       THEN **P**[**be_able′**(x,[**do′**(x, ...)])] ▷ **P**[**do′**(x, ...)]]

(60) is the basis for (19c) with its Q2 implicature.

---

[14] Sincerity condition on statements, if you will. See Allan (1994c).

[15] There is idiolectal and perhaps dialectal variation with respect to these relations. For instance, some people find contradictory *I had the ability to win but I wasn't able to win*. Others, like myself, do not.

(61)   *have the ability to* → $T_i[\lozenge[T_j[be\_able'(x, ...)]]]$

IF $T_j=P$

THEN $T_i[\lozenge[P[be\_able'(x,[do'(x, ...)])]]]] \;\triangleright\; T_i[\lozenge[P[\neg[do'(x, ...)]]]]$

(61) is the basis for (18f) with its Q1 implicature.

The reason that *Kim was able to win that race* ⊩ *Kim had the ability to win that race*, i.e. (19c) ⊩ (18f), despite their different implicatures, is that implicature is in part a function of the choice of words in an utterance: choosing the former indicates that the implicature of the latter does not apply. The same rule applies when *two* is used instead of *three*: *three* logically implies 'two' and *two* implicates 'no more than two', which is certainly not the implicature of *three*. The rule applies just as well to *emu* and *bird*: the Q2 implicature 'can fly' does not apply to *emu* despite the fact that *x is an emu* ⊩ *x is a bird*. It is therefore a regular effect of lexical choice that *Kim was able to win that race* does not implicate 'S does not know that Kim did win that race'.

(60) gives the semantics for (19c) and, like (19a-b), it includes a Q2 implicature in the lexicon; so let us consider the other examples of Q2 implicature in (19).

(19d)   Emma got pregnant and married George ▷ Emma got pregnant and then later married George

(19e)   Sam and Jack bought a house ▷ Sam and Jack bought a house together

And may conjoin all sorts of sentence constituents and whatever is conjoined is grouped together such that there is always some plausible reason for the grouping. With the exception of some conjoined NPs that I will refer to as NP-***com'**-Conjunction, the conjoined constituents are synonymous with a conjunction of sentences.

(62a)   Sue is short and slim ⊣∣∣⊢ Sue is short ∧ Sue is slim

(62b)   Joe cussed and spluttered ⊣∣∣⊢ Joe cussed ∧ Joe spluttered

(62c)   Eric was driving too fast and hit a tree ⊣∣∣⊢ Eric was driving too fast ∧ Eric hit a tree

(62d)   Miss Hardcastle always drove slowly and carefully ⊣∣∣⊢ Miss Hardcastle always drove slowly ∧ Miss Hardcastle always drove carefully

(62e)   Joe and Harriet are tall ⊣∣∣⊢ Joe is tall ∧ Harriet is tall

(62f)   Joe and Harriet have three kids ⫤⊩ Joe has three kids ∧ Harriet has
         three kids

(62a) groups two of Sue's salient physical characteristics. (62b) groups salient acts
for a particular occasion. (62c) groups related events. (62d) groups the adverbs of
manner. (62e) and (62f) each group Joe and Harriet according to a common characteristic. The nature of the grouping gives rise to a variety of implicatures. I will discuss only NP conjunctions and sentence (clause) conjunctions.

NP conjunctions are illustrated by (63), which is comparable with (62), and (64),
which is different.

(63)   Two and three are numbers ⫤⊩ Two is a number ∧ Three is a
         number

(64)   Two and three make five ⫣ Two makes five ∧ Three makes five

The difference is a function of the predicate. Given the conjunction NP_x and NP_y,
exemplified in (63), $[\![NP_x]\!]$ = x (to be read "the denotation of NP_x is ensemble x")
and $[\![NP_y]\!]$ = y. A revealing recipe-like paraphrase of (64) is: Take 'two$_x$' and take
'three$_y$', combine them (*com$'$(x,y)), and you get 'five$_w$', cf. *Mix flour$_x$ and water$_y$
to make paste$_w$*. *com$'$ is a ≥ 2-place predicate with a sense 'is added to, is mixed or
combined with, acts jointly or together with, is acted upon jointly or together with'.
The subject NP, $NP_z[NP_x$ and $NP_y]$, is formalised by (65):

(65) $\forall x,y,z[(x \cup y = z) \rightarrow \forall u[u \subseteq z \longleftrightarrow (u \subseteq x \vee u \subseteq y)]]$

(63$'$-64$'$) are informal and partial semantics for (63-64).

(63$'$)   **be$'$**(z,[**number$'$**(z)]) → **be$'$**(x,[**number$'$**(x)]) ∧ **be$'$**(y,[**number$'$**(y)])

(64$'$)   **make$'$**(z,w) → **make$'$**([*com$'$(x,y)],w)

Putting the pieces together:

(66) $NP_z[NP_x$ and $NP_y]$ → $[\![NP_x]\!]$ = x ∧ $[\![NP_y]\!]$ = y ∧ $[\![NP_z]\!]$ = z

         $\forall x,y,z[(x \cup y = z) \rightarrow \forall u[u \subseteq z \longleftrightarrow (u \subseteq x \vee u \subseteq y)]]$

         Where v and w are possibly null:

         [..[PRED(v,z,w)]..] → [..[PRED(v,x,w)]..] ∧ [..[PRED(v,y,w)]..]

                                           ∧ [..[PRED(v, [*com$'$(x,y)],w)]..]

         [..[PRED(v,z,w)]..] ▷ [..[PRED(v, [*com$'$(x,y)],w)]..]

         ELSE [..[PRED(v,z,w)]..] → [..[PRED(v, [*com$'$(x,y)],w)]..]

ELSE [..[PRED(v,z,w)]..] → [..[PRED(v,x,w)]..] ∧ [..[PRED(v,y,w)]..]

The sequence Φ ELSE Ψ ELSE Γ is an ordered sequence of senses: if sense Φ does not apply, try sense Ψ; if sense Ψ does not apply, then it must be sense Γ. The implicature indicates that wherever possible, NP conjunction is interpreted as NP-***com′**-Conjunction.

Because ***com′**(x,y) is loosely interpreted on a scale between fusion and co-temporaneous close proximity, it is the standard Q2 implicature of NP-Conjunction. Hence, the preferred implicature of (67), which is canceled by the adverbial in (68).

(67) Tom and Jo made tea ▷ Tom and Jo jointly made tea.

(68) Tom and Jo made tea on alternate days.

Note the loose interpretation of ***com′**(x,y) in (68).

(69a) Granny kissed Joe and Harriet ▷ the kissing took place at about the same time in about the same location and (CRED ≥ 0.6) for much the same reason

(69b) Susan was a teacher and a friend ▷ the descriptions are applicable at about the same time in about the same location and (CRED ≥ 0.6) for much the same reason

The degree of coordination required from conjoined actors (**do′**([***com′**(x,y)], ..) varies; in (70-71), the variation depends partly on the plural *bikes* versus the singular *tandem* and partly on encyclopedic data about bikes and tandems.

(70) Joe and Harriet rode their bikes down the road ⊮ They rode separate bikes

(71) Joe and Harriet rode their tandem to work ▷ Joe and Harriet jointly rode their tandem

If it is known that Joe's sister's name were Harriet, (72) would be infelicitous compared with (73) or *Joe and Harriet both* (or *each*) *have children*. The same holds for (19e), *Sam and Jack bought a house*, as for (72): in felicitous discourse, if Sam and Jack did not buy the house together, the implicature needs to be canceled by existing common ground or by explicit statement.

(72) Joe and Harriet have children ▷ Joe and Harriet have had children together

(73)   Joe and his sister have children ▷ (CRED ≤ 0.1) Joe and his sister
        have had children together

The transitive verb *kiss* logically requires a kissee, y in $do'(x,[kiss'(x,y)])$. In (74), where there are joint actors and the kissee is unspecified, the verb is rendered reciprocal.

(74)   Joe and Harriet kissed

        → $(do'([*com'(\textit{Joe, Harriet})],[kiss'([*com'(\textit{Joe, Harriet})],\varnothing)])$

        ⊩ Joe kissed something ∧ Harriet kissed something

(75)   For x = ⟦NP$_x$⟧ ∧ y = ⟦NP$_y$⟧

        NP$_x$ *and* NP$_y$ *kissed* ▷ $do'([*com'(x,y)],[kiss'([*com'(x,y)], \varnothing)])$

        $do'([*com'(x,y)],[kiss'([*com'(x,y)], \varnothing)]) \longleftrightarrow do'(x,[kiss'(x,y)])$

        $\wedge\ do'(y,[kiss'(y,x)])$

This explains a reciprocal interpretation of *kiss*; but it leaves unexplained why *Bonnie and Clyde killed* cannot be interpreted as 'Bonnie and Clyde killed each other'. Presumably, some verbs must be tagged as reciprocal verbs. On that unsatisfactory note, I conclude the discussion of *NP and NP* constructions.

On condition that Φ and Ψ are well-formed (combinations of) propositions expressed as well-formed conjunctions in English, (76) gives the semantics for *and*:

(76)   Φ *and* Ψ ⟷ Φ ∧ Ψ

There is in addition a series of implicatures. The two weakest implicatures result from discourse factors. The very weakest is that the only motivation for the sequence of Φ and Ψ is familiarity, topicality, or the like; e.g. when choosing between (77a-b).

(77a)   Every morning, Harry walks the dog, and George cleans the dishes.

(77b)   Every morning, George cleans the dishes, and Harry walks the dog.

The next weakest is that "Φ is backgrounding for Ψ".

(78)   There was once a rich young businessman, and he was very handsome.

(79)   While I was in London, I met a great actress; and I met Judi Dench.

(79), inspired by an example of Deirdre Wilson's, would violate the Gricean maxim of manner (a) if the great actress were Judi Dench, cf. *I met a great actress – Judi Dench*; (b) if S believed Judi Dench to be a great actress, cf. *I met two great actresses, one of whom was Judi Dench*. The most likely explanation for the sequence in (79) is that S is denigrating Judi Dench's acting ability against that of some so far unnamed great actress who sets the scene for further comment on Judi Dench. Without additional contextual information, speculation on examples like (78-79) is fruitless.

The remaining implicatures are more strictly motivated. The weakest among them is exemplified in (19d): $\Phi \prec \Psi$, which means 'Φ temporally precedes Ψ' and the sequence of utterance is iconic for the temporal sequence of the events referred to in Φ and Ψ. This temporal sequence is entailed by the next strongest implicature, which is "Φ has the consequence Ψ" or "Φ gives a reason for Ψ",[16] because **action $\prec$ consequence** as in (80-81).

(80)   Joe opened the bottle and drank the contents.

(81)   Mow the lawn and I'll give you $15.

The strongest implicature, "Φ causes Ψ", as in (82), entails the two aforementioned: because **cause $\prec$ effect**.

(82)   Flick the switch and the light comes on.

On the assumption that the strongest contextually possible implicature is conventionally deemed to hold, (83) gives the semantic structure of the propositional conjunction *and* (including those arising from NP conjunction, cf. (66)).

(83) Φ *and* Ψ $\longleftrightarrow$ $\Phi \wedge \Psi$

IF CRED($\neg\Phi \rightarrow \neg\Psi$) ≥ 0.9 $\wedge$ CRED(**cause**$'(\Phi,\Psi)$) ≥ 0.8

THEN Φ *and* Ψ $\triangleright$ Φ *causes* Ψ

ELSE IF CRED(**enable**$'([\mathbf{do}'(\varnothing,\Phi)],\Psi)$) ≥ 0.9 $\wedge$ CRED($\neg\Phi \rightarrow \neg\Psi$) ≥ 0.8

THEN Φ *and* Ψ $\triangleright$ Φ *enables the consequence* Ψ $\vee$ Φ *is a reason for* Ψ

ELSE IF CRED($\Phi \prec \Psi$) ≥ 0.8

THEN Φ *and* Ψ $\triangleright$ Φ *and then later* Ψ

---

[16] I have not succeeded in separating these systematically.

ELSE IF CRED(**enable′**(Φ,[**do′**(S,[**say′**(S,Ψ)]))) ≥ 0.8

THEN Φ *and* Ψ ▷ Φ *is background for* Ψ

ELSE Φ *and* Ψ ▷ Φ *is probably more topical or more familiar to
S than* Ψ

Note the following conditional relations:

(84)   Φ *causes* Ψ

→ Φ *is a reason for or enables the consequence* Ψ
→ Φ *temporally precedes* Ψ

Whether the discourse based implicatures are part of this sequence remains to be discovered. Consider (19d), *Emma got pregnant and married George*: it is false (CRED = 0) that Emma's getting pregnant causes her to marry George;[17] but it is quite probable (CRED = 0.75) that her marriage to George is a consequence of her being pregnant, whether or not George is the father-to-be. It is almost certain (CRED ≥ 0.9), even though defeasible, that Emma's pregnancy precedes her marriage. Out of any natural context of use it is not possible to determine whether or not saying *Emma got pregnant* is a background for going on to say that she married George. This aside, it has been possible to propose a (partial) lexicon entry for *and* which includes its Q2 implicatures.

(19f) is an example of conditional perfection (Geis & Zwicky 1971), i.e. a condition is interpreted as a biconditional:

(19f)   If you mow the lawn, (then) I'll give you $15 ▷ I'll give you $15
only if you mow the lawn

Literature on such sentences includes Geis & Zwicky (1971), Noordman (1979, 1985), Akatsuka (1986), van der Auwera (1986, 1997), König (1986), Dancygier & Sweetser (1997). (19f) has such paraphrases as (85-88).

(85)   Mow the lawn and I'll give you $15.

(86)   Don't mow the lawn and I won't give you $15.

(87)   Either you mow the lawn, or I won't give you $15.

---

[17] Perhaps this prevaricates over what counts as cause. To me, *Emma married George because she was pregnant* does not warrant a conclusion that pregnancy is a *cause* but only the *reason* for the marriage. In *Emma got pregnant because she loved George* the cause of pregnancy was not love, but copulation (or IVF).

(88)   I won't give you $15 unless you mow the lawn.

Conditional perfections are semantically $\Phi \rightarrow \Psi$ with the constraint that Ψ is a consequence of Φ, and therefore that $\Phi \prec \Psi$ (chronologically). Furthermore, they are typically advisives of one kind or another, e.g. in (89) (which Dancygier & Sweetser 1997 refer to as a *predictive conditional*) the advice is about a typical state of affairs; in (19f) or (90), Ψ is an inducement (Noordman 1985, Fillenbaum 1986); in (91) it is a deterrent; in (92) it is an off-record indication of disbelief.

(89a)   If it rains, we won't go hiking.

(89b)   It rains and we don't go hiking.

(89c)   Either it doesn't rain or we don't go hiking.

(90a)   If you stop crying, I'll buy you an ice-cream.

(90b)   You stop crying and I'll buy you an ice-cream.

(90c)   Either you stop crying or I don't buy you an ice cream.

(91a)   If you cry, I'll smack you.

(91b)   You cry and I'll smack you.

(91c)   Either you don't cry or I'll smack you.

(92a)   If you're the Pope, I'm the Empress of China.

(92b)   Yeah, you're the Pope and I'm the Empress of China.

(92c)   Either you're not the Pope or I'm the Empress of China.

(92) may not seem to be an instance of **action / event** $\prec$ **consequence**, but it can be paraphrased as 'the consequence of you calling yourself the Pope is that I shall call myself the Empress of China'. Not all conditionals are of this type; for instance, some have a protasis that establishes a felicity condition for S uttering the apodosis, but Ψ is not a consequence of Φ and there is no hint of conditional perfection.

(93a)   If you want a drink, there's beer in the fridge.

(93b)   If you don't mind me saying so, I think you've got the wrong end of the stick.

(93c)   If he's such a good husband, how come he's always out with the
        boys?

There is, therefore, no disjunctive version of the sentences in (93): none of (94)
make sense.

(94a)   *Either you don't want a drink or there's beer in the fridge.

(94b)   *Either you want a drink or there's no beer in the fridge.

(94c)   *Either you'll mind me saying so, or I think you've got the wrong
        end of the stick.

(94d)   *Either you don't mind me saying so, or I haven't got the wrong
        end of the stick.

Other conditionals have the sense 'even if Φ, nevertheless Ψ', but Ψ is not a consequence of Φ and, again, there is no hint of conditional perfection or the possibility of
a disjunctive version.

(95a)   If he offers a pay rise, still I'm going to quit.

        #Either he doesn't offer a pay rise or I'm still going to quit.

        #Either he offers a pay rise, or I'm still not going to quit.

(95b)   If I insult his wife, he doesn't defend her.

        #Either I don't insult his wife or he doesn't defend her.

        #Either I insult his wife or he defends her.

We now have a criterion for perfective conditionals because $\Phi \veebar \neg\Psi$ and $\neg\Phi \veebar \Psi$
have the same truth conditions as $\Phi \longleftrightarrow \Psi$ and $\neg(\Phi \veebar \Psi)$.

$\Phi\rightarrow\Psi$ encompasses the following examples of conditional perfection:

(96) $A \rightarrow B$ If you mow the lawn, I'll give you $15

(97) $\neg A \rightarrow B$ If you stop crying, I'll buy you an icecream[18]

(98) $A \rightarrow \neg B$ If you keep crying, I won't buy you an icecream

(99) $\neg A \rightarrow \neg B$ If you don't mow the lawn, I won't give you $15

---

[18] You stop crying $\rightarrow$ $\neg$[you cry].

The semantics is:

(100)   *If* Φ *(then)* Ψ ⟷ Φ → Ψ

  IF *If* Φ *(then)* Ψ ▷ (Φ∧Ψ) ∨ (¬Φ ∧ ¬Ψ)

  THEN *If* Φ *(then)* Ψ ▷ Φ *only if* Ψ

I will ignore other senses of *if...then* constructions to deal with the conjunctive para-phrases of perfective conditionals like (85) and the disjunctive ones like (87).

(101)   Φ *and* Ψ ⟷ Φ ∧ Ψ

  IF Φ *and* Ψ ▷ (Φ ∧ Ψ) ∨ (¬Φ ∧ ¬Ψ)

  THEN Φ *and* Ψ ▷ Φ *only if* Ψ

(101) should be added to (83), above the causative implicature. Since no formula can conversationally implicate itself, the first conjunct of the implicature in the second line of (101) is entailed and only its disjunction with the second conjunct is impli-cated.

(102)   ((Φ *or* ¬Ψ) ∨ (¬Φ *or* Ψ)) ⟷ (Φ ∧ Ψ) ∨ (¬Φ ∧ ¬Ψ)

  ((Φ *or* ¬Ψ) ∨ (¬Φ *or* Ψ)) ▷ Φ *only if* Ψ

The upshot of the semantics in (102) is that (87) has the structure in (103).

(103)   Mow the lawn and I'll give you $15 or don't mow the lawn and I won't give you $15

   Φ ∧ Ψ ∨ ¬Φ ∧ ¬Ψ

If this is correct, we need an explanation for the discrepancy between the hypothe-sised meaning and the impoverished superficial form of (87). The objection to S us-ing (103) in place of (87) is that it violates the second maxim of quantity by being more prolix than necessary just because the second conjunct is a conversational im-plicature of the first, as shown in (102). In (87) the disjunction is represented by just one conjunct from each side of the disjunctive connector. The four possibilities are:

(87)   Either you mow the lawn, or I won't give you $15.

(104)   Don't mow the lawn or I'll give you $15.

(105)   ?*I'll give you $15 or don't mow the lawn.

(106)   I won't give you $15 or you'll mow the lawn.

None of (104-106) is consistent with the meanings of (85-88). (105) is nonsense, and both (104) and (106) conversationally implicate that S does not want the lawn mown, which is contrary to the implicature of (87). Both (104) and (106) tie the consequence to non-action, again unlike (87). Logically, however, (87) and (104) have the same truth conditions, so the difference in meaning is due to implicature. In order to get the right meanings for each of them, the disjunctive version of the perfective conditional must present the first conjunct from the left side of (103) followed by the disjunctive connector *or*, and the final conjunct from the right side of (103).

I have been ignoring the fact that the left-conjunct, A, in A *and* B, ¬A *and* B, etc. normally has a second person addressee and is often imperative. When third person subjects do occur, as in (107), there is a strong preference for the *if* A *then* B construction to be used instead.

(107a) He does that again and he's fired.

(107b) It rains, and the game'll be canceled.[19]

Because the state of affairs is nonfactual in all of (85-92), a subjunctive paraphrase of the A clause is possible, though rarely natural, cf. (108-110). In (109) the subjunctive paraphrase substitutes for an *if* clause, disposing of *and*, and permitting clause sequence to be reversed as in (110). Note the subject-auxiliary inversion in (109-110).

(108) If you should mow the lawn, I'll give you $15.

(109) Should you mow the lawn, (then) I'll give you $15.

(110) I'll give you $15, should you mow the lawn.

Nonfactuality sanctions the use of *any* in sentences like (111).

(111) Eat any of those chocolates, and I'll smack you.

(112) Eat those chocolates, and I'll smack you.

(113) Eat those chocolates.

Each of a pair of conjuncts should be able to stand alone as an independent proposition; but the A clause of (111), *Eat any of those chocolates*, cannot stand alone without implying some kind of consequent.[20] Significantly it has the negative import

---

[19] Note the generics which, being law-like, are predictive: *It rains and the game is canceled, If it rains the game is canceled, It's fine or the game gets canceled.*

[20] The same holds for its paraphrase *Eat even one of those chocolates....*

made explicit in the prohibition of the disjunctive (114) – from which the A clause can stand alone as in (115).

(114)   Don't eat any of those chocolates, or I'll smack you.

(115)   Don't eat any of those chocolates.

The negative *Don't* cannot be omitted from (114) nor can it be inserted into (111). Although the A clause of (112) can stand alone, as in (113), the latter is a command or exhortation that H eat the chocolates; sentences (111-112), like (114), warn H not to eat the chocolates. This interdiction is carried by the first clause alone in (114), but is the joint product of the two conjoined clauses in (111-112). This is achieved by means of the inference (117) from the paraphrase of (111-112) in (116):

(116)   Do A and the consequence is the unwelcome B.

(117)   B is relevant because it is intended as a deterrent to doing A; ∴ "Don't do A".

It is the need to interpret from the two conjuncts of A *and* B (or ¬A *and* ¬B) taken together, that encourages the belief that the logical semantics for the A *and* B constructions is identical to the semantics of the *if* A *then* B construction. I reject this hypothesis because of the morphological difference between A *and* B and *if* A *then* B (etc.). Because the *if* A *then* B structure does not always give rise to an A *and* B pair we would require some plausible explanation for why it only occurs in the instances we have been discussing. On the analysis presented here, A *and* B constructions asymmetrically entail *if* A *then* B constructions and the fact that A *and* B comes to be interpreted as *if* A *then* B follows naturally, i.e. on general cognitive and pragmatic principles of semantic extension, from the fact that A *and* B is interpreted in appropriate contexts as A *and then (later)* B. Summing up: the morphological and circumstantial evidence favours the analysis I have given, whereas the suggestion that A *and* B is semantically identical to *if* A *then* B leaves the exceptional morphology unexplained.

I now turn to (19g).

(19g)   Jack ate the cookies ▷ Jack ate all of the cookies

The explanation for this arises from matters discussed with respect to (18d-e): the definite article is a species of universal quantifier (cf. Russell 1956). In the second line of (118), c is the ensemble of cookies and e is what Jack ate. In this case the ensemble is defined as a set by the plural quantifier, PL_Q.

(118) $P[[j=Jack]([\textit{the}\ x: x \subseteq [PL_Q\ y: \textbf{cookie}'(y)]](\textbf{do}'(j,[\textbf{eat}'(j,x)])))]$

   IF $c=\lambda y[PL_Q\ y: \textbf{cookie}'(y)] \wedge e = \lambda x[P[\textbf{do}'(j,[\textbf{eat}'(j,x)])]]$

THEN $\exists!x[x \subseteq c \cap e \to x = c] \wedge |c \cap e| > 1$

The final line of (118) says that *Jack ate the cookies* is true in the world and time spoken of only if there is exactly one set of cookies identical with the set of cookies which Jack ate, and its membership is greater than one. The implicature of universality arises from the use of the definite rather than the indefinite, which partitions an ensemble. It is relevant that the definiteness implicative scale is binary, <definite, indefinite>, and it overlaps a quantifier scale. Compare the two indefinites in (119):

> (119)   Jack ate { two / some } cookies ▷ Jack didn't eat all of the cookies

Jack ate the two cookies is only felicitous when these are the only two in the world and time being spoken of.

And now for the tricky business of negative scope.

> (19h)   I don't believe we've met ▷ We have not met

The most likely pronunciation for (19h) is *I don't believe we've MET* in which the syllable in **BOLDFACE SMALL CAPS** indicates accent (primary stress). In the right context, it is possible to say (120):

> (120)   I don't not believe that we've not met

It follows that the lefthand side of (19h) is at least three ways ambiguous (121-123), corresponding to different scope of the negative as indicated in the spoken medium by the accent. The prosodic and correlated scope effects on sentences subject to 'neg-raising' are surprisingly omitted from the otherwise comprehensive discussion in Horn (1978, 1989).

> (121)   It is not the case that I do believe that we've met
>
> ⊣∥⊢ I **DON'T** believe we've met ⟷ ¬[I believe that we've met]
>
> ⊩ (122) ∨ (123)

> (122)   I do disbelieve that we've met
>
> ⊣∥⊢ I don't be**LIEVE** we've met ⟷ I do ¬[believe] that we've met

> (123)   I (do) believe that we've not met
>
> ⊣∥⊢ I don't believe we've **MET** ⟷ I believe ¬[we have met]
>
> ⊩ We have not met

Why is (123) the implicature in (19h)? In fact, with respect to the spoken *I don't believe we've MET*, which is the least contextually constrained and therefore the most likely pronunciation, *we have not met* is not an implicature but an entailment! When the implicating sentence is decontextualised, as in (19h), it is an implicature, cf. (19a-b). Furthermore, S's belief that *we have not met* provides the most probable grounds for both the denial in (121) and the assertion of disbelief (122). These are more evident with other examples, e.g.

(124)   Sue doesn't believe the report that Jo and Sam are having an affair.

⊣⊪ Sue disbelieves the report that Jo and Sam are having an affair.

≢ Sue believes the report that Jo and Sam are not having an affair.

Nevertheless, the grounds for Sue's disbelief must either be that she attaches no credibility to the source of the report (whatever its content), or she believes Jo and Sam are not having an affair. Either way, there is the implicature in (125) – canceled if Sue finds all such reports incredible – which exactly complements the one in (19h):

(125)   Sue doesn't believe the report that Jo and Sam are having an affair
        ▷ Sue believes that Jo and Sam are not having an affair

Additional evidence comes from the location of a negative polarity item in the lowest clause. The scope of the negative is italicised.

(126)   Sue doesn't believe that Jo and Sam *met* { until after / before } Jo's mother died

        ⊣⊪ Sue believes that Jo and Sam didn't *meet* { until after / before } Jo's mother died

(127)   Sue dis*believes* that Jo and Sam met { *until after / ^{OK}before } Jo's mother died.

(128)   It is not the case *that Sue believes that Jo and Sam met { *until after / ^{OK}before } Jo's mother died.*

Even in (127-28), there is an implicature that Sue believes that Jo and Sam did not meet until after Jo's mother died, and this is a precondition on their felicitous utterance.

If *believe* is typical of Neg-Raising Verbs (NRV), and if the lexicon does contain an entry for the negative, the latter should incorporate the essence of the informal proposal in (129).

(129) NP_x *not* NRV NP_y [S] ▷ NP_x NRV NP_y ¬[S]

Let's turn to (19i):

(19i)   Jack backed a horse ▷ Jack backed a racehorse

(130)   Jack backed a horse into the cart ▷ The horse was not a racehorse

As shown in Allan (1995b) (to say nothing of works cited there), the verb *back* has developed through various metaphors arising ultimately from the human body part noun *back*. Moving an animal or a vehicle backwards, its rear end to the fore as in (130), is analogous to a human whose back aligns with their rear end. The expression *back (someone) (up)* meaning "give support to" arises directly from the journeying metaphor in which a person moves forward with their back oriented to the journey's origin and supporters follow at their leader's back. The cognitive image is probably boosted by the fact that, traditionally, humans and certain domestic animals carry heavy loads on their backs. In (19i), though, *back* is a nonmotional act.

(131)   x *backs* y → **do′**(x,[**cause′**(x,[y *go backwards*])])

ELSE x *backs* y → **do′**(x,[**support′**(x,[**do′**(y,∅)])])

do′(x,[**support′**(x,[**do′**(y,∅)])]) reads 'x supports y in some endeavour' and this is the relevant sense of *back* in (19i). If the implicature in (19i) is to appear in the lexicon, it will not be in the entry for *back*, but in the entry for *horse*, which looks something like (132).

(132)   *horse* ⟷ **horse′**(x) → **animal′**(x) ⊃ **mammal′**(x) ⊃ **equidae′**(x)

IF ∃y[**horse′**(y) ∧ **do′**(x, [**back′**(x,y)])]

THEN **do′**(x,[**support′**(x,[**do′**(y,∅)])])
       ▷ **do′**(x,[**bet′**(x,[**do′**(y,[**race′**(y)])])]) ∧ **racehorse′**(y)

ELSE IF x *backs the wrong horse*

THEN ∃y[T_i[**do′**(x,[**support′**(x,[**do′**(y,Φ)])])] ∧ T_j[¬[**do′**(y,Φ)])]] ∧ $T_i ≺ T_j$

The (first) IF condition of (132) admits collocation into the lexicon. Are such context-sensitive conditions on listemes permissible? I do not believe they are, because they depend upon a combination of listemes, not a single listeme. The next set of examples, based on (19j), are similarly iffy.

(133a-b) clearly contrast with (18d-e).

(133a)   Sam { dropped / waved } an arm ▷ The arm is his own[21]

---

[21] I ignore the unlikely possibility of *arm* being used for *armament* rather than a body part. It behooves me to explain why the use of the indefinite in (19j) has, loosely speaking, the opposite effect

(133b) Sam { broke / lost } an arm ▷ The arm is his own

Examples like (133a) are restricted to movement of a proper subset of body parts when change in its location is in focus (consider the possible ambiguity of *Sam shook a hand*: shook his own hand about; performed a greeting by shaking the hand of another). At best (133a) would be a context-sensitive rule such as:

(134)   x moves y ∧ y is a body part

   → **do′**(x,[a(n) y: **body_part′**(y)]([**move′**(x,y)])
        ∧ ∃z[**have′**(x,[**body_part′**(z)]) ∧ y ⊂ z])]

   ▷ y is x's body part

This would have to be located in a lexicon under a large number of either movement verbs or body part nouns; but neither seems appropriate. (134) characterises knowledge about a combination of listemes, not a single listeme.

There is a similar problem with (133b). Injury to or loss of a proper subset of a set of body parts gives rise to the implicature as shown; but representing this in the lexicon is at least as problematic as for (133a). The default interpretation is unaccusative: "something happens such that x suffers damage or loss to a body part". H must determine this from the combination of verb and body part NP. In fact (133) identifies the tip of a problematic iceberg, as indicated in (135). Unlike (133b), these normally name deliberate actions.

(135)   *x ameliorates the condition of a body part*

   a. Sam shaved a leg ▷ her own leg

   b. Sam plucked an eyebrow ▷ her own eyebrow

   c. Sam scratched an arm ▷ her own arm
       [also in the unaccusative injury sense]

Other acts affecting a body part refer to someone other than the actor, (136), as do other kinds of acts involving body parts, (137).

(136a) Sam tickled an arm ▷ not his own arm

(136b) Sam groped a thigh ▷ not his own thigh

---

from its use in (18d-e). An indefinite can only be used when the body part NP refers to a proper subset of the relevant body parts. A possessive definite can be used, e.g. *Sam broke his arm*, even though Sam has more than one arm. A detailed explanation is outside the scope of this paper, but briefly it is explicable in terms of the newsworthiness of the event; distinguishing which of Sam's arms it was is at best a secondary matter (see Allan 1986, forthcoming).

(136c) Sam kissed a gloved hand ▷ not his own hand

(136d) Sam kicked an arm ▷ not his own arm

(137) Sam { photographed / spotted } an arm ▷ The arm is not his own

The interpretations of (133-137) rely on knowledge about common human behaviours. For instance, it is common ground that people wave their arms for various purposes, and rare to wave anyone else's, consequently, the latter should be explicitly mentioned. If Sam were a window dresser and the arm referred to is that of a mannikin, this would need to be established as part of the common ground. Attending one's bodily comfort and appearance is the common ground in (135); but if context indicated that Sam is at work as a beautician she might well be plucking someone else's eyebrow. These are aspects of encyclopedic knowledge that will be called upon in computing the meanings of the combinations of listemes in (19h-j) and the associated examples.

Let us take a final example (on which see also Larrivée, this volume):

(19k) The driver stopped the car ▷ The driver applied the foot brake in order to stop the car

The driver could have used a handbrake to stop the car, so the implicature in (19k) is cancelable. In another scenario, the car could have been a child's pedal car with no brakes at all – which is consistent with the entailment in (138), but not the implicature in (19k).

(138) The driver stopped the car at time t_i

$\Vdash$ The car was in motion at t_{i-1} $\wedge$ the person controlling the car did something at t_{i-1} to cause the car to stop

$\Vdash$ The car did not stop because it crashed or ran out of petrol

Is it the semantic frame of *car* or its encyclopedia entry that carries the information that a car has a foot brake and a handbrake which serve different primary functions? The semantic specification of *car* in the lexicon will be a refined and expanded version of (139).

(139) $\textit{car} \longleftrightarrow \textbf{car}'(x) \rightarrow \lambda y[\textbf{vehicle}'(y) \wedge \textbf{wheeled}'(y) \wedge \exists z[\textbf{seat_for_the_driver}'(z) \wedge \textbf{face_front}'(z) \wedge \neg\exists w[\textbf{seat}'(w) \wedge \textbf{in_front_of}'(w,z)] \wedge \textbf{accommodate}'(y,z)]](x)$

▷ x has a motor and up to about six passenger seats; it has two wheels at each side for forward and backward movement.

(139) says nothing about any means of stopping or starting a car. The encyclopedia entry linked to *car* will contain information of the following kind:

(a) An account of the semantic links between *car, cart, carriage* and *carry* and of the growing salience of the 'automobile' sense of *car* during the 20th century.

(b) The principal function of a car is to transport people. A car is controlled by one of them, the driver.

(c) Description of the components of a typical car and of their functions. E.g.

   (i) The wheels of a car are rimmed by tyres that are typically pneumatic. The front wheels turn to direct the car as it moves. This turning is effected by the driver who changes direction by rotating the steering wheel inside the car.

   (ii) A car is typically propelled (and otherwise powered) by a motor, usually an internal combustion engine. The motor is started by an ignition switch, activated on most cars by a key.

   (iii) When running, the engine causes the wheels to move when the gears within the transmission are engaged. The speed of the running engine is controlled by an accelerator pedal operated by the driver.

   (iv) That the car's motion is stopped by applying brakes to the wheels. These brakes are controlled by the driver applying a foot brake. A handbrake holds the car from moving when it is parked.

   (v) Most cars have two rows of seats facing forward, the driver occupying a seat in the front row.

   ...

(d) Some car marques are: BMW, Ford, Lamborghini, ...

   ...

Despite the fact that a motor car's brakes are contingently inalienable, the weight of evidence suggests that their function within a car does not arise directly from lexical or semantic properties of the word *car*. Instead, it is something we know about the objects denoted by *car*. The Q2 implicature of (19k) must, therefore, derive from encyclopedic information about cars and the default means of stopping them.

In preceding sections I established the functions of a lexicon and an encyclopedia and described the relationship between them. I then defined Q1 and Q2 implicatures and endorsed their pragmatic status. In this section I have defended the claim that the Q1 and Q2 implicatures of listemes should be included among their semantic specification in the lexicon. An implicature identifies the default interpretations, i.e.

the *probable* meaning in the absence of constraints imposed by a particular context. IF, THEN, ELSE conditions sequence probabilities among implicatures in the lexicon. The standard implicatures must be learned by the language user along with the *necessary* sense(s) of the listeme. A strong argument for this innovation to the lexicon is a quantifier like *two. Two* necessarily means 'at least two'; but if you ask a lay population, they interpret it as meaning 'exactly two', its most probable meaning. This is a fact ignored only by an incompetent lexicographer. The vast majority of the lay population of English speakers assumes that *bull* denotes a male bovine. This is the standard implicature; there are bull elephants, bull hippos, bull whales, bull alligators, etc. each of which can be referred to simply as a *bull* when common ground makes use of the term unambiguous and cancels the implicature. To my mind, there is no doubt that Q1 and Q2 implicatures must be entered into the lexicon; and I have shown how this might be done for a variety of listemes. The implicatures that attach to collocations of listemes, however, are not located in the lexicon; like the meanings of the collocations themselves, they must be computed.

4. Key points

- I presupposed in this paper that there is a division of labour between the lexicon and the encyclopedia. The lexicon contains formal, morphosyntactic, and semantic specifications of listemes and the encyclopedia contains other kinds of information about listemes, e.g. their etymology, and information about the denotata of listemes.

- A second premise for this paper was that semantic specification in the lexicon should incorporate defeasible default (probable) meaning of a lexicon item together with the logically necessary components of lexical meaning.

- The defeasible default meaning is a conversational implicature; and, because such implicature is pragmatic and often based on encyclopedic knowledge, it seemed reasonable to suppose that implicature might be at the interface of lexicon and encyclopedia.

- Despite the fact that conversational implicatures are pragmatic entities, generalised quantity implicatures, as defined in section 2 (the only implicatures examined), are readily included in a lexicon entry.

- All the Q implicatures associated directly with a single lexicon item were readily and usefully incorporated into the lexical entry for the item, and there is no reason to expect that exceptions will be uncovered.

- Where the implicature arises from a combination of listemes, it cannot be included in the lexicon, but must be generated by the semantic component of the grammar.

- Where the implicature arises from encyclopedic information evoked by a semantic frame or script and not the semantic specifications of the lexicon entry, as in the case of (19k), it cannot be included in the lexicon.

References

Akatsuka, Noriko. 1986. "Conditionals are discourse-bound". In Elizabeth C. Traugott, Alice ter Meulen, Judy S. Reilly & Charles A. Ferguson (ed.), *On conditionals*. Cambridge: Cambridge University Press. 333-351.

Alford, Richard D. 1988. *Naming and identity. A cross-cultural study of personal naming practices*. New Haven: HRAF Press.

Allan, Keith. 1986. *Linguistic meaning* (2 vol.). London: Routledge & Kegan Paul.

Allan, Keith. 1994a. "Speech act theory. An overview". In Ron Asher (ed.), *Encyclopedia of language and linguistics*, vol. 8. Oxford: Pergamon Press. 4127-4138.

Allan, Keith. 1994b. "Speech act hierarchy, locutions, illocutions and perlocutions". In Ron Asher (ed.), *Encyclopedia of language and linguistics*, vol. 8. Oxford: Pergamon Press. 4141-4142.

Allan, Keith. 1994c. "Felicity conditions on speech acts". In Ron Asher (ed.), *Encyclopedia of language and linguistics*, vol. 3. Oxford: Pergamon Press. 1210-1213.

Allan, Keith. 1995a. "What names tell about the lexicon and the enyclopedia". *Lexicology* 1. 280-325.

Allan, Keith. 1995b. "The anthropocentricity of the English word(s) *back*". *Cognitive linguistics* 6. 11-31.

Allan, Keith. 1999. "The semantics of English quantifiers". In Peter Collins & David Lee (ed.), *The clause in English*. Amsterdam: John Benjamins. 1-31.

Allan, Keith. Forthcoming. *Semantics in a natural language*. Oxford: Basil Blackwell.

Atlas, Jay D.; Levinson, Stephen C. 1981. "It-clefts, informativeness, and logical form. Radical pragmatics (Revised standard version)". In Peter Cole (ed.), *Pragmatics (Syntax and semantics*, vol. 9). New York: Academic Press. 1-61.

Austin, John L. 1975 [1962]. *How to do things with words*. Oxford: Oxford University Press.

Barsalou, Lawrence W. 1992. "Frames, concepts, and conceptual fields". In Adrienne Lehrer & Eva F. Kittay (ed.), *Frames, fields, and contrasts*. Hillsdale: Lawrence Erlbaum. 21-74.

Boguraev, Branimir; Briscoe, Ted. 1989. "Introduction". In Branimir Boguraev & Ted Briscoe (ed.), *Computational lexicography for natural language processing*. London: Longman. 1-40.

Bunt, Harry C. 1985. *Mass terms and model-theoretic semantics*. Cambridge: Cambridge University Press.

Clark, Herbert H. 1996. *Using language*. Cambridge: Cambridge University Press.

Dancygier, Barbara; Sweetser, Eve. 1997. "*Then* in conditional constructions". *Cognitive linguistics* 8. 109-136.

DuBois, John W. 1980. "Beyond definiteness. The trace of identity in discourse". In Wallace Chafe (ed.), *The pear stories*. Norwood: Ablex. 203-274.

Fillenbaum, Samuel. 1986. "The use of conditionals in inducements and deterrents". In Elizabeth C. Traugott, Alice ter Meulen, Judy S. Reilly & Charles A. Ferguson (ed.), *On conditionals*. Cambridge: Cambridge University Press. 179-196.

Fillmore, Charles J. 1978. "On the organization of semantic information in the lexicon". In Donka Farkas, Wesley M. Jacobsen & Karol W. Todrys (ed.), *Papers from the parasession on the lexicon*. Chicago: Chicago Linguistic Society. 148-173.

Fillmore, Charles J. 1982. "Frame semantics". In Linguistic Society of Korea (ed.), *Linguistics in the morning calm*. Seoul: Hanshin. 111-137.

Fillmore, Charles J.; Atkins, Beryl T. 1992. "Toward a frame-based lexicon. The semantics of RISK and its neighbors". In Adrienne Lehrer & Eva F. Kittay (ed.), *Frames, fields, and contrasts*. Hillsdale: Lawrence Erlbaum. 75-102.

Frege, Gottlob. 1966 [1892]. "On sense and reference". In Peter Geach & Max Black (ed.), *Translations from the philosophical writings of Gottlob Frege*. Oxford: Blackwell. 56-78.

Gazdar, Gerald. 1979. *Pragmatics. Implicature, presupposition, and logical form*. New York: Academic Press.

Geis, Michael; Zwicky, Arnold. 1971. "On invited inferences". *Linguistic inquiry* 2. 561-566.

Givón, Talmy. 1984. *Syntax. A functional-typological perspective*, vol.1. Amsterdam: John Benjamins.

Grice, H. Paul. 1975. "Logic and conversation". In Peter Cole & Jerry L. Morgan (ed.), *Speech acts* (*Syntax and semantics*, vol. 3). New York: Academic Press. 41-58.

Hawkins, John A. 1978. *Definiteness and indefiniteness*. London: Croom Helm.

Hepworth, James; McNamee, Gregory (ed.). 1989. *Resist much, obey little. Some notes on Edward Abbey*. Tucson: Harbinger House.

Horn, Laurence R. 1972. *On the semantic properties of the logical operators in English*. Bloomington: Indiana University Linguistics Club.

Horn, Laurence R. 1978. "Remarks on neg-raising". In Peter Cole (ed.), *Pragmatics* (*Syntax and semantics*, vol. 9). New York: Academic Press. 129-220.

Horn, Laurence. 1984. "Toward a new taxonomy for pragmatic inference: Q-based and R-based implicature". In Deborah Schiffrin (ed.), *Meaning, form, and use in context. Linguistic applications*. Washington DC: Georgetown University Press. 11-42.

Horn, Laurence R. 1989. *A natural history of negation*. Chicago: University of Chicago Press.

Jackendoff, Ray. 1983. *Semantics and cognition*. Cambridge: M.I.T. Press.

Jackendoff, Ray. 1985. "Multiple subcategorization and the θ-criterion. The case of *climb*". *Natural language and linguistic theory* 3. 271-295.

Jackendoff, Ray. 1990. *Semantic structures*. Cambridge: M.I.T. Press.

Katz, Jerrold J. 1977. "A proper theory of names". *Philosophical studies* 31. 1-80.

König, Ekkehard. 1986. "Conditionals, concessive conditionals and concessives. Areas of contrast, overlap and neutralization". In Elizabeth C. Traugott, Alice ter Meulen, Judy S. Reilly & Charles A. Ferguson (ed.), *On conditionals*. Cambridge: Cambridge University Press. 229-246.

Kripke, Saul. 1972. "Naming and necessity". In Donald Davidson & Gilbert Harman (ed.), *Semantics of natural language*. Dordrecht: Reidel. 253-355. Republished (1980) as *Naming and necessity*, Oxford: Blackwell.

Lambrecht, Knud. 1994. *Information structure and sentence form. Topic, focus, and the mental representations of discourse referents*. Cambridge: Cambridge University Press.

Langacker, Ronald W. 1987. *Foundations of cognitive grammar*, vol. 1. *Theoretical prerequisites*. Stanford: Stanford University Press.

Lerdahl, Fred; Jackendoff, Ray. 1982. *A generative theory of tonal music*. Cambridge: M.I.T. Press.

Levinson, Stephen. 1983. *Pragmatics*. Cambridge: Cambridge University Press.

Levinson, Stephen. 1995. "Three levels of meaning". In Frank R. Palmer (ed.), *Grammar and meaning*. Cambridge: Cambridge University Press. 90-115.

Lewis, David. 1969. *Convention*. Cambridge: Harvard University Press.

Lewis, David. 1979. "Scorekeeping in a language game". *Journal of philosophical logic* 8. 339-359.

Lieberson, Stanley; Mikelson, Kelly S. 1995. "Distinctive African-American names. An experimental, historical, and linguistic analysis of innovation". *American sociological review* 60. 928-946.

Lyons, John. 1995. *Linguistic semantics. An introduction*. Cambridge: Cambridge University Press.

Moore, Judy; Harrison, Pamela; Monfries, Mark; Simon, Helen; Clarke, Cass; Best, Ray; Whelon, Rob; Simpson, Joni; Massey, Marjorie; Bradley, Rolfe. 1980. *The complete Australian gardener*. Sydney: Bay Books.

Noordman, Leonard G.M. 1979. *Inferring from language*. Berlin: Springer.

Noordman, Leonard G.M. 1985. "On contextual constraints of some conditional conjunctions". In Geer A.J. Hoppenbrouwers, Pieter A.M. Seuren & Anton J.M.M. Weijters (ed.), *Meaning and the lexicon*. Dordrecht: Foris. 302-307.

Pulman, Stephen G. 1983. *Word meaning and belief*. London: Croom Helm.

Pustejovsky, James. 1995. *The Generative Lexicon*. Cambridge: M.I.T. Press.

Putnam, Hilary. 1975 [1962]. "It ain't necessarily so". In his *Mathematics, matter and method. Philosophical papers*, vol. 1. Cambridge: Cambridge University Press. 237-249.

Quine, Willard V.O. 1960. *Word and object*. Cambridge: M.I.T. Press.

Russell, Bertrand. 1956 [1905]. "On denoting". In Robert C. Marsh (ed.), *Logic and knowledge*. London: Allen and Unwin. 39-56.

Schank, Roger C. 1982. *Dynamic memory. A theory of reminding and learning in computers and pople*. Cambridge: Cambridge University Press.

Schank, Roger C. 1984. *The cognitive computer*. Reading: Addison-Wesley.

Schank, Roger C. 1986. *Explanation patterns*. Hillsdale: Lawrence Erlbaum.

Schank, Roger C; Abelson, Robert P. 1977. *Scripts, plans, goals and understanding. An inquiry into human knowledge structures*. Hillsdale: Lawrence Erlbaum.

Schwartz, Stephen P. 1980. "Natural kinds and nominal kinds". *Mind* 89. 182-195.

Searle, John R. 1969. *Speech acts*. Cambridge: Cambridge University Press.

Searle, John R. 1979. *Expression and meaning. Studies in the theory of speech acts*. Cambridge: Cambridge University Press.

Shapin, Steven. 1994. *A social history of truth. Civility and science in seventeenth-century England.* Chicago: Chicago University Press.

Simpson, Ken; Day, Nicolas. 1993. *Field guide to the birds of Australia.* Melbourne: Viking O'Neil.

Sperber, Dan; Wilson, Deirdre. 1995 [1986]. *Relevance. Communication and cognition.* Oxford: Blackwell.

Stalnaker, Robert C. 1973. "Presupposition". *Journal of philosophical logic* 2. 77-96.

Stalnaker, Robert C. 1974. "Pragmatic presupposition". In Milton K. Munitz & Peter K. Unger (ed.), *Semantics and philosophy.* New York: New York University Press. 197-213.

Strawson, Peter F. 1950. "On referring". *Mind* 59. 320-344.

van der Auwera, Johan. 1986. "Conditionals and speech acts". In Elizabeth C. Traugott, Alice ter Meulen, Judy S. Reilly & Charles A. Ferguson (ed.), *On conditionals.* Cambridge: Cambridge University Press. 197-214.

van der Auwera, Johan. 1997. "Conditional perfection". In Angeliki Athanasiadou & René Dirven (ed.), *On conditionals again.* Amsterdam: John Benjamins. 169-190.

The role of domains in the interpretation of metaphors and metonymies[1]

William Croft

University of Manchester, Department of Linguistics, Manchester M13 9PL, United Kingdom
E-mail: W.Croft@man.ac.uk

0. Introduction

Consider the following sentence:

(1)   Denmark shot down the Maastricht treaty.

This sentence is generally taken to involve both metonymy and metaphor: the subject proper name *Denmark* is a metonymy for 'the voters of Denmark', while the predicate *shot down* is a metaphor for 'cause to fail'. After the fact this is all quite straightforward. But how does the listener know that this sentence is not about a

[1] This paper was first published in *Cognitive Linguistics* 4 (1993), pp. 335-370. Permission to reprint was granted by Mouton de Gruyter and is gratefully acknowledged. Apart from a few editorial changes, some additional footnotes and bibliographical updates, and a new afterword, the text is identical to that of the original paper. An earlier version of the latter was presented at the second International Cognitive Linguistics conference in Santa Cruz, California, in 1991. I am grateful to members of that audience, particularly George Lakoff and Eve Sweetser, for their comments, and to my semantics students, especially Tim Clausner, for many discussions of the ideas contained herein; and to Dirk Geeraerts, René Dirven and an anonymous reviewer for extensive and detailed comments that greatly improved the content of the paper. None of these people bear any responsibility for the content as presented, of course.

military act, or a particular piece of territory in Europe? The question this paper will address, though not fully answer, is: how are such "figurative" meanings constructed in a particular utterance? What leads speakers to not employ the basic or literal meanings of those words, or, if they do, to shift to the appropriate meaning?

This is a problem of semantic composition, that is, of the relation of the meaning of the whole to the meaning of the parts. Unlike the typical problems of semantic composition discussed in the formal semantic literature, where the meaning of the whole is at least in part determined by the meanings of the parts, the meaning of the parts here seems to be determined in part by the meaning of the whole. I will argue here that the "meaning of the whole" that affects the meanings of the parts is what I call the *conceptual unity of domain*: all of the elements in a syntactic unit must be interpreted in a single domain. In example 1, for instance, the domain is political activity.

Moreover, a large part (though not all) of what is going on in metaphorical and metonymic interpretation is adjustment of the domains of the component elements, and hence their meanings, to satisfy the conceptual unity of domain. I use the word *adjustment* here because the adjustment of domains is related to the conceptualisation phenomena that Langacker calls *focal adjustments* (Langacker 1987:ch.3). In section 1, I will describe a theory of word meaning and the role of domains in word meaning, taken largely from Langacker's model of cognitive grammar (Langacker 1987, 1991). In section 2, I will describe the role of domains in metaphor and metonymy, and argue that metonymy as traditionally conceived usually involves a more general phenomenon of polysemy that critically involves domains. In section 3, I discuss the relationship between metaphor and metonymy and semantic composition in cognitive grammar, arguing that metaphor applies to dependent predications and metonymy to autonomous predications (Langacker 1987:8.3). Finally, in section 4, I argue that the scope of the conceptual unity of domain is a dependent predication and the autonomous predications that it is dependent on, and that a listener's cognitive processing in "solving" the conceptual unity of domain requires reference to context.

1. Word meaning and domains in cognitive grammar

One of the central tenets of cognitive semantics is that the meaning of words is encyclopedic: everything you know about the concept is part of its meaning (Haiman 1980, Langacker 1987:4.2.1). From this it follows that there is no essential difference between (linguistic) semantic representation and (general) knowledge representation; the study of linguistic semantics is the study of commonsense human experience. Thus, that aspect of "pragmatics" which involves the employment of "world knowledge" or "commonsense knowledge", and even contextual knowledge (since the speech act context is part of our world knowledge, albeit a very specific piece of knowledge), becomes part of semantics.

Not surprisingly, taking seriously the encyclopedic view of semantics rather drastically alters our view of most of the outstanding problems of semantics (without necessarily solving them, however; but at least they look much more natural). Although in theory all knowledge about an entity is accessible – that is, the whole knowledge network is accessible – some knowledge is more central (Langacker 1987:4.2.2), and the pattern of centrality and peripherality is a major part of what distinguishes the meaning of one word from that of another. Langacker identifies four criteria for centrality: the extent to which knowledge of the concept applies to all entities categorised by the concept (*generic*), the extent to which knowledge of the concept applies to only those entities (*characteristic*),[2] the extent to which the knowledge is general knowledge in the speech community (*conventional*), and the degree to which the knowledge applies to the object itself as opposed to external entities (*intrinsic*).[3]

Understanding the meaning of a word in the encyclopedic view means entering the knowledge network at a certain point – more precisely, activating the network by activating it at a certain point or points:

> The entity designated by a symbolic unit can therefore be thought of as a point of access to a network. The semantic value of a symbolic unit is given by the open-ended set of relations (...) in which this access node participates. Each of these relations is a cognitive routine, and because they share at least one component the activation of one routine facilitates (but does not always necessitate) the activation of another. (Langacker 1987:163)

Thus, semantic space is the whole network of an individual's – and a community's – knowledge. This knowledge as a whole is not unstructured. Encyclopedic knowledge appears to be organised into experiential domains (Langacker 1987:4.1, Lakoff 1987, among many others). The notion of a domain is central to the understanding of metaphor and metonymy. In particular, it is critical to identify when one is dealing with a single domain or different domains. Despite its centrality, the notion of domain has not been delineated in detail. It is related to the notion of a semantic field, as in the field theories of Trier and others. This work has come under considerable criticism, not least because the notion of semantic field is left undefined:

> What is lacking so far, as most field-theorists would probably admit, is a more explicit formulation of the criteria which define a lexical field than has yet been provided. (Lyons 1977:267)

---

[2] These two criteria together define *cue validity* (Rosch 1978).

[3] Centrality is clearly closely related to prototypicality, in the sense of prototypical properties rather than prototypical instances of a category, as the reference to Rosch's analysis of prototypes suggests. However, centrality pertains to the organisation of knowledge in the mind, not the categorisation of individuals which both gave rise to that knowledge structure and employs that structure.

The most carefully worked-out description of domains is found in Langacker (1987), some of which is based on Lakoff & Johnson (1980); the description that follows makes explicit some assumptions that are implicit in those works. But to understand the notion of a domain, we must begin by describing a central aspect of a concept symbolised by a word, its division into a profile and base.[4] We will begin with Langacker's (1987:183-184) example of an arc of a circle. A concept, such as that of an arc, presupposes other concepts, in this case that of a circle. An arc is defined only relative to a circle; otherwise it would be merely a curved line segment. What we intuitively think of as the arc itself is the *profile*; the notion of a circle which it presupposes is its *base*. This idea is not totally new; one of its better-known manifestations is as a "frame" in artificial intelligence and linguistics. The concept of [ARC] is not just the profile but also the base; the concept is definable only relative to what it presupposes.[5] A circle itself is defined relative to two-dimensional space. The concept [CIRCLE] profiles that shape configuration, and has (two-dimensional) space as its base.[6] In other words, a concept can function as either a profile or as a base for another concept profile.

The profile-base relation is not the same as the central-peripheral relation discussed above with respect to the encyclopedic definition of word meaning. The base is that aspect of knowledge which is necessarily presupposed in conceptualising the profile. Peripheral knowledge is knowledge associated with a concept that is not as generic, characteristic, conventional, and intrinsic as more central knowledge. Peripheral knowledge is not presupposed knowledge, but additional, less central asserted knowledge. Of course, peripheral knowledge as well as central knowledge is organised in a profile-base fashion. This will be illustrated later.

Profile and base are conceptually interdependent. On the one hand, profiled concepts cannot be understood except against the background knowledge provided by the base. On the other hand, the base exists as a cognitively unified and delimited "chunk" of knowledge only by virtue of the concept or concepts defined with respect to it.

---

[4] What I am calling a *concept* is a semantic structure symbolised by a word; Langacker calls this a *predication*, and I will use these terms interchangeably. While there are concepts that do not – yet – have words that symbolise them, the notion of a concept is sufficiently difficult to identify independently of language that we will restrict ourselves to those that are already symbolised and therefore have a definite existence consecrated by the conventions of a language. Grammatical morphemes are also predications, of course; however, I will not be discussing them in this paper.

[5] Searle (1979) also argues for the necessary inclusion of background assumptions in the definition of a word.

[6] To be precise, it has shape as its base, and the concept of shape – not "a shape", but "shape" – is profiled in two-dimensional space. I return to this issue below.

A particular base is almost always the base for several concept profiles. For example, a circle is the base not only for [ARC], but also [DIAMETER], [RADIUS], [CHORD], etc. This is what makes the base a domain, in the intuitive sense: several different concept profiles have it as a base. We can now define a domain as *a semantic structure that functions as the base for at least one concept profile* (typically, many profiles). As Taylor (1995:84) notes:

> In principle, any conceptualisation or knowledge configuration, no matter how simple or complex, can serve as the cognitive domain for the characterisation of meanings.

We can say that the domain of a circle includes the concepts of an arc, a diameter, a radius, a chord, etc. A circle itself is in the domain of two-dimensional space (actually, shape). This demonstrates that a particular semantic structure can be a concept in a domain (when it is profiled), or a domain itself (when it is functioning as the base to other concept profiles). We return to this point below.

Space itself does not appear to be profiled in a domain that serves as its base. Instead, it emerges directly from experience (cf. Lakoff & Johnson 1980:ch.12). Langacker calls space a *basic domain*. Basic domains are concepts that do not appear to be definable relative to other, more basic concepts, at least in the commonsense or folk model of experience. There are a substantial number of such basic domains; in fact, a good idea of the basic domains there are can be found by examining the higher divisions of a good thesaurus.

Langacker calls a nonbasic domain an *abstract domain*. The notion of a circle, functioning as a base, is an example of an abstract domain. An abstract domain itself is a concept that presupposes another domain. The other domain need not be a basic one. I noted above that shape is more precisely the base for [CIRCLE]; the concept of [SHAPE] is in turn profiled in two-dimensional space.[7] One can have an arbitrarily deep nesting of abstract domains before reaching a basic domain. However, the base is usually taken to be just the domain immediately presupposed by the profiled concept. We will call this domain the *base domain*, or simply the base. Langacker (e.g. 1987:493) calls it the *scope of predication* (recall that a predication is a concept). He notes that the scope of predication (i.e. the base) "may sometimes constitute only a limited portion of relevant domains" (ibid.). The involvement of multiple domains in the definition of a concept will be discussed below.

The relation between an abstract domain and the base domain it presupposes is not a taxonomic relation (or, as Langacker calls such relations, a schematic one). It is a relationship of concept to background assumption or presupposition. This distinction is sometimes obscured by the English language. The word *shape* stands for the do-

---

[7] The other major concept profiled in space is [LOCATION].

main as a mass noun, but as a count noun (*a shape*) it is a more general or schematic concept subsuming [CIRCLE], [SQUARE], [TRIANGLE], etc. A more general or schematic concept is not the domain for the particular concept; in fact, it is itself profiled in the same domain as its particular concept. As will be seen below, it is not always easy to distinguish a taxonomic relation from an abstract-base domain relation.

Langacker (1987:150-151) argues that some domains involve more than one *dimension*. An obvious case is space, which involves three dimensions (some concepts, such as [CIRCLE], need only two dimensions for their definition; others need only one). Many physical qualities that are grounded in the experience of sensory perception, such as temperature and pitch, are one-dimensional. Others, such as color, can be divided into hue, brightness and saturation. Generally, dimensions of a domain are all simultaneously presupposed by concepts profiled in that domain. This is the critical point: a concept may presuppose several different dimensions at once.

In fact, a concept may presuppose several different domains. For example, a human being must be defined relative to the domains of physical objects, living things, and volitional agents (and several other domains, e.g. emotion). The combination of domains simultaneously presupposed by a concept such as [HUMAN BEING] is called a *domain matrix*. Langacker (1987:152) makes the important point that there is in principle only a difference of degree between dimensions of a domain and domains in a matrix. In practice, we are more likely to call a semantic structure a domain if there are a substantial number of concepts profiled relative to that structure. If there are few, if any, concepts profiled relative to that structure alone, but instead there are concepts profiled relative to that structure and another one, then those structures are likely to be called two dimensions of a single domain. The term *domain* implies a degree of cognitive independence not found in a dimension.

The domain structure presupposed by a concept can be extremely complex. We can begin by considering the domain of physical objects, commonly invoked as a basic domain. The physical object domain is in fact not a basic domain, but a domain matrix. It consists of the domains of matter (an object is made of matter), shape (since objects have a shape; even substances have a shape, although it is not fixed), and location (embodying the principle that two objects cannot occupy the same location). Matter is a basic domain but, as we noted above, shape and location are abstract domains based on space, which is a basic domain.

Physical objects are themselves very general. Let us now consider how one would define what seems to be a kind of physical object, the letter T. It is directly defined as a letter of the alphabet; its base (domain) is hence the alphabet. The alphabet is itself an abstract domain presupposing the notion of a writing system – it is not just an instance of a writing system, since the latter involves not just a set of symbols such as an alphabet but also the means of putting them together, including the order on a page, spaces for words, etc. The domain of writing systems in turn presupposes the activity of writing. The activity of writing must be defined in terms of human communication, which presupposes the notion of meaning – perhaps a basic domain, since the symbolic relation appears not to be reducible to some other relation – and of the visual sensations, since writing is communication via inscriptions visually perceived, rather than auditorily or through gestures. And since writing is an activity, the domains of time and force or causation (both basic domains, since force is a generalisation of causation, as argued by Talmy 2000:ch.I-7) are also involved in the domain matrix of writing, since the letter T is the product of an activity. Since it is a human activity, it presupposes the involvement of human beings. Human beings are living things with mental abilities such as volition, intention and cognition (themselves dimensions of the mental domain or, better, domains in the matrix of the domain of the mind). Living things in turn are physical objects endowed with life. A diagram exhibiting all of the basic-abstract domain relations presupposed in defining the concept of the letter T is shown in figure 1 (the basic domains are given in small capitals):

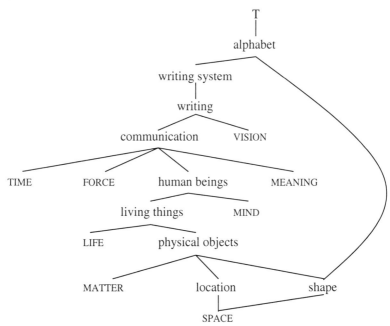

Figure 1: Domain structure underlying the concept of the letter T

Figure 1 demonstrates that it is incorrect to describe the concept of the letter T simply as belonging only to the domain of writing, as a typical informal theory of domains would most likely have it. The vast majority of concepts belong to abstract domains which are themselves profiled in complex domain matrices, often also abstract, and so ultimately presuppose a large array of basic domains, which I will call a *domain structure*.

It is not easy to distinguish profile-base relations from taxonomic ones (that is, type vs. instance). For example, is writing an instance of human communication, or is writing an instance of an activity that can only be understood in terms of the goals of human communication? I believe the latter is a more accurate description, and have described it as such. Likewise, since writing is an instance of human activity, human activity does not appear as a domain, but the various domains that it presupposes – time, change, force, volition – do appear, because anything presupposed by a human activity will be presupposed by any instance of it (cf. the discussion of the base of a circle and a shape above).

It is also difficult to determine direct vs. indirect reference to a domain. Recall that Langacker argues that the definition of an arc does not directly presuppose two-dimensional space, but rather it presupposes a circle which in turn presupposes two-dimensional space. Thus, an arc is not directly a two-dimensional object per se, but only such by virtue of being a part of a circle. Likewise, the letter T is not directly a shape, but only such by virtue of being a letter of the alphabet. But in fact, is the letter T a shape by virtue of being a letter of the alphabet, or by virtue of being the physical product of the activity of writing? I believe it is best described as the former, since the set of symbols is a set of shapes.

Another similar problem in this example is the location of the domain of mental ability. The activity of writing is a volitional, intentional activity, so it presupposes the domain of mental ability. But mental ability is presupposed by writing because writing presupposes human involvement, and the human involvement involves volition and intention.[8] Determining the exact structure of the array of domains upon which a profiled concept is based requires a careful working-out of the definitions of concepts, not unlike that carried out by Wierzbicka in her semantic analyses (see e.g. Wierzbicka 1987, 1988).

It is not clear from Langacker (1987) whether he considers the domain matrix of a concept to include only the base domains against which a concept is directly profiled or the entire domain structure underlying the concept profile. The example of the letter T demonstrates that, for many concepts, the domain structure can be quite

---

[8] There are actions that involve human beings, but do not require mental ability, for example seeing a person. But seeing something does not require that something to be a person; only activities inherently referring to mental abilities do.

It is also possible for other entities to write, e.g. for an animal to be taught to produce writing. This is a deviation from the idealised cognitive model (Lakoff 1987) of writing. An abstract domain is a conceptual structure, and Lakoff convincingly argues in his book (and elsewhere) that conceptual structures involve idealisation. Langacker (1987:150,fn.4) observes that an abstract schema is essentially an idealised cognitive model, which is in turn analogous to the notion of a frame. At any rate, the domain structure represents the presuppositions of the ideal case.

deep. There is some evidence that the notion of a domain matrix must include all of the domains in question. Consider the concepts [PERSON] and [BODY]. [PERSON] is profiled against the abstract domain of human beings. As the diagram above indicates, human beings are living things with certain mental abilities (recall the classic definition of man as a rational animal). Living things in turn are physical objects endowed with life. The concept [BODY] represents a person's physical reality (alive or dead). Its base is nevertheless still the abstract domain of human beings (or more precisely, animals), but it profiles the physical object domain in the domain structure underlying human beings. Contrast [BODY] with [SOUL], which profiles a nonphysical domain of a human being; or with [CORPSE], which profiles the physical object domain but also profiles a particular region in the life domain, namely [DEAD]. Another example is [KNEEL]. Only things with knees, or something resembling knees, can kneel; hence its base domain is (higher) animals – more precisely the base domain matrix includes animals as well as time and force, since kneeling is a process (see the matrix under "communication" in figure 1). However, it primarily profiles a particular posture, which is a spatial configuration of the object, and the domain of spatial configuration (shape) is quite deeply nested in the domain structure underlying [KNEEL].[9]

This is still not the end of the matter of describing the domain structure underlying a concept. Recall that meaning is encyclopedic. We have focused our attention only on the most central fact about the letter T, that it is a letter of the alphabet. Langacker calls the alphabet domain the *primary domain* of the concept, since it is the domain in which the most central facts about the concept are defined. However, there are other things we know about the letter T that are also quite central. It is the twentieth letter of the alphabet, which brings in the domain of a scale (ordering; a basic domain) and measurement, which in turn presupposes numbers, which in turn presupposes the notion of a unit of an entity. The letter T also corresponds to a linguistic sound, specifically a consonant which brings in the domain of sound sensation (another basic domain), vocal articulation (a very abstract domain), and (again) language or communication. And there is much more specific knowledge that is quite peripheral to its meaning, for example that it is the initial of my wife's last name, which presupposes a whole host of abstract domains based on other abstract domains and ultimately a wide range of basic domains.

Whether these other domains form part of the matrix of the concept of the letter T depends on whether the concept of the letter T profiles such things as the fact that it is the twentieth letter of the alphabet, it is the initial of my wife's last name, etc. Langacker does not precisely answer this question. In the passage quoted above, Langacker (1987:163) states that activation of a concept (presumably, its profile)

---

[9] [Editor's footnote] With the advent of so-called "kneeling buses" for travellers who need a little help getting on and off, the latter example may have to be revised. These buses owe their name to the fact that their front part can be lowered for easier access.

"facilitates (but does not always necessitate)" the activation of more peripheral knowledge about that concept. He later says that some routines (that is, pieces of knowledge) are sufficiently central to be activated almost every time (ibid.). This implies that the central-peripheral relation is defined in terms of necessitation vs. facilitation of activation; facilitation can perhaps be thought of as a priming effect. Other factors, such as contextual priming, presumably can convert "facilitation" of activation of peripheral knowledge to actual activation of that knowledge in particular speech events where that peripheral knowledge is relevant.

The activation of the base domain of a profiled concept, on the other hand, is presumably necessary, since the definition of a base domain is the semantic structure presupposed by the profiled concept. This implies that the whole structure given in the diagram is going to be activated. Langacker does not explicitly state this, but he does suggest that the profile-base relation is a matter of attention, in a generalised model of attention which includes multiple loci of attention, which in turn could be modelled in terms of intensity of activation (1987:188). One could extrapolate that the less direct the involvement of the domain in the definition of the concept, the less intense its activation will be when the concept is activated.

All of the above cognitive semantic structures – encyclopedic definitions, central vs. peripheral knowledge, profile and base, basic and abstract domains – are necessary for the definition of a single meaning of a word (Langacker 1987:164,fn.12). There is no apparatus given above for describing multiple meanings of a word. In a later chapter (viz. chapter 10), Langacker argues for a "schematic network" (cf. Lakoff's 1987 notion of a radial category) for describing different uses of a word which combines both classical and prototype notions. All uses of a single word are related through various types of extensions from an original meaning (original in the ontogenetic sense); in addition, a more schematic meaning subsuming many or all of the specific uses can arise and fit into the network. Metaphor and metonymy are two types of extensions of word meaning; they represent different uses of a particular word. I now turn to the role of domains in licensing these semantic extensions.

2. Domains, metaphor and metonymy

The term *metaphor* has been used for many different kinds of figurative language, depending in part on the theory of metaphor subscribed to by the analyst. I will examine the types of metaphors that are central to Lakoff & Johnson's (1980) theory, which can be illustrated by the contrast in the following two sentences:[10]

---

[10] Lakoff and Johnson describe a large class of phenomena as metaphors, some of which are probably better accounted for by other cognitive processes. For example, they describe a metaphor MORE OF

(2)   She's in the living room.

(3)   She's in a good mood.

Lakoff & Johnson employ a cognitive semantic model and analyse this type of metaphor as a conceptualisation of one domain in terms of the structure of another independent domain, that is, a mapping across domains. The two domains, the source domain and the target domain, do not form a domain matrix for the concepts involved. In this example, the use of *in* in (3) for the relation between a person and her emotional state does not mean that the speaker has constructed a profile for metaphorical *in* simultaneously encoding a spatial relation and an emotional relation. Only the emotional domain is profiled in (3); however, the emotional domain is conceptualised as having the same or similar structure to space by the use of the predicate *in*.

As we saw in section 1, if one accepts Lakoff & Johnson's theory of metaphor, as I do, one must be more specific as to what domain or domains are involved in a metaphor. I argue that the two domains being compared are base domains, that is, the bases of the profiled predication. In this case, the two domains are, as indicated in the informal description in the preceding paragraph, location and emotion, the base domains of the two uses of *in* in (2) and (3).[11]

In order to get an accurate description of a metaphor, the description of the metaphor has to be formulated in such a way that the two base domains are equated. For example, Lakoff & Johnson (1980:73) describe the following example as an instance of a metaphor they describe as AN OBJECT COMES OUT OF A SUBSTANCE:

(4)   I made a statue out of clay.

The metaphorical expression is *out of*. Its base domain in the metaphorical usage is creation (that is the meaning of *make* selected in this sentence); the literal meaning has motion as its base domain, so the metaphor can be phrased as CREATION IS MOTION. Of course, both of these abstract domains, creation and motion, have multiple domains in their base matrices; for example, motion involves time, change and location.

Likewise, one must be careful to define the metaphor in terms of the base domain of the words in question. This is not always easy. Consider the metaphor described by Lakoff & Johnson (1980:49) as LOVE IS A PATIENT; the following examples are theirs:

FORM IS MORE OF CONTENT (Lakoff & Johnson 1980:127), illustrated by the intensification represented in *He ran and ran and ran*; this is more likely to be an example of iconic motivation (Haiman 1983, 1985).

[11] Actually, *in* involves containment, so more than location is involved in the source domain.

(5)   This is a *sick* relationship.

(6)   They have a *strong, healthy* marriage.

(7)   The marriage is *dead* – it can't be *revived*.

(8)   Their marriage is *on the mend*.

(9)   We're getting *back on our feet*.

(10)   Their relationship is *in really good shape*.

(11)   They've got a *listless* marriage.

(12)   Their marriage is *on its last legs*.

(13)   It's a *tired* affair.

First, the metaphor is probably best described as LOVE IS A BODILY STATE. The words *sick, strong, healthy, listless* and *tired* all have a bodily state as the base. The phrases *back on our feet, in really good shape*, and *on its last legs* are themselves metaphors whose target domain is also bodily states. However, the words *dead* and *revived* are arguably profiled in the domain of life, which is one of the domains underlying the domain of living things which in turn underlies the domain of bodily states (see the domains underlying "human beings" in figure 1).[12] They are part of another metaphor, LOVE IS LIFE, which can generate other metaphorical expressions using words profiled in the domain of living things:

(14)   Their letters kept their love *alive*.

(15)   Her selfishness *killed* the relationship.

(16)   His effort to understand her *breathed new life into* their marriage.

Of course, LOVE IS A BODILY STATE and LOVE IS LIFE are metaphors coherent with each other, since bodily states presuppose the notion of life. However, the metaphors cannot be lumped together under something like LOVE IS A LIVING THING, since there are many other aspects of living things that are not metaphors for love, specifically those associated with the body (bodily activities such as spitting, sweating; or the body itself, e.g. its parts, etc.).

The role of domains in metaphor is quite central to the definition of that concept in Lakoff & Johnson's model. However, to be more precise about the phenomenon that

---

[12] One could argue that *alive* and *dead* are bodily states also, but they are clearly of a different kind from *listless* or *healthy*.

I am examining, I will use the term *domain mapping* to describe metaphor (though since in the Lakoff-Johnson model the two terms are virtually synonymous, I will continue to use the term *metaphor*). The role of domains in metonymy, on the other hand, is not direct, although it is more pervasive than has generally been noted, once a careful examination of the domain structure underlying a concept is undertaken.

The traditional definition of metonymy is a shift of a word-meaning from the entity it stands for to a "contiguous" entity (Ullmann 1957:232; cf. Lakoff & Johnson 1980:35 and Taylor 1995:122). Entities are contiguous because they are associated in experience (Lakoff & Johnson 1980:39-40). Lakoff & Turner (1995:103) argue that metonymy, unlike metaphor, "involves only one conceptual domain. A metonymic mapping occurs within a single domain, not across domains". However, as we have seen above, a concept is profiled against an often very complex domain structure or matrix, even if there is only one abstract domain as the base. In fact, in the next sentence, Lakoff & Turner switch to describing metonymy as a mapping within a schema (ibid.); the term *schema* is more amenable to describing a complex domain structure (cf. Taylor 1995:87). And Lakoff (1987:288) describes a metonymic mapping as occurring "within a single conceptual domain, which is structured by an ICM [idealised cognitive model]" – which Langacker equates with an abstract domain. Thus, the generalisation should be rephrased as "a metonymic mapping occurs within a single domain matrix, not across domains (or domain matrices)". Of course, the domain matrix possesses a unity that is created by experience – the real point of Lakoff's position.[13]

This is indeed the critical difference between metaphor and metonymy. Metaphor is a mapping between two domains that are not part of the same matrix; if you say *She's feeling down*, there is no spatial orientation domain in the matrix of the metaphorical concept of emotion being expressed; HAPPY IS UP involves two different concepts with their own domain structures underlying them. In metonymy, on the other hand, the mapping occurs only within a domain matrix. However, it is possible for metonymy, as well as for other lexical ambiguities, to occur across domains within a domain matrix. In this way, domains do play a significant role in the interpretation of metonymy.[14] I will now illustrate some examples of this role.

---

[13] René Dirven suggests that this characterisation will not distinguish between *Tea was a large meal for the Wicksteeds* (metonymy) and *Drinking Kriek-Lambiek is not just drinking, it is eating and drinking together* (metaphor). The first case is clearly metonymy, since the whole meal is profiled in a domain matrix that includes tea. However, drinking Kriek-Lambiek is profiled in a domain consisting of drinking and not eating; this is its source domain, and the target domain is the matrix of both drinking and eating.

[14] In some cases, domain mapping occurs between two domains, one of which happens to be in the matrix of the other. This appears to be what is going on with what Goossens (1990) calls "metaphor from metonymy", illustrated below:

Consider the following typical examples of metonymy:

(17)   Proust spent most of his time in bed.

(18)   Proust is tough to read.

(19)   *Time* magazine is pretty vapid.

(20)   *Time* took over *Sunset* magazine, and it's gone downhill ever since.

Sentences (17) and (19) are considered "literal", (18) and (20) "metonymic". However, in the encyclopedic view of semantics, the works of Proust and the company that produces *Time* magazines are part of the concepts of [PROUST] and [TIME-MAGAZINE] respectively. However, they are less central than the fact that Proust was a person and *Time* is a magazine, not least because they are quite extrinsic to the central concepts. The domain matrix of an encyclopedic characterisation of [PROUST] will include the domain of creative activity. Since Proust's claim to fame is that he is a writer, and the work produced is a salient element in the domain of creative activity, the metonymic shift is quite natural (and in fact, is quite productive). Nevertheless, the metonymic shift also involves a shift of domains within the domain matrix (schema, frame, script) for *Proust*. A similar argument applies to *Time magazine*: a secondary domain for magazines is that of the process of publication, in which the publishing company is a salient entity. The metonymy that shifts reference from the magazine to the company also shifts domains from the magazine as an object with semantic content to the domain of publication. We will call this conceptual effect *domain highlighting* (cf. Cruse 1986:53), since the metonymy makes primary a domain that is secondary in the literal meaning.

Domain highlighting appears to be a necessary though not sufficient condition for metonymy, which also involves shift of reference, at least in the most typical occurrences thereof. Thus, the relation between domain highlighting and metonymy dif-

---

(i)   "Oh dear", she giggled, "I'd quite forgotten".   (Goossens 1990:328)

(ii)   "Get out of here!" he thundered.

In these cases the usual interpretation is that the act of speaking takes on metaphorical properties of giggling and thundering. As Goossens observes, the metaphor applies to the message (as intended by the speaker) as well as the medium. I would analyse this as a domain mapping, but the source domain (sound) is one of the domains in the matrix of the target (speaking) – hence the appearance of being "metonymy".

Goossens' examples of "metonymy within metaphor", on the other hand, appear to be exactly that:

(iii)   She caught the minister's ear and persuaded him to accept her plan.
                                                            (Goossens 1990:334)

Ear is a metonymy for 'attention', and that metonymy is itself embedded in a metaphorical use of *catch*.

fers from that between domain mapping and metaphor, since domain mapping does appear to be definitional for metaphor. While domain highlighting appears to be a consequence of many if not all instances of metonymy, it also occurs in other types of lexical ambiguity that have not always been considered metonymy. Consider the following sentences:

(21)   This book is heavy.

(22)   This book is a history of Iraq.

The concept [BOOK] is profiled in (at least) two primary domains, the domain of physical objects and the domain of meaning or semantic content. In (21), the physical object domain of *book* is highlighted by virtue of the requirements of the predicate *heavy*. In (22), on the other hand, the semantic content domain of *book* is highlighted, again due to the requirements of the predicate *be a history of Iraq*.[15]

It is not clear that there are in fact two different entities being referred to in (21) and (22). From a conceptual point of view, however, the concept symbolised by *this book* is different in (21) and (22). It is not an example of metonymy in the usual sense of that term because the elements profiled in each domain are highly intrinsic; no reference is made to external entities. For both of these reasons, the word *book* is not always treated as metonymic, or even ambiguous, in these sentences.

Another oft-cited example illustrates the distinctness of the domains of space and physical material in characterising physical objects (see, for example, Cruse 1986:65, Taylor 1995:124):

(23)   I broke the window.

(24)   She came in through the bathroom window.

These two uses of *window* are usually analysed as an ambiguity; in the encyclopedic semantic view, they highlight the physical object and shape or topological domains of the concept [WINDOW] respectively. The interpretation of [WINDOW] as an opening in the shape domain is somewhat extrinsic because it makes crucial reference to what is around it – contrast the use of *window* to describe a physical object in a hardware store showroom – though it appears to be less extrinsic to the concept [WINDOW] than the publishing company and writings in examples (18) and (20) above. The existence of examples such as *window* in (23) and (24) suggests that there is a continuum between the clear cases of metonymy and the highlighting of highly intrinsic facets of a concept as in (21) and (22). The existence of this continuum suggests that domain highlighting plays a role in lexical ambiguities other than

---

[15] There is another reading of (21) which also refers to the semantic content domain, and which I will discuss below.

metonymy (assuming that one does not want to extend the term *metonymy* to the book and window examples).

It may not be the case that domain highlighting within the domain matrix of a word is involved in all cases of metonymy. In some cases, the shift of prominence of domains in the matrix is quite subtle, and sensitive to the semantics of the associated words. For instance, consider the following examples of synecdoche, a phenomenon usually subsumed under metonymy (Ullmann 1957:232, Lakoff & Johnson 1980:36; examples from Lakoff & Johnson 1980:36-37):

(25)   We need a couple of strong bodies for our team.

(26)   There are a lot of good heads in the university.

(27)   We need some new faces around here.

Since a part has the whole as its base domain, it appears that no domain selection is involved in these examples. But in fact in an encyclopedic characterisation of *body*, *head* and *face*, the domain matrix of each part is different, since each body part is associated with different human qualities and behaviours. The selection of bodies in (25) is sanctioned by the need to highlight the physical strength/ability domain underlying the domain of human beings; *heads* in (26) by the need to highlight the domain of human intelligence; while *faces* in (27) is a cross-linguistically widespread synecdoche for persons as a whole, the presence or absence thereof being what is the topic of (27) (cf. Lakoff & Johnson 1980:36-37). The synecdoche is in fact highlighting precisely the domain that is relevant to the predication. Compare (25-27) to (28-30), in which the choice of parts-for-whole is different. While a sentence such as (29) is interpretable, it does not mean the same thing as (26).

(28)   ??We need a couple of strong faces for our team.

(29)   ??There are a lot of good bodies in the university.

(30)   ??We need some new heads around here.

Another example of metonymy which involves a subtle shift in domain prominence is

(31)   I filled up the car.

In (31), it is understood that it is the gas tank that is filled, not the main body of the car. This interpretation is possible only because the phrase [fill up VEHICLE], without the substance indicated, is conventionally interpreted as 'fill up with fuel'; only by explicitly indicating the substance can it be interpreted as 'the interior of the car', and only by explicitly indicating the gas tank can it be interpreted as 'fill the gas tank' with some other substance than fuel:

(32)   I filled up the car with gasoline and set it on fire. [gas tank or interior of car]

(33)   I filled up the car with sand. [interior of car only]

(34)   I filled up the gas tank with sand.

The two meanings of *fill up* are profiled in two different domains: the more general meaning in the domain matrix of substances and containers (shape), and the more specific meaning in the more abstract domain of fuelling, which is based on the substances/containers domain as well as a domain of fuel-requiring mechanical objects. The interpretation of car as 'gas tank of car' involves the highlighting of the domain of fuelling in the domain matrix of [CAR] as well as a shift to the relevant part of the car; in fact, it is the highlighting of that domain by the predicate *fill up* that sanctions the shift of reference (at least when the conventional expression was first coined).

The analysis of metonymy in an encyclopedic theory of meaning, whether or not a secondary domain is highlighted in the process, casts a different light on a problem in semantic representation raised by Nunberg (1979). Nunberg presents an analysis of metonymy arguing from a non-encyclopedic view of semantics. Nunberg argues that there should be one "basic" denotation of a polysemous term, e.g. for *Proust*, *Time magazine*, and *window*. Metonymic uses are to be derived by a set of pragmatic functions that shift the meaning to the appropriate referent. Nunberg argues that the basic meaning is ultimately undecidable because any word (or at least, any noun) can be used to refer to the type of entity, a token of the type, and also the name for the entity, and a token of the name (the latter two are expressed orthographically with quotation marks, but are not phonologically distinct):

(35)   A cat is a mammal.

(36)   His cat is called Metathesis.

(37)   "Cat" has three letters.

(38)   "Cat" here has a VOT of 40ms. [referring to a spectograph of an occurrence of the word]

In the encyclopedic approach, there is no "basic" meaning; all metonymic meanings are present in the encyclopedic semantic representation. This is also true for the meanings which Nunberg finds ultimately undecidable. Any symbolised concept will have as part of its encyclopedic definition the phonological entity that symbolises it, and instantiations of the concept (more precisely, concepts of instantiations of the concept type).

This last question leads us to another problem of metonymy: where to locate it in the interaction of words and phrases in semantic composition, or to put it more generally, conceptual combination. The standard view is that metonymy represents an ambiguity (or pragmatic extension) of the noun, so that in (17-31) and (35-38), it is a question of the meaning of the noun phrase being shifted from its "basic" or "normal" meaning. Langacker (1984, 1987:7.3.4) argues for the opposite point of view: the ambiguity is in the predicate (in traditional terms), not the noun phrase (argument). Consider the following examples:

(39)   We all heard the [trumpet].   (Langacker 1987:271,ex.24a]

(40)   This is a striped [apple].

The traditional analysis is that the bracketed nouns symbolise 'sound of the trumpet' and 'surface of the apple' respectively, and *trumpet* and *apple* are ambiguous. Langacker argues that we should treat the noun phrases as really symbolising the entities they appear to be symbolising, namely the trumpet and the apple, and that the reference to the sound and to the surface is a characteristic of the predicate, so that *hear* can profile 'hear the sound of [noisemaking object]' and *striped* can profile 'striped surface of [three-dimensional opaque object]'. Langacker takes this position for (39) and (40) in order to avoid any syntactic derivational or transformational relation that would "delete" the *sound of [the trumpet]* and *surface of [the apple]*. Although Langacker does not discuss metonymy by name, (39-40) are closely related to prototypical instances of metonymy, and an active zone analysis for metonymy is in the spirit of the cognitive grammar view that there is a direct symbolic relation between word and meaning.

Langacker's argument in favour of this position notes the idiosyncrasy and conventionality of the ability of particular predicates to allow "metonymic" noun phrase arguments. For example, *hear* can also take an NP that symbolises the sound itself:

(41)   We all heard the sound of the trumpet.

Langacker describes the "metonymised" referent as the *active zone* of the entity symbolised by the argument NP. Thus, the sound produced by the trumpet, and the surface of the apple, are the active zones of the profiled entity, but do not match the profile of the entity itself.

While Langacker's alternative analysis seems reasonable for a number of examples such as those with perception verbs, there are other examples in which the traditional analysis seems more appropriate, and this suggests that a different approach to the question should be taken. For example, predicates describing the actions of na-tional governments virtually always allow the country itself to be the agent of the action:

(42)   Germany pushed for greater quality control in beer production.

(43)   The United States banned tuna from countries using drift nets.

(44)   Myanmar executed twenty Muslim activists.

Also, many of the same predicates allow the seat of government or the head of state to function as the agent; although some significant semantic differences are found so that interchangeability is not possible in all contexts, it is possible to use all three when it is actually the government (rather than the head of state alone) that makes the decision:

(45)   France / Paris / Mitterrand will hold a referendum on the Maastricht treaty.

It would seem odd to consider every action verb attributable to an act of government to be ambiguous between 'act of [a government]', 'act of the government located in and ruling [a country]', 'act of the government seated in [a capital city]', and 'act of the government led by [a head of state]'.[16]

In other cases, the metonymic extension is an idiosyncrasy of the noun, not the predicate:

(46)   I ate roast chicken for dinner.

(47)   *I ate roast cow for dinner.

One cannot argue that there is an ambiguity in *eat* so that it can mean 'eat the flesh of [an animal]', since (47) is unacceptable.[17] The word *chicken* must clearly be taken to stand for 'the meat thereof'. Nevertheless, there is a clear metonymic relation between chicken flesh and chicken "on the hoof" (to borrow a collocation from Nunberg), which is productive with less commonly eaten animals:

---

[16] The last interpretation, with the head of state, often is ambiguous, but that is because the predicates describing acts of governments can also describe acts of individuals, so that *Bush lobbied against the biodiversity treaty* can mean the US government, but can also mean (and is more likely to mean) Bush the individual.

[17] The unacceptability of (47) is due to the historical idiosyncrasy that English speakers appropriated Norman French words to symbolise 'the meat thereof' for cows, pigs and sheep (*beef, pork, mutton*). However, this does not make the synchronic situation any less idiosyncratic.

(48)   I ate grilled rattlesnake for dinner.

(49)   I ate roast tapir for dinner.

(50)   I ate pan-fried armadillo for dinner.

If it were not for the existence of examples such as (47), one might have argued that the metonymy resides in the predicate rather than in the noun.

To some extent, the issue of whether the metonymy can be localised in the predicate or in the noun is a red herring: the metonymy occurs by virtue of the collocation of the predicate and the noun, that is, the semantic composition of the two. The encyclopedic view of meaning supports this approach. One of Langacker's motivations for his analysis is to treat the surface object of *hear*, *the trumpet*, as the "real" object of the verb, without some syntactic transformation that claims that the underlying object of *hear* is the noun phrase *the sound of the trumpet*.[18] But in the encyclopedic view of the meaning of *trumpet*, the sound it produces is a quite salient (albeit somewhat extrinsic) aspect of the profiled concept. Conversely, part of the encyclopedic characterisation of *hear* is that objects produce sounds that people hear. Thus, one can have one's semantic cake and eat it too: (part of) the profile of *trumpet* is the object of *hear*, and (part of) the profile of what is heard is the object producing the sound.[19] The same is true of the act-of-government examples: a salient part of the profile of a country, a capital city, and a head of state in the encyclopedic definition of those concepts is the government that rules the country, is seated in the capital city, and is headed by the head of state, respectively. Of course, as I describe in more detail in the following section, it is the semantics of the predicate that highlights the relevant aspect of the encyclopedic profile of the concept symbolised by the noun; the metonymic interpretation arises only in the combination of noun and predicate.

---

[18] This is quite clear in Langacker (1984), in which he uses the same analysis to argue against a "Tough-movement" analysis as in *Hondas are easy to fix*. In the Tough-movement examples, easiness is being attributed to some inherent property of the surface subject, e.g. the make of automobile, and that property is described as 'easy to fix'.

[19] This is true of any sound produced by any sound-producing object, not just the intended sound of objects like trumpets whose purpose is to produce sound. The collocation of a noun symbolising an object with *hear* will result in the highlighting of any salient sound associated with the object: *I hear the boats on the canal* can refer to any sound produced by the boats – the horn, their splashing, gliding through the water, the people talking on them, etc.

3. Differences between domain mapping and domain highlighting

In the preceding section, Lakoff & Johnson's analysis of metaphor as domain mapping was adopted and it was argued that the source and target domains are the base domains of the "literal" and "figurative" concepts symbolised by the word. It was also argued that an essential part of metonymy is the highlighting of an aspect of a concept's profile in a domain somewhere in the entire domain matrix or domain structure underlying the profiled concept. Those analyses imply that a central aspect of figurative language is the manipulation of experiential domains in understanding and communication. In the case of metonymy, the manipulation of domains plays a significant role, but metonymy cannot be reduced to domain highlighting, and domain highlighting is found in other types of lexical ambguity for which the term *metonymy* may not be appropriate. I will henceforth use the terms *domain mapping* and *domain highlighting* to describe the semantic phenomena that are under examination in this paper. I will now explore under what circumstances one would expect to find domain mapping and domain highlighting in linguistic expressions.

Consider the following examples from chapter 6 of Lakoff & Johnson (1980), on one type of metaphor, and the subsequent examples from chapter 8, on metonymy; the figure of speech is italicised as in the original:

(51)   He's *in* love.

(52)   We're *out* of trouble now.

(53)   He's *coming out* of the coma.

(54)   I'm *slowly getting into* shape.

(55)   He *entered* a state of euphoria.

(56)   He *fell into* a depression.   (Lakoff & Johnson 1980:32)

(57)   He likes to read the *Marquis de Sade*.

(58)   He's in *dance*.

(59)   *Acrylic* has taken over the art world.

(60)   The *Times* hasn't arrived at the press conference yet.

(61)   Mrs. Grundy frowns on *blue jeans*.

(62)   *New windshield wipers* will satisfy him.   (ibid.:35)

A glance at these examples and many others suggests that metaphor is associated with predicates (not just verbs, but also prepositions and adjectives), and metonymy with nouns (hence the focus of Nunberg's paper on nominal metonymy). However, this initial hypothesis is simply incorrect. Examples (63-66) below involve domain mapping with nouns, and examples (67-70) involve domain highlighting with verbs:

(63)   mouth of a person, an animal, a bottle, a cave, a river
                                                        (Cruse 1986:72)

(64)   handle of a door, suitcase, umbrella, sword, spoon   (ibid.:74)

(65)   tree, phrase structure tree, family tree, clothes tree

(66)   cup [for drinking], acorn cup, resin cup, cup [for capstan], cup [golf
        hole], bra cup   (Dirven 1985)

(67)   She swore foully.

(68)   She swore loudly.

(69)   The vase fell quickly.

(70)   The vase fell far.

In examples (63-66), the different uses of *mouth, handle, tree* and *cup* are undoubtedly profiled in different domains, as the explicit or implicit nominal or genitive modifiers suggest. There is a resemblance in shape and function in all of the examples, resemblances which appear to be of the image-schematic kind characteristic of metaphors. These are generally agreed to be nominal metaphors, or at least a figurative phenomenon closely akin to metaphor which involves domain mapping in essentially the same way.

In examples (67-70), a verb which has more than one primary domain associated with it has one or the other domain highlighted by virtue of the adverb associated with it. In (67), the content of the imprecation is highlighted, while in (68) it is the sound volume that is highlighted. In (69), the time and change domains in the matrix underlying motion are highlighted, while in (70) it is the location/distance domain.

Although domain mapping and domain highlighting can occur with a word of any lexical category, there is a generalisation underlying the distribution of these two cognitive semantic phenomena. In (63-66), domain mapping is induced by the nominal/genitive dependents on the noun that is figuratively interpreted. In (67-70), domain highlighting is induced by the adverbial modifier to the verbal predicate. In order to formulate the distribution of domain mapping and domain highlighting, we must examine the cognitive grammar description of syntactic/semantic composition.

One of the criteria for the centrality of knowledge to a particular concept is its intrinsicness: the extent to which it refers to (or rather, does not refer to) entities external to that concept. Some concepts, however, inherently involve extrinsic entities; these are called *relational concepts*. The external entities that relational concepts "include" correspond roughly to the arguments of a predicate in formal semantics; examples include [EAT], which inherently makes reference to an eater, an item eaten, and to a lesser extent to the implement used by the eater in eating.[20] A relational concept contains only a schematic representation of the extrinsic entities associated with it, in our example the eater, the thing eaten, etc. *Things* (a technical term in cognitive grammar) are nonrelational concepts, however (Langacker 1987:6.1.1). Relational concepts are divided into *atemporal relations* and *processes*, which correspond roughly to those relational concepts that are construed as static (i.e. construed atemporally) and those that are construed as unfolding over time.[21] Things are the semantic structures symbolised by nouns, while relations are symbolised by verbs, adjectives, adverbs, and prepositions.

Syntactic/semantic composition, that is, symbolic composition in cognitive grammar, involves two aspects: what the semantic type of the resulting complex expression is, and how the component expressions are fitted together. The phrase *the fat book* and the sentence *The book is fat* symbolise two different semantic sorts: the phrase symbolises a thing, while the sentence symbolises a "state of affairs" (in cognitive grammar terms, an *imperfective process*). The two constructions differ (among other things) in their *profile determinant*, that is, the component element that determines the semantic type of the whole. In the phrase, *book* is the profile determinant, since it is also a thing (we are ignoring the semantic contribution of *the*). In the sentence, *book* is not the profile determinant; if we ignore the contribution of *be*, one could say that *(being) fat* is the profile determinant.[22] As can be seen by the different status of *book* and *fat* in the phrase and in the sentence, profile determinacy is a function of the construction into which words enter (Croft 1996).

This leaves the matter of how words are combined semantically. Relationality may appear to underlie semantic composition in cognitive grammar, but this is not precisely correct. In the canonical case of a main verb and the subject and object dependent on it, as in *Mara sings*, this appears to be the case: the subject is nonrelational, and the predicate is relational; the subject referent "fills the slot" for the singer in the relational semantic structure for *sing*. But what about *Mara sings beau-*

---

[20] In this respect the notion of a relational concept is richer than that of a predicate: less centrally involved extrinsic entities are part of the concept. In fact, one can add manner and other more peripherally involved entities to the entities inherently involved in the act of eating.

[21] For the purposes of this paper, it is not necessary to describe this distinction in detail.

[22] Cognitive grammar accommodates the fact that some expressions may have no profile determinant, or even more than one profile determinant (Langacker 1987:291-292).

tifully? Here *beautiful(ly)* is a relational structure with a "slot" for a process, and *sings* "fills that slot". The fact that *sings* is inherently relational is irrelevant to the combination of *sings* and *beautifully*. Thus, in one and the same sentence, *sings* is both an entity with "slots" to be filled, and a "filler" for another entity's "slot".

In one of Langacker's most insightful analyses of the relation between syntax and semantics, he argues that it is not relationality that governs symbolic combinations, but an independent phenomenon which he calls autonomy and dependence. In most grammatical combinations, one predication can be identified as the autonomous one and the other as the dependent one using the following definition: "One structure, D, is dependent on the other, A, to the extent that A constitutes an elaboration of a salient substructure within D" (Langacker 1987:300). Let us examine our example *Mara sings beautifully* with respect to this definition. *Mara* (that is, the semantic structure symbolised by *Mara*) does indeed elaborate a salient substructure of *sings*, namely the schematic singer in its semantic representation that makes it a relational predication (concept). Having compared *Mara* to *sings*, we must reverse this process and compare *sings* to *Mara*: does *sings* elaborate a salient substructure of *Mara*? The answer is "no", but it is not a categorical answer; after all, the semantic representation of *Mara* is encyclopedic, and part of the encyclopedic knowledge about Mara is that the speaker knows that Mara sings. But this is a very non-salient substructure of Mara. Hence, we can say that *sings* is dependent and *Mara* is autonomous, relative to each other.

Now let us compare *sings* and *beautifully*. *Sings* elaborates a salient substructure of *beautifully*, namely the schematic process that makes it a relational predication. But *beautifully* does not elaborate a salient substructure of *sings*, even though *sings* is relational. At best, *sings* has a not very salient substructure representing the manner in which the process is executed, and *beautifully* elaborates that; but that substructure is not nearly as salient in the semantic representation for *beautifully* as the substructure of *beautifully* that is elaborated by *sings*. So on balance *beautifully* is the dependent predication and *sings* is autonomous. Note that, by this analysis, *sings* is dependent relative to *Mara*, but autonomous relative to *beautifully*. Autonomy and dependence are relative notions, and that is exactly what is needed to describe this aspect of semantic composition.

We may now characterise the conditions under which domain mapping and domain highlighting occurs: domain mapping occurs with dependent predications, and domain highlighting occurs with autonomous predications. As the preceding discussion of *sings beautifully* demonstrates, "dependent" does not necessarily correspond with "relational" (verbs, adjectives, etc.), and "autonomous" does not necessarily correspond with "nonrelational" (nouns). Thus, there is no connection between metaphor/domain mapping and relational predications, or between metonymy (more precisely, domain highlighting) and nonrelational predications. This will account for the cases in (63-70). But let us begin with the "typical" cases, (51-62).

In (51-56), the metaphorical expressions are dependent on the subject and object – more precisely, the object of the preposition in all but (55); hence they are the ones subject to domain mapping. But in particular it is the autonomous expressions on which they are dependent that induce the domain mapping: *love, trouble, the coma, shape, euphoria* and *depression* are all profiled as states (physical or emotional) of a human being, and those expressions require the metaphorical interpretation of the container-based directional prepositions and verbs.

In contrast, in (57-62), the expressions that manifest domain highlighting are all autonomous relative to the main verbs which are dependent on them. And, conversely, the domain highlighting is induced by the dependent expressions in relation to which the italicised expressions are autonomous. For example, in (57), *read* requires that the object be understood as a text; in (60), *arrive* requires that the subject be interpreted as a person (or at least as an animal, but no animal is salient in the domain matrix of *Times*);[23] and in (62), *satisfy* requires that the subject be some completed event.[24] These examples all illustrate the principle to be discussed in section 4: that, in the grammatical combination of an autonomous and a dependent predication, the dependent predication can induce domain highlighting in the autonomous one, and the autonomous predication can induce domain mapping in the dependent one. Now let us turn to the other cases.

Examples (67-70) are straightforward: it is clear that the verb is autonomous relative to the adverb, and it is the adverb that induces the domain highlighting. Again, it is important to note that the word in question be autonomous relative to the word that is inducing the domain highlighting.

Examples (63-66) are more difficult, because an argument must be made that the nouns *mouth, handle, tree* and *cup* are dependent on their nominal/genitive modifiers, and can be so construed even when no such modifiers are present. This latter question will be discussed in section 4. *Mouth* and *handle* are what are called *relational nouns*, since they represent parts of wholes; it is those wholes which make up the genitive modifiers. Langacker (1987:185) argues that relational nouns such as part nouns do not profile the thing (in this case, the whole) that they are related to (what he calls a *landmark*); otherwise they would no longer be nouns/things. Instead, the landmark is a very salient substructure in the base. Of course, the structures in the base are part of the semantic structure of the concept (see section 1 above). On the other hand, the part elaborated by the head noun is not as salient a substructure of the whole symbolised by the genitive as the whole is for the part.

---

[23] There is another interpretation of *arrive*, as in *The Times arrived at my doorstep*, in which case the physical-object interpretation is possible. In fact, both interpretations are possible in both contexts (see examples 80-81 below), but the adjuncts favour one reading over the other.

[24] The other examples involve not just domain highlighting of the autonomous predications but also domain mapping (metaphor) in the dependent predications; we will return to this in a moment.

Thus, in the expression *the mouth of the river* (or *the river's mouth*, or *the river mouth*), *mouth* is on balance more dependent on *river*, and *river* is more autonomous relative to *mouth*. And it is *river* that induces the domain mapping for *mouth*.

The same argument can be applied to *handle* and other relational nouns; can it also be applied to *tree, cup* and other nonrelational nouns that have metaphorical interpretations? In the cases illustrated, the answer is "yes". In some of the examples, e.g. *bra cup*, the word is functioning as a relational noun (part/whole). In the examples *phrase-structure tree* and *family tree*, the modifying nouns essentially name the base domain of the head noun's profile. As such, they are in a relation very much like a part-whole relation: the base domain taken as a whole is a quite salient substructure of the profiled concept, while the profiled concept is not a very salient substructure of the base domain (on average, no more so than any other concept in the domain). In *clothes tree, clothes* elaborates a much more salient substructure of *tree* – the tree is made expressly for the purpose of hanging clothes – than *tree* does in *clothes*. An example like *acorn cup* is a closer call: the cup is "for" the acorn and so *acorn* elaborates a salient substructure for *cup*; but the acorn is often conceived of sans cup, and so *cup* elaborates a less salient substructure of *acorn*. While there appears to be no general principle by means of which we can say that the metaphorically interpreted noun is the dependent member, partly because the semantics of noun-noun compounding seems to be so open-ended (Downing 1977), it seems to be a not unreasonable hypothesis given the examples just discussed, and should be investigated further.

4. The unity of domain revisited

In the last section, I argued that domain mapping can take place with a dependent predication when the autonomous predication it is dependent on induces it; and domain highlighting can occur to an autonomous predication when the predication dependent on it induces it. The reason for this is that the grammatical combination of a dependent predication and the autonomous predication(s) it is dependent on must be interpreted in a single domain (or domain matrix). Consider again a simple example of metaphor and metonymy:

(71)   She's in a good mood. [= (3)]

(72)   Proust is tough to read. [= (18)]

In (71), the relational predication *(be) in* is interpreted metaphorically in the target domain of emotion. This renders the sentence semantically coherent because the subject of *be* and the complement of *in* are in the domain of emotion. In (72), Proust is interpreted metonymically because the complex predicate *be tough to read* requires an entity in the domain of semantic content, and the metonymic interpretation provides just such an entity in that domain.

In both of these cases, and in all such cases in general, there is an attempt to "match" the domain of the dependent predication and of the autonomous predications that elaborate it. Sentences such as (71) and (72) that do not match domains in the "literal" intepretations of the elements are not rejected as semantically incoherent. Instead, the listener attempts to interpret one or more elements figuratively, using metaphor or metonymy (or other cognitive processes that we have not discussed here). In other words, there is a background assumption on the part of the listener that sentences are semantically coherent. These background assumptions I call the "conceptual unities". The conceptual unity discussed in this paper is the unity of domain.

This account leaves two questions as yet unanswered: the scope of the semantic unit that requires conceptual unity, and the source of the required conceptual unity. We now take up these questions in turn.

It should be clear from our description of conceptual adjustments of domains that the scope of the unity of domain is the dependent predication and the autonomous predications it is dependent on, but no more. That means if a word enters into grammatical relations with more than one other word – for example, *sings* compared to *Mara* and *sings* compared to *beautifully* – it is possible that it will be interpreted in different domains for each of the grammatical relations it contracts.

The first example of this is illustrated by another problem that Nunberg (1979) found with his analysis of a basic and derived meanings for nouns that allow metonymy. In some examples, the basic and a derived meaning must be simultaneously attributed to a single occurrence of the word:

(73)   Cædmon, who was the first Anglo-Saxon poet, fills only a couple of pages in this book of poetry. [Nunberg 1979:167,ex.29]

The single occurrence of the word *Cædmon* is used to refer both to the person and to his works. This problem disappears in the encyclopedic view of metonymy. Both domains are present in the domain matrix of the complex. For the word *Cædmon*, more than one part of its domain matrix can be highlighted simultaneously. However, the triggers are found in different grammatical relations: *Cædmon* with respect to the nonrestrictive relative clause *who was the first Anglo-Saxon poet*, and with respect to the main clause *fills only a couple of pages in this book of poetry*. *Cædmon* is the autonomous predication in both cases, but relative to different dependent predications.[25]

---

[25] If one reverses the two clauses, the sentence is less acceptable:

The same is true of the following example, in which the main predicate highlights the physical object domain of the object NP, but its PP modifier highlights the semantic content domain:

(74)   I cut out this article on the environment.

Example (20), repeated below as (75), provides an example of the same phenomenon involving anaphora, with *Sunset magazine* referring to the company and anaphoric *it* referring to the magazine's content:

(75)   *Time* took over *Sunset magazine*, and it's been downhill ever since.

In fact, different modifiers (adjuncts) in a single phrase can highlight different domains of the head:

(76)   a thin, dog-eared monograph on hallucinogenic mushrooms of the
        Pacific Northwest

In (76), the two adjectival modifiers highlight the physical object domain of *monograph* and the prepositional phrase postmodifier highlights the semantic content domain. Here also, the predication *monograph* enters into two different grammatical relations with two different predications which are dependent on it.

If a predication is dependent on more than one autonomous predication, then the whole combination must obey the conceptual unity of domain:

(77)   I won't buy that idea.

Not only must *buy* be mapped into the domain of mental activity, but the subject *I* also has the domain of the mind highlighted (the person as a being with mental capacities, not a physical object, for instance). *Idea*, of course, has mental activity as its (primary) base domain.

We now turn to the second question, whether or not one can predict what the domain of the combination of a dependent predication and the autonomous predication(s) it is dependent on will be. It turns out that this is not decidable, because, not surprisingly, unexpressed contextual knowledge can enter into the semantic determination of the domain in which an utterance is interpreted.

(iv)   ?Cædmon, who fills only a couple of pages in this anthology, was the first
        Anglo-Saxon poet.

This is due to the fact that although both metonymic interpretations can be accessed from a single occurrence, one meaning is more established than the other (Cruse 1986:68-71). Nevertheless, an analysis of metonymy must still account for the fact that it is possible for the same linguistic expression to simultaneously highlight two aspects of the concept symbolised by that expression.

Either the autonomous or dependent predication in a grammatical unit can have its domain adjusted, via domain mapping or domain highlighting. In the simplest cases, such as (71) and (72), either the autonomous or the dependent predication is interpreted "literally" – that is, as the most intrinsic entity profiled in the concept's primary domain(s) – and the other element of the sentence has its domain adjusted. As (71) and (72) demonstrate, there is no a priori directionality, requiring either the autonomous or the dependent predication to be interpreted literally. In fact, both may be interpreted figuratively, as in (1), repeated here as (78), or (79):

(78)   Denmark shot down the Maastricht treaty.

(79)   Sales rose to $5m last year.

In (78), the domain of political force is highlighted in the subject NP, and there is a domain mapping in the main verb from weaponry to political action. In (79), the value (price) domain rather than the object, service etc. domain is highlighted in the subject NP, while there is a domain mapping in the verb from vertical motion to increase in quantity, specifically monetary quantity.

One could identify the object NPs *Maastricht treaty* and *$5m* in (78) and (79) as the source of the figurative interpretations of the subject and the verb, since they "literally" refer to the political activity and monetary value domains, respectively. However, it is not always possible to attribute the figurative interpretations of the parts of a construction to some "literally" interpreted element in the clause. In some examples, only contextual properties can provide the "source" of the figurative interpretations. Consider again the following example:

(80)   This book is heavy. [= (21)]

The profile of the concept symbolised by the word *book* inhabits two domains, physical objects and meaning (semantic content). However, the predicate *heavy* can be interpreted "literally" in the physical object domain, or it can be shifted metaphorically to the meaning domain. Thus, there are interpretations of both subject and predicate in both the physical object and meaning domains, and in fact this sentence is ambiguous out of context for precisely that reason. Another example of this is the following sentence:

(81)   The newspaper went under.

One interpretation of this sentence has both subject and predicate interpreted figuratively. Metonymy and metaphor interact to produce the interpretation 'The company producing the newspaper went bankrupt'. However, there is also another interpretation, 'The physical paper went under the surface of the water'; cf. *The boat went under.* Since one of the domains in the matrix of [NEWSPAPER] is that of physical objects, which undergo motion, which is the "literal" domain of [GO UNDER], this other interpretation is possible as well.

These examples demonstrate that the correct literal or figurative interpretations of the elements of sentences is not decidable from the elements of the sentence by themselves. The domain in which a predication is interpreted can be determined by context. This is possible because the autonomy-dependence relation is a relationship between semantic structures, which need not be overtly expressed in an utterance. A semantic structure symbolised by a word in a sentence can contract an autonomy-dependence relation with a semantic structure left unexpressed in the context. This is why the nominal metaphors in (63)-(66) can be interpreted metaphorically without the nominal modifiers upon which they are dependent being present in the utterance. For example, *cup* [for drinking, for a golf hole, for a capstan] is interpreted in whatever domain is prominent in the context of the speech event. In fact, an interpretation in any domain is possible, short of semantic incompatibility (and conventional limitations on the figurative interpretations of particular words and phrases). This is not surprising, considering that this is generally the case in semantic interpretation.

5. Conclusion

In this paper, I have argued that particular grammatical constructions, those that combine a dependent grammatical element with the autonomous elements it is dependent on, must be interpreted in a single domain (the unity of domain). This is a necessary part of the interpretation of such constructions, which include almost all of the common grammatical constructions, for example predicate-argument, head-modifier, noun-genitive, verb-adverb. In order to achieve the semantic coherence specified by the unity of domain, there must often occur an adjustment of the domains of the individual words in the construction. Domain adjustment is also a major factor, if not the major factor, in a significant portion of what are usually called *metaphors* and *metonymies*. In order to focus on this aspect of the interpretation of words, I have more precisely characterised the conceptual semantic phenomena that I have described as *domain mapping* and *domain highlighting* respectively. In the case of metonymy, it is particularly appropriate to choose a different term to describe the domain adjustment involved.

The conceptual unity of domain is one of at least three conceptual unities. The second is the unity of mental space, including "physical" space and time. A mental space is a conceptual construct that is used to describe the ontological status of entities and situations – e.g. a belief, a desire, a counterfactual hypothesis, or even reality at a particular location in time or space (Fauconnier 1994). Fauconnier (1994) describes in detail the types of conceptual mappings that are required in interpreting sentences in which predicates and arguments originate in different mental spaces, namely the variety of counterpart relations. Consider, for example, example (82), which builds a belief mental space M for Margaret's belief:

(82)   Margaret believes that her sister bought a car.

In (82), assume that Margaret has a sister in "reality" (R; that is, mutually believed space). The complement of *believes* must be interpreted in Mary's belief space M, so the phrase *her sister* must designate individuals in M, which the listener normally takes to be the counterparts of Margaret and her sister in M. Likewise, *a car* must be interpreted as designating an individual in M, whether or not there is a counterpart in R. The crucial point for us here is that all of the entities in the complement are interpreted in M, and if the "normal" interpretation of a linguistic expression is to an entity in a mental space other than M, e.g. Margaret in (82), it must be interpreted as referring to a counterpart in M to be coherent.

The third conceptual unity is that of selection (cf. the minor propositional act of selection in Croft 1990), in which predicate and argument must match in individuation, quantification or number (i.e. 'plexity', as defined by Talmy 2000:ch.II-1) and genericness (generic vs. specific, or type vs. token). These construals have been called granularity coercions (Hobbs 1989).[26] The necessity of the unity of selection is illustrated in the following examples:

(83)   She is resembling her mother more and more every year.

       [stative predicate construed as an inchoative process]

(84)   "Fresh walnut meats"

       [substance construed as a set of individuated objects]

(85)   Cats have whiskers.

       [bare plural construed as reference to a kind with generic predicate]

(86)   Cats were lounging on the patio.

       [bare plural construed as reference to a set of cats with specific predicate]

There is some reason to believe that the three conceptual unities (domain, mental space, selection) are the most important ones in imposing semantic coherence on an utterance. Langacker (1991:33) argues that both nominal and verbal structure involve three levels of organisation: the level of a concept type, manifested in a bare noun or bare verb stem; the level of a grounded instance of the type, manifested in a

---

[26] The unity of selection has been the topic of a considerable amount of work in formal semantics, but no satisfactory unified account has been presented as yet.

full nominal with determiner and a full finite clause; and an intermediate level of an instance of the type, corresponding to the grammatical unit at which quantification occurs. The conceptual unity of domain is at the level of the type: a concept type is defined against its base domain. The unity of mental space is at the level of a grounded instance of a type: grounding involves situating the instance with respect to speaker/hearer knowledge (Langacker 1987:126-127), which is modelled by mental spaces (Langacker 1991:97). Finally, the unity of selection is at the level of the instance, since it is at that level that individuation and quantification occur. The conceptual unities represent the requirement that dependent verbal predications must be semantically coherent with respect to the autonomous nominal predications that they are dependent on.[27]

In comprehending an utterance, the listener assumes the unities of domain, mental space, and selection, and attempts to interpret the sentence as conforming to those unities, employing metaphor, metonymy, granularity, counterpart relations, and other *focal adjustments* (Langacker 1987:3.3) where necessary. The listener is under a strong Gricean convention that the speaker is being semantically coherent, particularly at the lower levels of semantic composition, such as predicate-argument and head-modifier constructions. For that reason, the listener will generally try as much as possible to adjust the meanings of the parts to yield a coherent interpretation of the whole. The conceptual unities of domain, mental space, and selection are a significant part of what it means for an utterance to be coherent. This adjustment is how the interpretation of the parts is influenced by the meaning of the whole, as described in the introduction. If such focal adjustments do not yield sensible interpretations, or are conventionally prohibited due to the constructions and inflections involved, the listener may assume the sentence is incoherent. A better understanding of the specific types of coherence (the unities) will cast much more light on the "irregularities" of the process of semantic composition. Nevertheless, the process can never be made fully algorithmic. As we observed for the unity of domain, elements of an utterance interact with context, that is, conceptual structures already activated to various levels at the time of the speech event. This will be true for the other unities as well. But this fact is not surprising, and in fact should be of some comfort for those of us who believe that the expressiveness and flexibility of language is essentially open-ended.

---

[27] The notion of conceptual unity is very similar to the notion of "isotopie" (Greimas 1966, Rastier 1987). However, I am using "conceptual unity" to refer only to the three levels of organisation of a clause or phrase, whereas "isotopie" is used for a much wider range of phenomena of semantic coherence.

Afterword

The essay reprinted here provides a detailed explication of the notion of a conceptual domain in cognitive linguistics, and applies the concept of domain to the phenomena of metaphor and metonymy. Following Lakoff & Johnson (1980), I argued that a metaphor involves a mapping from a source domain to a target domain, whereas metonymy involves a shift from one domain in a domain matrix to another. The concept of a domain assumes a uniform and general representation of a speaker's encyclopedic knowledge of experience. In the encyclopedic view, knowledge of a concept differs in degree of centrality, not in kind ('dictionary' vs. 'encyclopedia'). In both metaphor and metonymy, knowledge of different degrees of centrality is involved in production and comprehension.

Metaphor involves a mapping of conceptual structures from the source to the target domain. While some metaphors are more general (schematic) than others, and some are more productive than others (see Clausner & Croft 1997), there is no dictionary-style separation of so-called linguistic meaning from encyclopedic meaning in our understanding of metaphors. For example, the understanding of the metaphor LOVE IS A BODILY STATE, in examples (5-13), requires an encyclopedic knowledge of both love and bodily states in order for a speaker to produce and understand the sentences in (5-13).

Domain shift, including metonymy, also requires the employment of encyclopedic meaning. The various domains combined in the domain matrix of a concept sometimes call forth relatively peripheral encyclopedic knowledge of the concept. The well-known metonymic mapping from a publication to the company that publishes it, illustrated in examples (19-20), is relatively peripheral knowledge (not being intrinsic). The contrast between the acceptable examples of synecdoche in examples (25-27) and the unacceptable examples (28-30) turns on relatively peripheral knowledge about salient functions associated with parts of the body and the functions of the groups or institutions with which the people possessing those parts of the body are associated.

The production and comprehension of metaphors and domain shifts is a linguistic process: a sentence would be semantically incoherent if it were not for the proper interpretation of its metaphorical and metonymic expressions. The phenomena of metaphor and metonymy provide strong evidence of the absence of a sharp distinction between 'dictionary meaning' and 'encyclopedic knowledge'.

Much has been written on metaphor and metonymy, and much continues to be written on both of those semantic phenomena and their linguistic consequences. In the rest of this afterword, I would like to focus on a recent analysis that touches on topics discussed in this paper. Both analyses have to do with metonymy.

Nunberg (1995) establishes a contrast between *reference transfer* and *predicate transfer*. Reference transfer is the cognitive shift from the referent of one expression to the referent of another expression. Nunberg (1995:110) gives (87) as an example of reference transfer:

> (87)   This is parked out back. [customer referring to key he has just given
>   to parking lot attendant]

Nunberg argues (ibid.) that the actual referent of the linguistic expression is the shifted referent (the car) and not the key. Evidence for this is that it is the shifted referent that determines the linguistic features of the demonstrative. For instance, in Italian, the following example uses masculine singular forms, in agreement with *il camion* ('the truck') and not with *la chiave* ('the key'):

> (88)   Questo [masc.sg.] è parcheggiato [masc.sg.] in dietro.

Reference transfer is a purely pragmatic phenomenon, that is, no linguistic conventions are involved. For this reason, it does not affect the analysis of metonymy in this paper.

Predicate transfer, on the other hand, as illustrated in (89), does involve linguistic conventions:

> (89)   I am parked out back.

In this case, Nunberg argues that the person, not the vehicle, is the argument of the predicate *parked out back*. He points out that, unlike reference transfer, in predicate transfer, the linguistic features are determined by the person, not the vehicle. For example, (90) is used when more than one person, including the speaker, have a vehicle parked out back, but not when one person has more than one vehicle parked out back:

> (90)   We are parked out back.

Nunberg (1995:111) describes predicate transfer in this example as follows: "the predicate *parked out back* contributes a property of persons, the property they possess in virtue of the locations of their cars". He argues that predicate transfer can take place with any sort of predicate. The examples in (89-90) illustrate transfer of a predicate in the grammatical sense, or a dependent predication in Langacker's terms. The following examples illustrate predicate transfer of a common noun, or an autonomous predication (Nunberg 1995:115):

> (91)   That french fries is getting impatient.

> (92)   They played lots of Mozart.

Examples (91-92) illustrate linguistic phenomena that indicate predicate transfer of the common noun rather than the predicate (dependent predication). In (91), the number of the demonstrative modifier and the auxiliary verb is determined by the person who ordered the french fries (singular), not by the french fries themselves (plural). In (92), the quantifier matches the uncountability of 'music by Mozart', not the countability of *Mozart*.

Nunberg's analysis corresponds closely to the discussion of Langacker's active zones vs. the traditional analysis of metonymy at the end of section 2 of this paper. Langacker's active zone analysis for examples such as *We all heard the trumpet* corresponds to Nunberg's analysis of predicate transfer in examples (89-90). That is, the metonymic shift is represented as part of the semantic structure of the dependent predication. The traditional analysis of metonymy corresponds to Nunberg's analysis of predicate transfer in examples (91-92). That is, the metonymic shift is represented as part of the semantic structure of the autonomous predication.

Both Nunberg and I argue that both types are found. This observation does not affect my hypothesis that metonymy involves the highlighting of a different domain than "normal" in the domain matrix of the autonomous predication. The difference between active zone / shift in the dependent predication and traditional metonymy / shift in the autonomous predication is with respect to which linguistic unit the highlighted domain is conventionally assigned to.

Nunberg's analysis however does affect which domain is the single domain which the entire phrase or clause is profiled in. In the case of predicate transfer for the dependent predication, as in (89-90), the domain of the overall expression is that of people and certain properties they possess, not vehicles and their locations. In contrast, the domain of the overall expression in (91) is people, not food, and in (92) is music performance, not people (composers).

Nunberg further argues that (in my terms) whole sentences can be restricted to conform to the unity of domain. It would take too much space to go through his argument in detail. Nunberg in essence argues that in the cases which I gave in the paper to argue that domain unity is restricted to a dependent predication and the predications it is dependent on all involve predicate transfer of the dependent predication. Thus, if multiple modifiers are used, they must all conform to the unity of domain (Nunberg 1995:120):

(93)   They serve meat from corn-fed / Arkansas / happy / beheaded chickens.

(94)   They serve corn-fed / Arkansas / ??happy / ??beheaded chicken.

In (94), *corn-fed* and *Arkansas* involve predicate transfer of the adjective. The unacceptability of *happy* and *beheaded* in (94) is due to the constraint on predicate transfer that the property transferred is of significance to the argument: "the meat from chickens may vary according to what they were fed, but not how they were slaughtered" (Nunberg 1995:120).

Likewise, the unacceptability of conjunction and nonrestrictive modification in (96-97), compared to (95), is due to the fact that *tied* has a transferred reading which "denotes the property that shoes acquire when their laces have been tied" (Nunberg 1995:123):

(95)   Billy's shoes were neatly tied but dirty. [the shoes are dirty, not the laces]

(96)   ??Billy's shoes were neatly tied but frayed.

(97)   Billy tied his shoes, which were dirty / ??frayed.

Nunberg (1995:124) argues that cases such as (98-99) represent a genuine ambiguity between transfer of the dependent predication – *be widely read* in (98) – and transfer of the autonomous predication – *Yeats* in (99):

(98)   Yeats is still widely read, though he has been dead for more than 50 years.

(99)   Yeats is still widely read, even though most of it is out of print.

Nunberg's observations, if they prove to be generally correct, are equivalent to substantially tightening the conditions for unity of domain to an entire sentence, not just each dependent predication within a sentence.

References

Clausner, Timothy C.; Croft, William. 1997. "Productivity and schematicity in metaphors". *Cognitive science* 21. 247-282.

Croft, William. 1990. "A conceptual framework for grammatical categories (or, a taxonomy of propositional acts)". *Journal of semantics* 7. 245-279.

Croft, William. 1996. "What's a head?". In Laurie Zaring & Johan Rooryck (ed.), *Phrase structure and the lexicon.* Dordrecht: Kluwer. 35-75.

Cruse, D. Alan. 1986. *Lexical semantics.* Cambridge: Cambridge University Press.

Dirven, René. 1985. "Metaphor as a means for extending the lexicon". In Wolf Paprotté & René Dirven (ed.), *The ubiquity of metaphor. Metaphor in language and thought.* Amsterdam: John Benjamins. 85-119.

Downing, Pamela. 1977. "On the creation and use of English compound nouns". *Language* 53. 810-842.

Fauconnier, Gilles. 1994 [1985]. *Mental spaces. Aspects of meaning construction in natural language.* Cambridge: Cambridge University Press.

Goossens, Louis. 1990. "Metaphtonymy. The interaction of metaphor and metonymy in expressions for linguistic action". *Cognitive linguistics* 1. 323-340. Revised reprint (1995) in Louis Goossens, Paul Pauwels, Brygida Rudzka-Ostyn, Anne-Marie Simon-Vandenbergen & Johan Vanparys, *By word of mouth. Metaphor, metonymy and linguistic action in a cognitive perspective.* Amsterdam: John Benjamins. 159-174.

Greimas, Algirdas-Julien. 1966. *Sémantique structurale. Recherche de méthode.* Paris: Larousse.

Haiman, John. 1980. "Dictionaries and encyclopedias". *Lingua* 50. 329-357.

Haiman, John. 1983. "Iconic and economic motivation". *Language* 59. 781-819.

Haiman, John. 1985. *Natural syntax.* Cambridge: Cambridge University Press.

Hobbs, Jerry. 1989. "Granularity". In Daniel S. Weld & Johan de Kleer (ed.), *Readings in qualitative reasoning about physical systems.* San Mateo: Morgan Kaufmann. 542-545.

Lakoff, George. 1987. *Women, fire and dangerous things. What categories reveal about the mind.* Chicago: University of Chicago Press.

Lakoff, George. 1990. "The invariance hypothesis. Is abstract reason based on image-schemas?". *Cognitive linguistics* 1. 39-74.

Lakoff, George; Johnson, Mark. 1980. *Metaphors we live by.* Chicago: University of Chicago Press.

Lakoff, George; Turner, Mark. 1989. *More than cool reason. A field guide to poetic metaphor.* Chicago: University of Chicago Press.

Langacker, Ronald W. 1984. "Active zones". In Claudia Brugman & Monica Macauley (ed.), *Proceedings of the tenth annual meeting of the Berkeley Linguistics Society.* Berkeley: Berkeley Linguistics Society. 172-188. Reprint (1990) in Ronald W. Langacker, *Concept, image, and symbol. The cognitive basis of grammar.* Berlin: Mouton de Gruyter. 189-201.

Langacker, Ronald W. 1987. *Foundations of cognitive grammar*, vol. 1. *Theoretical prerequisites.* Stanford: Stanford University Press.

Langacker, Ronald W. 1991. *Foundations of cognitive grammar*, vol. 2. *Descriptive application.* Stanford: Stanford University Press.

Lyons, John. 1977. *Semantics* (2 vol.). Cambridge: Cambridge University Press.

Nunberg, Geoffrey. 1979. "The nonuniqueness of semantic solutions. Polysemy". *Linguistics and philosophy* 3. 143-184.

Nunberg, Geoffrey. 1995. "Transfers of meaning". *Journal of semantics* 12. 109-132.

Rastier, François. 1987. *Sémantique interprétative*. Paris: Presses universitaires de France.

Rosch, Eleanor. 1978. "Principles of categorization." In Eleanor Rosch & Barbara Lloyd (ed.), *Cognition and categorization*. Hillsdale: Lawrence Erlbaum. 27-48.

Searle, John R. 1979. "Literal meaning". In his *Expression and meaning. Studies in the theory of speech acts*. Cambridge: Cambridge University Press. 117-136.

Talmy, Leonard. 2000. *Toward a cognitive semantics* (2 vol.). Cambridge: M.I.T. Press.

Taylor, John R. 1995 [1989]. *Linguistic categorization. Prototypes in linguistic theory*. Oxford: Oxford University Press.

Turner, Mark. 1990. "Aspects of the invariance hypothesis". *Cognitive linguistics* 1. 247-255.

Ullmann, Stephen. 1957 [1951]. *The principles of semantics*. Oxford: Blackwell.

Wierzbicka, Anna. 1987. *English speech act verbs. A semantic dictionary*. Sydney: Academic Press.

Wierzbicka, Anna. 1988. *The semantics of grammar*. Amsterdam: John Benjamins.

Part Three

WORDS, WORDS,

WORDS

Re-cycling in the encyclopedia[1]

Richard Hudson

*University College London, Department of Phonetics and Linguistics, Gower Street,
London, WC1E 6BT, United Kingdom
E-mail: dick@linguistics.ucl.ac.uk*

and

Jasper Holmes

*Rijksuniversiteit Groningen, Afdeling Engels, Postbus 716, 9700 AS Groningen,
The Netherlands
E-mail: j.w.holmes@let.rug.nl*

0. Introduction

The principle of "recycling" holds that (mental) concepts are "recycled" rather than
duplicated. On the one hand, a concept that is used outside language may be recycled as the meaning of a word (language-external recycling); and on the other, a
concept which serves as the meaning of one word may be recycled as part of the
meaning of another (language-internal recycling). The alternative in both cases is to
postulate a concept which is both similar in "content" but distinct in status (and
name). At one level, this is just a matter of common sense (Hudson 1985): why
should we, as learners, build two distinct concepts when one concept could do both

---

[1] We would like to thank Joe Hilferty and an anonymous reviewer for comments on an earlier version.

jobs? For example, if a child has a concept "bicycle" for dealing with the world (of bicycles), why should it construct a distinct concept for dealing with the word *BICYCLE*? Much more likely, surely, is that a single concept will be used for both purposes. Similarly, if a child has a concept "bicycle" for dealing with the word *BICYCLE*, why should it construct a further concept to fill the vehicle role in the meaning of the verb *CYCLE*?

However, this principle is clearly not self-evident because there are well-established intellectual traditions which deny it. Theories of meaning traditionally distinguish sharply between dictionary-meaning and encyclopedic information, which at least allows the interpretation that the concepts involved must be different: there must be one "bicycle" concept defined by the dictionary, and a different one defined by the encyclopedia. Another tradition that ignores the principle is practical lexicography, where different words are defined separately (often by separate lexicographers) without any attempt to build one word's meaning into that of the other. E.g., in the Collins Cobuild English Language Dictionary we find the following two definitions:

(1a)   **Skill** is the knowledge and ability that enables you to do something such as a job, game, or sport very well.

(1b)   Someone who is **skilful** at doing something does it well.

Does this mean that skill requires a higher level of competence ("... very well") than merely being skilful ("... well"), or that it is possible to be skilful at doing something which is not covered by the list of examples mentioned for skill? If the principle of recycling had been respected, the second definition would have included the word *skill* (e.g. "Someone who is skilful has a skill"). In view of these departures from the principle, it clearly needs to be supported by evidence.

The theory of recycling allows testable predictions. If a concept is involved in the definitions of two words, it should carry the same uncertainties of interpretation in both words. This seems to be true in at least some cases. For example, the meaning of *MOTHER* applies clearly in some cases, but less clearly in others where the traditional roles are divided between a birth-mother and a nurture-mother (Lakoff 1987:74-84). As predicted by recycling, exactly the same uncertainties arise in interpreting words such as *PARENT*, *GRANDMOTHER* and all the terms whose definitions build on "parent" – *AUNT*, *UNCLE*, *COUSIN* and so on (Hudson 1995:63-72). This supports the view that the definition of (for example) "parent" really is 'mother or father', where "mother" is exactly the same concept that is also the sense of *MOTHER*.

The purpose of this paper is to explore the concept "cycling", the sense of the verb *CYCLE* as used in sentence (2) (which is normal British usage):[2]

---

[2] It appears to be less familiar in America, where the verb *BIKE* is more commonly used (cf. below).

(2)   I cycled to work.

The discussion will provide further evidence for language-external recycling of concepts. If the same concepts which are linked to words are also linked to more general conceptual "frames", then in principle anything language users know about bicycles should be able to affect the linguistic behaviour of CYCLE.

However, our conclusion will not be that word meanings are simply non-linguistic concepts that have names. We shall show that the language itself imposes a structure of its own on the concepts, and argue that far from refuting the claim of recycling this is exactly what we should expect. The analysis will be couched in terms of Word Grammar (henceforth WG; cf. Hudson 1990, 1998).

1. Bicycles

The most obvious fact about cycling is that it typically involves a bicycle. (We return to atypical cases below.) Any analysis of Cycling must therefore recycle Bicycle.[3] It would be ridiculous to define the means of locomotion in cycling without any reference at all to Bicycle.

What, then, is a bicycle? This question has been answered at length by Wierzbicka (1985:104-123), whose discussion shows how much we all know about bicycles, and whose definition fills a whole page (ibid:112), of which we quote the first few lines:

(3)   A KIND OF THING MADE BY PEOPLE,

        it is made for one person to be able to go by means of it from one
        place to another

        faster than by walking and with less effort (...)

The definition is expressed in part in terms of a universal metalanguage containing a limited number of terms. Wierzbicka claims that this "Natural Semantic Metalanguage" reflects a "language-like innate conceptual system", and could in principle be used as the sole metalanguage for semantic definitions (Wierzbicka 1996:22).

We find this claim unconvincing. First, we notice that her own definition of Bicycle applies the principle of recycling by using terms which are not part of the universal metalanguage. The passage quoted includes *faster*, *walking* and *effort*, and in the later parts of the definition we find *legs*, *feet*, *hands*, *wheels*, *frame*, and *stick out*.

---

[3] From now on we shall use upper case initials when referring to the names of concepts, to save repeating the phrase *the concept "X"*. Words will continue to be written using small capitals.

Without these terms, the definition would have been much worse – not only impossibly long and tedious, but also less revealing.

However, more importantly, there is a fundamental conflict between her theory and the principle of recycling. Her aim is to define all concepts in terms of the same set of primitives, but this excludes recycling in principle. As we have just seen, WHEEL is included in her definition as a concession to practicality, but this presumably counts as a weakness in the analysis, when judged by her principle, whereas we consider it a strength. When the principle is applied rigidly, the result is surely a poor analysis. To take a simple example, her definition of Bicycle repeatedly refers to the pedals, but avoids using the term PEDAL because this is not part of the universal metalanguage. Consider the following extracts from later in the definition:

(4a)   it has two parts for the person's feet

which are attached to the frame near the bottom and which are connected with the wheels

so that by pushing these parts with one's feet one can cause the wheels to turn

(4b)   the parts for the feet are as small as they can be without being too small to support a person's feet

The definition leaves everything to the reader's linguistic and pragmatic skills, whereas a good analysis would surely make the link between the "parts for the feet" explicit by assigning them a single name within this definition.

Worse still, the ban on recycling prevents the definition of one concept from building on that of another concept. What about Pedal itself? It too needs a definition, but this will have to start from scratch, rather than building on the information about pedals in the definition for Bicycle. This is exactly the opposite of what recycling demands. We believe that the definition of Bicycle should refer to Pedal, so that each definition supports the other; and the reason why we believe this is not just for analytical brevity, but because we believe that knowledge is, in fact, integrated in this way.

Another theoretical claim that underlies Wierzbicka's analysis of Bicycle is that a distinction can be drawn between the "mental dictionary" and the "mental encyclopedia" (1985:113, 1996:335). This allows her to exclude a great deal of historical information which she finds in the Encyclopedia Britannica, on the grounds that most people know what a bicycle is without knowing about its history. This may well be true (though most people probably know a few things about the history), but what does the claim mean? As we commented earlier, one possible interpretation is that there are in fact two concepts, one of which acts as the meaning of BICYCLE while the other is the locus of the encyclopedic knowledge. But if that is the case, what is the relationship between these two concepts? Surely the whole point of the distinction is to distinguish different kinds of knowledge about the *same* concept? But if the same concept is involved in both kinds of knowledge (as we assume is the case), what does the distinction mean in psychological terms? After all, it is generally accepted that radically different kinds of knowledge may converge on a single concept – consider, for example, how different a lexeme's phonological structure is from its syntactic classification – so there is no general requirement that a concept's characteristics should be in some sense uniform. The issues that arise are too general and fundamental to pursue here, but we register serious doubts about this distinction.

So, what *is* a bicycle? As suggested for this very concept in Hudson (1995:24-28), we believe that Bicycle is part of a network of concepts that define each other, each concept being recycled in the definitions of others. As Wierzbicka's definition shows, the concepts relevant to Bicycle are of different types and have to do with at least the following: a bicycle's function, structure, mode of operation and size. We shall not attempt a "complete" definition simply because we do not believe this is a meaningful target. After all, if we are trying to model the knowledge of actual speakers, we must accept that different speakers have different amounts of knowledge.[4]

Here is an attempt at the beginnings of a prose definition:

> (5a) A bicycle has a frame, two wheels, a saddle, pedals, a chain and handlebars.

> (5b) A bicycle's rider sits on its saddle.

> (5c) A bicycle's rider holds its handlebars.

> (5d) A bicycle's rider pushes the pedals round.

> (5e) A bicycle's rider rides it.

This definition contains much less information than Wierzbicka's, so it is not fair to compare its length with hers; but it is fair to point out how its length is minimised by the repetition of single terms like PEDAL which will be defined separately. In fact, all the statements in (5) form part of the definitions of the other terms involved: just as Riding is part of the definition of Bicycle, so Bicycle is part of the definition of Riding. Circularity is avoided because neither concept is defined exclusively in terms of the other. The idea that concepts are defined by their relationships to other concepts is reminiscent of traditional "field theories" of semantics, but unlike those theories the notion of "contrast" plays no part here; a concept is defined by what it

---

[4] E.g., Wierzbicka reports that spokes are mounted tangentially, i.e. at right angles to the radius of the hub. Some people know this, others do not. One of us learned it from Wierzbicka.

"is" (i.e. by its positive links to other concepts) rather than by its contrasts with what it is not.

To further clarify this idea, consider (5b). This statement helps to define Bicycle by specifying that a bicycle is ridden by someone who sits on its saddle. It also helps to define a number of other concepts: Rider (one kind of rider sits on a bicycle's saddle), Sitting (one kind of sitting is the relationship between a bicycle's rider and its saddle) and Saddle (one kind of saddle is the part of a bicycle where the rider sits). Ultimately, the analysis of any one concept is complete only when every other concept in the (same) mind has been analysed. We shall partially satisfy this obligation for Riding, but we shall have to leave all the other concepts undefined.

2. Networks as flexible frames

One of the leading ideas in recent theorising about lexical semantics has been the idea that concepts are linked in complex structures called "frames". These are the foundation of the theory of Frame Semantics (Fillmore 1985, Fillmore & Atkins 1992), according to which a word's meaning is understood "with reference to a structured background of experience, beliefs or practices, (...) the background frames that motivate the concept that the word encodes" (Fillmore & Atkins 1992:77). The classic examples of frames are Commercial Transaction (background to Buying, Selling, Paying, Charging and so on) and Risk (background to the meanings of DANGER, VENTURE, GAMBLE, RISKY and other words, in addition to RISK itself). More generally, there are global theories of knowledge which claim that all knowledge is organised in terms of frames (Barsalou 1992).

One of the attractions of these ideas is the importance they give to relationships, in contrast with theories that merely recognise "associations" among concepts (what Barsalou calls "feature-list representations") – e.g. an association between Bird and Feathers, Wings, Eggs and so on. The structures we actually find are more like a bicycle frame, where each part has a definite (and rigid) relationship to each other part. Cognitive science has established that mere association is not enough, so we must pay attention to the specific relationships among concepts (Reisberg 1997:280-285). The essential characteristic of frames is that they define a set of more or less specific relationships among the concepts that they bring together – e.g. "buyer", "seller", "money" and "goods" in the frame for Commercial Transaction.

A more negative feature of frames is the implication that knowledge is divided into frame-sized packages, each with its own natural boundaries and identity. As Lehrer & Kittay (1992:16) point out, this raises serious analytical problems to which it is hard to see any solution: "How do we decide that terms belong to different semantic frames (...), rather than saying that they have different meanings within one frame (...)?". For instance, by claiming that Money is part of the Commercial Transactions frame, are we denying that it is part of the Wealth frame, the Banking frame or the Work frame? Similarly, Goods seems to belong just as much to Ownership as to Commercial Transactions. When boundaries are problematic, it is often worth considering whether they really exist and to look for a theoretical alternative in which the boundaries concerned play no part.

In this case, the alternative is the widely held view that knowledge constitutes a *network* (Reisberg 1997:257-303). A network can give the same information about relationships as frames, but without demanding any boundaries between parcels of knowledge. The difference between networks and frames is largely a matter of metaphor. In a frame analysis each concept is a box, whereas in a network it is a point or node. In both cases the concept is defined by its relationships to other concepts, but in a frame analysis the definition is contained in the box, whereas in a network it is just the totality of links from the concept concerned to other concepts. In a frame analysis it is possible to imagine a distinction between the "defining" relationships, contained inside the box, and other, descriptive or encyclopedic relationships, which are left outside; but such a distinction is impossible, in principle, in a network. Frame analysis raises the problem of frame boundaries defined by Lehrer & Kittay; network analysis does not.

Returning now to the definition of Bicycle, we can show how the prose definition given in (5) can be translated into a network. Each of the concepts named is represented by a node, and each relationship is a function which is represented by a labelled arrow that points from the argument to its value. Some of the nodes are labelled for convenience, but the labels are actually redundant, since every node is already defined uniquely by its relations to other nodes. Suppose we assume, to start with, that each verb-noun pair in the prose definition corresponds to just one relationship in the diagram. The result is shown in figure 1, which contains some relationships that are rather implausible, such as "sits on" and "pushes round". The diagram does not yet include all the information from (5): for example, it ignores the frame, the wheels and the chain. The main point, however, is that a concept may be shown as just one node on which several relationships converge, providing its "definition". Thus Bicycle is by definition the concept which stands in this particular set of relationships to Pedal, Handlebars, and so on, and the rider (shown by the unnamed dot) is defined by its relationships.

Various improvements to the network in figure 1 are possible. One unsatisfactory feature is the naive way in which the distinction between concepts and relationships is applied, based as it is directly on grammatical categories: nouns define concepts and verbs define relationships. Like many others (e.g. Jackendoff 1983:67), we believe grammatical class to be irrelevant to status in conceptual structure, so concepts may be defined by verbs as well as by nouns. Accordingly, we assume that the network will include concepts for "states of affairs" like Sitting (or Sitting-on) and Pushing (or Pushing-round) which can be exploited here. This gives us the network in figure 2.

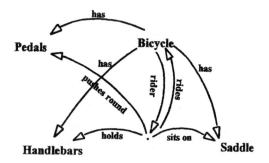

Figure 1

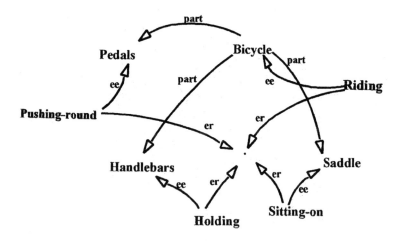

Figure 2

All the relationships are now rather general and drawn from a small list – in this case just Part (replacing the less informative Has), and the two provisional role names Er (for Sitter, Pusher and so on) and Ee. The diagram is more complicated than the first because single direct relationships (e.g. "sits on") have been replaced by pairs of relationships (Er, Ee) to a linking concept (Sitting-on). However, this price is worth paying for the benefit of a more homogeneous semantics. Instead of assuming that nouns map onto concepts and verbs onto relationships, we can assume that both kinds map onto concepts; and instead of assuming that noun meanings are defined by links whereas verb meanings are links, we can define both in the same way. Thus Sitting is a concept node linked to others (Posture, Vertical, Bottom, Seat, Weight, On and so on), and just like Bicycle, the concept Sitting is defined by the sum total of these links.

The unified view of word meaning illustrated here is rather uncontroversial among cognitive linguists, who would probably agree for example that the concept Arriving can be expressed equally well either by a verb or by a noun (*ARRIVE, ARRIVAL*) and most relationships double up as the sense of some noun (*DIFFERENCE, MIDDLE, RELATIONSHIP* and so on). Somewhat more controversially, however, we are not convinced by those like Wierzbicka (1988) and Langacker (1987) who argue that grammatical differences always indicate subtle semantic differences of "construal" which should affect the semantic structure. In our view, the sense of the verb *ARRIVE* is precisely the same concept as the sense of the noun *ARRIVAL*; they are exact synonyms (though semantic differences result, of course, from the effects of verb and noun inflections).

Our approach is therefore basically orthodox in relation to the tradition of cognitive linguistics, but it departs from the tradition of predicate logic by denying the simple mapping between syntax and semantics which underlies much of predicate logic; in this, however, it follows a widely accepted recent tradition which includes ACT-R (Anderson 1993), Conceptual Dependency analysis (Schank & Rieger 1974) and Conceptual Graphs (Sowa 1984). The assumption in predicate logic is that the semantic predicate is defined by the syntactic predicate (which includes at least the verb), and its arguments are defined by the syntactic subject and possibly other syntactic "arguments". For instance, *Pat sat on the bicycle* maps to something like "Sitting-on (Pat, the-bicycle)". The predicate and its arguments have quite different statuses in the logic – for example, the arguments may be variables, but this is (normally) not allowed for the predicate. In our analysis, in contrast, the semantic structure consists of three concepts (Pat, The-bicycle, Sitting-on) and two relationships (Er and Ee), each of which has an argument (Sitting-on) and a value (respectively Pat and The-bicycle). The two analyses are contrasted in figure 3. In spite of this fundamental difference, our analysis does preserve one of the assumptions of predicate logic, which is that concepts are not linked as equals (except in coordination). Wherever a pair of concepts is linked, the link "belongs" to one of them; for example, the Er link belongs to Sitting-on, not to the cyclist, because we know that Sitting-on needs an Er, a sitter (just as a grin needs a grinner, in spite of the Cheshire Cat); but a person need not be involved in Sitting-on, and only becomes a sitter by virtue of a link to Sitting-on. In the diagram this asymmetry is shown by the direction of the arrow, which goes from the owning concept (its argument) to the other concept, which is its value.

PREDICATE CALCULUS

Sitting-on (Pat, the-bicycle)

WORD GRAMMAR

Figure 3

In summary, then, grammatical word classes are not reflected in the semantics. As far as verbs and nouns are concerned, they are all linked permanently to at least one sense, and all senses have the same status: they are concepts which are linked in many different ways to other concepts. Instead of being divided into "frames", knowledge spreads without boundaries across the whole network. We must now address an important question for any network theory, which is how to distinguish the various links from one another.

The example just given might suggest that we are committed to searching for a very small set of primitive relationships such as Er and Ee, but this is not so. Indeed, as we shall show below, it is possible to interpret the label *er* either as the name of a constant (like the traditional Agent) or as a variable whose value depends on the owning concept – the rider of Riding, the sitter of Sitting and so on. As in Sowa's theory of Conceptual Graphs (conveniently summarised in Luger & Stubblefield 1993:368-378), we assume that a large number of relationships may be distinguished: rider, sitter, colour, name, meaning, pronunciation, and so on. This is helpful, even essential, if each concept is linked in many different ways to other concepts. For example, a word has a pronunciation, a spelling, a meaning, a word-class, a language, a style and perhaps other attributes, each of which is shown by a separate link, and each of these links must be distinguished from the others.

It is controversial to assume an open-ended list of relationships, because each one must somehow be defined; the same objection can be made of course to any set of concepts, but it is easier to see how non-relational concepts define each other. It is often objected that the attractions of a network approach presuppose a small, predefined list of relationships (Reisberg 1997:280-281), so we must ask how relationships are defined. The answer is that they are defined in just the same way as concepts: by their place in the total network, so the labels are strictly redundant. Firstly, a complex relationship can be defined in terms of simpler ones: for example, the Grandparent relationship can be defined in terms of Parent (Grandparent of X = Parent of Parent of X), and Rider-of (a direct link between the rider and the vehicle) in terms of Er, Ee and Riding, as shown in figure 4.

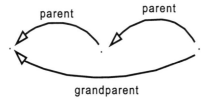

grandparent

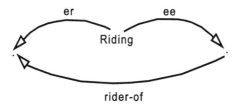

rider-of

Figure 4

The second way of defining relationships in the network is the same mechanism by which concepts are linked in an "Isa" hierarchy. So just as Dog isa Mammal, we can classify relationships: Parent isa Relative, Rider isa Er, and Rider-of isa User-of. In WG diagrams the Isa link is shown by a small triangle which rests on the supercategory and whose apex is linked by a line to the instance. Figure 5 shows how this system can also be applied to relationships. As far as the analysis of Bicycle is concerned, this means that we can define Rider as a derived relationship, based on the concept Riding and the two more basic relationships Er and Ee, and similarly for Pedaller, Holder and Pusher. If necessary we can even define specific variations on the Part relationship, such as "Saddle-of" and "Frame-of", in terms of the basic Part relationship plus the categories to which the things concerned belong.

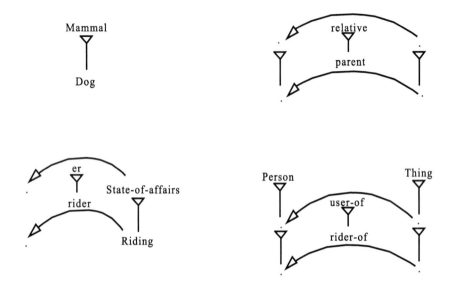

Figure 5

Such derived relationships may be needed in natural-language semantics for possessive constructions (e.g., *my nose* involves a relationship Nose-of), but they also have
two advantages in network analysis. First, they reduce long-distance relationships to
combinations of local relationships; for example, Grandparent establishes a direct
link between nodes which would otherwise be linked only indirectly, but once established this link may itself be used in defining other relationships (e.g. in this case,
Great-grandchild of X = Child of Grandchild of X). This has a bearing on the shape
of the network and seriously affects the way in which activation will spread from
node to node when the network is in use. Clearly the process of defining one relationship in terms of a chain of others is selective, because spreading activation is
selective; so it is important to discover the principles on which the selection is based.

The second advantage of recognising derived relationships is that they combine the
flexibility of a network with the internal specificity of a frame. Suppose a concept
has many different parts whose internal relationships are rigidly fixed; this internal
structure can easily be defined in a frame, but it can also be specified in a network
provided that the various parts can be distinguished from one another in terms of
their relationship to the whole – in other words, if they are defined "functionally".
This is made possible by derived relationships. Take the example Bicycle. If a network for Bicycle defines the functions Frame-of, Front-Wheel-of and so on, it can
then define the relationships among their values, as in figure 6, which shows the
spatial relationships among some of the parts. In this diagram, we use the two dimensions as an analog equivalent of true space, just as one might use the left-right

dimension to represent time; but unlike the left-right convention we assume that this picture is in fact a plausible approximation to our actual mental representation of Bicycle (some kind of mental image, rather than a truly propositional structure – "a pattern in the 2½-D sketch that is loaded from long-term memory rather than from the eyes"; Pinker 1997:286). It should be obvious how this network could be expanded to include the remaining parts.

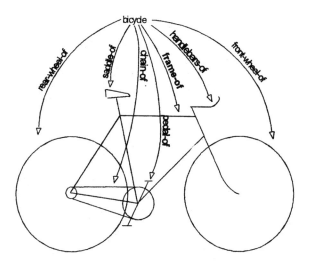

Figure 6

The analysis could be taken much further; for example, we could build an "Isa" hierarchy for all the objects (Bicycle, Pedal, etc), people (Rider) and activities (e.g. Riding, Holding), and provide fuller definitions of the parts in terms of their physical, interactional (e.g. force-dynamic) and functional properties. We could also discuss the status of non-typical bicycles by discussing the logic of default inheritance and the Best Fit Principle, which are central to WG theory. However, the main point that we have established is that the concept Bicycle can be fully defined by its relationships to other concepts, and that these relationships integrate the concept into a vast network which includes the totality of our conceptual knowledge. We shall now take this view for granted and move on to the definition of cycling.

3. Cycling as riding

The meaning of CYCLE is closely related to that of RIDE, so *ride a bicycle* is a close paraphrase. However, the two are not exact synonyms. The differences shall be explored in a later section; meanwhile, our task is to reveal the similarities.

If the senses of CYCLE and RIDE are the concepts Cycling and Riding, the first step is to show that Cycling is a kind of Riding – that Cycling isa Riding, as shown in figure 7, which also includes an Ee link (for the "ride-ee", the thing ridden) whose value isa Bicycle. In short, the diagram shows that cycling is riding a bicycle.

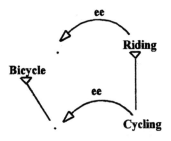

Figure 7

Of course, we know far more about Riding than the fact that it has an Ee. Riding is the sense of RIDE in examples like (6a) below:

(6a)   I rode the bicycle / *car / *plane / *boat.

(6b)   I drove the car / *bicycle / *plane / *boat.

(6c)   I flew the plane / *bicycle / *car / *boat.

(6d)   I sailed the boat / *plane / *bicycle / *car.

Clearly, Riding is restricted to certain kinds of vehicles – bicycles, but not cars or planes. Riding is not limited to bicycles, however: it is also possible with motorcycles and horses; indeed, horses are probably the default, as can be seen from the normal meaning of RIDE when used intransitively (e.g. *I go riding every evening*). What these three "vehicles" have in common is that the rider sits *on* them, not *in* them, so this is another fact that we can include: the rider is in the "on" relationship to the vehicle.

Thirdly, the rider is in control of the vehicle, in contrast with a different, intransitive, use of *RIDE* (followed by *in* or *on*), which we can call Mere-Riding. Though the preposition varies with the vehicle, *any* vehicle is possible in (7b) and (7c). This is further confirmation of the fact that a different sense is involved.

(7a)   I rode the bicycle / *bus / *ship / *train.

(7b)   I rode on the bicycle / bus / ship / train.

(7c)   I rode in the car / plane / boat.

If A rides on the back of B's bicycle, A is riding *on* the bicycle, but not riding it. If Riding involves being in control, it must be an example of Controlling, so Riding isa Controlling (as Cycling isa Riding). It must also isa Mere-Riding, because whenever you ride a bicycle you necessarily ride *on* it as well (and likewise for horses and motorcycles). Consequently, Riding isa Mere-Riding as well as Controlling: if you ride a bicycle, you ride *on* it and control it. All these relationships are shown in figure 8.

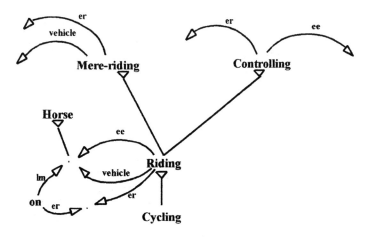

Figure 8 (the relationship labelled *lm* is Langacker's 1987 "landmark")

4. Language and concept formation

With part of the analysis in place, we can pause to consider a very general question: what role does language play in the learning of concepts? The principle of recycling predicts that language and general thinking share the same concepts: Bicycle is used not only in understanding the word BICYCLE but also in coping with bicycles in daily life. The question is whether these concepts are learned through language or through direct experience. Our most honest answer is that we (the authors) simply do not know, and cannot offer a well-developed theory of concept formation. However, some of the facts about the verb CYCLE are suggestive, and support the conclusion that some word meanings must be learned primarily on the basis of language, whereas others are probably learned primarily through direct observation. This conclusion is uncontroversial, but the relevant facts strike us as interesting.

It is easy to learn concepts for animals, foods and daily activities such as waking up, eating and walking simply by direct observation because the categories are clearly distinguished by bundles of cooccurring observable features (Rosch 1978:28). If concepts are defined by their links to other concepts, then a new concept is defined as soon as a unique bundle of links is established. It is likely that children learn the concept Bicycle in this way, since bicycles are so distinctive both visually and functionally. Similarly for Cycling. There is no reason to believe that either depends on the children's experience of the relevant word, provided they have direct experience of bicycles and of people cycling. The same is not true, however, of the concepts Riding, Driving, Sailing and Flying as illustrated in (6). Take Riding, which is applied to horses, bicycles and motorcycles:

(8)   I rode my horse / bicycle / motorcycle / *car / *boat / *plane.

This list of vehicles is motivated by the fact that in each case the rider sits *on* the vehicle, not *in* it, and the vehicle goes on land, not water or air. It seems, then, that the verb RIDE, at least as used in examples like (8), always has the same concept as its sense. Similar conclusions apply to the other verbs, so our minds must also contain the concepts Sailing and Flying. But how did we learn these concepts? It is possible that we might have arrived at this classification of "transported going" on the basis of direct observation, but many other classifications are equally easy to imagine: e.g., we might have made a fundamental distinction according to whether or not the vehicle had wheels, or a motor, each of which would have been different from the one that we actually have.[5] Nor can we assume that each concept is defined by the skill that it demands – riding a motorcycle requires some of the skills of driving and

---

[5] The criterion of wheels puts bicycles with cars, not with horses, and that of a motor puts motorcycles with cars, not with bicycles.

some of riding, and an ability to ride a horse scarcely generalises at all to riding a bicycle.

In short, the four-way division into Riding, Driving, Sailing and Flying is not "natural" and determined by the way the world is. Rather, we assume that it is learned largely on the basis of language: when we learned the verb *RIDE*, we created a concept for its sense on the basis of how we heard this verb used. This is a coherent concept definable by a single bundle of links to other concepts, but it is not an inevitable outcome of non-verbal experience. It is learned on the basis of experience, but verbal experience plays a crucial part, so our concept formation has been guided by the idiosyncracies of English. We assume that these in turn reflect the history of English society, going back to the days when Riding was exclusively tied to horseback, Driving to horse-drawn vehicles and Sailing to boats with sails and when Flying was defined by birds and insects. If this conclusion is correct, we might expect other languages to have organised this part of experience differently – as is indeed the case. E.g., in German, the verb used with bicycles is the same as for cars (*FAHREN*), and different from the one used with horses (*REITEN*).

Examples like these seem to us to support strongly the view that "knowledge of the world" and "knowledge of language" merge in a single network of knowledge to which both linguistic and non-linguistic experience can contribute. It is true that some concepts are relatively independent of language while others are relatively dependent on it, but there is no clear boundary between them, and no clear advantage in trying to draw one. We shall see further evidence for this view in the following sections.

5. Cycling as a manner of motion

Mere-riding in general (and cycling in particular) is a way of moving, so the analysis must relate it to the notion of moving. In this section, we look more closely at the concept Moving, and the four relationships that define it. All appear in figure 9.

The first two relationships, viz. manner and result, are inherited from higher categories: any event can have a manner, and many events other than moving may have results. Specific to Moving is the fact that there is a path, the end of which corresponds to the result. The path is a spatial relationship between three parts: a beginning, a middle and an end. Each of these isa Location: a relationship between a located (er) and a place (lm). The last part of the path, its end, is the same as the result of Moving, which is also a Location. Though the path and the result are closely connected as described, they must nevertheless remain separate. In (9), the second adjunct refers to the duration of the result; in (10), it refers to the movement's duration along the path.

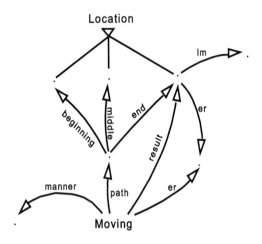

Figure 9

(9)   We went to Manchester for two days.

(10)   We went over the moors for two days.

Different kinds of Moving may be specified in terms of a *single* relationship, or in terms of a *combination*. (9) and (10) show that Going has a path as well as a result. Arriving is defined only in terms of its result (At), Rising in terms of its path (the end is Higher-than the beginning), Walking in terms of its manner (using the feet), Soaring in terms of both manner (rapid, uncontrolled) and path (as for Rising), Scramming in terms of both manner (rapid) and result (not here). A particular specification may be further detailed or overridden by the referents of syntactic dependents:

(11)   We arrived in Manchester.

(12)   He fell up the stairs.

(13)   My uncle can walk on his hands.

In (11) the result is further detailed, in (12) the default direction is reversed, and in (13) the default manner is overridden. This is possible only if the overriding specification is close to the default value. Walking on your hands counts as walking under the Best Fit Principle (Walking is the closest kind of locomotion available in the lexicon). Moving around on your belly counts as a kind of Crawling for the same reason.

Where a kind of Moving is *not* specified as to one of the relationships, that relationship is still inherited and can be expressed in syntactic structure. In (14) the result verb ARRIVE has path and manner adjuncts; in (15) the path verb RISE has manner and result adjuncts; and in (16) the manner verb CYCLE has path and result adjuncts.

(14)   We arrived by bicycle via Saddleworth.

(15)   The float suddenly rose out of the water.

(16)   We cycled over the moors to Manchester.

However, only those verbs that have a (compatible) lexically specified result may appear with certain result dependents:

(17)   We went in the park.

(18)   The float rose in the water.

(19)   We cycled in the sand pit.

Going has a result, identified by the referent of the preposition in (17). Rising and Cycling, by contrast, have no specific result, so the prepositions in (18) and (19) refer to the location of the respective activities. In order to specify the result of Rising, we must exploit the path relationship, by using a preposition like INTO. INTO, since it refers unambiguously to a path, can also force a directional interpretation onto CYCLE.

The above differences lie behind the widely recognised contrast between manner-of-motion and direction-of-motion verbs (Levin 1993:263-264, Slobin 1996). CYCLE is a manner-of-motion verb, Mere-riding a concept that defines motion in terms of manner rather than direction. The manner shared by all examples of Mere-riding is that the rider is carried by a vehicle; in contrast with (say) a load of coal, what the vehicle carries is a person. Thus, our definition of Mere-riding must relate it to the concepts Carrying, Vehicle and Person via the relationship Manner. Figure 10 shows the details.

The network in figure 10 could be paraphrased as follows: "You ride by being carried by a vehicle" or "When you ride you are carried by a vehicle". Notice how the role relations are reversed between carrying and riding, since the ride-er is the carry-ee, and the carry-er is the location of the ride-er. This example justifies treating the movement and its manner as two different events, in spite of the fact that they are simply different conceptualisations of the same event.

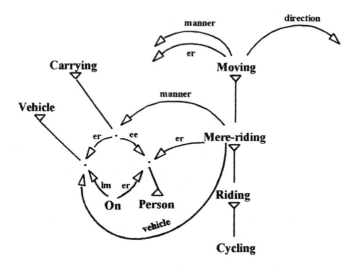

Figure 10

We could now go on to define Carrying as a combination of supporting and move-ment; for example, if you carry a tray, you support the tray and move at the same time, so the carrying isa both supporting and moving. However the analyses given so far already show how the concept can be defined "upwards" in relation to more general concepts. These higher-level concepts are relevant because of default in-heritance, so we now have a rich definition of Cycling which either by stipulation or by inheritance has the following characteristics:

(20a) Cycling isa Riding.

(20b) Cycling isa Mere-riding.

(20c) Cycling isa Moving.

(20d) The manner of Cycling isa Carrying.

(20e) The cycle-er of Cycling isa Person.

(20f) The vehicle of Cycling isa Bicycle.

(20g) The vehicle of Cycling is the carry-er of its manner.

(20h) The cycle-er of Cycling is the carry-ee of its manner.

(20i)   The cycle-er of Cycling is the Er of the On state whose landmark is its vehicle.

These facts are all represented formally in the network, so the prose versions are a direct translation of the network notation. The semi-formal metalanguage reads oddly, but should be comprehensible and can easily be turned into ordinary prose (with the technical terms and concept-names retained):

(21a)   Cycling is a kind of Riding.

(21b)   Cycling is a kind of Mere-riding.

(21c)   Cycling is a kind of Moving.

(21d)   Cycling involves carrying.

(21e)   A cyclist is a person.

(21f)   The vehicle used in cycling is a bicycle.

(21g)   In the carrying involved in cycling, the bicycle does the carrying.

(21h)   In this carrying, it is the cyclist that is carried.

(21i)   The cyclist rides on the bicycle.

6. Cycling as pedalling

We shall now consider cycling from a different perspective. One of the special features of cycling, as an example of riding, is that it is the only kind of riding in which the rider has to provide the energy.[6] A closely related feature is that it is only bicycles that have pedals; and the link between the features is that the pedals receive the rider's energy and help to turn it into forward movement.

Somewhat surprisingly perhaps, these characteristics of cycling may be reflected in the lexical relations of the verb CYCLE. The verb has the same stem as the noun, whose sense is Bicycle: thus (for those who have CYCLE meaning Bicycle) to cycle is to ride a cycle. The same is true of the lexemes BICYCLE and BIKE: to bicycle is to ride a bicycle, and to bike is to ride a bike. The same is not true, however, of other verbs of riding. For horses, we have no verb HORSE, nor, for Mere-Riding, do we

---

[6] Horse-riding may be energetic, but the energy produced by the rider is not what keeps the horse and rider moving forwards.

have verbs derived from CAR, WAGON, TRAIN, PLANE or any other kind of vehicle. Levin (1993:267-268) claims that most vehicle-nouns can be used as verbs, quoting examples such as BALLOON and BOAT, but our intuitions differ from hers, and we feel sure that even she could not use CAR or AUTOMOBILE as a verb. Admittedly, we can go boating (a pattern we shall consider below), but we can hardly boat to the next village. Even MOTORCYCLE and MOTORBIKE have no verb: you can cycle to the next village, but not motorcycle there. In short it is only verbs whose sense is Cycling that are "zero-derived" from a noun which names the vehicle.

On the other hand, there is a different area of vocabulary where this zero-derivation is very productive, and which may have provided the model for these exceptional lexemes. This is the semantic field which includes skating and skiing: when you skate you wear skates and when you ski you wear skis. The productivity of the system can be seen in neologisms like ROLLER-BLADE, which can be used either as a verb or as a noun. What these activities have in common is that the user provides the energy for forward movement through some kind of device fixed to their feet – let us call it (for want of an established term) "Foot-Powering". Admittedly, not all noun-verb pairs that define ways of moving fit this formula: exceptions include SKI-BOARD and SURF-BOARD, where the energy comes from elsewhere, and SLEDGE and TO-BOGGAN, where there is not even a device fixed to the feet. Nevertheless, the pattern may be clear enough to motivate the zero-derivation of Cycling verbs.

However suggestive it may be, though, the linguistic evidence does not show that Cycling isa Foot-Powering, even if there are enough similarities to justify the zero-derivation. The pattern is productive in skating and skiing, but not in cycling. We can ride a tandem, but when doing so we are not tandeming, and likewise for TRICYCLE and MONOCYCLE. The most we can assume is that Cycling shares some features with Foot-Powering which motivated the extension of the zero-derivation pattern – in the same way that it may perhaps have extended from skiing to ski-boarding and thence to surf-boarding, and from skiing to sledging.

Much more persuasive, however, is the analogy of a different verb in the field of cycling: PEDAL. This makes a close fit for Foot-Powering, both linguistically (to pedal is to use pedals) and conceptually, since it is the transmission of forward energy via a device fixed to the feet.[7] We can therefore conclude that the "pedalling" part of cycling isa Foot-Powering.

On a theoretical note, this is a clear example of the benefits of basing the analysis on a network rather than on frames. The analysis just suggested would be hard to express in frames because the frames for Riding and Foot-Powering are in general distinct, but show this small area of overlap. The frames cannot be simply combined by unification, but neither can either of them be treated as part of the other.

---

[7] The only uncertainty is whether pedals count as "fixed" to one's feet.

How, then, can we integrate Pedalling and Foot-Powering into the network for Cycling? The force-dynamic chain takes the energy from the rider's foot through the pedal (and chain) to the wheels, which convert the energy into forward movement. It is the forward movement of the bicycle that takes the rider forwards, so pedalling is only indirectly related to the rider's forward movement. Pedalling is not the manner of the cycling itself, but of its manner – it is the manner of movement for the bicycle, not for the cyclist. This is a happy conclusion, because Pedalling and Carrying would otherwise have been in competition as the value for the Manner function of a single concept. The solution, therefore, is to analyse Cycling as a kind of Riding whose manner is an example of Carrying whose manner is Pedalling.

The first step in the analysis is to focus on Pedalling. Unfortunately, as we have seen, this is itself a manner of motion like Skating and Skiing; so it has a manner of its own, which we shall call simply Pushing a device with the foot. This is the meaning of the verb *PEDAL*, as in (22).

(22)   We pedalled across the lake in the pedal-boat.

The analysis of Pedalling is shown in figure 11 as one example of Foot-Powering contrasting with (for example) Skating.

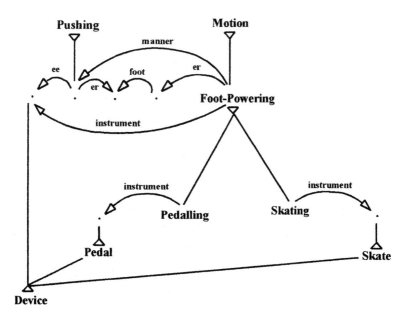

Figure 11

The next (and last) step is to show how the analysis of Pedalling is recycled as part of the analysis of Cycling. Ignoring the details that have already been covered in other diagrams, figure 12 shows the overall structure of Cycling. It shows that pedalling is an essential component of cycling. This seems to us correct; for example, if we had to describe someone free-wheeling down a hill we would use *RIDE* (or a verb such as *COAST*) rather than *CYCLE*.

(23)   I rode / *cycled down the steep hill without pedalling.

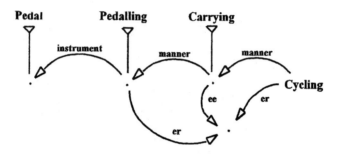

Figure 12

Pedalling is so important for Cycling that we may even be able to apply *CYCLE* to stationary exercise-bikes, where movement is obviously not relevant.

(24)   ?I cycle on the exercise-bike for half an hour every morning.

However, if this is possible, it must be a special use of *CYCLE* where the default Moving is overridden – depending on experience and entrenchment, either a nonce exception or a lexicalised sub-case of Cycle. The "cyclist" is still supported by the bike, so half of the definition of Carrying is still relevant, but it is not complete Carrying, nor is it complete Cycling.

What this section has achieved is to show that Pedalling is an important element of Cycling, which can be incorporated in a network definition in spite of the complexities caused by the fact that Pedalling defines the manner of the manner of Cycling.

7. Cycling as outdoor fun and indoor exercise

The analysis so far has focused only on the observable, physical aspects of Cycling – what the cyclist does, and what the results are in terms of movement. However we have ignored an important part of the activity, its purpose. Why do people cycle? The fact is, of course, that an infinite number of purposes are possible, and an ordinary sentence containing CYCLE leaves the choice completely open, so any of the continuations in (24) are possible:

(24)   I cycled to work

    a.   to save time.

    b.   to save money.

    c.   to keep fit.

    d.   to remind myself of my boyhood.

    e.   to outwit the police.

    f.   to win a bet.

    g.   to avoid the Martians.

However, there are two purposes which have been picked out for special linguistic treatment: fun and fitness. At least two grammatical patterns signal that an activity is being done for such purposes. We therefore assume that they belong together conceptually as different manifestations of a single super-purpose. In the absence of an established term we shall call it "Life-Enhancing", the point being that the activity is done for the benefit it does to the actor's emotional or physical well-being, and not for the specific results produced by the action.[8] In the case of cycling, this means that the cycling is done for fun or to improve fitness, rather than in order to get to the destination – indeed, there may not be a destination (as when cycling round a racetrack). The effect of these grammatical patterns, then, is to signal explicitly that what is normally just a by-product of the activity has been promoted to its main purpose.

The purpose of Life-Enhancing can be signalled by means of two different kinds of nominalisation. Both patterns are highly productive, so we shall start by exploring their use in domains other than cycling. One involves (once again) zero-derivation, but in this case the derivation of a noun from a verb. For example, WALK may be used as an ordinary common noun:

(26a)   I had a walk.

(26b)   I went for a walk.

(26c)   The walk did me good.

(26d)   I told them about my walk in the park.

---

[8] It would be interesting to speculate about the role of language in the development of this concept.

(26e)   What you need is a good walk.

If you walk to the kitchen to make a cup of coffee, you have not had a walk, less still gone for a walk. A walk is certainly an example of Walking, but it is walking whose purpose is not to reach a specific destination, but enjoyment. If you are invited to go for a walk, the route is open for negotiation and the destination may well be the same as the starting point. These observations suggest that the noun WALK has its purpose specified as Life-Enhancing. We do not know whether the verb has a default purpose (reaching the destination) or a completely unspecified purpose, though the result may be taken as the purpose in the absence of any other specification (it is the default).

The same seems to be true of all manner-of-motion verbs. A drive in the countryside aims at pleasure, not achievement, and likewise for a swim, a ride, a paddle, etc. However, complications arise with some verbs, one of which happens to be CYCLE and its synonyms. We cannot go for a bike or a bicycle; and presumably the reason for this is that as we pointed out earlier, the nouns BIKE and BICYCLE are already in use as the concrete nouns from which the verbs are derived – a bike/bicycle is what we ride on when we bike/bicycle.[9] Instead, we use a completely different noun, BIKE-RIDE. A bike-ride is certainly something one does for pleasure or fitness, and not just as a way to reach the destination: so when you cycle to work, you have not had a bike-ride. The choice of noun is not arbitrary, of course, if Cycling isa Riding, and BIKE-RIDE sits comfortably alongside HORSE-RIDE, DONKEY-RIDE and so on, as well as examples like TRAIN-RIDE which involve Mere-Riding rather than controlled Riding.

These verb-noun relations can be included in the network, but we must first explain how generalisable lexical relations can be handled. Since a network is purely declarative, there is no place for procedures which create one lexeme on the basis of another – e.g. a rule which creates an adverb by taking an adjective and adding -ly. Instead, relations between lexemes must be handled by named functions such as "noun-of" or "adverb-of"; thus QUICKLY is the adverb-of QUICK. The generalisation in this case is that the adverb-of an adjective shares the adjective's stem but also has -ly. In the case of zero-derivation, the two lexemes simply share the same stem. For verb-noun pairs where the verb is considered basic, the noun-of the verb has the verb's stem – hence the fact that WALK can be used either as a verb or as a noun.

As far as meaning is concerned, the derived lexeme also has a sense which is based on that of its source lexeme. As already indicated, we assume that a concept may act as the sense of either a noun or a verb, so the noun-of the verb may have exactly the

---

[9] This explanation is supported by a minor dialect difference between the two authors regarding the possible meaning of the noun CYCLE: it can have either a concrete meaning (Bicycle) or an abstract one, as in "go for a cycle", but not both.

same sense as the verb; we believe this is true of many nominalisations (e.g. AR-RIVAL, LOVE) but as the discussion above showed, it is not quite true of manner-of-motion verb-noun pairs like WALK, since the noun has the specific purpose of Life-Enhancing. This is the analysis presented in figure 13, which can be paraphrased as follows: the sense of a Mom ("manner of motion") verb is a motion which has a manner, and its noun (i.e. its nominalisation) has the same stem and almost the same sense, but its sense has the added feature of aiming at Life-Enhancement.

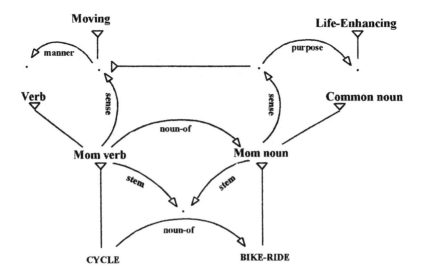

Figure 13

The other grammatical pattern that signals Life-Enhancing is illustrated by the following examples.

(27a) I went swimming with the kids.

(27b) Would you like to come flying?

(27c) We went mushroom-picking.

(27d) Please come paddling with me!

If you go swimming then you do it for fun or for fitness, and not to save your life. Therefore, you have not been swimming if you swim to the shore after being shipwrecked. Similarly for all the other examples; if you come flying, the destination is secondary, and most probably we will take off and land at the same place; if you go mushroom-picking, this is a pastime, not your way of earning a living; and so on.

Unlike the zero-derived nouns, manner-of-movement is only one of many possibilities, as illustrated by the example of mushroom-picking. Almost any activity which can be done for the sake of Life-Enhancing qualifies – fishing, painting, singing, etc. – but we cannot go (or come) working because Working conflicts fundamentally with the purpose of fun or fitness. However, there are some exceptions which we cannot explain: we cannot go cooking, eating, coffee-drinking, chatting or sleeping, however life-enhancing these activities may be. Nor can we explain why some examples of the grammatical pattern define traditional activities which were (and are) done as jobs: we would go harvesting, hay-making or fruit-picking for money rather than for fun or fitness. However the main point is that we can easily go or come cycling, and that when we do so we are doing it for fun or fitness.

The grammatical pattern is more complicated than the zero-derived nouns discussed earlier. Indeed, we cannot claim to understand the grammatical pattern fully, as will become clear below. Its first part is one of the verbs *GO* and *COME*, which have their normal senses as deictically restricted verbs of direction-of-motion. You can either go or come swimming according to the deictic status of the destination, the swimming-place. However, in this pattern it is not possible to define the destination more precisely in the usual way:

> (28a)   I went (*swimming) to the seaside.

> (28b)   I went *(swimming) at the seaside.

The normal possibilities for spatial location seem to be replaced by those of the second word: *at the seaside* is possible in (28b) because it depends on *swimming*, but the expected dependency between *went* and *to the seaside* in (28a) is suppressed. We cannot explain how this verb can have a deictically specified direction but does not allow a normal direction adjunct.

The other part of the pattern is the "ing-word", which is much harder to analyse. This is partly because it is hard to distinguish from two other constructions: the non-movement pattern in (29a) below, which has negative overtones, and the pattern in (29b) where the ordinary *GO* or *COME* is combined with a participial adjunct.

> (29a)   Don't go / *come saying anything you'll regret.

> (29b)   He went / came / walked (to the woods) humming his favourite tune.

Another problem is that it is quite unclear what kind of word the ing-word is. Examples like (30a) suggest that it may be a participle, i.e. a verb, but (30b) shows that it can be a noun or adjective, because there is no verb *MUSHROOM-PICK*, as can be seen from (30c).

(30a) We went picking mushrooms.

(30b) We went mushroom-picking.

(30c) *We mushroom-picked.

Because of these uncertainties we shall not try to suggest a proper analysis for the syntax of the ing-word, nor for the semantics of *GO/COME*, so the diagram in figure 14 is particularly provisional in syntax and in its treatment of the deictic meaning. In the semantics, "There" summarises the complex contrast between Going and Coming and is a reminder of the need to explain the ban on ordinary direction adjuncts that we saw in example (28a).

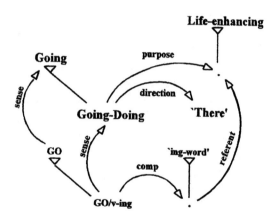

Figure 14

The details of the analysis are unimportant for our main point, which is the possibility of *go cycling* where the cycling has to be taken as something we do for fun or fitness. Like the zero-derivation pattern discussed earlier, this one defines the purpose as Life-enhancing, but as we have seen in (25) this is not the only purpose that can be forced on Cycling by the linguistic context. The flexibility of purpose suggests a semantic analysis of Cycling in which the purpose is left undefined, so that it can be filled in by the "construction meaning" as illustrated by the two constructions just discussed.

8. Conclusion

Although we have left some important threads dangling loose, we have been able to develop a reasonably insightful semantic analysis of Cycling which reveals its links to the notions Bicycle, Riding, Moving, Pedalling and a number of others for which there are no established names such as Life-enhancing and Mere-riding. The most important gap in the semantic analysis is the concept Cycle (as in *the cycle of the seasons*), which we think is probably closer to Pedalling than to Cycling.

While discussing Cycling, however, we have tried to establish a number of general theoretical principles which we now summarise in order to stress that this kind of work cannot be done in a theoretical vacuum; indeed, we feel that it depends on a general theory of cognition.

- Concepts are recycled rather than duplicated – for example, the concept Bicycle is referred to directly in the definition of Cycling, rather than represented in that definition by some other concept which is similar to it.

- Recycling means that the sense of one word may be recycled as part of the definition of another; so the concept Bicycle which defines Cycling is the same concept as the one that is the sense of the lexeme *BICYCLE*.

- If non-language concepts are recycled as word senses, and vice versa, language contributes to the defining of concepts in the same way as other kinds of experience do, with its contribution ranging from zero (e.g. Bicycle) to almost totality (e.g. Riding or, perhaps, Life-enhancing).

- Network notations reflect recycling by assigning to each concept a single point on which many different relationships converge.

- Networks are a better model for conceptual structures than frames are because they do not imply boundaries.

- Networks and recycling are hard to reconcile with the traditional distinction between encyclopedic and dictionary meaning, because a network allows no such modular distinctions and any concept defined in the dictionary would also be recycled as a focus of encyclopedic relationships.

References

Anderson, John R. 1993. "Problem solving and learning". *American psychologist* 48. 35-44.

Barsalou, Lawrence W. 1992. "Frames, concepts and conceptual fields". In Adrienne Lehrer & Eva F. Kittay (ed.), *Frames, fields and contrasts. New essays in semantic and lexical organization.* Hillsdale: Lawrence Erlbaum. 21-74.

Fillmore, Charles J. 1985. "Frames and the semantics of understanding". *Quaderni di semantica* 6. 223-253.

Fillmore, Charles J.; Atkins, Beryl T. 1992. "Toward a frame-based lexicon. The semantics of RISK and its neighbours". In Adrienne Lehrer & Eva F. Kittay (ed.), *Frames, fields and contrasts. New essays in semantic and lexical organization.* Hillsdale: Lawrence Erlbaum. 75-102.

Hudson, Richard. 1985. "Some basic assumptions about linguistic and non-linguistic knowledge". *Quaderni di semantica* 6. 284-287.

Hudson, Richard. 1990. *English word grammar.* Oxford: Blackwell.

Hudson, Richard. 1995. *Word meaning.* London: Routledge.

Hudson, Richard. 1998. *Encyclopedia of word grammar.* URL: http://www.phon.ucl.ac.uk/home/dick/papers.

Jackendoff, Ray. 1983. *Semantics and cognition.* Cambridge: M.I.T. Press.

Lakoff, George. 1987. *Women, fire and dangerous things. What categories reveal about the mind.* Chicago: University of Chicago Press.

Langacker, Ronald W. 1987. *Foundations of cognitive grammar*, vol. 1. *Theoretical prerequisites.* Stanford: Stanford University Press.

Lehrer, Adrienne; Kittay, Eva F. 1992. "Introduction". In Adrienne Lehrer & Eva F. Kittay (ed.), *Frames, fields and contrasts. New essays in semantic and lexical organization.* Hillsdale: Lawrence Erlbaum. 1-18.

Levin, Beth. 1993. *English verb classes and alternations. A preliminary investigation.* Chicago: University of Chicago Press.

Luger, George; Stubblefield, William. 1993. *Artificial intelligence. Structures and strategies for complex problem solving.* Second edition. New York: Benjamin/Cummings.

Pinker, Steven. 1997. *How the mind works.* London: Penguin.

Reisberg, Daniel. 1997. *Cognition. Exploring the science of the mind.* New York: Norton.

Rosch, Eleanor. 1978. "Principles of categorization". In Eleanor Rosch & Barbara B. Lloyd (ed.), *Cognition and categorization.* Hillsdale: Lawrence Erlbaum. 27-48.

Schank, Roger C.; Rieger, Charles. 1974. "Inference and the computer understanding of natural language". *Artificial intelligence* 5. 373-412.

Slobin, Dan. 1996. *Mind, code and text.* Unpublished manuscript, University of California, Berkeley.

Sowa, John. 1984. *Conceptual structures. Information processing in mind and machine.* Reading: Addison-Wesley.

Wierzbicka, Anna. 1985. *Lexicography and conceptual analysis.* Ann Arbor: Karoma.

Wierzbicka, Anna. 1988. *The semantics of grammar.* Amsterdam: John Benjamins.

Wierzbicka, Anna. 1996. *Semantics. Primes and universals.* Oxford: Oxford University Press.

Towards an operationalisation of the lexicon-encyclopedia distinction: A case study in the description of verbal meanings in Russian[1]

Eva Born-Rauchenecker

Universität Hamburg, Institut für Slavistik, D-20146 Hamburg, Germany
E-mail: e.born-rauchenecker@aston-online.de

The principle of fuzziness of meanings of a polysemous word is the crucial factor which determines its semantics. The fact that lexicographical descriptions do not reflect this state of affairs (trying instead to rid lexical entries of fuzzy examples) substantially distorts the impression one gains of the semantic structure of the words to be described. (Šmelev 1973; transl. E.B.-R.)

0. Introduction

This paper is not to be understood as a plea for a strict distinction between lexicon and encyclopedia, at least not at the level of our cognitive apparatus or at that of a

---

[1] Most of the work towards this paper was done at the Slavisches Seminar of the Universität Hamburg. I wish to thank Britta Wölpern, Horst Dippong, and Leon Jamei for reading through an earlier version and suggesting several improvements. I also acknowledge the input of an anonymous referee, as well as of the volume's editor, Bert Peeters.

cognitive model of it. It does intend to identify default-like principles that make it possible to distinguish the two domains, if and when a distinction is necessary. In my opinion, such principles are definitely required in semantics and especially in lexicography. Lexicographical analysis involves the study of the different contexts in which a word may be used; it often leads to the identification of polysemy, i.e. separate meanings of a word that are then to be described in a more or less specific manner. Traditional lexicographers generally assume that their definitions merely provide linguistic information, described by Schwarz (1992:92) as "Informationen, die für eine adäquate Verwendung sprachlicher Ausdrücke in einer Sprachgemein-schaft notwendig sind" ('information required for an appropriate use of linguistic expressions in a language community'). A cursory look through any dictionary shows that this is not necessarily true: the *Oxford Advanced Learner's Dictionary* (henceforth *OALD*), for instance, defines *yellow* as "the colour of gold or the yolk of a hen's egg", and *flower* as "that part of a plant that produces seeds" (among other things). The inclusion in a dictionary entry of encyclopedic information – at least that part of it that is conventionally shared by all the members of a language com-munity (this excludes individual associations, which are also part of encyclopedic information) – often seems to be unavoidable to allow for full understanding of a lexical unit.

One prominent linguist who treats encyclopedic knowledge as separate, and insists on describing it as far as possible, is Anna Wierzbicka. Among her stated aims is a desire to engage in lexicography using the semantic primitives of language itself, the basic building blocks (about sixty in recent research) for all our concepts, whatever language they belong to (for recent exemplification, cf. Wierzbicka 1996, 1997). While not avoided, polysemy is not postulated as being in the nature of things; its existence is acknowledged only if a simpler realistic description is impossible. The so-called two-level approach (see e.g. Bierwisch 1970, 1979, 1983; cf. also Taylor, this volume), on the other hand, distinguishes a purely linguistic domain consisting of formal rules and patterns, and an encyclopedic domain. Encyclopedic information is usually not described, and the notion of polysemy is avoided as far as possible.

Cognitive linguists such as Langacker (1987-1991) and Taylor (1995) categorically reject the "one form, one meaning" principle. For them, lexical knowledge and en-cyclopedic knowledge are generally defined as being the same: the lexicon is ency-clopedic by its very nature, which basically means that polysemy is taken for granted. A model in which linguistic knowledge and encyclopedic knowledge are undifferentiated would seem to be theoretically attractive and even plausible, espe-cially when the results of studies in ontogenesis and cognition are taken into ac-count. In lexicographical work, on the other hand, serious problems cannot be avoided unless a clear distinction is made.

Certainly, no difference between linguistic and encyclopedic knowledge is either mentioned in "traditional dictionaries" such as the *OALD*, the *Malyj Akademičeskij Slovar'* (henceforth *MAS*) of contemporary Russian, and so on, or maintained in the structure of the lexical entries found in these works. The consequences are immediately visible: lemmas are typically condemned to be nothing more than unstructured lists of word meanings, or rather contexts. Such lists provide a very poor representation indeed of any underlying polysemy. Especially for dictionary users, unstructured lists are as unsatisfactory as an extremely abstract definition that fits all (or at least all the literal) uses of a word and that may result from the non-differentiation of linguistic and encyclopedic knowledge.

There are of course cases where encyclopedic knowledge plays no role whatsoever. The definitions of relational terms such as *can* ('know how to do', as in *she can swim*) and *about* ('in no particular direction', as in *walking about the town*) obviously contain no encyclopedic component. Many more lexical units cannot be described in concrete terms without any encyclopedic information. Apart from colour terms such as *yellow* and natural kinds like *flower, cat, apple tree, gold, woman*, there are all the names of artefacts like *glass, kettle, telephone, car*, and quite a few more. Consider words such as *cat*, defined in the *OALD* as 'small, domestic, fur-covered animal often kept as a pet, to catch mice, etc.', or *telephone*, defined in the same dictionary as 'means, system, of transmitting the human voice by electric current, through wires (...) supported by poles (...), or by radio'. Often, pictures seem to be more useful than paraphrases of the kind just quoted to convey the meaning of a word. Pictures take over the function of paraphrases; however, neither could be considered good representatives of linguistic knowledge. The proportion of linguistic and encyclopedic information is not the same throughout: the encyclopedic part appears to be greater, for example, in the case of concrete nouns than in that of relational terms such as verbs or prepositions (cf. *apple* vs. *eat, window* vs. *through*, etc.). The easier it is to show what is referred to when one uses a word, the greater the number of encyclopedic components in the meaning of a word. Leiss (1986:80) correctly observes that definitions of referential terms in particular seem to require more detailed reference to our knowledge of the world than do definitions of relational terms. Each part of speech appears to obey its own "laws".[2]

A new type of dictionary has started to appear in the last two decades. The so-called "explanatory combinatorial dictionary" (for Russian, see e.g. Mel'čuk & Žolkov-skij's 1984 *Tolkovo-kombinatornyj Slovar'*, henceforth *TKS*) is based on Mel'čuk's Meaning-Text approach (e.g. Mel'čuk 1988). To the best of my knowledge, explanatory combinatorial dictionaries are the only ones that have attempted to make the distinction between linguistic and encyclopedic information explicit. They include an abundance of polysemic items, with each lemma containing a huge amount of information both on the syntagmatic and paradigmatic relations of lexical items. Most information provided is considered to be linguistic knowledge. In the *TKS*, encyclopedic information is usually given only in the lemmas of nouns.

---

[2] Sometimes, the same would seem to hold for subsets within particular parts of speech.

Unfortunately, as far as I can tell, syntagmatic and paradigmatic relations of the kind listed in the *TKS*, no matter how important they are for tracing the borderline between lexicon and encyclopedia in defining relational terms, are unable to contribute to the solution of the problem dealt with in this paper. Indications on the sort of constructions allowed by specific verbs are not very helpful either, and the same holds true for information derived from comparison across languages (i.e. contrastive analysis). Illustrated with English examples, the problem is the following: how do we know, i.e. which criteria help us decide that *eat an apple* and *eat an ice-cream* are two instances of one meaning, whereas *open a window, open a suitcase* and *open a debate* represent different meanings of the form *open* (for more on the latter, see Taylor 1992)? To appropriately deal with the polysemy or otherwise of relational terms, linguistic and encyclopedic components have to be distinguished. The work done in the Meaning-Text model has to be taken further. The present paper is one step in that direction; it looks at meaning variation in Russian verbs. An analysis of concrete verbs in Russian will illustrate the comprehensive nature of linguistic knowledge: a great deal of conceptual information that at first seems to be genuinely encyclopedic turns out to be lexical.

What follows may be construed as an invitation to further investigate linguistic knowledge, and first of all semantic rules such as those that govern the regular alternations established by Bierwisch (1983) for concepts like SCHOOL, MUSEUM, HOSPITAL, the regular polysemy of nouns, verbs, and adjectives established by Apresjan (1992), and the so-called functional operations of Lehmann (1996).

1. Counting meanings: monosemy, polysemy and homonymy

For an adequate linguistic description of semantic variation within lexical units (be it at a synchronic or a diachronic level), it is necessary 1) to assume the reality of polysemy, and 2) to differentiate linguistic and encyclopedic information: is a newly added meaning based on a semantic component of the initial meaning, or is it based on a connotation of the initial word? The investigation of principles of polysemy goes beyond linguistic description inasmuch as it also involves the search for cognitive principles (focusing, for instance, on "intrinsic" or "extrinsic" components of information, to use the terms proposed by Lehmann 1975).[3]

The dichotomy between linguistic and encyclopedic knowledge has been reformulated by some as the no less problematic trichotomy between monosemy, polysemy, and homonymy. The latter terms reflect the linguist's intuition that the different instances of a form are not equally related. The extremes are as follows: if token 1 and

---

[3] For arguments against a mere listing of lexical items in dictionaries without an account of the (supposed) principles of our cognition, cf. Born-Rauchenecker (1997).

token 2 turn out to be identical, the case at hand is one of monosemy (as in *eat an apple* vs. *eat a banana*); if token 1 and token 2 are totally unrelated, the case at hand is one of homynymy (as in *the gloss [of silk]* vs. *the gloss [of an article]*).

Since not all instances of variation are as simple as in the previous examples (cf., in section 0, the triplet *open a window, open a suitcase, open a debate*), the need for explicit criteria to justify the existence of polysemy as well as of diversity of relatedness of meanings becomes especially obvious. Or, as Taylor (1995:266-267) puts it:

> [I]f we allow the multiplication of the senses of a word, where do we stop? Since no two tokens of a word will refer to *exactly* the same situation, there will always be *some* difference between two instances of the same word. But how different do the instances have to be, in order for us to be sure that we are dealing with two distinct polysemes? Where, and on what grounds, do we draw the line between polysemy and contextual modulation?

In other words, how do we draw the line between polysemy and what some have called *monosemy*? Most of the well-known polysemy tests apply in clear-cut cases only. One such test, mentioned by Apresjan (1992:207), focuses on relational terms:

> 'The firewood in the fireplace and the neon lamps in the street **went out** almost simultaneously.' (...) [H]ad there been no contexts where both semantic components were realized simultaneously, there would be no reason to claim that 'to cease to burn' and 'to cease to emit light' coexist within one meaning.[4]

Taylor (1995:101-102) mentions another test to distinguish monosemy from polysemy. Presupposing, as does Apresjan (1992:195), that the distinction between monosemy and polysemy is equivalent to that between vagueness and ambiguity, he points out:

> An ambiguous sentence has more than one reading. It is thus possible, in principle, to assert one of the readings while denying the others. Thus one can readily assert that there is a *pig* (i.e. a gluttonous person) in the house, while denying the presence of a *pig* (i.e. a farm animal).[5]

---

[4] The co-existence of two meanings seems to be easier activated in the area of nouns: cf. Apresjan's (1992) example *Auditorija byla polnoj i šumela* 'The auditorium was filled and noisy', where two readings of the subject noun are combined (namely *auditorija₁* 'auditorium' and *auditorija₂* 'audience').

[5] Talking about polysemy, Apresjan (1992:195) argues that "the phenomena which give rise to it are rooted both in the grammar of the language (ambiguity of syntactic constructions) and in its lexicon (lexical ambiguity)".

Using the same example (*pig*), Aitchison (1994:60) observes that "'The farmer watched the *pig* feeding its piglets, and so did the foundry foreman' would be very odd if the foundry foreman was looking at a metal pig". There can be little doubt that she is right. But are we still dealing with polysemy (as she seems to assume)? Oddness does not necessarily have to be a result of polysemy. The two pigs have absolutely nothing in common with one another. This would have to be a case of homonymy.[6]

The limited validity of tests is clearly illustrated by Tuggy (1993), who claims that it is always possible to find contexts where apparently different lexical meanings of a word do fit together (cf. also Taylor 1995:289):

> 'I have been *painting*, and so has Jane' is wrong, if the speaker painted a house, and Jane painted a landscape. But what about the following sentence? 'When I'm *painting* I try to get the colour on evenly, and so does Jane'.

How, then, do we decide whether two tokens are identical, unrelated or somewhere in between? Some find polysemy where others still see monosemy, and homonymy is sometimes postulated in cases declared in other quarters to be clear instances of polysemy.[7] The only way out of the apparent quagmire is by way of definition:

(I)   If two instances of a form f have a single lexical definition in common, they are monosemes and belong to one lexeme (cf. e.g. Mel'čuk 1988);

(II)   If a rule (e.g. a pattern such as metaphor or metonymy) exists that can be mapped onto two instances of a form f, they are polysemes and belong to different lexemes (cf. e.g. Lehmann 1995);

(III)   If two instances of a form f do not have one lexical definition in common and if there is no rule that could be mapped onto them, they are homonyms.

Homonymy is not a phenomenon this essay will deal with any further. However, the case of polysemy and of monosemy is different. We shall consider them in the order in which they have just been mentioned. With respect to lexical polysemy, Lehmann (1995, 1996) builds on Apresjan's (1992:208) definition of meaning similarity. The definition runs as follows:

---

[6] Oddness may of course also be the result of a clash of styles, of unusual combinations, and the like.

[7] In Cruse (1986), we find the whole spectre of assumptions, from minimalist (e.g. Bierwisch, Wierzbicka) to maximalist positions (e.g. Haiman, Haas).

The meanings a_i and a_j of the word A are called similar if there exist levels of semantic description such that their definitions [...] have a *nontrivial common part*, and if it plays the same role with regard to other semantic components in definitions. [emphasis added]

A nontrivial part is a basic part in the lexical definition (a trivial one could be the component 'to cause' in definitions of causative verbs). Lehmann goes one step further by placing the nontrivial common part against a cognitive background. He lists a couple of so-called *functional operations* that are thought of as representing devices of human cognition; they are taken as an explanation of meaning change, both at the synchronical and the diachronical levels, for polysemy as well as for word formation: "Funktionale Operationen (FO) sind allgemeine Prinzipien, nach denen die Bedeutungen des Bedeutungsinventars einer Sprache verändert werden" 'Functional operations (FO) are general principles by which the meaning inventory of a language is changed' (Lehmann 1996:257).[8] The most important among them are listed below.

• *Modification*: the prototype of the motivating meaning is preserved, while one or more additional components are changed, e.g. *a human being > his cruelty suggests that he is less than human* (see *OALD*, s.v.).

• *Highlighting*: this device allows for the concept of a lexical unit to be structured according to the principle of figure and ground, or for an already structured concept to be given a new structure, e.g. *it is a banality to ask her to come > this was a conversation that was chiefly banalities* (see *OALD*, s.v.).

• *Recategorisation*: the referent of the motivating meaning belongs to a certain category A, whereas the motivated (derived) meaning has a referent in a category non-A (compare e.g. the meanings of *sickle* 'tool for lopping' vs. 'shape of the moon', which is a recategorisation from natural phenomenon to artefact).[9] Meaning change in verbs is often a result of Recategorisation of one or more arguments; still, verbal metaphors are not restricted to combinatorial effects, as shown by the following examples taken from *MAS* and from Apresjan & Páll's (*A/P*) Russian-Hungarian dictionary:

(1a)   glotat'$_{MAS-1b}$ (x, čaj) 'to swallow greedily (x, tea)' > glotat'$_{MAS-1c}$ (x, knigu) 'to devour greedily (a book)'

(1b)   goret'$_{A/P-1}$ (bumaga) 'to burn (a sheet)' > goret'$_{A/P-9}$ (molodoj čelovek) 'to burn emotionally (the young man)'

---

[8] FOs may be usefully compared to Bierwisch's (1983:87) *conceptual operations* or *schemes* (i.e. regular alternations).

[9] There are obvious similarities with the concept of mapping from a source domain onto a target domain as illustrated for instance in Lakoff & Johnson (1980).

(1c)   proglotit'$_{MAS-1a}$ (ded, piljulju) 'to swallow (grandfather, a pill)' > proglotit'$_{MAS-2a}$ (ded, obidu) 'to swallow (grandfather, the insult)'

(1d)   guljat'$_{A/P-1}$ (činovnik) 'to go for a walk (the civil servant)' > guljat'$_{A/P-3}$ (činovnik) 'to have a day / a few days off (the civil servant)'

The examples in (2) show that Modification, too, may be independent of combinatorial effects. This is not true in the case of Highlighting, as shown in (3).

(2a)   lit'$_{A/P-1b}$ (čaj) 'to pour (x, tea)' > lit'$_{A/P-3b}$ (sveči iz voska) 'to pour (x, candles of wax)'

(2b)   vzjat'$_{A/P-1}$ (studentka, knigu) 'to take (the student$_{fem}$, the book) > vzjat'$_{A/P-10}$ (studentka, knigu I v biblioteke) 'to borrow (the student$_{fem}$, the book I in the library)'

(3a)   Zvonar' bil$_{A/P-12b}$ v kolokol. 'The bellringer rang (hit) the bell' > Kolokola b'jut$_{A/P-13c}$. 'The bells ring'

(3b)   Devuška chorošo pišet. 'The girl writes well' > Ručka chorošo pišet. 'The pen writes well'

These few examples demonstrate that the semantic distance between initial meaning and derived meaning may differ across FOs, and even within. That is, lexicographical definitions resemble one another either to a greater extent, as in (3a), or to a lesser one, as in (1d). In each case, the distance between meaning₁ and meaning₂, between meaning₂ and meaning₃, between meaning₃ and meaning₁, etc., i.e. the deductive steps of the lexicographer, ought to be reflected in the lemma structure (cf. Born-Rauchenecker 1997, and the lexicographical practice of the *TKS*).

Moving on to monosemy now, the following principles may serve as guides for the discovery of the right sort of paraphrase for truly monosemic instances (cf., once again, the works of Apresjan and Mel'čuk): (i) paraphrases should, if possible, be constructed in accordance with the well-known principle of *genus commune et differentia specificae*; (ii) they must not be too abstract (i.e. the intended meanings must be recognisable as such);[10] (iii) they must be unambiguous, i.e. define only one lexical unit (and not for instance its synonyms as well) and rely on a well-defined meta-language; (iv) they must be valid for all instances belonging to the given meaning; (v) the distribution of a lexeme must be taken into account.

On top of all that, a further distinction within monosemy would appear to be useful, especially if we keep the necessities of practical lexicography in mind. There is

---

[10] Following this principle, paraphrases should, if possible, be based on our naive picture of the world (Russ. *naivnaja kartina mira*).

nothing new here: the practice of distinguishing what is mostly referred to as *variants* within a single meaning is well-known in lexicographical practice. Meanings are usually identified by means of, e.g., Arabic numerals; quite often, variants are "counted" as well, for instance by means of lower case letters (but as we have seen, further structuring of the lemma is needed).

A definition of the term *variant* is not easy to give. The one provided by Apresjan (1992:207) may be misleading. Monosemy is, according to this author, a case of "inclusive disjunction", that is, "if A = 'B or C', then A = 'either B or C, or both B and C'". In Apresjan's own example (*The firewood in the fireplace and the neon lamps in the street **went out** almost simultaneously*), A equals *go out*, and B and C are represented by *the firewood in the fireplace* and *the neon lamps in the street*. But what about cases where the combination of B and C together with A sounds relatively odd, although B and C do seem to belong to one definitional lexical paraphrase? Note the following contrasts:

(4a)   Peter opened the book.

(4b)   Peter opened the bottle.

(4c)   ?Peter opened the bottle and the book.

(4d)   ??Peter opened an expensive bottle of French red wine and the leather-bounded book of his friend.

In an attempt to broaden Apresjan's approach, I propose the following definition:

(IV)   If two instances of a form f cannot be (sufficiently) reflected in one lexicographical definition, and the semantic difference is not a matter of rule, but a matter of combination, then they are to be viewed as variants of one meaning.

(IV) is the first of the two main theses formulated in the present paper. The second one will follow in section 2. As suggested by the Roman numeral, the definition is to be added to the ones given above for monosemy, polysemy and homonymy. It may serve as the bridge that leads us back to our original concern, the dichotomy of linguistic and encyclopedic knowledge. We now have some good tools to pursue further work in this field. My concern in the present paper is with so-called "combinatorial encyclopedic effects", more particularly those that are produced by the combination of a concrete ("motoric") agentive verb and a concrete second argument. An abstract second argument can force a metaphorical meaning upon the verb; such cases will not be considered.[11]

---

[11] There are, of course, various other types of "encyclopedic effects". Apresjan (1992:195-196) gives the example in (i):

2. A case study in the description of Russian verbal meaning

The existence of widely divergent lemma structures for related words in the same dictionary, or for the same word in different dictionaries, provides stark evidence for the need to operationalise the distinction between lexicon and encyclopedia. Compare the respective lemmas of the verbs *otkryt'* 'open' and *zakryt'* 'shut' in *MAS*; without wishing to engage in cheap criticism of traditional lexicography, I must point out that cases such as this are not isolated.

(5a)　　(*MAS*)

　　　　1.a. otkryt' kastrjulju / rojal' 'to open the pot (saucepan) / the grand piano'

　　　　1.b. otkryt' banku konservov / butylku 'to open the can / the bottle'

　　　　2. otkryt' dver' / okno 'to open the door / the window'

　　　　3. otkryt' knigu / glaza / zontik 'to open the book / one's eyes / the umbrella'

　　　　(...)

(5b)　　(*MAS*)

　　　　(...)

　　　　3. zakryt' knigu / glaza / zontik 'to shut the book / one's eyes / the umbrella'

　　　　4.a. zakryt' kastrjulju / škaf / čemodan 'to shut the pot / the cupboard / the suitcase'

　　　　4.b. zakryt' okno / kryšku rojala 'to shut the window / the cover of the grand piano'

　　　　(...)

It is not hard to see that the various combinations involving *otkryt'* 'open' and *zakryt'* 'shut' on the one hand, and *kastrjulju* 'pot', *okno* 'window', etc. on the other hand, are grouped differently. Whereas arguments like POT and GRAND PIANO are listed within a single variant of *otkryt'*, this is not what happens in the case of *zak-*

(i)　　　The child, like a machine, opened its mouth, stuck out its tongue, breathed heavily, and the physician thought that the examination went perfectly well.

Although *breathe* is a non-intentional verb, it is interpreted as intentional in the context provided. Apresjan adds that this interpretation "is forced by encyclopaedic information concerning medical examination rather than lexical meanings of the words" (ibid.). As far as I am concerned, such effects are of minor interest here (for "situational effects" in general, see Reuther 1990).

ryt', where they appear with different variants within a single lexeme. Similarly, WINDOW and GRAND PIANO are listed within a single variant of *zakryt'*, but in the case of *otkryt'* they are considered different enough even to belong to two different lexemes. It is difficult to figure out where the combinations *zakryt' butylku* 'close the bottle' and *otkryt' čemodan* 'open the suitcase' belong.

The data in (6) and (7), based this time on a comparison between two dictionaries, show that the phenomenon is not restricted to verbs of opening and closing:

(6a)   (*MAS*)

1.a. brosit' čepčiki v vozduch / granatu / kamen' 'throw caps in the air / a grenade / a stone'

1.b. brosit' jakor' / nevod 'throw the anchor / a fishing net'

(6b)   (*A/P*)

1. brosit' šapki v vozduch / mjač / kamen' 'throw caps in the air / a ball / a stone'

3. brosit' jakor' / nevod 'throw the anchor / a fishing net'

(7a)   (*MAS*)

1.a. žarit' kartofel' / mjaso / rybu 'to fry potatoes / meat / fish'

1.b. žarit' kofe / semečki 'to roast coffee / seeds'

(7b)   (*A/P*)

1. žarit' kartofel' 'to fry potatoes'

2. žarit' kofe / semečki 'to roast coffee / seeds'

Clearly, the problem stems from the traditional lexicographical practice of defining the meaning of a concrete verb by describing the actions it denotes. Especially in the case of what, for the want of a better term, might be called "affecting verbs", the precise movements that a subject carries out are determined by the "affected object". If one were to try to list all the objects capable of being thrown or opened, it would be hard to group them satisfactorily. And if we were to list those groups in a dictionary as lexemes, we would bring linguistic and encyclopedic knowledge onto the same level. Instances such as these demonstrate the lack of a principled distinction between lexicon and encyclopedia in the field of lexicography. That no such distinction is made is one of the reasons for different results in lexicographical analysis.

Let us have a closer look at the material in (6) and (7). The examples with the verb *brosit'* in (8) illustrate the facilitating role that contrastive semantics may play to separate meanings. It should be obvious, though, that different meanings in one language (e.g. Russian) do not always correspond to different forms in another (e.g.

English). It is the task of a language-specific semantics to describe and explain the concepts and rules of the corresponding language.

(8a) Petr brosil mjač. 'Petr threw the ball'

(8b) Petr brosil jakor'. 'Petr threw the anchor'

(8c) Petr brosil prognivšuju grušu. 'Petr threw away the rotten pear'

(8d) Petr brosil svoju kurtku. 'Petr threw down his jacket carelessly'

Each single instance of the verb *brosit'* 'throw' in (8) is ambiguous. Apart from the suggested reading of (8a), namely 'Petr threw the ball', there exists a second reading reminiscent of (8c), namely 'Petr threw the ball away', and also a third (although perhaps uncommon) reading reminiscent of (8d), namely 'Petr threw down the ball carelessly'. In contrast, it is hard to imagine a reading along the lines of (8b), with Petr throwing the ball in the way anchors are thrown. And this is exactly the point where we have to realise the influence of encyclopedic knowledge. According to our knowledge of the world, it may be possible to throw a (not too heavy) anchor or a fishing net like a ball, but we normally expect anchors and fishing nets to be thrown the way they are supposed to be, unless there is situational or textual information that points in a different direction (e.g. two children playing with toys, with the first child asking the second to throw the [toy] anchor across).

Applying the lexicographical principles introduced above, we get the following structure for the verbal lemma *brosit'* 'throw':[12]

(9) BROSIT': X BROSAET Y =

I.1.a. With a forceful movement of the arm, X causes Y at t_0 to fly or to fall (up to t_0 X was holding Y in his hand(s), after t_0 X does not hold Y in his hand(s) anymore). *Petr brosaet kamen'* 'Petr throws a stone'

I.1.b. (?With a forceful movement of the arm,) X causes Y at t_0 to fall (up to t_0 X was holding Y in his hand(s), after t_0 X does not hold Y in his hand(s) anymore, but X does hold a rope (or cord) connected with Y). *Petr brosaet jakor'* 'Petr throws the anchor' [NB: World knowledge tells us that, to cause a movement of Y (e.g. an anchor), it need not be directly touched. In this case, X uses a special device.]

I.2. (?With a forceful movement of the arm,) X causes Y at t_0 to fly or to fall (up to t_0 X was holding Y in his hand(s), after t_0 X does not hold Y in his hand(s) anymore), but usually (in accordance with

---

[12] For the sake of simplicity the definition is given in English. Strictly speaking, only a Russian definition would be correct (see the lexicographical principles in Mel'čuk 1988).

established social practice) Y is not treated like that, and the speaker judges the treatment negatively. *Petr brosaet kurtku na divan* 'Peter carelessly_throws his jacket onto the sofa'

I.3. (??With a forceful movement of the arm,) X causes Y at t_o to fly or to fall (up to t_o X was holding Y in his hand(s), after t_o X does not hold Y in his hand(s) anymore), and X does not want to use Y any longer. *Petr brosaet jabloko v korzinu dlja musora* 'Peter throws_away the apple into the waste bin'

Brosit'$_2$ and *brosit'$_3$* both result from Modification of the motivating meaning *brosit'$_1$*. The referential prototype remains, but is enriched with further information: the derived meanings refer without any doubt to ways of throwing (this is what is called *genus commune*), but they are more specific than *brosit'$_1$* (*differentia specifica*). The meanings are grouped under a general heading I, due to further meanings of *brosit'* that are not considered here and have to be grouped under a heading II, because of the greater distance between motivating and motivated lexemes (compare *brosit' kurit'* 'to quit smoking').

The complexity of meaning structures becomes apparent especially when one tries to define meanings in a lemma. Why are the paraphrases of *brosit'$_{I.1.a}$* and *brosit'$_{I.1.b}$*, although different, considered variants of a single lexeme? On the basis of a comparison of their tokens, one can easily see that they are unambiguous. Apparently this is the best way to separate usage-variants from lexemes in a first analysis of the structure of a lemma (i.e., better than the similarity of lexicographical definitions and the type of semantic relatedness).[13]

Moving on from *brosit'* 'throw' to *žarit'* 'fry, roast', we find that the corresponding lemma in *TKS* confirms to our proposed operationalisation:

(10)   (*TKS*)

I.1.a. Segodnja Ivanovy žarili kartosku / rybu. 'Today the Ivanovs fried potatoes / fish'

I.1.b. Segodnja Ivanovy žarili semečki / kofe. 'Today the Ivanovs roasted seeds / coffee'

I.2. Segodnja Ivanovy žarili gusja / celogo barana. 'Today the Ivanovs grilled a goose/ a whole he-sheep'

---

[13] In *MAS*, *brosit' čepčiki v vozduch* 'throw caps in the air' and *brosit' jakor'* 'throw the anchor' belong to one lexeme: they are regarded as variants (see the lexicographical definitions above). This is in accordance with our principle that "if meaning change is a matter of object knowledge, we have variants of one lexemic meaning". In *A/P*, the same instances belong to different lexemes: they have a status I cannot endorse.

What exactly is entailed by the verb *žarit'* 'fry, roast' in the first meaning (I.1) depends on our encyclopedic knowledge of objects such as POTATOES, FISH, SEEDS, and so on: some of these objects are fried, others roasted. But the utterance *Segodnja Ivanovy žarili kartošku* does not necessarily refer to the frying of potatoes. Without further contextualisation, it is ambiguous: apart from being fried in a frying pan (I.1.a), potatoes may also be placed on a grill (I.2). Such ambiguity is once again symptomatic of linguistic knowledge and, in a next step, becomes an argument for the distinction of two discrete meanings (lexemes).

It is not surprising that in some cases the two knowledge spheres (lexical or linguistic knowledge vs. encyclopedic or world knowledge) coincide: knowledge of objects meets ambiguity, so to speak. An additional example involves the verb *žat'* 'press' (used with reference to either fruit or juice). Two meanings must be distinguished, namely 'apply one or more fingers to exert pressure on an object' vs. 'squeeze with the intended effect of producing juice'.

> (11)   Petr žal avokado. Ono bylo uže sliškom mjagkoe. 'Petr pressed the avocado. It was too soft already.' (cf. *A/P* 1)
>
> Petr žal apel'sin. Odin konečno daet ne očen' mnogo soka. 'Petr squeezed the orange. However, one orange does not produce much juice.' (cf. *A/P* 6)
>
> Petr žal apel'sin. 'Petr pressed / squeezed the orange.'

Once we know what avocados look like, we also know that they are unlikely candidates for juice-making. Typical fruits for this purpose include oranges and lemons. On the other hand, a sentence like *Petr žal apel'sin* 'Petr pressed an orange' is ambiguous, even more so than the above-mentioned utterance *Petr brosil jakor'* 'Petr threw the anchor'. This is because our encyclopedic knowledge of how we treat anchors is more specific then that of what we do with oranges. That slight difference between *žat'* 'to press' and *brosit'* 'to throw' illustrates once more the fuzziness of words and the limited validity of semantic principles. Ambiguity invites us to separate the tokens. I for one cannot think of a single lexicographical paraphrase that covers the two instances.

A/P is right in its treatment of the verb *čertit'* 'draw'. It has just one lexeme where *MAS* distinguishes no less than three; the differenciation appears to result from the fact that in some instances of *čertit'* one draws only a few lines, whereas in others the verb denotes an activity involving quite a number of linked, well-structured lines.

> (12a)   (*MAS*)
>
> 1.a. čertit' linii v tetradke 'draw lines in the exercise book'

2. čertit' plan doma / geografičeskie karty 'draw the plan of a house / geographic maps'

3. čertit' figuru / neskol'ko strok 'draw, sketch, write a figure / some lines'

(12b)　(*A/P*)

1. čertit' plan, schemu, grafiki, linii na peske, kartu, figuru na liste bumagi, tuš'ju 'draw a plan / a scheme / graphics / lines in the sand / a map / a figure on a sheet / with Indian ink'

There is no ambiguity, and therefore no need to distinguish more than one lexeme: the manner of drawing depends entirely on what is being drawn. In other words, our encyclopedic knowledge fills us in on the precise meaning of each verb-noun combination. This is not to say that a list of common instances (and of any language-specific combinatorial restrictions) is not important; for the foreign language learner it is crucial to have access to such lists, and any good dictionary must provide them.

Another example that demonstrates the well-known fuzziness of meaning is the verb *česat'* 'scratch, comb'. *A/P* and *MAS* present basically the same lemma structure:

(13a)　(*A/P*, *MAS*)

1. česat' lob / grud' / psa za uxom / spinu linejkoj / ranu 'scratch one's forehead / one's breast / the dog behind its ears / one's back with a ruler / a wound'

2. česat' volosy / golovu / borodu (grebnem) / belye kudri 'comb one's hair / one's head / one's beard (with a comb) / one's white curls'

From an English point of view, there is certainly an important difference between *česat'*₁ and *česat'*₂. FOREHEAD, WOUND, etc. do not match the selectional restrictions of *česat'*₂ 'comb'; similarly, HAIR, CURLS, etc. are not "compatible" with *česat'*₁ 'scratch'. This might indicate that, from a Russian point of view, there is no need to distinguish more than one lexeme: encyclopedic knowledge seems to provide all there is to know. The reality is not quite as straightforward, though. A few nouns do fit the two meanings of *česat'* and thus engender ambiguity:

(14)　česat' golovu / borodu 'scratch / comb one's head / one's beard'

I would be inclined to say that the best way to account for the above is by mentioning instances such as (14) in the lexical entries of both *česat'*₁ and *česat'*₂.

The more we compare different lemma structures in different dictionaries, the more obvious the need becomes for operational principles that will allow (i) a clearly spelled out meaning of a word with due respect for its possible fuzziness, (ii) a description that takes account of the word's part of speech and/or its lexical group af-filiation (verbs of movement, nouns denoting artefacts etc.), and (iii) (in accordance with the scientific orientation of linguistics) a duly articulated structure capable of falsification.

Logically, there are four different types of verb-noun combination. Illustrations are provided immediately afterwards.[14]

(i)   In type 1, the combination of V and N results in ambiguity. To de-scribe the ambiguity and keep incompatible meanings separate, two or more different lexical definitions are required. This is considered to be a clear case of lexical knowledge.

(ii)   In type 2, the meaning of V remains basically unaltered when a noun N_1 is replaced with a noun N_2 of the same semantic class (e.g. inanimates). Differences in denotation are a matter of encyclopedic knowledge.

(iii)   In type 3, the meaning of V remains basically unaltered when a noun N_1 is replaced with a noun N_2 of a different semantic class. This is again considered to be a clear case of lexical knowledge.

(iv)   In type 4, the meaning of V changes when a noun N_1 is replaced with a noun N_2 of a different semantic class. This is a clear case of rule application (e.g. Modification, Highlighting, or Recategorisa-tion).

Ad (i)

(15a)   Petr delil chleb. 'Petr divided / shared a loaf of bread.'

(15b)   Petr delil chleb (na kuski). 'Petr divided the loaf of bread (into pieces).'

(15c)   Petr delil chleb (s druz'jami). 'Petr shared the loaf of bread (with his friends).'

In (15a), the combination V + N can have more than one meaning (as indicated in the English translation). The example sentence is ambiguous. The two instances of *delit'* 'divide, share' are related through Modification: in each case, Petr breaks the bread into pieces, but in the latter the "motoric" meaning is so to speak enriched

---

[14] A more comprehensive study would have to look not only at these, but also at more complex com-binations. Questions to be answered include, e.g., how many verb lexemes are involved in the phrases *položit' bol'nogo v postel'* and *položit' bol'nogo v kliniku* 'put the sick man to bed / send the sick man to the hospital'.

with a social component. This means that the definitions are significantly different.[15] Other examples include *žarit' kartofel'* 'fry / grill potatoes', *brosit' jabloko* 'throw / throw away the apple', *česat' borodu* 'scratch / comb one's beard', etc.

Ad (ii)

(16a)   Petr položil brevno na zemlju. 'Petr put the beam down on the ground.'

(16b)   Petr položil korobku v karman. 'Petr put the box in his pocket.'

(16c)   Petr položil trubku. 'Petr put down the receiver.'

The arguments *brevno* 'beam', *korobka* 'box', and *trubka* 'receiver' are non-human and inanimate. How they are to be put (or put down) and in which position they find themselves afterwards is a matter of world knowledge (of beams and boxes and receivers); the differences need not be listed in a dictionary. Utterances such as (16c) are not ambiguous: wether the receiver rests in a horizontal or a vertical position depends on the sort of telephone (wall-mounted or table model), not on the verbal meaning. Other examples include *otkryt' čemodan / okno* 'open the suitcase / the window', *čertit' liniju / plan* 'draw a line / a plan', *est' ris paločkami / est' tarelku supa* 'eat rice with chopsticks / eat a bowl of soup'.

Ad (iii)

(17a)   Marina sprjatala knigu v škafu. 'Marina hid the book in the wardrobe.'

(17b)   Marina sprjatala druga v kvartire. 'Marina hid her boy-friend in her flat.'

The non-human argument *kniga* 'book' in (17a) is replaced with the human actant *drug* 'boy-friend' in (17b). The meaning of *sprjatat'* 'hide' is not affected by this substitution; its lexicographical definition remains unchanged. Other examples include *položit' knigu v sumku / bol'nogo v postel'* 'put the book in the bag / the sick man to bed', *dvigat' stulom / dvigat' pal'cem* 'move the chair (while sitting on it) / move one's finger'.

Ad (iv)

(18a)   Marina brosila mjač. 'Marina threw the ball.'

---

[15] A sentence like *Petr shared the bread with his friends* is not always meant literally. When it is not, we are dealing with an occurrence of *pars pro toto* and/or of recategorisation (compare uses like *delit' radosti i goresti* 'share happiness and sorrow'). At first sight, such uses could be taken to be variants within a single lexeme. Further investigation is however required.

(18b)   Marina brosila druga. 'Marina finished the relationship with her
        boy-friend.'

As in (iii), a human argument is replaced with a non-human argument. The difference is that the meaning now changes significantly: the instances belong to two different lexemes and cannot possibly be gathered·under one lexicographical definition.
The meaning change demonstrated here is a result of rule application, and more specifically of Recategorisation. An example of Modification would be *česat' spinu
linejkoj / česat' volosy grebnem* 'scratch one's back with a ruler / comb one's hair
with a comb'.

Type (ii) is the most interesting one from our point of view: nowhere else are the
problems inherent in the count of meanings of a verb greater than they are here.
Dictionaries are likely to present quite different lemma structures for all types, but
especially so for type (ii).

It is obviously not possible to establish *a priori* lists of second argument nouns for
each type. Consider the following lists ("sets"):

$M_1 =$ {frozen chicken, bike, picture, bottle of milk, book, house, watch,
          budgie, island, star, ...}

$M_2 =$ {ball, stone, hat, shoe, bottle, book, TV, ...}

$M_3 =$ {Motorrad 'motorbike', Roller 'scooter', Fahrrad 'bicycle', Auto
          'car', Laster 'lorry', Traktor 'tractor', ...}

$M_4 =$ {motorbike, scooter, bicycle, ... }

$M_5 =$ {car, bus, lorry, tractor, ...}

Each verb selects its own list members. M_1 represents members of the class
EVERYTHING THAT CAN BE BOUGHT, M_2 members of the class EVERYTHING THAT CAN
BE THROWN, and M_3 members of the class ALLES WAS MAN FAHREN KANN. There is
no single class in English that corresponds to the latter. Two classes are required,
namely EVERYTHING THAT CAN BE RIDDEN (cf. M_4) and EVERYTHING THAT CAN BE
DRIVEN (cf. M_5). What seemed to be purely encyclopedic knowledge (cf. EVE-
RYTHING THAT CAN BE BOUGHT) turns out to be linguistic information (cf. EVE-
RYTHING THAT CAN BE RIDDEN VS. ALLES WAS MAN FAHREN KANN). The exact labels
for the lists are EVERYTHING THAT CAN BE CORRECTLY COMBINED WITH *buy*₁,
EVERYTHING THAT CAN BE CORRECTLY COMBINED WITH *throw*₁, EVERYTHING THAT

CAN BE CORRECTLY COMBINED WITH GERMAN *fahren*₁, and so on.[16] Variable amounts of encyclopedic knowledge are still involved: encyclopedic information plays an important role in the definition of verbs such as *otkryt'* 'open' because the way things are opened varies according to their nature.

Since *a priori* lists for verb-noun combination types cannot be established, different meanings of a verb have to be listed on the basis of the different argument types it may select. It is not a straightforward task, though, to determine what exactly is to be considered an argument type. [+ human], [– human], [+ animated], [– animated], [+ artificial], [– artificial], etc. are the sort of features traditionally used to briefly characterise argument types. But how are we supposed to classify *okno* 'window', *butylka* 'bottle' and *čemodan* 'suitcase' in the context of the verb *otkryt'* 'open'? The well-known structuralist feature analysis is certainly very useful in investigations of metaphor, but for our purposes it appears to be too rough or simply inadequate (due to its binarity). For example, *drug* 'friend' and *mjač* 'ball' are easily contrasted in terms of the feature [± animated]; but this opposition carries no information regarding the number of meanings of the verbs they may be combined with (*sprjatat' mjač / sprjatat' druga* 'hide the ball / hide one's boy-friend', *brosit' mjač / brosit' druga* 'throw the ball / finish the relationship with the boy-friend'); cf. also the opposition between *linija* 'line' and *plan* 'plan' ([± complex]) or between *spina* 'back' and *kudri* 'curls' ([± hair]) and its importance when it comes to deciding the number of meanings of *čertit'* and *česat'*.

Some verbs have more specific selectional restrictions than others: they are the easiest ones to define. Verbs with relatively weak selectional restrictions are obviously a different matter: it is quite hard to find a non-tautological category-title for the nouns that could serve as second arguments for *buy, paint, open*, etc. Furthermore, it is important to emphasise that in principle meta-language and object-language have to be the same (cf. Mel'čuk 1988). Only then could it be guaranteed that the complex concepts used in definitions are compatible with the semantic specifics of the object-language. This means that a lexicographical definition can only operate with the concepts available in the object-language. If a language does not offer a hyperonym for DOOR, LID, TOP, CAP, COVER (which we would need to define the literal instances of *otkryt'* 'open' using one paraphrase), it is virtually impossible to construe a single comprehensible definition. Besides, were such a comprehensive definition to be offered, the question would arise wether this is the correct way of capturing the meaning(s) of a lemma. Of course, lexicography consists in making abstractions on the basis of the instances of a word (which is actually equivalent to the acquisition of the vocabulary of one's mother tongue). But if the abstractions go further than the

---

[16] There seems to be a considerable amount of tautology involved here, but the difficulties in separating the various levels (BUY vs. *buy*) are not confined to the topic at hand; they are in fact a basic problem in semantics.

concepts of a language allow, what happens to the psychological reality of the given lexicographical entry? In my opinion, neglecting the limits of the object-language in meta-language leads to a situation where the differing semantic structures of different languages are ignored for the sake of a lexicographical meta-language, irrespective of the object-language.

The preceding remarks lead to the second main thesis of this paper:

> (V)   More important than the need for a definition capturing all instances of a lexeme is the need for functional devices (FOs) separating the meanings of a word.

Thus far, several principles or criteria have been identified for the purpose of separating linguistic from encyclopedic knowledge, i.e. lexemic meanings from variants: they are (i) ambiguity, (ii) meaning transferability, and (iii) FO formulation. Applying each of these to our chosen example, the verb *otkryt'* 'open', we find for instance:

Ad (i)

No ambiguity arises in the case of *otkryt' kastrjulju* 'open the pot' vs. *otkryt' butylku* 'open the bottle' vs. *otkryt' dver'* 'open the door'.

Ad (ii)

A door cannot be opened in the same way as, say, a bottle: there is no meaning transferability between these two instances.

Ad (iii)

Among the various instances, no rule that has the status of a FO can be formulated.[17]

The net result of the analysis is a set of rather different instances of a single lexeme. The reason for this is to be found in the existence of referential differences at the level of the second argument, or rather in the encyclopedic knowledge connected with *kastrjulja* 'pot', *butylka* 'bottle', *dver'* 'door'. The best way to reflect this in a lexicographical description seems to be through a list of typical instances (which thus fulfil the role of variants; for the *MAS*-structure of the lemma see (5a) above).[18]

---

[17] Each principle may behave differently with different verbs. In the case of *otkryt'*, the ambiguity test and the transfer test are stronger than the FO-formulation test.

[18] Depending on the object that is being opened, the combination V + N sometimes allows a further optional argument denoting an instrument (e.g. *otkryt' butylku štoporom* 'open a bottle with a corkscrew'). Examples where such an optional argument undergoes meaning change (as in *open the door with a key*) are not considered here. I also wish to point out that the proposed dictionary entry in (19) is by no means "final". It is a first and modest attempt at accounting for the meaning of the verb *otkryt'* in a principled way. I am not very pleased with the precise phrasing in I.1.c, but find it hard to come up with a better alternative.

(19) OTKRYT': X OTKRYVAET Y =

I.1.a. X removes the cover or stopper Z (mostly placed in a horizontal position) of a three-dimensional object Y. *Nataša otkryvaet kastrjulju / konservy / butylku* 'Nataša opens the pot / the can / the bottle (*lit.*)'

I.1.b. X pushes away the outer side (mostly placed in a vertical position) of an object Y, categorised as two-dimensional, that is part of another object Z (while the inner side of Y remains in place). *Nataša otkryvaet dver' / okno / rojal'* 'Nataša opens the door / the window / the grand piano'

I.1.c. X takes apart the two (or more) outer sides of an object (while the inner sides stay together). *Nataša otkryvaet knigu / glaza / zontik.* 'Nataša opens the book / her eyes / the umbrella'

To further illustrate the power of the operationalisations, let us have a look at another verb, namely *snjat'* 'take down, take off, remove'. Typical instances are:

(20a) *A/P 1, MAS 1*

Ol'ga snjala jaščik / trubku / knigu s polki. 'Ol'ga took down the box / picked up the receiver / picked the book from the shelf'

(20b) *A/P 2, MAS 1 & 2*

Ol'ga i Igor' snjali koleso / štory$_{MAS\ 1}$ / pautinu$_{MAS\ 1}$ / polki so sten. 'Ol'ga and Igor' removed the wheel / the curtains / the spider web / the shelves from the wall'

(20c) *A/P 3, MAS 3*

Ol'ga snjala pal'to / kol'co / šljapu / čechly s mebeli. 'Ol'ga took off her coat / her ring / her hat / removed the cover from the furniture'

(20d) *A/P 4, MAS 4*

Ol'ga snjala kožuru s apel'siny / snjala verchnij sloj / kožicu s kolbasy. 'Ol'ga took the peel off the orange / took the upper layer off / took the skin off the sausage'

The various second arguments in (20b), (20c), and (20d) appear to make up lexical categories: keeping in mind the necessity to insure that the labels we chose are not too general, let us call them THINGS THAT ARE FIXED, THINGS PEOPLE WEAR, and ALL SORTS OF COVER. The instance *Ol'ga snjala čechly s mebeli* 'Ol'ga removed the cover of the furniture' is in my opinion not a token of the meaning shown in (20c), as in *A/P* and *MAS*, but of that shown in (20d).

Again we have different combinations of a concrete verb and concrete second arguments. But how many meanings do we have? The structures of *A/P* and *MAS* are
nearly identical, but are they correct? To clarify this, I shall now apply the principles
of operationalisation:

(i) Are the various instances (lexically) ambiguous?

(ii) Is the specific meaning of an instance transferable?

An utterance like *Ol'ga snjala trubku* in (20a) appears to be phraseological, because
the notion of a direction of movement is absent. Nevertheless, the utterance is well
placed within (20a), even though in a dictionary a short comment would certainly be
useful. Exactly like the other instances cited in (20a), *Ol'ga snjala trubku* may be
ambiguous: 1. 'Ol'ga picked up the receiver', 2. 'Ol'ga removed the receiver (because the telephone is out of order)'. Checking the instances in (20b) to (20d) for
ambiguity, we find that an utterance such as *Ol'ga snjala štory* is ambiguous, too.
On the one hand it could mean that the curtains are hanging at the window and Ol'ga
is taking them off, for instance because they are dirty and need washing. On the
other hand the curtains may be lying (folded up) on a shelf in a shop and Ol'ga is
taking them down to buy them. The same is true of *Ol'ga snjala pal'to*, which refers
either to Ol'ga taking off her coat, or to Ol'ga taking down a coat (e.g., from the top
of a wardrobe). It might be argued that *Ol'ga snjala kožuru* in (20d) is ambiguous as
well because, without the additional phrase *s apel'siny*, it is not clear if Ol'ga is re-
moving the peel from the table or the peel from the fruit. Of course, out of context,
the latter interpretation is certain to be highly preferred.

Thus, roughly speaking, all the instances in (20b) to (20d) are ambiguous: all of
them can be interpreted as having the meaning described in (20a). It follows that the
meaning of (20a) is easy to transfer. Transferring the meaning of the examples in
(20a) to the constructions in (20b) leads to a reconceptualisation of objects like
wheels and curtains (from fixed to non-fixed). A transfer in the opposite direction
may be more problematical, because fixed boxes or books are less common. The
possibility of a meaning transfer from (20c) to (20b) suggests once again that an instance such as *Ol'ga snjala pal'to* is ambiguous between 'take off one's coat' and
'take down the coat (e.g., from a hook on the coatstand)'. The latter may be thought
of as similar to taking down curtains. A transfer the other way round (ignoring the
second argument *čechly* 'cover (of furniture)'; see above) is almost impossible. The
meaning 'take off a ring' in (20c) cannot be transferred to the meaning 'take the peel
off the orange', and vice versa. A transfer from (20c) to (20b) is difficult to carry
out, because fixed rings, hats, etc. are again not very typical.

(iii) Which FO, if any, can be reconstructed?

Without a doubt, the meanings of the tokens of *snjat'* 'take down, take off, remove'
in (20) are interrelated. As there is no mapping between categories, Recategorisation

may be excluded. The prototype of the primary meaning illustrated in (20a) is given in (21):

(21)   (object Y is at the top of Z, and) a person X gets object Y by lifting it off and taking it down.

This prototype is lost in all the other instances; Modification may therefore be excluded as well. What remains in all cited instances is that before lifting Y, Y is in contact with Z, and after lifting Y, Y is no longer in contact, but the movement top-down is out of focus in (20b) to (20d). I shall take this as evidence for Highlighting. It will be clear, though, that the notion of FOs requires further investigation. As far as I can tell, a projection of a FO onto the different meanings of (20b) to (20d) is not possible, which means that the suggestions from the ambiguity-test and the transfer-test have proved to be right.

As a result of operational principles (i), (ii), and (iii), we get the following lemma-structure:

(22)   I.1. Ol'ga snjala jaščik / knigu s polki. 'Ol'ga took down the box / the book from the shelf'

I.2.a. Ol'ga i Igor' snjali koleso / štory$_{MAS\ 1}$ / pautinu$_{MAS\ 1}$ / polki so sten. 'Ol'ga and Igor' removed the wheel / the curtains / the spider web / the shelves from the wall'

I.2.b. Ol'ga snjala pal'to / kol'co / šljapu. 'Ol'ga took off her coat / her ring / her hat'

I.2.c. Ol'ga snjala kožuru s apel'siny / snjala verchnij sloj / čechly s mebeli / kožicu s kolbasy. 'Ol'ga took the peel off the orange / took the upper layer off / removed the cover from the furniture / took the skin off the sausage'

The methodology adopted to structure the meanings of the verb *otkryt'* 'open' (or *snjat'* 'take down') is representative and can easily be applied to other verbs of the same type that are equally likely to be articulated in a misleading way in traditional lexicography (with encyclopedic information placed at the same level as linguistic information). Compare (listed are only instances that are judged as two lexemes or classified in different ways in *MAS* and/or in *A/P*): *čertit' liniju – čertit' plan* 'to draw a line – to draw a plan'; *bit' ego kulakami – bit' kulakom po stolu* 'to hit him with one's fists – to hit the table with one's fist'; *brosit' mjač – brosit' jakor'* 'to throw a ball – to throw the anchor'; *dvigat' stulom – dvigat' pal'cem* 'to move the chair (while sitting on it) – to move one's finger'; *pisat' bukvy – pisat' pis'mo* 'to write (small and capital) letters – to write a letter'; *položit' brevno / den'gi v karman / trubku* 'to lay (down) the beam / to put money in one's pocket / to put down the receiver'; *krutit' koleso – krutit' golovoj* 'to turn the wheel – to move one's head in circles'; *ryt' zemlju – ryt' kanal* 'to dig the ground – to dig a drain', *stavit' knigu v škaf – stavit' posudu na stol* 'to put the book in the cupboard – to put the crockery on the table', etc.[19]

3. Conclusion

In this paper, I have argued that, in semantics and especially in lexicography, default-like principles enabling a distinction between linguistic/lexical and encyclopedic knowledge to be made are definitely required. I have described the role of encyclopedic knowledge in lexicographical definitions of concrete verbs, and I have suggested three operationalisations to separate encyclopedia from lexicon in the domain of lexicography. The three operationalisations are as follows:

(i)   "if a phrase is ambiguous, then two meanings are involved"

       ($\rightarrow$ linguistic knowledge)

       "if a phrase is not ambiguous, then only one meaning is involved"

       ($\rightarrow$ encyclopedic knowledge)

(ii)   "if meaning transfer is possible, then two meanings are involved"

       ($\rightarrow$ linguistic knowledge)

       "if meaning transfer is not possible, then only one meaning is involved"

       ($\rightarrow$ encyclopedic knowledge)

(iii)   "if application of a Functional Operation (FO) is possible, then two meanings are involved"

       ($\rightarrow$ linguistic knowledge)

       "if application of a FO is not possible, then only one meaning is involved"

       ($\rightarrow$ encyclopedic knowledge)

---

[19] Sometimes, a lemma reflects the genesis of a meaning. The verb *položit'* originally meant 'lay down', and *stavit'* 'put in a vertical position'. Neither possessed the variant meaning 'to put somewhere' without any indication of the position of the affected object. Thus, at a synchronic level, the varying meanings seem to be a matter of combination, not a matter of the verbal meaning itself. Incidentally, *MAS*'s structure of the uses of *položit'* is *položit'*$_1$ and *položit'*$_2$, whereas the uses of *stavit'* are presented as variants (and hence are listed under one number). Also, sometimes a change of object coincides with a change of the situational gestalt (i.e., a change of the aspectual partner), e.g. *ryt' zemlju* 'dig the ground' is a process, *ryt' kanal* 'dig a drain' an event. For this kind of fuzziness of meaning and the regular alternations of gestalt, see Lehmann (1997).

5. References

Aitchison, Jean. 1994 [1987]. *Words in the mind. An introduction to the mental lexicon.* Oxford: Blackwell.

Apresjan, Yuri D. 1992. *Lexical semantics. User's guide to contemporary Russian vocabulary.* Ann Arbor: Karoma.

(*A/P* =) Apresjan, Jurij D.; Páll, Erna. 1982. *Russkij glagol – vengerskij glagol.* Budapešt: Tankën'vkiado.

Bierwisch, Manfred. 1970. "Semantics". In John Lyons (ed.), *New horizons in linguistics.* Harmondsworth: Penguin. 166-184.

Bierwisch, Manfred. 1979. "Wörtliche Bedeutung. Eine pragmatische Gretchenfrage". In Günther Grewendorf (ed.), *Sprechakttheorie und Semantik.* Frankfurt: Suhrkamp. 119-148.

Bierwisch, Manfred. 1983. "Semantische und konzeptuelle Repräsentation lexikalischer Einheiten". In Rudolf Růžička & Wolfgang Motsch (ed.), *Untersuchungen zur Semantik.* Berlin: Akademie-Verlag. 61-99.

Born-Rauchenecker, Eva. 1997. "Überlegungen zur Verbpolysemie und ihrer Lexikographie". In Jana Schulze & Eduard Werner (ed.), *Linguistische Beiträge zur Slavistik aus Deutschland und Österreich. V. JungslavistInnen-Treffen Bautzen 1996.* München: Sagner. 34-66.

Cruse, D. Alan. 1986. *Lexical semantics.* Cambridge: Cambridge University Press.

Lakoff, George; Johnson, Mark. 1980. *Metaphors we live by.* Chicago: University of Chicago Press.

Langacker, Ronald W. 1987-1991. *Foundations of cognitive grammar* (2 vol.). Stanford: Stanford University Press.

Lehmann, Volkmar. 1995. "Rekategorisierung und interne Struktur von Kategorien (Die Beispiele Aspekt und Metapher)". In Klaus Harer & Helmut Schaller (ed.), *Festschrift für Hans-Bernd Harder zum 60. Geburtstag.* München: Otto Sagner. 303-319.

Lehmann, Volkmar. 1996. "Die Rekonstruktion von Bedeutungsentwicklung und -motiviertheit mit Funktionalen Operationen". In Wolfgang Girke (ed.), *Slavistische Linguistik 1995.* München: Sagner. 255-289.

Lehmann, Volkmar. 1997. "Grammatičeskaja derivacija u vida i tipy glagol'nych leksem". *Trudy aspektologičeskogo seminara filologičeskogo fakul'teta MGU im M.V. Lomonosova*, vol. 2. Moskva: Izd-vo Moskovskogo universiteta. 54-68.

Leiss, Elisabeth. 1986. "Das Lexikon ist keine Enzyklopädie. Antwort auf J. Ziegler, LB 93 (1984)". *Linguistische Berichte* 101. 74-84.

MAS. 1981-84. *Malyj Akademičeskij slovar' russkogo jazyka v chetyreh tomah*. Second edition (4 vol.). Moskva.

Mel'čuk, Igor A. 1988. "Semantic description of lexical units in an explanatory combinatorial dictionary. Basic principles and heuristic criteria". *International journal of lexicography* 1. 165-188.

Mel'čuk, Igor A.; Žolkovskij, Alexander K. 1984. *Tolkovo-kombinatornyj slovar' russkogo jazyka. Opyt semantiko-sintaksiceskogo opisanija russkoi leksiki*. Vienna: Wiener Slawistischer Almanach. Referred to in the text as *TKS*.

Reuther, Tilmann. 1990. "Semantik und Situation. Zur Bedeutung einiger russischer Verben der Fortbewegung". In Walter Breu (ed.), *Slavistische Linguistik 1989*. München: Sagner. 259-267.

Schwarz, Monika. 1992. *Einführung in die kognitive Linguistik*. Tübingen: Francke.

Šmelev, Dmitrij N. 1973. *Problemy semantičeskogo analiza leksiki (na materiale russkogo jazyka)*. Moskva: Nauka.

Taylor, John R. 1992. "How many meanings does a word have?" *Stellenbosch papers in linguistics* 25. 133-168.

Taylor, John R. 1995 [1989]. *Linguistic categorization. Prototypes in linguistic theory*. Oxford: Oxford University Press.

TKS. Cf. Mel'čuk & Žolkovskij (1984).

Tuggy, David. 1993. "Ambiguity, polysemy, and vagueness". *Cognitive linguistics* 4. 273-290.

Wierzbicka, Anna. 1996. *Semantics. Primes and universals*. Oxford: Oxford University Press.

Wierzbicka, Anna. 1997. *Understanding cultures through their key words*. Oxford: Oxford University Press.

Knowledge *of* words versus knowledge *about* words: The conceptual basis of lexical relations[1]

M. Lynne Murphy

School of Cognitive and Computing Sciences, University of Sussex,
Brighton BN1 9QH, United Kingdom
E-mail: lynnem@cogs.susx.ac.uk

0. Introduction

In the Beginning (of Generative Grammar), there was (lexical) Chaos. But it did not last long. In the same year that Chomsky (1965:84) wrote that the lexicon is "an unordered list", James Deese's book *The Structure of Associations in Language and Thought* (Deese 1965) paved the way for several theories of a semantically organised lexicon. Models such as Adrienne Lehrer's semantic fields (Lehrer 1974) and the "psycholexicographical" WordNet lexical database (G. Miller 1990) posited a lexicon ordered by semantic relations such as synonymy, antonymy (or contrast), and hyponymy.

Sometimes such theories, following Deese, saw the semantic relations among words as providing basic structures that constrain (or even constitute) the lexical represen-

[1] I am grateful to Bert Peeters and two anonymous reviewers for feedback on an earlier draft of this paper, and to the Baylor University (Waco, Texas) Research Council for grant support during Fall 1998. The arguments contained herein are expanded and their implications more fully addressed in Murphy (forthcoming).

tation of meaning. In more recent work, Lehrer (1992) and G. Miller (1998) make more modest claims about the semantic potential of lexical networks and claim that only a small number of semantic relations, including antonymy and synonymy, are properly lexical. However, the idea that the lexicon can or should be organised on semantic grounds persists, as does the notion that relation on definitional grounds is separable from relation on encyclopedic grounds (Mettinger 1994).

In this paper, I argue that semantic relations among words are *not* represented in the lexicon. This argument rests on common assumptions about the division of labor among lexicon, grammar, and conceptual knowledge, and on facts about lexical relations phenomena that force an extralexical treatment of semantic relations. Thus, by this argument, no matter how much (if any) semantic information the lexicon contains, information about a word's synonyms or antonyms is part of encyclopedic knowledge.

Arguments for semantic organisation of the lexicon are presented in section 1, after which they are critiqued in section 2 as being insufficient to account for the rich and variable uses of semantic lexical relations. Section 3 presents the means to account for these relations without recourse to lexical organisation. In this treatment, relations among words are generated through two interrelated and general cognitive principles and constitute conceptual knowledge about words, rather than linguistic knowledge of them. In section 4, the implications of this treatment are examined. Not only does it account for behaviour in psycholinguistic experiments (e.g., free word association tests), but it also allows for a variety of factors to come into play in judgements of word-relatedness. The model accounts for different levels of context-sensitivity or rigidity in antonymic pairings or synonymic groupings, since the relations may be learned through experience or derived from other concepts. In my conclusion (section 5), I show these findings to be compatible with a variety of current positions on whether semantic content can be represented in the lexicon.

1. Initial evidence for semantic relations in the lexicon

The assumption that semantic relations among lexical items are fixed in the lexicon seems to follow quite naturally from the position that they appear to be fixed in the mind. Before arguing against this assumption, let us look at the evidence that lexical relations are indeed mentally fixed. Essentially, two types of arguments have supported that position.

The first argument relies on behaviour in psycholinguistic experiments, especially the free word-association task. In such experiments, subjects hear or read a single word stimulus and must give an automatic one-word response. In school-age children and adults, responses are very often related to the stimulus by paradigmatic lexical relations, especially antonymy, synonymy, or hyponymy. So, for example, the typical response to *black* is an antonym, *white* (74.5% in the 1952 Minnesota norms, Jenkins 1970), and the second most common answer, *dark*, is a near-synonym. Considering the number of idioms and compound words that begin with *black* and the number of black things in the world, it is remarkable that more subjects did not give syntagmatically related responses (e.g., *widow, bird, board, sheep, jack, mood, flag, Monday*) or other conceptually related responses from different grammatical or semantic categories (e.g., *mourning*). However, not all stimuli evoke such consistent responses. For example, the top response for *trouble* (*bad*) was given by only 8.83% of respondents in the Minnesota norms. And not all stimuli evoke paradigmatically related responses, even within a single grammatical category or semantic field. For example, while in the case of *table* the set-contrastive relation *table-chair* had the highest association rate of any item in the Minnesota norms (83.25%), the top response for its fellow furniture name, *bed*, was *sleep* (57.93%), rather than a related member of the furniture category. Thus, the work of explaining word association responses is not finished if we posit lexical representation of semantic relations. Theories of lexical organisation must also explain why certain words have more consistent responses than others, and why not all words within a syntactic or semantic category evoke the same types of responses.

The second argument advanced in favour of the thesis that semantic relations are relations in the lexicon focuses on the two most salient such relations, i.e. synonymy and antonymy. Whereas semantic relations should be relations among meanings (rather than among words *per se*), synonymy and antonymy are found to be based on properties of the words themselves (rather than on properties of the corresponding concepts or denotata, for instance). They qualify as relations among words, rather than among the concepts that the words refer to, and so it is often argued that they are relations in the lexicon. Synonymy is a relation between two words that represent the same concept. Since only one concept is represented by the words, synonymy cannot be a relation among the concepts that the words represent and is therefore definitionally a relation among words (or some subset of their senses, see section 2.1). Antonymy is a slightly trickier case. The concepts represented by two words must be in opposition for antonymy to exist, but semantic opposition is not a sufficient condition for antonymy. For example, *hate* is the antonym of *love*, but its synonyms (*abhor, despise, detest*) are not antonyms of *love* (we might say they are opposites of *love*, but not antonyms of it). The special privilege of some oppositional pairings over pairings of their synonyms is evident not only in word association tests, but also in corpus studies that reveal much greater than chance rates of co-occurrence of traditional antonym pairs, in contrast to pairings involving their synonyms (Charles & Miller 1989). I will call these typical antonym pairings (e.g., *high-low, black-white, love-hate*) canonical antonyms, and other types of examples (e.g., *hate-adore, blue-red*) non-canonical opposites. Thus, antonymy is a relation between two words, not simply between two meanings. We can contrast this to the case of hyponymy, where if *sedan* is a hyponym of *car*, then it is necessarily also a hyponym of *auto*.

In brief, evidence from word association tests and corpus studies indicates that some words stand in set relations to each other. This leads to the assumption that particular associations are represented in the mind. In the case of antonymy and synonymy, words themselves, not just the concepts they map to, are related. Thus, it is assumed that these relations must be represented in our store of word knowledge, the lexicon.

2. Evidence against semantic relations in the lexicon

The relations revealed by free word-association tasks are not always relations between either meanings of words or words as such, and thus cannot be used in evidence for or against lexical organisation. For instance, *bird* is the top response to *eagle* in the Minnesota norms, but the type-token relation this reflects is not so much a relation among words as a relation among the denotata of the words (eagles are birds). Similarly, the set-contrastive relation between *table* and *chair*, although not a type-token relation, may well be a relation among denotata rather than among words (chairs are often found in the vicinity of tables).

Still, it is clear that relations among lexical items exist and that the very regular and automatic co-occurrence of certain pairs is evidence that they may have special status in the mental representation of language. However, any leap to the conclusion that these relations are therefore represented in the lexicon is premature. The following subsections outline some of the reasons why that leap should not be taken. The discussions tend to focus on antonymy, because it is the more complex relation.

2.1. Polysemy

While antonymy and synonymy are not just relations among concepts, neither are they relations among words, since they involve specific senses of words. For instance, *car* and *automobile* are not semantically equivalent – they are only synonyms to the extent that they have senses or uses that are semantically equivalent. *Car* is a synonym of *automobile* when it is used to refer to four-wheeled, engine-propelled road vehicles made to carry a few people, but not when it is used to refer to a railroad car or an elevator car. Similarly, antonymic relations vary by sense. For example, the antonym of *dry* is typically wet, but the opposite of *dry wine* is *sweet wine*, not **wet wine*.

The examples presented here may actually be cases of homonymy, such that different lexical items rather than senses within single lexical items are contrasted. But if we were to use antonymic or synonymic relations as a test for homonymy, the size of the lexicon would explode. In addition to dry_1 in *a dry towel*, we would need dry_2

to account for its antonymic relationship with *moist* (but not *wet*) in the context of *a dry cake*, and *dry₃* to account for its antonymic relationship with *oily* (but not *wet*) in *dry problem skin*, and *dry₄* to account for its antonymic relationship with *productive* in *a dry cough*. Murphy & Andrew (1993) further demonstrate the context-specificity of antonymy, providing experimental evidence that antonyms of adjectives vary according to the nouns that the adjectives modify. For example, the opposite of *fresh* in *fresh fish* is different from the opposite of *fresh* in *fresh bread* or *fresh shirt*. Thus, antonymy does not seem to relate lexical entries or sense entries in the lexicon, but instead it relates specific applications of words. Trying to treat these relations within the lexicon involves a great (if not impossible) amount of counter-intuitive and counter-productive replication of lexical information.

If we try to account for single words that have a variety of antonyms by claiming that antonyms relate sense entries rather than word entries, then we also create a problem for words that have a number of senses, but only one antonym. If each sense has its own relations to synonyms and antonyms, our treatment of lexical relations does not properly generalise about words that have the same synonyms or antonyms for a number of senses. For example, if *long* has different senses when it describes ropes, lives, or the English vowels [aj] and [ej], then each of those sense representations needs to be linked to the antonym *short*. Thus, it is difficult to make a workable model of a lexicon that is organised by antonymy and synonymy, because semantic relations are both sensitive and insensitive to sense differentiations.

2.2. Binarity

The feasibility of organising the lexicon on the basis of paradigmatic semantic relations is further called into question by the failure of theories that choose this tack to explain why antonymy is typically a *binary* relation, whereas other relations regularly involve more than two words (or meanings) at a time. Some models, such as WordNet, hold that binary contrast is basic to the lexicon, and thus do not properly capture the non-binary nature of other contrasts. Others, such as Lehrer's semantic field theory, treat contrast as basic, allowing binary contrasts to be predicted by the availability of vocabulary within a field's structure. Neither of these approaches can satisfactorily explain how binary opposition and non-binary contrast can co-exist within the same semantic field. They fail to justify why, apart from the contrast set *sweet-sour-bitter-salty*, certain binary oppositions involving those words do appear, but not others. For instance, the contrast set supports oppositions such as *sweet-sour* or *sweet-bitter*, but *bitter-salty* or *salty-sour* are far less likely to be contrasted on their own.

One approach that has difficulties with larger sets is Lehrer's semantic field theory, which arranges words into contrast sets, with antonymy arising quite naturally where only two words are involved. However, in the semantic field in Figure 1, *happy*, which belongs to a larger set of emotion terms, is placed in an *antonymic* relation with *unhappy* at the top level and in a *contrast* relation with *unhappy*'s hyponyms, *sad, angry,* and *frightened,* on the lower level. There is no recognition of the fact that one of the so-called contrast relations (*happy-sad*) is in fact as privileged (or 'canonical') as the antonymic relation (*happy-unhappy*), as demonstrated by word association and natural language oppositions. The relation *happy-sad* is not even treated as a case of antonymy. Instead, one privileged relation is being promoted at the expense of the other. Just how the antonymy of *happy-sad* can be represented without doing something entirely arbitrary to the field structure is not at all clear.

happy	unhappy		
	sad	angry	frightened

Figure 1: A semantic field representation for selected emotion terms

Larger contrast sets do not always include privileged pairs. Outside a particular context (such as colour theory or traffic signal systems), one is hard-pressed to argue that any of the basic chromatic colour terms (*red, blue, orange,* etc.) has a single antonym. For the WordNet architecture, which organises the adjective lexicon around antonymic pairings of basic-level adjectives, this creates a problem: how to deal with adjectives that are in larger contrast sets.

To illustrate, let us look at colour terminology in more detail. WordNet treats the basic colour terms as non-basic words: instead of contrasting colours to each other, the current version (1.6) opposes the terms *chromatic* and *achromatic,* and the colour names are coded as linking to *chromatic* by the similarity relation (K. Miller 1998). Figure 2 illustrates the latest WordNet representation of the colour set.

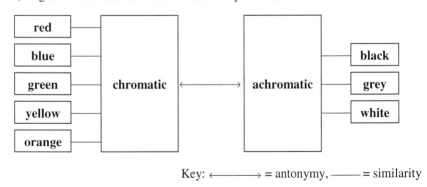

Key: ⟷ = antonymy, ⎯⎯ = similarity

Figure 2: Colours in the WordNet adjective lexicon

Hence, in order to account for the lexical relations among colour terms while using binary antonymy as an organisational principle, WordNet must treat non-basic vocabulary as if it were basic.[2]

A second oddity in WordNet has to do with basic-level adjectives that do not have a clear antonym. Because antonymy is a basic organisational principle in the WordNet adjective lexicon, dummy antonyms must be inserted in some cases where no antonyms exist. For example, *not-angry* exists as a lexical item in WordNet because there is no form **unangry* (K. Miller 1998).

2.3. Productivity

If semantic relations are predictable, they should not be included as arbitrary information in the lexicon. One indication that they are predictable is if they are the results of productive processes. That is, if we can create new instances of synonymy or antonymy, then there must be some relational mechanism that predicts these relations. Thus, evidence of new antonymic pairings is partial evidence against lexical representation of such relations.[3]

The productivity of synonymy is obvious: if we invent a new English word that represents (to some extent) the same thing that an existing English word represents, then the new word is automatically a synonym of the older word. The binary nature of antonymy, on the other hand, makes it seem less productive. If one antonym exists for a word, there should be no room for a second. Occasionally a single word sense does have two canonical opposites, e.g. *happy-sad* and *happy-unhappy*. The negating prefixes, *un-*, *iN-*, and *non-* allow some productivity in antonym-making. While *un-* and *iN-* are semantically restricted, *non-* is completely productive, allowing any adjective or noun to have an antonym. However, at least in some cases, antonymy created by *non-* seems more akin to phrasal negation than to most cases of canonical antonymy, since canonical antonyms (including *happy-unhappy*), unlike phrasal negation and antonymy created by *non-*, typically refer to two states rather than one. If we say that some people are either happy or unhappy, then we know which of two states those people are in. But if we say that they are either happy or non-happy, we only know what *single* state they are either in or not in.[4]

The productivity of antonymy can be seen to be at work in items that only have opposites in specific contexts. Even though *red* has no canonical antonym, it has sev-

---

[2] This is rather ironic, considering that the notion of 'basic' level terminology comes to us from the study of colour terms in Berlin & Kay (1969).

[3] If, apart from that, we can show that the new relations were predictable from and in fact predicted by the same relational principle that was responsible for the established relations, the job is finished (cf. sections 2.5 and 3.2).

[4] See Horn (1989) for discussion of the differences and similarities among various types of affixal and phrasal negation.

eral opposites in particular contexts.[5] For people who know colour theory, every colour has two opposites; in pigments, the opposite of *red* is *green*, and for light, the opposite of *red* is *cyan*. In semiotic systems, the colour red (and thus the word *red*) has other antonyms: for traffic signals, it is green; in Chinese and Japanese culture the opposite of red ('good fortune') is white ('bad fortune'). But even outside such scientific and semiotic systems, English speakers can come up with viable opposites for *red* and explain how they did so, whether it is *blue* (because red and blue go together) or *black* (because red and black oppose each other on a checkerboard) or some other colour. While the more technical term *antonym* is reserved for the prototypical or canonical cases, the near-synonym *opposite* is used for any type of contrast, including those that are more context-dependent or debatable, as in the comic strip dialogue in (1).

(1)   Mr. Dithers: Why do you always say the opposite of whatever I say? If I say right, you say left! If I say bad, you say good! If I say red, you say brown!

          Dagwood: Brown isn't the opposite of red... I think blue is.

In fact, the category of 'opposites' is so broad that it can even apply (on non-semantic grounds) to proper names. In the conversation in (2) (reported by Georgia Green, personal communication), the name Tom Jones is the opposite of Engelbert Humperdinck because they represent extremes on the scales of commonality and complexity for names.

(2)   (Parents explaining to daughter why pop singer Engelbert Humperdinck named himself after a 19th century composer.)

          Mother: You know, to call attention to himself, and differentiate himself from the competition.

          Father: The other guy that sang the same kind of music went by the name Tom Jones. As a name, Engelbert Humperdinck is the opposite of Tom Jones.

---

[5] Some readers may feel that the colour terms are different from other contrast sets, and not worth discussing as having opposites. But the difference is often overstated. It is true that there are no context-independent binary oppositions within the chromatic colour set, unlike, say, in the emotion set (*happy-sad*). However, rejecting antonymy within the colour set on the basis that there is no good-bad contrast (context-independent binary oppositions, unlike colour terminology, generally oppose what is 'good' or positive to what is 'bad' or negative: *happy* vs. all the other emotions, *sweet* vs. all the other tastes, etc.) is not a legitimate move. Not all antonyms involve such a contrast, e.g. *hot-cold*. The non-existence of morphological opposites for the colour terms (**unred* vs. *unhappy*) is also not relevant: the achromatic colours, which do include the antonym pair *black-white*, cannot take the *un*-prefix either (**unblack, *unwhite*).

Non-canonical opposition among members of contrast sets, opposition of non-semantic characteristics, and other cases of context-based opposition are *not* accounted for by theories of a semantically organised lexicon.[6] Elimination of these categories may seem appropriate, since they do not have the same canonical status that antonymy has. Non-canonical opposition might be a pragmatic (conceptual) matter, while canonical antonymy might be a lexical (linguistic) matter. However, antonymy is an example of opposition. If one (viz. opposition) is excluded from the lexicon, so should the other (viz. antonymy), especially since they are both productive, and therefore predictable, hence not at their place in the lexicon.

The phenomena of canonical antonymy and context-dependent opposition seem interrelated for several reasons. Both are binary relations. Both can represent relations among words, not just relations among meanings (as the proper name example shows). Opposition usually, like antonymy, involves semantic contrast. And antonymy, like opposition, is affected by context, at least to the extent that it is through context that we can identify the relevant sense of a word in order to determine its appropriate opposite, as in the case of *dry*. Because antonymy is an example of opposition, it also seems that the two relations should share the same source, in other words, they should come to be by similar processes. Since one is retained and the other rejected, this is not acknowledged in semantic field and WordNet models. They treat lexical relations (including antonymy, but not opposition) as primitive elements of lexical organisation. Since antonymy is considered to be a somewhat arbitrary relationship in the WordNet view (in that it involves word forms, not just meanings), antonymic links in the lexicon would have to be learned through experience, such as the experience of antonyms co-occurring in utterances at greater than chance rates. In contrast, the non-canonical oppositions would have to be invented.[7] Such unrelated treatment of antonyms and opposites may neglect generalisations that can be made across the wider range of semantic relations among words.

2.4. Prototypicality

In the previous section, a distinction was made between canonical and non-canonical relation pairs. What was left out of the picture, quite deliberately, is the fact that, among the non-canonical and perhaps even the canonical examples, some pairings are better than others. This is true for synonymy, since lexical items may be argued to be "better" or "best" synonyms for other lexical items, as in example (3).

---

[6] WordNet accounts for some of the non-canonical opposites by noting 'indirect' antonym relations among items whose synonyms are direct antonyms. In Figure 2 above, *chromatic* and *achromatic* are direct antonyms, and *red* and *grey* are indirect antonyms.

[7] While indirect antonymy in the WordNet structure accounts for some cases of non-canonical opposition, it does not account for others, such as opposition within contrast sets.

(3)   You could become landed gentry which I think would be the best
        synonym for proprietor.

        (*Notes on the New Jersey Proprietors,* Edward Ball Group, 1995-
        1997; http://www.altlaw.com/edball/propnote.htm)

Similarly, we acknowledge better and worse opposites or antonyms, as in (4).

(4)   The phrase being tossed around (...) was "Pain is temporary, pride
        is forever". Except that I had heard it before as "Pain is temporary,
        pride is permanent", which I liked better (...) because "permanent"
        is a better antonym for "temporary".

        (http://is.dal.ca/~susanhal/results/97/imc97.html)

Cruse (1994) has noted that lexical relations show prototypicality effects. Basic-
level words in canonical antonym pairs (*big-little, black-white, night-day*) are perceived as more prototypical examples of antonymy than other antonym pairs.
Herrmann et al. (1986) report that, when asked to rate word-pairs on their degree of
antonymy, subjects (on average) rated all the following pairs as exemplifying a high
degree of antonymy, but *hot-cold* was rated more antonymic than *immaculate-filthy*,
which, in turn, was rated more antonymic than *brilliant-retarded*.

Of course, there could be many reasons for these prototypicality effects, but they
seem to indicate that a mere co-indexing or linkage between related lexical sense
entries is insufficient to account for variations in relatedness.

2.5. The predictability of antonymy

The main argument for specifying antonymic relations in the lexicon is that canonical antonymy seems to be lexically idiosyncratic. Thus, the argument goes, semantic
principles cannot determine antonymy, since if they could, the canonical antonyms
big-little (for instance) would not sound better to us than the non-canonical pair
large-little. But if antonymy is the result of a productive process, then we should be
able to predict which pairings are antonymous and which are not. Antonymy can be
shown to be predictable if we look more deeply and broadly at the data. Using the
size adjectives as illustration, the deep view involves examining the alleged synonymy of *large-big* and *small-little* more carefully. The broad view involves taking
non-semantic information into account.[8]

Murphy (1995) demonstrates that it is not surprising that *big-little* and *large-small*
(and often *big-small*) are antonyms, while *large-little* are not, since the antonymic
pairs provide better examples of semantic opposition than *large-little* does. Semantic

---

[8] The size adjectives are a constant feature of the argument: cf., e.g., Gross et al. (1989), Charles &
Miller (1989), Gross & Miller (1990), Justeson & Katz (1992), K. Miller (1998).

opposition involves similarity of meaning but for one crucial difference (see 3.2). *Large-little* have more than one difference between them, since not only do they represent different extremes on the size scale, but they also differ in what they measure. As shown in (5) below, *large* (like *small*) measures (a) quantities and (b) gestalt size, while *little* (like *big*) can be used (b) for gestalt size, (c) for synaesthetic effect, (d) to express metaphoric size (e.g., importance or complexity), and (e) to express emotive content. In addition, *big* and *small* have sense-types in common, in that they both are used for (d) metaphor and (f) one-dimensional size (in this case, height).

(5a) **quantity:**   We've received a {large / *big / small / *little} amount of mail.

(5b) **gestalt:**   They own a {large / big / small / little} dog.

(5c) **synaesthesia:** It let out a {*large / big / ?small / little} squeal.

(5d) **metaphor:**   They made a {*large / big / small / little} mistake.

(5e) **emotive:**   What a cute {*large / big / *small / little} dog!

(5f) **1-D size:**   He is {*large / big / small / ?little} for his age.

Thus, well-devised semantic principles would not predict that *big* and *large* have the same antonyms, since *big* and *large* are not true synonyms and neither are their potential antonyms, *little* and *small*.

Looking broadly at the predictability of antonymy, Murphy & Andrew (1993) and Cruse (1994) point out that when the basic size adjectives are similar in sense, they may still differ in register. For example, *big* and *little* are preferred in talk to small children, while *large* and *small* predominate in the *Wall Street Journal* (Murphy 1995). Other non-semantic criteria also affect the "fit" of antonyms. Good antonyms are those that match on as many criteria as possible while maintaining semantic opposition. Thus, the members of good antonym pairs are similar in their grammatical category (*sad-happy* vs. *sad-joy*) and level of commonality (*dead-alive* vs. *dead-vital*), and may have the same base morpheme (*happy-unhappy*, *colourful-colourless*), same level of morphological complexity (*happy-sad*, *asleep-awake*), or even the same rhyme scheme (which, to the linguistically sophisticated, may represent morphological or historical similarity, e.g. *arid-humid*, *ascend-descend*).[9] Section 3 introduces means by which non-semantic similarities can play a role in antonymic opposition.

---

[9] A lexical system like WordNet, which assumes antonymy to be somewhat arbitrary, essentially treats the non-semantic similarities among antonym pairs (which partially account for the pairing of those words) as historical accidents.

2.6. Summary: Why lexical relations are not in the lexicon

Sections 2.1 to 2.5 highlighted the following problems for treating semantic relations (antonymy and synonymy) as represented in the lexicon.

1. While different word senses can have different antonyms and synonyms, not all senses of a single word differ in what antonyms and/or synonyms they take. Thus, treating lexical relations as relations among senses is unsatisfactory because it fails to make generalisations across word senses.

2. Binary relations are required for antonymy, although contrast relations among many items exist as well, and a single lexical item may be in both antonymic and contrast relations with other words. Lexical treatments do not account for the co-existence of these relation-types: they privilege one type or the other, and they do not explain the preference for binary contrast in antonymy.

3. Lexical relations are products of productive processes. Since models of semantically organised lexicons represent canonical lexical relations as special, they do not account for the similarities between canonical and non-canonical relations.

4. Lexically related pairs of words vary in the strengths of their relations. Thus, the theoretical mechanism that accounts for lexical relations must do better than to link words by relations that are simply [+antonymic] or [+synonymic].

5. Lexical relations are predictable by semantic and non-semantic criteria. On the assumption that only arbitrary information is included in the lexicon, lexical relations should not be represented as basic lexical information.

At this point, it is worthwhile to examine our terminology, since the terms *semantic relations* and *lexical relations* are somewhat misleading. While antonymy and synonymy depend on semantic relatedness, they may indicate non-semantic relatedness as well. And while they involve lexical items, the relations themselves are not specified in the lexicon. I persist in using the terms (since I know of no better ones) but I distinguish between them. *Semantic relations* are those relations that are defined by similarity or difference in the semantic characteristics of the words. 'Lexical relation' is a broader category that includes any relations that hold between words, based on any relational criteria. Thus, in addition to lexical relations on semantic grounds (opposition, synonymy, hyponymy, etc.), we might speak of the relations between lexical items that rhyme or that are transitive verbs, and so forth. While the focus here is on paradigmatic semantic relations in particular, the treatment proposed in the next section can be generalised to account for members of any lexical paradigm.

3. The extralexical origins of semantic relations among words

If we take seriously the postulated division of labour between linguistic (lexical and grammatical) and conceptual mental modules, an extralexical treatment of lexical relations is necessary, since lexical relations do not contribute toward linguistic competence, as discussed in 3.1. (And if we do not accept modularity, then a cognitive account of lexical relations is still in order.) Using some general principles of cognition in section 3.2, we see that an extralexical treatment of lexical relations is both possible and theoretically economical.

3.1. Lexical modularity

The modularity of the linguistic faculty (see Chomsky 1980) has been questioned in recent years by a variety of theorists (see Levinson 1997 for a summary of arguments). For the time being, though, we shall assume that linguistic modularity is generally feasible and that the linguistic module has two sub-modules: one lexical, the other grammatical. (I will return to this assumption in section 5.) With reference to lexical items, the contents of the two linguistic sub-modules may be specified as follows:

1. *Only arbitrary information that contributes to linguistic competence is included in lexical entries.*

2. *Non-arbitrary facts about a lexical item that contribute to linguistic competence can be derived from rules in the grammar and the word's lexical entry.*

3. *Information that is predictable from world knowledge and pragmatic and/or cognitive principles is not represented in the linguistic sub-modules.*

In addition to these premises about the contents (and non-contents) of the linguistic modules, we can identify similar premises about world knowledge. Premise 4 is a conceptual counterpart for lexical premise 1, and premise 5 is a conceptual counterpart for grammatical premise 2.

4. *Non-linguistic arbitrary information is represented in the conceptual realm.* The "conceptual realm" is not a well-defined theoretical construct as yet, but it is obvious at least that if the mind is modular, then some module (or some number of modules) is responsible for the representation of non-linguistic knowledge. And it is obvious that some of this knowledge concerns apparently arbitrary facts. The fact that cherries are red is, to botanically-innocent me, an arbitrary fact about cherries.

5. *Non-arbitrary information about the (non-linguistic) world can be derived from arbitrary (and other non-arbitrary) information about the world and general principles of cognition.* Thus, inferences can be thought of as the products of a conceptual 'grammar'.

While various theoreticians posit various internal structures and processes for the linguistic and conceptual modules, these five assumptions are basic to most modularised theories of language and conceptualisation. In addition, nearly everyone agrees that the lexicon cannot house all the information that is necessary in order to use words in semantically meaningful and pragmatically appropriate ways. In other words, lexical-semantic competence in a language is not wholly dependent upon information and structures in the lexicon; the conceptual realm must be involved in the production and interpretation of meaningful utterances.

Given these assumptions, the following question arises: "Where is the dividing line between linguistic and non-linguistic knowledge?" A default dividing line is statable as: "If it's about language, it's linguistic; if it's about the world, it's conceptual". However, this default fails to recognise that our language is a part of our world. In addition to linguistic knowledge *of* words, we may acquire conceptual knowledge *about* words, in other words metalinguistic knowledge about words. Thus, three types of knowledge are relevant to a discussion of the lexicon and the linguistic-conceptual divide:

1. Lexical knowledge, or knowledge *of* words;

2. Conceptual knowledge relating to words, or knowledge *about* words;

3. Conceptual knowledge relating to the denotata of words, or knowledge *of/about* the world.[10]

The distinction between lexical and conceptual word knowledge is necessary if we want to take seriously our first premise about the lexicon: viz. that the lexicon stores only information that is *both arbitrary and relevant to linguistic competence*. It does not store any *non-arbitrary* information which is relevant to linguistic competence (syntax, phonology, morphology), and neither does it store any arbitrary information which does not meet the competence criterion. Certain information about words is just not relevant when we speak of the lexicon. For instance, I know that *tern* is common in crossword puzzles, and that *condonation* was accidentally left out of the most recent South African English dictionary, and that *facetious* has all the English vowels in alphabetical order, and that my mother hates it when I use the word *puke*. Where is that information stored? Even though much of it is arbitrary, it is certainly not contributing to my competence in producing and parsing English sentences. So, no one (as far as I know) would want to claim that these types of facts are represented in my lexicon. It follows that these facts must therefore be mentally represented elsewhere, more particularly in the way that other world knowledge is made accessible, i.e. as concepts. Thus, we must distinguish between the knowledge that

---

[10] Someone interested in broader issues of cognition and concept formation might want to subdivide the third category in a variety of ways. This is no doubt legitimate, but it is also irrelevant to the problem at hand. A further subdivision has therefore not been pursued.

allows me to competently use a word like *tern* in a sentence and the knowledge that I might use in having a conversation about the word. Hence, in addition to a lexical entry for *tern*, I have a conceptual representation of the word *tern*, as well as some conceptual representation of terns (the birds, not the words). In essence, the word-form *tern* has both a sense that refers to birds, and a sense that refers to itself.

A new question now arises: Which facts about words are included in lexical knowledge and which are conceptual knowledge about the words? This brings up a thorny problem for linguistic theory-making. When we, as linguists or as speakers of a language, reflect upon words, our reflection is not a lexical process; it is a conceptual process and therefore the objects being reflected upon are our perceptions of the words, and the objects with which we are doing this reflecting are the concepts we have of the words.[11] As is made evident by the inherent difficulty of creating dictionaries or grammars, semantic and other linguistic knowledge is not directly available to our rational processes. Thus, when we think about words in the lexicon, we are always at least one step removed from the object of our study: we make inferences about words, rather than observations of lexical entries. To use a phonemic example, when thinking about the word *cat*, I know it has three sounds, but there is no reason to believe that this fact is lexically represented. What is more likely represented in the lexicon is the fact that the word has the sounds /k/, /æ/, and /t/, in that order. In observing the word, I have made the inference that its sounds are three in number, and this fact is not relevant to my actual use of *cat* as a piece of language: there is no reason to believe that the lexicon can count to three. Thus, in reflecting upon the word *cat*, I perceive the word and conceptualise it (or make use of my conceptualisation of it). The preceding claims are probably not controversial, but acknowledgement of the distinction between lexical and conceptual word-knowledge is necessary in accounting for some phenomena that traipse the lexical-conceptual divide.

Thus, knowledge about words is part of knowledge about the world. Knowledge about the world includes facts that we store in memory (e.g., my memory of someone telling me that *condonation* was left out of the dictionary) and knowledge that is derived from other things we know (e.g., knowing that *cat* has three sounds derives from knowing how to count and how to pronounce *cat*). Within this conceptual knowledge, we have knowledge of how categories relate to one another, as we have already seen with the case of type-token relationships (an eagle is a type of bird). Some of this relational knowledge is likely part of how the concept for a category is represented (a concept of eagles that is not related to the concept of birds is a rather impoverished eagle-concept). But these relations among concepts can also be forged

---

[11] Robinson (1997:253) discusses in detail this dilemma of what he calls "objective theories of language and cognition", with reference to pragmatic principles.

anew, as when we form ad hoc conceptual categories like 'skirts that will go with my new green blouse' (see Barsalou 1983, 1992).

Whether all lexical entries must have corresponding conceptual representations depends in part on one's treatment of lexical meaning (see section 5). One could have a conceptualisation of a word without a lexical entry for it. For instance, I learned at a Scrabble ® game tournament that *hili* is an English word (at least as far as the rules of the game permit). So, I know that *hili* is a word, that it is English, and that it is worth seven points, but I cannot use it in a sentence (unless I use it to refer to itself) – I do not know how to pronounce it, what it means, or even what part of speech it is. If I were to learn how to use the word, I would acquire a new lexical item and add new information to the old concept I already have for that word.

From these theoretical assumptions and linguistic facts, it is just a short step to positing that lexical relations are extralexically represented in the conceptual realm. Knowing that *cold* is the opposite of *hot* is something I know about these two words. So, when I call up my conceptual knowledge of *cold*, I call up memories and make inferences that allow me a detailed picture of what I know about *cold*: that it is the opposite of *hot*, that it rhymes with *gold*, that it has four letters, that it can be an adjective or a noun. Knowing that *cold* is the opposite of *hot* need not be involved in my knowledge of the meaning of either of the words or in my use of the words individually (see section 5). The implications of 'extralexical lexical relations' are discussed in section 4, but before getting to those, we need a typology and a means by which to derive these relations.

3.2. Relational principles and types of lexical relations

Two cognitive principles can generate all of the types of lexical relations mentioned above. I will call these principles Relation by Contrast and Relation by Opposition, although they apply more generally than to just the semantic relations of contrast and opposition, since they can contrast or oppose more than just semantic material. A Relation by Contrast (henceforth RC) holds among the members of a set iff the members of the set have all the same contextually relevant properties but one. A Relation by Opposition (henceforth RO) holds among the members of a set iff a) the set has exactly two members, and b) the members of the set have all the same contextually relevant properties but one.

RC, then, is a principle of 'minimal difference',[12] and RO is a subtype of RC, in that it is a principle of 'minimal difference among pairs'.[13] As noted in section 2.2, lexi-

---

[12] Minimal difference has been noted by many others in discussing antonymy, including Clark (1970), Hale (1971), Gundel et al. (1989), and Grandy (1992). Clark posits a number of rules in addition to his "Minimal Contrast Rule," including a Marking Rule, a Category Preservation Rule, and a Feature-Deletion or -Addition Rule. Gundel et al. use the term *minimally different* to describe the

cal treatments of antonymy do not explain why binary pairs are privileged, and neither does RO. However, as a general conceptual relation principle rather than a specifically lexical principle or feature, it accounts for a wider range of phenomena. Any explanation of why binarity is privileged in cognition is a more powerful explanation than an account of why just antonymy is binary. It is certainly beyond the scope of this discussion to explain binarity in all its forms, but it seems clear that the prevalence of binarity is a general problem for cognition, rather than a specific linguistic problem. Semantic lexical relations are not the only area in which binarity is the norm in language. Linguistically, sentential negation and affixal negation also reflect a bivalent schema, and categorisation is often into two opposing categories even when more than two possible categories exist (thus, Aristotle's Law of Excluded Middle).[14] In addition, in discussing the relationship between language and gesture, McNeill (1997:199) notes that "thinking in terms of differences, and creating fields of opposition in order to have the differences be meaningful, is a general capacity of human thinking and not just contrasts embodied in the lexical system". Thus, binary opposition is so widespread in the cognitive system that it is unenlightening and inelegant to treat it as simply being stipulated in the lexicon.

Neither RO nor RC make any reference to criteria for judging similarity or difference, other than to say that 'relevant' criteria be applied. Because of this, they are general enough to account for any of the lexical relations mentioned in this paper, since, for different lexical relations, different criteria are relevant. Hence, all relations are cases of minimal difference, but they may differ in what objects they are relating and on what criteria they are contrasting them. Semantic relations are those in which the information that is relevant to minimal difference is semantic in nature. Synonymy and semantic contrast are applications of RC. Phonetic form is rarely relevant to semantic relations, but it is relevant to the various phonetic lexical relations, such as rhyme and alliteration. Grammatical paradigms represent another type of lexical relation. Each of these relations is a subrelation of RC, and their particular requirements for minimal difference are summarised in table 1. All of these relations are relations among concepts, so when relations relate words, they are not relating lexical entries, but they are relating concepts of words.

---

difference between the marked and unmarked members of an antonym pair. My application of the term is more general, to include other types of relations.

[13] It could actually be the other way around, so that Opposition is the more basic relation, and Contrast is the result of repeated application of Opposition. In fact, we often seem to come to contrast by way of opposition. For instance, I might say "*Sofa* and *divan* are synonyms of *couch*", rather than saying "*Sofa, couch,* and *divan* are synonyms". In the former case, we have put *couch* into a binary relation twice: *couch-sofa* and *couch-divan*. In the latter case, we treat them as one contrast set: *couch-sofa-divan.*

[14] See Murphy (1997) for a discussion of how sexual orientation labels have evolved in order to preserve binary category distinctions.

Relation	Relates	Similarity	Incompatibility	Example
synonymy	word concepts	intensional meaning, grammatical category, register, etc.	word form	*couch : sofa, divan : settee : davenport...*
semantic contrast	categories	semantic category, level of categorisation	reference	*north : south : east : west*
rhyme[15]	word forms	ending sounds	beginning sounds	*how : now : cow : bow : brow ...*
alliteration	word forms	beginning sounds	ending sounds	*brown : brow : brie : broke : brig ...*
grammar paradigm	word forms	lexeme, inflectional category type (e.g., tense, number, case)	inflection	*break : broke : bro-ken*

Table 1: Instantiations of Relation by Contrast

The "Similarity" column in table 1 is incomplete, and not every lexically related pair will be similar on all the listed criteria, since RC only requires similarity in contextually relevant properties. In some contexts, for instance, register is not relevant to synonymy. But we acknowledge as "better" synonyms those that are similar on as many counts as possible.

ROs are different from RCs in that the first step to achieving opposition is having a two-member set. In cases where the set has more than two possible members, they are whittled down to two by making more and more properties relevant to the relation. By treating lexical relations as relations among word concepts, both linguistic form and semantic properties are available as material for choosing "better" antonyms. Thus, although I have listed antonymy and semantic opposition as two types of relations in table 2, they are really the same relation. The only difference is that in so-called antonymy the form of the word becomes relevant in order to exclude other potential antonyms.

---

[15] There are many types of rhyme, for which there are more specific relation criteria. Here, I have only given my layperson's definition of rhyme.

Relation	Relates	Similarity	Incompatibility	Example
antonymy	word concepts	semantic category, level of categorisation, register, phonetic form, morphological complexity	reference	*ascend : descend*
semantic opposition	categories	semantic category, level of categorisation	reference	*rise : descend* *scotch : soda* *cat : dog*
hyponymy	categories	semantic category	level of categorisation	*bird : [robin,* *swift, swan...]*
meronymy	categories	same object	completeness	*house : [floors,* *windows, walls,* *roof, doors...]*

Table 2: Instantiations of Relation by Opposition

No reference is made to the type of words that can or cannot enter in a relation of antonymy or opposition. Thus, I do not follow Lyons (1977), who refers to antonymy only where there are pairs of opposed gradable antonyms. Indeed, *scotch* and *soda* can be antonyms on the grounds that they are the two noun members of the set phrase *scotch and soda*, or they can be opposites on the grounds that they refer to things that are similar by virtue of being in the same drink and minimally different by virtue of being different ingredients in the drink. In the opposition category, we also have pairs like *cat* and *dog*, which are minimally different in that they are the two members of the set of common domesticated animals that are kept in houses, but not in cages. Note, however, that in particular contexts the relevant opposite of *cat* may be *kitten* (or even *human*, for that matter).

Hyponymy and meronymy (also included in table 2) are cases of binary opposition rather than contrast, in that they contrast a set of one to a set of many.[16] Since RO requires the items in the relation to be as similar as possible (given the context), the

---

[16] We might be able to consider hyponymy and meronymy contrastive relations if we extended the relations to more than two levels. Thus, an example of hyponymy would be *animal-bird-eagle-bald eagle*, and an example of a meronymic set might be *state-city-street-block-lot*. I have not tried to include these in table 1 because the terms *hyponymy* and *meronymy* are usually only applied to bilevel relations, not multilevel relations.

best hyponyms are only one level of categorisation away from their hyperonyms, and parts are better meronyms than subparts.[17]

Theorists with a taxonomical bent have identified subtypes of antonymy, hyponymy, meronymy, and other relations. In the present treatment, different types of antonymy (or other relations) may arise due to two factors: the characteristics of the items in the relation or the contextual definition of 'relevant' characteristics for similarity or difference. For instance, the difference between complementary (*dead-alive*) and contrary (*big-little*) antonyms (Lyons 1977) is that the first type is a relation among non-gradable states and the latter is among gradable states. The difference between equipollent (*hot-cold*) and polar antonyms (which display more marked/unmarked distributional differences, e.g. *long-short*; Cruse 1986), is that the scale on which the polar antonyms are measured has an inherent starting point (e.g., 0 inches), while the equipollent scale extends indefinitely in either direction (Bierwisch 1989).[18] Different types of meronymy, e.g., object-functional part, group-member, artefact-ingredient (Chaffin et al. 1988), come about because different types of parts are relevant to different kinds of things, and different kinds of parts are relevant to different situations.

Another differentiation among types of relations comes from the assumption that we can differentiate semantic and pragmatic relations, thus assuming a dictionary-encyclopedia division in which the dictionary includes a basic thesaurus. Mettinger (1994) distinguishes between opposition on purely semantic grounds ('systemic' opposites), e.g., *high-low*, and opposition that requires access to encyclopedic information ('non-systemic' opposites), e.g., *wavy-straight, oral-rectal*. As in the other instances of oppositional taxonomy, both of these types of opposition can be accounted for as relations between word concepts rather than between lexical entries. The fact that *wavy-straight* is a more context-specific relation (since it applies specifically to hair and not to oceans) does not entail that *high-low* is a lexical rather than conceptual relation. If meaning resides outside the lexicon (as many argue it should; cf. section 5), then the derivation of both types of antonym pair is a derivation performed on knowledge *about* words, not knowledge *of* words. Even if there is semantic representation in the lexicon sufficient to contrast *high-low*, the fact that

---

[17] The description of meronymy in table 2 is the least satisfactory of the group, since "completeness" is not a very good description of the difference between whole and part (a part can be complete on its own). Part of the problem in formulating this description is the asymmetricality of the relation. While a part of a hammer is a handle, a handle is not necessarily a part of a hammer (it could be part of a shovel). So, the handle is part of the hammer-concept, but hammers are not necessarily part of the handle-concept.

[18] In later work, Cruse also comes to the conclusion that his types of antonymy are predictable on semantic grounds, but his scalar apparatus differs from Bierwisch's. See Cruse (1992) and Cruse & Togia (1995).

they are canonically antonymic is still knowledge about the words, and therefore extralexical knowledge (see section 4.2).

In brief, lexical relations can be subdivided among as many categories as we like, but they all can be reduced to being examples of RCs or ROs.

4. Implications

Accounting for lexical relations as conceptual knowledge *about* words, rather than lexical knowledge *of* words, is consistent with the facts about lexical relations phenomena. So far, we have seen that this treatment allows non-semantic information to affect semantic relations and that it can generalise lexical relations to being of two general types, contrastive or oppositional, depending on how many items stand in relation to one another.

An obvious benefit of this approach is that the lexicon is left unorganised, and thus the lexicon does not involve lexical gaps that need to be filled simply because our hypothesised lexical architecture says they should be there. Thus, the lexicon contains no *unangry*. The opposite state from angriness may be represented in our conceptual knowledge, but since it is not associated with a particular lexical item, it does not provide an antonym for *angry*. Thus, the antonym of *angry* is just not one of the things we need to know to use or talk about the word *angry*.

Further facts about lexical relations phenomena, and the implications for treating them as knowledge *about* words, are discussed below.

4.1. Polysemy and metaphor

Lehrer (forthcoming) points out that if a basic sense of a word is in a semantic relation with another word, that relation can be extended to other senses of the word. For example, the basic temperature sense of *hot* contrasts with *cold*. While the opposite of the 'illegally acquired' sense of *hot* is not *cold*, they too can be contrasted if enough context is given, as in (6).

> (6)   He traded in his hot car for a cold one. (Lehrer forthcoming)

Lehrer uses (6) to argue that antonymy relates words (not meanings) and that at least some of these relations are mentally fixed (not derived). However, given the distinction of lexical and conceptual word-knowledge assumed here, the possibility of extending the uses of opposed words exists without claiming that those oppositions are part of our lexical knowledge of the words. In this case, the speaker chooses not to elect a semantically appropriate opposite for this sense of *hot* (such as *legal*), but instead to exploit what he and the hearer know about the word *hot*: that it is the canonical opposite of *cold*. The speaker can then use *cold* in a novel way, making a pragmatic implicature based on the common knowledge that *hot* means 'illegally acquired', that *hot-cold* are opposites (and are being semantically opposed in this context), and that semantic opposition involves minimal difference in meaning (thus the only possible relevant meaning for *cold* is 'legally acquired'). Thus, the extra-lexical account of lexical opposition is consistent with the fact that words, not just meanings, can be in established contrastive relations, but it does so without claiming that these facts are represented in our lexicons.

4.2. Canonical and non-canonical relations

The contrast between canonical and non-canonical relations may be accounted for by the fact that our knowledge about the world, and hence about words (as part of the world), is composed of both remembered facts and derived inferences. Canonical antonyms (like *up* and *down*) and similar binary lexical relations (like the automatic relation of *scotch* and *soda*) may be the type of remembered fact that is represented in the conceptual store.[19] Since a canon of antonym pairs is drilled into (at least American) children in early education, there is reason to believe that some canonical antonym pairs are remembered, rather than derived, relations. Nearly 30 years later, the *Up and Down* song, sung by the Sesame Street muppet Harry Monster, still goes through my head.

But it is also possible that these antonyms are canonical because they are more pro-totypical antonyms, owing to the commonality and relative semantic equivalence of the words involved. Thus, I may know the fact that *up* is the antonym of *down* either because I was taught this fact once and now remember it, or because I initially de-rived the antonymic relation myself, by realising that the two words stand for things that are minimally different. The *up-down* relation became part of my antonym canon when my first experiences of its antonymy (either independently-derived or taught) were reinforced by further experience of *up-down* antonymy, including anto-nym lessons in kindergarten and on Sesame Street and exposure to co-occurrences of the words in utterances.

This account explains more facts about antonym acquisition than are explained by Charles & Miller (1989), who argue that the primary source of antonymic associa-tions is the experience of the antonymic words co-occurring in utterances, or by Justeson & Katz (1991), who add that the antonymic words must also be substitut-able for one another (i.e., they should occur in the same types of syntactic environ-ments). These claims are based on the fact that antonymous adjectives co-occur within sentences at much greater than chance rates, but the corpora they use to prove

---

[19] How memories are represented is far beyond the scope of this paper. The only point that is relevant here is that there is a difference between things we know because we learned them once (either by being told about them or by figuring them out) and things that we know because we figured them out anew from other facts.

this point are of adult, written language, and thus not the best data for exploring how antonymy is acquired. Murphy (1998), on the other hand, investigates co-occurrence in three diary studies of children in the CHILDES Database (MacWhinney 1995). Children aged 2-5 also use both members of antonym pairs at higher than chance rates within turns, although their parents may not use the same antonyms at such high rates of co-occurrence. This may indicate that children are aware of antonym pairings even before they have been explicitly taught about antonyms.[20] Charles & Miller's claim that antonym co-occurrence is the source of antonymy fails to explain why the pairs originally began co-occurring. The present treatment uses the relational principles to account for the preference for particular pairings, but also acknowledges the role of co-occurrence in making antonym pairings more memorable, and thus part of the antonymic canon that an individual knows.

4.3. Syntactic variability

The above-mentioned corpus studies assumed that antonymic co-occurrence involves semantically opposed members of the same grammatical category. But Fellbaum (1995) shows that sameness of grammatical category is not a necessary feature of co-occurring antonyms, since zero-derived and morphological variants on the members of antonym pairs also co-occur at greater than chance rates. For example, not only do the verbs *begin-end* and the nouns *beginning-end* occur at greater than chance rates, but also *begin* (N) and *endless* (Adj), and *beginning* (N) and *end* (V). Fellbaum (1995:289) concludes that "[r]egardless of their syntactic category, words expressing semantically opposed concepts tend to be used together in the same sentences". But if only a semantic contrast were involved, there might be little reason to prefer pairing *begin-end* over *start-end*. The forms of the words seem relevant, but the grammatical category does not. In a relatively acontextual search for a 'good' antonym for *begin* (such as in creating a thesaurus or responding to a word-association stimulus), we would consider sameness of grammatical category as relevant to the relation, because grammatical category differences reflect some semantic differences, and because only by considering grammatical category could we whittle down the contrast set to two. In a sentential utterance context, on the other hand, grammatical category becomes less relevant, since the speaker must use words that are appropriate to the syntactic structure of the sentence. The relation principles allow contextual variation in the relevant criteria for sameness and difference in antonymic judgements, which means that there is no problem: the grammatical category of the words can be ignored. By treating the relations as relations among concepts, we can account for the co-occurrence of *begin-endless* and *beginning-end (V)*

---

[20] The relative poverty of the diary data does not allow for a definite conclusion on this matter, since the recorded material includes only short periods of unstructured family interaction, and does not include other types of input to the child or input from the child's prelinguistic period. However, the ease with which very young children use antonymic pairs and the lack of evident adult modelling of those pairs are suggestive. We return to young children's knowledge of antonyms in section 4.4.

by assuming that our concepts of words are not as strictly differentiated as our lexical entries. So, while we have reason to believe that *begin* and *beginning* are separate lexical items (since they differ in form and part of speech, and since the nominalisation of *begin* with *-ing* is somewhat arbitrary), they may not be so differentiated in our conceptualisation of them, since concepts are notoriously fuzzy-edged. Since I know that *begin* is the antonym of *end*, if my concept of the word *end* represents a prototype category, then *endless* may be a less prototypical example of the *end* category, and thus not an ideal antonym for *begin* in a word-association task, but an acceptable contrasting term in another context, and a much better opposite for *begin* than for *start*.

4.4. Paradigmatic shift

As noted above, children below school age use antonyms contrastively in utterances, just as adults do. But children and adults differ in their responses to word-association stimuli: children tend to respond syntagmatically (Brown & Berko 1960), giving a word that would go with the stimulus in a sentence. For example, in responding to *black*, children tend to give nouns for black things: e.g. *crayon, cat, bird* (Entwisle 1966). After they enter school, children increasingly answer as adults do, preferring antonyms, synonyms, hyponyms, and the like. McNeill (1966) refers to this as the *paradigmatic shift*. A possible reason for the shift in responses after school-age is that associations among word pairs are reinforced in the types of literature and activities common in (at least American) kindergarten classrooms. Indeed, Ervin-Tripp (1961) found that children whose school experience included antonym and synonym substitution exercises gave paradigmatic responses to word association stimuli, in contrast to an earlier study, done before such exercises were popular, in which 9- to 12-year-old children used as many syntagmatic responses as kindergartners.

In interpreting word association results, it is hard to tell what exactly is being associated: the words or the concepts evoked by those words. In the present treatment, concepts are being associated in either case: the concepts about the reference of the word, or the concepts about the words themselves. Sometimes, it is clearly the word forms that are being related, as when rhyming responses are given (*high-try*). And in cases where canonical responses are given, it also seems to be the words that are contrasted, since synonyms of the canonical responses are much rarer responses. In syntagmatic responses like *black-crayon*, it is less likely that the word concepts (and not the concepts represented by the words) are being associated. Instead it seems that the thought begun with the first word is completed with the second word. Perhaps school experience and literacy are associated with paradigmatic responses because they encourage people to form theories of words. As language speakers, we can get along fine without reflecting on the qualities of words; we use words in order to reflect upon the things that the words represent. But in learning to read, we begin to notice things about words and their written form: commonalities among them that allow us to remember how to spell them, similarities in form that help us to remember the meaning of difficult words, and so forth. And as we get older and become more literate, we may gain exposure to types of rhetorical communication that exploit similarities and differences among words. Perhaps the type of metalinguistic awareness that results from literacy makes older children and adults more apt to perceive the words themselves as the stimuli in a word-association task, rather than reacting to just the meaning of the word.

4.5. Linguistic relativism and universality

If binary antonymic relations are represented as arbitrary information in the lexicon, we may be tempted to think of these arbitrary linguistic pairings as encouraging or enforcing a binary categorisation of experience. Thus, theories in which the lexicon is organised by semantic relations seem to take a side on linguistic relativism: the fact that (what are assumed to be) arbitrary lexical facts are mirrored in other cognitive behaviour is proof that language influences thought. Furthermore, if, as John Lyons claims, "every language is a unique relational structure" (1977:231), we should expect to find quite a bit of diversity among the linguistically relative conceptual systems and what they represent as related.

On the other hand, if the binary categorisation of experience is predicted by more general cognitive mechanisms and antonymy is just another example of binary contrast of concepts (as argued in section 3.2), then it is just as likely (if not more) that contrasting word pairs simply reflect contrasting concepts. This is supported by the fact that lexical relations are consistent cross-culturally. Word-association tests have shown marked similarities in the types of associations made by speakers of various languages (see e.g. Rosenzweig 1961). Where word association differences exist across cultures, they can be attributed to specific cultural differences, rather than differences in the semantic structures of the languages (Szalay & Windle 1968). For example, the previously mentioned case of 'red-white' opposition in East-Asia is not due to particular linguistic representations of the words for 'red' and 'white'. It is due to the fact that red and white symbolise certain things in those cultures, and their symbolic meanings are contrasted. Most prototypical antonymic pairings are quite steady across cultures (where there is a word for 'long' its opposite can be translated as 'short'), indicating that the meanings are determining the relations, and not that the relations are arbitrary.[21]

---

[21] Cruse (1986, 1992) claims that antonymic relations differ among languages, noting that French *chaud-froid* differ from English *hot-cold* in that they are not in an equipollent relation and that German *gut-schlecht* translates into English as *good-poor* rather than *good-bad*. Murphy (1995) notes that the French examples are better treated as equivalents of English *warm-cool* and that the differences in the semantic distribution of *bad* and *schlecht* are not indicative of differences in type of relation among the languages, but instead examples of the same relation applying in languages with slightly different vocabularies.

5. Conclusion: The (ir)relevance of lexical relations

As discussed in sections 3 and 4, an extralexical treatment of lexical relations has many implications for our understandings of antonymy, synonymy, and other relations. However, the view of lexical relations promoted here says precious little about the lexicon itself. In theoretically moving lexical relations out of the lexicon, most of the vigorously debated questions about word meaning and the lexicon are left unanswered. But not answering the question is a step toward answering it. What has been established here is that facts about lexical items that may seem to be relevant to debates about the lexicon are, in fact, not relevant. Theorists must therefore look elsewhere to support any argument that the lexicon has semantic content, or that it is organised, or that the lexicon exists as a module of a modular language faculty. In the earlier sections of this paper, I assumed that both lexical knowledge *of* words and conceptual knowledge *about* words exist. Approaching the problem from that side allowed us to see that in order to be true to the ideal of a modular lexicon, we must not make that lexicon account for lexical relations phenomena. If, on the other hand, one wants to argue that there is no semantic lexicon or no lexicon, an extralexical treatment of lexical relations is a step toward explaining lexical phenomena without recourse to a modular lexicon. By way of conclusion, I offer some thoughts on how this treatment of lexical relations interacts with various positions on where or whether the dividing line between language and conceptualisation can be drawn.

The view presented here is consistent with several views on whether the lexicon has semantic content, but inconsistent with the view that lexical relations phenomena prove anything about the semantic content of the lexicon. In other words, the arguments presented here are consistent with any theory of the lexicon that is not dependent upon paradigmatic lexical relations or with any theory that does not posit a semantic, modular lexicon. Obviously, any theory in which conceptual and lexical structures are not differentiated will hold that relations among words are part of our general world knowledge. Theories that hold that the lexicon has no semantic content thus interact well with the treatment of lexical relations presented above.

Arguments that the lexicon includes semantic relations are de facto arguments that the lexicon has semantic content. For some, e.g., WordNet in its earliest days, the semantic relations were the total semantic content of the lexicon. Since associations among words have proven insufficient to the task of differentiating lexical senses (G. Miller 1998), a semantically organised lexicon is not a semantically self-sufficient lexicon. Thus while the treatment presented here is incompatible with theories in which lexical relations determine the semantics of words, it is not clear that such theories need to be taken seriously.

An extra-lexical treatment of lexical relations can co-exist with lexical semantic theories that provide some sort of non-relational skeletal representation of meaning in the lexicon. For example, theories involving semantic primitives (e.g., Katz &

Fodor 1963, and to a lesser extent, Wierzbicka 1996) may claim to account for lexical relations (on the basis of minimal difference among the feature specifications or primitive descriptions of words), but their accounts of lexical relations will be insufficient for those relations that are more dependent on context to determine minimal difference. However, these theories' ability to account for lexical meaning is not affected by whether or not lexical relations are derivable within the lexicon. As argued above, conceptual knowledge about words would still be needed for independent reasons, and we can assume that the meanings of words (although not necessarily in the same form that they are represented in the primitive-based lexicon) would be accessible for the derivation of lexical relations in the conceptual realm (since without the ability to map words to concepts, the notion of lexical linguistic modularity is pointless). While some may assume that lexical relations are necessary for the semantic description of contrary or complementary adjectives, the semantic structures of gradable adjectives are the same, whether or not they have lexicalised opposites, since having a word for *large* is not dependent upon having a word for *small*, and having a word for *short* is not dependent upon having a word for *long* (see Dixon 1982). Thus, representing some semantic information in the lexicon does not entail lexical representation of antonymy, synonymy, and the like.

Nunberg (1978) holds that word meanings are not fixed in the lexicon but are pragmatically inferred, based on conventional ("normal") beliefs about what a word can be used to mean and further limited by the context. Although he did not phrase the problem this way, the normal beliefs about word use are essentially knowledge about words. So, in this understanding of word meaning, one thing I know about *hot* is that people in my community normally use it to refer to temperature. Another thing I know about *hot* is that it is contrasted with *cold*.

Jackendoff (1997 and elsewhere) proposes that knowledge of lexical items is contained in three interfacing representational modules: Phonological Structure (PS), Syntactic Structure (SS) and Conceptual Structure (CS).[22] Without wanting to put words in Jackendoff's theory, I note the following. Since he does not differentiate semantic and conceptual knowledge (it is all the same and it belongs in CS), semantic lexical relations are not part of the strictly linguistic realm: they must involve the conceptual structure. The existence of several sources of knowledge about words does not prevent there being concepts about words, which are based on our perceptions of words and how they are used. Our perceptions of words and their uses are perceptions of information that has its source in PS, SS, and CS, but because we can perceive the outputs of PS and can gain some SS information about words by observing their syntactic placement and morphological qualities, we can conceptualise words based on those perceptions. Thus, lexical relations as relations between words

---

[22] What I have been calling the *conceptual realm* is a more general category than Jackendoff's CS.

(not just between meanings) can have access to more than just semantic information in CS.

Pustejovsky's (1995) *Generative Lexicon* model states that a theory of lexical meaning must account for relations such as antonymy, synonymy, hyponymy, and meronymy (Pustejovsky 1995:23-24), and that a Lexical Inheritance Structure "identifies how a lexical structure is related to other structures in the dictionary, however it is constructed" (ibid.:58). Unfortunately, after saying this, the author never returns to the topic of paradigmatic relations. Thus, it is not at all clear whether antonymy and synonymy actually need to be represented in the generative lexicon, or whether, as Fodor & Lepore (1998:273) presume, these terms are included in Pustejovsky's goals for the lexicon because of the "tendency among lexical semanticists to think that synonymy, antonymy, hyponymy, and the like must be bona fide lexical phenomena because, after all, linguists have spent a lot of time studying them".

Because we do not have direct access to knowledge in the lexicon, we cannot conclude from the evidence presented above that the lexicon is completely unorganised. We can conclude that lexical organisation is not what we are talking about when we talk about antonyms or other paradigmatic relations. The lexicon may indeed be organised in some way to facilitate lexical access, but that is irrelevant to our discussion of "good" and "bad" antonyms, word association games, and the like. Corpus studies may be used to argue that the lexicon is organised by antonymy and that ease and economy in lexical access is the cause of the frequent co-occurrence of antonyms. However, there are obvious pragmatic sources for the high rates of antonym co-occurrence: the more minimal the difference between two contrasting lexical items, the more striking the contrast between them will be; the more familiar the opposition (in the case of canonicals), the more likely that the audience will appreciate the contrast. In order to make their points, speakers naturally prefer more effective (and affective) opposites. Fellbaum (1995) points out that some of the co-occurring antonyms in her study involve an emphatic redundancy (as in *The bombs dropped on Japan were to end a war, not to start one*; Fellbaum 1995:296), a humorous style (e.g. *hate the lovable Irish*; ibid.:296), or reference to a change of state (e.g. *throw light into the dark corners*; ibid.:297).

In the debate about whether mental dictionary and mental encyclopedia can be separated, this paper has focused on the status of the mental thesaurus. As such, I have argued that thesaurus information is encyclopedic, not definitional. Thus, the paradigmatic relations among words evident in thesauri, word association tests, and rhetorical parallelism do not entail paradigmatic organisation of the lexicon. While the model presented here is vague in terms of the structures of concepts, it is convincing to the extent that it shows that semantic relations among words are best represented as metalinguistic knowledge that is not resident in the organs of linguistic competence.

References

Barsalou, Lawrence W. 1983. "*Ad hoc* categories". *Memory and cognition* 11. 211-227.

Barsalou, Lawrence W. 1992. "Frames, concepts, and conceptual fields". In Adrienne Lehrer & Eva F. Kittay (ed.), *Frames, fields, and contrasts. New essays in semantic and lexical organization*. Hillsdale: Lawrence Erlbaum. 21-74.

Berlin, Brent; Kay, Paul. 1969. *Basic color terms. Their universality and evolution*. Berkeley: University of California Press.

Bierwisch, Manfred. 1989. "The semantics of gradation". In Manfred Bierwisch & Ewald Lang (ed.), *Dimensional adjectives. Grammatical structure and conceptual interpretation*. Berlin: Springer. 71-261.

Brown, Roger; Berko, Jean. 1960. "Word association and the acquisition of grammar". *Child development* 31. 1-14.

Chaffin, Roger; Herrmann, Douglas J.; Winston, Morton. 1988. "A taxonomy of part-whole relations. Effects of part-whole relation type on relation naming and relation identification". *Cognition and language* 3. 1-32.

Charles, Walter G.; Miller, George A. 1989. "Contexts of antonymous adjectives". *Applied psycholinguistics* 10. 357-375.

Chomsky, Noam. 1965. *Aspects of the theory of syntax*. Cambridge: M.I.T. Press.

Chomsky, Noam. 1980. *Rules and representations*. New York: Columbia University Press.

Clark, Herbert H. 1970. "Word associations and linguistic theory". In John Lyons (ed.), *New horizons in linguistics*. Baltimore: Penguin. 271-286.

Cruse, D. Alan. 1986. *Lexical semantics*. Cambridge: Cambridge University Press.

Cruse, D. Alan. 1992. "Antonymy revisited. Some thoughts on the relationship between words and concepts". In Adrienne Lehrer & Eva F. Kittay (ed.), *Frames, fields, and contrasts. New essays in semantic and lexical organization*. Hillsdale: Lawrence Erlbaum. 289-306.

Cruse, D. Alan. 1994. "Prototype theory and lexical relations". *Rivista di linguistica* 6. 167-188.

Cruse, D. Alan; Togia, Pagona. 1995. "Towards a cognitive model of antonymy". *Lexicology* 1. 113-141.

Deese, James. 1965. *The structure of associations in language and thought*. Baltimore: Johns Hopkins University Press.

Dixon, Robert M.W. 1982. "Where have all the adjectives gone?" In his *Where have all the adjectives gone? and other essays in semantics and syntax.* The Hague: Mouton. 1-62.

Entwisle, Doris R. 1966. *Word associations of young children.* Baltimore: Johns Hopkins University Press.

Ervin-Tripp, Susan M. 1961. "Changes with age in the verbal determinants of word-association". *American journal of psychology* 74. 361-372.

Fellbaum, Christiane. 1995. "Co-occurrence and antonymy". *International journal of lexicography* 8. 281-303.

Fodor, Jerry A.; Lepore, Ernie. 1998. "The emptiness of the lexicon. Reflections on James Pustejovsky's *The Generative Lexicon*". *Linguistic inquiry* 29. 269-288.

Grandy, Richard E. 1992. "Semantic fields, prototypes, and the lexicon". In Adrienne Lehrer & Eva F. Kittay (ed.), *Frames, fields, and contrasts. New essays in semantic and lexical organization.* Hillsdale: Lawrence Erlbaum. 103-122.

Gross, Derek; Fischer, Ute; Miller, George A. 1989. "The organization of adjectival meanings". *Journal of memory and language* 28. 92-106.

Gross, Derek; Miller, Katherine J. 1990. "Adjectives in WordNet". *International journal of lexicography* 3. 265-277.

Gundel, Jeanette; Houlihan, Kathleen; Sanders, Gerald. 1989. "Category restrictions in markedness relations". In Roberta Corrigan, Fred Eckman & Michael Noonan (ed.), *Linguistic categorization.* Amsterdam: John Benjamins. 131-147.

Hale, Kenneth L. 1971. "A note on a Walbiri tradition of antonymy". In Danny D. Steinberg & Leon A. Jakobovits (ed.), *Semantics. An interdisciplinary reader in philosophy, linguistics and psychology.* Cambridge: Cambridge University Press. 472-484.

Herrmann, Douglas J.; Chaffin Roger; Daniel, Margaret P.; Wool, Robert S. 1986. "The role of elements of relation definition in antonym and synonym comprehension". *Zeitschrift für Psychologie* 194. 133-153.

Horn, Laurence R. 1989. *A natural history of negation.* Chicago: University of Chicago Press.

Jackendoff, Ray. 1997. *The architecture of the language faculty.* Cambridge: M.I.T. Press.

Jenkins, James J. 1970. "The 1952 Minnesota word association norms". In Leo Postman & Geoffrey Keppel (ed.), *Norms of word association.* New York: Academic Press. 1-38.

Justeson, John S.; Katz, Slava M. 1991. "Co-occurrences of antonymous adjectives and their contexts". *Computational linguistics* 17. 1-19.

Justeson, John S.; Katz, Slava M. 1992. "Redefining antonymy. The textual structure of a semantic relation". *Literary and linguistic computing* 7. 176-184.

Katz, Jerrold J.; Fodor, Jerry A. 1963. "The structure of a semantic theory". *Language* 39. 170-210.

Lehrer, Adrienne. 1974. *Semantic fields and lexical structure*. Amsterdam: North Holland.

Lehrer, Adrienne. 1992. "A theory of vocabulary structure. Retrospectives and prospectives". In Martin Pütz (ed.), *Thirty years of linguistic evolution*. Amsterdam: John Benjamins. 243-256.

Lehrer, Adrienne. Forthcoming. "Gradable antonymy and complementarity". In D. Alan Cruse, Franz Hundsnurscher, Michael Job, Peter R. Lutzeier (ed.), *Handbook of lexicology*. Berlin: Walter de Gruyter.

Levinson, Stephen C. 1997. "From outer space to inner space. Linguistic categories and non-linguistic thinking". In Jan Nuyts & Eric Pederson (ed.), *Language and conceptualization*. New York: Cambridge University Press. 13-45.

Lyons, John. 1977. *Semantics*, vol. 1. Cambridge: Cambridge University Press.

MacWhinney, Brian. 1995. *The CHILDES project. Tools for analyzing talk*. Hillsdale: Lawrence Erlbaum.

McNeill, David. 1966. "A study of word association". *Journal of verbal learning and verbal behavior* 5. 548-557.

McNeill, David. 1997. "Growth points cross-linguistically". In Jan Nuyts & Eric Pederson (ed.), *Language and conceptualization*. New York: Cambridge University Press. 190-212.

Mettinger, Arthur. 1994. *Aspects of semantic opposition in English*. Oxford: Clarendon.

Miller, George A. 1990. "WordNet. An on-line lexical database". *International journal of lexicography* 3. 235-244.

Miller, George A. 1998. "Foreword". In Christiane Fellbaum (ed.), *WordNet. An electronic lexical database*. Cambridge: M.I.T. Press. xv-xxii.

Miller, Katherine J. 1998. "Modifiers in WordNet". In Christiane Fellbaum (ed.), *WordNet. An electronic lexical database*. Cambridge: M.I.T. Press. 47-67.

Murphy, Gregory L.; Andrew, Jane M. 1993. "The conceptual basis of antonymy and synonymy in adjectives". *Journal of memory and language* 32. 301-319.

Murphy, M. Lynne. 1995. *In opposition to an organized lexicon. Pragmatic principles and lexical semantic relations.* Unpublished PhD dissertation, University of Illinois at Urbana-Champaign.

Murphy, M. Lynne. 1997. "The elusive bisexual. Social categorization and lexicosemantic change". In Anna Livia & Kira Hall (ed.), *Queerly phrased. Language, gender, and sexuality.* New York: Oxford University Press. 35-57.

Murphy, M. Lynne. 1998. "Acquisition of antonymy. Evidence from child input and output". Paper presented at the Annual Meeting of the Linguistic Society of America, New York.

Murphy, M. Lynne. Forthcoming. *Semantic relations and the lexicon.* Cambridge: Cambridge University Press.

Nunberg, Geoffrey. 1978. *The pragmatics of reference.* Bloomington: Indiana University Linguistics Club.

Pustejovsky, James. 1995. *The Generative Lexicon.* Cambridge: M.I.T. Press.

Robinson, Edward A. 1997. "The cognitive foundations of pragmatic principles. Implications for theories of linguistic and cognitive representation". In Jan Nuyts & Eric Pederson (ed.), *Language and conceptualization.* New York: Cambridge University Press. 253-271.

Rosenzweig, Mark R. 1961. "Comparisons of word association responses in English, French, German, and Italian". *American journal of psychology* 74. 347-360.

Szalay, Lorand B.; Windle, Charles. 1968. "Relative influence of linguistic versus cultural factors on free verbal associations". *Psychological reports* 22. 43-51.

Wierzbicka, Anna. 1996. *Semantics. Primes and universals.* Oxford: Oxford University Press.

Formal versus encyclopedic properties of vocabulary: Evidence from nominalisations[1]

Heidi Harley

University of Arizona, Department of Linguistics, Douglass 200E,
Tucson, AZ 85721, USA
E-mail: hharley@u.arizona.edu

and

Rolf Noyer

University of Pennsylvania, Department of Linguistics, 619 Williams Hall,
Philadelphia, PA 19104-6305, USA
E-mail: rnoyer@babel.ling.upenn.edu

0. Introduction

Ever since Chomsky (1957) discussed *Colorless green ideas sleep furiously*, it has been evident that grammatical well-formedness of expressions is distinct from their being appropriate for use in a normal speech situation. In this paper, we seek to

[1] An earlier version of this paper was published in Heidi Harley (ed.), *Papers from the UPenn / M.I.T. roundtable on argument structure and aspect* (*M.I.T. working papers in linguistics* 32, 1998), under the title "Licensing in the non-lexicalist lexicon. Nominalizations, vocabulary items and the encyclo- paedia".

clarify the dividing line between the formal properties underlying grammatical well-formedness and the encyclopedic (real-world) knowledge that informs attitudes about pragmatic anomaly. We adopt a radically anti-lexicalist approach to grammar, following proposals of Halle & Marantz (1993) and Marantz (1997a). We detail how formal and encyclopedic properties are differentiated in this theory, and more specifically how vocabulary items are formally licensed for use, irrespective of their meaning properties. We then illustrate the advantages of our preferred theory through an analysis of English derived nominalisations.

In the first part of the paper, we introduce this alternative theory of grammar, Distributed Morphology, in which the functions of the lexicon as it is commonly assumed are distributed among various components of the grammar. We differentiate between a *vocabulary*, which lists phonological expressions that can be inserted into syntactic structures, and an *encyclopedia*, which associates phonological expressions with meanings. Second, we propose formal properties for what we call *vocabulary items*, which determine their proper distribution in sentences; these properties are intended to replace the lexicalist mechanisms of "theta-roles" and "selection". Formal properties of vocabulary items determine (in part) whether a given expression is *grammatically well-formed*, but encyclopedic properties influence speakers' judgements about *appropriate use* of expressions.

Having made explicit how the distinction between grammatical well-formedness and appropriate use is to be captured formally, we go on to examine some of the classic arguments for lexicalism from Chomsky's (1970) study of English nominalisations. We build on a revisionist interpretation of Chomsky (1970) offered in Marantz (1997a), according to which the presumed arguments for an autonomous lexicon taken from Chomsky (1970) are not well-founded. We attribute the anomaly of the expression #*John's growth of tomatoes* not to syntax or to the formal properties of the vocabulary item *grow*, but rather to encyclopedic knowledge.[2] Given the syntactico-semantic structure of nominalisations and transitive clauses that we adopt, a subject of a transitive clause is interpreted as agentive, while a subject of a nominalisation *may be* construed as agentive provided the encyclopedic properties of the nominalisation permit this interpretation. Since the encyclopedia asserts that growing is a spontaneous activity (internally-caused in the sense of Levin & Rappaport Hovav 1995), the subject of the nominalisation of *grow* is neither entailed to be nor pragmatically construed as the agent. Hence we attribute this variety of anomaly to a combination of encyclopedic knowledge and the types of semantic entailments which certain syntactic structures provide. We then show that where ill-formedness of an expression is not due to formal properties but rather to pragmatic anomalies associated with encyclopedic knowledge, speakers' reactions to sentences containing

---

[2] Throughout this paper, # is used to signal pragmatic anomaly. * is reserved for downright ungrammaticality.

nominalisations vary when the context of utterance is appropriately modified, and are best characterised as gradient. Finally, we briefly review how our proposed division between grammatical and encyclopedic knowledge might be extended to handle cases of structural "coercion" of meaning, in which sentence structure forces interpretations which are encyclopedically inappropriate.

1. Theoretical background

1.1. Lexicalism versus Distributed Morphology

Theories of syntax emerging from Chomsky (1981) and following work rely on a lexicon to construct morphophonologically complex objects (i.e. words) which form the atoms of syntactic representation. For example, the lexicon produces words like *the, barbarians, destroyed* and *city*, and each of these words has a categorial status and certain needs which must be met in order for the word to occur in a well-formed expression such as *The barbarians destroyed the city*. These needs are formalised in a variety of ways, but include the argument-taking properties (theta-roles) of items and their requirements regarding position in the clause (case-requirements). For example, *destroyed* requires both an agent subject and a patient object; phrases such as *the barbarians* or *the city* must occur in certain positions in the clause where they receive "case", licensing their appearance. In such theories, which we will call here *lexicalist,* rules occurring within the lexicon relate stems to words and words to words by modifying either their morphophonological form or their argument-taking properties, or both (Lieber 1980, Selkirk 1982, Di Sciullo & Williams 1987). Lexicalist approaches commonly assume that syntactic categories such as N, V, A are in a relatively simple relationship to morphological (form) categories *noun, verb, adjective*: put simply, syntax is defined as the constituent structure of strings of words.

Distributed Morphology (henceforth DM), a theory of the architecture of the language component outlined in Halle & Marantz (1993, 1994), Marantz (1995, 1997a) departs radically from the above. Syntax is not (solely) a theory of the constituent structure of word strings since words are not equated with syntactic terminals; neither are the types of syntactic terminals equated with morphological classes. Rather, phrase-markers are constructed freely out of abstract categories defined by universal features, including such "functional" features as tense, number, person, definiteness and so forth. Phonological expressions called *vocabulary items* (henceforth VIs) are inserted into syntactic structures at spell-out after syntactic operations. A phonologically annotated syntactic representation is then interpreted in consultation with the encyclopedia, along with universal semantic mechanisms. Encyclopedia entries give the interpretation of VIs, potentially in very specific contexts and in combinations. The encyclopedia may contain expressions of varying size (phrasal idioms, words, sub-words); accordingly, there is no commitment to any correlation between the size of constituents associated with specialised meanings and the size of constituents manipulated by syntax. An overview appears in figure 1.

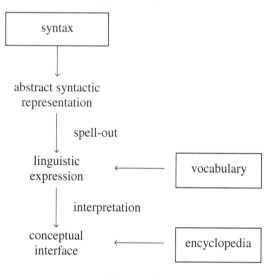

Figure 1

1.2. Structural meaning

The revised view of grammar depicted in figure 1 requires a serious reconsideration of the theory of argument-structure alternations, since there no longer remains any lexicon in which morphophonological expressions having related argument structures can be related. Consider a transitivity alternation verb such as *melt*:

(1a)   The sun melted the snow.

(1b)   The snow$_i$ melted t$_i$.

In a lexicalist theory, the lexicon produces two verbs, viz. *melt$_1$*, which is intransitive, and *melt$_2$*, which is transitive. Each has distinct role-assigning abilities and hence projects distinct syntactic structures. The lexicon is responsible for creating both verbs and relating the two.

In DM however, there is no lexicon, and there exists only a single VI *melt*. Whether *melt* is interpreted transitively or intransitively depends on the syntactic structure into which it is inserted: when *melt* is inserted into the structure in (1a), the interpretation is transitive; inserted into (1b), *melt* is intransitive.

Following Marantz (1997a) and along the lines of Construction Grammar (Goldberg 1995 and references therein), we assume that a syntactic structural description imposes a particular canonical meaning. For example, the transitive structure of (1a) forces an interpretation in which the sun is doing whatever is being done, while the snow is what is undergoing whatever is being done. The unaccusative structure in (1b) forces an interpretation according to which the snow is again undergoing what is being done. We call this aspect of the meaning of a sentence its *structural semantics*. The addition of VIs fills out the meaning of the sentence by detailing the nature of the arguments and predicates involved, but, we assume, such a 'filling out' must always remain consistent with the structural semantics imposed by the syntactic construction itself.

Gleitman (1990) and colleagues (Naigles et al. 1993, Gleitman et al. 1996) have proposed that children begin to acquire the meaning of verbs by attending to the "frames" or syntactic contexts in which these verbs occur. As Gleitman shows, the syntactic context or "frame" is much more informative to the child for the purposes of learning novel forms than the speech-situation.

1.3. Structural coercion and its limitations

Not every VI may be inserted into any structure. Compare (2) with (3):[3]

(2a)   Chris thought the book to Martha.

(2b)   The bridge exploded the engineers.

(3a)   The red under did not five lunch.

(3b)   James put yesterday.

The ditransitive structure in (2a) has a canonical interpretation: the subject (*Chris*) is an agent, the direct object (*the book*) is a theme and the indirect object (*to Martha*) refers to a goal. Although a verb such as *think* does not normally appear in this type of ditransitive structure, interpretation remains possible, provided it respects the various role assignments. In other words, interpretation is subject to the *structural coercion* of the meaning of the verb *think*. To the extent that the sentence has any meaning, Chris must be engaging in teleportation or telepathic dictation and Martha is the recipient of a book, as information or as object. Other interpretations may be possible, but in any of them, Chris is doing the thinking and Martha is getting the book. In (2b), the interpretation that must be given is that the bridge is causing the exploding (a thing bridges do not normally do), while the engineers are being blown

---

[3] In order not to pre-empt the discussion which follows, we abstain for the moment from using the anomaly (#) and ungrammaticality (*) markers introduced a moment ago.

to bits. While both sentences in (2) require a bit of imagination for a felicitous interpretation, it is only our knowledge (or expectations) about real-world events that
render them peculiar.

The sentences in (3), however, are different in an important respect. (3a) would
make sense only if *the red under* were somehow capable of being a subject and if
five were somehow capable of being a verb. However, this is not the case. (3b)
would only be possible if *put* denoted an action whose expression *does not* require
both a theme and a location. It is the precise nature of this difference that we are
concerned with in this paper. Specifically, we propose a theory of *licensing* which
states the grammatical conditions under which VIs can be inserted into syntactic
structures. According to this proposal, the sentences in (3) are marked by the grammar as ill-formed (*) and uninterpretable under any circumstance because the VIs
under, five and *put* are not appropriately licensed. Their underlying syntactic structures are however unobjectionable: they are the same structures that occur in perfectly ordinary sentences such as *The tall man did not eat lunch* or *James swam
yesterday.*[4] In contrast, the sentences in (2) are not ill-formed: they are merely pragmatically anomalous (#).

Exploring the nature of the licensing conditions will allow us to propose a clear dividing line between sentences which are ungrammatical for structural reasons (because their VIs are unlicensed) and sentences which, while grammatical, are deviant
only owing to the real-world (encyclopedic) knowledge that speakers possess about
the felicitous use of VIs. In recent experiments, Lidz (1997) has shown that children's "frame-compliance", i.e. their ability to adapt to structural coercion of meaning, has specific limitations. In particular, Lidz shows that utterances which contain
the appropriate frame for a verb like *think* (which takes a CP complement) are not
interpretable if, instead of *think*, an unaccusative motion verb like *fall* (which normally takes a DP internal argument) is inserted (cf. *The giraffe falls that the zebra
jumps*). That is, the licensing conditions of *fall* are not met in such a frame, and no
interpretive coercion is possible. We interpret these data as supporting our proposed
division. Where licensing conditions are met, structural coercion is possible with
pragmatic anomaly; where licensing conditions are not met, the result is outright ill-
formedness.

---

[4] Obviously, if there was no recognisable underlying syntactic structure (as in *Red not the under did
lunch five*), the result would be ungrammatical as well.

2. Formal properties of syntactic categories and vocabulary items

2.1. Two kinds of syntactic category: f-nodes and l-nodes

We adopt the view that syntactic terminals fall into two classes. The first class, which we call *f-nodes*, consists of feature bundles for which the speaker normally has no choice as regards vocabulary insertion; the VIs which fill them are *f-morphemes*. For the second class, which we call *l-nodes*, a speaker's choice of VI (*l-morpheme*) is not determined in advance and has truth-conditional force.[5] For example, in (4), the VIs *the, -ed,* and *a,* are completely determined by the grammar for the speaker, given a syntactic structure containing appropriate f-nodes with such features as [definite], [past] and [indefinite]. The choice of the VIs *cat* and *mouse* is not so constrained; the speaker might equally have chosen *shark* and *fish*.

> (4a)   The cat chased a mouse.

> (4b)   The shark chased a fish.

> (4c)   The fish chased a shark.

It is clear that there are different flavours of functional projections: these projections are composed of different features (representing, for example, different tenses or numbers etc.) which are selected from a fixed class provided by Universal Grammar. The difference between a number node representing 'singular' and one representing 'plural' is visible to the syntax throughout the derivation. Similarly, the node representing the functional category ("little") v will have a set of UG-provided light verbs which may fill it, including (but not necessarily limited to) CAUSE, BECOME, and BE; these light verbs will be present as syntactic features from the beginning of the derivation (*Merged* in the terminology of Chomsky 1995) and they will be visible throughout.

The first question which we explore in this paper is whether or not there are also different flavours of l-nodes: whether there are l-nodes specified, for example, for transitivity or category. We will argue that in fact no l-node is ever specified for category: there is only one type of l-node, whose categorial status is defined by its syntactic context. This we refer to as the l-node hypothesis.

---

[5] The reader should not scan too deeply into the significance of the names *f-node* and *l-node*, although it is not unreasonable to assign a rough implication of 'functional' to f-node and a rough implication of 'licensed' to l-node.

(5)   *The l-node hypothesis:*

Categories for which spell-out is not deterministic are not distinguished in syntax.

Corollary: Syntax does not manipulate categories such as N, V or A.

The view that certain linguistic entities acquire their "noun" or "verb" status by their context rather than through inherent specification is hardly new, and can be found originally in Sapir (1921), as well as in Chomsky (1970) and elsewhere. What we hope to accomplish here is to lay out the logical consequences of this view within a particular approach.

Although we suppose that there is only one l-node type, the VIs which may be inserted at a given l-node have licensing conditions associated with them specifying the syntactic environment in which they may appear. Thus there is no such thing as a fundamentally transitive l-node, or a fundamentally nominal or verbal l-node. L-nodes appear in whatever syntactic context the derivation creates for them, and then VIs are inserted which are compatible with this context.

There is thus a fundamental difference between the insertion of VIs at l-nodes and insertion at f-nodes. The f-nodes are fully specified for features and hence the VIs which may fill them are in *competition*, in the sense of Panini, as discussed in Halle & Marantz (1993, 1994) and Noyer (1997). The l-nodes, however, are not so specified, and the VIs which may fill them are not in competition. Rather, we propose that a given VI is *licensed* by appearing in a syntactic context compatible with its requirements. As we will see, licensing environments are necessarily local, in a strict sense, preventing conditioning of an l-morpheme's insertion by f-nodes which are not in the immediate morphosyntactic environment.

2.2. L-nodes and their environments

As an example of the type of entity which an l-node must be, let us consider the composition of some fairly straightforward verbs under a split-VP approach to verbal formation like that adopted in Travis (1994), Kratzer (1996), Harley (1995), Chomsky (1995) and (in a slightly different sense) Hale & Keyser (1993). In this type of VP syntax, (agentive) external arguments are generated in the specifier of a light verbal head which is projected separately from a lower, basic verbal head. In the current illustration, the two heads project vP and VP, respectively. The light verbal head of the vP is a functional projection with a very limited inventory of meanings.[6] When the verb is a simple agentive transitive, like *kiss* or *destroy*, the little v

---

[6] Indeed, Harley (1995) maintains that v may only mean three different things, BE (stative), and CAUSE and BECOME (both eventive and configurationally determined). It is not crucial for our pur-

which selects the external argument is clearly something realising the UG feature CAUSE. Consider the necessary meaning which the lower V must have in order to combine with the CAUSE morpheme and produce the meaning *destroy*:

(6) *destroy* - CAUSE = "destroyed" (resultant state)

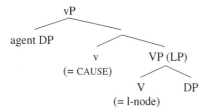

The lower V, denoting the resultant state of the action identified by the composite overt verbal form, is in fact an l-node. The verbal character of the combined form results from the combination of an l-node which is a functional projection of v and its attendant meaning. From now on, we will notate VP as LP to emphasise that it derives its verbal character by appearing in a vP context, rather than from any inherent categorial specification.[7]

Similarly, verbs such as *grow* or *explode* in their transitive uses must have l-nodes denoting something like 'resultant state' which combine with the CAUSE morpheme to produce the transitive verb in sentences like those in (7):

(7a) John grows tomatoes.

$[_{vP} [_{DP} \text{John}] [_{v'} \text{CAUSE} [_{LP} \text{grown} [_{Dp} \text{tomatoes}]]]]$

(7b) The demolition team exploded the casino.

$[_{vP} [_{DP} \text{The demolition team}] [_{v'} \text{CAUSE} [_{LP} \text{exploded} [_{Dp} \text{the casino}]]]]$

On their intransitive uses, as in (8), the light verb morpheme heading little v must be something like HAPPEN or BECOME, with no agentive argument in its specifier:

(8a) Tomatoes grow.

$[_{vP} \text{BECOME} [_{LP} \text{grown} [_{DP} \text{tomatoes}]]]$

poses here whether or not this is in fact the entire inventory of possible feature specifications for v or if there are a few more; there is general agreement in the literature that at least CAUSE and BECOME are possible realisations of v, whatever other possibilities exist. See, however, the discussion of suppletion in section 4.2 below.

[7] LP will later be seen appearing in a nominal context.

(8b)   The balloon exploded.

[_{vP} BECOME [_{LP} exploded [_{DP} the balloon]]]

The same l-node as in the transitive cases, designating the resultant 'grown' or 'exploded' state, combines with the little v morpheme to produce the final verbal form. Essentially, l-nodes can freely appear in any verbal environment: below any vP, with or without a specifier, with or without a complement. The syntax generates any syntactically well-formed structure, and when vocabulary insertion takes place at PF any VI which is compatible with the generated structure may be inserted at the l-node. We term this the 'prix fixe' approach to argument structure: from a given "Numeration" (i.e. collection) of initial bundles of features and l-nodes, the syntax creates legitimate structures, which then are filled with appropriate VIs.

To make this notion clearer, consider the "menu" in (9). Each structural position corresponds, so to speak, to a course; one item from a list of possibilities may be chosen to fill each structural position. Some slots have the possibility of not being filled or realised at all, reflected in {Ø} being a possible "selection" for that slot.[8]

(9)   Prix Fixe Verbal Argument Structure

   a. Specifier of vP: one of the following:

         i)   Ø

         ii)   DP (including empty categories)

   b. v head: one of the following:[9]

         i)   HAPPEN / BECOME

         ii)   CAUSE

         iii)   BE

---

[8] There does not seem to be a possible verb class which takes *no* arguments at all, although this is a logical possibility, given that examples of verbs with empty complement slots, empty internal subject slots (Spec,VP) and empty external argument slots (spec,vP) exist. Some other syntactic requirement must force the appearance of at least one argument, and cause derivations consisting only of an l-node combining with vP to crash. A plausible candidate for such a requirement is the Extended Projection Principle, which must be satisfied higher in the functional projections of the sentence by some argument. Of course, as elsewhere expletives are inserted to satisfy the EPP, one could imagine that such a verb class could exist with expletive subjects. Possibly, weather verbs are an example. On the other hand, it is entirely conceivable that the correct theory of expletives will entail that every true expletive must have an associated argument which will replace the expletive at LF, and that the weather verb expletives are not true expletives at all. The current proposal is compatible with either result.

[9] There may be other v nodes as well; see section 4.2 for some speculations.

c. Specifier of LP: one of the following:

                              i)   Ø

                              ii)   DP

d. L head: l-node

e. Complement of LP: one of the following:

                              i)   Ø

                              ii)   DP

There will also of course be choices for filling the Tense head, for example, {past, present} or an Aspectual head {perfective}, etc.; we abstract away from the higher functional projections for the present discussion.

Table 1 below displays the various choices for the slots in the above schema and a suggestion for an example of a vocabulary item which could appear in each configuration. This is *not* intended to be a definitive characterisation of English verb classes; rather, it should be viewed as an illustration of how this type of system might function; we will leave specific problems of class membership for future work.

Verb	Spec,vP	v	Spec,LP	L	Comp,LP
give	DP	CAUSE	DP	l	DP
destroy *grow* (tr)	DP	CAUSE	Ø	l	DP
jump	DP	CAUSE	Ø	l	Ø
learn	Ø	BECOME	DP	l	DP
grow (intr) *arrive*	Ø	BECOME	Ø	l	DP
know	Ø	BE	DP	l	DP
tall (?)	Ø	BE	Ø	l	DP

Table 1

Note that choosing BE or BECOME as v head will preclude the possibility of having an argument in Spec,vP (since neither BE nor BECOME selects an external argument), while CAUSE will force the appearance of an agent/initiator DP in Spec,VP: this is the only genuine sense in which argument selection plays a role in this system. Note further that since linear relations play no role in the syntax, there can be no distinction between an LP with just a complement and an LP with just a specifier, as the sisterhood relation between the head and its single argument will be identical in both cases after Merge has applied. Here, for convenience, we have noted all such examples as having just a complement, leaving the Spec,LP position empty.

Granted this sort of approach is desirable, in that it allows the syntax to freely generate structures, the question arises how to constrain the insertion of VIs in a principled way, so that they are not permitted to appear in inappropriate syntactic contexts, e.g. *John knew Mary the book. We explore the solution to this problem in section 2.3 below. Further, if we wish to extend the process of free generation of structures, followed by insertion of appropriate VIs to non-verbal contexts, and thus maintain our non-lexicalist stance, we must account for the facts of the nominalisation paradigm addressed by Chomsky (1970). Why is it possible to say *John grows tomatoes* and *Tomatoes grow*, but not #*John's growth of tomatoes*? Similarly, why is it possible to have both *The city's destruction* and *The army's destruction of the city* but not #*The city destroys*? This is addressed in section 3.

2.3. Licensing of vocabulary items

To capture the restrictions on insertion contexts for VIs realising the l-node, we propose that each VI is listed with a set of licensing requirements. These licensing requirements effectively replace the standard notion of "category". If a VI is listed as [+cause], for example, then it will be well-formed only if inserted in the complement to the CAUSE "flavour" of v. We say that the VI "needs" CAUSE. If a VI is listed as [−cause], then it is *not* well-formed when occurring under CAUSE: we then say that the VI "shuns" CAUSE. Because a [+cause] VI appears only in the context of CAUSE, it will necessarily have an external argument, following the discussion of selection of external arguments above. Note, however, that this selection is only *indirect*; the VI may not specify directly that it requires a specifier of little v, only that it requires a particular type of little v to raise to.

A VI may be *underspecified* for a given syntactic possibility, permitting it to appear with or without that particular syntactic element. An item which is specified as [±v], for example, may appear in the context of v or in some other context: it may, for instance, appear in an l-node which is sister to a determiner or some other nominal element. When that happens, it will be realised as a noun rather than as a verb. Such a VI neither needs nor shuns v. Similarly, a VI may be specified as appearing in the context of one or more DPs (that is, selecting one or more internal arguments).

We suggest that a VI may be specified for [±v], [±be], [±cause], [±DP$_1$] and [±DP$_2$], at least.[10] Eventive v types are divided into BECOME and CAUSE, distinguished by a

---

[10] As discusssed in section 4.2 below, there may in fact be a large number of possible realisations of v (GO, APPL, etc.). If so, it is perhaps necessary to posit specifications for each one, such as [±go].

[±cause] feature. The [±be] feature can be interpreted as expressing stativity vs. eventiveness, that is, a [–be] VI may be further specified for type of event with [±cause], while a [+be] VI is necessarily non-eventive, hence [–cause]. Other implications between features are more straightforward; if a VI is specified for [–v], then obviously it may not be specified for [+cause], etc. In table 2, we provide examples of VIs with their licensing information and associated encyclopedic content.[11]

	Phonology	Licensing environment	Encyclopedia
a.	sink[12]	[±v],[+DP],[±cause]	what we mean by *sink*
b.	big	[–v],[+DP]	what we mean by *big*
c.	open	[±v],[+DP],[±cause]	what we mean by *open*
d.	destroy	[+v],[+DP],[+cause]	what we mean by *destroy*
e.	arrive	[+v],[+DP],[–cause]	what we mean by *arrive*
f.	grow	[+v],[+DP],[±cause]	what we mean by *grow*

Table 2

So far, then, we have concluded that it is feasible to permit the syntax to generate any possible verbal structure, given the constraints of Merge. The insertion of VIs at appropriate terminal nodes will be conditioned by the information listed under "licensing environment" with each VI. Now we address the question of how we can characterise the behaviour of particular VIs in non-verbal syntactic environments.

3. Nominalisations and argument structure

How does this approach to argument structure and lexical insertion permit an account of the nominalisations discussed in Chomsky (1970) and alluded to above? Does the difference encoded above between *grow* and *destroy* permit a characterisation of the fact that the possessor of nominalised *grow* cannot be interpreted as an

---

[11] Of course this is not intended to be an exhaustive characterisation of English verb classes, but rather an illustration of the mechanisms necessary to make this approach feasible.

[12] The question of how *sink* and *open* differ such that in the non-verbal environment *open* is realised as an adjective (requiring nominalising morphology to become nominal) and *sink* is realised as a noun (requiring participle morphology to become adjectival) is a thorny one. For the moment, we will assume that they do *not* differ, and the realisation or not of overt morphology in these other environments does not reflect on their fundamental structure. This seems intuitively wrong, but we will adopt it as a temporary position for the purposes of this discussion.

agent, while the possessor of nominalised *destroy* may be so interpreted? Below, we argue that in fact, in nominal contexts, the interpretation of the possessor as agent or theme is not in fact determined by the subcategorisation information we encode above, but by our real-world (encyclopedic) knowledge about the meaning of the roots in question. The pragmatic anomaly of *#John's growth of tomatoes* is the result of the interaction of our real-world knowledge about growing with our knowledge of the possible interpretations for an argument in Spec,DP.

3.1. "Derived" nominalisations

Let us consider yet again the empirical issue raised by the data in (10) below:[13]

(10a)   Tomatoes grow.

       The growth of the tomatoes

       The tomatoes' growth

(10b)   John grows tomatoes.

       #John's growth of tomatoes

       #The tomatoes' growth by John

(10c)   #The crop destroyed.

       The crop's destruction

(10d)   The insects destroyed the crop.

       The insects' destruction of the crop

       The crop's destruction by the insects

Let us assume (following Marantz 1997a) that nominalisations are created by inserting VIs into a terminal node governed by D, exactly as verbs are created by inserting VIs into a terminal node governed by v. This structure is illustrated in (11) below.

(11)

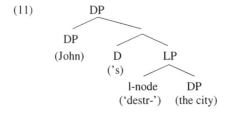

---

[13] The discussion in this section is based largely on that of Marantz (1997a).

The VI will be inserted into the l-node, exactly as for the verbal context illustrated above, and morphological allomorphy/readjustment rules will spell out DESTROY as *destruct* and add the nominalising suffix *-ion*.

In the verbal context, whether or not a VI may appear in the unaccusative environment or the causative environment is determined by its licensing feature [±cause]. GROW is indifferent to whether the v to which it raises is [+cause] or [–cause], hence it may appear in either environment (10a,b). DESTROY, however, requires that its licensing v be [+cause], and hence it has no intransitive variant (10c). Exactly the reverse situation obtains in the nominal context. DESTROY may appear with either its agent or its theme in the specifier position of the nominalised form (10d), while GROW may appear only with its theme in the specifier position of the nominalised form (10a,b). Do we then need to posit a similar feature for the nominal form? That is, do we assume that D has flavours, like v, which select for agents or themes in its specifier, and assign subcategorisation features to roots in the same fashion as for the verbal environment?

It is clear that this cannot be the correct approach. The specifier of D may certainly contain an agent or theme, but it may also contain possessors or other associated arguments, e.g. locations. This is never true of the specifier of v, which may only contain agents. Further, if the argument structure of nominalised forms was arbitrarily feature-determined in this way, we would expect that the appearance of agents in the verbal form would vary independently of the appearance of agents, themes or other arguments in the specifier of the nominal form. The fact that the grouping of properties correlates with particular encyclopedic/semantic characteristics, as we shall show below, would be unexpected on such an approach.

Marantz (1997a), following Levin & Rappaport Hovav (1995), notes that there is an essential difference between the type of causation in transitive verbal GROW and that which occurs in verbal DESTROY. Growing is an activity which must be internally caused; in *John grows tomatoes*, John is merely facilitating the growth of tomatoes which occurs spontaneously. Destruction, on the other hand, must be externally caused; things do not destroy spontaneously. In *The insects destroyed the crops*, the insects are acting directly to bring about a result that would not occur by itself. Roots like DESTROY require a direct causer to initiate the event in question.

If, Marantz suggests, the interpretation of arguments in the specifier of D is left open, defaulting, perhaps, to something like 'possession' but able to take on shades of meaning according to the encyclopedic content of the complement of D, the possible interpretations of the specifier of D in the examples in (10) above can be argued to fall out purely from the nature of the roots DESTROY and GROW, rather than from some structural or featural aspect of these roots. That is, if a VI denotes an event which requires the action of an external causer to occur, like DESTROY, the specifier of D in a nominalisation containing DESTROY may be interpreted as that external causer. If a VI denotes an event which requires no external causer to occur, e.g. a spontaneous or internally caused event like GROW, then the external causer interpretation is not available for the element in the specifier of DP; only the internal causer argument (which of necessity is also the theme) may appear in that position.

The question still arises, of course, as to why the "facilitator" role present in transitive verbal GROW is not a possible interpretation for the specifier of D. We will consider and dismiss one explanation of this phenomenon in the following section.

3.2. Variable-behaviour roots

Where do the "shades of meaning" which determine the interpretation of the Spec,DP argument come from? Two possible sources are imaginable. The first is the licensing or subcategorisation information that each VI brings along, specifying the optionality or necessity of CAUSE when in the verbal context. The other possibility is that it is our real-world knowledge about whether or not an event can occur spontaneously that determines our ability to interpret Spec,DP as an external causer.

The first solution is by far the simplest. If the specification [+cause] exists in the licensing information of a given VI, then the external causer reading is available for the specifier of DP: the [+cause] requirement entails that the action cannot occur spontaneously and hence an external causer is necessary for the initiation of the event. Further, this would provide an explanation for the unavailability of the 'facilitator' interpretation in the GROW case: any verb which does not have the [+cause] specification, as is the case for verbs of the GROW class, will not have any causer interpretation, facilitator or otherwise, licensed for the specifier of DP; only the universally available theme interpretation is possible in these cases. However, as we show below, the existence of a class of variable-behaviour verbs casts doubt on this approach to the availability of an external causer interpretation. Rather, we will argue that real-world, encyclopedic information must license the interpretation of Spec,DP.

In (12), we give examples of roots that participate in the inchoative/causative alternation, yet allow an external causer interpretation for the Spec,DP argument in a transitive nominalisation as well as the internal, spontaneous interpretation in the intransitive nominalisation. That is, these verbs behave both like GROW and like DESTROY.

      (12a)   The balloon exploded.

                The balloon's explosion

      (12b)   The army exploded the bridge.

                The army's explosion of the bridge

(12c) Wealth accumulated.

The wealth's accumulation

(12d) John accumulated wealth.

John's accumulation of wealth

(12e) Jim and Tammy Faye separated.

Jim and Tammy Faye's separation

(12f) The teacher separated the children.

The teacher's separation of the children

(12g) The German principalities unified in the 19th century.

The principalities' unification in the 19th century

(12h) Bismarck unified the German principalities.

Bismarck's unification of the German principalities

Since these VIs undergo the inchoative/transitive alternation, it must be the case that they are marked [±cause] in their subcategorisation information for the verbal environment, just like GROW. Yet, unlike GROW, they allow a transitive nominalisation. The suggestion above, that the availability of a transitive nominalisation depends upon a [+cause] marking on the VI, cannot therefore be maintained for these roots. It is conceivable that we could posit for this class two homophonous roots, one marked [±cause] which is spontaneous, and the other marked [+cause] which is of necessity externally caused, but this duplication of effort seems unattractive, to say the least. Part of the goal of the morphosyntactic enterprise undertaken here and in other DM-inspired work is to shift the burden of interpretation as much as possible from the syntax to the general conceptual/semantic interface; multiple homophonous semantically distinct VIs would fly directly in the face of that enterprise.

All the information that the speaker needs to know regarding the fact that these verbs can behave like members of both the GROW class and the DESTROY class is available in the Encyclopedia. That is, the speaker knows that these roots denote events that may occur spontaneously, like growing, or that may be truly externally caused, like destroying. GROW, in its current usage, may never be truly externally caused, and hence it may not participate in a transitive nominalisation, but UNIFY, as of German principalities, may either be spontaneous or truly externally caused, hence its variable behaviour. This knowledge is part of the real-world knowledge of the speaker about the meaning of the root, not part of the grammaticised subcategorisation information needed to ensure that the VI does not appear in an inappropriate syntactic context.

The fact that a root's behaviour may be conditioned by the particular theme which is inserted confirms the correctness of this observation. Our real-world knowledge tells us that there are some things, like dust, which are much more likely to accumulate spontaneously than to be accumulated on purpose by some external causer. When we choose such a theme, ACCUMULATE behaves like a spontaneous VI of the GROW class, losing its ambiguity, as in (13). It is not that the syntactic subcategorisation requirements of the VI have changed, but simply that our knowledge about the ac-cumulation of dust tells us that it is wildly unlikely for an external causer to initiate that action.

(13a)   Dust accumulated on the table.

(13b)   The accumulation of dust on the table

(13c)   #John's accumulation of dust on the table

A similar point can be made when the causer in the verbal form cannot be a true ex-ternal cause, but rather plays a facilitator's role like the subject of the transitive *John grows tomatoes*. If it is pragmatically clear that the causer in the verbal structure may not be a true external causer, it may not appear as the subject of a transitive nominalisation, as illustrated in (14).

(14a)   Adultery separated Jim and Tammy Faye.

         #Adultery's separation of Jim and Tammy Faye

(14b)   The Cold War separated E. and W. Germany.

         #The Cold War's separation of E. and W. Germany

(14c)   The 19th century unified the principalities.

         #The 19th century's unification of the principalities

These judgements are somewhat variable from speaker to speaker. Since we argue that the licensing of the transitive nominalisation depends on encyclopedic or real-world knowledge, this is hardly surprising: it is reasonable to assume that one speaker might think the Cold War could truly externally cause something, and that another speaker might think the opposite. It would, however, be surprising under the conjecture that the interpretation of these sentences depended upon the syntactic specifications of the roots, which presumably do not vary between two speakers who agree that these roots do participate in the inchoative/causative alternation.[14]

---

[14] The editor of this volume, Bert Peeters, feels there is a difference between (14a) on the one hand, and (14b,c) on the other hand, which may well have an impact on the judgements made by individual native speakers. The Cold War and the 19th century refer to the time frame during which East and

Essentially, then, we argue that these structures are not ungrammatical, in the sense of being syntactically ill-formed. Rather, for a majority of speakers, they are pragmatically anomalous: nothing that they know about the meaning of these VIs allows them to construct a "normal", i.e. agentive, interpretation. An ungrammatical sentence would be one in which a VI was not licensed by the syntactic context in which it found itself, e.g. *John grows tomatoes the garden*. In such a sentence, the insertion of a dyadic verb into a triadic context produces a truly ungrammatical structure.

We have argued that the behaviour of a VI when nominalised depends on the encyclopedic information associated with that VI, not on its syntactic specifications. Although it is possible to categorise verbs as in (15) below, these categorisations do not follow from syntactic considerations, and are therefore predicted to be subject to gradience and variation. Nevertheless, this rough classification does inform speaker judgements regarding appropriate use and interpretation of vocabulary.

(15)   *Three classes of verbs*

   a.   Internal Causation: the action is always dependent on the argument undergoing the change of state. (Also called spontaneous)

   b.   External Causation: The action must be instigated by an argument other than the one undergoing the action.

   c.   Underspecified: The action may causally originate either with the object of the action or with another argument.

4. Further issues

In section 2.3, it was proposed that VIs may be specified as requiring certain f-nodes in their local environment in order to be licensed for insertion: this is a strictly grammatical property of a VI. In addition, in section 3.2 it was claimed that the encyclopedic (extragrammatical) meaning of a VI also imposes certain restrictions on the readings which speakers can associate with a given syntax. We now consider the extent to which these distinct devices overlap in their function.

To a certain extent, the licensing restrictions represent the grammatical analogues of certain meaning properties of VIs. VIs representing end states of externally caused

---

West Germany were separated, and the German principalities unified, respectively. Nothing of the sort applies to (14a), where adultery is not a time frame. It is interesting to note a similar pattern in the case of the corresponding compounds: (14b,c) are fully acceptable once the *'s* is dropped (cf. *the Cold War separation of E. and W. Germany, the 19th century unification of the principalities*), whereas (14a) (*adultery separation of Jim and Tammy Faye*), while rather anomalous, is not syntactically ill-formed.

events (DESTROY) require CAUSE for insertion when verbal; but VIs representing end states of spontaneously occurring events (GROW) do not necessarily forbid CAUSE. While certain encyclopedic properties of a VI are sometimes correlated with certain formal licensing properties in this way, their relationship is not necessarily a direct one. Understanding the nature of this mismatch is crucial, we believe, to understanding the contribution of encyclopedic knowledge versus structural semantics in the interpretation of expressions.

Indirect relations between licensing requirements of VIs and their encyclopedic properties is not limited to verbs. We consider here several further examples.

4.1. Some further cases of structural coercion

First, consider the distinction between mass and count nouns. Under normal circumstances, embedding under a number word makes mass readings of nouns unavailable:

> (16)   #I had three cheeses for breakfast.

Since the encyclopedia entry for *cheese* includes the information that cheese does not typically come in discrete countable chunks or types, the structural meaning in (16) and the encyclopedic information are in conflict. Structural coercion forces the reading in which three types or pieces of cheese are involved.

To the extent that a VI denotes a necessarily uniform and indivisible substance, count noun syntax leads to severe anomaly:

> (17)   #I saw three oxygens in the kitchen.

Encyclopedic knowledge of the meaning of *oxygen* prevents any *reasonable* interpretation of (18). We propose then that (17) has the same status as:

> (18)   #John's growth of tomatoes

Both (17) and (18) are grammatically well-formed. (17) can mean only that I saw three 'pieces' of oxygen, or three entities meeting the description 'oxygen'. (18) can mean only that John is in some relationship to an event of tomato growing, for example the event of tomato-growth that John was just speaking about.[15] But what counts as a potential relationship is heavily influenced, if not in actual practice constrained, by encyclopedic properties. Put differently, *to the extent that* the Encyclopedia says that growing is an event which occurs spontaneously and without an agent, *John* cannot receive the agent interpretation in (18). Similarly, *to the extent*

---

[15] We ignore here noneventive readings of the nominalisation, such as one in which John is literally sprouting a growth of tomatoes from his body.

that oxygen is a uniform and indivisible substance, there can be no count interpretation in (17).

A similar example can be drawn from stage-level and individual-level predication.[16]

(19)   #Mary sometimes has green eyes.

The example in (19) is anomalous because the predicate *have green eyes* is normally an individual-level predicate (barring use of coloured contacts, etc.). The cooccurrence of such a predicate with a modifier like *sometimes* forces the stage-level reading. On our view, there is no reason to localise the stage-level or individual-level difference in a particular formal feature present in syntax or in the licensing conditions for VIs. Speakers judge (19) anomalous owing to encyclopedic knowledge only, and (19), like (17) and (18), is grammatically well-formed.

4.2. Aplastic vocabulary items and suppletion

Like the verbs discussed earlier, certain "nominal" VIs must be licensed by local f-nodes. For example, pluralia tantum such as *scissor(s), measle(s), blue(s), trouser(s),* or *Olympic(s),* when governed by D (i.e. nominal), can be inserted only when in a local relation with a [plural] f-node.

(20)   *measle* ⟷ l-node / governed by D, ___ + [plural]

Following Embick (1997), we can call such VIs *aplastic* (unbendable) because they refuse to adapt to syntactic environments which others of their morphological form class normally do. Can licensing statements such as those in (20) be used to express the distribution of suppletive allomorphs such as *wen(t), worse,* or *bett(er)*? As we show below, suppletive alternants cannot be considered aplastic in this sense, given our earlier assumptions.

Following Halle & Marantz (1993), we assume that *destroy,* for example, is changed to *destruct-ion* in the nominal context in a post-syntactic "readjustment component". The readjustment component performs a variety of functions including the partial modification of the phonological forms of stems, as well as the insertion of morphemes which are not present in syntax.[17]

(21)   *destroy* ⟷ *destruct-* / when governed by D

Such readjustment rules, proposed in Chomsky & Halle (1968), have always been problematic inasmuch as no clear criteria were available to separate rule-related

---

[16] We thank Mimi Lipson for pointing out the relevance of this phenomenon.

[17] On post-syntactic morpheme-insertion rules, see Embick (1997).

pseudo-suppletive morpheme alternants such as (*destroy* ~ *destruct-*) from truly suppletive pairs such as *bad* ~ *worse*, for which no rule was postulated. No interesting theory of readjustments could be proposed, since any theory that permitted / bæd / to be respelled as / wərs / could presumably do anything.

In the framework adopted here, pseudo-suppletive pairs like *destroy* ~ *destruct-* reflect single VIs which are related by readjustment rules. Truly suppletive pairs however reflect distinct VIs which are not related by readjustment.

In recent work, Marantz (1997b) notes that if truly suppletive alternants are distinct VIs, then they must be f-morphemes in the sense defined earlier. Suppose, for example, that *worse* and *bad* are two distinct l-morphemes with the following licensing conditions (we leave aside the precise specification of an adjectival environment):

(22a)   *worse* ⟷ l-node / ___ + [comparative]

(22b)   *bad* ⟷ l-node

Worse will have the correct distribution, since it will be licensed only in the comparative environment. *Bad* however will also be available in this environment, since the licensing conditions on *bad* cannot specify 'not in the environment of [comparative]'. Nothing then will prevent the grammar from freely generating **badder* as an alternative to *worse,* just as the grammar will generate *shark* as an alternative to *cat.*

Given our assumptions, for truly suppletive pairs to be in a relation of competition, they must be competing for f-nodes. If in turn f-nodes are defined by universal features, it follows that there must be an f-node for every truly suppletive pair, and that truly suppletive pairs must therefore reflect the spell-out of universal syntactico-semantic primes. In (23), the prime which in English we spell as *bad* ~ *worse* is represented as BAD:

(23a)   *worse* ⟷ BAD / ___ + [comparative]

(23b)   *bad* ⟷ BAD

Marantz argues that it is no accident, then, that true suppletion is limited to general concepts, and never occurs in VIs reflecting specific cultural artefacts.[18]

---

[18] This of course remains an empirical question. In terms of learnability, as Marantz suggests, given a space of universal conceptual primes, the child can associate two phonologically unrelated VIs with some cell in that space. But without this pre-given structure, the child has no way of determining that two phonologically unrelated alternants do not in fact denote two different sorts of objects (or predicates).

If Marantz's hypothesis is correct we have two significant results. First, a theory of readjustment rules becomes a possibility, since any pair of morpheme alternants that reflects a cultural artefact must be pseudo-suppletive and not truly suppletive. Second, the class of f-nodes must be larger and more extensive than previously assumed. If *go ~ wen(t)* realises an f-node, then this f-node GO can presumably be mentioned as a licenser for some class of l-morphemes, for example, certain verbs of motion. Just as we have seen transitivity alternations depending on the underspecification of [±cause], so we might expect more subtle alternations involving [±GO] and other such f-nodes implicated by suppletive pairs. We feel that a reappraisal of lexical verb classes along these lines is an urgent topic for future research.

5. Conclusion

In the l-node hypothesis, we proposed that there is in fact only one l-node, whose syntactic status is always determined by its local relation with f-nodes.[19] It follows from this that notions such as "noun" and "verb" are purely derivative in syntax, although potentially significant morphophonologically. We provided a "menu" of simple syntactic structures which may be generated from a small inventory of syntactic primes, providing a fragment of the space of syntactic possibilities relevant for vocabulary insertion.

Second, we argued that the distinction between l-nodes and f-nodes derives from different conditions on the insertion of VIs at these nodes. Insertion at f-nodes is subject to *competition*: the most highly specified VI available is inserted in an f-node (Halle & Marantz 1993, 1994). Insertion at an l-node, however, is subject to conditions of *licensing*: any VI which meets certain conditions can be inserted in the structure.

If there is but one type of l-node and vocabulary insertion at l-nodes is constrained by licensing, it follows that argument structure alternations arise when VIs may be licensed in more than one syntactic structure, that is to say, when a VI's licensing conditions are underspecified. For example, the verb *sink* is licensed both in a transitive and in an unaccusative syntax. Section 2 provided a preliminary list of verbal VIs typed according to their licensing privileges.

In section 3 we reconsidered the argument that the behaviour of nominalisations demands a lexicon, as many researchers have assumed since Chomsky (1970). Fol-

---

[19] It is conceivable that l-nodes are subcategorised by syntactico-semantic properties such as event/entity, animacy etc., which are eventually matched up with specific VIs at Insertion. While the possibility that such information is syntactically represented on l-nodes exists, it is beyond the scope of the present discussion, so we do not examine this question here.

lowing Marantz (1997a), we argued that pairs such as *growth ~ grow* involve the same VI GROW but in different syntactic contexts. We further argued that expressions such as *#John's growth of tomatoes* are not strictly speaking ungrammatical, since all VIs are licensed. We attribute the anomaly to semantics alone: the encyclopedic meaning of GROW is not *by itself* capable of assigning a causer role to *John*, and, because the syntax of nominalisations contains no CAUSE projection, the "desired" (i.e. agentive) reading cannot be obtained. *#John's growth of tomatoes* is thus on a par with *#Sincerity admires John*: both expressions are equally grammatical and equally (un)usable under normal conversational circumstances.

Finally, we considered implications and extensions of our proposals. First, we argued that *#John's growth of tomatoes* has the same status as *#I saw three oxygens in the kitchen* or *#Mary sometimes has green eyes*. In each case, encyclopedic properties conflict with structural meanings, introducing interpretive anomalies. Following Marantz (1997a), we also suggested that truly suppletive allomorphy occurs only for f-morphemes. If correct, the class of f-nodes is considerably enlarged and includes such elements as BAD, GOOD and GO, among others. Insofar as argument structure alternations depend on the specification of licensing f-nodes, we predict that there should exist further classes of alternations dependent on this expanded inventory. Confirmation of this hypothesis awaits further study.

References

Chomsky, Noam. 1957. *Syntactic structures*. The Hague: Mouton.

Chomsky, Noam. 1970. "Remarks on nominalization". In Roderick A. Jacobs & Peter S. Rosenbaum (ed.), *Readings in English transformational grammar*. Waltham: Ginn. 184-221.

Chomsky, Noam. 1995. *The minimalist program*. Cambridge: M.I.T. Press.

Chomsky, Noam; Halle, Morris. 1968. *The sound pattern of English*. New York: Harper & Row.

Di Sciullo, Anna-Maria; Williams, Edwin. 1987. *On the definition of word*. Cambridge: M.I.T. Press.

Embick, David. 1997. *Voice and the interfaces of syntax*. Unpublished PhD dissertation, University of Pennsylvania.

Gleitman, Lila R. 1990. "The structural sources of verb meaning". *Language acquisition* 1. 3-55.

Gleitman, Lila R.; Gleitman, Henry; Miller, Carol; Ostrin, Ruth. 1996. "'Similar' and similar concepts". *Cognition* 55. 321-376.

Goldberg, Adele E. 1995. *A construction grammar approach to argument structure.* Chicago: University of Chicago Press.

Hale, Kenneth L.; Keyser, Samuel Jay. 1993. "On argument structure and the lexical representation of syntactic relations". In Samuel Jay Keyser & Kenneth L. Hale (ed.), *The view from building 20.* Cambridge: M.I.T. Press. 53-109.

Halle, Morris; Marantz, Alec. 1993. "Distributed morphology and the pieces of inflection". In Samuel Jay Keyser & Kenneth L. Hale (ed.), *The view from building 20.* Cambridge: M.I.T. Press. 111-176.

Halle, Morris; Marantz, Alec. 1994. "Some key features of distributed morphology". In Andrew Carnie, Heidi Harley & Tony Bures (ed.), *Papers on phonology and morphology (M.I.T. working papers in linguistics* 21). Cambridge: M.I.T. working papers in linguistics. 275-288.

Harley, Heidi. 1995. *Subjects, events and licensing.* Unpublished PhD dissertation, M.I.T.

Kratzer, Angelika. 1996. "Severing the external argument from its verb". In Johan Rooryck & Laurie Zaring (ed.), *Phrase structure and the lexicon.* Dordrecht: Kluwer. 109-137.

Levin, Beth; Rappaport Hovav, Malka. 1995. *Unaccusativity. At the syntax-lexical semantics interface.* Cambridge: M.I.T. Press.

Lidz, Jeffrey 1997. "Constraints on the syntactic bootstrapping procedure for verb learning". Unpublished manuscript, University of Pennsylvania.

Lieber, Rochelle. 1980. *The organization of the lexicon.* Unpublished PhD dissertation, M.I.T.

Marantz, Alec. 1995. "A late note on late insertion". In Young-Sun Kim, Byung-Choon Lee, Kyoung-Jae Lee, Hyun-Kwon Yang & Jong-Yurl Yoon (ed.), *Explorations in generative grammar.* Seoul: Hankuk. 396-413.

Marantz, Alec. 1997a. "No escape from syntax. Don't try morphological analysis in the privacy of your own lexicon". In Alexis Dimitriadis, Laura Siegel, Clarissa Surek-Clark, and Alexander Williams (ed.), *Proceedings of the 21st annual Penn linguistics colloquium (U. Penn working papers in linguistics* 4:2). 201-225.

Marantz, Alec. 1997b. "'Cat' as a phrasal idiom. Stem suppletion, or the arbitrariness of the sign". Talk given at the University of Paris VIII.

Naigles, Letitia; Gleitman, Henry; Gleitman, Lila R. 1993. "Children acquire word meaning components from syntactic evidence". In Esther Dromi (ed.), *Language and cognition. A developmental perspective.* Norwood: Ablex. 104-140.

Noyer, Rolf. 1997. *Features, positions and affixes in autonomous morphological structure*. New York: Garland.

Sapir, Edward. 1921. *Language. An introduction to the study of speech*. New York: Harcourt, Brace and World.

Selkirk, Elisabeth O. 1982. *The syntax of words*. Cambridge: M.I.T. Press.

Travis, Lisa. 1994. "Event phrase and a theory of functional categories". In Païvi Koskinen (ed.), *Proceedings of the 1994 annual conference of the Canadian Linguistic Association*, vol. 2 (*Toronto working papers in linguistics*). Toronto: University of Toronto. 559-570.

Part Four

GRAMMAR

Grammar, the lexicon, and encyclopedic knowledge: Is there such a thing as informational encapsulation?[1]

Joseph Hilferty

Universitat de Barcelona, Departament de Filologia Anglesa i Alemanya,
Gran Via de les Corts Catalanes 585, 08007 Barcelona, Spain
E-mail: hilferty@lingua.fil.ub.es

0. Introduction

In linguistic theories that adopt a stringent modular perspective, the relationship between grammar and world knowledge is, at best, highly indirect. Such frameworks take it as a matter of doctrine that grammatical knowledge and world knowledge are fundamentally different in nature and do not come into direct contact with each other. Thus, in order to keep the two from intermingling, it is conjectured that, whatever the actual architecture of the mind might be, grammatical knowledge and world knowledge are at least one interface removed from one another (cf. Jackendoff 1997). Cognitive segregation via faculty psychology, one might call it.

---

[1] I would like to thank two anonymous referees for their helpful remarks, as well as Chet Creider, Maria Josep Cuenca, Mar Garachana, Dick Hudson, Paul Kay, Anna Poch, and And Rosta for discussions (and disagreements) on various parts of this material. Special thanks must also go out to Javier Valenzuela, who critiqued this paper (several times!), and to Bert Peeters for giving me the needed extra time to get the project off the ground. Portions of this article were read at the 6è Col·loqui Lingüístic de la Universitat de Barcelona (Barcelona, 21 December 1998) and co-presented with Javier Valenzuela at the 5th International Cognitive Linguistics Conference (Amsterdam, 14-19 July 1997).

Without a doubt, research assumptions are shaped and colored by what one expects to find. Analysts who start off with the preconceived idea that language is a modular system will find it less than immediately obvious that, in a given case in point, extragrammatical knowledge and syntax are interacting in an intimate fashion. But such cases do occur, and are noticeable only if one keeps an unprejudiced eye on the data (cf. e.g. Croft 1995, Lakoff 1991). Hence, there is at least some reason to believe that the mind is not tightly partitioned off into a tidy myriad of "knowledge boxes". The mind has internal structure, to be sure, but this internal structure leaks.

1. Three definitions of linguistic modularity

Modularity is a tricky subject. The perplexity of the matter, which has caused many misunderstandings throughout the years, stems from one simple, yet thorny, fact: modularity means different things to different people (cf. Müller 1996b). To start with, neuroscientists and behavioral scientists ascribe different meanings to the concept (cf. Bates 1994, Elman et al. 1996), and this makes it important not to confuse the two perspectives. For the neuroscientist, *modular* means "neurologically structured", in the sense that certain sets of brain cells are known to specialise (e.g., for certain visual stimuli, etc.) and, hence, may not be equally involved in all cognitive functions. For the behavioral scientist, the term refers to a much stronger claim of self-contained autonomy of certain domain-specific processes. It is the latter, clearly controversial, claim that will be examined here.

Since the early 1980s, starting with the publication of Chomsky (1980a, 1980b), several definitions of modularity have been put forth in the behavioral sciences, thus creating a polysemous notion. One oft-used sense, due to Newmeyer (1983), is a strictly linguistic definition: it draws on the existence of exceptions, which are claimed to provide proof of the arbitrary relationship between syntax, on the one hand, and semantics and discourse functions, on the other. A second sense, which comes up occasionally in the cognitive science literature, embraces domain specificity as its crucial feature. Finally, a third sense emerges from a set of criteria postulated in Fodor's (1983) seminal work, *The Modularity of Mind*. I take up each of these definitions in turn.

1.1. Exceptions

At the heart of Newmeyer's (1983) thesis for modularity is the observation that the syntactic form of a linguistic expression does not necessarily follow completely and predictably from its semantics. The lack of fit between syntax and semantics is therefore said to constitute clear proof that grammar is an autonomous module. Put more simply, in Newmeyer's opinion, exceptions to a rule provide evidence of the modular nature of a system, in this case, grammar. Or, put even more simply still, there must be a grammar module, because syntax cannot be reduced wholesale to semantic considerations.

Despite widespread belief to the contrary (see, e.g., Culicover & Jackendoff 1997), this argument is less than watertight. Take, for instance, the following examples:

(1a)   Sarah gave the charity fund raiser twenty dollars.

(1b)   *Sarah contributed the charity fund raiser twenty dollars.

In line with Newmeyer's reasoning, the fact that both *give* and *contribute* have similar semantics yet make use of different subcategorisation frames is supposed to demonstrate conclusively that syntax is autonomous from semantics. But does irregularity really prove modularity? I think not.

The rationale behind Newmeyer's assumption is, in my view, specious, since a proponent of nonmodular syntax could easily turn Newmeyer's argument on its head and take the opposite tack: the high degree of semantic-syntactic predictability that occurs in natural language shows that syntax is undoubtedly not autonomous. Consider, for example, the following paradigmatic relationship:

(2a)   Bill went to San Francisco.

(2b)   Bill walked to San Francisco.

(2c)   Bill ran to San Francisco.

(2d)   Bill swam to San Francisco.

(2e)   Bill flew to San Francisco.

(2f)   Bill drove to San Francisco.

(2g)   etc.

Here, it could be argued that the high degree of predictability is the direct result of semantic considerations. So, even if Newmeyer's claim were in some sense illuminating, modularity would at best be a statistical concept that depends directly on the ratio of rule-following instances to exceptions.[2]

Both views are plainly wrongheaded, however. The problem with such positions is that they embody what is aptly called the *type-predictability fallacy*. As Langacker has noted on a number of occasions (cf. Langacker 1988a, 1988b, 1990a, 1990b,

---

[2] Of course, the former would always outnumber the latter, if only because exceptions are by definition less numerous than rule-following instances.

1991), this fallacy confuses two logically distinct matters: the types of elements needed for the grammar and the predictability of their behavior. That is, recognising that irregularities exist in grammar does not inevitably force the conclusion that grammar is not a set of form-meaning pairings. It just means that some rules are not fully productive and nothing more. Perhaps such cases might have to be treated in terms of prototypicality and lower-level generalisations (cf. Goldberg 1992, 1994, 1995, Taylor 1998), but unless a lack of productivity equates with modularity (which seems extremely doubtful), then the only conclusion one can draw from Newmeyer's definition is that it is fallacious.

1.2. Domain specificity

The second characterisation of modularity often found in the literature simply portrays it as the equivalent of domain specificity. While this is no doubt a much-accepted view, especially among theorists interested in going beyond linguistic structure (see, e.g., Jackendoff 1992, Pinker 1997), it is to all intents and purposes a very weak version of modularity. In fact, in many ways, it is quite arguably the weakest version of modularity possible, for the simple reason that it is also the most powerful. Let me explain.

While it is perhaps undeniable that domain specificity is a necessary constituent of modularity (see section 1.3. below), it is rather improbable that it is constitutive of the notion itself. As Fodor (1983:52) puts it:

> Chess playing, for example, exploits a vast amount of eccentric information, but nobody wants to posit a chess faculty.

Domain specificity is obviously too weak a constraint, because just about anything could be modular on this definition. In fact, given such a broad concept of modularity, virtually all concepts would probably have to be modules. Consider, for instance, the following passage taken from a recent relevance theory article (Carston 1997:45):

> [Sperber (1994, 1996)] suggests that central thought processes are quite generally modular, that thought can be accounted for by a large network of conceptual modules whose domains crosscut those of the peripheral perception modules; there must, of course, be myriad intricate connections of pathways between such micro-modules. So, for instance, you might have a conceptual module for CAT; this module would receive and process information about cats via the visual, auditory, tactile, olfactory and linguistic modules. As well as storing newly received CAT information, it might send on representations to other conceptual modules, say a more general ANIMAL concept module.

Clearly, the view that domain specificity equates with modularity is, at the very least, quite questionable, since it could easily accommodate such dubious theoretical constructs as a "cat faculty" or even a "Teletubbies faculty". Thus, paradoxically, it is precisely the catchall character of this version of modularity that makes it too powerful a notion: it simply casts its net too wide to be useful.

So, just because people naturally subdivide their knowledge into domains, this does not mean that domain-specific knowledge is modular perforce. For if this were true, many unlikely candidates for "modularitydom", ranging from Bartlett (1932) and Piaget (1926) to Lakoff (1987) and Rumelhart (1980), would, upon revision, become modularists.[3] Hence, understood as domain specificity, the term *modularity* cannot distinguish between a modularist position and a nonmodularist position. Plainly, then, such a definition carries little substance, because it turns the concept into no more than a buzz word signifying allegiance to a certain school of (grammatical) thought.

1.3. Informational encapsulation

Fodor (1983:47-101) employs a more elaborate strategy than the previous two in defining modular systems of the mind. As is well known, he sees modular systems as exhibiting some nine properties (see also Reboul, this volume). Briefly, these are:

(i)   domain specificity (cf. section 1.2);

(ii)   mandatory operation (also known as *obligatory firing*; i.e., modules are reflexlike);

(iii)   limited conscious access;

(iv)   fast performance;

(v)   informational encapsulation;

(vi)   shallow outputs (i.e., modules do not interact with background knowledge);

(vii)   dedicated and fixed neural architecture (i.e., neurological localisation);

(viii) specific breakdown patterns (i.e., dissociations);

(ix)   a characteristic ontogenic course (i.e. characteristic sequencing and pace of development).

Because of the tentative (and perhaps speculative) nature of these criteria, it seems reasonable to assume that, even now, almost twenty years later, they are not to be taken as constituting necessary and sufficient conditions. Whatever the status of these properties, Fodor makes it clear that point (v), informational encapsulation, is

---

[3] This scenario is not nearly as hypothetical as it might seem on first thought, since Newmeyer (1996) clearly endorses the revisionist position I am describing when he characterises Talmy Givón, George Lakoff, and Ronald Langacker as supporters of linguistic autonomy.

the most important trait of modular systems. I shall therefore make no attempt at an exhaustive survey of each of the remaining claims.[4] I have no qualms with counting informational encapsulation as modularity and can see no counterargument that would make it a debatable definition. Given this assumption, my task will be to present counterevidence to the claim that syntax is informationally encapsulated. As we shall see, such data can be found if only one looks for them.

2. Grammar, the lexicon, and encyclopedic knowledge

We are now in a position to concentrate on the next part of our story. The lexicon has traditionally been considered to be a "component" of language, separate from both grammar and world knowledge. In the course of the last twenty years, however, it has become increasingly clear that such a neat distinction cannot be upheld. On the one hand, Haiman (1980) and others have placed the lexicon-encyclopedia distinction in serious doubt, arguing that encyclopedic information is part of the lexicon.[5] On the other hand, work in quite a few linguistic approaches, most notably cognitive grammar (Langacker 1987, 1990a, 1991) and construction grammar (Fillmore & Kay 1999, Goldberg 1995, Kay 1997), has made it especially plain that a clean division between grammar and the lexicon is also doubtful (for a review of the psycholinguistic evidence, see Bates & Goodman 1997).

This naturally prompts the following question: is syntax informationally encapsulated from semantics and world knowledge? This is a question that most hardcore modularists would answer affirmatively without a second thought. However, as Maratsos & Matheny (1994) have pointed out, strict syntactic autonomy from meaning structures has always been a problematic assumption. Taken in its strongest form, this would entail that syntax could never have an effect on semantics. Of course, even since the early days of generative grammar, it has been readily accepted that syntax can affect meaning (e.g., logical-form interface relations such as scope, structural ambiguity, word order, and the like). Hence, the strongest form of informational encapsulation has never been recognised by Chomskyan generative grammar.

In this section I adduce a counterexample to the weaker claim of syntactic modularity, viz., that grammar is a self-contained system that is insensitive to semantic constraints and encyclopedic-knowledge structures. What I aim to show is that world

---

[4] For discussions of points (vii), (viii), and (ix), see Bates (1994), Elman et al. (1996), Maratsos & Matheny (1994), Müller (1996a).

[5] See, e.g., Barsalou (1993), Fillmore (1975, 1985), Hilferty (1997), Hudson (1984, 1990, 1995), Lakoff (1987) and Langacker (1987).

knowledge plays a vital role in constraining a particular case of "lexical syntax": that of bare-NP complementation of Spanish *tener* 'have'. This counterexample and others like it (cf. e.g. Lakoff 1991, Croft 1995) pose a threat for the integrity of information-encapsulated syntax, even in its attenuated form, because they show that syntactic distributions can be directly affected by nonsyntactic structures.

2.1. Spanish tener 'have' and bare-NP complementation

In many languages (e.g., English or Spanish), it is not usually recognised that singular count nouns can be maximal projections (i.e., nominal constituents that can stand on their own in argument positions).[6] However, at least in a subset of those languages, there appear to be some core- and non-core-grammar data which show that this *is* a possibility. To my mind, probably the most interesting case has to do with a specific type of bare-nominal complementation manifested by Spanish *tener* 'to have'.[7] An example of this phenomenon can be found in (3):

> (3)   ¿Tienes   coche?
>
> *Have-2nd/sg car*
>
> 'Do you have a car?'

Now, the fact that a singular count noun such as *coche* 'car' can be used as a perfectly legal complement is a little strange, because (as alluded to above) most verbs do not sanction this complementation pattern:

> (4a)   *¿Ves   coche?
>
> *See-2nd/sg car*
>
> 'Do you see car?'

> (4b)   *¿Sabes   conducir coche?
>
> *Know-2nd/sg drive   car*
>
> 'Do you know how to drive car?'

In light of examples such as (4), the analyst might be content just to write it down to the whims of convention and be done with it. This would be a deficient analysis, however, because not all bare singular count nouns can be complements of *tener*. For example, under normal circumstances (in asking for change, for instance) it would be highly unusual for *moneda* 'coin' to appear as a complement of *tener*, even though its morphosyntactic features coincide with those of *coche* 'car'.

---

[6] For a critical discussion of maximal projections, see Kornai & Pullum (1990).

[7] See Hilferty & Valenzuela (2000) for a formalisation of the following discussion.

(5a)   ?*¿Tienes   moneda?

        Have-2nd/sg coin

        'Do you have coin?'

(5b)   ¿Tienes   monedas?

        Have-2nd/sg coins

        'Do you have any coins?'

Why should this be? The answer, we shall see, is actually quite straightforward if a nonmodular perspective is adopted, that is, if the syntax is allowed to make reference not only to constraints on form, but also to matters of semantic construal and general-knowledge structures.

The problem at hand is not nearly as enigmatic as it might appear at first blush. However, in order to solve the puzzle of *tener*'s bare-NP complementation, it will be necessary to invoke our encyclopedic knowledge about possessions. Spanish, it seems, makes use of a very general idealised cognitive model (in the sense of Lakoff 1987),[8] which has two distinct logical possibilities for possession: one in which possessions are typically held in numbers larger than one, and another in which the entity in question is normally possessed in amounts of just one. These two idealised views of possessions place constraints on the form of *tener*'s complements, so that not just any bare count noun can be maximal.

As proof of the above claim, consider the following examples:

(6a)   ¿Tienes   marido?

        Have-2nd/sg husband

        'Do you have a husband?'

(6b)   *¿Tienes   maridos?

        Have-2nd/sg husbands

        'Do you have husbands?'

It is abundantly clear that in Western societies women are supposed to have only one husband at any point in time. Given this particular detail of our encyclopedic knowledge, it follows then that the bare count-noun complement of *tener* should appear in the singular. As the examples in (6) show, this is in fact the case.

---

[8] Idealised cognitive models are essentially equivalent to what Fillmore (1975, 1985) has called *frames* and Langacker (1987, 1990a, 1991) has called *cognitive domains*.

Now, consider the opposite situation, in which a singular count noun would generally be thought of as unacceptable:

(7a) *¿Tienes   hijo?

          Have-2nd/sg child?

          'Do you have child?'

(7b) ¿Tienes   hijos?

          Have-2nd/sg children?

          'Do you have children?'

Here, the complement must take the plural as its number value in order to be a maximal constituent. This stems from the fact that, in our idealised conception of kinship relations, the traditional nuclear family is normally thought of as having more than one child (though, given the low birthrates of recent times, things may be changing). Obviously, such data constitute solid evidence for the claim that the idealised cognitive model of possession plays a key role in the complementation of *tener*.

Considerations such as these are highly significant to the overall argument of this paper, because they show that a syntactic property such as maximality is not impervious to facets of background knowledge. Be this as it may, it might be objected that there are certain count nouns that can appear as either plural or singular. Such is the case of examples (8):

(8a) ¿Tienes   bolis?

          Have-2nd/sg pens

          'Do you have pens?'

(8b) ¿Tienes   boli?

          Have-2nd/sg pen?

          'Do you have a pen?'

Crucially, however, they would not be equally appropriate in all situations: (8a) would be suitable if the speaker were a customer at a stationary store, whereas (8b) would not. Conversely, (8b) would be completely acceptable if the speaker were inquiring whether the hearer needed a pen, whereas (8a) would probably be rather forced in such a situation (unless of course several pens were needed). So, instead of being an exception to the analysis, these examples actually conform to it.

Up till now I have only made reference to more or less conventional uses of *tener* + bare NP. There are, however, "unconventional" uses that do not fit canonical idealised cognitive models of possession. In such cases, it is necessary to resort to the notion of an *ad-hoc* idealised cognitive model (cf. Hilferty & Valenzuela 2000). Take, for instance, example (9):

(9)   ¿Tienes   moneda?

       Have-2nd/sg coin

       'Do you have a coin?'

As discussed above, an example such as this might, at first sight, seem rather odd, since it contradicts our tacit knowledge about possessing coins: people usually carry more than one coin with them. Nonetheless, it is not very difficult to imagine a situation that could override this conventional cognitive model, and thus convert (9) into a perfectly acceptable utterance. An appropriate context could, for instance, be that of a person who offers a coin to a friend in order to use a shopping cart at a supermarket or a locker at a bookshop. Such usage possibilities are not very remarkable; they simply reflect our natural ability to construct *ad-hoc* categories (cf. Barsalou 1983, 1991). Hence, what we do in such cases is to create an on-line idealised cognitive model, which is contingent on the demands of the discourse context.

Before moving on, it is important to stress that the importance of the present counterexample to the thesis of autonomous syntax is not merely that encyclopedic knowledge can affect a morphosyntactic feature such as number. Rather, its significance goes much deeper than that: it shows that it is possible for idealised cognitive models to play a central role in stipulating whether bare count-noun complements can be construed as syntactically maximal or not. To put it another way, whether or not a bare count noun can stand as a complement of *tener* depends on whether or not it meets the conditions of number placed on it by world knowledge. This of course violates the autonomy thesis, since maximality is generally deemed to be a purely syntactic feature par excellence (as in, e.g., X-bar theory). Clearly, the fact that grammar is not immune to outside constraints is a severe blow to the conception of syntax as a modular system.

2.2. Rebutting the rebuttals

Most functionalists would of course find the above to be very compelling evidence against syntactic autonomy. A hard-nosed modularist might take another view of things, however. As Lakoff (1991) notes, a defender of the autonomy thesis might contend that such counterexamples are not really counterexamples at all, because the offending cases could be said to be merely unacceptable, rather than ungrammatical.

This response would miss the mark entirely. To argue (as does Newmeyer 1991:103-104) that semantics acts as a filter for blindly generated syntactic structures essentially renders modularity-theoretic accounts of syntax unfalsifiable. In point of fact, such a response takes the autonomy of syntax to be an axiom, and not a matter of contention to be established empirically. There thus could not be such a thing as a counterexample to modularity. Unfortunately, I know of no evidence suggesting that people spontaneously produce grammatically correct patterns of linguistic symbols lacking grounding in either sound or meaning. In the absence of persuasive evidence to the contrary, invoking the competence-performance distinction fails to deal with the problem at hand, because, in short, the manœuvre robs modularity of any empirical content it might otherwise have.

Of course, a staunch modularist might very well see falsifiability as a secondary issue and insist on forcing the point that syntactic and semantic well-formedness are not the same thing. The argument would no doubt be predicated on the assertion that surely just about everyone this side of 1957 agrees that grammaticality can be dissociated from acceptability. For instance, semantic, not syntactic, concerns are what filters out a sentence such as:

(10)   *I ate the drink.

Due to the breach of selectional restrictions, the semantics of such a sentence is anomalous, even though the syntactic pattern it adopts is itself impeccable. So, while a sentence may be grammatically well-formed, it may be rejected on the grounds that it is semantically (or pragmatically) unacceptable.

This is probably undeniable (cf. Langacker 1988b). However, I do not think that the case presented in the previous section (section 2.1) is entirely analogous to that of a sentence such as (10). Indeed, there is a telling difference: to repair the problem in (10), one would have to change a whole word; in the case of *tener*, on the other hand, one would merely have to change the complement's number inflection. Accordingly, the motivation behind these corrections is different in each case: in (10), the aim is to resolve the semantic clash between *ate* and *drink*; with regard to *tener*'s complement, the inflectional adjustments are meant to remedy problems of maximality. In short, the two cases are not completely parallel to one another: in one case, semantics is not affecting syntax; in the other it is.

Certainly, the "semantic filter" argument is not the only strategy that could be exploited to salvage modularity. Another conceivable reaction to a counterexample such as the bare-NP complementation of *tener* might be to take the matter out of the hands of linguists and place it in the care of psycholinguists. This tactic would no doubt have the effect of reframing the question: it would no longer be a matter of *if* semantic and contextual information can integrate with syntactic information, but rather *when* it does so. That is, according to the tenets of modular syntactic theory, sentences are supposed to be parsed first on independent structural principles and then assigned a semantic representation. Under this reinterpretation of the issue, it is conceivable that semantic information could play a major role in constraining distributions, but only after the autonomous parser had done its job.

The problem with this response is that there is no real consensus among psycholinguists working in the area of syntactic processing that sentence parsing actually works in a modular fashion (for reviews, see Carpenter et al. 1995, Mitchell 1994, Tanenhaus & Trueswell 1995). So, to accept the claim of a modular syntactic parser uncritically would be just a case of begging the question, especially since Marslen-Wilson & Tyler (1987) have presented on-line psycholinguistic evidence showing that discourse context can have a facilitating effect on sentence parsing.[9] In any event, the onus is on modularity theorists to show that counterexamples such as the one discussed herein are first processed, both receptively and in production, as pure form and then fleshed out semantically. The intimate connection between syntax and semantics (including world knowledge) in such cases suggests that modularists have their work cut out for them.

3. Conclusion

Is there such a thing as informational encapsulation? This of course is still very much an open question and I do not pretend to know the answer. No doubt, it could turn out to be true. But so long as there are data that go unexplained by modular theories of grammar, the burden of proof to dispel the illusion of interactionism (if it is in fact an illusion) falls to the proponents of syntactic modularity.

As things stand, modularity simply cannot be taken as an established fact in grammar, no matter what received wisdom currently presumes.[10] If syntax really is informationally encapsulated from nonsyntactic processes, then it is up to modularists to present the corroborating evidence: ignoring counterexamples to the autonomy thesis simply does not shed any light on the matter, let alone prove the point. The modularity of grammar is an empirical question that needs to be established, not begged.

References

Barsalou, Lawrence W. 1983. "*Ad hoc* categories". *Memory and cognition* 11. 211-227.

---

[9] See Dabrowska (1997) for an interesting argument against syntactic modularity on the basis of an off-line experiment.

[10] Actually, I am unaware of any evidence that establishes the correctness of informational encapsulation in any domain of cognition, even vision (which by almost all accounts is very modularlike).

Barsalou, Lawrence W. 1991. "Deriving categories to achieve goals". In Gordon H. Bower (ed.), *The psychology of learning and motivation. Advances in research and theory*, vol. 27. New York: Academic Press. 1-64.

Barsalou, Lawrence W. 1993. "Flexibility, structure and linguistic vagary in concepts. Manifestations of a compositional system of perceptual symbols". In Alan F. Collins, Susan E. Gathercole, Martin A. Conway & Peter E. Morris (ed.), *Theories of memory*. Hillsdale: Lawrence Erlbaum. 29-101.

Bartlett, Frederick C. 1932. *Remembering. A study in experimental and social psychology*. Cambridge: Cambridge University Press.

Bates, Elizabeth A. 1994. "Modularity, domain specificity and the development of language". *Discussions in neuroscience* 10. 136-149.

Bates, Elizabeth A.; Goodman, Judith C. 1997. "On the inseparability of grammar and the lexicon. Evidence from acquisition, aphasia, and real-time processing". *Language and cognitive processes* 12. 507-584.

Carpenter, Patricia A.; Miyake, Akira; Just, Marcel Adam. 1995. "Language comprehension. Sentence and discourse processing". *Annual review of psychology* 46. 91-120.

Carston, Robyn. 1997. "Relevance-theoretic pragmatics and modularity". *UCL working papers in linguistics* 9. 29-53.

Chomsky, Noam. 1980a. *Rules and representations*. New York: Columbia Univerity Press.

Chomsky, Noam. 1980b. "Rules and representations". *The behavioral and brain sciences* 3. 1-15.

Croft, William. 1995. "Autonomy and functionalist linguistics". *Language* 71. 490-532.

Culicover, Peter W.; Jackendoff, Ray. 1997. "Semantic subordination despite syntactic coordination". *Linguistic inquiry* 28. 195-217.

Dabrowska, Ewa. 1997. "The LAD goes to school. A cautionary tale for nativists". *Linguistics* 35. 735-766.

Elman, Jeffrey L.; Bates, Elizabeth A.; Johnson, Mark H.; Karmiloff-Smith, Annette; Parisi, Domenico; Plunkett, Kim. 1996. *Rethinking innateness. A connectionist perspective on development*. Cambridge: M.I.T. Press.

Fillmore, Charles J. 1975. "An alternative to checklist theories of meaning". In Cathy Cogen, Henry Thompson, Graham Thurgood, Kenneth Whistler & James Wright, *Proceedings of the first annual meeting of the Berkeley Linguistics Society*. Berkeley: University of California. 123-131.

Fillmore, Charles J. 1985. "Frames and the semantics of understanding". *Quaderni di semantica* 6. 222-254.

Fillmore, Charles J.; Kay, Paul. 1999. *Construction grammar*. Stanford: CSLI.

Fodor, Jerry A. 1983. *The modularity of mind. An essay on faculty psychology*. Cambridge: M.I.T. Press.

Goldberg, Adele E. 1992. "The inherent semantics of argument structure. The case of the English ditransitive construction". *Cognitive linguistics* 3. 37-74.

Goldberg, Adele E. 1994. "Another look at some learnability paradoxes". In Eve V. Clark (ed.), *Proceedings of the twenty-fifth annual child language research forum*. Stanford: CSLI. 60-75.

Goldberg, Adele E. 1995. *Constructions. A construction grammar approach to argument structure*. Chicago: University of Chicago Press.

Haiman, John. 1980. "Dictionaries and encyclopedias". *Lingua* 50. 329-357.

Hilferty, Joseph. 1997. "Mothers, lies, and bachelors. A brief reply to Wierzbicka (1990)". *Word* 48. 51-59.

Hilferty, Joseph; Valenzuela, Javier. 2000. "Maximality and idealized cognitive models. The complementation of Spanish *tener*". *Language sciences* [in press].

Hudson, Richard. 1984. *Word grammar*. Oxford: Blackwell.

Hudson, Richard. 1990. *English word grammar*. Oxford: Blackwell.

Hudson, Richard. 1995. "Identifying the linguistic foundations for lexical research and dictionary design". In Donald E. Walker, Antonio Zampolli & Nicoletta Calzolari (ed.), *Automating the lexicon. Research and practice in a multilingual environment*. Oxford: Oxford University Press. 21-51.

Jackendoff, Ray. 1992. *Languages of the mind. Essays on mental representation*. Cambridge: M.I.T. Press.

Jackendoff, Ray. 1997. *The architecture of the language faculty*. Cambridge: M.I.T. Press.

Kay, Paul. 1997. *Words and the grammar of context*. Stanford: CSLI.

Kornai, András; Pullum, Geoffrey K. 1990. "The X-bar theory of phrase structure". *Language* 66. 24-50.

Lakoff, George. 1987. *Women, fire, and dangerous things. What categories reveal about the mind*. Chicago: University of Chicago Press.

Lakoff, George. 1991. "Cognitive versus generative linguistics. How commitments influence results". *Language and communication* 11. 53-62.

Langacker, Ronald W. 1987. *Foundations of cognitive grammar*, vol. 1. *Theoretical prerequisites*. Stanford: Stanford University Press.

Langacker, Ronald W. 1988a. "Autonomy, agreement, and cognitive grammar". In Diane Brentari, Gary Larson & Lynn MacLeod (ed.), *Papers from the 24th regional meeting of the Chicago Linguistic Society*, vol. 2. *Parasession on agreement in grammatical theory*. Chicago: University of Chicago. 147-180.

Langacker, Ronald W. 1988b. "An overview of cognitive grammar". In Brygida Rudzka-Ostyn (ed.), *Topics in cognitive linguistics*. Amsterdam: John Benjamins. 3-48.

Langacker, Ronald W. 1990a. *Concept, image, and symbol. The cognitive basis of grammar*. Berlin: Mouton de Gruyter.

Langacker, Ronald W. 1990b. "The rule controversy. A cognitive grammar approach". *CRL newsletter*, June, Article 4-3-1.

Langacker, Ronald W. 1991. *Foundations of cognitive grammar*, vol. 2. *Descriptive application*. Stanford: Stanford University Press.

Maratsos, Michael; Matheny, Laura. 1994. "Language specificity and elasticity. Brain and clinical syndrome studies". *Annual review of psychology* 45. 487-516.

Marslen-Wilson, William D.; Tyler, Lorraine K. 1987. "Against modularity". In Jay L. Garfield (ed.), *Modularity in knowledge representation and natural language understanding*. Cambridge: M.I.T. Press. 37-62.

Mitchell, Don C. 1994. "Sentence parsing". In Morton Ann Gernsbacher (ed.), *Handbook of psycholinguistics*. San Diego: Academic Press. 375-409.

Müller, Ralph-Axel. 1996a. "Innateness, autonomy, universality? Neurobiological approaches to language". *Behavioral and brain sciences* 19. 611-631.

Müller, Ralph-Axel. 1996b. "The epigenesis of regional specificity". *Behavioral and brain sciences* 19. 651-660.

Newmeyer, Frederick J. 1983. *Grammatical theory. Its limits and its possibilities*. Chicago: University of Chicago Press.

Newmeyer, Frederick J. 1991. "O, what a tangoed web they weave...". *Language and communication* 11. 97-107.

Newmeyer, Frederick J. 1996. "Müller's conclusions and linguistic research". *Behavioral and brain sciences* 19. 641-642.

Piaget, Jean. 1926. *La représentation du monde chez l'enfant*. Paris: Alcan.

Pinker, Steven. 1997. *How the mind works*. New York: Norton.

Rumelhart, David E. 1980. "Schemata. The building blocks of cognition". In Rand J. Spiro, Bertram C. Bruce & William F. Brewer (ed.), *Theoretical issues in reading comprehension. Perspectives from cognitive psychology, linguistics, artificial intelligence, and education.* Hillsdale: Lawrence Erlbaum. 33-58.

Sperber, Dan. 1994. "The modularity of thought and the epidemiology of representations". In Lawrence A. Hirschfeld & Susan A. Gelman (ed.), *Mapping the mind. Domain specificity in cognition and culture.* Cambridge: Cambridge University Press. 39-67.

Sperber, Dan. 1996. *Explaining culture. A naturalistic approach.* Oxford: Blackwell.

Tanenhaus, Michael K.; Trueswell, John C. 1995. "Sentence comprehension". In Joanne L. Miller & Peter D. Eimas (ed.), *Speech, language, and communication.* San Diego: Academic Press. 217-262.

Taylor, John R. 1998. "Syntactic constructions as prototype categories". In Michael Tomasello (ed.), *The new psychology of language. Cognitive and functional approaches to language structure.* Mahwah: Lawrence Erlbaum. 177-202.

Encyclopedia-lexicon distinctions in Jingulu grammar[1]

Rob Pensalfini

University of Queensland, Department of English, Brisbane, Qld 4072, Australia
E-mail: r.pensalfini@mailbox.uq.edu.au

0. Introduction

Encyclopedia entries and lexical items are not in one to one relationships. This seems like a fairly innocuous, even facile, claim if one is merely thinking about such things as idiom chunks, where several lexical items combine to give rise to a single noncompositional encyclopedic meaning. However, the claim is neither innocuous nor facile when taken to the level of word structure. The Jingulu language of Northern Australia provides a striking example of this claim. Roots in Jingulu are not able

---

[1] The ideas and analyses herein are based on those found scattered over some 350 pages in my doctoral dissertation (Pensalfini 1997). They owe a lot to comments, questions, and discussions raised by many of my colleagues and teachers at the Massachusetts Institute of Technology and the University of Chicago, by participants at ConSOLE V (December 1996) and the M.I.T. Australian Linguistics Circle (January 1997), and audiences at the University of Western Australia and Carleton College. In particular I would like to thank Mark Baker, Bob Dixon, Ken Hale, Morris Halle, Michael Kenstowicz, Beth Levin, Alec Marantz, David Nash, Rachel Nordlinger, Bert Peeters, Norvin Richards, Jay Rifkin, Jerry Sadock, Jane Simpson, and Cheryl Zoll. Sadly, I cannot blame any of these people for any errors, omissions, or heresies which remain. I was partially supported in my theoretical research by a Hackett studentship from the University of Western Australia, and in my field research by grants from the Australian Institute for Aboriginal and Torres Strait Islander Studies, Papulu Apparr-kari, and Diwurruwurru-jaru, and by assistance from the Institute for Aboriginal Development and Gurungu Council.

to stand alone as words, but must instead combine with some other morpheme. The roots themselves are encyclopedically rich but seem to have no formal grammatical standing, while the elements with which they combine are rich in formal grammatical features but bleached of encyclopedic meaning.

This article argues for a distinction between two kinds of syntactic positions: those which can host encyclopedic features and those which can host only formal features. The distinction accounts for a range of syntactic, morphological, and phonological phenomena in Jingulu. The analysis, cast in the terms of the Distributed Morphology (DM) framework (Halle & Marantz 1993, Marantz 1996), crucially distinguishes between vocabulary items which contain encyclopedic information (which are semantically 'contentful') and those which convey purely formal features (and are semantically 'bleached').

In section 1 we see how verbal words are constructed in Jingulu, and that what an English speaker might want to call a 'verb' is in fact an interaction between two morphemes, not necessarily adjacent, within the Jingulu verbal word. These two morphemes are analysed as a formal verb and an encyclopedically laden category-less root. This interaction most closely resembles an obligatory 'light verb' strategy, and is argued to arise from a ban on encyclopedic features in positions which are reserved for formal features. In section 2 this analysis is extended to Jingulu nominals. We then turn, in section 3, to an analysis of Jingulu vowel harmony, which affects both verbs and nominals, and which defies analysis using traditional morphological category labels. The analysis proposed here rests on the notion that the encyclopedically laden category-less roots are uninterpretable as formal objects unless they undergo syntactic merger with some formal (but semantically bleached) element. In the final section, the rigorous separation of encyclopedic and formal features into separate vocabulary items is shown to be the source of Jingulu's extremely nonconfigurational syntax, and similar divisions are held up as the source of nonconfigurational syntax generally.

1. The structure of Jingulu verbs

Verbs are the most morphologically complex of all words in Jingulu, conveying information about person and number of subject and object as well as tense, aspect, mood, polarity, direction of motion, and nature of state or action. Fully inflected verbs are able to stand alone as clauses, with all other parts of speech optional in a grammatical sentence.

1.1. Description

(1a-g) provide a variety of inflected verbs each of which constitutes a fully grammatical Jingulu sentence.[2]

(1a) Ngiji-wunyu-nyu-ju.
see-3dl-2O-DO
Those two can see you.

(1b) Ambaya-nu.
talk-DID
He spoke.

(1c) Ngaba-nga-jiyimi.
have-1sg-COME
I am bringing it.

(1d) Maya-narna-yi.
hit-3fS1O-FUT
She will hit me.

(1e) Miyi-ji!
hit-NEGIMPV
Don't hit it!

(1f) Mindi-rruku.
1dlInc-CAME
You and I came.

---

[2] The following abbreviations have been used throughout the paper:

1, 2, 3	first, second, third person
sg, dl, pl	singular, dual, plural number
S, O	subject, object
Inc, Exc	inclusive, exclusive reference
m, f, n, v	masculine, feminine, neuter, vegetable gender
NOM, ACC, ERG, DAT, GEN	nominative, accusative, ergative, dative, genitive case
LOC, ALL, ABL	locative, allative, ablative role/case
FOC, EMPH	contrastive focus, emphasis
DEM	demonstrative
FUT, DIST	future, distant past tense
HAB	habitual aspect
IRR, IMPV	irrealis, imperative mood
INV, REFL	inverse, reflexive/reciprocal morpheme
THRU, NOML	intensifier/adverbialiser, nominaliser (suffixes)

(1g)   Ya-ardi.

        3sg-HAB

        He used to do it.

The verb word commonly (as in (1a-e)) begins with a morpheme which is glossed
by use of a verb in English. For this reason alone, traditional morphological accounts
of Jingulu (see Chadwick 1975 for example) have considered this morpheme to be
the verb or verb stem, though I refer to it as a 'root', and will argue that it has no
categorial status whatsoever. This morpheme is followed by a subject marker (null
when the subject is third person singular, as in (1b)), and an object marker (as in
(1a), null when the object is in the third person, as in (1c)). Certain combinations of
subject and object trigger agreement by way of a fused morpheme which represents
features of both subject and object (as in (1d)).[3] Agreement marking is always followed by a final element which encodes tense, sometimes aspect and/or mood, and
direction of motion. This final element is the only obligatory part of the verb, and
(1f-g) demonstrate verbs which lack an initial root morpheme. However, the final
element is morphologically a suffix, and therefore must always be preceded by either an initial root (1b, e), or agreement markers (1f). While third person singular
subject marking is usually null, there are overt forms (/ya/ and /ka/) which are used
only if null agreement would strand the final element without a preceding host
within the verb (1g). I argue in the following section that it is this final element
which is the true syntactic verb of the Jingulu clause.

1.2. Will the real Verb please stand up?

The final element encodes not only inflectional properties such as tense, mood, and
aspect, but also distinctly verbal notions such as direction of motion or activity. The
latter fall into three broad classes, corresponding to the English verbs *come* (2), *go*
(3) and *do / be* (or 'motion-neutral', as in (4)). As can be seen from (2-4), the final
element is fully suppletive: its form cannot possibly be predicted on the basis of
other elements of the paradigm. For the full paradigms, see Chadwick (1975) or
Pensalfini (1997).

        (2a)   Ya-**jiyimi** bininja.

                3sg-COME man

                The man is coming.

---

[3] Note that fused agreement morphemes for situations involving a third person subject and first
person object vary according to the gender of the subject. This is the only instance in which Jingulu
verbal morphology is sensitive to gender features.

(2b) Ya-**ngku** ngurrarrungka.
3sg-WILL_COME tomorrow
He'll come tomorrow.

(2c) Ya-**miki** murdika-mbili.
3sg-CAME car-LOC
He came in a car.

(2d) Larrba ngirri-**mardiyimi**.
previously 3plExc-CAME(DIST)
We came here long ago.

(3a) Nga-**ardu**.
1sg-GO
I'm on my way.

(3b) Nga-**rriyi**.
1sg-WILL_GO
I'll go.

(3c) Nga-**rruku** idajku.
1sg-WENT yesterday
I went (there) yesterday.

(4a) Wayabij nya-**ju**.
tired 2sg-DO
You are tired.

(4b) Ngindi-mbili nga-**nu**.
here-LOC 1sg-DID
I did it here.

(4c) Wurraka-na ya-**yi**.
3plGEN-M 3sg-FUT
He'll do it for them.

(4d) Yukulurrubi ya-**marriyi** nginimbili.
grass_species 3sg-DID(DIST) here
Yukulurrubi used to be here.

Equivalents of other English verbs in Jingulu are constructed by combining one of these final elements with an initial root to form a verbal word which includes the agreement markers. Different combinations of root and final element can yield different English verbs in translation, as illustrated in (5).

(5a)   Ngaba-nga-ju karnarinymi.
        hold-1sg-DO   spear
        I have a spear.

(5b)   Ngaba-nga-rriyi   karnarinymi.
        hold-1sg-WILL_GO spear
        I'll take a spear.

(5c)   Ngaba-jiyimi karnarinymi.
        hold-COME   spear
        He's bringing a spear.

(5d)   Ngaruk baka-nga-rriyi.
        dive-1sg-WILL_GO
        I'll dive down.

(5e)   Ngaruk baka-nga-yi arduku.
        dive-1sg-FUT   carefully
        I'll submerge (something) carefully.

In (5a-c) the root /ngab-/ 'hold' is combined with three different final elements to yield the translations 'have', 'take', and 'bring'. In (5d-e) the choice of final element affects the transitivity of the clause, and thus whether the root /ngaruk bak-/ is to be translated as 'dive' or 'submerge'.

Jingulu also allows 'verb drop', though this is more correctly characterised under the present analysis as 'root drop'. Root-less clauses are the only way to express English notions such as 'come' and 'go', though roots can 'modify' these by supplying information as to the manner of coming and going. Compare the sentences with roots in (6) to the root-less clauses of (7).

(6a)   Jirrkiji-mindu-wa.
        run-1dlInc-WILL_GO
        You and me will run (off).

(6b)   Ngaja-nya-ana-ju.
        see-2sg-1O-DO
        You can see me.

(6c)   Anikiya-nya-ju.
       do_what-2sg-DO
       What are you doing?

(7a)   Ya-ardu kardarda ya-jiyimi.
       3sg-GO always 3sg-COME
       He's always coming and going.

(7b)   Ya-angku.
       3sg-WILL_COME
       He will come.

(7c)   Kara-mbili nga-ju.
       fog-LOC 1sg-DO
       I'm in the fog.

(7d)   Jangu wurru-ju.
       nothing 3pl-DO
       They're doing nothing.

(7e)   Nam wunyu-ju.
       stuck 3dl-DO
       They're stuck together.

(7f)   Ajuwara manyan nya-nu? – Ngindi-mbili nga-nu.
       where sleep 2sg-DID DEM-LOC 1sg-DID
       Where did you sleep? – I did it there.

Root-less clauses are primarily used to express coming and going (7a-b), or in tandem with other words to create clauses with predictable meanings (in (7c) with a case-marked nominal, and in (7d-e) with adverbials); they can also be used when the root meaning is understood, in 'root ellipsis' constructions (cf. the second clause in (7f)).

Further evidence that the agreement markers are associated with the final element and not the root comes from the appearance of a few extremely rare cases (two sentences out of a corpus of some three and a half thousand) when a fully inflected word intervenes between the co-verbal root and the rest of the verb:

(8a)   **Kibardki** ibilka-rni **nya-yi** ngardajkala-rni, nginda
       bathe water-FOC 2sg-FUT big(m)-FOC that(m)
       bunungkurru-mbili miji-ngurri-nu kurdijalaka.
       billabong-LOC get-1plExc-DID mussel

Wherever there's enough water for you to bathe, we would have gotten mussels in that billabong.

(8b)   **Ambaya** ngaya **nga-nu** Warranganku-mbili.
        speak   1sgNOM 1sg-DID Beetaloo-LOC
        I spoke about Beetaloo.

In these cases the agreement markers are found prefixed to the final element, and not suffixed to the root.

It seems reasonable, then, on descriptive grounds alone, to consider the final element of the Jingulu verb-word to be the syntactic verb. I will refer to this element as the 'core verb' or 'light verb'. Like the verb in light verb constructions in English and other languages, it is semantically bleached, carrying all of the verbal morphology and retaining only one or two purely formal distinctions (e.g., in the case of Jingulu, direction of motion). One important difference is that in Jingulu *all verbs* in Jingulu involve a light verb, and *all verbs* containing a co-verbal root involve merger of a syntactically complete clause with the formally vacuous root. Such structures are familiar, even common, in English (consider the range of light verb constructions such as 'give (something) a look / listen / taste / try / shot / feel', 'have a look / listen / burl / run / swim'), but in Jingulu the construction is *obligatory*. Another difference is that Jingulu's obligatory light verb strategy seems highly unusual when compared to that of Indo-European languages, where the combination of formal verbal and encyclopedic predicate features into one item is the norm.[4] Within the broad spectrum of Australian languages, Jingulu represents an extreme of the tendency which many languages have toward the use of light verbs and encyclopedically rich co-verbal elements in tandem. The co-verb plus light verb structure is the main way of expressing predication in Gurindji, where the complement of light verbs is somewhat bigger than in Jingulu (some thirty versus Jingulu's three). Even in Warlpiri, which has a large class of verbs, the use of co-verbs in tandem with inflecting verbs is very common (Ken Hale, personal communication).

Among Australian languages employing a light verb strategy, there is wide variation with respect to the nexus between co-verb and core verb. In some languages, the co-verb is tightly bound to the complex containing the light verb (as it is in Jingulu), while in other languages the co-verb behaves like an independent word, more freely ordered with respect to the complex containing the core verb (Capell 1979b). In the latter type of language, the co-verb might best be viewed as an adverbial element, containing some categorial information. In Minimalist terms (Chomsky 1993), it is not as dependent on other elements for its LF interpretability as is the Jingulu co-verb.

---

[4] My use of the notions "formal verbal" and "encyclopedic predicate" is further explained in section 1.3.

1.3. Theoretical motivation for the structure

The above description of Jingulu verbal clauses appeals to the notion of encyclopedic knowledge outlined by Marantz (1996). A lexical item, Marantz notes, following late GB and Minimalist assumptions, encodes three distinct kinds of features: phonological, formal, and (real-world) semantic. The term *real world semantic* (or *encyclopedic*) is used to distinguish these features from 'formal' semantic features which enter into the computational system or which (in Minimalist terms) are relevant in deriving LF representations from numerations of lexical items. Formal features are exactly those which the computational system makes use of in deriving sentences from bundles of features. According to Marantz, the computational system has access to only these features, and is therefore unable to distinguish, for example, 'cat' from 'dog', 'walk' from 'run', as these distinctions are properties of encyclopedia entries, wherein real world semantic features are stored. Real world semantic distinctions are made by interpretive and conceptual modules, and not by the computational system of the language faculty. Marantz claims that the domains of encyclopedic and formal features are distinct and that words which are considered 'verbs' in English, for example, consist of two nodes, a root node comprising only encyclopedic features and thus not possessed of a formal syntactic category and a categorial node consisting of the head's formal features. Evidence for this claim is not as readily apparent for English as it is for languages where verbs and nouns have distinct morphological forms, but Jingulu provides an extreme example in its verbal system, where formal and encyclopedic features of verbs are separated from one another by other material (the agreement markers).

In Jingulu, the root contains all and only the encyclopedic features of the predicate, while the formal features (tense, aspect, mood, direction of motion, argument structure) are found within the final element, the core verb. In other words, real world semantic, or encyclopedic, content is *not* found in the core verb, but rather in the co-verbal root which optionally precedes the (core) verb and its agreement markers. While the root is what English speakers might recognise as a verb, it is really a category-less element modifying the true syntactic (core) verb. This division of encyclopedic and formal features is motivated in Jingulu by a complete ban on encyclopedic knowledge in the core V position, so that it can only ever be filled by the three encyclopedically blanched syntactic verbs 'come', 'go', and 'do / be' (inflected for tense, mood and other formal properties).

Another of Marantz' (1996) predictions is borne out by Jingulu. Marantz predicts that suppletion should only ever be found in purely syntactic positions (those positions in which only formal features are allowed), observing that cross-linguistically, verbs with meanings like 'do', 'be', 'go' and 'come', and nominals with meanings like 'person' or 'thing' or pronouns commonly have suppletive forms. Both nominal and verbal roots in Jingulu only ever vary predictably, while both agreement markers and final verbal elements are highly suppletive (see Chadwick 1975 or Pensalfini 1997 for details of the agreement system).

The co-verbal root (or semantic predicate) in Jingulu is therefore syntactically deficient, containing encyclopedic knowledge but no grammatical features. In order to
appear in a sentence it must be phonologically prefixed to a syntactic clause, which
contains the true verb and the agreement markers. Syntactically, the category-less
root merges with a clause to create a verbal clause. Being devoid of syntactic verbal
features, a root which fails to merge with an IP complement will not meet LF interface conditions (being a category-less element and therefore formally uninterpretable) and a derivation containing such an unmerged root will crash.

If the merger of a particular clause (argument structure) with a particular root (thematic structure) yields an uninterpretable result, the sentence crashes at the interpretive interface (LF), despite being syntactically well-formed as far as the computational system is concerned. In practice, there are very few such uninterpretable sentences. The sentences in (9) demonstrate that Accusative objects are possible even
with predicates that would translate as intransitive in English as long as there is an
interpretation available. Where there is no feasible interpretation, as in (9c), the
sentence is rejected by speakers as 'making no sense'.

> (9a)   Dardu-nama ya-jiyimi   **ngarru**.
>   *many-time   3sg-COME 1sgACC*
>   They all came to me.

> (9b)   Ya-marriyimi,   marlarluka-rni wanyma-marriyimi **ngarnu**,
>   *3sg-WENT(DIST) old_men-ERG   walk-WENT(DIST)   3sgACC*
>   dunjuwa-kaji ya-marri,   warrijki-rni.
>   *burn-THRU   3sg-DID(DIST) ghost-FOC*
>   The people would take him and cremate him, the deceased one.

> (9c)   */# Bininja manyan ka-ju **ngarru**.
>   *man   sleep   3sg-DO   1sgACC*
>   The man is sleeping (at) me.

That even root-less clauses display a variety of argument structures suggests that
Jingulu verbs are vague with respect to case assigning properties, rather than that
roots somehow affect the argument/case properties of verbs.

As we have seen (cf. section 1.2), the present analysis is well-motivated on purely
descriptive grounds. I would like to argue that, for *theoretical* reasons as well, it is to
be preferred over an analysis which gives the structure of the Jingulu verb as
[Verb(stem) + Agreement + Tense/Aspect] (as suggested, for instance, in Chadwick
1975). Baker (1996a) notes that in morphologically rich languages, particularly
those of the polysynthetic sort, the configurational structure apparently lacking in
the structure of the clause is found (reflected) in the morphological structure of the
head word. This is basically a revision of the observations that led to the formulation

of the Mirror Principle (Baker 1985).[5] Under the [Verb(stem) + Agreement + Tense/Aspect] analysis, Jingulu inflection appears contrary to these observations. The agreement markers would be suffixes to the verb, with the subject marker closer than the object marker. Under this analysis, the Head Movement Constraint (Travis 1984, from which the Mirror Principle effect derives) drives us to an underlying structure like that in (10), wherein the subject (external argument) is closer to the verb than the object (internal argument) is, violating a supposed universal principle of grammar.

(10)

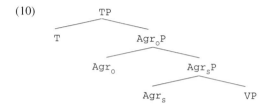

On the other hand, under the analysis I am proposing, the verb-word consists of the (optional) co-verbal root followed by a verb with agreement prefixes. The structure of the Jingulu verb word would therefore be as shown in (11) (based on the universal clause architecture proposed in Chomsky 1993). The core V raises to Agr_O, creating a complex head $[Agr_O\text{-}V]$, then this new head adjoins to T, where the V features of Tense (and possibly Aspect and Mood, though I remain agnostic as to whether these require their own functional heads) are checked. Finally the complex head $[T\text{-}Agr_O\text{-}V]$ raises and adjoins to Agr_S. This inflected verb merges into a phonological word with the adjacent category-less root. The verbal, tense, aspectual and mood features are spelled out on the suppletive core verbs, while the agreement features on the head are spelled out by the agreement markers. T is able to cause allomorphy in the core V because T governs V within the inflectional complex (as required by Halle & Marantz 1993).

---

[5] This observation, and Baker's work following from it, is in a sense an attempt to formalise the long-standing observation that some languages are morphologically driven while others are syntactically driven. Within Lexical Functional Grammar (LFG), this idea has been formalised by saying that in some languages argument information comes from the morphology while in others it comes from the syntax, and two distinct formal levels are proposed (see, for example, Nordlinger 1997, Nordlinger & Bresnan 1996). The two formal approaches differ in that Baker's, by positing just one level of morphosyntactic representation, seeks to explain Mirror Effects by saying that the order of morphemes in a word derives from the relative positioning of syntactic heads and general principles of syntactic movement and incorporation.

(11)

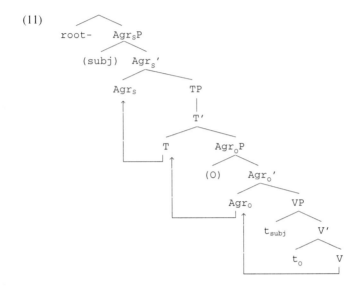

2. The structure of Jingulu nominals

The structure in (10) is central to an understanding of Jingulu syntax and vowel harmony as well as word structure, as we shall see in sections 3 and 4. However, Marantz' (1996) analysis of categorial membership and the role of syntactic heads applies just as much to nominal as to verbal words. Jingulu nominals are not as complex as Jingulu verbs, but the analysis of the word as consisting of a category-free (encyclopedically rich but formally vacuous) element combining with a category head (containing formal features but semantically bleached) extends quite readily to nominals.

2.1. Description

Jingulu nominals (a morphosyntactic class which subsumes the semantic/pragmatic classes of noun and adjective) generally inflect for case, and optionally for number and animacy. Nominals belong to one of four genders which, for convenience, shall be called 'masculine' (general animate), 'feminine' (specific animate), 'vegetable' (specific inanimate) and 'neuter' (general inanimate). The basis for division of nominals into genders is primarily semantic: 'masculine' includes words whose referents are male higher animates or lower animates in general; 'feminine' consists of words for female higher animates or lower animates which are perceived as unusual (stinging creatures, animals atypical of their class); 'vegetable' includes any long or pointed object as well as most vegetable foods and thorny plants; 'neuter' contains words for all other inanimates. As shown in (12), modifiers and nouns which can refer to a number of these gender classes have different forms, depending on the gender of their referent.

(12a) bininja ngamula, wawa   kurlukurla
       man   big(m)   child(m) small(m)
       big man, small boy

(12b) nayurni ngamulirni, wiwirni kurlukurlirni
       woman big(f)   child(f) small(f)
       big woman, small girl

(12c) darrangku ngamulu, kijurlurlu kurlukurlu
       tree   big(n)   stone   small(n)
       big tree, small rock

(12d) kingmi   ngamulimi, karrijbi kurlukurlimi
       rainbow big(v)   road   small(v)
       big rainbow, small road

Modifying nominals, such as *ngamulu* 'big' and *kurlukurlu* 'small' in (12), take an inflectional suffix which depends on the gender of their referent. Words which can have referents in more than one gender class, such as *wawa* 'child' also have forms which differ in the same way as different adjectival forms.[6] Words which do not vary in gender (such as *bininja* 'man', *kijurlurlu* 'rock', or *kingmi* 'rainbow') still show an overwhelming tendency to end in a phoneme string which is determined by their gender. Simplifying somewhat, masculine nominals are characterised by a final *-a*, feminine by a final coronal plus *-i*, general neuter by a final *-u*, and vegetable by a final labial plus *-i*.

2.2. Extension of the verbal analysis

Extending the account from section 1, I propose that nominal words be viewed as also consisting of a category-less, but encyclopedically rich, root merged with a nominal category head, which bears the formal features of the noun, including gender, number, and animacy (13). It is fairly uncontroversial to claim that gender morphology in Australia, such as the gender endings of Jingulu, arose historically from the morphophonological simplification of classifier words; cognates can be found

---

[6] The feminine form for 'child', *wiwirni*, is entirely predictable from the masculine *wawa*. The vowel alternation in the root is due to vowel harmony, discussed in detail in section 3.

between bound gender morphemes in some languages and nominal classifier words
in languages which still use them (Capell 1979a). Classifier words are an excellent
example of morphemes which have become semantically bleached, so that their
function in a clause is purely formal and not to convey the kind of information about
the world that encyclopedically laden items do. It is common for such semantically
bleached vocabulary items to become morphophonologically reduced to clitics and
affixes over time.

(13)

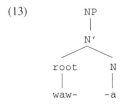

Under a structure such as (13), the gender morphology itself 'heads' the noun
phrase, which is to say that all the formal categorial information about the noun
phrase is carried on the inflection, and none on the root, which is itself of no category.

2.3. Predictions of the analysis

Both nouns and verbs in Jingulu, under the analysis proposed in this article, consist
of category-less roots combining with semantically bleached formal categorial
heads. This parallel between the major categories of nominal and verb will be instrumental in the analysis of Jingulu vowel harmony in section 3, but there are several other predictions of the analysis which I wish to address now.

First of all, if a nominal, for whatever reason, does not appear with a gender suffix,
it should not be able to participate in clausal syntax, since it lacks interpretable formal features. Remarkably, Jingulu personal names seem to fall into exactly this
category. Personal names do not display the same behaviour as other nominals with
respect to gender inflection. As mentioned above, each gender has a characteristic
ending, which here is analysed as a nominal head.

Personal names, which it would be culturally inappropriate to cite, show no such
regularity. While most personal names end in a vowel, there is no correlation between final vowel and gender for names. Personal names can therefore be considered category-less words which are not able to be affixed to nominal heads (gender
endings). As a result, they are not able to form syntactic nominals, and are never
found with gender endings or with any other suffixes such as case and focus markers. Speakers never produced sentences with personal names in them, and rejected
such sentences when I produced them. The only ways in which personal names can
be used in Jingulu is either as vocatives (though this is considered extremely impo-

lite and only used when chastising someone) or as dislocated elements, separated from clauses by a very significant intonation break (greater than the usual dislocation structure). Within clauses, kinship terms and skin names are used to refer to people.

The other prediction to be addressed here relates to the category-free status of roots. If the roots themselves are devoid of syntactic category information, we might well expect that a given root should be able to combine with either a nominal or a verbal head in order to produce either a noun or a verb, without the need for category-changing derivational morphology. In fact this is only true to a very small extent. Roots referring to transitory states (stage-level predicates), such as /bardakurr-/ ('well') and /marliy-/ ('sick'), are able to form either verbs or nominals (adjectives), as demonstrated in (14a).[7] However, roots referring specifically to entities can not form verbs and those referring to activities can not form nominals, as shown in (14b-c).

(14a) nominal: Marliyi-rni nga-ju.
　　　　　　　　sick-f　　　1sg-DO
　　　　　　　　I am sick.　　[ego: female]

　　　　verbal:　Marliya-nga-ju.
　　　　　　　　sick-1sg-DO
　　　　　　　　I am sick.　　[ego: any gender]

(14b) nominal: Ngunbuluka wurru-ju.
　　　　　　　　doctor　　　3pl-DO
　　　　　　　　They are doctors.

　　　　　　　　*Jarrkaja wurru-ju.
　　　　　　　　run　　　3pl-DO
　　　　　　　　They are runners / running.

(14c) verbal: *Ngunbuluku-wurru-ju.
　　　　　　　　doctor-3pl-DO
　　　　　　　　They are doctors / doctoring.

　　　　　　　　Jirrkiji-wurru-ju.
　　　　　　　　run-3pl-DO
　　　　　　　　They are running.

---

[7] However, the two main dialects of Jingulu differ as to which strategy is preferred. The Warranganku dialect prefers the verbal strategy and the Kuwarrangu dialect prefers nominals in these situations. Nonetheless, both options are grammatical in both dialects (Pensalfini 1997).

On closer inspection, however, this disparity is to be expected. While the encyclope-dic roots may not carry any formal categorial information, they do carry real world semantic knowledge which must be compatible with the formal features of the syn-tactic heads with which they merge. A root such as /ngunbuluk-/ ('doctor') would include information which makes it clear that a word containing this root refers to an entity, and this encyclopedic information combined with the formal features of a verb would produce an object which is uninterpretable with respect to its real world semantics. Similarly, the root /jarrkaj-/ ('run') would be specified as referring to a type of activity, which is not compatible with the formal features of a nominal head. Stage-level predicate roots do not specify reference to either entity or activity, and are therefore compatible with either nominal or verbal heads.

Under this account, derivational morphemes such as /jkal/, demonstrated in (15), are seen as encyclopedically, not formally, 'contentful' vocabulary items which alter the real-world semantics of the root.

> (15a)   Jama-rniki-rni murdika ngirrma-nu.
> *this(m)-ERG   car   fix-DID*
> He fixed the car.

> (15b)   Jama-rniki-rni ngirrma-jkal-a murdika-rna.
> *this(m)-ERG   fix-NOML-m   car-DAT*
> He's a mechanic.

The 'nominalising' suffix /jkal/ extends the meaning of a 'co-verbal' root from an action to an entity associated with the performance of that action. It is not a 'cate-gory-changing' morpheme as such, but alters the real world semantics of the root so as to make it compatible with a different set of categorial heads.

3. Jingulu vowel harmony

In the next two sections we will see how the structures proposed in sections 1 and 2 provide us with powerful tools for analysing the thornier issues of Jingulu grammar. In this section we consider vowel harmony, found among nouns and verbs alike, and find an elegant solution in terms of syntactic merger in order to satisfy interpretabil-ity requirements on initially category-less roots.

3.1. A brief description

Jingulu displays regressive vowel height harmony (suffixes trigger harmony in roots) in both nominal and verbal words. Suffixes triggering harmony must not only contain a high vowel and be adjacent to the root, but must also belong to a specific morphosyntactic paradigm.

In Jingulu, both nominal and verbal roots (the open classes) exhibit harmony, but each under different morphosyntactic conditions. Common to both is the phonological process. The presence of a [+high] vowel (/i/ or /u/) in an affix of a particular class (to be defined) causes adjacent low vowels in the root to become [+high]:[8]

(16a)	warlaku	+	/-rni/	→	warlakurni
	dog		f		'bitch'
(16b)	ngamula	+	/-rni/	→	ngamulirni
	big		f		'big (fem)'
(16c)	ankila	+	/-rni/	→	ankilirni
	cross cousin		f		'female cross cousin'
(16d)	kunyarrba	+	/-rni/	→	kunyirrbirni
	dog		f		'bitch'
(16e)	bardarda	+	/-rni/	→	birdirdini
	younger brother		f		'younger sister'
(16f)	ngaja	+	/-mindi-yi/	→	ngijimindiyi
	see		1dlInc-FUT		'we will see'
(16g)	ngarrabaja	+	/-wurru-nu/	→	ngirribijiwurrunu
	tell		3pl-DID		'they told (it to him)'

In (16a) the final vowel of the root is already [+high], so there is no change. If the final vowel of the root is the non-high vowel (/a/), it becomes [+high] (/i/), as in (16b-f). Adjacent non-high vowels in the root are also changed to [+high], as demonstrated in (16d-f). In (16d) the last two vowels in the root both change from /a/ to /i/, and in (16e-f) all of the vowels in the root change from /a/ to /i/. If the root contains a [+high] vowel, however, non-high vowels preceding it (to its left) never change to [+high], so in (16c) the first vowel does not change to /i/ because an un-

[8] The effect of vowel harmony in Jingulu is striking, with the distinction between two of its three vowels collapsing wherever harmony takes place. Some lexical distinctions can be lost as a result. For instance, the masculine kinship terms *baba* and *biba*, meaning 'older brother' and 'son' respectively, both have the feminine form *bibirni*, which therefore means both 'older sister' and 'daughter'.

derlyingly [+high] vowel (/i/) intervenes between it and the suffix triggering harmony.

Jingulu harmony can thus be viewed as the spreading of the feature [+high] from a suffix vowel into the root. Spreading continues until an underlying [+high] vowel (/i/ or /u/) is encountered in the root, and no further. This can be explained if we view the vowel system of Jingulu as consisting of the following feature bundles (phonemes):

(17)   /a/   =   [+vocalic, -round]

        /i/   =   [+vocalic, -round, +high]

        /u/   =   [+vocalic, +round, +high]

Harmony spreads the [+high] from a triggering position to the left until it encounters a previously specified [+high], which it does not cross. The phonetic component fills in [-high] as the height value for all vowels which are not phonologically specified as [+high]. The vowel that surfaces as /a/ is underlyingly unspecified for height (see Beckman 1995:54 and references therein for further arguments).

The forms in (16) are derived thus:

(18a)   warlaku   +   /-rni/   →   warlaku-rni
            | | | |
          [+hi]   [+hi]   [+hi][+hi]

(18b)   ngamula   +   /-rni/   →   ngamuli - rni
            | | | \
          [+hi]   [+hi]   [+hi][+hi]

(18c)   ankila   +   /-rni/   →   ankili-rni
            | | | \
          [+hi]   [+hi]   [+hi][+hi]

(18d)   kunyarrba   +   /-rni/   →   kunyirrbi-rni
            | | | \
          [+hi]   [+hi]   [+hi]   [+hi]

(18e)   bardarda   +   /-rni/   →   birdirdi-ni
                                | \
                              [+hi]   [+hi]

(18f) ngaja + /-mindi - yi/ → ngiji - mindi - yi

         | | |

       [+hi][+hi][+hi]   [+hi][+hi][+hi]

(18g) ngarrabaj + /-wurru - nu/ → ngirri biji - wurru-nu

         | | |

      [+hi][+hi][+hi]   [+hi] [+hi][+hi]

In nominals, it is the gender affixes which contain /i/ that trigger harmony. Recall from section 2 that Jingulu has four genders, each of which has a characteristic ending. These endings are taken to represent the nominal heads, bearing the formal features of the nominal category, which combine with the root to form nominal words.

When the feminine or vegetable endings appear on a nominal, harmony is induced in the root as described above. Examples can be found in (16) as well as in (19) below.

(19a) walanja + /-rni/ → wilinji-rni

     goanna (male)   *f*   'goanna (female)'

(19b) mamambiyaka + /-mi/ → mamambiyikimi

     soft (masc)   *v*   'soft (veg)'

One question that arises is why the characteristic neuter ending /-u/ does not induce harmony (given that subject agreement morphemes containing /u/ do induce harmony in co-verbal roots). The only possibility which suggests itself is that the neuter form of nominals does not involve suffixation of a high vowel, but rather that the final /u/ is present in the root, and the N head in these instances is null. Thus the requirement that the trigger for harmony be across a morpheme boundary from the target is not met, and no harmony occurs.

There is evidence beyond mere theoretical convenience for this assumption. The (general) neuter gender contains the greatest proportion of irregular forms (members not ending in the characteristic gender ending *-u*). The genders that do induce harmony, feminine, and vegetable show the greatest regularity, with very few members not ending in the characteristic coronal or labial plus *-i*. The feminine and vegetable genders are also the smallest and semantically most restrictively defined (the most marked). Furthermore, words borrowed into the neuter class from other languages (typically Mudburra, Kriol, or English) are less likely to undergo regularisation to a form ending in the characteristic vowel than are words borrowed into other classes. Irrespective of the possible historical status of final *-u*, this evidence supports a synchronic analysis in which the formal nominal head is null in the neuter form.

Gender endings are the only suffixes which induce harmony in nominal roots. Number markers and case markers containing high /i/ do not induce harmony:

(20a) bardarda-ni   (vs birdirdini)
       younger brother-ERG   ('younger sister')

(20b) jikaya-mbili
       lake-LOC

(20c) wawa-bila   (vs wiwirni)
       child-dl(animate)   ('girl' (child-f))

(20d) mamambiyaka-bila   (vs mamambiyikimi)
       soft-dl   ('soft-v')

As number and case suffixes always follow gender suffixes (N heads), nominal harmony can simply be defined as taking place across the boundary between the root
and the immediately following suffix.

Harmony in verbal roots is not so easily described. It is triggered by non-singular
subject agreement morphemes, and also by the imperative of motion /-yirri/ and the
negative imperative /-ji/. These triggers all contain [+high] vowels (/i/ or /u/) in their
first syllable, and appear in bold-face in (21).

(21a) Ngangarra ngaja-nga-ju.
       wild_rice   see-1sg-DO
       I can see wild rice.

(21b) Ngangarra ngiji-**ngurru**-ju.
       wild_rice   see-1pllnc-DO
       We can see wild rice.

(21c) Ngiji-**kunyi**-ju ngangarra?
       see-2dl-DO   wild_rice
       Can you two see the wild rice?

(21d) Mankiya-ju ambaya-ju.
       sit-DO   talk-DO
       He's sitting down talking.

(21e) Nyami-rni   ngaya   mankiyi-**mindi**-ju,
       2sgNOM-FOC 1sgNOM sit-1dllnc-DO
       marrinjku imbiyi-**mindu**-ju.
       language talk-1dllnc-DO
       You and I are sitting, talking language.

(21f) Nginirniki dika maja-nga-yi kurlukurlu.
       this(n)   fat   get-1sg-FUT small(n)
       I'll get a little bit of this fat.

(21g) Ngunu   buba miji-**yirri**!
       Dem(n) fire   get-GOIMPV
       Go get some firewood!

(21h) Ngarrabaja-mi jamaniki-rni marliyi-**ngirri**-ju!
       tell-IRR   this(m)-FOC sick-1plExc-DO
       Tell that person that we're sick.

(21i) Ngirribiji-**ji** ngininiki-rna.
       tell-NEGIMPV this(n)-FOC
       Don't go spreading this around!

In (21a) the root appears in its unharmonised form, [ngaja], as the subject marker contains the non-high vowel /a/. The forms in (21b-c) show the same root appearing with a subject marker containing a [+high] vowel: this results in the root surfacing as [ngiji]. The root in (21d) shows no harmony as the subject is third person singular (null agreement), while in (21e) the same roots appear with a subject marker containing a [+high] vowel, and so harmony is induced. Note once again that the first /a/ of the root /mankiya/ is unaffected because the underlying [+high] vowel in the root blocks the spread of the suffix's [+high] beyond it. In (21g) harmony is induced by the Imperative of motion /-yirri/; the same root is shown in its unharmonised form in (21f). The unharmonised form of the root /ngarrabaja/ in (21h) contrasts with the form in (21i), where harmony is triggered by the negative imperative /-ji/.

Other verb suffixes containing [+high] vowels, such as second person object agreement /nyu/, the Irrealis marker /mi/ (usually used as an imperative), and the Inverse marker /ni/, do not trigger harmony, even when immediately adjacent to the root:

(22a) Wawa-rni ngaja-nyu-nu.
       child-ERG see-2O-DID
       The child saw you.

(22b) Kuka   maja-mi!
       grandfather get-IRR
       Get Grandpa!

(22c) Ngangarra ngaja-mi!
       wild_rice   see-IRR
       Look at the wild rice!

(22d)   Kijurlurlu-ngkami ngaja-ni-ngurru-ju.
        stone-ABL   *see-INV-1plInc-DO*
        He sees us from the rock.

There are rarely occurring forms of some non-singular subject markers which have /a/ as their first vowel (and seem to only ever occur in conjunction with the irrealis marker /mi/), and these do not trigger agreement. Contrast (23c-d) as different ways of saying the same thing.

(23a)   Yabanju maja-**wanya**-mi dunjuwa-kaju wanyu-mi!
        small(n) get-2dlIMPV-IRR burn-THRU   2dl-IRR
        You two get a little fire going!

(23b)   Kunyiyirrini dalk baja-**anya**-mi!
        2dlERG   pull-2dlIMPV-IRR
        You two pull this!

(23c)   Ngaja-**arru**-mi!
        see-2plIMPV-IRR
        Look, you mob!

(23d)   Ngiji-**wurru**-mi!
        see-3pl-IRR [9]
        Look, you mob!

In summary, all of the suffixes that trigger harmony in verbs have [+high] vowels as their leftmost vowel, but not all suffixes that contain [+high] vowels are able to trigger harmony, even if they occur immediately adjacent to the root.

The difference between the morphemes which trigger harmony and those which do not is that members of the former group (subject agreement, /-yirri/ and /-ji/) are always adjacent to the root and other inflectional material can never intervene. As demonstrated in (24a-b), /-yirri/ and /-ji/ can not co-occur with subject agreement, while object marking (24c) and the irrealis/imperative marker /-mi/ (24d-e) can both be preceded by overt subject marking.

---

[9] In conjunction with Irrealis /mi/ in its imperative function, third person regular agreement forms of the appropriate number are used. This strategy is not uncommon cross-linguistically. Regular conjugations in Italian, for example, use third person singular indicative forms for second person singular (familiar) imperative.

(24a) *Miji-wurri-yirri!   /   *Miji-kurri-yirri!
       get-3pl-GOIMPV /   *get-2pl-GOIMPV*
       Go and get it, you mob!

(24b) *Ngirribiji-kunyi-ji!   /   *Ngirribiji-wunyi-ji
       tell-2dl-NEGIMPV   /   *tell-3dl-NEGIMPV*
       Don't you two tell anyone!

(24c) Ngiji-ngirri-nyu-nu kunyaku.
       see-1plExc-2O-DID 2dlACC
       We saw you two.

(24d) Arduwa-nama kunyila langalanga-nya-mi.
       slow-time   2dlNOM think-2sg-IRR
       Just think about it first.

(24e) Ngunya-arna-mi kungka.
       give-1O-IRR   another(n)
       Give me another one!

The resulting generalisation is that, for both nominals and verbs, the suffixes which trigger harmony are those suffixes which contain [+high] vowels and which can not be preceded in the word by any phonological material that is not part of the root. Other suffixes containing [+high] vowels do not trigger harmony, even when no material intervenes between them and the root.

3.2. Formal analysis

An analysis of this phenomenon in formal terms is not straightforward. Clearly, phonological adjacency between trigger and target is not sufficient. However, an analysis which allows null morphemes to block the spread of phonological features creates more problems than it solves. The process of feature spreading appears to be sensitive only to phonological information: it is blocked only by the presence of a specific vowel feature, and is not blocked by the presence of consonants, so it is difficult to see how phonologically absent material could block spreading.

If the structures proposed for verbal and nominal words in sections 1 and 2 are correct, the problem posed by Jingulu vowel harmony reduces to a case of apparent mismatches between structures in the phonology and the morphosyntax at the right edge of roots. This is illustrated for verbal roots in (25). According to the analysis in section 1, the core verb is the final element of the verbal word, which bears tense, aspect and mood features and which, with the exception of the imperatives of motion and negation, occurs in conjunction with agreement markers. The root lacks a syntactic category in and of itself, and hence always appears in conjunction with a light verb. Harmony takes place within the first bracketed constituent of the phonological structure (the constituent which contains the root).

(25)   constituency

syntactic	phonological
[[root][Agr_S-Agr_O-V]]	[[root-Agr_S][Agr_O-V]]
[[root][IMPV]]	[root-IMPV]

I argue that there is no mismatch or bracketing paradox involved, but rather that head movement in the syntax creates structures like those in the right hand column of (25). Recall that roots in Jingulu are syntactically deficient, bearing no categorial features, and must merge with a syntactic head in order to be recognised by the computational system. Verbal clauses have the underlying structure in (26).

(26)

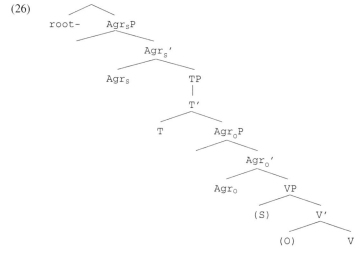

To satisfy the root's need for syntactic category features, the nearest syntactic head must raise and merge with the root, as in (27). This provides the root with formal features which allow it to remain at LF as a licit object. Agr_S is the closest head to the co-verbal root, and rises to merge with the root. The notation in (27) suggests that this merger precedes the raising of V through the functional heads (Agr_O, T, and (trace of) Agr_S). This is one possible derivation, and essentially the one adopted below. Another possible derivation would be for Agr_S to excorporate from the complex head [Agr_S-T-Agr_O-V] formed by the raising of V through the functional heads. This is notationally more complex, but essentially makes no difference to the analysis.

(27)

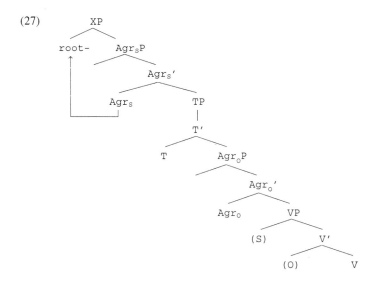

The V in imperatives of motion and negation does not project Agr or T heads (recall that these Vs never occur with agreement), and so the nearest head to the root is the V itself. The structures indicated in the second column of (25) are a result of the root attracting and merging with the nearest head. The harmony domain can thus be defined as that node which contains the root following this merger. Some examples from (21) are explained in these terms in (28).

(28a) (from (21b))

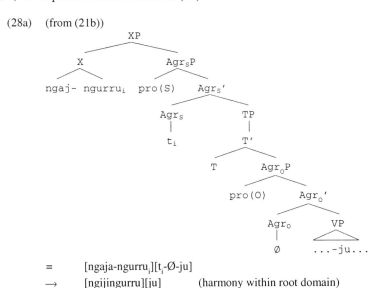

=   [ngaja-ngurru_i][t_i-Ø-ju]

→   [ngijingurru][ju]   (harmony within root domain)

(28b)   (from (21d))

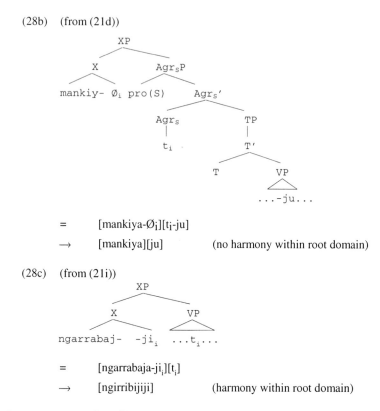

    =   [mankiya-Øᵢ][tᵢ-ju]
    →   [mankiya][ju]   (no harmony within root domain)

(28c)   (from (21i))

    =   [ngarrabaja-jiᵢ][tᵢ]
    →   [ngirribijiji]   (harmony within root domain)

The Inverse construction, illustrated by (22d), does not induce harmony because, as argued in Pensalfini (1997), the Inverse marker /-ni-/ does not occupy the subject node, but rather is a 'filler' morpheme which is inserted to host object agreement and verbs under certain circumstances (namely when there is a third person subject and a non-third person object). An argument in favour of analysing the Inverse marker as a morpheme that is not associated with a syntactic head is the fact that the appearance of inverse marking never affects the syntax of the clause in any way. Its presence or absence determines a choice of morphemes according to principles laid down in Pensalfini (1997), but its presence or absence does not affect case marking on overt nominals, transitivity, or grammaticality.

(29)   (from (22d))

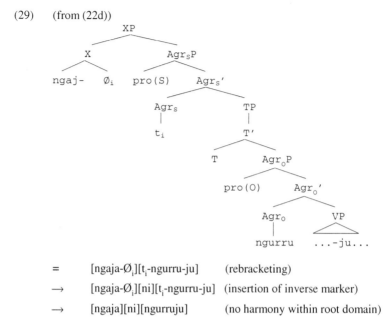

=   [ngaja-Øᵢ][tᵢ-ngurru-ju]   (rebracketing)
→   [ngaja-Øᵢ][ni][tᵢ-ngurru-ju] (insertion of inverse marker)
→   [ngaja][ni][ngurruju]   (no harmony within root domain)

Turning our attention now to nominal harmony, we see that there is always adjacency between a nominal root and the gender marker (N head). A nominal like *wawarni* ('boy-ERG') therefore has a structure like that in (30a), while *wiwirni* ('girl-NOM') has the structure in (30b). N heads are phonologically suffixes and can not appear independently of roots. In (30) the case-marker is assumed to head its own projection KP, and takes NP as a complement. All overt nominals in Jingulu are either KPs or PPs.

(30a)

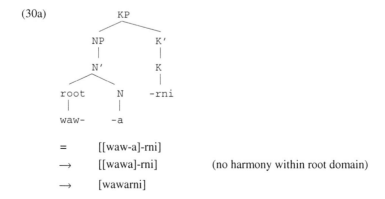

=   [[waw-a]-rni]
→   [[wawa]-rni]   (no harmony within root domain)
→   [wawarni]

(30b)

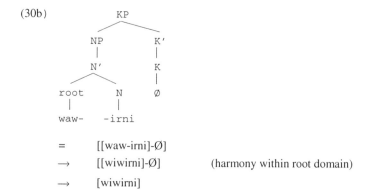

    =   [[waw-irni]-Ø]
    →   [[wiwirni]-Ø]   (harmony within root domain)
    →   [wiwirni]

No head movement is required for nominals since the nominal root and the N head enter the computation as sisters. The domain of harmony is within the N' headed by the gender affix.

The analysis outlined in this section describes a system wherein a root that is a potential target for harmony forms a phonological domain with the nearest syntactic head, a potential trigger. This domain is formed in order to satisfy syntactic computational requirements: to provide a syntactically vacuous but semantically rich element to participate in the syntax by having it merge with the nearest syntactically laden (but semantically bleached) element. The trigger and the target must both be within that domain in order for harmony to occur. In Jingulu, the domain thus formed is only relevant to feature spreading, including harmony and the surface realisation of linking vowels (a distinct but similar process to harmony, possibly best described as ablaut, discussed at length in Pensalfini 1997), but not to other phonological processes such as stress assignment.

4. Jingulu syntax

In this section, the distinction between encyclopedic and formal features is used to explain Jingulu's highly nonconfigurational syntax, and to suggest an analysis for nonconfigurationality cross-linguistically.

4.1. A selective history of derivational approaches to nonconfigurationality

This section should not be read as a history of theoretical approaches to nonconfigurational syntax. It is merely a summary of analyses, within a specific formal approach, which are seen to be direct precursors of the analysis to be presented in subsequent subsections of this article. There is a wealth of alternative analyses in a variety of frameworks, the most prominent of which are discussed in Pensalfini (1992 and forthcoming). Some are also criticised in Pensalfini (forthcoming).

Nonconfigurational languages have long challenged the basic structural ideas of derivational theories of syntax, such as that employed in this article. Apparently lacking any surface relations which reflect underlying predicate and argument structure, nonconfigurational properties have been held to include free word order, discontinuous nominal constituents, extensive null anaphora (pro-drop), and lack of asymmetry between subject and object arguments (Hale 1980, Jelinek 1984, Marácz & Muysken 1989, Baker 1996a,b among others). Many authors working in a derivational generative framework have noted the apparent correlation between nonconfigurational properties and rich inflection, particularly rich verb agreement.

Jelinek (1984) was the first to formalise the general approach adopted in this article within the derivational generative tradition. Jelinek suggests that, in nonconfigurational languages of the 'Warlpiri type' (free word order, discontinuous NPs, extensive null anaphora, rich agreement system), the agreement markers themselves are the arguments, with optional case-marked NPs adjoined to the clause, modifying (construed with) one of the arguments. Any number of adjoined case-marked NPs might be construed with the same argument, thus giving rise to apparently discontinuous NPs.

The strongest evidence against this approach to nonconfigurationality came from languages which exhibit many canonically nonconfigurational properties (free word order, discontinuous NPs, extensive null anaphora, no apparent binding asymetries), yet lack agreement altogether. Jiwarli is a case in point (cf. Austin 1999, Austin & Bresnan 1996).

Across several works (e.g. Baker 1996a,b), Baker has proposed two broad types of nonconfigurational languages, which I will call polysynthetic (head-marking) and dependent-marking.[10] In both of these types, argument positions are obligatorily occupied by null elements, and overt nominals are, as Jelinek (1984) had suggested, adjoined to the clause.

In polysynthetic nonconfigurational languages, assignment of thematic roles by a predicate is only possible if the predicate contains a morpheme coindexed with the argument position to which the role is being assigned (Baker's 1996a Morphological Visibility Criterion). This can be achieved in one of two ways: incorporation of NP into the argument position, or an agreement morpheme in the role-assigning word coindexed with the argument position. If an argument is incorporated, the argument position is occupied by a trace. If the agreement strategy is adopted, Baker argues that the agreement morpheme absorbs case in much the same way as passive morphology does in English (Baker et al. 1989). An overt NP in argument position

---

[10] The terms 'head-marking' and 'dependent-marking' are due to Nichols (1986).

would now be ruled out by the Case Filter, which means that argument positions can only be occupied by *pro*, which, Baker argues, does not require case (Baker 1996a).

In these languages, overt NPs are linked to argument positions by dislocation. Overt NPs in languages of this type examined by Baker, notably Mohawk (North America) and Mayali (Northern Australia), certainly show properties of dislocated phrases. For a start they are not case-marked. Cross-linguistically, dislocated NPs tend to surface in the default case of the language. Dislocated pronouns in English occur in the Accusative case (for example: ***Him**, I think he's the one who sang last night*), and Accusative is the default case in English, as can be seen from single word utterances and coordinate NPs (for instance: *Who's there? – **Me!**; [You and **them**] can all go together*). In most languages of the world, however, the default case is Nominative (or Absolutive or unmarked), which means that all dislocated NPs will surface as unmarked, irrespective of which argument they are construed with. As dislocation involves a bijective relationship between dislocated elements and argument positions, only one dislocated NP can be construed with any argument, and these languages lack discontinuous NPs as a result.

In dependent-marking languages, on the other hand, Baker (1996b) argues that thematic role assigners are not case assigners, and can therefore not support overt NPs in their argument positions. Overt NPs are linked to the *pro* arguments by secondary predication. Because any number of NPs can serve as secondary predicates to the same argument position, and secondary predicates can be adjoined to a clause in any order, apparently discontinuous NPs are generated in these languages. I say 'apparently discontinuous NPs' because they are in actual fact separate NPs construed with a single (null) argument.

Baker's work makes some startlingly accurate predictions, and is ingenious in suggesting a link between morphological strategy (head- versus dependent-marking) and certain nonconfigurational properties (NP discontinuity in particular). However, its reliance on case-assigning properties as the source of nonconfigurationality leads us to expect that the two sources of nonconfigurationality (case absorbed in polysynthetic languages, deficient case assignment in head-marking nonconfigurational languages) are quite distinct, and that a nonconfigurational language will display the characteristics of one or the other type.

4.2. Jingulu as a mixed type nonconfigurational language

Jingulu, however, displays a combination of polysynthetic and dependent-marking nonconfigurational properties, and yet is even more extreme in apparently allowing verbs (roots) to be dropped freely. Like both Mohawk and Jiwarli, Jingulu displays free constituent order (31) and allows any or all arguments to be null (32).

(31a)   Uliyija-nga ngunja-ju   karalu.   [SVO]
        sun-fERG   burn-DO   ground
        The sun is burning the ground.

(31b)   Uliyijanga karalu ngunjaju.   [SOV]

(31c)   Ngunjaju uliyijanga karalu.   [VSO]

(31d)   Ngunjaju karalu uliyijanga.   [VOS]

(31e)   Karalu uliyinanga ngunjaju.   [OSV]

(31f)   Karalu ngunjaju uliyijanga.   [OVS]

(32a)   Jama-ni   warlaku-rni dajba-nana-nu.
        that(m)-FOC dog-ERG   bite-3sgS1O-DID
        That dog bit me.

(32b)   Banybila-nga-nu ibilka karrinbiyi.
        find-1sg-DID   water tree_water
        I found tree water.

(32c)   Kird baja-nga-nu.
        break-1sg-DID
        I broke it.

(32d)   Umbuma-ngarna-nu.
        sting-3fS1O-DID
        It stung me.

In (32a) there is no overt nominal corresponding to the object, while in (32b) it is the subject that is not represented overtly. Both subject and object are left unexpressed (by overt nominals) in (32c-d).

The presence of subject and object agreement markers following the verbal root is obligatory (recall from section 1 that agreement with third person singular subjects and all third person objects is null), which might lead us to conclude that Jingulu is polysynthetic. However, free word order is also found with nominal predications, where there are no morphemes in the clause which can be linked to arguments of the predicate. The sentences in (33) were checked with native speakers and found to be acceptable equivalents, and equivalent orders of nominal predicate, subject, and modifier of subject are found in texts.

(33a)   Ngarri-na-ni   kirda ngunbuluka.
        1sgGEN-m-ERG father doctor
        My father is a doctor.

(33b)   Ngarrinani ngunbuluka kirda.

(33c)   Ngunbuluka ngarrinani kirda.

(33d)   Ngunbuluka kirda ngarrinani.

(33e)   Kirda ngarrinani ngunbuluka.

(33f)   Kirda ngunbuluka ngarrinani.

Another property of Jingulu which distinguishes it from polysynthetic nonconfigurational languages is the appearance of apparent discontinuous NPs (multiple non-
adjacent coreferent nominals). This is supposed to be a property of dependent-
marking nonconfigurational languages like Jiwarli. The boldfaced nominals in each
of the sentences of (34) refer to the same entity.

(34a)   **Mardilyi** karrila   **jamarniki-rni**!
        sickly(m) leave_it(IMPV) this(m)-FOC
        Leave this old sickly fellow alone!

(34b)   **Ngamurlu** ngayi-rni   **jurrkulu-rna** ambaya-nga-yi.
        big(n)   1sgNOM-FOC creek-DAT   speak-1sg-FUT
        I'm telling you about the big creeks.

(34c)   **Ngunu** maja-mi ngarru **darrangku**.
        DEM(n) get-IMPV 1sgACC stick
        Get me that stick.

(34d)   **Murrkulyi** miyi-ngirru-nu   **karruji**.
        three   kill-1plExc-DID spider
        We killed three spiders.

(34e)   **Darduwala-rni** maja-ni-ngurru-ju **wajbala-rni**.
        many_people-ERG get-INV-1plInc-DO whitefella-ERG
        Lots of white people took photos of us.

(34f)   **Jiminiki bikirra nyambala** kurdarlyurru ka-ju   **bikirra-rni**.
        this   grass   DEM(n)   green(n)   3sg-DO grass-FOC
        The grass is green.

The most natural analysis for these constructions is one which involves multiple
predications on *pro* arguments, as Baker (1996b) argues for Jiwarli, rather than generating the nominals within a single NP. More than one demonstrative referring to a
single argument is not only permissible, but in fact an extremely common strategy
(see (34f) and (35)). It is also common to find a pronoun with the same reference as

an overt nominal (35f) or a nominal repeated in a clause (34f). This makes it unlikely that these words were generated together within a single NP and somehow split up at a later stage in the derivation (such as by scrambling). Once again, words referring to the same entity in the sentences of (35) are given in bold type.

(35a) **Jama-ni   ngininiki-ni** bulurukuji.
that(m)-ERG this(n)-ERG   bee_bush[11]
This is a bee bush.

(35b) **Jamaniki-ni** ibilka-rdi   **nyambala** kurranjiyaji.
this (m)-FOC water-HAB DEM(n)   shallow
This water is shallow.

(35c) **Jimi-na   nyambala** warrka-nu balarrjuwa-nu.
that(m)-FOC DEM(n)   fall-DID   smash-DID
It fell and smashed.

(35d) Dakani   **jiminiki-ni** larrba **nyambala.**
leave_it(IMPV) this(n)-FOC old   DEM(n)
That one's old, leave it!

(35e) **Nyinda-rni** kurrnyu **nyambala** ilykinya-nga-rriyi.
DEM(m)-FOC skin   DEM(n)   cut-1sg-WILL_GO
I must skin this one.

(35f) Nyami-nga nayu-nga   ngaba-ju **kunyaku kujkarrabilarni**
DEM(f)-ERG woman-ERG hold-DO 2dlACC   two(m)
bayiny-bila.
man-dl(animate)
That woman has you two men.

As previously mentioned, this behaviour is more typical of a Jiwarli type (secondary predication) language. However, the presence of pronominal-like agreement elements within the verbal word is not the only similarity between Jingulu and dependent-marking polysynthetic languages. While free nominals most commonly bear overt case markers (as in Jiwarli), Jingulu optionally allows nominals in clause-peripheral positions to appear in default case (nominative for pronominals, absolutive (unmarked) for other nominals), irrespective of the argument they represent (as

---

[11] Masculine demonstratives are permitted with nominals of all genders. For an analysis of this and related phenomena in Jingulu, see Pensalfini (1999).

in (36)). These nominals are usually set off from the rest of the clause by an intonation break.

(36a)   **Dilkurni nginaniki**, kakuwi darra-ardi.
        kite   this(f)   fish   eat-HAB
        The white-breasted kite eats fish.

(36b)   Lamurrangkurdi darra-ardi, **ngindi   barnibukarri**.
        stinking_turtle   eat-HAB   that(m) hawk
        The hawk eats stinking turtles.

(36c)   **Jama-bili-na**,   birri-wunya-na-miki marluka-yili-rni.
        that-dl(ANIM)-FOC visit-3dl-1O-CAME   old_man-dl-ERG
        Those two old people came to see me yesterday.

(36d)   **Kunyuurlu**, nyambala-nayi miyi-wurru-nyu-ju kunyaku.
        2dlNOM   DEM(n)-INDEF hit-3pl-2O-DO   2dlACC
        You two, they hit you two as well.

(36e)   **Nginyila**,   nginda-rni   wawa miyi-wurru-na-ju nginyaku.
        1dlExcNOM DEM(m)-FOC   boy   hit-3pl-1O-DO   1dlExcACC
        They hit me and the boy.

(36f)   **Kurraala**, dajba-ni-kurru-nu murrkunbala.
        2plNOM   bite-INV-2pl-DID   three_people
        It's bitten you three.

(36g)   **Nginda**, duku-nga-rri   ibijinku-ngka.
        DEM(m) sit-1sg-WILL_GO shade-ALL
        I'm going to sit in that shade.

(36h)   Lilingbi-nga-ju nginirniki-rni linku-mbili, **mangarli**.
        hurt-1sg-DO   this(n)-FOC   chest-LOC   chest
        My chest hurts here.

(36i)   Kalyurrunga-rni-mbili kibardka-nga-rriyi, **kalyurrunga**.
        water-FOC-LOC   swim-1sg-WILL_GO water
        I'll have a swim in the water.

The bold-face nominals in (36a-c) are expected to appear with ERG suffixes, referring as they do to animate subjects of transitive predicates, but instead appear in the unmarked ABS form. The pronominals in (36d-f) all refer to objects of transitive verbs and therefore are expected to appear in the Accusative, but instead appear in the Nominative (note that the objects in (36d-e) are also referred to by pronouns in Accusative forms). In (36g-i) the unmarked nominals are construed with elements that are in non-core (semantic) cases. In each of these cases the appearance of the nominal in an 'unexpected' case is dependent on its being clause-peripheral.

These facts suggest that dislocation of NPs, such as Baker has proposed for polysynthetic nonconfigurational languages, is also an option in Jingulu. Dislocated nominals appear at clause boundaries, outside the positions occupied by secondary predicates, most likely in [Spec, CP] given that dislocation and wh-questions are mutually exclusive (Pensalfini 1997). Dislocation is assumed to involve an operator-variable relationship between the dislocated nominal in clause-peripheral position and *pro* in the argument position. A *pro* that enters into such a relationship with a dislocated nominal can still have nominals predicated of it by Baker's (1996b) secondary predication.

It would appear, then, that Jingulu uses a combination of dislocation and secondary predication in order to express overt nominals that are construed with null arguments. The choice of strategy can therefore not follow directly from a difference between case properties of thematic role assigners, and there is no clear distinction between head-marking and dependent-marking kinds of nonconfigurationality.

4.3. Nonconfigurationality as the result of bans on encyclopedic features in certain core positions

This section proposes an alternate source for nonconfigurationality, while still maintaining Baker's (1996a, b) insights into the mechanics of nonconfigurational syntax. This is essentially an extension of the idea in section 1 that certain syntactic positions are closed to encyclopedic features. In section 1 (and 3) we saw that all the apparently aberrant properties of Jingulu words are easily explained by assuming that different morphological domains are mandated for formal features and for encyclopedic features. I want to suggest that nonconfigurationality is also the result of encyclopedic information being barred from certain syntactic positions, in particular core argument (subject and object) positions, in nonconfigurational languages.

In these languages, argument positions can only be filled by encyclopedically vacuous material, namely *pro* or traces. Overt nominals, laden as they are with encyclopedic features, must occur outside of the core IP, either as wh-moved or dislocated elements in [Spec, CP] or adjoined to IP. The choice of strategies for construing overt nominals with arguments is independent of the requirement which forces nonconfigurational syntax, and therefore the choice of dislocation versus secondary predication is essentially free (and, as in Jingulu, a language may utilise both options).

The claim with regard to Jingulu, then, is that Jingulu does not allow encyclopedic features to occupy the core verbal node (section 1) or any argument positions (this section). The entire core clause in Jingulu is sacrosanct to formal computational information alone, with semantically rich elements restricted to the periphery of the syntactic clause. If this seems strange at first, it might be well to consider a language of the opposite type from the perspective of a language like Jingulu. English allows encyclopedic information into all core positions, verb and arguments, and as a result has a highly restrictive syntax. Formal elements must combine in narrow and specific ways, and if encyclopedic features are inextricably bound up with formal features, not only might the computation be cluttered up by the presence of much irrelevant material, but the binding of encyclopedic features to formal ones greatly restricts freedom of word order and the ability to drop or add (encyclopedically rich) elements at will.

4.4. *A note on the typology of configurationality*

If the approach to nonconfigurationality outlined in the previous subsection is correct, the source of nonconfigurational behaviours lies in the separation of encyclopedic and formal features into different lexical items. At one extreme we have the highly configurational English, which allows encyclopedic information in both syntactic predicate and argument position, while at the other end is Jingulu, with its prohibition on encyclopedic information in core verbal and argument positions, and with its resultant free word order, null anaphora, discontinuous nominal expressions, and verb-(root-)drop.

However, the analysis predicts the existence of other types of languages. One, the most commonly identified 'nonconfigurational' type, is nonconfigurational with respect to the behaviour of nominal expressions, but not with respect to verbs. Warlpiri, Mohawk, and Jiwarli, three of the most discussed nonconfigurational languages, would all fall into this type. In these languages, encyclopedic information is allowed in core verbal position, but is not allowed in argument positions. Another type is exemplified by the Papuan language Kalam, and possibly also by Welsh (Jerrold Sadock, personal communication) and Basque (Beth Levin, personal communication). In these languages, encyclopedic information is allowed in argument positions, giving rise to fairly restricted word order, no NP discontinuity, and limited null anaphora, while the core syntactic verb may not host any encyclopedic information, which results in a light-verb structure for all verbal clauses.

The ramifications of such an analysis on a theory of nonconfigurationality are discussed in detail in Pensalfini (forthcoming). That article examines a number of different configurational types, with examples coming from a wide range of (primarily Australian) languages, and shows how restrictions on encyclopedic information in certain syntactic positions combines with choices regarding how overt adjuncts are to be construed with argument positions to give rise to the wide array of configurational types discussed in the literature on nonconfigurationality.

5. Conclusion

The distinction between encyclopedia and lexicon is crucial to an understanding of Jingulu grammar. Jingulu distinguishes between morphemes which contain encyclopedic information and morphemes which are purely formal (free of encyclopedic features). It employs this distinction rigorously. Encyclopedically laden morphemes are barred from core syntactic positions, those positions which are crucial to the syntactic computation, and are relegated to the periphery of the syntactic clause. This has immediate ramifications for both word structure (morphophonology, morphology) and phrase structure (syntax, morphosyntax).

Those vocabulary items which convey purely encyclopedic information are categorially vacuous, and must merge with elements which have categorial content in order to create well-formed LF representations. The exact details of this merger are explored in sections 1-3, and are used to explain the structure of Jingulu words from morpheme order to vowel harmony.

At the level of the phrase, the different domains of encyclopedic versus purely formal vocabulary items give rise to nonconfigurational syntax. Items which provide encyclopedic information about argument referents may not occupy argument positions, and so other strategies are required to allow them to be construed with the arguments. The choice of strategies was shown in section 4 to be independent of the source of nonconfigurationality. The analysis presented in section 4.3 is intended to supplant previous explanations of nonconfigurationality within the derivational generative tradition.

Without a division of vocabulary items into those which represent encyclopedia entries and those which are purely formal, Jingulu offers several challenges to the generative linguist. The facts of vowel harmony seem quite independent of the nonconfigurational phrase structure of the language, and the order of morphemes within the verbal clause appears to be an independent anomaly. In this article I have shown that all of these phenomena follow from the division of labour in Jingulu morphology between core and peripheral positions in the clause, where core positions are the domain of formal features and peripheral positions the domain of encyclopedic features.

References

Austin, Peter. 1999. "Word order in a free word order language. The case of Jiwarli". Unpublished manuscript, University of Melbourne.

Austin, Peter; Bresnan, Joan. 1996. "Nonconfigurationality in Australian aboriginal languages". *Natural language and linguistic theory* 14. 215-268.

Baker, Mark. 1985. "The mirror principle and morphosyntactic explanation". *Linguistic inquiry* 16. 373-416.

Baker, Mark. 1996a. *The polysynthesis parameter*. Cambridge: Cambridge University Press.

Baker, Mark. 1996b. "Notes on dependent-marking-style nonconfigurationality in Australian languages". Unpublished manuscript, McGill University, Montreal.

Baker, Mark; Johnson, Kyle; Roberts, Ian. 1989. "Passive arguments raised". *Linguistic inquiry* 20. 219-251.

Beckman, Jill N. 1995. "Shona height harmony. Markedness and positional identity". In Jill N. Beckman, Laura Walsh Dickey & Suzanne Urbanczyk (ed.), *Papers in optimality theory* (*University of Massachusetts occasional papers*, 18). Amherst, Mass.: GLSA. 53-75.

Capell, Arthur. 1979a. "Grammatical classification in Australia". In Stephen A. Wurm (ed.), *Australian linguistic studies*. Canberra: Pacific Linguistics C54. 141-228.

Capell, Arthur. 1979b. "Classification of verbs in Australian languages". In Stephen A. Wurm (ed.), *Australian linguistic studies*. Canberra: Pacific Linguistics C54. 229-322.

Chadwick, Neil. 1975. *A descriptive grammar of the Djingili language*. Canberra: Australian Institute for Aboriginal Studies.

Chomsky, Noam. 1993. "A minimalist program for linguistic theory". In Kenneth L. Hale and Samuel Jay Keyser (ed.), *The view from building 20*. Cambridge: M.I.T. Press. 1-52.

Hale, Kenneth L. 1980. *The position of Warlpiri in a typology of the base*. Bloomington: Indiana University Press.

Halle, Morris; Marantz, Alec. 1993. "Distributed morphology and the pieces of inflection". In Kenneth L. Hale & Samuel Jay Keyser (ed.), *The view from building 20*. Cambridge: M.I.T. Press. 111-176.

Jelinek, Eloise. 1984. "Empty categories, case, and configurationality". *Natural language and linguistic theory* 2. 39-76.

Marácz, Laszlo; Muysken, Pieter (ed.). 1989. *Configurationality. The typology of asymmetries*. Dordrecht: Foris.

Marantz, Alec. 1996. "'Cat' as a phrasal idiom". Unpublished manuscript, M.I.T.

Nichols, Johanna. 1986. "Head-marking and dependent-marking grammar". *Language* 62. 56-119.

Nordlinger, Rachel. 1997. *Constructive case. Dependent-marking nonconfigurationality in Australia*. Unpublished PhD dissertation, Stanford University.

Nordlinger, Rachel; Bresnan, Joan. 1996. "Nonconfigurational tense in Wambaya". Paper presented at the Grenoble LFG conference, August 1996.

Pensalfini, Robert. 1992. *Degrees of freedom. Word order restrictions in Pama-Nyungan*. Unpublished honours dissertation, University of Western Australia, Perth.

Pensalfini, Robert. 1997. *Jingulu grammar, dictionary, and texts*. PhD dissertation, M.I.T.. Distributed by *M.I.T. Working Papers in Linguistics*.

Pensalfini, Rob. 1999. "Optional disagreement and the case for feature hierarchies". In Sabrina Billings, John Boyle & Aaron Griffith (ed.), *Proceedings of the 35th annual meeting of the Chicago Linguistics Society*, vol. 2. *The panels*. Chicago: University of Chicago.

Pensalfini, Rob. Forthcoming. "Towards a typology of configurationality". *Natural language and linguistic theory*.

Travis, Lisa. 1984. Parameters and effects of word order variation. PhD dissertation, M.I.T. Distributed by M.I.T. Working Papers in Linguistics.

Part Five

FURTHER AFIELD

Lexical and encyclopedic knowledge in an *ab initio* German reading course[1]

Susanne Feigenbaum

University of Haifa, Department of French, Mount Carmel, Haifa 31905, Israel
E-mail: suzanf@research.haifa.ac.il

0. Introduction

The acquisition of lexical items belonging to a foreign language (FL) has long been considered secondary to the acquisition of its syntax. However, in recent years, interest in the lexicon has been renewed for at least two reasons. First of all, it has become clear that vocabulary does not develop automatically. Its growth depends on the time that is available to the learner and the effort put into it. It has been shown that passive lexical knowledge cannot be wilfully put to active use if it is not systematically integrated into FL learning (cf. Laufer 1992, 1997, 1998). Secondly, the minimal vocabulary requirements of many educational programmes concerned with the communicative aspect of language learning have proven unsatisfactory. The present article deals with the reading strategies of learners who are *not* required to actively learn any vocabulary, and argues that world knowledge may *support* but not *replace* lexical knowledge. Even with the support of contextual inferences based on world knowledge, communication by means of deficient vocabulary is severely hampered.

---

[1] I wish to express my appreciation to the editor of this volume, Bert Peeters, for his most valuable comments and his careful revision of the manuscript.

My observations are based on a pilot study involving 25 students at the University of Haifa during their last semester in an *ab initio* reading course in German. Like other similar courses, this one involves four semesters of study and prepares beginners to read academic texts. Towards the end of the course, students have reached a stage where they are expected to successfully read texts drawn from the humanities.[2] The teaching focuses on grammatical items and on morphological and syntactic characteristics, but less on semantic contents. Conscious vocabulary training is practically absent. To make up for this lack, students work with a bilingual dictionary.[3]

In general terms, a programme without vocabulary tasks looks encouraging to the learner, because it indicates that one may progress without having to memorise. It delivers good results during the first two semesters, i.e. at beginners' level. But at a more advanced level vocabulary-related mistakes become more frequent and are often frustrating. This is primarily because the number of words students would have to look up in their dictionaries increases with the difficulty of the texts. If too many new words surface in a text in short succession, learners simply refrain from opening the dictionary, unless it is unavoidable. Unfortunately, increased reliance on the grammar of the interlanguage may lead to faulty identification of words (because of the existence of so-called false friends and the possibility of false interpretations brought about by polysemy) as well as to inadequate reconstruction of the message.[4] In addition, apart from the number of new words, there is the issue of their growing complexity. Learners of German, a language known for its particularly challenging morphological structure and its high rate of polysemy, have to struggle with numerous compounds and derivatives, i.e. words not necessarily listed in their dictionaries. The majority of errors here stem from mistaken identification of morphemes, either because learners simply do not recognise them or because they presume that they stand for something different from what they really mean. Laufer (1997) has studied this phenomenon, referring to it as *deceptive transparency* (DT).

On first inspection, errors resulting from polysemy and DT appear to have a similar cause. In both instances, it is believed that the meaning of a word is 'y', whereas in fact it is 'x'. A closer look reveals that different learning strategies are involved. On the one hand, DT is context-free. It occurs when knowledge of the learner's L1 or another previously learned FL interferes with the understanding of the structure of specific lexical items. Polysemy, on the other hand, is context-related. It requires awareness that a word has more than one meaning, but it also demands experience with context evaluation.

---

[2] On the level of text types, see Rogolla & Rogolla (1985), or Brandi & Momenteau (1992).

[3] Reading at a high level of proficiency should be independent of the dictionary, but the same does not hold at lower levels.

[4] It must be noted, though, that only 7% of the errors committed by the pilot group are caused by false friends.

direct, as unambiguous, as the one between the (Saussurean) dyadic sign and its concept. FL words become mere signifiers, and the corresponding L1 concepts become signifieds. Because it is perceived as being solid, i.e. consisting of dyadic signs that are constant and definite once they are acquired, FL learners prefer to remain within the realms of LK. It is based on a limited set of items and rules that may be memorised and learnt. As a result, it is fairly easy to determine how long it takes to acquire the basic vocabulary of a target language.[8]

Unfortunately, FL learners soon find that words exist with more than one referent and therefore more than one equivalent in L1. Imagine a learner encountering the German word *Wende*. Dictionaries provide E. *turning* as an equivalent, which is appropriate for a philosophical text. In the case of a political text, the learner would be better off looking up the word in an encyclopedia, where it is included on the strength of its referring to a period in recent German history (i.e. reunification of East and West in 1989-1990). While L1 speakers are able to hit upon the relevant interpretation without much likelihood of error, FL learners can hardly be expected to know when to consult the encyclopedia instead of the dictionary.

Interpretation seems to call for a more elaborate model than the Saussurean. The Peircean model (after C. S. Peirce; cf. Hartshorne & Weiss 1965) includes a third element, called the Interpretant, which links the signifier to the signified. In a dyadic sign model, where signifier and signified are two sides of the same coin, apprehension is instantaneous. In a triadic model, where information flow is mediated by the Interpretant, apprehension implies duration. Another feature of the triadic sign implying duration is that it is susceptible to growth: signs provoke reactions, which in turn become signs. Eco (1985) describes this process as follows: "If I hear a sound in an unknown language and I realise that this sound produces outrage with everyone, I may infer that it has an unpleasant meaning. Thus the behaviour of other speakers is an Interpretant of the Interpretant of the sound." Reference (in general) is established inferentially, by selection of the appropriate Interpretant. Interpretants are mental in nature and include experience, habits and context. That is, they include EK.

2.2. Learning stages in L1 and in FL

As pointed out, language acquisition takes place in stages, each of which has its own semiotic characteristics. Each stage shapes LK and EK in its own particular ways. As a general rule, in discussing the various stages, I shall first describe some aspects relevant for L1 before moving on to those concerning FL.

---

[8] In contrast, it seems unlikely that we will ever be in a position to establish precisely the amount of EK competent speakers have at their fingertips or how fast they accumulate it.

Stage 1: Emotions

L1

The first instances of meaning are like impressions. According to Peirce, they are established by the so-called Emotional Interpretant. The earliest encounter with language occurs through the phonological module. Fernald (1994) points out that infants identify linguistic units mainly in affective contexts, like the one created by maternal prosody. Researchers have further emphasised that children use their first words as "names" for objects and persons (Bloom 1994:7). Dad is *Dad* and their favourite toy is *Toy*. This usage of nouns as private names implies rigid reference to real-world entities. It is therefore possible to say that, in stage 1, LK's phonological module (the only one that has started to develop) overlaps with rigid EK.

FL

During the emotional period of getting started in a FL, textbooks help learners to become acquainted with the universe of the target language. Pronunciation and intonation are introduced. Vocabulary introduced at this stage supports the one-to-one principle. Often, textbooks organise lessons around central protagonists, with whom one becomes familiar on a personal basis. This is an opportunity to teach typical names, like "Peter Martens" or "Fritz Wenzel", as well as names of countries and their capitals.[9]

Stage 2: Dynamics

L1

After a highly emotional period, the interface between LK and EK is gradually built up as names turn into common nouns. Crucial for learning words is frequent exposure to the language. Still, at this stage, the interface remains fuzzy since early words like *mother*, *table* or *water* function as names. They refer to objects that the child can identify with. The tangible nature of this kind of meaning explains why infants learn words more easily when somebody points the corresponding objects out to them. Baldwin (1994) calls this the "word-world" relation. I shall call it an indexical relation. Indexical signs have a Dynamic Interpretant. An important characteristic of this indexical stage is the principle of exclusive reference: children assume that there are no two words for a single object. On the other hand, they may use the same word for several objects, provided the latter are somehow associated. As for EK, throughout the dynamic learning stage, a fuzzy interface lies between the rigid and the personal types.

---

[9] I am taking Neuner et al. (1986, 1988) and Van Eunen et al. (1989) as a basis for my analysis.

FL

At stage 2 of the foreign language acquisition process, lexical items also belong to the fuzzy interface between rigid and personal EK. On the one hand, they describe the ways of life of the speakers of the target language, and are therefore part of personal EK. On the other hand, they are associated with rigid EK, because lexical items are quantitatively limited and more names are added (e.g. of universities, towns, countries, or famous athletes). At the level of LK, morphological and syntactic structures are developed.

Stage 3: Logic

L1

From about one and a half years until the age of seven, children complete the acquisition of basic vocabulary. At the same time, they learn to rely on morphology and syntax, which will enable them, among other things, to distinguish common nouns (*This is a sib*) from proper names (*This is sib*) (cf. Bloom 1994:18). Words that were formerly apprehended as tokens are now used as types and may designate more than one concept (e.g. the verb *take*, where one has collocations such as *take out*, ~ *off*, ~ *apart*, ~ *time*). All these instances of linguistic behaviour are coherent with the symbolic aspect of the sign and the mental nature of the Logical Interpretant. In addition, they imply the existence of a *strict separation* (rather than a fuzzy interface) on three different levels: between LK and EK, between the modules of the lexicon, and between rigid and personal EK.

FL

Many FL methods emphasise that a language needs to be grasped with constant reference to the specific culture of the people who speak it. I think this is an overstatement: learners at stages 1 and 2 are not yet ready for this sort of approach. At stage 3, vocabulary related to the arts, literature, politics and society still belongs to personal EK. In addition, it is necessary to develop all the modules of LK. Grammatical structures are progressively refined, complex sentence syntax is put into practice, and special attention is paid to word formation (e.g. compounds and affixes). FL learners become aware of additional meanings to some of the words they learn, especially in collocations and idioms. They discover, for instance, that *Schwein haben* does not mean 'have a pig' but 'be lucky'.

Stage 4: Culture

L1

Adult grammar develops after the age of seven until approximately the age of eleven. Morphological structures become more complex, speech may be self-repaired and metalinguistic conscience is further developed (Karmiloff-Smith 1994:578). Children may use proper names in narrative anaphora, and their semantics reaches higher levels of precision. Words from science, history, and the like serve as a bridge between LK and cultural EK. Yet sign action does not stop there, but may develop under the influence of personal and cultural experience. Typically, the stage 4 age group tends to enrich narratives with confabulations based on world knowledge, as reported by Schmidlin (1996). For that reason, I shall refer to the stage 4 Interpretant as the Enriched Interpretant.

FL

Stage 4 includes the upper intermediate and advanced levels. The students in my test group have not reached this stage. Textbooks at this level attempt to bring the learner to near-native competence in all grammatical modules, by using authentic texts and situations.

2.3. Problems faced by the learner

In L1 acquisition, moving from stage 1 (Emotion, rigid EK) to stage 4 (Culture, cultural EK) takes about eleven years. This is a long time span, which can hardly be equalled in the case of FL acquisition. Programmes for adults in particular are much shorter.[10] The question is *whether* the itinerary may be cut short. A closer look at my test group suggests that there are severe implications. Table 2 shows how the task-goal flow is adapted to suit the particular circumstances.

Semiotics	Linguistic module	Prompts
The Emotional Interpretant	Phonology & Morphology	Scan the word
The Dynamic Interpretant	Morphology & Syntax	a) Recognise its morphological structure b) Retrieve its meaning in the dictionary c) Assess the syntactic environment
The Logical & Enriched In-terpretants	Semantics & Pragmatics	Adjust

Table 2: FL reading strategies

---

[10] There would generally be very few takers if courses were longer: not alone do adults believe that learning languages requires little time, they also do not have enough time to learn them.

Confronted with a text, FL learners gradually move from the unknown to the known by translating lexical items. Certainly, during the first two semesters (stages 1 & 2), reading strategies are employed which are appropriate and successful, because texts are elementary. Words are compatible with the first two Interpretants. Vocabulary is restricted and repetitive. Learners remain at the back of textbook writers' minds: all words used are as unambiguous as possible, and polysemy is avoided. But after one year, when the basics of stage 3 have not yet been internalised, learners are confronted with elaborate academic texts. These are completely different. Words are no longer limited to those commonly used in textbooks, and there are many more different words in every single text. Naturally, the discrepancy between learner vocabulary and required vocabulary is immense.

A direct effect of the shortened itinerary is a deficiency in *sight vocabulary*. The latter consists of words that are recognised when encountered in a text, although they are not part of the active vocabulary. When a rather solid portion of the text is familiar, learners are in a better position to guess the meaning of unknown words. According to Laufer (1997), sufficient sight vocabulary is a prerequisite for successful guessing.

Another negative effect is the difficulty to differentiate common nouns (LK) and proper names (rigid EK). Recall that by the time young L1 learners reach stage 4 (culture) they possess a lexical base. On encountering a new word that is not part of the basic lexicon, they may infer that it is a name (because names are not in the basic lexicon). In contrast, FL learners cannot make the same sort of inference. As I have said before, their basic lexicon is in the dictionary. If a new word cannot be found there, learners have to check whether it is a compound or a derived word, a conjugated form or a proper name. Needless to say, this is a burdensome task. The FL learners in my study, in particular, appear not to have established an Enriched Interpretant yet, and are faced with a considerable hurdle.

It could certainly be argued that university students should develop cognitive strategies that allow them to reconstruct the context. Furthermore, their general education should help them detect private names. Finally, they should be able to use their L1 competence and their experience from former language learning. With respect to the last point, researchers who specialise in tertiary language acquisition have indeed reached the conclusion that positive interaction of the sort just described does take place: there is evidence that fast *grammatical* progression is relatively problem-free.[11] My own research provides further confirmation, with syntax being the lowest source of errors. Surprisingly, there is no evidence to suggest anything similar in the area of vocabulary learning. For learners who find themselves struggling with higher degrees of lexical complexity, previous FL experience does not carry any advantage. L1 competence cannot be accessed automatically when a second or a subsequent

---

[11] Kallenbach (1998) reports opinions of learners to that effect.

language is being learned. Newport (1994) has pointed out some typical problems for adults, which are independent of previous FL experience. For instance, due to the maturational constraint, adults do not learn languages as well as children, even if they have enough time available. Furthermore, adults have serious difficulties analysing complex lexical structures. I shall take up this point in the paragraphs on morphology in section 3 below.

Briefly, reading FL texts above the appropriate level imposes a burden on vocabulary, and it also puts the learner into a state of general uncertainty that affects the whole decoding activity. Foreignness is attributed to the whole system, mistakes are transported from one module to the other, and incongruous translations are liberally altered to fit personal interpretations.

3. Errors

Since, as I have argued, the construction of LK advances gradually with the development of EK, the interaction between the two kinds of knowledge is governed by time constraints. If there is not enough time to develop each stage of EK, LK cannot function properly; vice versa, EK is jeopardised without sufficient LK. The question is whether shortcomings in one kind of knowledge adversely affect the other kind of knowledge situated at the same level. Would it be true to say that insufficient rigid EK, for instance, would impair the grammar of the Dynamic Interpretant, and insufficient cultural EK the grammar of the Logical and the Enriched Interpretants? This hypothesis is difficult to sustain, because the lexical modules are constantly developing, and some are present at all levels of EK (cf. table 3).

Age	FL level	Phon	Sem	Morph	Synt	EK
0 - 1 ½	1 - 2	x	x			Rigid
1 ½ -7	3	x	x	x	x	Personal
7 - 11	4	x	x	x	x	Cultural

Table 3: The formation process of LK and EK

Rather, the interaction between LK and EK is such that the slightest error may cause errors of all kinds. An error which occurred in the phonological module, for example, may have consequences for rigid EK, but may also affect all types of EK. To better appreciate the extent and nature of error propagation, recall that the components of the lexicon are modular. As such, they may interact directly with EK, or indirectly by way of another module. The following itinerary looks probable:

- When starting to scan, readers activate the phonological module.
- If they successfully apply the phonological rules, they go on to the morphological module.
- In case of error, there are two possibilities: (a) the error interacts directly with EK, or (b) it is transported into the morphological module.
- The same happens throughout the other modules.

The following paragraphs describe what types of errors occur in each module. Table 4 summarises the proportion of each type against the total.

Syntax	6%
False friends	7%
Scanning	22%
Polysemy	31%
Morphology	34%
Total	**100%**

Table 4: Types of errors

3.1. Phonetics

The first of the reading strategies applied is to scan the signifiers in an attempt to grasp letters or groups of letters, and their relationship with sounds. It is used when reading texts in L1 as well as FL. Adult textbooks propose various ways to transfer the reader's competence in L1 into the target language. As is well known, optical perception is either holistic or analytical. Many textbooks take this into account, favouring either the holistic approach by concentrating on words, or the analytical one by concentrating on individual signs (Wirbelauer 1983, Rogolla & Rogolla 1985).

With its reduced number of digraphs and diacritic marks, German is usually not considered difficult in this respect. Nevertheless, our tests show that 22% of reading errors are initiated by scanning. Many of them occur as a result of negative transfer from L1 (Hebrew) or L2 (English), either at the level of the consonant-vowel system, or as a result of incongruity between holistic and analytical perception.

An example of L1 interference involving *consonants* concerns the letter batches < ch >, < sch >, and < h >, especially when combined with < s > or < t >. As I have shown elsewhere, Israeli students tend to ignore or to confuse these (Feigenbaum 1993). Some of the affected words are given in (1).

(1a)   *Gesicht* 'face' vs. *Geschichte* 'history'

(1b)   *waschen* 'wash' vs. *wachsen* 'grow'

(1c)   *verzeihen* 'forgive' vs. *verzeichnen* '[to] register'

A possible explanation is that in standard Hebrew there is only one graphical representation for the fricatives [s] and [š] and that a morpheme-final [t] combined with an initial fricative or affricate (/s/, /š/, /ts/) produces a cluster in which the order of the two elements is reversed.[12]

Examples of L2 interference involving *vowels* are easy to find. Standard Arabic and Hebrew have no graphical representation for vowels. This void in the native competence is filled by phonological patterns acquired within L2. Thus, < ei > and < ie > are frequently confused, as in (2):

(2a)   *erhielt* 'received' vs. *erhellt* 'lit'

(2b)   *Ziel* 'goal' vs. *Zeile* 'row, lign'

Other errors stem from the fact that < u >, often pronounced in English as [ʌ] (in words such as *cut, but,* etc.), is mistaken for < a > or < o >, which in English may sound similar. Words thus confused include those in (3).

(3a)   *Gefühle* 'feelings' vs. *Gefallen* 'favour'

(3b)   *Rückschau* 'retrospective' vs. *Rockshow* 'rock show'

Added umlauts may also be classified here:

(4a)   *schon* 'already' (interpreted as *schön* 'beautiful')

(4b)   *Buchsee* (a name, interpreted as *Büchse* 'box')

Sometimes, all factors are combined, as when *Künstler* 'artist' is read as *Kanzler* 'chancellor', *manchen* 'many' as *Menschen* 'people', *sieht* 'sees' as *zeigt* 'shows'.

Finally, ignoring or inverting graphical signs may be linked to inappropriate scanning behaviour. L2 English has prepared Israeli students to treat graphical signs holistically, because of a poor match between letters and sounds. For many, it is therefore puzzling to switch to the analytical reading required by German, and to match

---

[12] This typically happens in the case of reflexives, where the prefix < hit > is added to the simple verb, as in the case of < slk > (i.e. [silek]), simple form meaning 'remove', which in the reflexive becomes < histlk > (i.e. [histalek] 'leave').

every letter with a phoneme. Endings (of individual letters or of batches) are particularly vulnerable to being overlooked. The following are often confused:

(5a)   *machte* (simple past of *machen* 'make') vs. *Macht* 'power'

(5b)   *geweiht* 'dedicated' vs. *Geweih* 'horns'

(5c)   *gewisse* 'certain' vs. *gewiss* 'certainly' vs. *Gewissen* 'conscience'

(5d)   *Formel* 'formula' vs. *formell* 'formally'

(5e)   *grau* 'grey' vs. *Grauen* 'dawn'

(5f)   *spätestens* 'at the latest' vs. *spätesten* 'the latest'

(5g)   *gegründet* 'founded' vs. *gegrünt* 'flourished'

(5h)   *als* 'when' vs. *alles* 'everything'

(5i)   *uneingeschränkt* 'unlimited' vs. *uneinig* 'in disagreement'

(5j)   *Stunden* 'hours' vs. *Studenten* 'students'

3.2. Morphology

The largest share of errors in my pilot study (34%) concerns the morphological module. The figure confirms the reality of the maturational constraint, mentioned earlier. Newport (1994) points out that adults choose to learn words as unanalysed wholes rather than to relate them to their respective morphological structures. And this is exactly what happened to my students in many instances.

Holistic scanning. Recall that the holistic behaviour described in the phonological module leads to a relaxed attitude towards letters. In the morphological module it leads to a tendency to neglect affixes: a word is grasped without its prefix (examples (6a-d)) or its suffix (example (6e)).

(6a)   *Hingelenkt* 'guided in this direction' (interpreted as *Gelenk* 'joint')

(6b)   *gestellt* 'put [past participle]' (interpreted as *Stelle* 'place')

(6c)   *herleiten* 'derive' (interpreted as *leiten* '[to] guide')

(6d)   *Verurteilung* 'condemnation' (interpreted as *Teilung* 'partition')

(6e)   *Täter* 'offender' (interpreted as *Tat* 'deed')

The examples above represent errors that occurred while a text was being scanned. Other holistic errors occur during dictionary consultation. Learners may not find a word even though it is included. A majority of students in my test group struck trouble with the word *Frühling* 'spring [one of four seasons]'. This is not at all surprising, given the way it is listed in Lavi's (1980) German-Hebrew dictionary (as follows: *Frühjahr n, ~ling m* (-s; -e)). Native speakers of German who wish to find the Hebrew equivalent for *Frühling* will not be puzzled by the fact that the suffix *-ling* can be combined with the modifier *früh*. They know, of course, that *Frühjahr* will lead them to the answer.[13] With German as the target language, one expects *Frühling* to be mentioned separately. This expectation is met in Inbal (1987), where *Frühjahr* and *Frühling* appear on successive lines.

Inconsistency. Newport (1994) mentions another pattern following from the maturational constraint. Adult understanding of morphological structures is inconsistent. Adults may use a morpheme correctly on one occasion and err the next. This is often observed in the case of the modifier-head construction of compounds.[14] Israeli students frequently, though not systematically, apply the order head-modifier typical of their L1 Hebrew or Arabic (11% of the total error rate). Deceptive transparency (24%), on the other hand, is the reason behind the mistaken interpretation of complex lexical structures. At least part of the material is interpreted transparently, as shown in examples (7a-c).

> (7a)   *keineswegs* 'by no means' (interpreted as *kein Weg* 'no way')

> (7b)   *weismachen* 'make believe' (interpreted as *weise machen* 'make wise')

> (7c)   *Sprichwort* 'proverb' (interpreted as *spricht* 'speaks')

DT and phonetic factors may be combined:

> (8)   *Künstlern* 'artists' (dative, plural)
>
>   Phonological error: the Umlaut is ignored
>
>   Morphological error: the suffix is read as a lexical morpheme
>
>   False interpretation: 'students of the arts', i.e. *Kunst-lern* ('arts-learn')

---

[13] The opacity of the above representation contrasts with the fact that in the same dictionary suffixes are normally found on the line following the main entry, whereas additions on the same line concern compounds.

[14] The problem is widespread, as is well known. Many FL studies deal with compound order; for French vs. German, see e.g. Platz-Schliebs (1997).

Overgeneralisation. The third and last feature of Newport's maturational constraint observed in my pilot group is the overgeneralisation of acquired patterns. Here are some of the data:

(9a)   *Rezeption* 'reception' (interpreted as *Rezept* 'recipe'; the suffix *-ion* does not always alter the reference of the derivational base, cf. /act = action/ or /oblige = obligation/)

(9b)   *einige* 'a few' (interpreted as *einigen* 'unify'; the case suffix *-e* is mistaken for a verb suffix)

(9c)   *heranwachsender* 'adolescent' (interpreted as 'more mature'; the case ending *-er* is mistaken for a comparative suffix)

(9d)   *bedenken* 'consider' (interpreted as *Gedanken* 'thoughts'; insepara-ble verb prefixes are often referentially redundant)[15]

3.3. Syntax

In reading courses such as the one reported here students are permitted to reproduce in L1 any syntactic structure belonging to the target language, as long as intelligibil-ity prevails. Therefore, my study does not take sentence structure into consideration. The few remaining reading mistakes attributed to syntax (6% of the total error rate) involve polysemous words that acquire an invariant meaning through their structural position. For instance, a word may be an attribute when preceding a noun, as in (10a), or when following an attributive verb, as in (10b), but it may be an adverb when preceding an adjective, as in (10c):

(10a)   Er trank das *ganze* Glas 'He drank the entire glass'

(10b)   Das Glas blieb *ganz* 'The glass remained entire'

(10c)   Das Glas war *ganz* zerschlagen 'The glass was entirely shattered'

In the first two sentences, the position of the attribute *ganz* 'entire' is superficially and structurally identical. However, in the third sentence, its position is ambiguous. Though superficially following the verb, *ganz* structurally precedes the adjective *zerschlagen* and is now an adverb meaning 'entirely'. No wonder, then, that to some of my students the third sentence made no sense at all. Indeed, how could a glass be at the same time 'entire' and 'shattered'?

---

[15] I have shown elsewhere that verb prefixation, especially with prefixes such as *be-* etc., represents an important source of errors (Feigenbaum forthcoming).

Another case worth mentioning is that of the German complementiser *zu*. It mostly causes problems when occurring as an infix:

> (11a)   *festzustellen* (cf. *feststellen* 'observe'), interpreted as *Festzug stellen* 'establish a festive procession'

> (11b)   *auszudrücken* (cf. *ausdrücken* 'express'), interpreted as *aus, zu-drücken* 'press together and out'

Zu occupies the fuzzy interface encountered in the other modules. The data demonstrate the student's shortcomings in syntax; on the other hand, they illustrate the modular functioning shown in table 1. Various phenomena which follow from the maturational constraint are also seen to be at work here. In the first example, the learner adhered to a holistic reading of *fest-zu*, which resulted in *Festzug*. In the second example, the affixes were analysed inconsistently.

3.4. Semantics

The second largest category of mistakes results from *polysemous* words which cannot be disambiguated through their structural position (31%). Selecting one meaning over the other is a decision-making process I shall discuss in the following section. Here I examine how the immediate context may lead learners towards a false solution because of errors made in other lexical modules. In example (12), the error can be traced from phonology to morphology and then to semantics:

> (12)   *ein vierblättriges Kleeblatt* 'a clover with four leaves'
>
> Phonological error: the long [e:] in *Kleeblatt* is read as a short [e]
>
> Morphological error: the compound noun is read holistically as *Kleb-blatt* 'sticker'
>
> Semantic error: the base *blatt* in the word *blättrig* is translated as 'sheet' instead of 'leaf'
>
> False interpretation: 'a sticker consisting of four sheets'

The Logical Interpretant is responsible for mistakes like this. According to Sperber & Wilson's (1995) relevance theory and Kempson's (1988) interpretation theory, meaning is not exclusively created by the code but it also depends on inference. Obviously, to speak of a sticker with four leaves would be incongruous. The only acceptable inference for *Klebblatt* is 'sheet'.

Another example is provided in (13). Once again, the principle of relevance is behind a reading error observed in my test group. The error has to do with the word *Mädchen*, which is polysemous between 'little girl' and 'young girl'.

(13)   *Ein zweieinhalbjähriges Mädchen fiel vom dritten Stock.*
'A little girl of two and a half fell down from the third floor'

The incorrect interpretation (see below) is triggered not by an error flow between modules but by the way in which the word features in bilingual dictionaries (e.g. Lavi 1980). The first translation (/na'arah/) is followed by the information "*(Kind)* = /yalda/". Only an experienced FL learner understands that at the age of two and a half, *Mädchen* and *Kind* have the same referent. My student, on the other hand, decided that the meaning of the sentence had to be 'A young girl of twelve and a half fell down from the third floor'. The learner's decision to interpret *Mädchen* as meaning 'young girl' was reached on the often observed assumption that the first meaning listed in the dictionary is the only one. Hebrew /na'arah/ refers to a young girl, whereas a girl of two and a half is a child (/yalda/). Consequently, the age was increased to suit the Hebrew referent of /na'arah/. The principle of relevance led the learner's EK2 to interfere with the semantics of the target language.

4. The components of EK

In the task-goal flow, I situated EK in a filtering position between the first and the final translation of FL terms. However, as we have seen, with regard to reading strategies, we must pay special attention to rigid EK. Names lend real-world reference to texts, and they are part of the referential chain. Therefore, they *belong* to the vocabulary. Personal and cultural EK, by contrast, *accompany* the vocabulary. This means that the precise reference of a lexical item also depends on context.

4.1. What to do with names

I have mentioned the grammatical separation of names from common nouns with the help of graphical signs or syntax. In German, where all nominals, be they names or nouns, are written with a capital, and where the absence of an article is common outside the area of names, the usefulness of such marks is limited. Recall also that without sufficient sight vocabulary learners tend to classify names as common nouns and analyse them according to the rules of word formation or conjugation; hence interpretations such as the following ((14a) is a case of deceptive transparency, (14b) one of overgeneralisation):

(14a)   *Münchenbuchsee* (the home of the painter Paul Klee), interpreted as *München-Büchse* 'boxes of Munich'

(14b)   *Oberitalien* 'upper Italy', interpreted as an individual's name

4.2. The filtering function of EK

Earlier on, personal and cultural EK, which do not belong to vocabulary, but *accompany* vocabulary acquisition, were inserted into the FL learning stages as follows: personal EK was invoked at stage 3 (logical) and cultural EK at stage 4 (enriched). I now propose to reexamine them within the adjustment strategies shown in table 5.

Personal & Cultural EK	Semantics & Pragmatics	a) Examine context and/or co-text
		b) Accept instant solution (or not)
		c) Continue search for solution
		d) If found, go to (e); if not, repeat (c)
		e) Adjust

Table 5: Adjustment strategies

Before we open the discussion on context interaction, which is situated within the Logical/Enriched Interpretants, it may be helpful to recall that another evaluation mechanism exists within the Dynamic Interpretant (cf. table 2). That kind of interpretation is based on grammatical rules. For instance, the semantic error in example (12) (*Klebblatt* instead of *Kleeblatt*) could have been avoided if the immediate grammatical context had escaped contamination. Likewise, one would expect morphological errors concerning place names (cf. (14a-b)) to be redressed by the presence of spatial prepositions. Such inferences are indeed often applied, but they do not provide a safety net. For instance, names of persons frequently appear in subject position, and one may therefore infer that a subject that is not listed in the dictionary is a personal name. This assumption is open to overgeneralisation, as in the case of example (15):

> (15)   *Besass er auch keine Bildung…*
>
> Correct interpretation: 'Although he did not have any education…'
>
> Morphological error: *besass* is not understood as a form of the verb *besitzen* 'possess, have'
>
> False interpretation: 'Besass had no education'

Context evaluation, by means of personal and cultural EK, should tell the learner whether the instantly reached grammatical solution is relevant or not. EK is expected to make up for any shortcomings at the level of LK. With respect to the errors described above, could it be that the learner did not follow the adjustment strategies to the end? Did the learner refrain from feeding back the contextual information to the sign for purposes of verification? The distinction made by Eco (1985:18) between *co-text*, i.e. the textual web in which a specific word appears, and *context*, i.e. the extra-textual field of reference, will help us reach the answer.

Co-text failure. Often a faulty interpretation is not incoherent with regard to the co-text. This is true for many errors described before. The interaction of homonyms is yet another example (homonyms are words found in the dictionary that are different from those that were being looked up):

> (16a)   *Die Polizei hat ihn frei gelassen* 'The police let him free' (*gelassen* is the past participle of the verb *lassen*), interpreted as 'The police remained calm' (*gelassen* is an adjective meaning 'calm')

> (16b)   *Viele von uns hast Du schon übergesetzt* 'Many of us you have already brought to the other side' (*hast* is the 2nd person singular of the present of the verb *haben*), interpreted as 'You have brought us hastily to the other side' (*Hast* is a noun meaning 'haste'; the information conveyed by the lower case initial is ignored, for reasons indicated above)

In both cases, the learner stopped at point 2 of the adjustment strategies. (16a) was taken to mean that the police remained calm because the thief was in prison. The faulty interpretation of (16b), on the other hand, did not conflict with the rest of the text.

Having examined passive EK, let us now look at active interactions. These are cases where the learner goes on to points 3-5 in table 5. The co-text is being fed back, albeit with a poor result. To begin with, recall that modules may interact with each other or directly with EK. An example of the latter kind of interface is given by the word *Künstler* 'artist', falsely interpreted as *Kanzler* 'chancellor' because of phonological interference. The *Kanzler* reading was supported by the fact that the text treated an aspect of German history. A second example takes us back to the syntactic module. As I have said, the immediate grammatical context can clear up polysemy, as in the case of the contradiction between "entire" and "shattered". Yet componential features do not always provide a clue. The succession of *weit* and *offen* in the following sentence failed to provide negative feedback:

> (17)   *Die Tür war weit offen.*
>
> Correct interpretation: 'The door was wide open'
>
> Syntax error: confusion of superficial and structural order.
>
> False interpretation: 'The door was wide and open'

(17) was part of a text about architecture, which led the learner to accept a mistaken reading, on the assumption that *weit* 'wide' referred to the size of the door. In other words, the co-text fed the syntactic error forward.

Context failure. The instances of filtering described above as occurring at the levels of rigid EK and/or personal EK may also occur at the level of cultural EK. Typically, though, cultural EK filtering occurs when the interpretation of an item is primarily supported by the extra-linguistic context. 'Primarily supported' means that neither the sentence structure nor the co-text impact upon the interpretation. In the example below, the cultural EK of L1 (the history of Israel) interacts with the cultural EK of the target language (German history):

(18)   *Literatur: Erinnerungen an die Gruppe 47. Vor 50 Jahren traf sich erstmals die Gruppe 47, der bedeutendste Autorenkreis der Nachkriegsliteratur.*

Correct interpretation: 'Literature: Remembering Group 47. 50 years ago took place the first meeting of Group 47, the most important circle of authors of post-war literature'

Polysemy: *Literatur* is understood as meaning 'professional literature', rather than 'literature as art form'

Polysemy: *Gruppe* is interpreted as 'team of pioneers'

Decision: *-krieg-* 'war' is interpreted as Israel's War of Independence

False interpretation: '50 years ago took place the first meeting of Group 47, the most important team of pioneers mentioned in the literature after the War of Independence'

Clearly, this is an extremely loose translation. However, this sort of translation shows that once EK has filtered a piece of information the lexicon hardly intervenes to make any repairs.

Wild and calculated guessing. So far I have presented an uninterrupted task-goal flow with EK being invoked to reach Goal 2 (the final translation). Quite often things do not happen that way. Experienced learners can conceptualise a final outcome and feed it back.[16] If necessary, they can repair irrelevance. It is correct to say that they will search until they find a solution that is satisfactory at least to them; the adjustment strategies sketched in table 5 do not present any *intrinsic* hurdles. However, inexperienced learners are unable to follow the same path. They cannot feed back a final outcome because of insufficient EK to conceptualise such an outcome in the first place. To establish text coherence, which according to the principle of relevance must be maintained, they simply feed forward whatever conclusions they have

---

[16] This is what happens in the think-aloud protocol established with students of French in Platz-Schliebs (1997). These learners check whether an L2 compound like *bloc-notes* has an equivalent in L1. If not, they create a phrase which relates to the context.

reached. Sometimes their decisions create the impression of unsuccessful guessing, as in the following examples:

(19a)   *Er wurde in allen Gesellschaften gefeiert.*

Correct interpretation: 'He was celebrated in all the circles'

Semantic error: unsuccessful selection of the equivalent for *Gesellschaft* ('society', but also 'circle').

False interpretation: 'He worked in many societies'

(19b)   *Zwei Tage erwog ich, wie ich die Reise am geschicktesten machen sollte.*

Correct (though literal) interpretation: 'I pondered for two days how I should undertake my travel in the cleverest way'

Scanning error: *wie* 'how' interpreted as 'why'

Holistic reading: *geschicktesten* 'cleverest' interpreted as *Geschick* 'destiny'

False interpretation: 'I pondered for two days why destiny obliged me to travel'

(19c)   *Er war das Ziel von manchen schönen Augen.*

Correct (though literal) interpretation: 'He was the target of many beautiful eyes'

Scanning error: *manchen* 'many' interpreted as *Menschen* 'people'

False interpretation: 'His aim was to find people with beautiful eyes'

Much may be gained from examining misreadings like these with due reference to dictionary strategies, to the relevance principle, and to the grammar of the interlanguage. For instance, the first equivalent in Lavi (1980) for *Gesellschaft*, used in (19a), is 'society'. Examples (19b) and (19c) are caused by error transfer from one module to another.

In light of all this, it must be asked whether EK is really as constructive for reading comprehension as many researchers believe. On the one hand, it seems obvious that polysemic words cannot be disambiguated out of context (cf. Bensoussan 1992). On the other hand, context alone does not provide the answer, as may be gathered from the above and as has been said by other researchers (cf. Laufer 1997). The high error rate observed in my study as a result of polysemy indicates that learners often fail somewhere around step 3 of the adjustment strategies, because there is nothing that would initiate a renewed evaluation. Learners are in no position to repair grammatical errors or to evaluate the co-text. Therefore, EK3 often takes over in the wrong direction.

5. Summary

I have investigated the interaction between LK and EK by analysing the reading strategies of university students in an *ab initio* reading course in German. It has not been my aim to blame failure at either level (LK or EK) on insufficient teaching in either field. Rather, my aim has been to show that the two fields of knowledge can be delineated, even though in FL teaching they should be constantly integrated.

Owing to the high cognitive demands and the short learning period of their programme, my test group presents a showcase for the fact that language learning implies the constant development of all types of knowledge, even at an age when one would expect part of it to be already established. One of the difficulties learners suffer is that words are dynamic entities. Even adults with FL experience find themselves in a situation where they are taking initial steps in language acquisition. Whereas competent speakers and more experienced learners possess sufficient vocabulary to select among multiple meanings, the less advanced learners cannot weigh up several possibilities. First, the short learning period they have benefited from does not provide them with sufficient sight vocabulary; secondly, they are not grammatically schooled to explore all the indications in the dictionary, so usually they choose the first entry. As a result, text translations often appear as confabulations rather than adequate solutions.

Since my error analysis is based on a relatively small sample, this study does not pretend to provide a compelling picture. Nevertheless, it seems to me that two points have become clear. First, adults apply every means to maintain intelligent text coherence. They weigh their solutions against the co-text, and if the latter does not provide any useful indications they adjust it (according to the principle of relevance) as a function of their knowledge of the world. This knowledge is mostly based on their own culture and need not correspond to the one implied by the text. Secondly, because learners trust their own EK more than their LK of the FL, they are lenient towards their interpretation of words, and they also apply the rules they have learnt in an inconsistent fashion. This explains why mistakes are made, not only against rules at an advanced FL level, but at all levels. The error rates for scanning, for morphology, and for semantics are not very different.

References

Baldwin, Dare A. 1994. "Infant contributions to the achievement of joint reference". In Paul Bloom (ed.), *Language acquisition. Core readings*. Cambridge: M.I.T. Press. 129-153.

Bensoussan, Marsha. 1992. "Learners' spontaneous translations in an L2 reading comprehension task. Vocabulary knowledge and use of schemata". In J.L. Pierre Arnaud & Henri Béjoint (ed.), *Vocabulary and applied linguistics*. London: Macmillan. 102-112.

Bloom, Paul. 1994. "Overview. Controversies in language acquisition". In Paul Bloom (ed.), *Language acquisition. Core readings*. Cambridge: M.I.T. Press. 5-48.

Brandi, Marie-Louise; Momenteau, Barbara. 1992. *Lesekurs für Geisteswissenschaftler*, vol. 1 & 2. München: Klett.

Diament, Henri. 1998. "Les difficultés inhérentes à l'enseignement de la littérature francophone en Israël". Manuscript, University of Haifa.

Duden. 1980. *Rechtschreibung der deutschen Sprache und der Fremdwörter*. Mannheim: Bibliographisches Institut.

Eco, Umberto. 1985. *Lector in fabula*. Paris: Grasset.

Feigenbaum, Susanne. 1993. "Lernergrammatik und täuschende Transparenz im Deutschunterricht". In *X. internationale Deutschlehrertagung. Deutsch als Fremdsprache in einer sich wandelnden Welt. Thesenband*. Leipzig: Herder-Institut. 180.

Feigenbaum, Susanne. Forthcoming. "Präfigierte Verbformen in der Wortschatzarbeit und in Leseübungen". In Sigrid Dentler, Britta Hufeisen & Beate Lindemann (ed.), *Tertiärsprachen. Empirische Untersuchungen*. Tübingen: Stauffenburg.

Fernald, Anne. 1994. "Vocalizations to infants as biologically relevant signals". In Paul Bloom (ed), *Language acquisition. Core readings*. Cambridge: M.I.T. Press. 51-94.

Hartshorne, Charles; Weiss, Paul (ed). 1965. *Collected papers of Charles Sanders Peirce*. Cambridge: Harvard University Press.

Hornby, Albert S.; Reif, Joseph A. 1978. *Oxford student dictionary for Hebrew speakers*. Tel Aviv: Kernerman & Kahn.

Inbal, Shimshon. 1987. *Neues Handwörterbuch Deutsch-Hebräisch; Hebräisch-Deutsch*. Jerusalem: Zack.

Kallenbach, Christiane. 1998. "'Da weiss ich schon, was auf mich zukommt'. L3-Spezifika aus Schülersicht". In Britta Hufeisen & Beate Lindemann (ed.), *Tertiärsprachen. Theorien. Modelle. Methoden.* Tübingen: Stauffenburg. 47-57.

Karmiloff-Smith, Annette. 1994. "Innate constraints and developmental change". In Paul Bloom (ed), *Language acquisition. Core readings.* Cambridge: M.I.T. Press. 563-590.

Kempson, Ruth M. 1988. "On the grammar-cognition interface. The principle of full interpretation". In Ruth M. Kempson (ed.), *Mental representations. The interface between language and reality.* Cambridge: Cambridge University Press. 199-224.

Klinkenberg, Jean-Marie. 1996. *Précis de sémiotique générale.* Bruxelles: De Boeck.

Kripke, Saul. 1980. *Naming and necessity.* Oxford: Blackwell.

Laufer, Batia. 1992. "How much lexis is necessary for reading comprehension?". In: J.L. Pierre Arnaud & Henri Béjoint (ed.), *Vocabulary and applied linguistics.* London: Macmillan. 126-132.

Laufer, Batia. 1997. "The lexical plight in second language reading. Words you don't know, words you think you know, and words you can't guess". In James Coady & Thomas Huckin (ed.), *Second language vocabulary acquisition.* Cambridge: Cambridge University Press. 20-34.

Laufer, Batia. 1998. "The development of passive and active vocabulary in a second language. Same or different?". *Applied linguistics* 12. 255-271.

Lavi, Jaacov. 1980. *Handwörterbuch Deutsch-Hebräisch.* Tel Aviv: Achiasaf (Langenscheidt).

Marello, Carla. 1996. "Les différents types de dictionnaires bilingues". In Henri Béjoint & Philippe Thoiron (ed.), *Les dictionnaires bilingues.* Louvain-la-Neuve: Duculot. 31-52.

Meyers grosses Handlexikon. 1985. Mannheim: Bibliographisches Institut.

Neuner, Gerd; Scherling, Theo; Schmidt, Reiner; Wilms, Heinz. 1986. *Deutsch Aktiv neu 1A.* Berlin: Langenscheidt.

Neuner, Gerd; Scherling, Theo; Schmidt, Reiner; Wilms, Heinz. 1988. *Deutsch Aktiv neu 1B.* Berlin: Langenscheidt.

Newport, Elissa L. 1994. "Maturational constraints on language learning". In Paul Bloom (ed.), *Language acquisition. Core readings.* Cambridge: M.I.T. Press. 543-560.

Platz-Schliebs, Anja. 1997. "Sprachliches und konzeptuelles Wissen beim Erschlies-
sen von L2-Komposita". *Zeitschrift für Fremdsprachenforschung* 8. 245-266.

Rey-Debove, Josette; Rey, Alain. 1993. *Le nouveau Petit Robert*. Paris: Dictionnaires Le Robert.

Rogolla, Hanna; Rogolla, Willy. 1985. *German for academic purposes*. Berlin:
Langenscheidt.

Saussure, Ferdinand de. 1968 [1916]. *Cours de linguistique générale*. Edition
critique de Rudolf Engler. Wiesbaden: Harrassowitz.

Schmidlin, Regula. 1996. "Wortschatz- und semantische Entwicklung im Grund-
schulalter". *Scolia* 9. 249-273.

Sperber, Dan; Wilson, Deirdre. 1995 [1986]. *Relevance. Communication and cognition*. Oxford: Blackwell.

Van Eunen, Kees; Gerighausen, Josef; Neuner, Gerd; Scherling, Theo; Reiner,
Schmidt; Wilms, Heinz. 1989. *Deutsch Aktiv neu 1C*. Berlin: Langenscheidt.

Wirbelauer, Hejny. 1983. *Lesekurs Deutsch*. Berlin: Langenscheidt.

Augmenting linguistic semantics descriptions for NLP: Lexical knowledge, encyclopedic knowledge, event structure[1]

Victor Raskin

Purdue University, Natural Language Processing Laboratory, W. Lafayette,
IN 47907-1356, USA
E-mail: vraskin@purdue.edu

Salvatore Attardo

Youngstown State University, Department of English, Youngstown, OH 44555-3415,
USA
E-mail: sattardo@cc.ysu.edu

and

Donalee H. Attardo

formerly of Carnegie Mellon University, Center for Machine Translation,
Pittsburgh, PA 15213, USA

[1] This paper was first published in *Machine Translation* 9 (1994), pp. 81-98, under the title "Augmenting formal semantic representation for NLP. The story of SMEARR", and is reprinted with kind permission from Kluwer Academic Publishers. The title used here is that of the original technical report (Purdue University, 1991, TR17-PNLPL-91). Apart from a few editorial changes, some additional footnotes and bibliographical updates, the text is identical to that of the original paper.

0. Introduction

In our BISFAI '89 paper (Raskin 1990), we outlined and justified a program for transposing linguistic semantics (LS) descriptions into meaning representation for natural language processing (NLP), or NLP semantics (NLPS). The program has now been implemented as SMEARR, a pilot SHAREABLE MEANING ANALYSIS AND REPRESENTATION RESOURCE, briefly described in section 2, and further justification of the approach precedes the description (section 1). In the process of implementing SMEARR, we have developed a methodology for augmenting, extending and enriching LS descriptions for NLPS, a process which has put the matters of the involved formalisms in the center of our agenda – this is dealt with in section 3. The single most important formal and conceptual issue involved in the formal and substantive makeover of LS descriptions for NLPS is event structure, a notion which has been crucial for NLPS for quite some time and which semantic theory is now slowly and somewhat erratically discovering; event structure is briefly discussed in section 4. The "back" effect of the formal and substantive requirements of NLPS on LS is addressed in the conclusion (section 5).

1. By way of (passive-aggressive) justification

It is perhaps appropriate to comment right at the outset how the SMEARR approach relates to the current shift in machine translation (MT) and NLP in general to empirically-based studies. This is an empirically-based study in linguistic semantics, primarily in lexical semantics. As such, it is congruent with such recent works in lexical semantics as, for instance, Levin (1993), Nirenburg & Levin (1992). The empirical reality underlying the study is natural language meaning as perceived by the native speaker and seen through the prism of recent semantic theories by their best proponents and practitioners and as adjusted for NLP purposes by a group of researchers combining linguistic theory with NLP practice.

This paper does not contain a description of an implemented or partially implemented NLP system for a toy domain. Instead, it offers a system combining lexical acquisition software with a sizable ready-made dictionary. It contains a clear methodology of extending, extrapolating, and porting this system to any real-life domain and sublanguage for which an MT or NLP system is needed. The system is partially justified on the following grounds. First, the semantic-network frame-based slot-and-filler approach has recommended itself as the most promising semantic one in the last decade or so of revived knowledge-based MT and artificial intelligence (AI) in general. The approach is based on the 3-dictionary (concept, analysis, and generation) framework developed by Nirenburg & Raskin (1987a,b), and, accordingly, the slot names are language-independent concepts while the fillers can be also concepts or actual lexemes of a language, depending on the type of the dictionary developed – this should perhaps allay the ontological concerns of those who are still nervous, along with Lewis (1972:170) some two decades ago, about the bogey man of translating "markerese into markerese". The fillers of the slots actively anticipate other constituents of the sentences in which the words corresponding to the entries are likely to occur, thus rendering the SMEARR dictionary effectively parsing-ready. The entries incorporate high-quality semantic intuition of native speakers, assisted and systematised by a theory-based and computerised methodology.

The temporary funding unpopularity of a straightforward semantic approach like this will not render it less crucial for effective MT, NLP, and AI. A deep, dedicated, and systematic semantic description, complete with the discovery of its rules and regularities, may fly in the face of some recent attempts to define such semantics out of existence by carving it into syntactic semantics as part of syntax (see, for instance, Frawley 1993 for a recent monumental effort in this direction and a review of it in Raskin 1994) and into non-systematic, minimalistic, idiosyncratic word-specific lexicon information as, basically, part of morphology, while leaving the semantic rules to vaguely defined and rather disinterestedly dismissed formal, perhaps truth-conditional semantics (see, for instance, Chierchia & McConnell-Ginet 1991). But it is our strong conviction that linguistic semantics, as we see it, will not blow over or go away as the central problem of both linguistic theory and practice and of MT, NLP, and AI. (Those unable to accept this eventuality should not perhaps read on.)

Obviously, though, the proof of the pudding is in the eating, and no eating as such is described in the paper. Nor do we think it possible to do semantic research in NLP exclusively by designing small NLP systems that use some limited semantic information. All we are hoping to offer here is an attractive recipe for a semantic module which we have every possible reason to think will work out in a variety of empirical studies. Both we ourselves and others, we hope, will be able to see what modifications our results will undergo in the actual working systems.

2. Description of SMEARR

Semantics remains the worst bottleneck in NLP. Extracting meaning from input text has not been done well enough to ensure the human-like degree of text understanding, which severely limits the effectiveness of text processing systems such as MT and information retrieval as well as that of natural language interfaces. Most existing NLP systems use some variation of such methods of meaning representation as conceptual dependencies (see, for instance, Schank & Riesbeck 1981), feature analysis (e.g. Ahlswede 1985), or "commonsense-based" predicate-calculus formulae (Woods 1967 was probably the first example). These methods usually provide rather crude semantic interpretation, often resulting in unresolved ambiguities and incorrect and/or insufficient inference. More sophisticated methods, such as preference semantics (e.g. Wilks 1975, Wilks & Fass 1984), require much more semantic analysis and are rarely implemented. This applies equally to such other sophisticated approaches as discourse analysis (e.g., Grosz & Sidner 1986, Reichman 1985, Tucker et al. 1986) or case-based reasoning (e.g. Kolodner 1984), primarily because they all require much finer granularity of meaning representation, i.e. a deeper and more subtle semantic analysis than NLP has been able to provide. Much recent work in NLPS, including ours, has been based on the semantic network approach derived from knowledge representation schemata *à la* Quillian (1968), Bobrow & Winograd (1977), Brachman (1979), Brachman et al. (1985), or Brachman & Schmolze (1985).

Practical implementation of meaning representation of any reasonable complexity and sophistication in NLP is very time- and effort-consuming. It involves a considerable amount of handcarving each individual entry, or "brute force" (see Jacobs 1991). Trying to tap the available resources for avoiding this, people have been attempting to extract NLP meaning representations from machine-readable dictionaries (MRD) (e.g. Boguraev et al. 1989, Calzolari 1991) and large corpora.

We started this work with a claim that semantic descriptions accumulated over the last three decades in the first-string work in linguistic semantics constitute the fourth resource for computational lexicography (along with brute force, MRDs, and corpora) and, more generally, for NLPS. Moreover, it is likely that this resource should be activated to do successful work with the other three resources. Thus, brute force, if uninformed by linguistic semantics, may lead to substandard *ad hoc* descriptions; non-semantic methods of extracting useful semantic information for NLP from MRDs may yield only very limited results; and without a sound semantic hypothesis on collocation, anaphora, and other syntagmatic relations, corpora – no matter how large – may not come through for NLPS either.

Given the lack of well-defined theory of linguistic semantics, utilising the high-quality LS descriptions produced in the field seems to be the most efficient way of tapping the resource, especially since – in an important way, if not literally – linguistic semantics has left no semantic stone unturned: it is reasonable to assume, even though hard to ascertain, that LS descriptions cover every semantic fact of at least better explored languages. At the end of the day (or, at least, later in the day), we still support the claim we started from. We discovered, not at all unexpectedly, that the high-quality LS descriptions were not directly portable into NLPS. We have focused, accordingly on the transfer formulae, and this is where reformalisation, augmentation, and enrichment of the entries have to take place. In some cases, the resulting SMEARR entries bear little non-trivial similarity to the LS description it may have started from. We continue to believe, however, that a much more detailed and explicit SMEARR entry was still informed by the LS description.

Descriptive work in linguistic semantics has been primarily of an illustrative nature. Developing a theoretical, often polemical argument, the author usually provides the description of a meaning informed by this argument and implies that this description is representative of many similar ones. Such descriptions have two major advantages over typical meaning representations in NLPS. They are:

- informed by some theory and, therefore, not *ad hoc*;

- executed by people skilled in linguistic description.

On the other hand, the disadvantage of LS descriptions for NLP is that they are:

- often executed in unfamiliar and inaccessible formalisms;

- less explicit than required by NLPS;

- meant as (representative) examples rather than to cover all the meanings of the language, and their extrapolability is strongly implied.

Accordingly, work with LS descriptions as the fourth resource for NLPS must consist of:

- replacing the formalism with one favoured by NLP;

- augmenting the descriptions;

- providing the descriptions of the missing "similar" items.

All of this has been implemented in SMEARR. The initial corpus of 450 high-quality LS descriptions was collected from over 600 post-1960 publications in linguistic semantics. It was then transposed into a formal ILT/Tamerlan notation (ILT = INTERLINGUA TEXT; see also Nirenburg et al. 1989; for a much earlier and less elaborate version, see Nirenburg et al. 1987) of a slot-and-filler nature which assigns a frame to each entry. Each frame is a node on an elaborate simple-inheritance *isa* tree hierarchy which, at this point, goes well beyond a limited domain (for a glimpse of the upper 5-6 levels of the hierarchy, see Nirenburg & Raskin 1987). Most entries in SMEARR are verbs or nouns, represented as processes or objects, respectively. The PROCESS and OBJECT frame templates are given below, with the slot names in Roman face and with the italicised material describing the value of the required filler.

Common Part of the PROCESS and OBJECT Templates:

(*word or other entry one of whose meanings the frame represents*

    (ref *bibliographic reference of the LS description, if any*)

    (def *LS description reproduced*)

    (lost-info *information, if any, lost in transposition*)

    (opinion of transcriber *text of opinion, if any*)

    (comment of transcriber *text of comment, if any*)

(isa mother node)

(subworld domain)

(syn list of synonyms of the entry)

PROCESS Template: **OBJECT Template:**

(consists-of *subprocesses*)   (consists-of *parts*)

(agent *animate*)   (subject-of* *process*)

(patient *animate recipient*)   (object-of** *process*)

(object *inanimate*)   (part-of *whole*)

(time *value in hardwired*** scale*)   (material *from material-set*)

(instrument *inanimate or process*)   (size *value in hardwired scale*)

(location *place*)   (colour *from colour-set*)

(proximity *value in hardwired scale*) (mass *from mass-set*)

(condition *timed event*)   (instrument-of** *process*)

(goal *future event*)   (condition *timeless event*))

(effect *future event*))

* if animate

** if inanimate

*** see below, in the paragraph after next, on hardwiring

Besides the templates, there are quite a few recurring nodes:

- 'cause X' is used with two events; the syntax is

  (cause (event1 event2)),

  where event1 is the cause of event2

- 'judge' is used to encode a value judgement done by either an agent or a patient anywhere into a frame, e.g.:

  (action judge)

  (agent agent)

  (patient patient)

  (object object)

  (quality value),

meaning an agent with regard to a patient assigns a certain judgemental quality value (hardwired below) to an object.

- 'have-authority' is used to denote a hierarchical situation between an agent and a patient, anywhere in a frame, e.g.,

    (state have-authority)

    (agent agentX)

    (patient patientX)

Hardwiring is a technical term used to indicate ranges of values arbitrarily selected to represent a continuum as a discrete set. These have been developed and implemented so far:

Parameter/Value	-5	-4	-3	-2	-1	0	1	2	3	4	5
Time			re-mote past	past	im-medi-ate past	now	im-medi-ate future	future	re-mote future		
Quality	ultima-tely bad	extre-mely bad	very bad	bad	sort of bad	neu-tral	sort of good	good	very good	extre-mely good	ultima-tely good
Size			min-uscule	very small	small	aver-age	big	very big	enor-mous		
Age			infant	child	adoles-cent	adult	mid-dle-aged	eld-erly	very old		
Quantity				much less	less	norm	more	much more			
Loudness			extre-mely quiet	very quiet	quiet	nor-mal	loud	very loud	extre-mely loud		
Pitch			extre-mely low	very low	low	nor-mal	high	very high	extre-mely high		
Proximity						loca-tion of agent	close to agent	not close to agent			

An example each of a PROCESS and an OBJECT frame follows (here and below, the homogenised indentation often distorts the hierarchical order of slots, which is, of course, rigorously maintained by parentheses):

(*convince*

    (ref Lakoff 1972:593)

(def CONVINCE: cause to come to believe)

(lost-info none)

(opinion none)

(isa communication-action)

(sbw world)

(consists-of speaking-action writing-action...)

(agent1 human)

(patient1 human)

(time 0)

(precondition

    (event1

       (state1 -believe)

         (agent2 patient1)   ;patient1 does not believe

         (object1 eventX))   ;eventX (i.e. some event)

        (time -1))

(effect

    (event2

       (state2 believe)

       (agent3 patient1)

       (object1 eventX)

       (time 1))

(cause (event0 event2))   ;agent1 causes patient1 to believe event2

(syn *persuade*))

(*nose*

    (ref Wierzbicka 1985:80)

    (def NOSE: part of the body sticking out in the middle of the face)

    (lost-info sticking out in the middle of)

    (opinion dependent on too many other concepts)

    (isa head-part)

    (sbw world)

    (consists-of nostrils tip bridge nasal-passages hair mucus)

(object-of blow scratch pick run ...)

(instrument-of sneeze sniff smell...)

(part-of face)

(material cartilage tissues)

(size size-set)

(shape shape-set)

(colour colour-set)

(mass mass-set)

(syn snout beak))

A lexical database (LD) with entry frames like the ones above constitutes the main part of SMEARR. SMEARR has been implemented in the Texas Instruments Explorer II environment on a FrameKit 1.5 basis in Common Lisp. It is designed to function, among other things, as an expert system in NLP semantics, especially on parsing-ready lexicons. The transparent notation (dispensable at will by the translation module – see 6 paragraphs below on the MT module in SMEARR) and straightforward non-partisan methodology render the resource truly polytheoretical and shareable for all needing to develop an NLPS module. It helps also that SMEARR is in the public domain. When brought to full capacity, SMEARR will contain around 5,000 English lexical entries. A parallel Russian lexicon has been partially implemented, and work on Spanish has been conducted on a smaller scale, primarily within the contrastive linguistic approach.

Besides LD, SMEARR has the following auxiliary modules:

- ONTOS-F, an interactive lexical acquisition tool;

- LDBMS, lexical database management system;

- NLI, natural language interface for LDBMS;

- MT, a limited ILT → English machine translation module;

- HELP, online help documentation;

- TUTOR, an online tutorial.

ONTOS, a general-use interactive tool for the acquisition and maintenance of lexical databases was conceived outside of SMEARR by Nirenburg & Raskin (see fragments of the "isa" tree hierarchy in Nirenburg & Raskin 1987:281, examples of typical frames in ibid:280-282, and screen dumps of working sessions with ONTOS, adding leaves to the tree, in ibid:283-285). It has been implemented and augmented to the current degree of convenience of use and sophistication of assistance and management by Nirenburg's team at Carnegie Mellon University (see Nirenburg et al. 1988). We have further improved and augmented it for the task of transposing LS descriptions into the SMEARR database by adding the powerful and easily accessible FrameBuilder module (Attardo 1990, 1991, 1993), thus creating ONTOS-F.

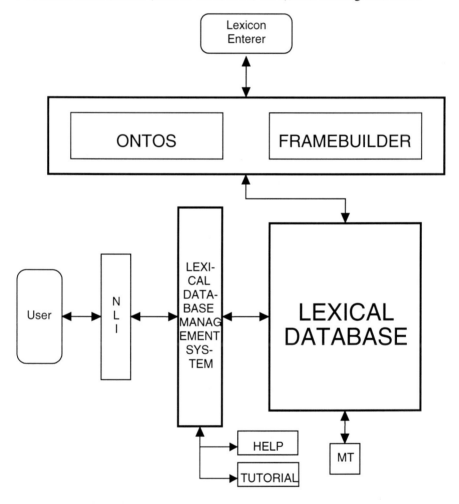

LDBMS provides menu-based access to the SMEARR database by word classes, individual words, and kinship (such as being siblings) between an input word and a word described in the database. Normally, if asked for the meaning(s) of a word, LDBMS will deliver one or more frames for it contained in the database. If the description is not yet in the database, it provides a few useful alternatives – thus, for *convince*, if it were not contained in the database, the menu would offer information on:

- a typical verb frame as shown above as a default offering for any verb clue;

- the entry for *remind* because of a syntactic similarity: like that verb, *convince* is used in the NP₁ V NP₂ *of* NP₃ type of phrase (cf. Postal 1971);

- the entry for *persuade/dissuade* because of a partial synonymy (cf. Lakoff 1972);

- the entry for "influence verbs," a great-grand parent of convince in the *isa* hierarchy.

LDBMS performs a number of functions with the frames with regard to their place in the hierarchy and/or other frames:

Function	*Input*	*Output*
MOTHER	Entry	The mother node of entry
SHOW	Word	The frame for the corresponding node
GET-FILLER	Slot	Filler
GET-FILLER-WITH-INHERITANCE	Slot	Filler with all the values, if any, inherited from the entry node's ancestor
FILL-FRAME	Word	The frame for the corresponding note, just as in SHOW, but with all the inherited values added
DESCENDANTS	Node	Tree with the input node as root
CHILDREN	Node	List with the input node as mother
IS-ANCESTOR	Node	Checks if a specified word is among the entry node's ancestors, and if so, shows the appropriate tree
SIBLING	Node	List with the sibling nodes under the entry node's mother
LOWEST-COMMON-ANCESTOR	2 nodes	Finds the lowest common ancestor and displays the tree
DYNASTY	2 nodes	Displays the path from a specified ancestor to a specified remote descendant
SYNONYM	Slot/Filler	Frames which include a specified slot/filler
SHOW-SYN	Node	List of nodes present in the hierarchy from the entry node's syn slot
SEARCH	Slots/Fillers	Frames having a specified combination of slots and/or fillers

NLI is a natural language interface which translates an inexperienced SMEARR user's input in plain English into one of the LDBMS functions above. Thus, the user may ask, "What's the meaning of *convince*, and NLI will correctly translate it into 'SHOW *convince*'; SMEARR will then execute this command and display the frame. NLI is designed to recognise all the reasonable paraphrases of English input corresponding to each of the SMEARR functions.

MT is a small machine translation system within the resource which translates the frames into standardised English for the benefit of a user who objects to the notation. Thus, the *convince* frame above will be translated by MT into this notation-free entry: "*convince* is an action of communication, which includes speaking, writing, etc. It is performed by a human agent and addressed to another human agent. Its precondition is that before the act of convincing, the person to be convinced does not believe something. Its effect is that after the act of convincing, that person believes it."

HELP contains documentation for all the components of SMEARR, and TUTOR includes two series of 5 tutorial sessions introducing the user to SMEARR. An additional section of tutorial contains 14 short lessons on the use of FrameBuilder.

3. Augmenting and reformalising the entries

Initially, the SMEARR project aimed only at locating the LS descriptions in the literature and transposing them into a machine-readable semantic notation, powerful enough to accommodate all the subtleties of LS descriptions. However, the transposition process revealed that the LS descriptions, even those reputed to be the most formal and well-defined, were not formal, well-defined, consistent, or rich enough to be used as they were for NLP purposes. Therefore, an *augmentation task* was added to the original project, which had the purpose of:

- filling the systematic "gaps" in the LS descriptions that the transposition process had revealed; and

- enriching the LS descriptions wherever required by the higher standards NLP analysis.

The augmentation task became the central part of the project, especially at the later stage when the instrumentation goals had been achieved.

In general, LS descriptions have been found to be generalised, illustrative, and requiring intuitive input from the user's intuition, even if claiming that they did not. Often LS descriptions focus on a canonical, archetypal meaning of the item, without links to its other uses. The following observations have resulted from the transposition and development of about 700 augmented, parsing-ready lexical entries, most of them verbs and nouns.

Concepts, not meanings. Most of the LS descriptions deal with concepts rather than with linguistic entities. Thus, no information on syntactic or semantic valencies, such as phrasality or collocation is typically given. The contents usually constitute or aspire to constitute the "logical form" of the described item so that the description tends to be language-independent. SMEARR descriptions supply all the missing information, going well beyond Mel'čuk's (e.g. 1979) non-superfluous lexical functions in that regard.

Depth/Explicitness. The major draw-back of many LS descriptions lies in their reliance on impoverished and implicit formalism, usually some form of predicate calculus. They typically use a no-name argument structure and *ad-hoc* predicates which are too primitive in structure but too complex and undefined conceptually, e.g., Fillmore's (1971) RESPONSIBLE in *accuse* below:

LS:

   accuse [Judge, Defendant, Situation (of)] (Performative)

   Meaning: SAY [Judge, 'X', Addressee]

   X = RESPONSIBLE [Situation, Defendant]

   Presupposition: BAD [Situation]

      (Fillmore, 1971:282)

SMEARR:

(*accuse*

      (isa speaking-action)

      (subworld world)

      (consists-of communication-action)

      (agent1 human)

      (patient1 human)

      (precondition

            (event1

                  (action1 actionX)

                        (agent2 patient1)

                        (time -2))

            (event2

                  (action2 judge)

                        (agent3 agent1)

                        (patient2 patient1)

                        (object1 (agent1 action1))

```
            (quality < 0)(time -1)))
    (event3
        ((action3 believe)
            (agent4 agent1)
            (object2 (actionX
                (agent2 patient1)))
                (time 0))))
    (time 0))
```

The SMEARR entry uses a large number of standard slots, each defined ostensibly through the predetermined ranges of values; it also puts a much higher premium on the conceptual simplicity of the description, rather than on its brevity or illusory logical primitiveness. The nesting parentheses may be not particularly human-friendly but they are most certainly LISP-friendly.

Deixis. In the process of transposition, Jackendoff's (1983) *approach* 'coming near' had to be augmented with additional spatial information to distinguish it from 'moving towards' and additional temporal information to mark the change of location over time. This and similar temporal data, along with those on speaker- and speaker-postulated-observer-related deixis, are typically needed to augment LS descriptions. For this purpose, SMEARR resorts to hardwiring time, quality, proximity, and a few other deictic parameters as predetermined ranges of numerical values.

LS:

approach: [event GO ([thing X], [path TOWARD ([thing Y])])])]
     (Jackendoff, 1983:184)

SMEARR:

(*approach*
        (isa motion-action)
        (sbw world)
        (has-as-part go)
        (agent animate)
        (patient object)

```
(precondition
    (loc agent 0)
    (loc patient 2)
(effect
    (loc agent 0
    (loc patient 1)))
```

Overdetermination. Many LS descriptions overdetermine reality by focusing on one possible realisation of meaning rather than on the general case. Thus Wierzbicka (1988) describes *dissuade* and many similar verbs in terms of 'saying', whereas one can be dissuaded in writing, by someone's action, etc.

LS:

X dissuaded Y from doing Z ==>
   Y thought this: 'I want this: I will do Z'
   after that, X said this to Y: I know this: you think this: 'I will do Z'
   I say: this is not a good idea (not a good thing)
   I say this because I want this: you will not think this
   because of this, Y did not think this after that
      (Wierzbicka 1988:40)

SMEARR:

(*dissuade*
    (isa communication-action)
    (sbw world)
    (consists-of speaking-action writing-action)
    (agent1 human)
    (patient1 human)
    (time 0)
(precondition
    (event1
        (action1 want)
            (agent2 patient1)   ;the patient wants to do something
            (object (event2
```
```

```
           (action2 actionX)
               (agent3 patient1)
               (time >0))))
       (goal -event1)))                    ;that the patient does not want to do it
```

Grain size. As already mentioned, LS descriptions are often found to be too general and to rely on implicit disambiguating knowledge of the reader. SMEARR has to distinguish between related but distinct meanings (e.g. *book* as a physical object and *book* as a mental object, the contents of the physical object), and often has to do so by giving a more detailed description (finer grain size) of the meaning. We are working on an additional variable-depth analysis (VDA) module for SMEARR which will modify its entries to a given grain size, from the smallest, GS1, to the largest, GS5. The entries shown throughout this paper are GS2 or GS3. VDA raises a number of complex issues which we will not go into in this paper. In the heart of it lies a standard methodology of deepening or shallowing an entry as per fillers in two additional specially introduced slots.

4. Event structure

This is the latest theoretical angle of our exploration of the augmenting process. As the examples of SMEARR entries above demonstrate, both the noun and verb entries in the SMEARR database are presented as components of a typical event in which their referents participate. The noun and verb templates present an essentially similar event structure, though with different emphases and degrees of detailisation.

Even more interestingly, the explicit characterisations of whole additional events, often temporally and/or causally contiguous to the "main event," are routinely used in lieu of what would have amounted to very complex predicates in the LS descriptions, to describe the preconditions, goals, and effects of the entry. Those events may involve other events needed to characterise them, thus leading to complex nestings (the entry for *argue* below contains 9 (!) conjoined and embedded events).

```
(argue
    (isa talk)
    (sbw world)
    (agent1 human)
    (patient1 human)
    (time 0)
```

```
(preconditions
   (event1
      (action1 believe)
         (agent2 agent1)              ;agent1 believes something
         (object1 (event2 eventX))
         (time < 0))
   (event3
      (action2 believe)
         (agent3 patient1)            ;patient1 does not believe it
         (object2
   (event4 -event2))
         (time < 0)))
(goal                                 ;goal may be optional; may overdetermine
   (event5                            ;the entry by arguing to persuade
      (action3 cause)
         (agent4 agent1)              ;the agent tries to
         (patient2 patient1)
         (time 0)
         (object3                     ;make the patient
   (event6
      (action4 believe)              ;believe
         (agent5 patient1)
         (time 0)
         (object4
   (event7 event2)))))               ;object1
   (event8
      (action5 cause)                 ;the patient tries to make
         (agent6 patient1)
         (time 0)
         (object5
   (event9
      (action6 believe)              ;the agent believe
```

```
          (agent7 patient1)
          (time 0)
          (object6
   (event10 -event2)))))))                    ;not event2
```

This emphasis on events has an ontology-based foundation (see Raskin 1990) as well as far-reaching theoretical ramifications, especially for LS. In fact, the concept is slowly and somewhat erratically creeping into LS (see, for instance, Partee 1991).

5. Conclusion

As we have shown, in order to be usable in NLPS, LS descriptions have to be reformalised on a much more rigorous basis, augmented, expanded, and enriched. In this light, the question arises as to whether the LS descriptions, with their fragile and deficient formalisms and impoverished "primes", are good for LS itself. This brings up a very controversial and difficult issue of the scope of lexical knowledge. Are our augmented, enriched, parsing-ready SMEARR entries still lexical in nature or are they "lexical plus"?

The question seems to be more important for lexical theory *per se* than for computational lexicology (a somewhat extreme stand on that was taken in Raskin 1990), because an NLP system, which needs enough information for adequate processing, may not particularly care as to where that information came from. In lexical theory, however, it is important to carefully delimit the lexicologist's responsibility, and failure to do so will lead to unlimited polysemy and dangers of both under- and overspecification. There are other long-ranging consequences of distinguishing or not distinguishing, more generally, between linguistic knowledge, stemming from one's native competence, and non-linguistic, encyclopedic, world knowledge going beyond that (cf. Raskin 1985).

Our current hypothesis is that lexical knowledge is a range from a minimum to a maximum value. The minimum lexical knowledge is what is shared by all native speakers, including those with zero encyclopedic knowledge on the subject, and it severely limits the number of possible inferences from an utterance. As the lexical knowledge is enriched by further links and connections, the number of possible inferences grows. At a certain maximum value, a cut-off takes place, and any further increase of knowledge is world knowledge, no longer lexical. Both the minimum and the maximum values are hard to determine, but the former seems to be conceptually clearer (see Raskin 1978), while the latter seems to be more easily validated by more abstract, metatheoretical arguments (see Raskin 1985). A proper formalisation of these generalisations is one of our current challenges.

We believe that in NLP the same range between the minimum and maximum meanings must be taken care of by VDA, the variable-depth-analysis module (see Nirenburg and Raskin 1986 for the initial discussion). Depending on the needs of an NLP system, you analyse and represent meaning more deeply, to a finer grain size, and make more inferences, or less deeply, to a larger grain size, and make do with fewer inferences. It is clear that the amount of inferencing should be exactly right for the system to achieve its goals.

Work in NLP semantics sheds an important light on formal linguistic semantic theory. For years, we have been writing and talking about the influence of linguistic semantics on computational semantics (see, for instance, Raskin 1987). This idea has motivated and informed our current research from the start. One important result of this research is that the "back" influence of NLP semantics on linguistic semantics turns out to be at least as important.

Afterword (by Victor Raskin)

A decade has elapsed since the bulk of the work on SMEARR was implemented, even though the article appeared, of course, later. The 1990s saw an impressive breakthrough in computational semantics: the stuff Nirenburg and I preached and practiced, with very few others, in the 1980s, bucking the trend of almost exclusively syntactic work in NLP, became the mainstream effort in the field. This also explains perhaps while our earlier work on the distinction between linguistic and encyclopedic information, which was and is of more practical importance to computational semantics than to theoretical semantics, had no resonance in the 1980s.

It is still incorrect to say that many in the NLP community do "brute force" semantics but many now do work on ingenious techniques around it, such as tagging-cum-statistics approaches, rather than ignoring or disdaining any attempt to handle meaning altogether. More importantly, the ontological foundation of SMEARR stopped being a bizarre maverick direction. Ontology is now a respectful and common approach to NLP. It is still not recognised by everybody but it is no longer a mark of the outcast from the NLP community.

SMEARR folded into what is now known as the MikroKosmos ontology (see, for instance, Mahesh & Nirenburg 1995, Mahesh 1996, Nirenburg & Raskin 2000; also http://crl.nmsu.edu/Research/Mikrokosmos), the largest ontology for NLP developed on an explicit principled basis with the help of semi-automatic acquisition tools and ready to use, share, and expand, if necessary. The first high-quality knowledge- and meaning-based system of machine translation between several pairs of languages was implemented on the basis of this ontology under the MikroKosmos project. Several other NLP systems for information extraction, summarisation, retrieval, and others were implemented on the same basis.

What was mentioned briefly in the conclusion of the paper became much clearer. By handling meaning ontologically, we capture accurately the delicate balance between linguistic and encyclopedic information – keeping them distinct, on the one hand, and using them simultaneously and harmoniously in the process of analysing and generating text.

The ontology is a tangled hierarchy of concepts, each with a set of slots and fillers, such as semantic roles for processes or parts for objects. It captures language-independent knowledge and serves as a basis for the lexicons of each particular language. Each lexical entry in such a lexicon either points to a concept, or constrains a concept, or relates to a filler in a slot for a concept. Thus, the English verb *speak* may point to the ontological concept SPEAK; *whisper* will be defined in terms of the same concept with a low value for volume specified in the appropriate slot; and *soft*, in the sense of low speech volume, will be defined in terms of that filler value.

The ontology is, then, where encyclopedic knowledge resides. The hierarchy of concepts is actually insufficient for capturing all of that. The ontology is also associated with scripts for complex events, such as the merger of two banks, as well as with a set of "remembered instances", such as the actual merger of some specific banks at a certain time. The specific lexicons for natural languages are the repositories of purely linguistic knowledge but they do also evoke minimum encyclopedic information. What is much clearer now is that no speech act is possible without some recourse to encyclopedic information because hardly any linguistic meaning is possible without it. It is still true, however, that more encyclopedic information, especially about pertinent remembered instances, enhances understanding, but the still problematic "minimal" understanding of an utterance involves a non-zero minimum of encyclopedic information. In other words, there are, apparently, no sentences devoid of encyclopedic information. This does, of course, throw into question again whether the distinction is worth maintaining.

Let us look at a simple sentence like *There are twenty people in the room*. Our knowledge of what room is indicated in the sentence is of an encyclopedic nature (and coincides, not accidentally, with the existential presupposition for the sentence). We may possess additional encyclopedic information, such as our knowledge that the room is a classroom, where a certain class meets at the time of speech. If we know further that 30 people are enrolled in the course, the sentence has an additional pragmatic meaning of a low attendance. The point is, however, that even the absolutely minimal understanding of the sentence involves some encyclopedic knowledge.

We believe, therefore, that what we call the two static resources, the ontology and the lexicons, actually capture the intricate nature of the distinction between linguistic and encyclopedic information. The separateness of the resources underscores the validity of the distinction. The involvement of both in semantic analysis and generation emphasises the fact that the two kinds of information cannot be completely divorced – they have to work together in every single utterance in a natural language.

References

Ahlswede, Thomas E. 1985. "A tool kit for lexicon building". In William Mann (ed.), *Proceedings of the Association for Computational Linguistics (ACL) 23rd Annual Meeting*. Chicago: University of Chicago. 268-276.

Attardo, Donalee H. 1990. *Making linguistic semantics work for natural language processing*. Unpublished MA thesis, Purdue University.

Attardo, Donalee H. 1991. "FrameBuilder. A tool for computational lexicography". Paper presented at ACH/ALLC '91 (Arizona State University, Tempe).

Attardo, Donalee H. 1993. "Reason-based heuristics for meaning analysis". *Literary and linguistic computing* 7. 48-63.

Bobrow, Daniel; Winograd, Terry. 1977. "An overview of KRL, a knowledge representation language". *Cognitive science* 1. 3-46.

Boguraev, Branimir; Byrd, Roy J.; Klavans, Judith L.; Neff, Mary S. 1989. "From structural analysis of lexical resources to semantics in a lexical knowledge base". In Uri Zernik (ed.), *Proceedings of the first international lexical acquisition workshop*. Detroit: International Joint Conference on Artificial Intelligence. Supplement.

Brachman, Ronald J. 1979. "On the epistemological status of semantic networks". In Nicholas V. Findler (ed.), *Associative networks. Representation and use of knowledge by computers*. New York: Academic Press. 3-50.

Brachman, Ronald J.; Fikes, Richard E.; Levesque, Hector J. 1985 [1983]. "KRYPTON. A functional approach to knowledge representation". In Ronald J. Brachman & Hector J. Levesque (ed.), *Readings in Knowledge Representation*. Los Altos: Kaufmann. 412-429.

Brachman, Ronald J.; Schmolze, James G. 1985. "An overview of the KL-ONE knowledge representation system". *Cognitive science* 9. 171-216.

Calzolari, Nicoletta. 1991. "Lexical databases and textual corpora. Perspectives of integration for a lexical knowledge base". In Uri Zernik (ed.), *Lexical acquisition. Exploiting on-line resources to build a lexicon*. Hillsdale: Lawrence Erlbaum. 191-208.

Chierchia, Gennaro; McConnell-Ginet, Sally. 1991. *Meaning and grammar. An introduction to semantics*. Cambridge: M.I.T. Press.

Fillmore, Charles J. 1971. "Verbs of judging". In Charles J. Fillmore & D. Terence Langendoen (ed.), *Studies in linguistic semantics*. New York: Holt, Rinehart & Winston. 272-296.

Frawley, William. 1993. *Linguistic semantics*. Hillsdale: Lawrence Erlbaum.

Grosz, Barbara J.; Sidner, Candace L. 1986. "Attention, intentions, and the structure of discourse". *Computational linguistics* 12. 175-204.

Jackendoff, Ray. 1983. *Semantics and cognition*. Cambridge: M.I.T. Press.

Jacobs, Paul S. 1991. "Making sense of lexical acquisition". In Uri Zernik (ed.), *Lexical acquisition. Exploiting on-line resources to build a lexicon*. Hillsdale: Lawrence Erlbaum. 29-44.

Kolodner, Janet L. 1984. *Retrieval and organizational strategies in conceptual memory. A computer model*. Hillsdale: Lawrence Erlbaum.

Lakoff, George. 1972. "Linguistics and natural logic". In Donald Davidson & Gilbert Harman (ed.), *Semantics of natural language*. Dordrecht: Reidel. 545-665.

Levin, Beth. 1993. *English verb classes and alternatives. A preliminary investigation*. Chicago: University of Chicago Press.

Lewis, David. 1972. "General semantics". In Donald Davidson & Gilbert Harman (ed.), *Semantics of natural language*. Dordrecht: Reidel. 169-218.

Mahesh, Kavi 1996. *Ontology development for machine translation. Ideology and methodology* (*Memoranda in computer and cognitive science* MCCS-96-292). Las Cruces: New Mexico State University Computing Research Laboratory.

Mahesh, Kavi; Nirenburg, Sergei. 1995. "A situated ontology for practical NLP". In *Proceedings of the AJCAI-95 workshop on basic ontological issues in knowledge sharing*. Montreal: International joint conference on artificial intelligence.

Mel'čuk, Igor A. 1979. *Studies in dependency syntax*. Ann Arbor: Karoma.

Nirenburg, Sergei; Levin, Lori. 1992. "Syntax-driven and ontology-driven lexical semantics". In James Pustejovsky & Sabine Bergler (ed.), *Lexical semantics and knowledge representation*. Berlin: Springer. 5-20.

Nirenburg, Sergei; Monarch, Ira; Kaufmann, Todd. 1988. *ONTOS. A knowledge base acquisition and maintenance system*. Pittsburgh: CMT Internal Memo, Carnegie Mellon University.

Nirenburg, Sergei; Raskin, Victor. 1986. "A metric for computational analysis of meaning. Toward an applied theory of linguistic semantics". In *Proceedings of the XIth international conference on computational linguistics (COLING '86)*. Bonn: University of Bonn. 338-340.

Nirenburg, Sergei; Raskin, Victor. 1987. "The subworld concept lexicon and the lexicon management system". *Computational linguistics* 13. 276-289.

Nirenburg, Sergei; Raskin, Victor. Forthcoming. *Principles of ontological semantics*. Cambridge: M.I.T. Press.

Nirenburg, Sergei; Raskin, Victor; Tucker, Alan. 1987. "The structure of interlingua in TRANSLATOR". In Sergei Nirenburg (ed.), *Machine translation. Theoretical and methodological issues*. Cambridge: Cambridge University Press. 90-113.

Nirenburg, Sergei; Raskin, Victor; McCardell, Rita. 1989. "Ontology-based lexical acquisition". In Uri Zernik (ed.), *Proceedings of the first international lexical acquisition workshop*. Detroit: International Joint Conference on Artificial Intelligence. Paper 8.

Partee, Barbara H. "Adverbial quantification and event structures". 1991. In Laurel A. Sutton, Christopher Johnson & Ruth Shields (ed.), *Proceedings of the 17th annual meeting of the Berkeley Linguistics Society*. Berkeley: Berkeley Linguistics Society. 439-456.

Postal, Paul M. 1971. "On the surface verb 'remind'". In Charles J. Fillmore & D. Terence Langendoen (ed.), *Studies in linguistic semantics*. New York: Holt, Rinehart & Winston. 181-270.

Quillian, M. Ross. 1968. "Semantic memory". In Marvin Minsky (ed.), *Semantic information processing*. Cambridge: M.I.T. Press. 216-270.

Raskin, Victor. 1978. "Presuppositional analysis of Russian, 1. Six essays on aspects of presupposition". In Victor Raskin & Dmitry Segal (ed.), *Slavica Hierosolymitana*, vol. 2. Jerusalem: Magnes. 51-92.

Raskin, Victor. 1985. "Linguistic and encyclopedic information in text processing". *Quaderni di semantica* 6. 92-102.

Raskin, Victor. 1987. "What is there in linguistic semantics for natural language processing?". In Sergei Nirenburg (ed.), *Proceedings of Natural Language Planning Workshop*. Blue Mountain Lake: RADC. 78-96.

Raskin, Victor. 1990. "Ontology, sublanguage, and semantic networks in natural language processing". In Martin C. Golumbic (ed.), *Advances in artificial intelligence. Natural language and knowledge-based systems*. Berlin: Springer. 114-128.

Raskin, Victor. 1994. Review of Frawley (1993). *Language* 70. 552-556.

Raskin, Victor; Attardo, Donalee H.; Attardo, Salvatore. 1991. "The SMEARR semantic database. An intelligent and versatile resource for the humanities". Paper presented at ACH/ALLC '91 (Arizona State University, Tempe, March 1991).

Raskin, Victor; Attardo, Salvatore; Hughes, Donalee. 1989. "On variable-depth NLP semantics. Transposition of high-quality semantic descriptions into ILT". W. Lafayette: Purdue University, PNLPL-TR-5-89.

Raskin, Victor; Attardo, Salvatore; Hughes, Donalee; Stede, Manfred. 1989. "Linguistic-semantics-based resource for meaning representation". W. Lafayette: Purdue University, PNLPL-TR-6-89.

Reichman, Rachel. 1985. *Getting computers to talk like you and me.* Cambridge: M.I.T. Press.

Schank, Roger C.; Riesbeck, Christopher K. 1981. *Inside computer understanding.* Hillsdale: Lawrence Erlbaum.

Tucker, Alan; Nirenburg, Sergei; Raskin, Victor. 1986. "Discourse, cohesion, and semantics of expository text". In *Proceedings of the XIth international conference on computational linguistics (COLING '86).* Bonn: University of Bonn. 181-183.

Wierzbicka, Anna. 1985. *Lexicography and conceptual analysis.* Ann Arbor: Karoma.

Wierzbicka, Anna. 1988. *The semantics of grammar.* Amsterdam: John Benjamins.

Wilks, Yorick A. 1975. "Methodology in AI and natural language understanding, and primitives and words". In Roger C. Schank and Bonnie Nash-Webber (ed.), *Proceedings of the first conference on theoretical issues in natural language processing (TINLAP-1).* Cambridge: Bolt, Beranek & Newman. 38-41.

Wilks,Yorick A.; Fass, Dan. 1984. "Preference semantics, ill-formedness and metaphor". *American journal of computational linguistics* 9. 178-187.

Woods, William A. 1979 [1967]. *Semantics for a question-answering system.* New York: Garland.

Author index

Abelson, R.P., 4, 51, 105, 114, 184, 216
Ahlswede, T.E., 465, 483
Aitchison, J., 296, 315
Akatsuka, N., 200, 213
Allan, K., 4, 13, 15, 19, 26-27, 31-32, 37-38, 44, 146, 169-217
Anderson, J.R., 105, 107, 110, 267, 288
Andrew, J.M., 321, 327, 347
Apresjan, Y.D., 294-296, 298-300, 315
Armstrong, S.L., 72, 92
Asher, N., 62, 93
Atkins, B.T., 4, 10, 45, 184, 214, 264, 289
Atlas, J.D., 169, 177, 188, 213
Attardo, D.H., 43, 463-86
Attardo, S., 43, 463-86
Austin, J.L., 179, 214
Austin, P., 421, 430

Baker, M., 393, 402-403, 421-422, 424, 427, 430
Baldwin, D.A., 442, 459
Bally, C., 164, 166
Barsalou, L.W., 89, 93, 101, 105, 110, 184, 214, 264, 289, 332, 345, 382, 386, 388-389
Bartlett, F.C., 105, 110, 381, 389
Barwise, J., 59, 93
Bates, E.A., 378, 382, 389
Battig, W.F., 104, 114
Baumgärtner, K., 25, 44
Beckman, J.N., 410, 430
Bensoussan, M., 457, 459
Berko, J., 340, 345
Berlin, B., 323, 345
Bierwisch, M., 7, 12, 35-36, 44, 115-118, 121-124, 126, 133, 135-139, 292, 294, 296-297, 315, 336, 345
Blakemore, D., 60, 93

Bloom, P., 442-443, 459
Bobrow, D., 466, 483
Boguraev, B., 175, 214, 466, 483
Bolinger, D., 26-30, 34, 44
Born-Rauchenecker, E., 7, 15, 18, 31, 39-40, 291-316
Bosch, P., 37, 44
Bouchard, D., 148, 167
Bouillon, P., 21, 24, 50
Brachman, R.J., 466, 483
Brandi, M.-L., 436, 459
Bresnan, J., 403, 421, 430-431
Briscoe, T., 175, 214
Brown, R., 324, 340, 345
Brugman, C., 116, 139
Bunt, H.C., 189, 214

Calzolari, N., 390, 466, 483
Capell, A., 400, 406, 430
Caplan, D., 72, 74-76, 93
Carpenter, P.A., 388-389
Carroll, J., 104, 110
Carston, R., 380, 389
Cavazza, M., 28, 40, 43-44
Chadwick, N., 396, 401-402, 430
Chaffin, R., 336, 345
Chambers, S.M., 98, 111
Charles, W.G., 319, 326, 338-339, 345
Chierchia, G., 465, 483
Chomsky, N., 5, 30-31, 44, 117, 133, 317, 329, 345, 349-351, 355-356, 360-361, 369, 371-372, 378, 382, 389, 400, 403, 430
Clark, H.H., 177, 214, 332, 345
Clausner, T.C., 219, 251, 254
Coltheart, M., 98-99, 110
Cooper, W., 163, 167

Croft, W., 37-39, 116, 137, 139, 219-256, 378, 383, 389
Cruse, D.A., 102-103, 110, 121, 139, 232-233, 240, 246, 254, 296, 315, 326-327, 336, 341, 345
Cuenca, M.J., 11, 44
Culicover, P.W., 137, 139, 379, 389
Cummins, S., 149, 167
Curtiss, S., 85, 93

Dabrowska, E., 388-389
Dancygier, B., 200-201, 214
Deane, P.D., 105, 110
Deese, J., 317, 345
Di Sciullo, A.-M., 351, 372
Diament, H., 439, 459
Dirven, R., 3, 38, 44-45, 122, 139, 231, 240, 254
Dixon, R.M.W., 343, 346
Downing, P., 244, 255
DuBois, J.W., 191, 214
Durkin, K., 132, 139

Eco, U., 3, 32-34, 45, 441, 454, 459
Elman, J.L., 100, 111, 378, 382, 389
Embick, D., 369, 372
Entwisle, D.R., 340, 346
Ervin-Tripp, S.M., 340, 346

Fass, D., 466, 486
Fauconnier, G., 4, 45, 248, 255
Feigenbaum, S., 1, 42-43, 435-461
Fellbaum, C., 339, 344, 346
Fernald, A., 442, 459
Fillenbaum, S., 201, 214
Fillmore, C.J., 3-10, 19-21, 23, 34, 45, 105, 111, 184, 187, 214, 264, 289, 382, 384, 389-390, 475, 484
Fodor, J.A., 3, 26-28, 30, 32-34, 47, 64, 82-83, 85, 93, 108, 111, 343-344, 346-347, 378, 380-381, 390
Forster, K.I., 98-99, 100, 111
Frawley, W., 3, 11-13, 45, 465, 484
Frege, G., 172, 214
Fuchs, C., 166-167

Gabbay, D., 161, 167
García, E., 126, 139
Garnham, A., 99, 111
Garrod, S.C., 105, 113
Gazdar, G., 181, 214

Geeraerts, D., 4-5, 14, 45-46, 102, 111, 130-131, 134-135, 139
Geiger, R.A., 13, 46
Geis, M., 200, 214
Gelman, S., 72, 93
Gilhooly, K.J., 104, 111
Givón, T., 191, 214, 381
Gleitman, L.R., 72, 353, 372
Godard, D., 21, 46, 68, 93
Goddard, C., 3, 13-15, 46
Goldberg, A.E., 353, 373, 380, 382, 390
Goodman, J.C., 382, 389
Goossens, L., 231-232, 255
Grandy, R.E., 332, 346
Greimas, A.J., 22, 46, 250, 255
Grice, H.P., 38, 46, 55, 58, 61-63, 169, 176-177, 188, 199, 215, 250
Gross, D., 326, 346
Grosz, B.J., 466, 484
Gundel, J., 332, 346

Haas, M., 296
Haiman, J., 3-5, 8, 11-13, 17, 22, 29, 33-34, 46, 220, 229, 255, 296, 382, 390
Hale, K.L., 332, 346, 356, 373, 421, 430
Halle, M., 24-25, 46-47, 350-351, 356, 369, 371-373, 394, 403, 430
Harley, H., 24-25, 39, 41-42, 47, 349-374
Hartshorne, C., 439, 441, 459
Hatakeyama, K., 17, 47
Hawkins, J.A., 191, 215
Heim, I., 62, 93
Herrmann, D.J., 326, 345-346
Herskovits, A., 116, 126, 139
Herweg, M., 116, 118, 123-125, 139
Hilferty, J., 4, 11, 41-42, 44, 377-392
Hobbs, J., 249, 255
Holmes, J., 18, 39, 259-290
Horn, L.R., 169, 181, 190, 206, 215, 323, 346
Hornby, A.S., 440, 459
Hudson, R., 18, 39, 47, 259-290, 377, 382, 390

Inbal, S., 440, 450, 459
Inchaurralde, C., 34-36, 97-114

Jackendoff, R., 30, 47, 135-136, 139-140, 161, 163, 167, 169, 183-184, 186-188, 215, 265, 289, 343, 346, 377, 379-380, 389-390, 476, 484
Jacobs, P.S., 372, 466, 484
Jakobson, R., 126, 140

Jayez, J., 21, 46-47, 68, 93
Jelinek, E., 421, 430
Jenkins, J.J., 319, 346
Jespersen, O., 165, 167
Johnson, M., 14, 48, 130, 140, 222-223, 228-231, 234, 239, 251, 255, 297, 315
Justeson, J.S., 326, 338, 347

Kallenbach, C., 445, 460
Kamp, H., 62, 93
Kampis, G., 109, 111
Karmiloff-Smith, A., 389, 443, 460
Katz, J.J., 3, 20-21, 26-30, 32-34, 47, 170, 215, 342, 347
Katz, S.M., 326, 338, 347
Kay, P., 323, 345, 382, 390
Keesing, R.M., 5-6, 11-12, 47
Keil, F., 72, 93
Kempson, R., 61, 93, 452, 460
Keyser, S.J., 356, 373
Kiefer, F., 36, 44
Kittay, E.F., 214, 264-265, 289
Kleiber, G., 2, 21, 47, 103, 111
Klinkenberg, J.-M., 12, 19, 21-23, 27, 37, 47-48, 439-440, 460
Kolodner, J.L., 466, 484
König, E., 200, 215
Kornai, A., 383, 390
Kövecses, Z., 14, 48
Kratzer, A., 356, 373
Kripke, S., 86, 93, 172-175, 215, 439, 460

Lakoff, G., 3-6, 11, 14, 33-34, 48, 57-58, 93, 102, 105, 112, 116-117, 120, 126, 140, 221-223, 226, 228-231, 234, 239, 251, 255, 260, 289, 297, 315, 378, 381-384, 386, 390, 469, 473, 484
Lambrecht, K., 191, 215
Lang, E., 35, 116, 123, 125, 138, 140
Langacker, R.W., 3-4, 10, 13-14, 36, 48, 97-98, 104, 112, 115-118, 120-126, 128-129, 131, 133, 135-136, 140, 175, 215, 220-224, 226-228, 231, 236, 238, 241-243, 249-250, 252-253, 255, 267, 273, 289, 292, 315, 379, 381-382, 384, 387, 391
Larrivée, P., 19, 37, 145-167, 210
Laufer, B., 435-436, 445, 457, 460
Lavi, J., 440, 450, 453, 457, 460
Leech, G., 31, 49
Lehmann, V., 294, 296-297, 314-315
Lehrer, A., 15, 49, 214, 264-265, 289, 317-318, 321, 337, 347

Leiss, E., 30-31, 49, 293, 316
Lepore, E., 344, 346
Lerdahl, F., 184, 215
Levin, B., 277, 280, 289, 350, 363, 373, 464, 484
Levin, L., 464, 484
Levinson, S.C., 169, 177, 181, 188, 213, 215-216, 329, 347
Lewis, D., 176, 178, 191, 216, 465, 484
Lidz, J., 354, 373
Lieber, R., 351, 373
Logie, R.H., 104, 111
Luger, G., 268, 289
Luscher, J.-M., 61, 94
Lyons, J., 177, 216, 221, 255, 335-336, 341, 347

MacWhinney, B., 339, 347
Mahesh, K., 481, 484
Manning, J., 132, 139
Marácz, L., 421, 431
Marantz, A., 24-25, 34, 46-47, 49, 350-351, 353, 356, 362-363, 369-373, 394, 401, 403-404, 430-431
Maratsos, M., 382, 391
Marconi, D., 29, 49
Marello, C., 439, 460
Markman, E., 72, 93
Marslen-Wilson, W.D., 32, 49, 100, 112, 388, 391
Matheny, L., 382, 391
McClelland, J.L., 100, 111
McConnell-Ginet, S., 465, 483
McCusker, L.X., 98, 112
McNeill, D., 333, 340, 347
Mel'čuk, I.A., 293, 296, 298, 302, 309, 316, 475, 484
Mervis, C., 72, 94
Mettinger, A., 318, 336, 347
Meyer, D.E., 99, 112
Miller, G.A., 317-319, 326, 338-339, 342, 345, 347
Miller, K.J., 322-323, 326, 346-347
Minsky, M.L., 4, 49, 105, 112
Mitchell, D.C., 388, 391
Moeschler, J., 61, 94
Momenteau, B., 436, 459
Montague, R., 180
Moravcsik, J., 161, 167
Morton, J., 98-99, 112
Müller, R.-A., 378, 382, 391
Murphy, G.L., 321, 327, 347

Murphy, M.L., 19, 39-41, 317-348
Muysken, P., 421, 431

Naigles, L., 353, 373
Nelson, K., 101, 112
Nerlich, B., 2, 39, 49
Neubauer, F., 17, 49
Neuner, G., 442, 460
Newmeyer, F.J., 378-381, 386, 391
Newport, E.L., 446, 449-451, 460
Nichols, J., 421, 431
Nirenburg, S., 19, 49, 464, 467, 471, 481, 484-485
Noordman, L.G.M., 200-201, 216
Nordlinger, R., 393, 403, 431
Noyer, R., 24-25, 39, 41-42, 47, 349-374
Nunberg, G., 38, 70, 94, 235, 237, 240, 245, 252-254, 256, 343, 348
Nuyts, J., 5, 49

Ortony, A., 50, 105, 113
Osgood, C., 103, 112

Paivio, A., 104, 112
Páll, E., 297, 315
Partee, B.H., 480, 485
Pattee, H.H., 109, 112
Patterson, K.E., 98-99, 112-113
Peeters, B., 1-52
Peirce, C.S., 439-442
Penrose, R., 109, 113
Pensalfini, R., 41-42, 393-431
Perry, J., 59, 93
Petöfi, J.S., 17, 49-50
Piaget, J., 381, 391
Pinker, S., 271, 289, 380, 391
Pires de Oliveira, R., 4, 14, 50
Platz-Schliebs, A., 450, 456, 461
Postal, P.M., 26, 33, 47, 473, 485
Pribram, J.K., 36, 108-109, 113
Prideaux, J., 109, 113
Prinz, J.J., 105, 110
Pullum, G.K., 383, 390
Pulman, S.G., 174, 216
Pustejovsky, J., 3, 19-21, 23-24, 34-35, 50, 55-56, 60, 63, 65-71, 73, 78-82, 85, 87-89, 91-92, 94, 136-137, 140, 148-149, 167, 175, 216, 344, 348
Putnam, H., 174-175, 216

Quillian, M.R., 466, 485
Quine, W.V.O., 28, 50, 180, 216

Quinlan, P.T., 104, 113

Rappaport Hovav, M., 350, 363, 373
Raskin, V., 1, 3, 17-19, 26, 34, 36, 42-43, 49-50, 463-486
Rastier, F., 22, 33, 50, 250, 256
Reboul, A., 1, 19-21, 24, 34-36, 55-95, 381
Récanati, F., 146, 167
Reddy, M.J., 36, 50, 98, 113
Reichman, R., 466, 486
Reif, J.A., 440, 459
Reisberg, D., 264-265, 268, 289
Reuther, T., 300, 316
Rey, A., 439, 461
Rey-Debove, J., 439, 461
Reyle, U., 62, 93
Rieger, C., 267, 289
Riesbeck, C.K., 465, 486
Robinson, E.A., 331, 348
Rogolla, H., 436, 447, 461
Rogolla, W., 436, 447, 461
Rooth, M., 161, 167
Rosch, E., 70, 72, 94, 103, 113, 117, 140, 221, 256, 274, 289
Rosen, R., 109, 113
Rosenzweig, M.R., 341, 348
Ross, J., 163, 167
Rudzka-Ostyn, B., 13, 46, 255, 391
Rumelhart, D.E., 105, 113, 381, 392
Russell, B., 205, 216
Ruwet, N., 37, 51

Sandra, D., 137, 140
Sanford, A.J., 105, 113
Sapir, E., 356, 374
Sartori, G., 99, 113
Saussure, F. de, 126, 440-441, 461
Scarborough, D.L., 99, 114
Schank, R.C., 4, 51, 105, 114, 184, 216, 267, 289, 465, 486
Schmid, H.-J., 3, 51
Schmidlin, R., 444, 461
Schmolze, J.G., 466, 483
Schreuder, R., 116, 118, 123, 139
Schulze, R., 116, 132, 140
Schvaneveldt, R.W., 99, 112
Schwartz, S.P., 174, 216
Schwarz, M., 116, 141, 292, 316
Searle, J.R., 34, 51, 118, 141, 179, 216, 222, 256
Seidenberg, M.S., 99, 114
Selkirk, E.O., 351, 374

Sewell, D.R., 105, 110
Shewell, C., 99, 113
Sidner, C.L., 466, 484
Silingardi, G., 29-30, 51
Slobin, D., 277, 290
Šmelev, D.N., 291, 316
Sowa, J., 267-268, 290
Sperber, D., 59, 62, 89, 94-95, 179, 217, 380, 392, 452, 461
Sprengel, K., 31, 51
Stachowiak, F.-J., 27, 35, 51
Stalnaker, R.C., 177, 217
Strawson, P.F., 180, 217
Stubblefield, W., 268, 289
Sweetser, E., 200-201, 214
Szalay, L.B., 341, 348

Talmy, L., 4, 214, 225, 249, 256, 381
Tanenhaus, M.K., 388, 392
Taylor, J.R., 7, 12, 15-17, 19-20, 34-36, 51, 115-141, 170, 223, 231, 233, 256, 292, 294-296, 316, 380, 392
Thompson, H., 5, 48
Togia, P., 336, 345
Toglia, M.P., 104, 114
Tomasello, M., 137, 141
Travis, L., 356, 374, 403, 431
Trier, J., 221
Trueswell, J.C., 388, 392
Tucker, A., 466, 486
Tuggy, D., 102, 114, 131-133, 141, 296, 316
Tulving, E., 101, 114
Turner, M., 231, 255-256
Tyler, L.K., 388, 391

Ullmann, S., 231, 234, 256
Ungerer, F., 3, 51

Valenzuela, J., 377, 383, 386, 390
van der Auwera, J., 200, 217
van der Sandt, R., 37, 44
Van Eunen, K., 442, 461
Van Langendonck, W., 39, 47
Verspoor, M., 3, 45
Victorri, B., 166-167

Weiss, P., 439, 441, 459
Wierzbicka, A., 3, 11-18, 20, 34, 39, 51-52, 105, 114, 136-137, 141, 226, 256, 261-263, 267, 290, 292, 296, 316, 343, 348, 470, 477, 486
Wilks, Y.A., 466, 486

Williams, E., 351, 372
Williams, J.N., 132, 141
Wilson, D., 59, 61-62, 89, 94-95, 179, 199, 217, 452, 461
Wilson, N.L., 28-30, 32, 52
Windle, C., 341, 348
Winograd, T., 466, 483
Winters, M., 134, 141
Wirbelauer, H., 447, 461
Woods, W.A., 465, 486
Wunderlich, D., 116, 118, 125-126, 134, 141

Ziegler, J., 30, 52, 316
Žolkovskij, A.K., 293, 316
Zweigenbaum, P., 28, 40, 43-44
Zwicky, A., 200, 214

Subject index

ability (English), 183, 192-195
acceptability, 25, 182, 237, 251, 385-387
access code, 98
access route, 98
accidence, 4, 12
accuse (English), 475
acquisition, 16, 101, 133-134, 137, 148, 338, 353, 438, 441, 443-444, 454
acquisition tool, 471
ACT Model, 105, 107
activation, 9-10, 32, 71, 73, 76-77, 100, 104-105, 107-108, 132-133, 135-136, 211, 221, 227-228, 250, 270
active zone, 121-122, 125, 236, 253
ACT-R, 267
agraphia, 77
AI, *see* artificial intelligence
allotopy, 21-22
almost (English), 146, 151-153, 162
ambiguity, 28-29, 56, 59, 65-66, 70, 99, 209, 231, 233, 236-237, 239, 247, 254, 295, 302, 304-307, 310, 312-314, 366, 465
analytic, 4, 12, 28-29; *see also* synthetic
antonymy, 40-41, 317-328, 332-344
aphasia, 74, 75, 76, 77, 74-78, 104
approach (English), 476
argue (English), 478
argument structure, 41, 60, 65-66, 68, 73, 79, 85, 89, 91, 267, 358, 361-367, 371-372, 402, 475
articles (definite and indefinite), 191-92
artificial intelligence (AI), 4, 10, 18-19, 28, 33, 222, 392, 464-465; *see also* cognition, artificial
assertion, 61, 154

autonomy, 4, 99-100, 117, 145, 185, 220, 242-248, 250, 252-254, 350, 378-379, 381-382, 386, 388; *see also* modularity

bachelor (English), 27
back (verb, English), 208
bare-NP complementation, 42, 383-387
base, 121, 222-224, 226, 228-231, 234, 239, 243-244, 246, 250
Best Fit Principle, 271, 276
bicycle (English), 39-40, 260-265, 267, 269-275, 277-279, 281, 284, 288
binarity, 321-23, 328
bird (English), 183-185, 188
bit' (Russian), 313
body parts, 208-10
brosit' (Russian), 301-304, 307-309, 313

cancellation. *See* defeasibility
canonicity, 338-339, 344
categorisation, 72, 79-81, 117, 136, 221, 311, 333-336, 341
centrality, 103, 121, 221-222, 228, 241, 251; *see also* peripherality
čertit' (Russian), 304-305, 307, 309, 313
česat' (Russian), 305, 307-309
circularity, 263
climb (English), 183-186
coercion
  structural, 351, 353-354, 368-369
  type, 21, 23-24, 65, 67-69, 82, 86, 88
cognition
  artificial, 19, 35-36, 42, 55-56, 63-65, 70-71, 85, 92; *see also* artificial intelligence
  natural, 19, 35-36, 55-56, 63-65, 70-73, 78, 81-82, 84-86, 92

Cognitive Grammar, 36, 63, 116-117, 122, 126, 133, 137, 215, 220, 236, 240-241, 382
Cognitive Linguistics, 2-6, 9-14, 33-36, 38-41, 63, 71, 102-103, 116-117, 251, 267
cognitive routine, 104
Cognitive Semantics, 4, 220
coherence, 17, 31, 248-250, 456, 458
cohesion, 17, 486
common ground, 169, 176-179, 183, 185, 197, 210, 212
complementary existential value, 157, 159-163, 165
compositionality, 60-61, 65-68, 81-82, 85-86, 88-90, 109, 122, 220, 236, 238, 240-242, 250
computational semantics, 481
concept vs. word, 35, 60-61, 63-64, 71, 73, 78, 89-90
concepts
    ad hoc, 56, 89-91, 332
    generic, 62, 70, 86-91
    specific, 56, 87-91
Conceptual Dependency Analysis, 267
conceptual graphs, 267-268
conceptual unity, 220, 245-246, 248-250, 253
conceptual vs. procedural content, 60-62
conceptualisation, 72, 121, 129, 136, 220, 223, 229, 330-332, 340, 342
conditional perfection, 200-205
conduit metaphor, 36, 98, 100, 103
conjunction, 195-200
connectionism, 36, 100, 105, 107-109
connotation, 101, 103, 294
Construction Grammar, 353, 373, 382
context failure, 456
contextual modulation, 121, 295
contingent properties, 6
contrast, 66, 263-264, 317, 321, 324-325, 328, 332, 333-339, 341, 344; *see also* opposition
contrast set, 319-322, 325, 333, 339
convention, 130, 178
conventionality, 130, 250
convince (English), 469
core, 12, 102, 126, 138, 427; *see also* periphery
core definition, 72-73, 79-86
core verb (= light verb), 67, 355-357, 394, 400-401, 403, 415, 416, 428
co-text failure, 455
co-verb, 399-403, 408, 411, 416
credibility, 180, 207

credibility metric, 181
cue validity, 221
cultural kind terms, 15
cycling (English), 39, 259-261, 271-275, 277-284, 286-288

deceptive transparency, 436, 450, 453
defeasibility (= cancellation), 38, 149, 150, 177, 180, 182, 185, 188, 197, 200, 207, 210, 212
definitional knowledge, 6
definitional properties, 6
deixis, 476
delit' (Russian), 306, 307
denotation, 12, 101-103, 171, 174, 196, 306
dependence, 220, 241-248, 250, 252-254
dependent-marking languages, 421-422, 424-425, 427; *see also* head-marking languages
Discourse Representation Theory (*DRT*), 62-63
disjunction, 190, 203, 299
disjunctive conditional, *see* conditional perfection
dislocation, 407, 422, 427
dissuade (English), 477
distinguisher, 26-27; *see also* marker
Distributed Morphology (*DM*), 2-3, 24-25, 39, 41-42, 350-352, 365, 394
domain, 38, 115, 121-122, 124, 128-129, 219-256, 297, 381, 384; *see also* root domain
domain annexation, 38
domain highlighting, 38, 232-235, 238-240, 242-248, 253
domain mapping, 38, 231-233, 239-240, 242-243, 247-248
domain matrix, 38, 224-226, 229, 231-232, 234-235, 239, 243-245, 251, 253
domain specificity, 82-83, 378, 380-381, 389
domain structure, 224, 226-227, 231, 239
double dissociation, 64-65, 74, 82, 84
DRT, see Discourse Representation Theory
dual route, 99
dvigat' (Russian), 307, 313
Dynamic Semantics, 63
dyslexia, 76-77, 99

ee (Word Grammar), 266-269, 272
ensemble theory, 189
entailment, 38, 150, 180, 185, 192-193, 199, 203, 205, 350
entrenchment, 282
er (Word Grammar), 266-269, 275, 277-279

errors, 446-453
  morphological, 450, 449-452, 454, 458
  scanning, 447-450, 457-458
  semantic, 452-454, 457-458
  syntax, 451-452, 455
essence, 4, 12
essential properties, 6
essentialism, 71-72, 84
est' (Russian), 307
even (English), 146, 151-153, 162-163, 165
event structure, 66, 68, 79, 91, 464, 478, 463-486
exceptions, 378-380
explicit vs. implicit communication, 61-62
extension, 58, 60, 62, 89, 128-129, 131, 135, 236-237; cognitive extension, 101-102; *see also* intension

false friends, 436, 447
falsifiability, 386-387
family resemblance, 103
FCS, see File Change Semantics
feature spreading, 410, 413, 415, 420
File Change Semantics (FCS), 62-63
filler, 242, 418, 464-465, 467, 473, 478, 482; *see also* slot
f-node, 355, 356, 367, 369, 370, 371, 372; *see also* l-node
focus, 37, 146, 150-154, 156-166; conceptual focus, 125
foreign language acquisition, 42-43, 135, 435, 437-438, 443-446, 454, 458
frame, 2, 4, 9-10, 18, 33, 38, 105, 184, 210, 213, 222, 226, 232, 261, 264-266, 268, 270, 280, 288, 384, 464, 467, 469, 471-474
Frame Semantics, 9, 264
frame template, 467-468, 478
FrameNet (Fillmore), 10
functional operations, 294, 297-298, 310, 312-314; *see also* highlighting, modification, recategorisation

Generative Grammar, 24, 34, 317, 373, 382
Generative Lexicon, 3, 19-21, 35, 56, 63, 65-70, 78, 82, 85-86, 88, 92, 344
Generative Linguistics, 63
go (English), 170, 178, 184, 187, 285-287
grain size, 478, 481
grammaticality (= grammatical well-formedness), 5, 41, 60-61, 66-69, 349-351, 354, 358, 360, 367-369, 372, 386-387, 402, 429

grammaticality vs. truth-conditionality, 61
granularity, 249-250, 466
guessing, 445, 456-457

hardwiring, 468-469
Head Movement Constraint, 403
head-marking (= polysynthetic) languages, 402, 421-425, 427; *see also* dependent-marking languages
highlighting (as a "functional operation"), 297-298, 306, 313
Holographic Brain Theory, 36, 108-109
homonymy, 56-57, 65-66, 81, 89, 130, 148, 294, 296, 299, 320, 455
hyperonymy, 40
hyponymy, 40, 103, 317-318, 320-321, 328, 335-336, 340, 344

idealised cognitive model (ICM), 4, 105, 226, 231, 384-386; ad-hoc idealised cognitive model, 386
identification procedure, 72-73, 79-86
illocutionary point, 179
image-schema, 102; *see also* schema
implicature, 37-38, 62, 104, 338; *see also* quantity implicatures
implicit vs. explicit communication, 61-62
incidental properties, 6
indeterminacy. *See* underdetermination
inference, 34, 37, 42-43, 59, 61-62, 84, 89, 104, 120, 162, 177-179, 184, 187-188, 190, 192, 205, 329, 331-332, 338, 435, 441, 445, 452, 454, 466, 480-481
informational encapsulation, 42, 82-83, 100, 123, 377-392
informativeness principle, 169, 177, 188
inheritance
  default, 271, 275, 277-278
  lexical, 344; *see also* lexical inheritance structure
instantiation, 128-137
intension, 60, 62, 89, 334; cognitive intension, 102; *see also* extension
interactivity, 99-100
Interpretant, 441-446, 452, 454
Inverse, 413, 418
isa (Nirenburg), 467-468, 470-471, 473, 475-478
isa (Word Grammar), 269, 271-273, 275, 278, 280, 284
isotopy, 21, 22, 250

krutit' (Russian), 314

landmark, 120, 124, 166, 243, 273, 279
lcp (lexical-conceptual paradigm), *see* meta-entry
lemma, 73, 79-82, 88, 91, 293, 298-300, 302-303, 305, 308-310, 313-314
lexical conceptual paradigm, *see* meta-entry
Lexical Functional Grammar (LFG), 403
lexical gaps, 337
lexical inheritance structure, 66, 79, 91; *see also* inheritance, lexical
lexical relations, 40, 279, 284, 317-348
LFG, see Lexical Functional Grammar
licensing, 25, 41, 228, 350-351, 354-356, 360-361, 363-364, 366-372
light verb, *see* core verb
listeme, 31-32, 37, 170, 173, 175-176, 208-213
l-node, 355-360, 362-363, 369-371; *see also* f-node

machine translation (MT), 2, 19, 464-465, 471, 474, 481
malapropism, 76
manner of motion, 275-281, 285-286
marker, 26-28, 160, 351, 353, 396, 398-403, 406, 411, 413-415, 418-419, 421, 423, 425; *see also* distinguisher
markerese, 465
maturational constraint, 446, 449-452
maximal projection, 383
Meaning-Text model, 293-294
measure function, 188
memory
    declarative, 105
    episodic, 101
    long-term, 101, 271
    production, 105
    semantic, 101, 104
    short-term, 101
    working, 105
mental space, 4, 38
meronymy, 335-336, 344
meta-entry (= lexical-conceptual paradigm, lcp), 67-68, 78, 81
metalanguage, 186, 261-262
metaphor, 2, 8-9, 14, 17, 34, 37-38, 98, 103-104, 127-129, 134, 186, 208, 219-256, 265, 296-297, 299, 309, 327, 337-338, 486
metonymy, 37-38, 120, 122, 124, 126, 128, 219-256, 296

MikroKosmos, 481
minimal difference, 332-333, 338, 343
Minimalism, 400-401
Mirror Principle, 403
model, 9-10
modification (as a "functional operation"), 297-298, 303, 306, 308, 313
modularity, 40, 42, 64-65, 74, 82-85, 88-89, 108, 117, 123, 136-137, 288, 329-332, 342-343, 377-382, 386-388, 401, 465, 471-472, 478, 481; *see also* autonomy
monosemy, 126, 294-296, 298-299
morphological errors, *see* errors
Morphological Visibility Criterion, 421
mother (English), 57-58, 260
MT, *see* machine translation

name bearer, 171, 174-176
names
    personal, 406
    proper, 13, 86-87, 90-92, 162, 164-165, 170-176, 191, 324-325, 438-439, 442-443, 445, 453-454
natural kind terms, 11-13, 15, 67, 72, 170, 173-174, 293
natural language processing (NLP), 42-43, 214, 463-486
Natural Semantic Metalanguage, 261
negation, 146, 150, 153-162, 164-165, 190, 206-207, 323, 333
network, 16, 39, 100, 103-105, 107-109, 129-133, 165, 170, 175, 221, 228, 263-265, 268-271, 275, 277, 279-282, 284, 288, 380, 464, 466
network model, 36, 115-141
NLP, *see* natural language processing
nominalisation, 283, 285, 340, 349-374
nonconfigurationality, 42, 394, 402, 420-422, 424, 427-429
nose (English), 470

object schema, 125
objectivism, 6
obligatory firing, 82-83, 381
only (English), 146, 151-153, 162-163
ontology, 480-482
operationality, 63-64, 70
opposition, 40, 103, 309, 319-328, 332-338, 340-341, 343, 344; *see also* contrast
otkryt' (Russian), 300-301, 307, 309-311, 313
overdetermination, 164, 477
overgeneralisation, 451, 453-454

overspecification, 43, 480

paradigmatic shift, 340-341
parallel distributed processing (PDP), 36, 108
paraphrase, 147, 196
part-whole relation, 39, 103, 106, 244
PDP, *see* parallel distributed processing
pedalling (English), 40, 262-263, 279-282, 288
perfective conditional, *see* conditional perfection
peripherality, 12, 103, 221-222, 227-228, 251; *see also* centrality
periphery, 12, 138; *see also* core
phonological stress, *see* prosodic stress
pisat' (Russian), 313
plexity, 249
položit' (Russian), 306-307, 313-314
polysemy, 40, 43, 55-59, 66-68, 70, 78, 81, 89, 102, 115-116, 120, 122-126, 130, 135, 147-148, 166, 220, 235, 291-297, 299, 320, 337-338, 378, 436, 445, 447, 451-452, 455-457, 480
polysynthetic languages, *see* head-marking languages
predicate logic, 267
predicate transfer, 252-253
predication, 121, 222, 229, 234, 248
autonomous, 220
dependent, 220, 242-247, 252-254
scope of, 223
predictability, 323, 325, 326-329, 336
preference conditions, 169, 183-185, 187
presupposition, 5, 33, 61, 104, 223, 482
priming, 99-100, 228
'prix fixe' approach, 358
procedural vs. conceptual content, 60-62
productivity, 25, 232, 237, 251, 280, 283, 321, 323-326, 328, 380
profile, 121, 222-231, 233, 235-236, 238-241, 243-244, 247, 253
profile determinant, 241
prosodic stress, 151-152, 154, 156, 158, 161-162, 164
prototype semantics, 2, 12, 126
prototype theory, 103
prototypicality, 117, 126, 132, 134, 149, 221, 228, 236, 313, 324-326, 338, 340-341, 380; *see also* typicality
psychological reality, 16, 131-133, 137, 310

Q implicatures, *see* quantity implicatures

qualia structure, 21, 24, 66-70, 73, 79, 81-82, 85, 88, 91
quantifiers, 156-159, 161-165, 189-191, 205, 212, 253; restrictive quantifiers, 188
quantity implicatures, 169-217; *see also* implicature
quantity maxims, 38, 169, 176, 203

recategorisation (as a "functional operation"), 297, 306, 308, 312
recycling principle, 39, 259-263, 274, 282, 288
reference transfer, 252
referential terms, 31, 293
Relation by Contrast (RC), 332-335, 337-338
Relation by Opposition (RO), 332-337
relational terms, 31, 40, 293-295
relativity (linguistic), 341
Relevance Theory, 55, 58, 63, 380, 452, 457
remembered instance, 482
riding (English), 263-264, 268-269, 271-275, 277-282, 284, 288
rigid denominator, 439
rigid designator, 86, 173-175
root domain, 417-420
run (English), 131-133
ryt' (Russian), 314

sarcasm, 165
saturation, 164, 166
scanning errors, *see* errors
scenario, 10, 105
scene, 2, 8-10, 33
schema, 9-10, 102, 105, 129-130, 226, 231-232, 466; *see also* image-schema, object schema
schematicity, *see* instantiation
script, 2, 4, 33, 38, 105-106, 184, 213, 232, 482
SDRT, *see* Segmented Discourse Representation Theory
secondary predication, 422, 425, 427-428
see (English), 173, 175, 177-178, 182, 184, 187
Segmented Discourse Representation Theory (SDRT), 62-63
selective binding, 21, 24, 82, 86
semantic errors, *see* errors
semantic field theory, 221, 263, 317, 321, 325
semantic fields, 280, 317, 319, 321-322
semantic primitives, 135, 262, 292, 342

semantic relations, 177, 317-337, 341-342, 344

semantic space, 103, 221

semanticality, 66-70, 79, 387

Sense Enumeration Lexicons (SELs), 66-67, 81

sense-spectrum, 103

set theory, 189

shallow output, 82-83, 381

sight vocabulary, 445, 453, 458

similarity, 129, 132, 296, 303, 322, 327-328, 333, 334, 336

size adjectives (English), 326-327

slip of the tongue, 76

slot, 241-242, 358-359, 464-465, 467, 469, 473, 476, 478, 482; *see also* filler

SMEARR, 43, 463-467, 471-478, 480-481

snjat' (Russian), 311, 312, 313

some (English), 182, 189-190

specification
  formal, 32, 170, 175, 186
  morphosyntactic, 170, 175, 186
  semantic, 170, 174-175, 188, 210-212

sprjatat' (Russian), 307, 309

stage-level predicate, 407-408

stavit' (Russian), 314

stop (English), 147, 150, 210

superschema, 130

suppletion, 357, 369-373, 396, 401, 403

synaesthesia, 327

synecdoche, 37, 39, 234, 251

synonymy, 29, 40-41, 65, 185, 267, 317-321, 323, 325-328, 333-334, 340, 342-344, 473

syntactic merger, 394, 400, 402, 408, 416-417, 429

syntactic movement, 156, 158

syntax errors, *see* errors

synthetic, 4, 12, 29; *see also* analytic

tener (Spanish), 42, 383-387

testability, 63-64

text processing, 17, 465, 485

Theory of Mental Representations, 87, 90

tip-of-the-tongue phenomena, 76

TRACE model, 100

translation, 445

truth-conditionality vs. grammaticality, 61

two-level model, 7, 35-36, 115-141, 292

type-predictability fallacy, 379

typicality, 71-72, 79, 84; *see also* protypicality

UG, *see* Universal Grammar

um (German), 125

underdetermination, 58-60, 62, 121, 129, 164, 166; *see also* underspecification

underspecification, 37, 41, 43, 178, 360, 367, 371, 480; *see also* underdetermination

ungrammaticality, *see* grammaticality

Universal Grammar (UG), 137, 355, 357

vagueness, 58, 295

variant, 40, 133, 299, 301, 303, 307, 310, 314, 339

versatility, 59

vocabulary item (VI), 2, 24-25, 41, 349-356, 358-372, 394, 406, 408, 429

vowel harmony, 394, 404-406, 408-420, 429

walk (English), 184, 187, 283-285

want + noun (English), 149-150

well-formedness, *see* grammaticality, semanticality

Word Grammar (WG), 2, 39, 261, 269, 271

word vs. concept, 35, 60-61, 63-64, 71, 73, 78, 89-90

WordNet, 317, 321-323, 325, 327, 342, 347

X-bar theory, 386

zakryt' (Russian), 300-301

žarit' (Russian), 301, 303-304, 307

žat' (Russian), 304

Language index[1]

Arabic, 448, 450

French, 22, 89, 148, 155-159, 237, 341, 450, 456

German, 125, 275, 308-309, 341, 435-461
Gurindji, 400

Hebrew, 440, 447-448, 450, 453

Italian, 252, 414

Jingulu, 41-42, 393-431

Jiwarli, 421-422, 424-425, 428

Kalam, 428

Mayali, 422
Mohawk, 422, 428

Russian, 291-316

Spanish, 41-42, 104, 383-387

Warlpiri, 400, 421, 428
Welsh, 428

---

[1] For languages other than English only. Individual English words are listed in the subject index.